BASIC CHASSIS, SUSPENSION AND BRAKES

INTRODUCTION

Cover Photography, **John Gates**
Cover Coordination, **Eric Rickman**

PETERSEN AUTOMOTIVE BOOKS

LEE KELLEY/Editorial Director
SPENCE MURRAY/Automotive Editor
DAVID COHEN/Managing Editor
SUSIE VOLKMANN/Art Director
LINNEA HUNT-STEWART/Copy Editor
RAYMOND HARPER/Copy Editor
LINDA SARGENT/Copy Editor
FERN CASON/Editorial Coordinator

PETERSEN PUBLISHING COMPANY

R.E. PETERSEN/Chairman of the Board; **F.R. WAINGROW**/President; **ROBERT E. BROWN**/Sr. Vice President, Publisher; **DICK DAY**/Sr. Vice President; **JIM P. WALSH**/Sr. Vice President, National Advertising Director; **ROBERT MacLEOD**/Vice President, Publisher; **THOMAS J. SIATOS**/Vice President, Group Publisher; **PHILIP E. TRIMBACH**/Vice President, Financial Administration; **WILLIAM PORTER**/Vice President, Circulation Director; **JAMES J. KRENEK**/Vice President, Manufacturing; **LEO D. LaREW**/Treasurer; **DICK WATSON**/Controller; **LOU ABBOTT**/Director, Production; **JOHN CARRINGTON**/Director, Book Sales and Marketing; **MARIA COX**/Director, Data Processing; **BOB D'OLIVO**/Director, Photography; **NIGEL P. HEATON**/Director, Circulation Marketing and Administration; **AL ISAACS**/Director, Corporate Art; **CAROL JOHNSON**/Director, Advertising Administration; **DON McGLATHERY**/Director, Advertising Research; **JACK THOMPSON**/Assistant Director, Circulation; **VERN BALL**/Director, Fulfillment Services

Despite the ballyhoo from Detroit automakers at new-model time about how this or that is new, great or innovative, many parts of the modern car remain almost ageless. That is, changes are slow and evolutionary rather than revolutionary. Among the systems on a car that go almost unchanged from one year to the next are the chassis, suspension and brakes. Brakes, as a case in point, have undergone little change in design or operation since the hydraulic system was laid down in the early Thirties. Of course, disc brakes are relatively new, but since they appeared in widespread usage in the early Sixties, they haven't changed much either.

Suspensions have evolved slowly, too, from the time our manufacturers settled on the independent front/solid rear axle system along about 1949. Exceptions to all of this do come along occasionally, of course, but we think you have the gist by now.

This is by way of explaining why this 4th edition of *Petersen's Basic Chassis, Suspension & Brakes* contains no real surprises. It isn't because Detroit has been lax in these areas; it's more a case of systems that are so highly refined that there's virtually no room for improvement.

The real intent of this book, though, is to help car owners who might not be at all versed in chassis, suspension and brakes get to know and understand their cars' underpinnings. If this sounds at all dull, then consider that increased tire life, extended brake use, and even improved fuel economy can result from a few at-home adjustments or simple replacement of parts. And because these could have a desirable effect on your wallet, the contents of this book are well worth studying.

**BASIC CHASSIS,
SUSPENSION & BRAKES NO. 4**

Copyright©1977 by Petersen Publishing Company, 8490 Sunset Blvd., Los Angeles, CA 90069. Phone: (213) 657-5100. All rights reserved. No part of this book may be reproduced without written permission. Printed in U.S.A.

**Library of Congress Catalog
Card No. 74-78892**

ISBN 0-8227-5021-X

CONTENTS

DESIGNING A CHASSIS 4
THE FRAME 10
ENERGY ABSORBING BUMPERS 20
THE FRONT END 24
WHEEL ALIGNMENT 42
SPRINGS AND TORSION BARS 48
SHOCK ABSORBERS 56
THE STEERING SYSTEM 62
POWER STEERING SYSTEMS 70
KEYS TO BETTER HANDLING 76
BRAKE HYDRAULICS 84
DRUM BRAKES 96
OVERHAULING DRUM BRAKES 106
HIGH PERFORMANCE BRAKE LINING 114
DISC BRAKES 118
DISC BRAKE CALIPER REBUILDING 130
POWER BRAKE UNITS 134
WHEELS AND TIRES 140
DRIVESHAFTS AND U-JOINTS 150
THE REAR END 160

FRONT-DRIVE SYSTEMS

ELDORADO/TORONADO 174
FORD FIESTA 180
DODGE OMNI/PLYMOUTH HORIZON 186

Designing A Chassis

A chassis is your car's underpinnings; a far more intricate assembly than just a pair of rails with wheels.

What is a chassis, anyway? What job is it supposed to do? Turns out that the answers depend entirely on the kind of car you're talking about. Each automotive category poses its own special challenges to the designer/builder, challenges that depend on what the car's user wants and how much he's willing to pay for it.

So what do various designers demand of a chassis? Let's take a look:

Detroit designer: "I consider the frame and body as inertia masses, free to move with respect to the suspension and each other. We use computers to predict their movements and help us locate and design mounts and linkages. In addition, my cars must pass rigid new federal safety standards."

European designer: "I require the stiffest yet lightest possible main unitized structure as a rigid platform for my new all-independent suspension. My customers won't mind a 'busy' ride if I give them good handling."

Road racing designer: "For me the basic structure is something to hold the engine, driver and fuel bags and to pick up the suspension loads."

Drag racing designer: "It has to be light, but not too light, and I don't need suspension as long as the chassis can flex a bit—but not too much."

For some car makers the chassis and suspension *are* the car, and for others they're just a means of putting power on the road. Then there are infinite combinations of these approaches, making car chassis a far more varied and intricate subject than engines, for example; or transmissions. That's why good chassis men are really hard to find!

FRAME DESIGN

In the old days the "classic" chassis was the twin-channel-rail frame of a Model A or a Chevy 6, connected to solid axles and leaf springs, the whole thing making up a structure so flexible you couldn't tell whether the springs or the frame were bending more. Today the "classic" approach to frame design is quite different. It's typified by the European approach mentioned above, calling for a basic frame/body that's exceptionally stiff, both in bending and in twisting (they're entirely different; think of a rubber hose). The idea is that only with a stiff main structure can you expect to be able to get the right handling and ride effects from your springs and suspension.

The logical descendant of the twin-rail frame is the twin-tube design, representing a big improvement in resistance to twisting. Most of Detroit's frames today are basically twin parallel tubes, with the tubes squared-off in sections so they'll fit better into the body sills. During the '50's we saw the first wide-spread use of multiple-tube frames in race cars and European models, welded up of many small-diameter tubes to form a bridge-like structure usually called a "space frame," because it derived its high strength from its enclosure of a lot of space.

Space frames evolved naturally in the drag racing world. Some of the finest examples can be seen on today's funny cars. These are solid space frames with high strength in both beaming and twisting. On a dragster, on the other hand, tube frames are stiff in beaming (considering the long wheelbases) but almost completely unbraced from side to side to allow twisting flexibility, which hopefully will keep as many wheels as possible on the ground.

And then there's the "monocoque" frame. This literally means "single shell." A true monocoque, like an Atlas or Saturn booster or an Apollo spacecraft, has all its strength in its outer surface skin. Internal bulkheads and supports are added, but theoretically only to prevent the skin surfaces from buckling and bending prematurely under load.

If you'll bear the above definition in mind, you'll realize that very few cars of any kind can be said to have true monocoque body/frames. There are several good reasons for this:

1. Doors have to be cut through the skin, for people to get in and out.

2. Especially in racing cars, there has to be fast and easy access to all the internal machinery.

3. The most important reason of all: The frame structure of a car is subjected to an incredible number of different kinds of loads, in different directions, at different frequencies, and of sizes that are often almost completely unknown. Compared to a car, the structure of a missile or an airplane is absurdly simple.

But weight-conscious designers have arrived at compromises between tube-type and monocoque frames

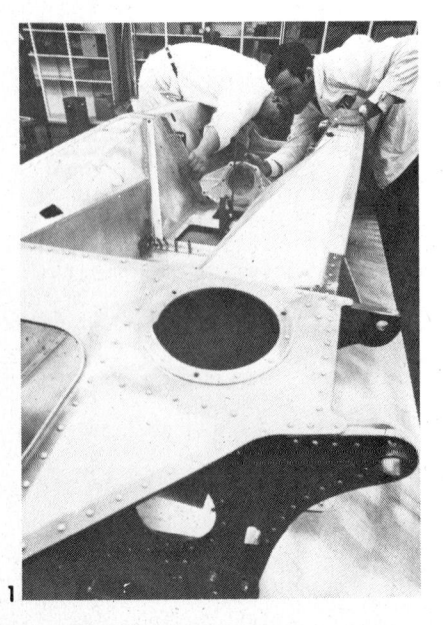

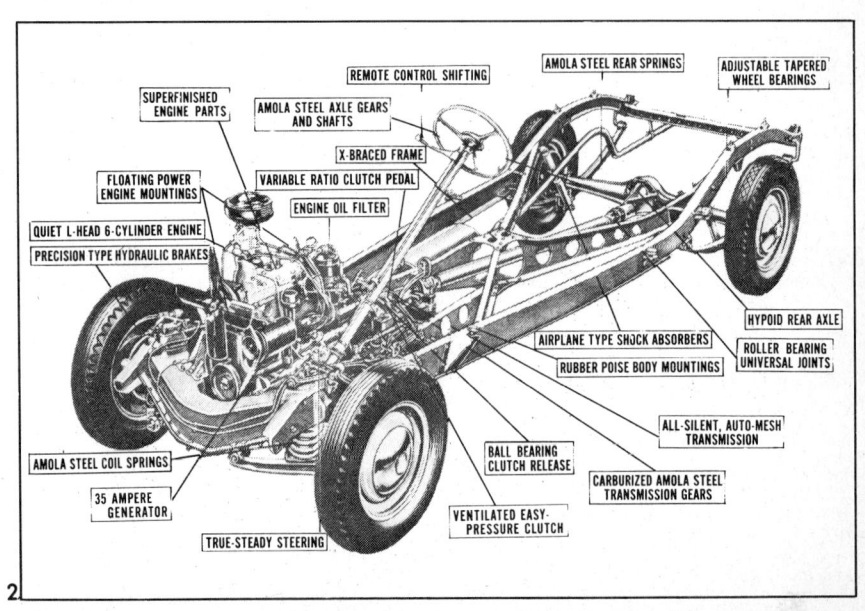

4/CHASSIS, SUSPENSION & BRAKES

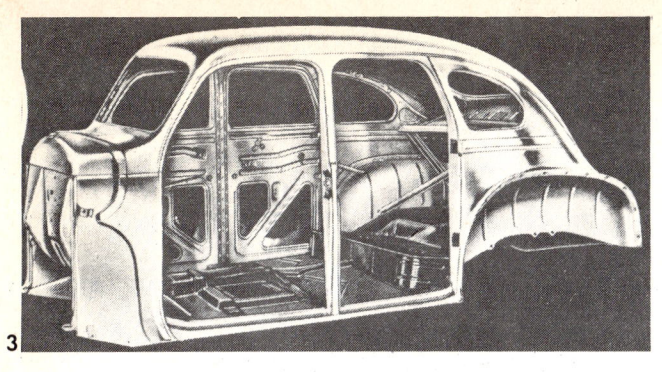

1. Both production and racing cars call on the chassis designer to use the least weight with maximum effect. Engineers here are studying stress and component placement on an STP race car built of stressed aluminum.

2. This pre-war Plymouth chassis is typical of the X-braced frames of the era, but featured advances like independent front suspension, open drive line and tube-type shocks.

3. First with hydraulic brakes in 1928, Plymouth was also ahead in body construction. Welded shell of this all-steel '40 model anticipated the unit-construction auto makers would all turn to eventually.

4. Modern passenger car chassis all use box-section frames with several crossmembers for the heavy results of today's styling. Note also the number of rubber body-to-frame pads for smoothness and quiet stability.

5. Truck chassis like this Blazer are the only applications you're likely to see still using the open channel frame like pre-war cars, and they have to be quite large in cross-section to do the job.

6. Race car chassis design must be executed with strength, simplicity and above all, light weight in mind. Most accomplish this with tubing.

that have been aptly described today as "multicoque."

Many European enclosed passenger cars are more monocoque than multicoque, carrying lots of stresses through the pillars and roof as well as through the platform floorpan. From the biggest Mercedes-Benz and Rolls-Royce down through the smallest Fiat, cars overseas have switched over almost entirely to integral body/frame construction.

In contrast, the trend in the U.S. may be back toward separate bodies and frames, or at least partial frames. Integral construction is retained on Ford's smallest cars (Maverick, Falcon and Mustang), on the entire Chrysler Corp. line, and in modified form on the Camaro and Firebird. American Motors is staying with it too. But GM returned to separate frames for its intermediates, after trying integral, and Ford is now doing the same thing with Lincoln. They're doing it because they just haven't been able to get that ultimate plush feeling of isolation from the road that's achievable only, they feel, with a separate frame and a body rubber-mounted to it.

For these American car structures no effort is made to achieve radically high stiffness. Size for size, an American body/frame car is about one-half to two-thirds as stiff, under twisting forces—as its European counterpart. Exceptional stiffness sometimes requires design compromises like thick pillars, a high trunk threshhold and fenders which are welded to the body instead of being removable for individual replacement.

"TUNING" FOR RIDE

American designers have decided to build cars that give and work with vibration inputs, instead of resisting them with high stiffness. Car structures are analyzed in scale model form, using plastic replicas of body panels that react to stresses just like sheetmetal and show high stress points visually. Such models are vibration-tested in small-scale rigs before the completed prototype cars are wrung out on torture benches like Chevy's tape-controlled road simulator, which has hydraulic rams under the wheels so powerful they could throw an Impala high into the air.

Through tests like these, all the rubber in the car is "tuned" to give the chassis the best possible ride behavior and feel over most of the roads on which it will be operated. Engine mounts aren't just engine mounts; they're "springs" that control the motion of the most important vibrating mass in the front of the car. And if weight is needed where it isn't found, the engineers add it artificially, as they did on certain Lincoln and Camaro convertibles, with carefully positioned, bolted-on weights.

All this rubber isolation and adjustment is dedicated to the prevention of any awareness by driver and passengers that there's a bumpy road beneath them. Yet—and this is one of the most challenging compromises of chassis design—to achieve good handling it's necessary to have very exact guidance of the wheels by the chassis, and a very direct communication channel to the driver so he knows what's happening down where the rubber meets the road. Surprisingly, both needs can be met. Most simply, it's done by connecting body/frame/suspension by rubber bushings which are made very flexible when moved up and down, yet very stiff when moved from side to side. As you may have noted if you've driven any of the latest Motor

CHASSIS, SUSPENSION & BRAKES/5

Designing A Chassis

City offerings, Detroit engineers used more rubber isolationing in body and suspension mountings this year than ever before, searching for the ultimate "quiet-ride"

The design and placement of these rubber isolation mounts is one of the finest arts being practiced in Detroit today. But for racing it's all wasted effort. When a stock car or Trans-Am car is prepared, for example, the first thing a mechanic does is to replace all the rubber bushings with metal-to-metal joints and substitute aluminum shims for the rubber body mounts. And then a big tubular roll cage is welded in to add still more to the stiffness of the body/frame. This step is especially important with cars like the Camaro, Firebird and Mustang II, which have a small subframe at the front.

What chassis designers seek, then, is an ideal combination of softness up-and-down and stiffness side-to-side. It's no surprise that they demand exactly the same combination of their tires. An average car tire, Firestone points out, is nothing more than some angry air surrounded by 11 lbs. of mixed synthetic and natural rubber, 6 lbs. of carbon black, 2½ lbs. of petroleum oils, 2½ lbs. of cord material, 1 lb. of steel in the bead wire, and a few ounces of sulphur, chemical accelerators and anti-oxidants. Somehow it's all put together in a way that works.

TIRES

The tire is the chassis designer's first line of defense against the transmission of road jolts to the car's occupants. He wants low inflation pressures, flexible tread surfaces and supple sidewalls to soak up highway irregularities. For high speeds and good handling, however, a tire needs moderately high pressures, and a tread surface that stays firm and flat and as closely aligned as possible to the plane of the wheel, which means the sidewalls can't be too flexible. A tire, then, is subject to exactly the same design compromises as go into the car's chassis.

Car designers agree fully that the single most influential factor in a car's sheer grip on the road, its maximum speed in a corner, is its tire design. This is especially true when the road is wet and slippery. With today's wide-tread tires, the grooves in the pattern design have to be especially wide to allow water to escape, to prevent "Hydroplaning," to let the rubber get to the road.

THE ROLE OF SUSPENSION

It's pretty obvious that the suspension is another valuable tool in the chassis designer's bag of tricks for improving a car's ride. That's the reason cars were equipped with suspensions in the first place, inheriting them from horse-drawn carriages. But

1. The term chassis means a lot more than a frame, and the modern Detroit high-performance car generally has heavy-duty components throughout, rather than just a big engine in a standard "marshmallow" chassis.

2. The original Mustangs had this type of platform frame. While it relied on the body for strength, it was not a completely unit-body car.

3. Large stampings welded together made for a strong chassis for the Corvette, necessitated by lack of rigidity in the fiberglass body.

4. The first principle of chassis construction, employed dramatically in racing cars, is that triangular sections are the best compromise in weights vs. strength vs. space.

5. The modern rear-engined race car chassis considers aerodynamics and mechanical components first priority and driver space and comfort second.

6. German BMW uses a platform type chassis with a separate body but no separate frame. The running gear is attached to the sheetmetal "tub."

7. Whether race car or passenger car, when you're designing a unit-construction without a frame, the placement of engine and suspension mounts becomes critical for stress.

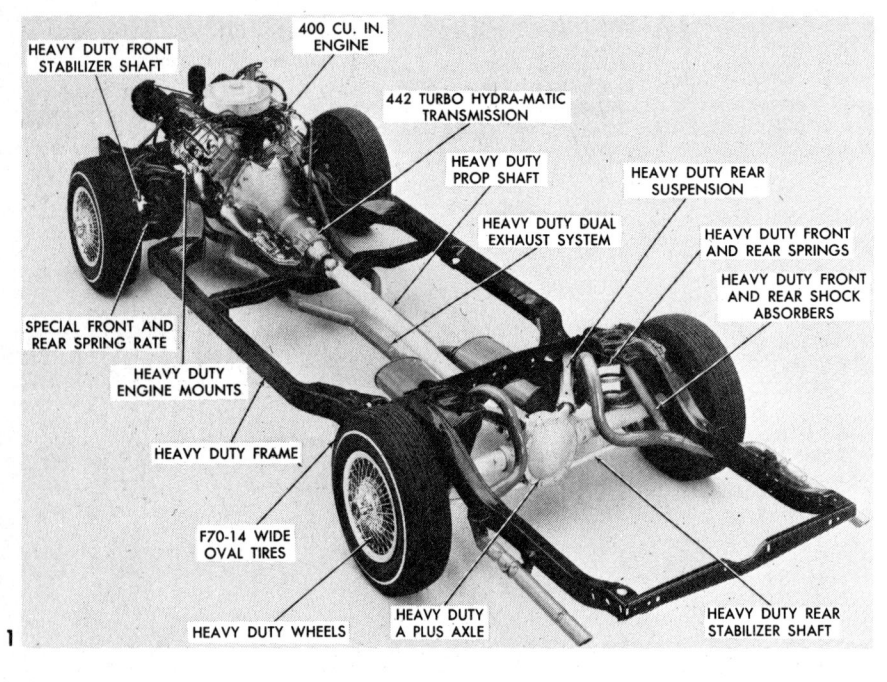

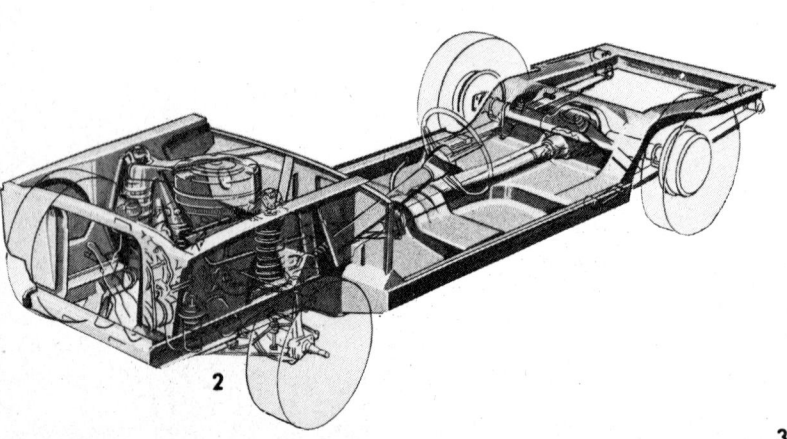

6/CHASSIS, SUSPENSION & BRAKES

now they're just as important in determining the quality and character of a car's handling. Look at it this way: As we said before, tire design mainly decides how well a car can grip the road. Suspension design, on the other hand, has more to do with the way the car feels as it enters and leaves corners, how stable it is on straights, and how driveable and safe it is at or near the absolute limit in a turn.

As you control a car with the steering wheel, you're changing the angles of the front wheels to try to get it to go in the desired direction. While you're doing that, the wheels are doing a little steering of their own. Depending on how the car is leaning or dipping on its springs, the suspension linkage is tilting and turning the wheels in subtle ways the designer has figured out, compensating for faults or enhancing virtues of his chassis. He may turn the rear axle slightly, in response to the way the rear springs are angled, or cause the front wheels to turn a little more or less than you intended them to. All these things—it's well worth noting—cannot be done with a car that has no suspension, or only a very primitive setup, between the wheels and the frame.

A few years ago, Buick stirred some excitement when it changed the classic front suspension layout. Trying to come up with a new layout to suit the needs of power-steered big cars, the engineers tried 10 different locations for the inner pivots of the wishbone arms. The one they finally chose has a low roll center—the point around which the geometry causes the front end of the car to pivot in roll—3 ins. below the ground surface instead of 2 ins. above.

Buick's layout gives positive camber as the wheel bounces upward, and goes more negative on the rebound. Theoretically this should reduce the front end's cornering grip, but Buick found the difference wasn't measurable, especially with the fine grip today's wide tires give anyway. And the new geometry stabilizes the car on bumps, slows the car's roll motions, and by actual measurement reduces side-to-side head tossing by 46% on a bumpy road! It looks like there's still room for improvement in one of your car's oldest chassis design features.

Front suspension on drag racers? Judging by the rudimentary systems used on rail dragsters, and by tests that have been run with no suspension at all, their super-long torsionally-flexible frames make real front springing irrelevant. This may not, however, remain true indefinitely. From their birth, the funny cars have posed suspension problems with their relatively short wheel-bases and stiff frames. Almost all of them have solid front axles guided by radius rods to the rear, with very simple steering linkages—so simple that some of them have to feed in some unwanted steering when the front end of the chassis rises and falls. For the funny cars, the independent front end has to be the way to go, but it has been tried in only a few cases.

At the rear of the American car it's

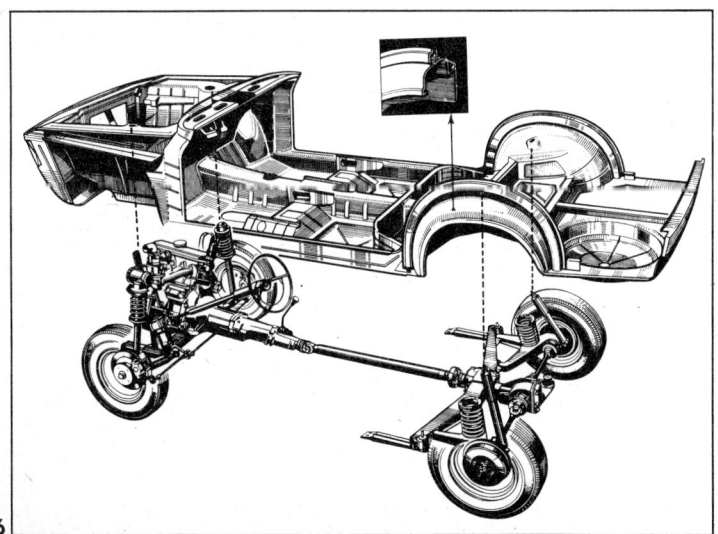

CHASSIS, SUSPENSION & BRAKES/7

Designing A Chassis

rare indeed to see anything other than a solid axle. With the demise of the Corvair, the Corvette remains the only U.S. production car with an independent rear suspension. In 1963 there were three independent rear suspension cars—the Corvette, Corvair, and Tempest. This may indicate that there isn't any real chance for widespread adoption of independent rears on American cars in the immediate future.

SPRINGS AND SHOCKS

Some time ago, designers realized that there's nothing special about a spring—as a spring—for a chassis, as long as it's designed so it doesn't start collapsing after it's been used for awhile. Torsion bars are still very much in the picture, on many imports, on Chrysler Corp. products, and on GM's front-drive models. At the rear, Ford's experimental Techna used special laminated-leaf torsion bars, a type used by VW for many years and tried, then rejected, by Oldsmobile for the Toronado. Torsion bars are used when other types would be in the way, as in a front-drive layout, when the designer wants to feed the spring reaction forces into some remote part of the frame, when they work out well with a certain suspension design, as at the front ends of rail dragsters, and when the factory making the car has a lot of torsion bar production capacity.

Coil springs today are far and away the most popular choice of builders for passenger cars, and for racing cars too. They're easy to make, easy to mount and adjust, and free of any of the internal friction effects of conventional multi-leaf springs. By variable-pitch winding, coils can be given a progressive-rate effect, which can help keep a car's ride height level in spite of varying loads.

Torsion bars, set up so they run across the chassis, and attached to the suspension with trailing links, have been showing up on many circle track cars the last few years. Some of these same cars have crossbars in the rear, too, with a leading link setup. Bars have one big advantage over coil and leaf springs, in that height adjustments can be made just by turning a screw. The same adjustment on a coil or leaf spring involves a considerable amount of work with spacers or new springs. There is no doubt that torsion bars work well. The main reason they have not appeared on more American cars is probably the cost of the changeover.

Spring and shock stiffness depend, first of all, on the weight of the car they support and the distribution of that weight. The curb weight alone is not as influential as the weight variation between a full and empty car. The effect of this variation is to make it a lot easier to design a good-handling 2-seater sports car than a good-handling 6-seater sedan with room for 300 pounds of luggage overhung behind the rear wheels. Springs that give a good ride with a lightly-loaded car are far too soft to handle bumpy roads when there is a full load.

Solutions to the load-compensation problem are well in hand. Variable-rate springs help. Funny cars, of course, practice a different kind of compensation. Instead of changing the spring rates they can move the engine back and forth to suit different traction conditions. Maybe Detroit just hasn't thought of that solution as yet!

A WORD ON WEIGHT

Where does a car designer want to put most of the weight? He wants it as low as he can get it, to start with. A low center of gravity directly im-

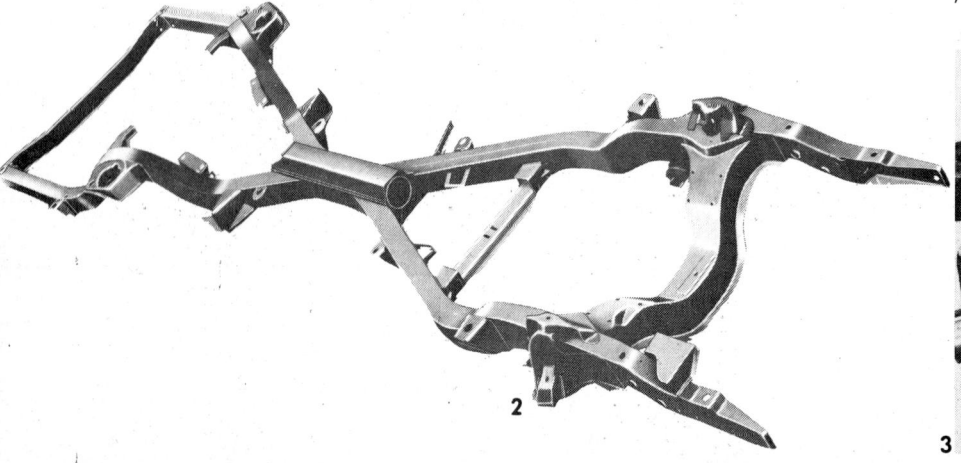

8/CHASSIS, SUSPENSION & BRAKES

Diagram labels (Dodge cutaway)

- **DASH PANEL**
  - Cowl Side Silencer
  - Plenum Silencer
  - Dash Liner
  - Wiring Disconnect Seal
- **DOOR AND WINDOW SEALS**
- **ROOF SILENCERS**
- **REAR SHELF PAD**
- **REAR DEFOGGER SEAL**
- **TRUNK COMPARTMENT LINER**
- **C-PILLAR BARRIER WITH SEALED PERIMETER**
- **HOOD PADS** (Optional)
- **REAR QUARTER PANEL DEADENER**
- **ENGINE**
  - Vibration Damper
  - Intake Manifold Pad
  - Air Cleaner
  - Spool Type Engine Mounts
- **DOOR**
  - Panel Deadener
  - Perimeter Seal
- **POWER PLANT BENDING DAMPER**
- **FLOOR PAN**
  - Undercoating (Optional)
  - Wheelhouse Silencer Pads
  - Jute Pads
  - Mastic And Pad
- **STEERING COLUMN**
  - Flexible Coupling
  - Seals
  - Support Plate Silencer
- **VIBRATION DAMPER**
- **SILENCER PAD**
- **ISOLATED FRONT SUSPENSION**
- **ISO-CLAMP REAR SPRINGS**
- **PROPELLER SHAFT VIBRATION ABSORBER**
- **RUBBER SUSPENSION BUSHINGS**
  - Struts
  - Sway Bar
  - Upper Control Arm
  - Lower Control Arm
  - Shock Absorbers
  - Rear Spring Front Eye
  - Rear Spring Shackle
  - Torsion Bar Rear Anchor
- **EXHAUST SYSTEM**
  - Laminated Exhaust Pipe
  - Modified Muffler Interior
  - Hangers
  - Resonator

---

1. Unit-construction in race cars is usually referred to as monocoque, in which the body or outer skin is actually a structural part of the chassis. The type shown here is a monocoque, but a separate fiberglass body is used for aerodynamics.

2. The rigid, X-type frame on the '58 Chevy allowed a low floorpan for easy passenger entry and room, but afforded little protection for an impact from the sides.

3. Today's chassis are comprised of welded sections made from complex stampings. Design parameters must now include "controlled crushability" to meet federal crash standards.

4. A monocoque has definite advantages in strength and light weight, but there are sometimes problems in accesibility and vulnerability.

5. The unique hull of the monocoque Ford GT's of a few years back used "sandwich" panels of aluminum with expanded honecomb metal inside for high strength with low weight.

6. Monocoques are not often seen in drag racing because of expense, but Mickey Thompson's 1969 car was a beautiful experiment in aluminum.

7. As if chassis designers didn't have enough to think about, today's buyers want luxury-car quiet and smoothness, too. Rubber insulators are being used increasingly as part of this "silent treatment."

---

proves the cornering of any car and reduces forward weight transfer on braking. This rule is made to be broken in the stock car drag racing classes, where more weight transfer to the rear wheels is obtained by *raising* the center of gravity as much as possible.

Then, it's great to have at least a reasonable amount of weight on the driving wheels. The cars with the best reputations for traction on poor surfaces, and for fine performance on the race track, have well over half their weight on the driving wheels. With a conventional American sedan, it's not easy to shift weight rearward. Ford gave it a try with the Techna, which has aluminum radiators, and all the major accessories at the rear of the engine, instead of the front. They were very pleased to get 45% of the car's weight on the rear axle.

With a rear engine, of course, the job gets done right. Competition cars can have as much as 80% of their weight on the rear wheels, even more with rearward transfer under acceleration. Front drive also provides excellent traction and stability for the highway, but the fact that weight is shifted *away* from the drive wheels under power is a fatal racing disadvantage. Why not combine both and have drive for all four wheels? A year or two ago, 4-wheel drive showed the promise of great things in Indy and road race cars, but has been legislated out of contention in most racing associations, like the turbine. It was tried at Indy with the turbine car, and Lotus tried it in the Formula cars. As more is learned about it, however, 4-wheel drive may come back on the racing scene. Four-wheel drive has made remarkable strides in public acceptance with the new, but not completely proven, "full-time" 4-wheel drive, which shows that the engineers are working on the concept and a lot of interesting new changes are taking place. But the chances of seeing 4-wheel drive on any passenger car are slim. Such radical innovations are too costly for most car owners. But there's always a chance that some new and interesting design will sneak off the end of an assembly line. Who ever would have thought that Cadillac and Olds would produce thousands of front-wheel-drive cars?

And maybe the safety and anti-pollution efforts of the government are not so restrictive after all. If engines are going to put out fewer horses, then we might end up with lighter, more exciting chassis. At least, we can hope that's what happens.

CHASSIS, SUSPENSION & BRAKES/9

The Frame

The real "backbone" of your car, the frame is the basis of everything else your car embodies.

In its simplest form, a frame can be comprised of two parallel rails that run the length of the car, with the suspension, mechanical components, and body bolted to them or to crossmembers running between them. This type was used for many years with great success, since it was both easy and inexpensive to manufacture. In many cases the completed chassis could be driven without the body attached since the body was a separate structure that was merely bolted on top of the frame rails.

By the '30's cars had become somewhat more sophisticated, with styling and speed becoming major sales features. It was soon realized that the additional strength required for a good-handling chassis frame carried with it the burden of increased weight—which in turn required a more powerful engine to pull it around.

The biggest problem was that of frame flexing due to the lack of torsional stiffness in the channel section rails that were used. On uneven surfaces, the out-of-line condition caused by the twisting chassis would drastically affect the stability of the vehicle. And if, for instance, one wheel was parked on a curb while the others were in the street, the doors would not open. A solution to this was the boxing of the frame rails—a move that would actually increase the strength approximately 500 times. Unfortunately this required fabricating each rail and therefore increasing the cost over the previous stamped type. Eventually, GM developed a seamless box section rail that made it more economical but, initially, they were welded together from two separate pieces.

All was well in the frame department for many years and then, as the trend went to lower, longer cars, new problems developed. If the body were set atop the frame, the lower profile would severely limit head room and seating position. The body had to be closer to the ground but the frame rails could not intrude into the passenger compartment. The only solution was a "swayback" type of frame that dipped down close to the ground in the area to be occupied, was pinched in at the front to clear the front wheels, and kicked up in the back to pass over the rear axle. With the frame rails now twisting and turning in order to clear all the running gear components and satisfy the space requirements, the problems encountered with the old-fashioned straight rails seemed minor by comparison. How could adequate strength be built into such a serpentine-like structure without the added penalty of excessive weight?

Many manufacturers decided they would rather switch than fight, and tooled up for unit construction. In the late '40's, the Nash and Hudson people had committed themselves to this type of design, as had many European small car manufacturers. Chrysler and DeSoto had tried it in the mid-'30's and dropped the idea. Lincoln Zephyrs of the same period had also been frameless, but discontinued the technique after several years of production.

Unit-body construction is, in its simplest form, a body to which the suspension and powertrain is attached. It does away with the need for a frame. There are several variations, but in general the body is comprised of a series of stamped panels that are welded together to form one unit. Usually, there is a platform-type floor pan that runs from the rearmost part of the car to a point at the approximate location of the firewall. Forward of the firewall, fabricated struts pass on either side of the engine to form a mount for both the engine and the front suspension. The platform stamping includes small ribs to aid structural rigidity and break up

10/CHASSIS, SUSPENSION & BRAKES

resonant frequencies that would transform the unit into a big bass drum.

The platform by itself is still prone to twist, since it is fabricated of relatively lightweight material. The strength necessary in the completed unit will come from various sections to be welded to it. A dashboard-firewall section, that may also include portions of the front wheel wells, adds considerably to the torsional stiffness of the platform. In many cases this section will also tie into the engine/suspension struts for added rigidity. As the remaining panels are welded into place, they will, one by one, eliminate local weaknesses and add to the total rigidity of the unit. In essence, the unit-construction car is a bridge; the floorpan represents the roadway, and the body panels form the superstructure—each one doing

1. While construction of channel or box frames usually requires only arc welding in simple configurations, a unit-body chassis means thousands of strategic electric spot welds.

2. Up until the early 1930's, most cars had simple straight-rail frames of open channel with straight cross-members. These were subject to flex but adequate for the powerplants and road speeds of the day.

3. This cutaway of a '66 Fairlane is typical of unit-type construction. Note the number of places the thin sheetmetal is formed into pockets, ribs and channels, for strength.

4. Factory engineers use plastic prototypes of chassis to sort out structural and handling problems. This Chevrolet engineer is using a strobe light to check frame dynamics.

5. Cross-sectional views around this '58 Chevy central-X or "wasp-waist" frame show how modern frames are made of folded, welded sheetmetal.

6. The frames on many newer cars are reduced to just subframes, used up front to attach suspension and the engine, but Olds Toronado returned to a full frame in 1971 to regain a quieter, more controlled ride.

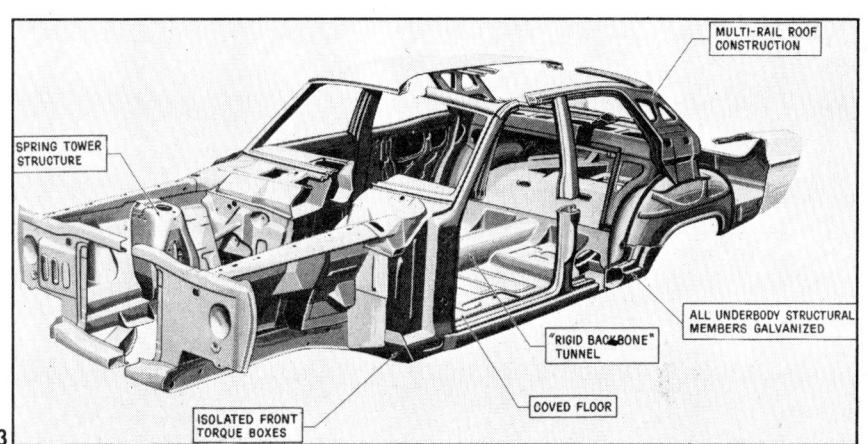

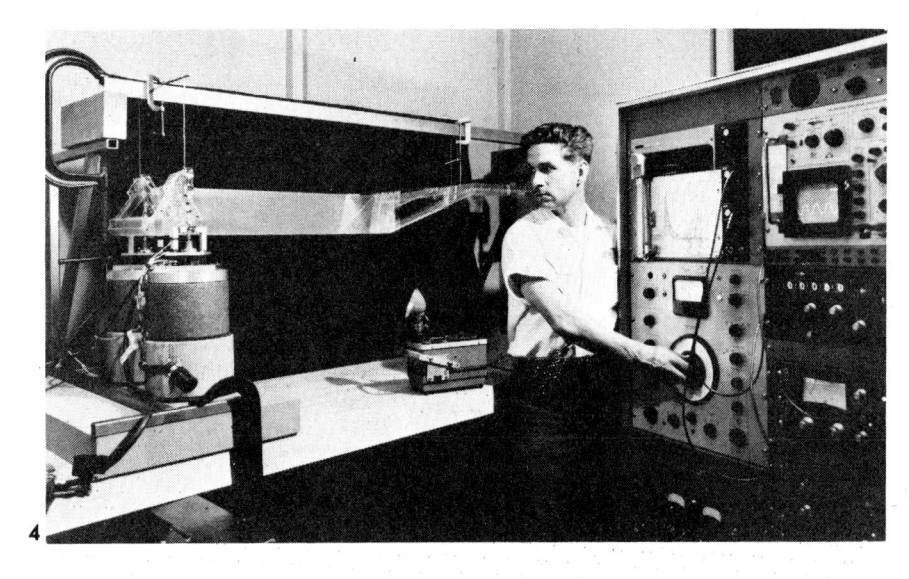

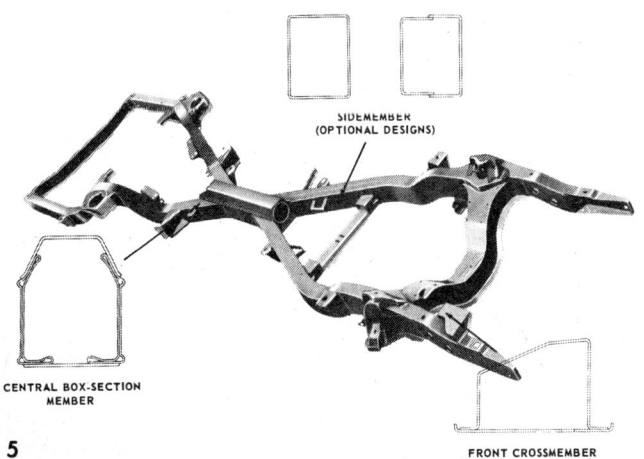

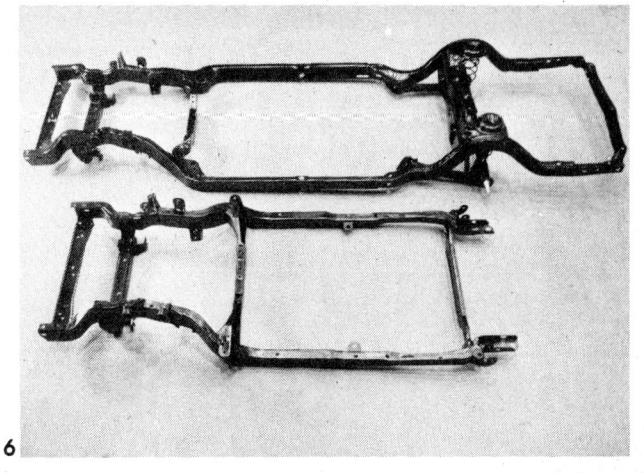

CHASSIS, SUSPENSION & BRAKES/11

The Frame

a specific job, and combining to form a rigid twist-free structure.

It was felt by many that the unit-construction method offered more than just the elimination of the frame proper. Potentially, the ride could be improved because of the increased torsional rigidity; body noise and rattles could be eliminated because of the all-welded construction; lower floors and wider bodies could be made much more easily; and greater safety to the passengers was thought to be a side benefit that would help sales.

All of these advantages looked good on paper so the major manufacturers committed themselves to the unit-construction concept in the mid-'50's. But they had all either overlooked or minimized the importance of several critical areas that would eventually force some of them to return to the separate frame for the large majority of their models.

NOT "THAT" EASY

It soon became apparent that the lower weight expected from this type of construction was not to be realized. In virtually every case where a manufacturer changed a specific model from a separate frame to unit-construction, the completed vehicle was heavier. The theoretical advantage of being able to use lighter material was offset by the need for additional bracing, webbing and gussets, especially in convertibles. In addition, increased road noise required the use of more sound-deadening material—the unit-construction Lincolns and Thunderbirds used 350 pounds of the stuff.

Major style changes were more difficult—and more expensive—since the entire unit structure had to be modified. With the separate frame the stylists could redesign the major body components and bolt them to an existing chassis assembly. With the trend in the late '50's being toward lower and longer cars, the problem of being married to a particular design that was too high for next year's needs was cause for great concern. Even minor changes in overall dimensions required major changes to the basic structure. It was just too expensive to be practical.

One of the biggest problems had already presented itself in the lack of interchangeability among different models in the same line. A 2-door sedan and a 4-door sedan required an entirely separate unit-body. With a conventional frame the center section could be lengthened or shortened to suit, but the unit-construction technique required additional tooling, along with that old bugaboo of mass

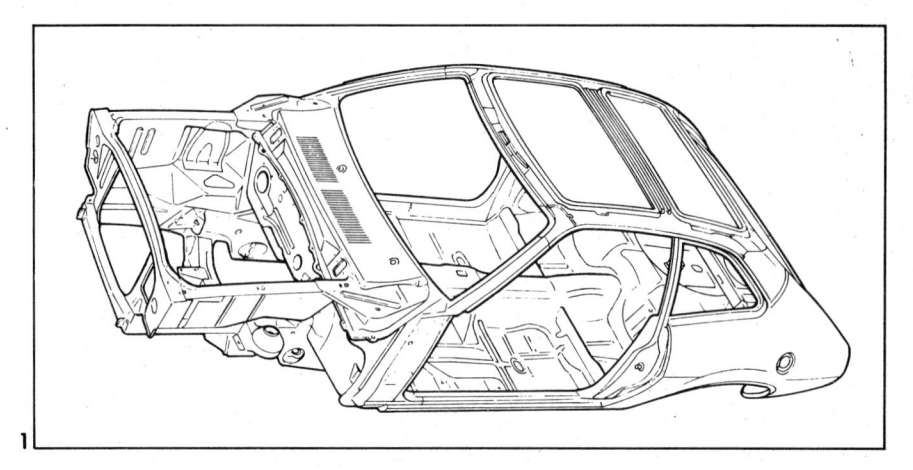

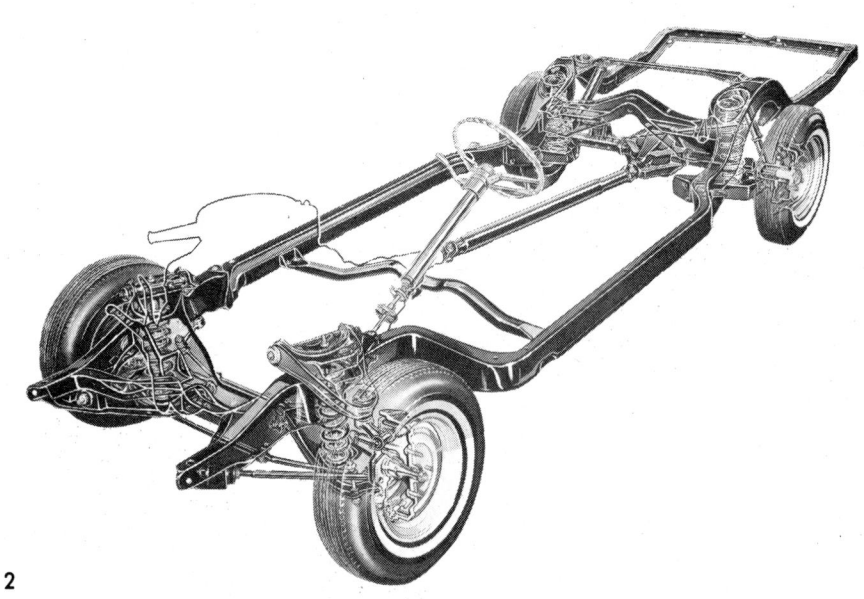

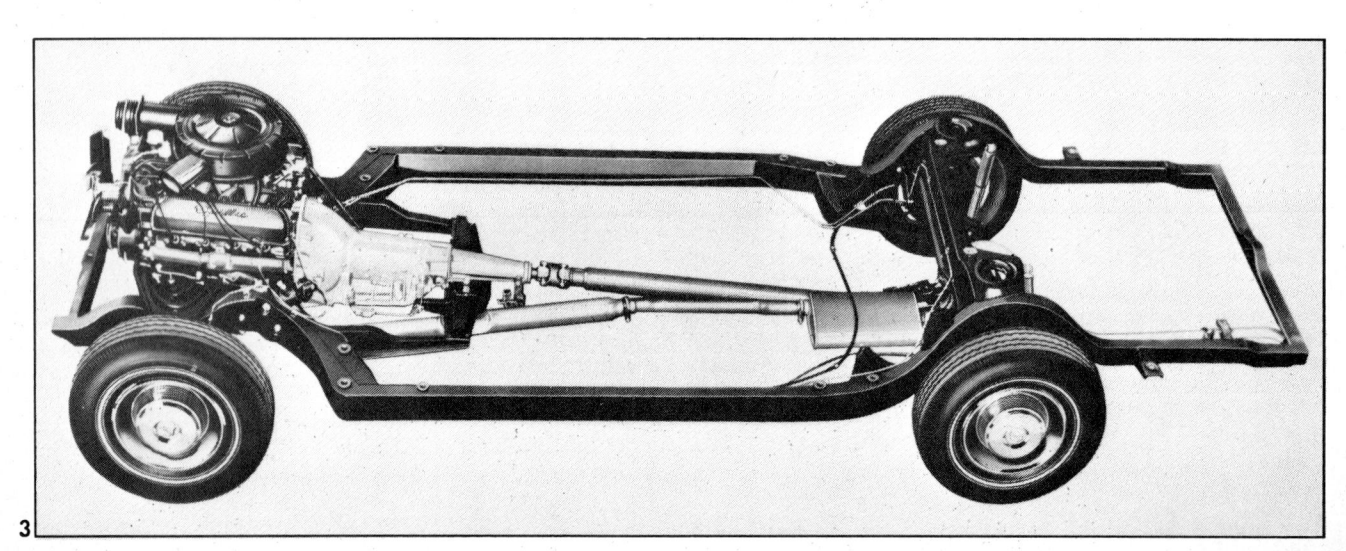

12/CHASSIS, SUSPENSION & BRAKES

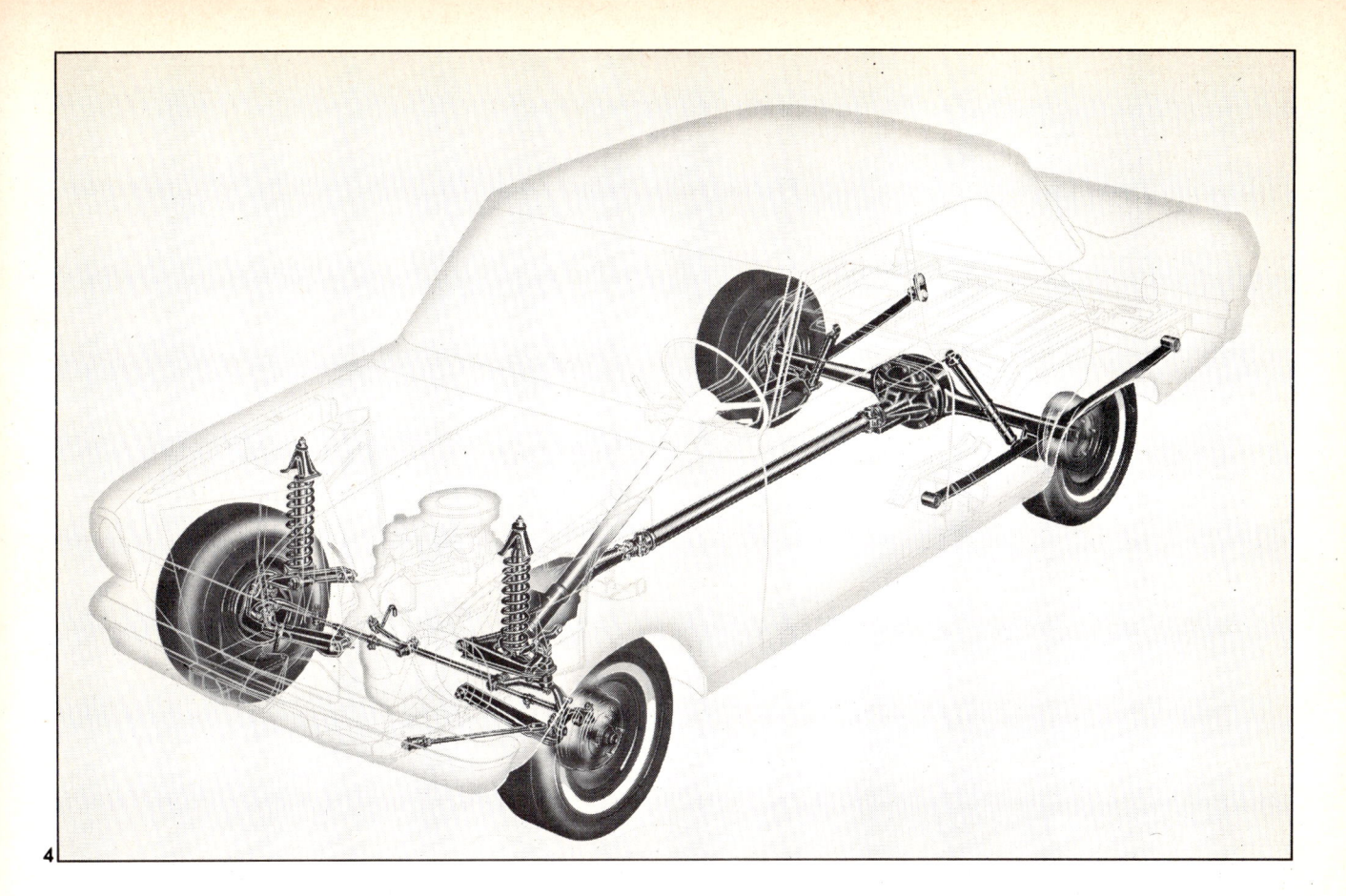

1. Ford Pinto illustrates current type of unit-body construction with "halo" roof for rollover protection.

2. Today's full-size cars use full frames pinched in at the front and rear wheels, and made of formed and welded box sections.

3. When Cadillac went to a perimeter frame in 1965 (like other automakers), it was their first new frame in nine years, with new engine mounting and wider tread. Note how transmission crossmember mounts up front rather than to the sides of the frame.

4. Dependability and freedom from rattles are some of unit-construction advantages. The Chevy II (now Nova) was so built as far back as 1962.

5. Changes that were new in this '69 Mercury frame included mounting the tranmission crossmember up front; an extra crossmember out in front for front bumper support, and an extension behind rear axle for body and rear bumper support.

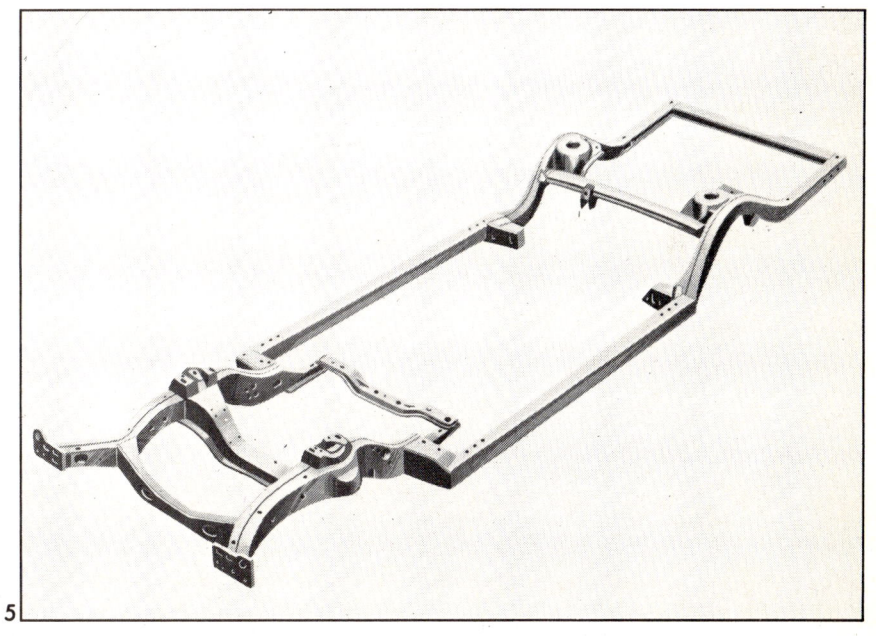

production—additional expense

Although the anticipated freedom from body rattles for longer periods was realized, under-body corrosion was more of a problem due to the thin sheetmetal. This was taken care of by dipping the body in special primer, but was another item that upped the cost. As good an idea as unit construction is on paper it is a long way from being the ideal production situation from Detroit's point of view.

This does not mean that unit construction is not as good as a separate frame and body combination. Quite the contrary, the unit-construction idea is most practical in particular vehicle applications. It is generally agreed in Detroit, by both word and action, that unit construction is the way to go with vehicles having a wheelbase of approximately 110 ins. or less. Many of the compacts of the last five years bear out this contention, as do imports like the Volkswagen.

However impractical the unit-construction technique proved itself to be for the larger model cars, the old problem of making a conventional frame strong while keeping the roofline low had not been solved. What's more, since the time of going to unit construction the trend was to even lower cars than had caused the switch in the first place. The only answer was an entirely new concept—one that would incorporate the best features of not only the separate frame but also unit construction.

The problem was still the same. In order to satisfy the trend to rooflines

CHASSIS, SUSPENSION & BRAKES/13

The Frame

that were becoming lower at the rate of ½-in. per year, the floor of the passenger compartment had to be closer to the ground than the conventional rail frame would allow; but separate frames seemed to be a necessity. In 1957, Cadillac made a breakthrough with a frame they dubbed a "cruciform" construction. It was a simple X with a center section that could be lengthened to increase the wheelbase in the longer models. There were no side rails at all, and the floor in the rear seat area could be lowered below the frame rails by providing footwells on either side of the cross point of the X. The front seat floor could not be lowered quite as much as the rear, but could still provide improvements over previous designs. The frame was extremely rigid and served to lower the silhouette while retaining the ability to enter the passenger compartment easily.

Over at Ford some good ideas had come out of their brainstorming sessions. By 1958, they were ready with the first of their "coke bottle" frames. Termed a perimeter frame, it took the form of a coke bottle by going around the outside of the passenger compartment and having only a single crossmember to support the underside of the transmission. With the area between the rails nothing but empty space, the passenger compartment floor could be lowered as much as styling dictated. The rails had to pinch in at the front to provide clearance for the front wheels, and therefore limited front leg room somewhat, but this was part of the price to be paid for the low look. That the occupants had to step over the frame rail to get in was of little concern since safety was a big thing at the time and the ad boys touted it as providing added protection in the event of a side collision—which in fact it did.

For the next couple of years there were no big advancements, although there were innumerable variations on the two concepts. It was 1961 when the big change came. A new concept that was to revolutionize the art of building frames was put into production by GM.

Called a torque box perimeter frame, it reversed all previous thinking on frame design. For years the engineers had strived to provide a frame that was as rigid as possible, feeling that any twisting would make the car unstable. GM engineers felt that controlled flexibility could still provide adequate stability and at the same time absorb some of the rougher road shocks.

Comprised basically of a perimeter frame running around the passenger compartment, with separate subframes to attach the suspension components, the innovation is the method used to weld the frame sections together. Fabricated sheetmetal boxes that have "built-in" flexibility attach the rails under the four corners of the passenger compartment and absorb shocks from the suspension system. The body attaches directly to the main perimeter frame, forming a rigid structure necessary in that area to assure that the doors always open and the glass stays in place under rough conditions. For years it was not uncommon for some vehicles to continually crack windshields when the vehicle was driven over rough roads. The body unit must remain as rigid as possible at all times if this is to be prevented, but the remainder of the frame structure can be relatively flexible through the use of torque box construction.

Ford made a slightly different attack on the problem by incorporating torque boxes in the Fairlane unit body in 1964. Not a true unit body since it had a light perimeter-type frame that was welded to the underside of the unit body for the necessary rigidity, the torque boxes were nevertheless a part of an all-welded unit that, when completed, did not have a separate frame. They combined the theoretical benefits of both types of construction and had one of the best riding and quietest of the unit-body types. The only price they paid was some added weight.

As in so many other fields, the search for the ideal has brought about several acceptable methods. If there was a best way, everyone would be using it. As it is, the methods will vary with the intended use—and ultimate cost—of the vehicle in question. The separate frame versus unit-construction controversy will continue, and innovations will be incorporated in the existing designs, all to the increased comfort and added safety of the car owner.

RACING

Designs for racing share some of the problems of the mass-production frames for passenger cars, but fortunately for the racing frame designer, the majority of the compromises are eliminated. Foremost, a racing frame must have torsional rigidity and be as

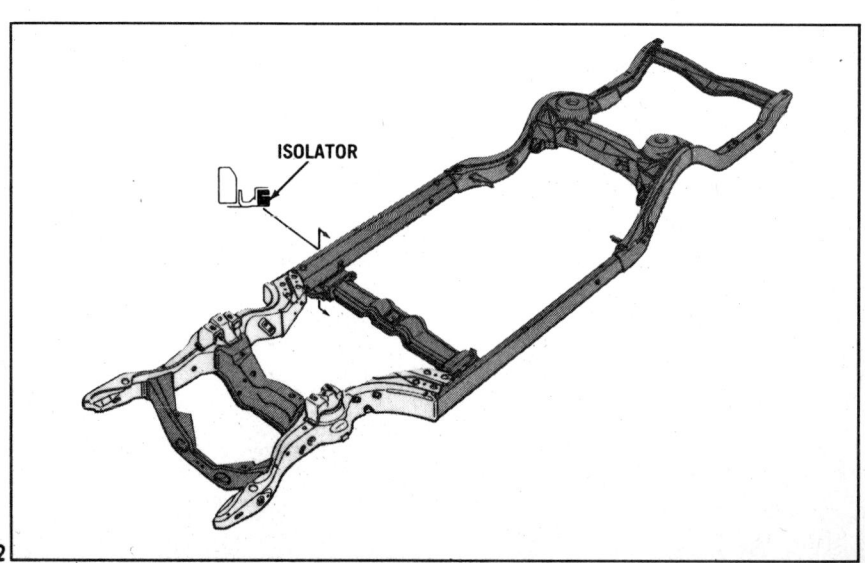

14/CHASSIS, SUSPENSION & BRAKES

light as possible. All else is secondary. Ease of manufacture, component accessibility and driver comfort must all be considered, but strength and light weight will win out in the event of any conflict. Several Italian cars of not so long ago were of such a design that frame tubes had to be cut out every time the engine was removed and welded back in after the engine was reinstalled. Not a good method for mass-production vehicles.

Frames comprised of a series of tubes have been around for a long time. Early efforts were generally with two parallel tubes that ran the length of the car with the engine/transmission and the driver sitting between the tubes and the suspension attached on the outside at each end. Due to its limited torsional rigidity and excessive weight it gave way in later years—first to a multi-tube, and then a space frame.

Multi-tube frames were essentially four main tubes with diagonal bracing between them. They were an improvement over the 2-tube versions in rigidity but sacrificed much of the advantage by increasing the vehicle's total weight. They were, after all, two parallel tube frames, one on top of the other.

The space frame was a concept that was new only to the automobile industry. Aircraft manufacturers had long relied on multi-tube construction that placed each tube under either tension or compression. Bending loads were isolated from the tubes by placing other tubes in a different plane that would accept the loads under the same conditions. Also important was that space was encompassed not by *squares* of tubing but

1. This 1973 Olds Cutlass frame is a good example of how complex frame shapes have become since "controlled crush" and side-impact protection became necessary criteria.

2. Siderails on the '73 Thunderbird frame are separate pieces slipped inside the front and rear sections and welded in place. This permits a strong siderail without the rest of the frame becoming too heavy.

3. Car buyers always demand more and more quiet from a car, so they can better enjoy their stereo radio, and engineers keep finding more ways to use rubber isolation bushings, especially on cars with subframes up front, which tend to be noisier.

4. This '50's Porsche racer frame is typical of a lightweight "space" frame with triangulated sections for rigidity without a lot of weight.

5. Drag racing chassis only have to take stresses of straight-line races, so they're not as "spacey" as a road racer, but this funny car chassis takes 1500 hp, weighs only 90 lbs.!

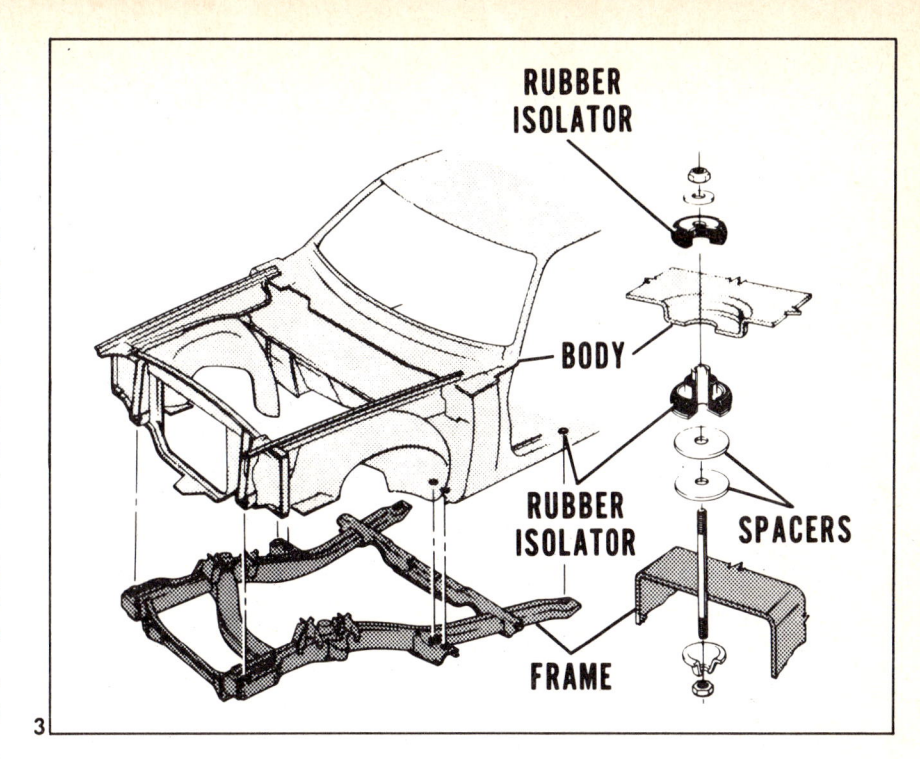

CHASSIS, SUSPENSION & BRAKES/15

The Frame

triangles, which offered much greater strength.

In single-seater racing cars it is an easier job to provide a strong, lightweight tubular space frame than it is in the more sophisticated 2-seater sports car. Regulations for sports cars require that there be operable doors as well as seating accommodations for a passenger. In addition, there are necessary components such as electrical equipment and spare wheels that further complicate the arrangement of the tubes. In the mid-'50's the complication reached an all-time high when the Maserati "birdcage" sports-racing car was built. The frame was constructed of literally hundreds of short, small diameter tubes, each supposedly having a vital job in the total rigidity of the frame. It was successful, but marked the end of an era that was soon to be replaced by a technique that brought with it a new automotive term—monocoque.

Monocoque construction was also borrowed from the aircraft industry, which through the years has probably made as many contributions to auto safety as to flying safety. Essentially, the technique is to distribute the loads imposed by the suspension throughout the entire body of the car. Each section or panel functions much as the tubes do in a space frame, in that they are placed in either a tension or compression condition and assist each other where necessary. The only frame structure that exists is in the form of connecting subframes to which vital components such as engine or suspension are attached.

The monocoque type of construction opens the door to the use of exotic materials. Steel, aluminum, magnesium, titanium, and fiberglass are all candidates since the strength of the unit comes more from the shape than from the materials used. The individual panels can be welded, riveted or, as in the case of fiberglass, bonded together. The monocoque also opened up new fields of automotive engineering which brought aircraft designers and chemists into the picture:

In accomplishing a functional monocoque frame, the vital areas can be formed in a box shape that will double as storage area for gasoline containers. What would otherwise be unusable space then contributes to the low overall weight and dimensions of the modern racing car. Look at the size difference between today's rear-engine cars and their front-engine predecessors.

In operation there are both advantages and disadvantages with this type of design, other than the obvious advantage of light weight and high torsional rigidity. In the event of an accident they are considerably stronger in and around the cockpit area, since the entire structure is strong. As stated, tubular frames concentrate their strength in areas that will be subjected to twisting forces from the tires. Any collision will quite likely exert forces in areas that are weak and prone to bend, since no loads were anticipated in any directions other than from the suspension. The monocoque is like an egg—strong in practically any plane and therefore less prone to collapse during a high-speed collision.

On the other hand, any damage done to the "tub," the jargon used for the main monocoque section, will usually require replacing it with a new one. This one fact could be enough to keep the true monocoque out of the passenger car field for a long time to come, although regular unit-construction cars aren't particularly easy to repair either.

Drag racing has developed its own technology over the years and, although it may appear rather basic at first, it gets technically interesting as more is learned. In the beginning, it was a simple matter of bolting a big engine into as light a frame as could be found, fitting some larger tires, and "gassing" it. But these days things are a lot more sophisticated. Special frames of strong, lightweight material support engines that develop over 1500 hp and exceed 230 mph in the ¼-mile.

For the all-out drag racing car,

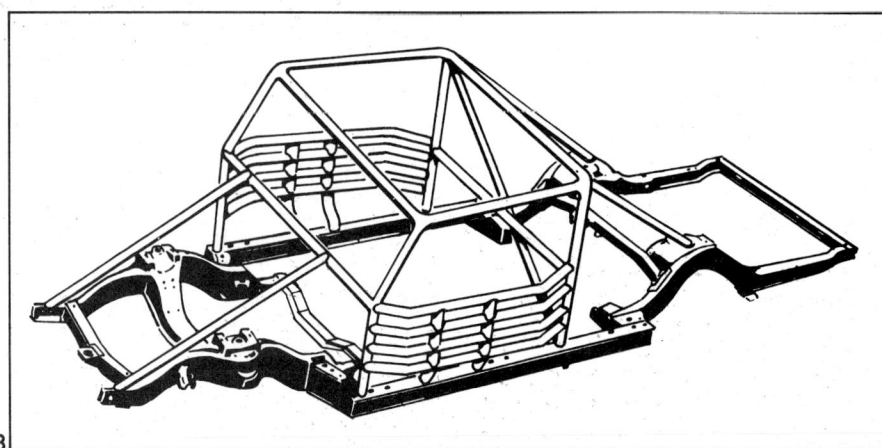

16/CHASSIS, SUSPENSION & BRAKES

evolution has brought forth a pretty standardized "slingshot" configuration. For many years this design had the engine just ahead of the rear axle and the driver actually behind the rear axle, but master innovator Don Garlits changed everything a few years back when he proved that the "rear-engined" configuration was the way to go. With the spindly front end and motorcycle-type wheels reaching far out in front, the cars look rather awkward, but in fact aren't, as is evidenced by the small number of accidents with these cars. It's also a tribute to dragster chassis design that when a rare accident occurs, it is even rarer that the driver is injured. While the main rails may look flimsy, the cage around the driver must pass stringent safety specs.

The frame that holds the working parts together is the result of a compromise between traction and stability. The engine is positioned far back in the frame to place a large portion of the vehicle weight over the driving wheels. However, if the weight is too far back, the front wheels will rise off the ground when the car accelerates. When this happens, steering control is lost and the driver will waste precious time by letting off the throttle momentarily. This is one of the reasons Garlits went to the so-called "rear-engined" design. Actually the engine is in just about the same location as the traditional slingshot, but now the driver is in *front* of the engine. This puts a little more precious weight on the front wheels, giving the driver much greater visibility and increased protection from fire.

Long wheelbases, often longer than 200 ins., are an attempt to overcome

1. Pro Stock drag cars are usually built from small unit-body cars, and for strength and driver safety must be gutted and fitted like this Vega with a new chassis/cage welded in from the inside and tied into the body and front end structure.

2. Underside of Grumpy Jenkins' Pro Stock Vega shows how much the car is supplemented by tubing supports.

3. Even full-size cars need bracing for racing like NASCAR, but more for driver protection at 200 mph than for actual frame stiffening.

4. Grand National NASCAR machines are generally built almost from the ground up, bracing in some places and saving weight in others. This is the Bud Moore shop in South Carolina.

5. One place where some stiffening is desired is on the front end, to tie the roll cage into the frame and support suspension modifications.

6. Race car chassis building is a fascinating challenge, trying to get lightness, strength and all your components, including driver, into the least possible space.

CHASSIS, SUSPENSION & BRAKES/1

The Frame

the tendency of the front wheels coming off the ground, while still placing enough weight over the rear wheels for traction. Since the whole car is actually pivoting on the rear axle under heavy acceleration, the front wheel assembly acts as a weight on the end of a lever. The longer the lever (the wheelbase), the more tendency for the front wheels to stay on the ground where they can steer the car.

Fortunately for the drag frame builder, his creations do not have to withstand the many sideloads that are the cause of frame twist in cars that must turn corners and travel over bumpy roads. It will, except on rare occasions, be loaded in only one direction. Therefore the frame need only withstand the tendency of the rear axle to want to turn with the wheels, and at the same time keep everything in alignment so that the car will go straight. An oversimplification perhaps, but these are the main considerations when a dragster frame is designed and built.

In the past there has been a lot of controversy over which of two basic dragster frame designs to use. Both types are at a casual glance the same, but one is intentionally flexible while the other is as rigid as possible. The arguments for both are convincing, but the performance differential is negligible. Both work well.

Proponents of the "flexi" types feel that the thin line between maximum traction and wheelstands can be broadened if the mass of the engine is allowed to move independently of the front wheels. To accomplish this they "build in" flexibility by either mounting the engine on pads that merely rest on the frame rails or leaving out otherwise vital connecting tubes so that the frame will bow in the middle as the car accelerates. Hopefully, the tendency of the engine to turn around the axle is satisfied but the flexibility keeps the front wheels on the ground. This compromise is said to increase traction, yet retain control.

Those of the old school prefer to build their frames as rigidly as possible and concentrate their efforts on putting the horsepower to the ground. Take your pick; they both go fast.

The subject of frames is one that has filled countless books, so we do not expect to cover it to everyone's satisfaction in one chapter of a "basic" book. Rather we have attempted to make the reader aware of what exists in this facet of the vast, complicated world of auto engineering.

18/CHASSIS, SUSPENSION & BRAKES

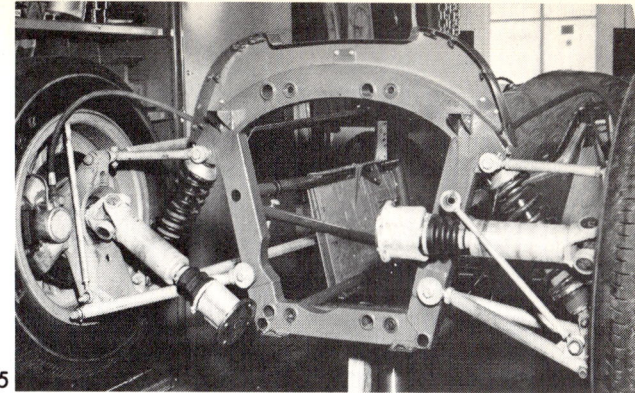

1. Monocoque frame designs like this Mickey Thompson funny car from 1969 are built like boat hulls, with the outer skin stressed as a vital part of the chassis. This can offer very light weight with stiffness.

2. With this rear-engined dragster as with any tube-frame race car, enclosing space in triangular areas is the key to necessary rigidity.

3. No matter how light you want a race car, the engine and suspension attachment points have to be extra strong, such as at the rear end on this Pro Stock Duster.

4. It's important with a monocoque frame to spread the load of engine or suspension attachment over a wide area, such as with the aluminum plate on this trans/rear end.

5. When a frame is built of light tubing, stronger bulkheads usually have to be provided to support the component attachment loads.

6. Both the tension and compression loads have to be accounted for in designing a frame. Note the tubing braces on these coil/shock mounts to take some load off the circular frame hoop and to prevent bending.

7. Sometimes it's desirable for ease of maintenance or repair on complex frames to have some sections removable, although this must be done right in order not to reduce the strength or safety of the car.

8. Drag racers often go overboard in search of a lighter frame, and this "Swiss cheese" frame is a good example of a bad practice.

CHASSIS, SUSPENSION & BRAKES/19

Energy Absorbing Bumpers

Everybody bows to legislative demands, but each car maker arrives at a solution in a different way.

The various "impact" bumpers used on today's crop of cars are the result of much hue and cry a few years back by bureaucrats who began demanding safety in almost everything we see, do and touch. When some type of bump absorption was demanded of Detroit by passage of the Federal Motor Vehicle Safety Standards, our car makers took their usual divergent paths to develop systems that would allow up to a 5 mph frontal "crash" (2½ mph in the rear) without damage to certain vulnerable body and chassis components. Although much of the blame for these requirements was laid on the insurance companies, Safety Standard MVSS-215 says nothing about sheet metal damage, which is what we all tend to think of occurring after a 5 mph bump. In fact, most bumps of this magnitude do visible body damage which can be repaired at or below the deductible clause amount stipulated in the average car owner's policy. In other words, if damage to the extent of $75 worth of body repair occurred, and a person's deductible was $100, then he'd never file an insurance claim and the insurance company would never hear of the claim.

What the do-gooders were after was a method of eliminating damage, in accidents of up to 5 mph in a head-on situation against an immovable barrier, to: "Lamps and reflective devices; hood, trunk and doors; fuel and cooling systems, and the exhaust system." Actually, they're trying to save us from ourselves by eliminating, or at least reducing, the possible consequences of driving the car after a minor collision, with a leaky exhaust pipe, a cracked fuel fitting, or headlights that point all kittywampus instead of where they're supposed to.

Although MVSS-215 specifies what musn't be knocked askew in a slow 5 mph bumper-bender, it leaves the design and hardware of the system entirely up to the car manufacturers. And that in the long run naturally makes things more complicated than they really need to be. Chevrolet, for example, uses two entirely different systems in its current lineup of cars, rather than the easier expedient of having one method common to all models.

When a car collides with a stationary object, the kinetic energy in the form of the car's forward motion must somehow be absorbed or converted into some other form of energy which is harmless. If a bumper were attached to a car frame by coil springs, the springs would absorb the "collision" energy as they were compressed. But since the springs must

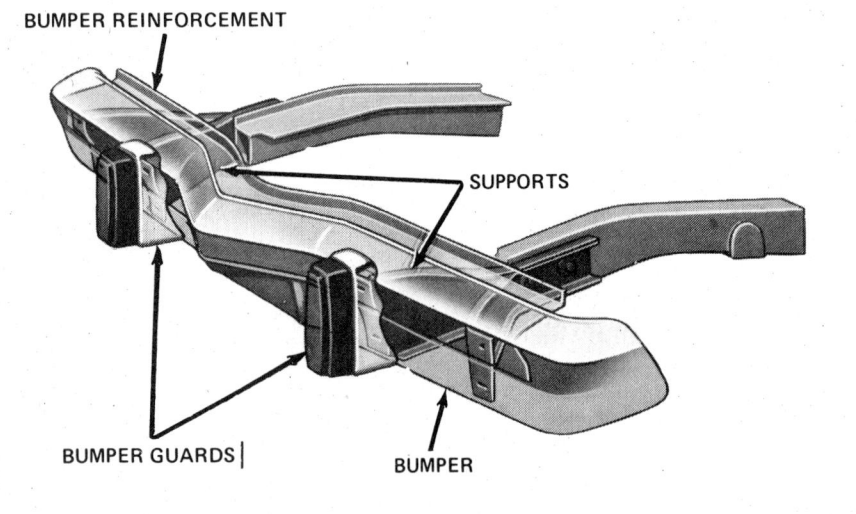

1. Chrysler Corp.'s interum bumper system was fairly straightforward; bumper supports were attached to car frame with bolts through slotted holes. A 5 mph impact would allow the bumper to slide back the depth of the holes. But—it took a body man to return the bumper to forward position.

2. Damaged Plymouth bumper removed from driver education car. This one was either hit slightly harder than the proverbial 5 mph, or the hit was off center. Either way, sheetmetal damage occurred.

3. Three bolts in slotted holes secure each bumper support and its attachment arm to the frame. Slots, according to theory, are long enough for rearward bumper movement of a 5 mph impact—providing bolts are torqued to exact specifications.

4. Undamaged side of bumper shows support (A) fastened about ¾-in. shorter than attachment arm (B). Slotted holes line up perfectly.

5. New for '74 is Chrysler's impact bumper cylinders which function almost like shock absorbers. System is used on Chrysler's larger cars.

6. Ford's '73 bumper system viewed on a car minus its front-end sheetmetal. Channel-like bumper attaching arm can be "rammed" back into receiver which is secured to frame. They are rubber-bonded together, so after the impact rubber will return to its normal shape thus pushing bumper back to its normal attitude.

somehow get rid of the energy, they'd recoil back to their normal attitude and, in so doing, would reverse the direction of the car—at least, in theory. There you'd be, with your dome against the steering wheel or windshield due to the necessary reversal of the car's direction.

Obviously, the collision force must be somehow absorbed, then somehow dissipated slowly if the method is to be at all practical.

One of the systems in widespread use, utilizes two cylinders which serve as the attaching hardware between bumper and frame. They are similar to ordinary piston-type shock absorbers, but with an exception. While a shock absorber can be compressed by hand, it will stay collapsed where you let go of it. The bumper energy absorber, on the other hand, will always return to maximum extension.

DESIGN IN ACTION

The energy absorber (see diagram) consists of two main components; a cylinder tube and a piston tube. The cylinder tube, which is filled with hydraulic fluid, has a small orifice at one end. Beyond the orifice is a free-floating piston which is contained within the second part of the unit, the piston tube. The free piston could move back and forth within its tube, except that the piston tube is pressurized with an inert gas which forces the piston down against the orifice. When the absorber is compressed, hydraulic fluid is forced from the cylinder tube through the metering orifice and presses against the free piston. Since hydraulic fluid cannot be compressed, but a gas is, the piston is forced to move inside the cylinder, further compressing the gas. In effect, the one cylinder telescopes into the other, increasing the pressure of the gas. This action is the gradual absorption of kinetic energy and its transfer into heat energy which is then dissipated through the walls of the absorber unit. Now, even though we've gotten rid of the heat, the absorber will return to its original extension as the pressurized gas forces the piston back again which, in turn, returns hydraulic fluid to the cylinder tube through the metering orifice.

You can't get inside one of these energy absorbers, since they are pressurized at the factory and then sealed in one of several ways depending upon the manufacturer. This is necessary to prevent anyone trying to gain access—which could be very harmful since the gas is under a considerable psi load.

If, in repairing a car which has suffered damage in an accident, it is found that the energy absorber was bent, or for some other reason will not re-extend itself fully, the absorber should be thrown away *after* the gas pressure is released. This is accomplished by drilling a very small hole through the body of the piston cylinder, un-crimping one of the sealed ends, or by whatever method stated in the pertinent factory shop manual.

If the absorber has returned to its full extension after a severe bump, it should be checked to see if its further operation has been impaired. Again, the factory shop manual will explain how this can be done, but basically the procedure is: face the car squarely in front of a brick wall or some other immovable barrier. Turn the ignition off, place in Park (if its an automatic trans), and set the handbrake. Place a hydraulic or mechanical jack between the bumper and the wall and apply enough pressure to compress the absorber at least ⅜-in., using an accurate measuring device (as a 6-in. ruler) to detect travel. Next, relax the jack and check to see if the absorber returns to its original position. If it does, fine; it's fully oper-

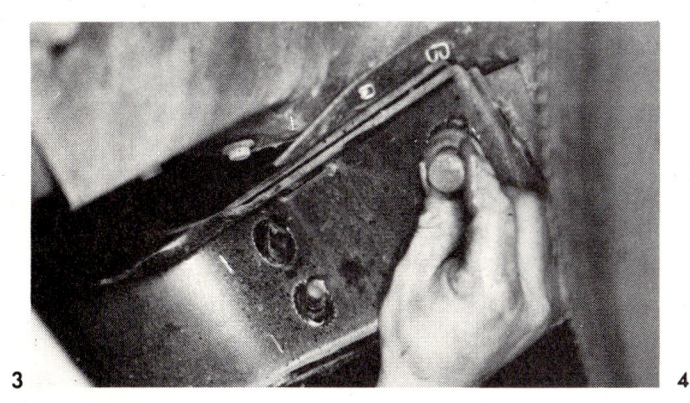

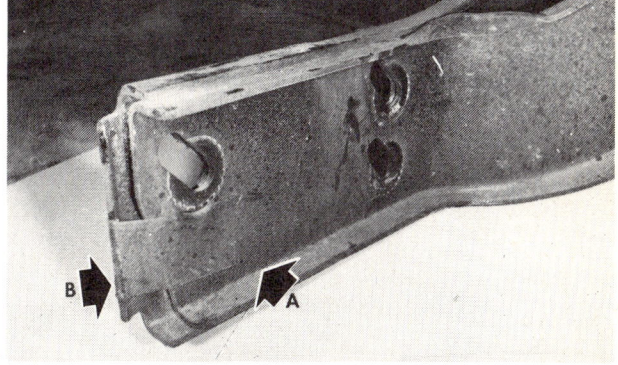

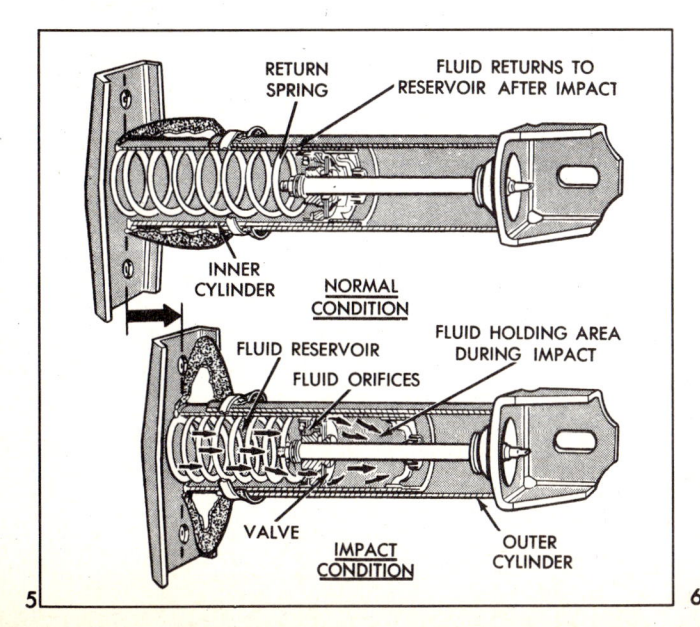

CHASSIS, SUSPENSION & BRAKES/21

Absorbing Bumpers

able. But if not, release the internal gas pressure by the method recommended in the shop manual *before* removing the absorber and discarding it. This type of energy absorber is perhaps the most complex in terms of hardware and function and is used on most GM cars as well as both the AMC car line and Jeeps.

The Chrysler energy absorber works along the same basic principle, paralleling the construction of a conventional shock absorber but with the ability to re-extend itself once it is compressed. Chrysler's version also uses hydraulic fluid which, when the absorber is compressed, is forced through small orifices to control the rate of compression. But instead of the fluid pushing against a piston, which in turn compresses a gas, Chrysler merely transfers the fluid from the front tube to the empty rear one. Return of the unit to its normal extension is simply handled by a coil spring, located inside the cylinder tube and which is compressed as the unit telescopes. The force of the spring pushes the unit to its normal extension and the fluid returns to the cylinder tube through this action, when the input energy (i.e. the "crash") has been relieved.

RECOVERY INS AND OUTS

These two types of impact energy absorbers are known as "recoverable"; that is they return fully to their extended position (if they're not damaged) and are ready for another bump.

Easier for the car manufacturer to produce, but more expensive for the car owner to repair (or have repaired), are the *non-recoverable* devices. One type is found on certain Chrysler models. The brackets that attach the bumper to the frame have slotted holes in the frame end. Similarly slotted holes are on the frame rails. When the brackets are assembled to the frame at the factory, bolts are placed through the corresponding slotted holes, and each bracket pulled forward as far as the slots will allow. The bolts are then torqued to a precise spec. Upon collision, the slots allow the bracket to slide rearward for the combined length of the slots; or about 3 ins. The system is designed to "bottom" the slotted holes against the bolts upon a full 5 mph impact. Smack harder than this, though, and you'll either shear the bolts and find the bumper buried somewhere in the grille or radiator; or if the bolts hold, the frame will buckle. Either way, extensive damage will result and the bumper will not return to its original position without the aid of a bodyman. But, the system does meet the Federal specs under the controlled crash situation, and that's all that's required.

Though the Safety Standard MVSS-215 was put into effect in time for the '73 car model year, some manufacturers foresaw its coming and rushed into production with some interim bumper systems for '72. One was the Pontiac device which consists of two telescoping channels and contains a series of fluted urethane cushions under partial compression. They "collapse" under impact, but supposedly expand back to their "as-

1. Rear view of Ford's telescoping supports reveals the rubber biscuits that are bonded to the I-beam and the channel in which it slides.

2. Top view of Ford casing and I-beam ram shows redesign of frame rail (A) and contoured wedge plate (B) which applies preload to prevent vibration and movement on rough roads.

3. The GM system is the most exotic of all such devices and has been in use for several years on most GM cars as well as American Motors products. Two beefy shock absorber-like cylinders tie bumper to frame. Units telescope inward, return to neutral position.

4. Cutaway of GM energy absorber shows relationship of components; much like a conventional shock absorber except it has capacity to re-extend itself after telescoping.

5. GM's energy absorbers, shown in this drawing installed on an AMC Jeep, can be checked for proper operation after an impact. Vehicle is firmly parked facing some kind of sturdy object, jack used to force the bumper back while mechanic measures the distance. When jack is released, bumper should return the same distance. An accurate ruler should be used. If cylinders don't respond, they must be discarded after release of internal gas pressure.

6. A body man may run across one of these some day and wonder what it is, since impact bumpers didn't come along until '73, and this is from a '72. Well, it's an intermediate step GM took with Pontiac to provide a "sort of" impact bumper. It was used only during the one year.

7. GM's absorbers mount to sturdy brackets; this is an Olds Cutlass. If impact is greater than 5 mph, this will "give" and is difficult to align.

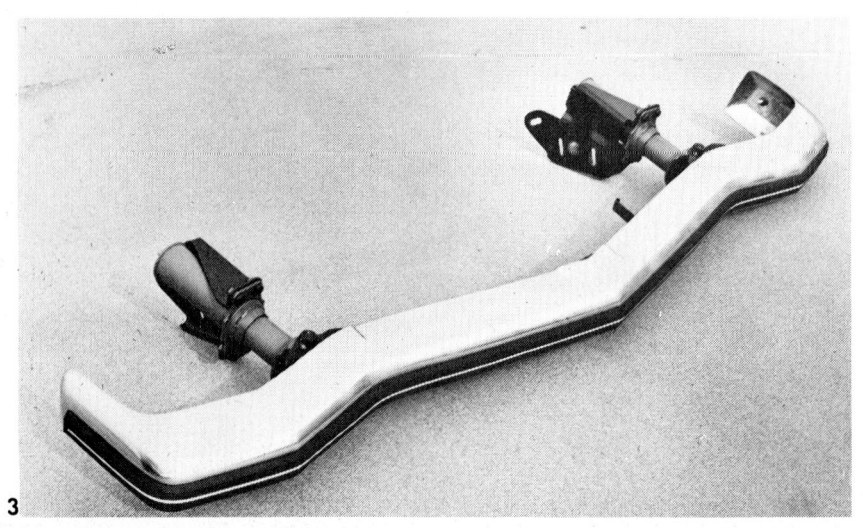

22/CHASSIS, SUSPENSION & BRAKES

installed" shape, or at least to about 95% of their former shape.

Different, yet vaguely similar, was Ford's early-on recoverable system. It, too, used telescoping brackets wherein the channel attached to the bumper could be "rammed" back into the receiver which attached to the frame. The pieces are bonded together with rubber. When the unit is telescoped, the rubber has enough elasticity to allow about 3 ins. of travel, which is what a 5 mph bump would produce. Then the rubber would assume its original shape, thus re-extending the bumper to its original location.

Other forms of non-recoverable bumper impact systems are with us today, each requiring its own techniques for repair, replacement or, if not damaged in a crash, then returned to fully expanded shapes. However, further legislation is afoot to eliminate these expensive-to-fix devices, and in the future we may well expect to find all bumpers federally required to be *fully* recoverable after impacts—even exceeding the present 5 mph limit.

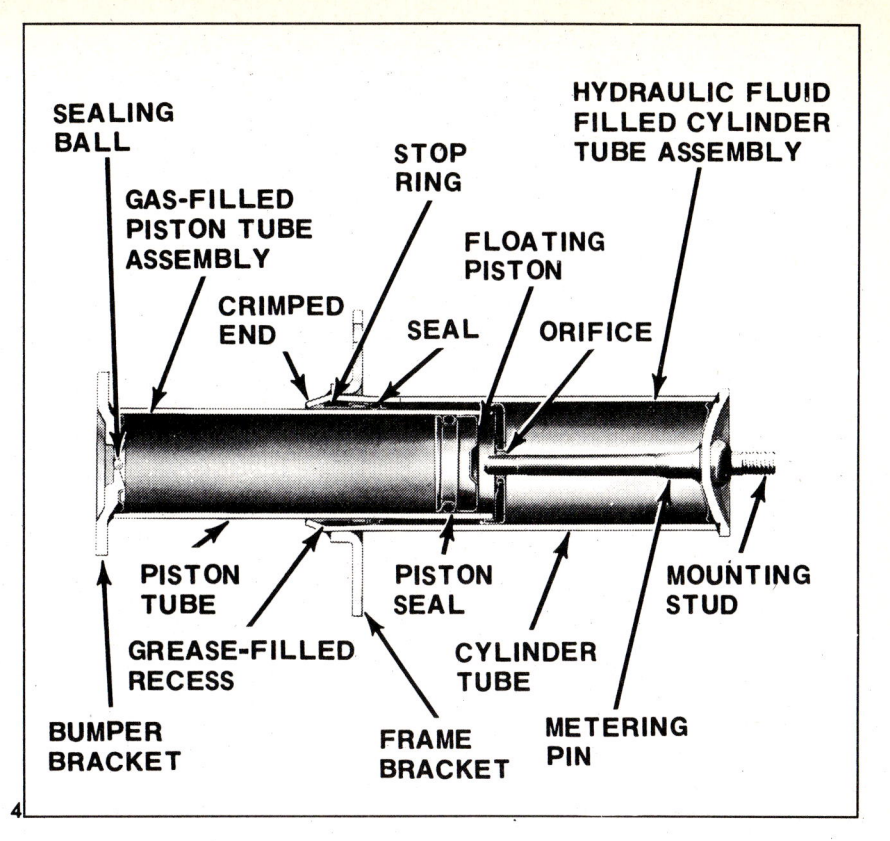

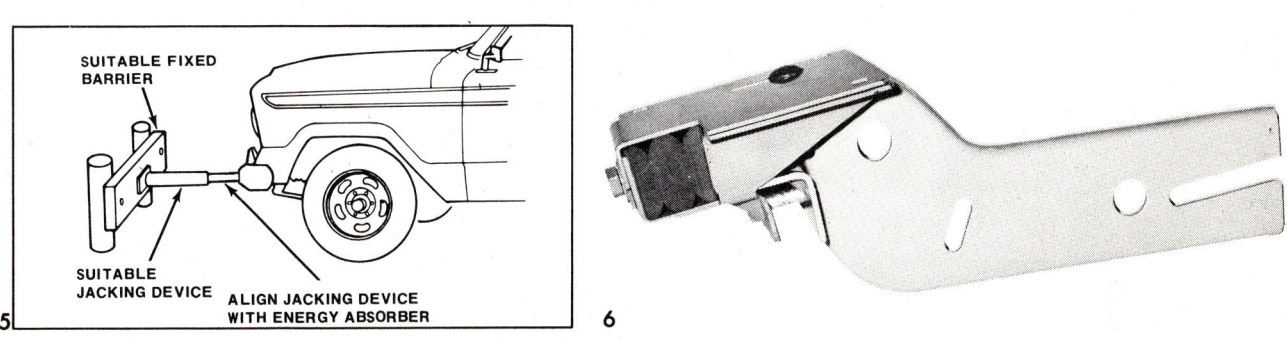

CHASSIS, SUSPENSION & BRAKES/23

The Front End
Knowing why and how your front suspension works will give you a new appreciation of your car.

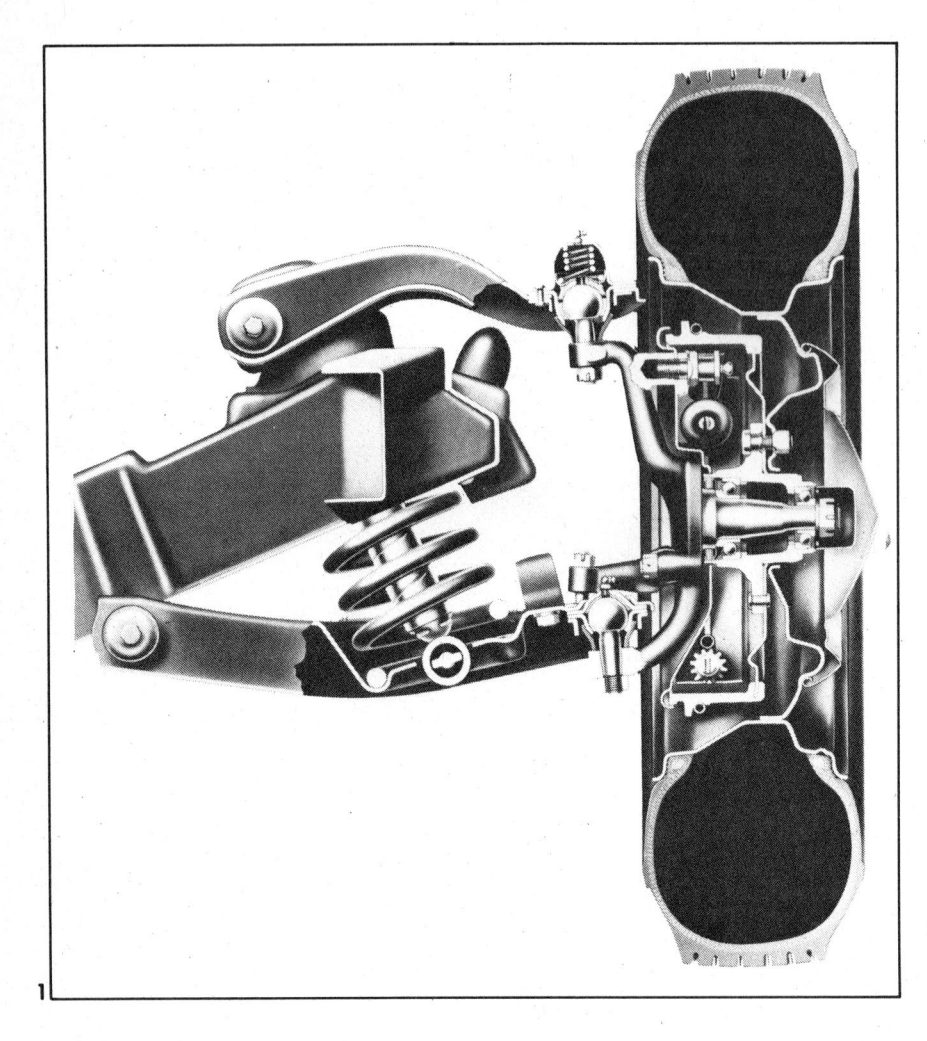

Most of the difficulties that occur in an automobile suspension will probably have something to do with the front end. The ball joints, steering linkage, alignment, or wheel bearings seem to cause more trouble than a kid with a sharp stick on a newly cemented sidewalk. The problem exists not because the front ends on cars today are poorly designed, but mainly because cars have to be able to both stop and go around corners. If a car were a two-wheeled, horse-drawn cart, steered by reins, then there wouldn't be any front end problems. All you would have to do is replace the 4-legged turning device as it wore out, although that might be often, depending on the life of a horse.

The automobile chassis and front end evolved from the horse-drawn wagon, which was easy to design because the whole front axle pivoted in the middle. The brakes were on the rear wheels, which didn't result in any startling whoa-power, but at least would keep the horse from wandering off with the wagon.

A pivoting front axle won't work on any vehicle that has front wheel brakes. The slightest imbalance between braking effort of the two front wheels would send the car darting from left to right like a rabbit escaping a fox. We have to have brakes on the front wheels and we must be able to steer the car when the brakes are applied. Because of those limitations the designer of front ends has ulcers. But he has done a good job on the modern automobile. However, front ends remain a weak point, even after 70-plus years of development, simply because there are so many pivot points, linkages, and bearing surfaces to wear and get out of adjustment.

If we are to have any reliability of operation so that when we turn the steering wheel we know the car is going to aim down a side street instead of climbing the sidewalk or running into a building, then all of the monkey motion on a modern front end is absolutely necessary. We know that pivoting the axle in the middle won't work because of the braking problem, so how about keeping the axle in one place and pivoting each wheel on the end of it? In the earliest cars that was the way to go,

1. This is typical of a late-model Detroit independent front end, with two unequal-length control arms to support the spindle and a coil spring with shock inside for dampening.

2. Without kingpin inclination, we have the condition on top which will pull the steering wheel right out of the driver's hands when he steps on the brakes. Note that when kingpin inclination line and tire and wheel centerline do not intersect at the road, the distance they are apart is called the scrub radius.

3. Besides showing the various types of ball-joint suspensions, schematic from McQuay-Norris also shows the recommended jack locations, types of alignment, and tolerances.

4. Before any independent front end can be aligned, all of the vital parts must be inspected for their condition and safety.

24/CHASSIS, SUSPENSION & BRAKES

All Ball Joint Suspensions fit into One of these FOUR Categories

Type with Studs Facing Each Other
(Coil Spring Between Control Arms)

Replace lower ball joints when axial movement exceeds .050" or radial movement exceeds .250".

Replace upper ball joints when stud shows any looseness.

Correct jack location for checking ball joint looseness with short pry bar under tire.

AXIAL MOVEMENT CHECK
Axial movement is up and down play. Check for it by jacking up front-end and using a short pry bar under the tire to move the wheel up and down.

RADIAL MOVEMENT CHECK
Radial movement is in and out play. Check for it by jacking up the front end and moving the tire in and out at top and bottom by hand.

Upper ball joint has built-in spring.
Steering knuckle or spindle forging is between ball joints.
Lower ball joint carries car weight.

Type with Both Studs Pointing Down
(Coil Spring Between Control Arms)

Replace lower ball joints when axial movement exceeds .050" or radial movement exceeds .250".

Replace upper ball joints when stud shows any looseness.

Correct jack location for checking ball joint looseness with short pry bar under tire.

Upper ball joint has built-in spring.
Steering knuckle or spindle forging fastens below each ball joint.
Lower ball joint carries car weight.

Type with Both Studs Facing Each Other
(Coil Spring Above Upper Control Arm)

Replace lower ball joints when axial movement exceeds .050" or radial movement exceeds .250".

Replace upper ball joints when stud shows any looseness.

Correct jack location for checking looseness with short pry bar under tire.

Upper ball joint carries car weight.
Steering knuckle or spindle forging is between ball joints. (Ramblers have trunnions instead of ball joints.)
Lower ball joint has built-in spring.

Type with Both Studs Facing Each Other
(Torsion Bar Suspension)

Replace lower ball joints when axial movement exceeds .050" or radial movement exceeds .250".

Replace upper ball joints when stud shows any looseness.

Correct jack location for checking joint looseness with short pry bar under tire.

Upper ball joint has built-in spring.
Steering knuckle or spindle forging is between ball joints.
Lower ball joint carries car weight.

Labels: WHEEL SPINDLE, UPPER BALL JOINT, UPPER CONTROL ARM, SHIM, SHOCK ABSORBER, IDLER ARM, STEERING SHAFT, WORM GEAR, SPRING, RELAY ROD, TIE ROD, TIE ROD SLEEVE, LOWER CONTROL ARM, LOWER BALL JOINT, SPINDLE STEERING ARM, PITMAN ARM

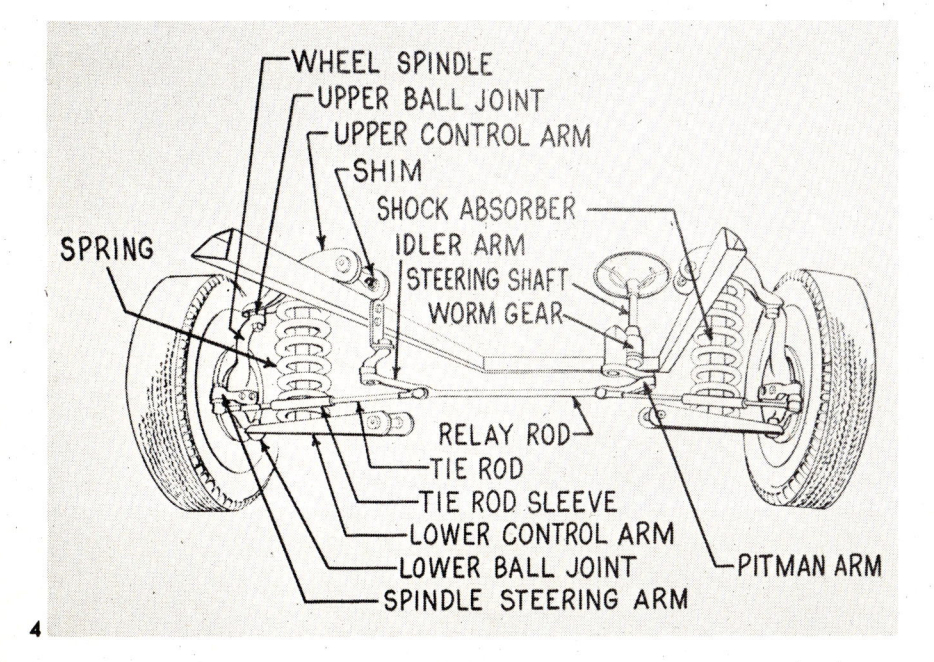

and the simple straight front axle—with kingpins as the pivot points—is still being used.

KINGPINS

An axle itself can be an I-beam, a tube, or any length of iron that is strong enough to hold up the car. At each end of the axle are parts known as the spools. They look just about like a wooden thread spool and are cast in one piece with the axle so that the holes are vertical. A kingpin goes down through the middle of each spool and acts as a pivot point for the steering knuckle, which is a kind of yoke that goes over the spool. Attached to the steering knuckle is a spindle which is really a short axle that supports the wheel bearings. Axles with spools on their ends and yokes on the steering knuckles are technically called "reverse Elliott" design. The obsolete design wherein the axle itself has the yoke and the steering knuckle has only a single pivot point is called "Elliott." Most cars in the early days of the industry started out with the Elliott and then went to the reversed Elliott. In all reversed Elliott designs, the kingpin is held in the spool at the end of the axle by a clamp or tapered bolt, and the steering knuckle turns on the kingpin.

With the kingpins, steering knuckles, spindles, and wheels mounted at the ends of our axle, all we have to do is put a tie-rod between the two steering knuckles so that the wheels will not try to go down the road in two directions at once. Also we run a drag link from the steering gearbox over to one steering knuckle and then we have a front end that will support the car through the springs bearing down on the axle, which we hope will

CHASSIS, SUSPENSION & BRAKES/25

The Front End

give us some control over the car as we go down the road.

KINGPIN INCLINATION

Control is the big problem in a front end and this is why there have been so many different designs brought out. No matter how good a front end is, it can't be perfect, so there probably will continue to be many different designs coming out as long as cars run loose on the streets and not on rails. If you look at the illustration of the kingpin in the end of the axle it doesn't look too complicated. It is locked into the axle with some kind of a wedging-type bolt, and the steering knuckle pivots on both ends of the kingpin so that the car can be steered. The problem is in figuring out the amount of side-to-side slant to put into the kingpin. Should the kingpin sit vertically, lean out or lean in? The lean of the kingpin across the car is called kingpin inclination. This does not take into consideration any of the angle of the kingpin in a fore and aft direction. That is something else we'll take up later.

Many of the early cars did not have any kingpin inclination at all. The pin was straight up and down. You can see that when steering the wheel with a kingpin that is straight up and down, the wheel will be forced to rotate as it steers because the pivot point is not in line with the contact point of the wheel where it touches the ground. If the wheel has to rotate when it is steered, this means that the action of the brakes is going to resist the turning of the wheel. So the harder you step on the brakes the harder it is going to be for you to steer the car. To solve this problem the kingpin is inclined inward at the top and outward at the bottom, so that a line drawn through the pin will point exactly through the contact point of the tire with the road. The result is that the car wheels are not forced to rotate during steering; they merely pivot in place, providing you have enough muscle in your arms to turn the steering wheel. The effort in steering is necessary because the tire has a lot more contact with the ground than a single point. Because only one point on the tread is the pivot center, then the rest of the tire contact area must be scrubbing or dragging along. The wider the tire, the greater this scrubbing action.

If you think about it, you will realize that kingpin inclination also causes the car to rise slightly as the wheels are turned from the straight-ahead position, which increases steering effort. Other factors in the front end, such as caster, may cancel out or increase some of the lifting of the car due to kingpin inclination. It's all tied in together. We study the different front end factors separately, but each one has an effect on the other when you are driving down the road, and camber is least effective of them all.

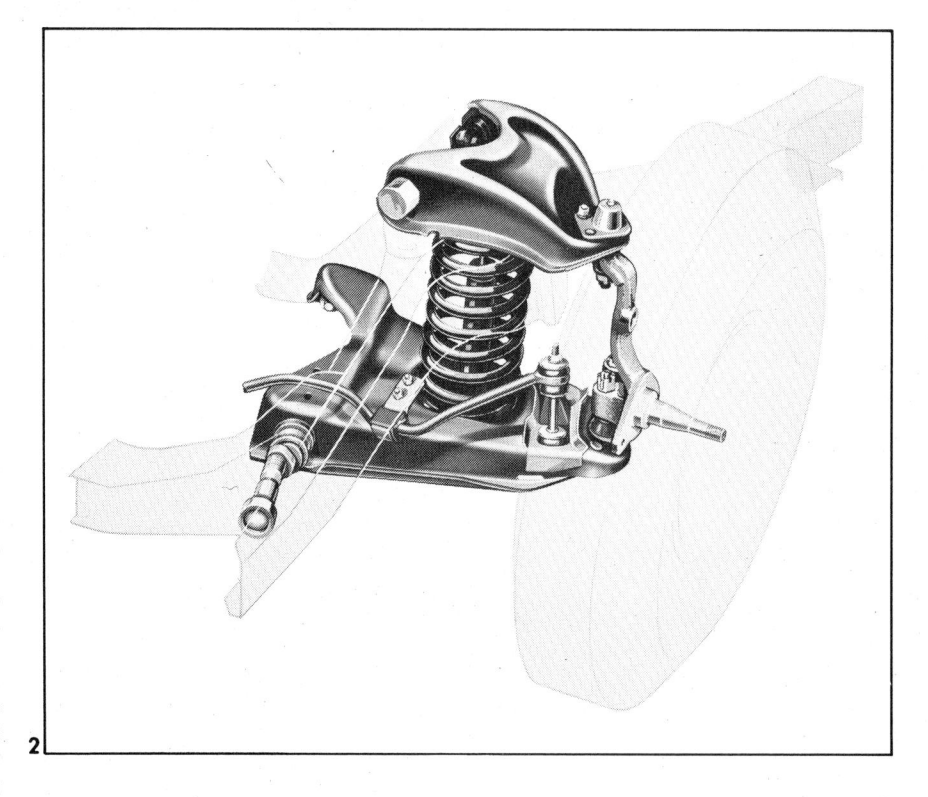

CAMBER

The wheels on a car may look as if they are sitting perfectly straight up and down but actually they aren't. The lean of the wheel either in or out at the top is known as camber. If the wheel leans out, it has positive camber. If it is straight up and down, the camber is zero and if it leans in we have negative camber. Many reasons have been advanced as to why camber is necessary. In the old days of narrow tires the right amount of camber would cause the weight of the car to be carried mainly by the larger inner wheel bearing. The outer wheel bearing was smaller and was there merely to keep the wheel securely in position and alignment. The weight was carried mostly on the larger inner wheel bearing because the spindle is stronger nearer its base. If too much weight were allowed to act on

26/CHASSIS, SUSPENSION & BRAKES

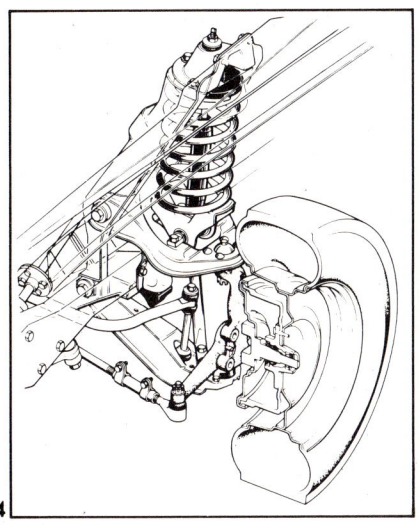

1. The '54 Chevrolet front end here was one of the last American designs to have independent action, but still use kingpin-type spindles.

2. Notice on this '62 Ford suspension how straight the A-arms appear; on late-models the upper arm is much more sloping for a better camber curve through its travel.

3. Typical of those suspensions on which the spring is mounted above the upper A-arm is this '65 Comet.

4. The AMC Gremlin also features the spring above the upper A-arm, and with a pivoting mount on the arm and rubber bushing at top to reduce road noise and dampen vibrations.

5. Earlier AMC's like this '64 used quite different A-arms, spindle and mount. Note the large "cone" to hold the coil spring in place.

the outer wheel bearing, the spindle might break off, and sometimes it did. Another reason for camber was to bring the force of the car weight directly in line with the curvature of the wheel spokes, which were dished for strength.

None of the old reasons for designing camber into a front end are really valid today. We have stronger spindles, better bearings, and tires so wide that if you tipped them enough to get most of the weight to bear on the inner wheel bearing, you'd have the tire running down the road on one edge. The result is that a lot of cars today have so little camber that it is practically nonexistent. Toe-in, however, is another measurement that is still very much with us.

TOE-IN

If you were up in the air where you could get a flying saucer view of the front end and also had X-ray eyes so that you could see through the fenders and all the sheetmetal, you would be Superman. And you could probably see that the front of the tires are closer together than the rear. Toe-in is set by lengthening or shortening the tie-rods and it is designed into a front end to take care of the slight bending of the steering linkage caused by the forward motion of the car. You actually don't have any toe-in when the car is running down the road. The linkage bends slightly and the wheels straighten out.

For many years front end designers thought that toe-in was needed to counteract positive camber. A wheel with positive camber has a tendency to do its own steering. A right wheel wants to go right and a left wheel wants to go left. Of course, the wheels can't do this, but in trying to do so they scrub rubber off the tires. Toe-in was thought to counteract the effect of camber and make the wheels go straight down the road without leaving half the rubber on the asphalt. It sounds convincing, but it just ain't so.

When combined with the angle of the steering arms the way they are attached to the steering knuckle, toe-in also results in the proper amount of toe-out on turns. Whenever a car is put through a turn the inside wheel is further along the turn than the outside. Therefore, the inside wheel has to be turned a greater number of degrees relative to the car frame than the outside wheel. This is not true in the case of a wagon with the axle pivoted at the midpoint because both wheels are at the same relative point of travel around their respective circles. When the wagon pivots, one wheel comes back and the other wheel goes forward, thus keeping them both on the same radius line. This doesn't happen in a car, so the inside wheel has to pivot through a greater angle than the outside. In order to make it all work out right, a line drawn through the center point of the kingpins and also through the center point of the ends of the steering arms will meet in the middle of the rear axle of the car. Then with the proper amount of toe-in, the wheels will toe-out on turns so that the center of the circle about which they are turning coincides with the circle the rear end is making.

This is known as the Ackerman principle, or Ackerman effect.

CHASSIS, SUSPENSION & BRAKES/27

The Front End

All of this sounds as if it were very carefully planned out so that the tires are going to turn perfect circles at all times and that no rubber will be wasted by being scrubbed off against the pavement. The truth of the matter is that toe-out on turns is only perfect at one angle of turn. Anything sharper or more gradual results in one or both of the tires being scrubbed sideways a certain amount. It is possible to design a front end that will give a perfect turning radius for every degree of turn but it is much more complicated than anything we have today, and a heck of a lot more expensive, too. Most of our driving is done in a straight line and, as a result, front ends work very well. How easily they work from the driver's standpoint is determined largely by the amount of caster, which has the widest range of any front end specification.

CASTER

As if we haven't talked about enough angles already, we now have one more, and that is caster—the lean of the kingpin to the front or rear of the car. If the kingpin leans to the rear we have positive caster; if it leans to the front the caster is negative. Most cars have positive caster (very similar to the front wheel of a bicycle) so that they will be stable when the car is running down the road. Positive caster gives a trailing effect to the wheel because the steering axis intersects the road ahead of the tire contact point. The extended front end of a chopper motorcycle is an example of extreme positive caster.

If caster were the only consideration, a car with zero caster would stay in a turning circle until the driver took it out. If he let go of the steering wheel, the car would not make any effort to return to a straight path.

Negative caster gives a leading effect to the front wheels because the steering axis intersects the road behind the tire contact point. A car with extreme negative caster would be so unstable that you couldn't drive it unless you held the steering wheel in a death grip. Relax a little and every little bump in the road would cause it to go into a turn, if caster were the only consideration.

Caster is not the only factor in a front end, and that is the reason we can drive a car with zero or negative caster without any trouble. With zero or negative caster our steering wheel will return to the straight-ahead position because of steering axis inclination. Because of the inclination of the steering axis, we are actually raising the car when we turn the steering wheel. The weight of the car tends to make the wheels straighten out, and so we have a steering wheel that comes back to the straight-ahead position when we let go of it.

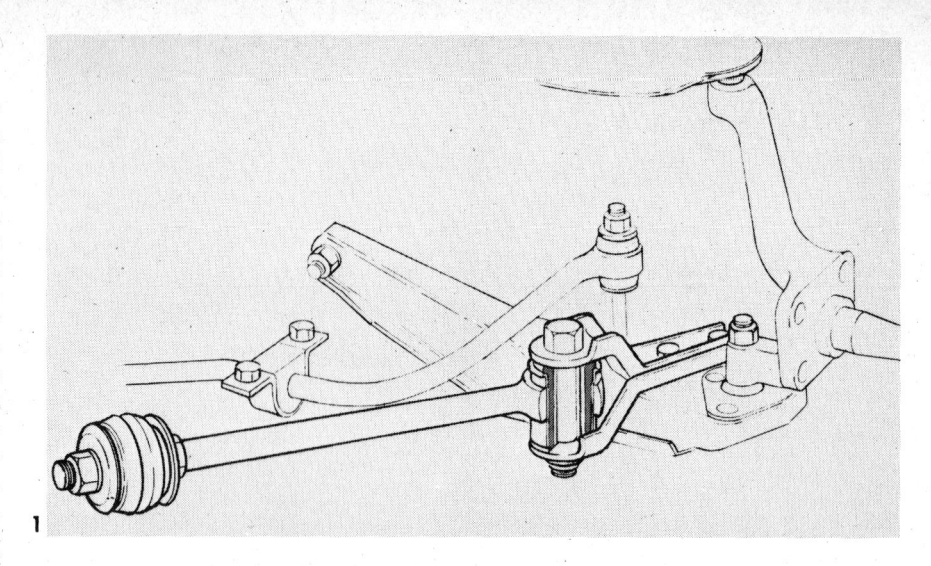

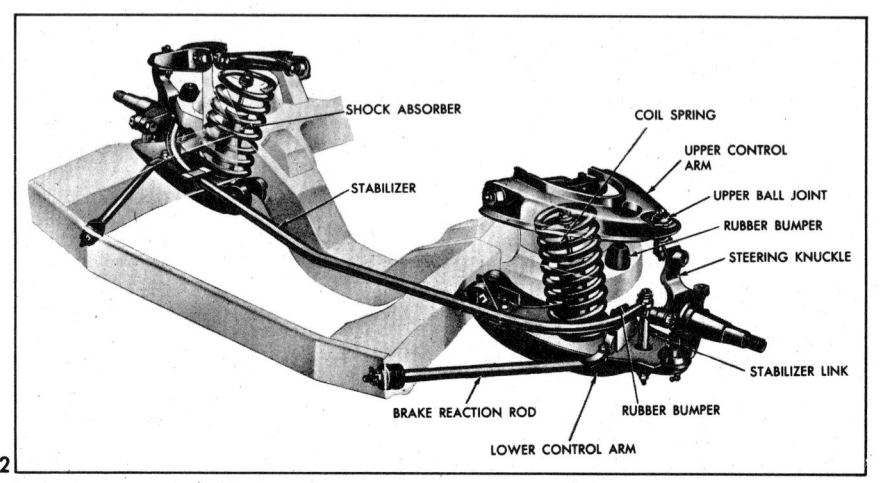

Most cars have positive caster because it makes the car travel in a straight line without any effort on the part of the driver. The more positive caster there is in a front end the greater the tendency for the car to travel in a straight line, and also the greater the effort required to turn the steering wheel. The amount of caster in a front end depends greatly on personal preference. More positive caster will give greater stability at high speed highway driving and require less driver attention to what's happening. Less positive caster or even negative caster will give a much easier steering car but one in which the driver is required to pay attention to the road at all times because the car may have a tendency to wander

So far we have talked about straight axles, but everything we have discussed also applies to the functions of the independent front end. But first . . .

SPRUNG/UNSPRUNG WEIGHT

One of the great fallacies in trying to understand suspension systems is due to the widespread but erroneous belief that the springs hold the chassis and body of a car *up*. The proper way to think of it, though, is that the springs push the wheels *down*, through the weight of the chassis and body. Look at it this way: If no weight other than that of the wheel and tire were exerted on the tire, it would tend to leave the road surface when it encountered a bump or rut at speed, returning to earth relatively slowly but landing with a resounding crash. If more weight is placed on the tire, it will return sooner, and if the weight is great enough, it won't leave the ground at all—the ideal situation.

The greater the relative weight difference between the sprung part of the suspension (axle, steering linkage, spindle, brake, wheel, tire, etc.), and the unsprung part (chassis, body, passengers, etc.), the sooner the tire will return to earth, if it leaves it at all. Ideally, if there was no unsprung weight, only sprung weight pushing down on the tire, the car's ride on even a rough road would be like driving on a glass top table. This is why many race car designers place as much of the wheel and steering components on the chassis (as the brakes) leaving less mass to bounce

28/CHASSIS, SUSPENSION & BRAKES

1. Stabilizing strut rods aren't new anymore, but the Cougar's articulated strut, with rubber bushings at each end, was new to Detroit when first introduced. Slight forward or back motion is possible for a smoother ride over bumpy streets.

2. Most new front ends are equipped with both brake reaction rods (strut rods) and an anti-sway stabilizer bar to reduce roll on corners.

3. Proper lubrication is important to get the maximum life out of your front-end components. Consult your owners manual for frequency and lube every place you see a grease fitting.

up and down with the tire. Surface adhesion, so necessary to absolute vehicle control, is thereby improved since more of the car's total weight is pushing down on the springs which, in turn, push the tires down against the ground.

INDEPENDENT FRONT ENDS

For many years every car on the road had a straight axle and it was more or less accepted that there wasn't any better way to attach the front suspension to an automobile. However, all throughout the years of straight axle automobiles, engineers realized that it was not the best design. When one wheel on a straight axle moves up or down because of bumps or ruts in the road, the other wheel also moves a little bit because the two wheels are tied together. A certain amount of this movement is translated to the automobile, resulting in a rough ride. Also, one wheel may be gripping the road perfectly, keeping the car where it's supposed to be going, but if the other wheel is bouncing around on a rougher portion of the road it can disturb the road adhesion of the wheel that's doing its job, so that the car doesn't handle. Too, the straight front axle has to be heavy in order to be strong, and the heavier it gets the harder it is to control when it starts bouncing around. Sooner or later somebody was bound to come up with a front end that would get rid of that big heavy straight axle.

So many cars have come and gone over the years that we don't know who had the first independent front end in the United States. But the most famous was probably Chevrolet with its knee action. It appeared first in the mid-'30's and was thought to be a marvelous development with its shock absorber and spring in a large housing filled with fluid. The disadvantage was the unsprung weight which was actually greater than it would've been with a solid axle. Also, it was a complicated mechanism that always seemed to be wearing out, or developing leaks at best. In the later '30's the term "knee action" was applied to any car with independent front end and coil springs, but Chevrolet gets the credit for coining the word and starting the trend to coil spring front ends.

Independent front ends on passenger cars are usually designed with a long arm on the bottom and a short arm on the top. When the wheel moves up and down it stays in the same place on the road but leans in or out. If the arms (called A-arms) were of equal length, then the wheel would stay perfectly vertical as it moved up and down, but the tire would scrub back and forth across the road surface. The short and long arm suspension is the way to go if you want any kind of tire life. In 1969, Buick made one of the first advances in front-end design since before WW II. By positioning the A-arms at a slightly different angle, the wheel leans out—when the spring is compressed—instead of in. This gives a little more stability when going around corners, and plenty of resistance to side winds (which can cause a lot of trouble in some cars.)

Trucks, in some ways, are way ahead of cars when it comes to different suspension designs. Ford's double beam is actually two straight axles, each axle being pivoted at the opposite side of the car from the wheel it supports. With the long pivot the result is very little camber change as the spring is compressed. Ford gets the benefit of independent front-end suspension with the toughness and durability of straight axle I-beam.

For many years all independent front ends were similar in design, using the A-arm type of construction. Each arm looked like an A, lying flat, with the point attached to the steering knuckle support and the wide end attached to the car with a bushing at each leg. Of course, the wider the A was spread, the greater the stability and durability of the front end. A different approach to the problem of stability and wearing in the A-arm type of front end is the strut rod design. When a strut rod is used, the bottom arm is no longer an A-arm, but just a control arm with a single point mounting or two bushings that are so close together they have the effect of a single point on the car. The outer end of the bottom control arm is attached to the steering knuckle with a ball joint.

When you have a single point mounting on the inner end of the bottom arm, something else has to be provided to hold the arm in alignment so that it won't be torn off the car the first time the wheel hits a bump. This extra part is called a strut rod. It attaches to the bottom arm near the steering knuckle and runs forward to a point on the frame. Strut rod design on front ends has been used on everything from compacts to Cadillacs. When the mounting point of the strut rod on the frame uses rubber bushings, the strut rod gives a little when the wheel hits something in the road. This "give" results in less road shock being transmitted to the frame of the car and, hence, a better ride.

CHEVY'S MONTE CARLO

At this point in our discussion the reader should be beginning to see why suspension systems are not updated or revised every model year, like front end sheetmetal or exterior color options. It's far too complex a matter, and once a design is finalized for production it's a safe bet the engineers will leave well enough alone for a good long time.

Buick, as we noted, made a fron-

The Front End

tend "breakthrough" for '69. For '73, Chevrolet announced a whole new concept (for them) of handling and ride control, achieved by an all-new front suspension layout that provides the Monte Carlo with, if not a sports car feel, at least an expensive import car feel. Here's how it came about.

John DeLorean, Chevy's General Manager (at the time that serious thinking began on the Division's offerings for the '73 model year), has a thing for Mercedes (he drives one himself), something unthinkable for a division General Manager a decade ago. But John DeLorean recognized certain qualities in the 300 SEL 6.3 that could add much to his product, provided they could be distilled and incorporated in the Chevrolet line without embarrassment. As an engineer not blinded by the glossy public relations maintained by the automotive establishment, he set out to achieve this kind of blend. But let's get one thing straight right now—the Monte Carlo is no Mercedes, yet it does exhibit a heavy degree of the thinking that originally created the 300 SEL 6.3, which some will tell you was the world's best car, bar none.

The pundits are right about one thing—the Mercedes has a character and quality that American mass production could never hope to duplicate (especially at a popular price), but then, who wants to simply copy another's work? The essence of the business is to take that which works best for the other fellow and apply it in a unique way, just as Kodak sold countless millions of Instamatic cameras by enclosing its film in a plastic cartridge for drop-in loading. This is nothing new or earth-shaking—Minox had been doing it for decades—but Kodak added a few fillips of its own for the mass market.

In a similar manner, Chevrolet set out to determine the desirable characteristics of the Mercedes in question by running a complete suspension analysis with the specific intention of duplicating the German's handling characteristics, but with a somewhat softened ride for the American market. Chevrolet Engineering just happens to have one of the most expensive and sophisticated analyzers available to sort out and isolate what makes any car tick, while simulating whatever kind of driving or road condition you care to name. Like other "miracles" of modern technology, all that's required by this device is that its users dial in the proper actuating program and then toast each other with a cup or two of coffee while the machine drives and evaluates the car in question, spouting forth countless long sheets of graph paper filled with data that drives engineering staffs to ecstasy. Older race car designers might just sneer at the use of a machine to analyze a suspension/handling design problem, but the elements at play are far more delicate and subtle than most would ever concede. Camber curves, stabilizer rates, compliance caused by linkage movement and bushing compression, sideview swing arm slope—these are only a few of the factors involved in the complicated world of suspension geometry and can no longer be figured by the seat of the pants—it's a machine's world—if we like it or not.

What the analysis turned up was an engineering accomplishment revolving around a rather large caster angle, a particular degree of well managed compliance and a high-effort steering gear. Of necessity, this is an oversimplification, but DeLorean's people translated it into 5° of positive static caster (the '72 Monte Carlo had zero caster), a revised sideview swing arm slope, high-effort power steering and steel-belted radial tires. Sounds simple enough, but there were several interlocking problems that complicated the reality of combining the Mercedes "speed feel" with an American touch.

To open the game, power had to be added to the steering to compensate for the higher effort, and a steering damper was used to alleviate steering wheel vibration. These helped to overcome problems caused by the high caster angle, but it was apparent that as the Mercedes handling owed *much* to the use of radials, other problems would arise. Radials *do* give a better road feel to steering while increasing traction and providing higher cornering force, but they *also* tend to give a somewhat harsher ride at lower speeds than do conventional bias-ply tires, and this sort of thing has been a "no-no" in Detroit philosophy for many years now—the soft and tender American derriere must be protected. Radials also tend to wander more from a straight line than bias-ply tires, but the increased static caster added a self-aligning torque that offset this particular disadvantage.

The real problem with using radial tires rested in low speed harshness, and traditional Detroit thinking would

1. Rather than the simple one-piece tie-rod of beam-axle days, a modern independent front end uses a relay rod and idler arm to allow the split tie-rods to pivot at the same point as the suspension's A-arms.

2. There's a right and wrong way to do everything, including adjusting wheel bearings. They should be done with a torque wrench to factory specs and then backed off for cotter pin.

3. Several of GM's lines changed the instant center points and the camber curves in 1969 to improve directional stability. In the arc that the wheel travels, positive camber increases as the wheel moves up, leaning the wheel to the outside.

4. Ball joints can break, usually with disastrous results. The danger signs are cracks around the hole where the stud comes out.

5. As with tie-rod ends, old ball joints can be a bear to get loose from their socket. This tool eases the job, works on rod ends, too.

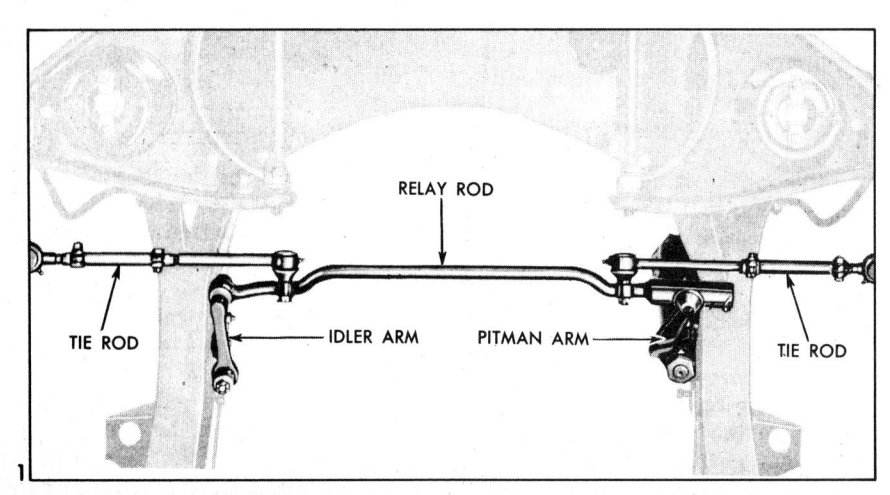

30/CHASSIS, SUSPENSION & BRAKES

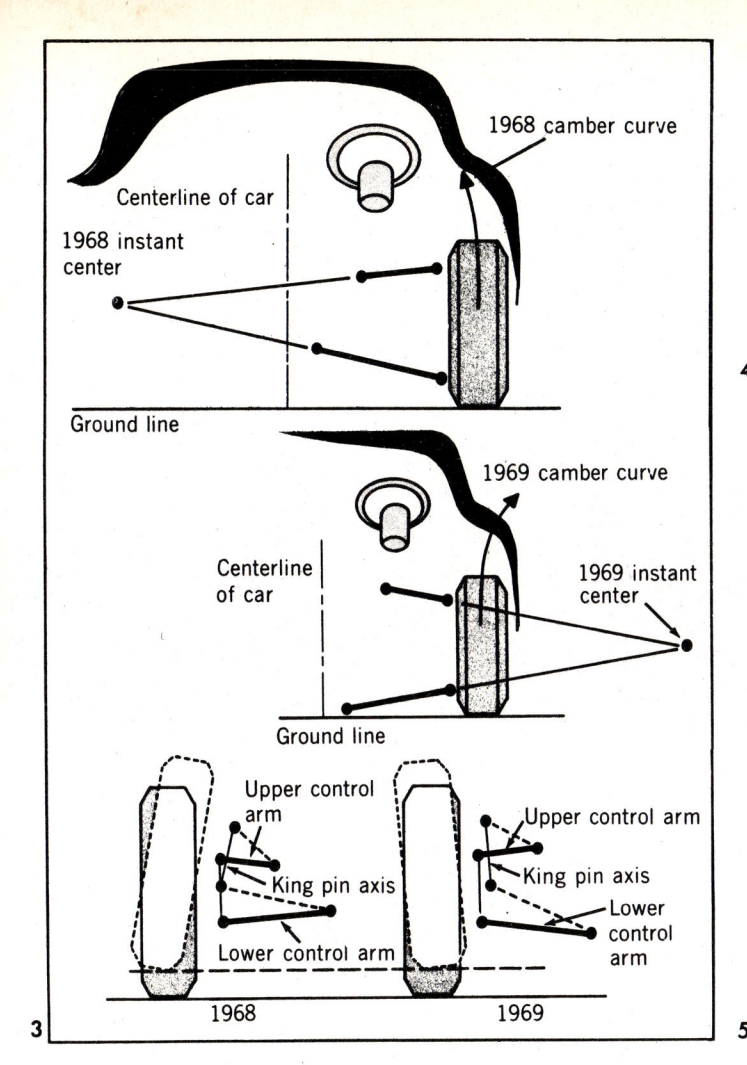

Figure 3: Camber curve diagrams comparing 1968 and 1969 suspension geometry, showing centerline of car, instant center, ground line, upper control arm, king pin axis, and lower control arm.

Figure 4 & 5: (photographs)

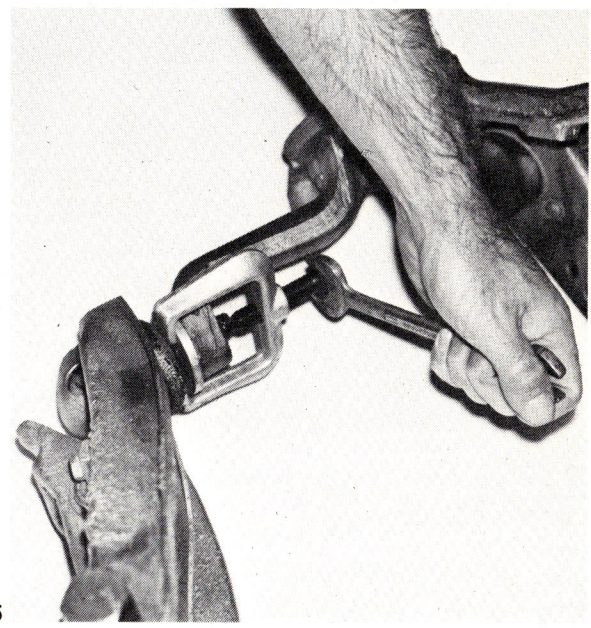

have resorted to adding more rubber to the suspension. All of which brings us in a rather oversimplified way to the beginning once more, for adding more rubber would have destroyed the much-sought-after compliance. The answer to this problem seemed to rest in a revision in the sideview swing arm slope. For those whose knowledge of suspension ends with tie-rods and stabilizer bars, this is the angle at which the two control arms (upper and lower) attach to the frame in relation to each other. The point at which the plane of the control arms intersect to the rear is the sideview swing arm; the slope of a line from that point to the wheel center is the slope angle. In recent years, Chevrolet has used a 2° negative slope, but in the Monte Carlo it becomes a full 6° negative angle.

Arriving at a decision to go this route, Chevrolet engineers found that the resulting suspension could better absorb bumps, while requiring less compliance in the rubber bushings. This in turn made it easier to "tune" the bushings for handling. Retuning the rubber was carried out throughout the car as body mounts were redesigned for better noise and roadshock isolation. Chevy engineers had found that the rubber mounts themselves were guilty of transmitting road noise, so they flattened the body mount compression rate by building a void in the center of the mounts. Cracking the problem of the rather unique power-assisted steering box used on the 300 SEL proved a bit tougher, but Chevrolet decided on a variable ratio unit with less overall effort, slightly reducing the Monte Carlo's ratio from the previous Chevy constant 17.5:1 ratio to 15.0:1 at center and 13.0:1 full right or left. Variable ratio gives a conventional steering response in straight-ahead driving, but when the steering wheel is turned beyond 40° in either direction from center, the ratio changes as the shorter sector teeth produce a greater pitman arm movement, turning the front wheels more rapidly with a correspondingly reduced steering wheel turn. The end result is that a good deal of the Mercedes steering feel was actually transferred to the Monte Carlo, along with a strong feel of where the center of travel is.

Finishing touches were added by foregoing independent rear suspension in favor of a rigid axle, increasing suspension travel almost a full inch, with coil springs and shocks all the way around, and front and rear stabilizer bars, giving the Monte Carlo a fairly stiff roll rate with a suspension that refuses to bottom out even when the car is fully loaded. Engineering the Monte Carlo was a feat of the first magnitude in the midst of outdated preconceptions, but getting it past the cost accountants and into dealer showrooms across the nation intact proved to be an equal if not more formidable challenge.

RUBBER BUMPERS

On any type of front end, even the old straight axle, you will see rubber bumpers mounted on the frame. A driver who keeps his car on smooth pavements and takes it easy will never use the bumpers throughout the life of the car. But if the car is driven through ruts and deep holes, or over curbs, then the rubber bumpers may keep something from being broken because they are the last resort before the front end crashes into the frame. Springs are usually variable rate, meaning that they exert more pressure as they are compressed, but in order to design a spring that will give a decent ride, the springs must be soft enough to allow the suspension to move. If your rubber bumpers

CHASSIS, SUSPENSION & BRAKES/31

The Front End

are worn out from bottoming the suspension too much and too often, either your springs are weak, you're carrying too much load in the car or you're driving just too darn hard.

Whether you drive hard or easy, the front end is controlled by the steering linkage, which is a bunch of rods that connect the steering box to the steering knuckles.

STEERING LINKAGE

On a straight axle, the only linkage required is a tie-rod and a drag link. The tie-rod attaches to the steering arms which are usually part of the steering knuckles. Somewhere on the tie-rods will be some kind of a sleeve and lock nut adjustment for adjusting toe-in. On one of the steering knuckles will be an extra arm or perhaps an extra hole on the steering arm where the drag link is attached. Drag links can run fore and aft or across the car, depending on the design of the steering. The simple tie-rod and drag link steering linkage was used for many years, but when independent front ends came in, the engineers found out that you couldn't run a tie-rod between the steering knuckles and still maintain the independence of each front wheel. With a simple tie-rod between the steering knuckles on an independent front end, the up and down movement of one wheel would pull the other wheel around with it. The answer was to go to a type of double tie-rod design without any drag link, wherein the tie-rods pivoted at approximately the same point that the A-arms did.

Chevy and Plymouth solved the problem by using a peculiar-looking pitman arm on the steering box which had two holes in it. Each hole supported a link to its own front wheel, so theoretically the tie-rod and drag link were the same piece of metal. A later development was center steering, wherein a large bell-crank was mounted on the front crossmember and connected through a drag link to the pitman arm on the steering box. From the large bell-crank a tie-rod went to each front wheel. It was called center steering because, although the steering box was mounted on the left frame rail—the same as any other car—the actual steering action came from the bell-crank mounted directly in the center of the front crossmember The theory was to get the pivot points of the tie-rods closer to the actual pivot points of the bottom A-arms.

Center steering was eventually discarded for the system that is used now on practically every automobile, wherein a large center link (relay rod) is used with an idler arm. The pitman arm is attached to one end of the center link and the idler arm to the other, with the idler arm pivoting on the right frame rail. Then the two tie-rods are mounted somewhere near the center portion of the center link. Some cars reverse the arrangement, putting the pitman arm and idler mounting points in the middle of the center link and the tie-rods out on the end. Other variations in design are brought about by power steering installations. But almost all cars today are based on the center link and idler arm design. Similarity of design also appears in other parts of the front end, as in ball joints, which are almost universally used.

BALL JOINTS

Car enthusiasts have a great resistance to change. Whenever a new design comes out they automatically feel that it must not be as good as what used to be. Most mechanics and enthusiasts felt the same way when ball joints first appeared. They figured that nothing could be as strong or as good as the old-fashioned kingpin. Actually nothing is as strong or as good as a ball joint front end. It's just better, no matter how you look at it. With kingpins, the outer ends of both A-arms must be connected by a spindle support. The support is mounted in bushings at the end of each A-arm and each bushing is a wear point. The spindle (steering knuckle) is mounted on the spindle support and rotates on the kingpin which gives us two more wearing points. The result is we have two grease fittings on the spindle for greasing the kingpin bushings and maybe three or four grease fittings at the ends of the A-arms to grease those bushings.

In a ball joint front end the steering knuckle and its support are made in one piece. The ball joints not only give the spindle freedom to move up and down, pivoted on the ends of the

1. *The most common method used to remove ball joint studs or tie-rod ends from their sockets is with a forked tool driven by a hammer.*

2. *When you don't have access to either a puller or a "pickle fork," you can sometimes loosen the stud by hitting the side of the socket with a hammer, so that the socket temporarily relaxes on the stud.*

3. *Although not designed to fix a ball joint worn beyond tolerances, Shimmy Stop can be used to used to get back that new-car-tight feeling. Compound squirts into joint through grease fitting, then hardens.*

4. *A worn ball joint such as at left has play that produces wobble in the front wheels. Shimmy-Stop is said to fill up the clearances and eliminate wobble and poor steering.*

5. *Ball joints are probably the most critical component in your front end. In 1973, Oldsmobile introduced a wear indicator in their ball joints. The indicator, like a collar around the grease fitting, sinks in when the ball joint is worn.*

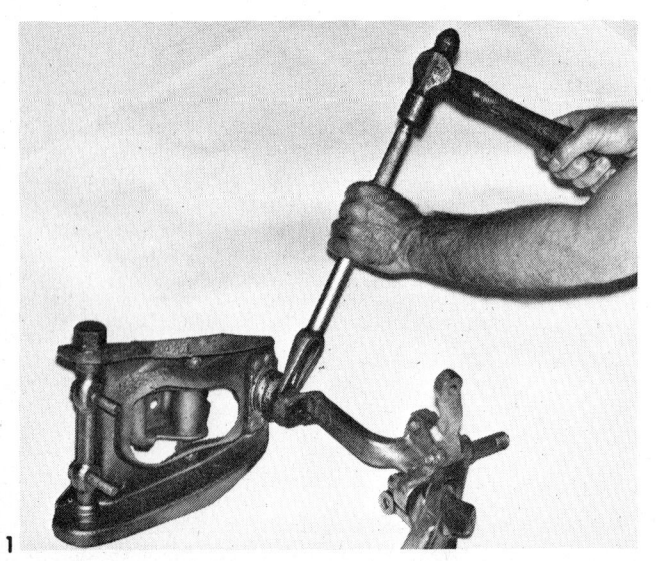

32/CHASSIS, SUSPENSION & BRAKES

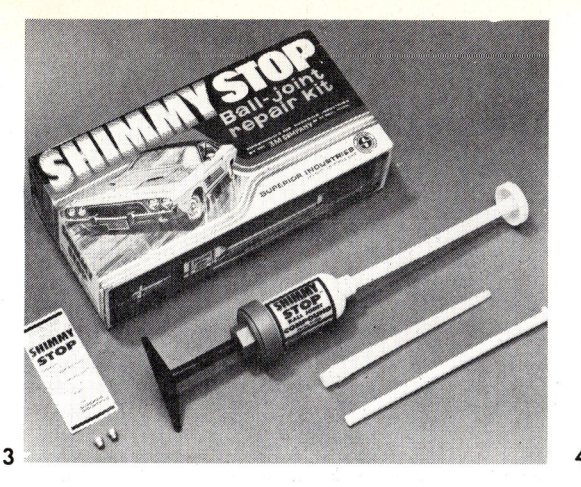

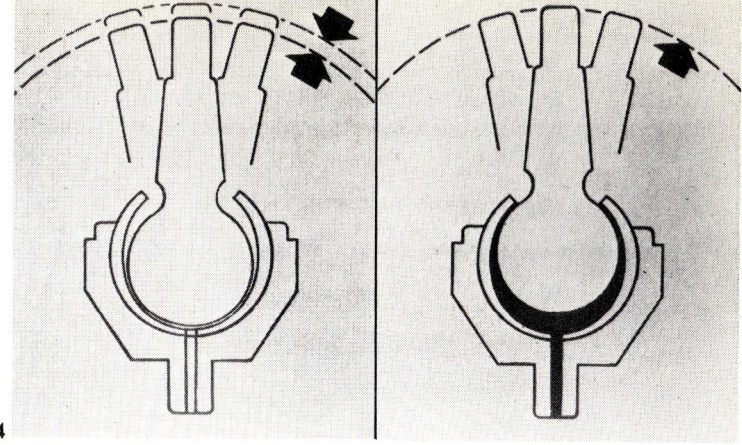

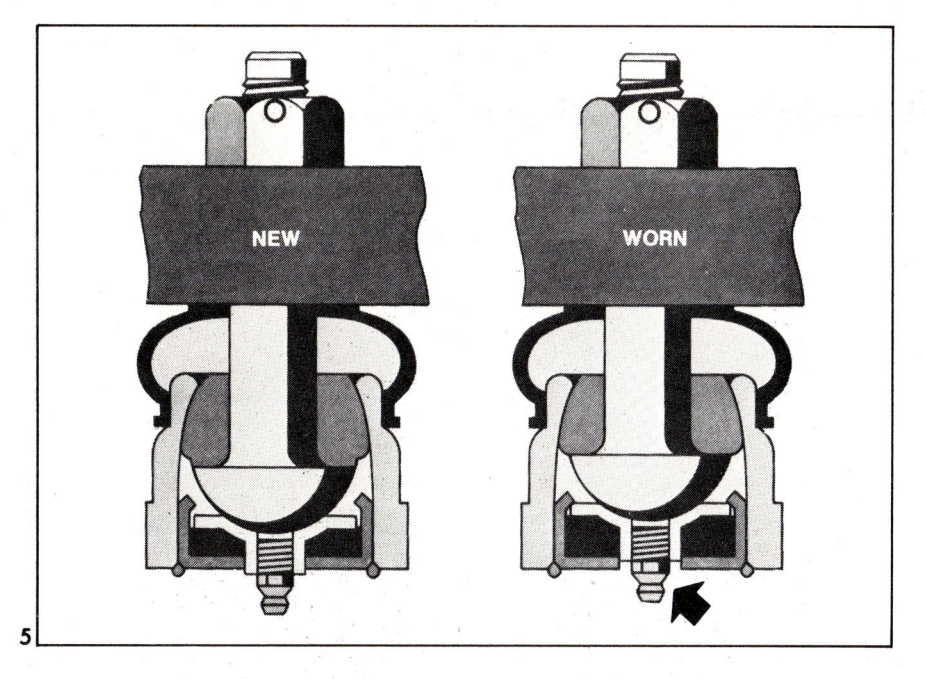

A-arms, but also allow it to be turned so that the car can go through a corner. The result is only two wear points and we have reduced quite a bit of the unsprung weight by getting rid of the separate spindle and spindle support. Another bonus realized with a ball joint suspension is the attaching of the brake anchor. In a properly designed front spindle for use with ball joints, the brake anchor will be attached to the spindle instead of the backing plate as on a kingpin front end. Thus a lot of vibration and brake noise caused by flexing backing plates are eliminated.

On a ball joint front end there are no kingpins, so you can't very well talk about kingpin inclination. Instead, the proper term is steering axis inclination, which is exactly the same as kingpin inclination without the kingpin. Kingpin inclination is the lean of the kingpin, and steering axis inclination is the lean of a line drawn through both ball joints. That line will intersect the road at the same point as the tire, just as a line drawn through the kingpin will.

One disadvantage of ball joints is in the way they are attached to the control arms. It seems as if the manufacturers have done their best to make it difficult for anybody who wants to replace a ball joint. Some are riveted to the arm, some are pressed in (requiring shop equipment for their removal), and some are screwed in. But even some of the ones that are screwed in are designed so that an ordinary socket wrench will not fit them, and they require special tools to get the old joint out and to screw the new one in. It's too bad that ball joints couldn't be made as simply as tie-rod ends, which we'll cover next.

TIE-ROD ENDS

The tool companies used to sell a socket with a large blade that would fit into a tie-rod or drag-link end and could be used for adjusting it. Nowadays, mechanics probably wouldn't even know what the tool was if you handed it to them, because tie-rods and drag links are nonadjustable and are thrown away when they wear out. Some tie-rod ends on modern cars need to be lubricated, but others are made with a type of rope or fiber in the end that keeps tension on the ball without the necessity of periodic lubrication. A good rod end will not have any play. If you can feel any slack in it while it's on the car, or if when it is removed you can rock the stud back and forth easily without any resistance, then the rod end is worn out and should be replaced. Rod ends are not used everywhere on the car that they could be. A good example is the sway bar that uses rubber bushings instead.

STABILIZERS AND SWAY BARS

When one wheel drops into a hole in the road the shock can sometimes be felt throughout the entire car. A way to minimize this shock is to attach a U-shaped bar to the frame of the car with each end attached to the outer part of the lower A-arm. As long as both front wheels go up and down at the same time, the bar has no effect on how the car rides or handles. But if one wheel drops into a deep hole, the bar will twist and restrain the wheel from falling all the way into the hole. Also, when the wheel hits the bottom of the hole, the shock of the wheel being pushed back up toward the car is softened by the twisting of the bar. It is called a stabilizer bar.

Stabilizer bars also resist leaning of the car while it is going through a corner. Anytime one wheel tries to move without the other wheel, the stabilizer bar is twisted and resists this unequal movement. The stabilizer bar sounds as if it might louse everything up on the front and make it work kind of backwards. The designers go to all the trouble to make an independent front end and then tie the front wheels together with a bar. Stabilizer bars do a good job, however; they dampen any excessive movement of the front wheels and result in better ride and better handling.

Terminology has become rather confused on stabilizers and sway

CHASSIS, SUSPENSION & BRAKES/33

The Front End

bars. Some stabilizers are actually called sway bar ride stabilizers. Strictly speaking, a sway bar is just a single bar attached to either the rear or the front end at one side of the car and to the frame of the car at the other side. They were used on early Fords with cross springs because the arrangement of shackles on a cross spring allows the frame of the car to move sideways without moving the front or rear end. The rear ends of many coil spring suspended cars also use sway bars. The reason for making the sway bar so long is to eliminate the chance of any normal movement of the front or rear end in an up and down direction affecting the frame of the car. A short bar would have more of a tendency to lift the frame when the rear or front end went up and down. Stabilizers and sway bars are usually mounted with some type of rubber bushing and the rubber itself acts as a restrainer to prevent any excess movement. In fact, rubber bushings probably do a better job on stabilizers and sway bars than a precision ball-type of joint would do. Rubber bushings should not be lubricated. We'll know why when we discuss front-end lubrication.

FRONT-END LUBRICATION

One of the quickest ways to ruin a tie-rod end, and even some ball joints, is to put an air-operated grease gun on the fitting and let the thing fire away like a machine gun. The pressure that an air-operated grease gun puts out is tremendous and it's easy to balloon the seals or break them so that they allow water or road dirt to enter. In some designs of tie-rod ends, the cap on the bottom of the socket is made of a thin sheetmetal and it can actually be pushed clear out of the socket by too vigorous application of an air-operated grease gun.

When using any grease gun, hand- or power-operated, the fitting should be wiped off beforehand and the grease applied slowly until it begins to ooze out of the joint from under the seal. How much grease you force through the seal depends upon how extravagant you feel. Actually all that is necessary is to apply the grease to the fitting until it just begins to ooze out of the other end of whatever it is you are greasing.

If you look carefully at the end of a clean grease fitting you will see a small ball check that is there to keep out water and dirt. Because the ball checks don't always work correctly, and because every time a man with a grease gun in his hand sees a fitting he feels an obligation to shoot it, the manufacturers have left out grease fittings in a lot of the late model cars, replacing them with rubber or metal plugs. If you remove the plugs and put grease fittings in for a periodic lubrication, you must take the grease fittings out again and put the plugs back. Leaving the grease fittings in is inviting disaster.

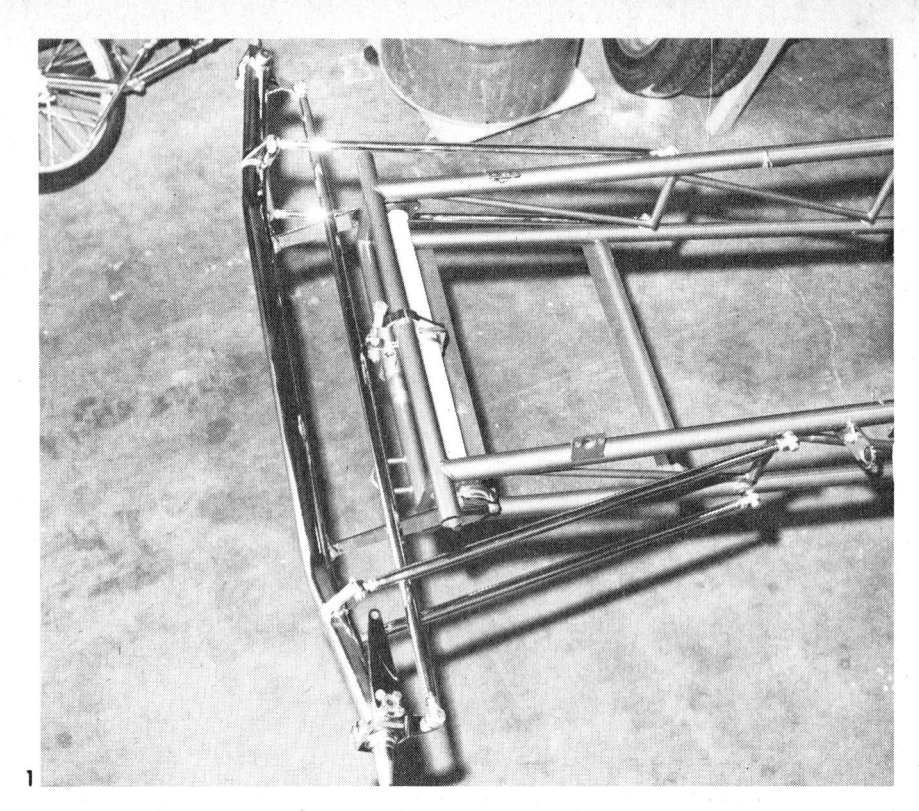

When you do grease your car you should not use any old grease that you happen to have lying around the garage. Pennzoil engineers have informed us that modern greases are specially compounded for extended-interval lubrication. The wrong kind of grease will not give protection against wear. Most greases nowadays are black which means that molybdenum-disulphide has been added to them as well as other additives that increase their quality.

If you buy any grease, read the can. If it doesn't say that it's for extended-interval lubrication or something similar (such as being compounded for late-model cars), then don't use it. Extended-interval grease can also be used successfully on earlier models. However, you can get into trouble when you grease springs with it. If an older car has leaf springs and you have been greasing it with ordinary grease, the use of the moly-type grease may result in spring sag because the moly is so slippery.

The only places on a front end that

34/CHASSIS, SUSPENSION & BRAKES

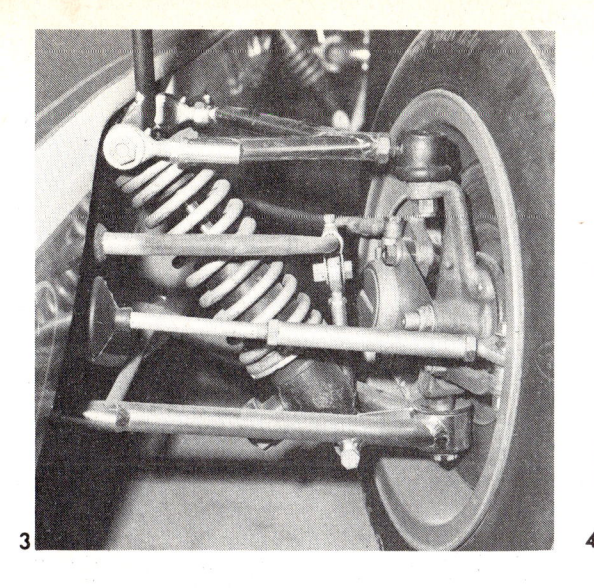

1. Dragster front ends have always been simple tube axles with cross-leaf spring or torsion bar. Even more simple are the new rear-motored cars where front end has no suspension at all, it's bolted on!

2. A few drag racers have gone to scratch-built independent front ends for better handling on rough tracks, but most stick with the old straight axle and let the chassis flexing be the suspension of the car.

3. By contrast, the cornering done by road racers requires that a front end be sophisticated, rugged and supremely adjustable to the track.

4. Racers don't add weight unless they absolutely have to. Looking at the beefy joints and uprights on a formula car gives you an idea of the brutal loads they encounter.

should be lubricated are those that have grease fittings or grease fitting holes. Rubber bushings on sway bars, shock absorbers or ride stabilizers should not be lubricated because they depend on friction to work right. If you lubricate them they will slip, and if they slip they wear out much faster than if they were dry. In most cases this applies to rubber bushings used in spring eyes and shackles also. The final authority is the manufacturer's recommendation. If he says grease it, then do it, but make sure you use the right kind of grease. Petroleum products and rubber don't get along too well. Any rubber lube or silicone-type lubricant is OK to use for rubber.

There's nothing complicated about greasing a front end if you work carefully, slowly and use the right lubricants. However, it's a little bit complicated when you get a 4-wheel-drive front end.

FRONT ENDS THAT PULL

Toronado and its elegant relative, Cadillac Eldorado, are considered so different because they have front-wheel drive, but there's more to it than that. Most people don't realize that these are the only General Motors cars with torsion bars on the front end. The layout of the front-end design is immediately recognizable as an ordinary independent suspension with upper and lower A-arms and a stabilizer bar. The difference is that the spindle is free to turn in a bearing and is driven by a short axle shaft coming from the differential mounted between the two front wheels. Unfortunately the drive-shafts run right between the two A-arms in the exact place where it would be nice to put a front spring. It's obvious that the designers went to torsion bars because they didn't have any other choice. The bars work off a lower A-arm and run parallel to the frame rails, being anchored at a crossmember behind the engine. This type of front wheel drive is so similar to a regular independent suspension front end that it really doesn't present any more problems, at least as far as the front end itself is concerned. The axles, U-joints, and the bearings supporting the spindles are another story that we won't go into here.

A more usual type of 4-wheel-drive front end, at least on American vehicles, is the kind that looks just like a rear end, except that the wheels steer. At each end of the axle housing is a large ball socket that looks as if it would allow the front wheels to flop in any direction. Inside the ball socket is a divided kingpin, which is set up with kingpin inclination the same as any normal front end. The kingpin must be divided so that the U-joint can be placed right at the pivot point. Camber and kingpin inclination are ordinarily built into the axle, and cannot be changed. If either camber or kingpin inclination is wrong because of bent parts, it is recommended in most cases that the parts be replaced. Replacing parts on any front end is not something that you do quickly and easily just before you go out for the evening. Most front-end repairs require special tools and careful workmanship.

FRONT-END REPAIRS

The only right way to fix front-end parts is to replace them. Every once in a while somebody comes out with a spring-like gadget that can be attached to a worn-out front end and supposedly make it operate just as good as new. The spring gadgets will eliminate excessive play but, because of the extra spring pressure, the parts will progress rapidly from a normal worn-out condition to the point where they are completely shot and may be dangerous. The only right way to go is to replace what's worn out with new parts.

Separating a tie-rod from the tapered hole that the stud fits into has been done for years with a pickle fork and a hammer. This is still the quickest and easiest way to loosen a tie-rod, providing you take the nut off before you start beating away. The only problem is that any metal or rubber dust seal at the top of the tie-rod is usually ruined when the pickle fork is used. If you are replacing the tie-rod end because it is worn out, then the damage done to the seal by the pickle fork doesn't make any difference because the new tie-rod will have a new seal. If you are removing a tie-rod end that you are going to have to put back, it might be a good idea to look in the tool company's catalogs under their screw-type pullers. They usually have one that can be used for separating tie-rods without any resultant damage to the dust seals.

Another method (which we don't like even though it's used by many mechanics), is the big hammer technique. If you put some tension on the end, back up the steering arm with a

CHASSIS, SUSPENSION & BRAKES/35

The Front End

sledge or big hunk of iron, and then whack the tapered hole with a hammer, you will momentarily distort the hole so that the rod end will pop out. It works, but it's brutal.

Idler arms can be renewed in many different ways. You can buy an original equipment arm, a replacement arm with bronze bushings or a ball bearing kit that will go in the original arm, taking the place of the rubber bushings that came on the car. The ball bearing kit is best but also expensive, so it all depends on how much money you want to spend and how long you are going to keep the automobile.

Idler arm kits are usually installed on the bench, after removing the idler arm from the car. When installing the ball bearing kit you may have difficulty on some makes of cars getting the old rubber bushings out of the arm. Special screw-type pullers are made for removing the old rubber bushings but most mechanics use a large vise, a punch and a hammer to drive the bushings out. Once the old bushings are out, the arm is cleaned up and the new ball bearing kit is easily installed. It will probably last longer than the rest of the automobile because it is adjustable for wear. If necessary, the wear adjustment can be used to put a pre-load on the bearings, which will help to eliminate wander if you have a car that steers too easily. This pre-load should not be misused, however. If your car has excessive wander, the trouble is probably in the front-end alignment and you should not attempt to correct that condition by putting a lot of pre-load on an adjustable idler arm.

Kingpin renewal is a major operation involving removal of everything attached to the end of the axle. It should not be necessary to disassemble the brakes in any way. You can just unbolt the backing plate from the spindle and remove the whole backing plate, brake, and hydraulic cylinder assembly without even disconnecting the hydraulic brake hose. Don't let the backing plate hang on the brake hose. It should be fastened securely underneath the fender while you're working on the spindle.

Most kingpins have a locking bolt of some kind that locks the kingpin to the spool on the end of the axle or knuckle support. Once the locking bolt is removed, the kingpin should come out readily, but rebuilding a rusty junkyard unit may require dynamite! After you get the spindle off the car it's easy to drive out the old bushings and drive in new ones. If the new bushings do not have holes

36/CHASSIS, SUSPENSION & BRAKES

plenty of automotive machinists and lots of pin-fitting hones around. It will pay you to hunt up a man who is willing to do the job right.

Properly fitted kingpins will result in a spindle that will flop from side to side with the slightest touch of your hand, and yet when you lift up and down on the extreme end of the spindle you will not be able to feel any play whatsoever. Pins fitted with reamers or other types of tools result in a certain amount of play, because the reamer removes more metal than is necessary to get the pin through the hole. In fairness to old-time mechanics we admit that some of them were expert with a reamer and could do a darn good job of fitting kingpins. In fact, they used to fit piston pins with the same reamer. However, we will put a honed kingpin fit up against a reamer job anytime and there isn't any doubt in our mind as to which would have the better fit.

After the spindle is assembled to the end of the axle you may have a certain amount of play up and down, which means that the spindle is sliding along the kingpin. If you have purchased a kingpin kit of high quality you will find little shim washers which are used between the spindle and the spool to take up the play. It's possible to turn out a kingpin job that you can really be proud of if you take the trouble to do it right.

Replacing ball joints is much easier than putting in a set of kingpins if you have a few special tools. Ball joints can be installed without disconnecting or removing any of the brake mechanism on most cars. The main problem you will have in working on ball joints is getting the old joint off the A-arm. It seems the car makers have done everything they can to make it as difficult as possible. Some joints are reveted to the arm, some are screwed in but require a special socket, and others are pressed in. Some of the pressed-in joints can be replaced by a joint that screws into the arm, cutting its own threads as it goes. The riveted joints are usually replaced with bolts. Screwed-in joints go right back in the same place, providing the threads in the A-arm are still good.

The first time you do a ball joint replacement job, you will probably wonder how you are ever going to get as far as removing the joint from the control arm, because you can't even get the tapered stud out of the steering knuckle. Sometimes a pickle fork will work, but in most cases a special puller must be used, and it will have to be coaxed a little with a few gentle taps from a 40-lb. hammer. A consultation with somebody who has already done a similar job

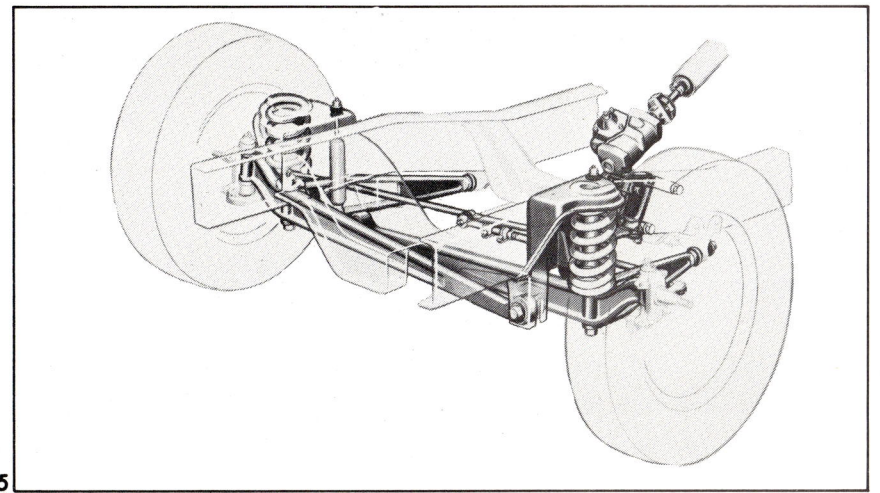

1. The road racer front end has to be built so that attachment loads are spread over the monocoque frame, and so that braking forces don't make the low-slung chassis "dive."

2. The NASCAR Grand National stock cars are that in name and body only, as the frame is reinforced and fitted with custom springs, A-arms and a torsion bar, and using two or three shocks per wheel is not uncommon.

3. Chassis on the Oldsmobile F-85 uses new "pivot-poise" linkage for smooth front spring action. The ball joints are "purgeable," in that they can be regreased without damage.

4. Most A-arms today are actually not attached square to the chassis, as this shot demonstrates. The idea is for the wheels to travel back as they move up, for better ride.

5. An unusual front end that's in between a beam axle and independent is Ford's twin I-beam system used on pickup trucks. Wheels are sprung independently but use sturdy beam arms for long life and load capacity.

for the grease to enter from the grease fitting, these holes must be drilled. After the bushings are in place and the new grease holes drilled, you are ready to fit the kingpins to the bushing. If you really want a good job of kingpin fitting, take the spindles and the kingpins to an automotive machinist and have him fit the pins on his Sunnen hone.

You don't have to use a hone to fit your kingpins to the bushings. An adjustable reamer, a nonadjustable reamer, a rat-tail file or even a paring knife will probably do the job, but there's a difference between just getting the kingpin to fall through the hole and making the pin fit the bushings the way it should. Beware of nonadjustable reamers made for Ford kingpins. These have been sold for many years and probably will be on the market for many years to come, but for some unexplainable reason they aren't the right size. There are

CHASSIS, SUSPENSION & BRAKES/37

The Front End

will save you many hours of anguish. Also, the hammer method we mentioned for tie-rod ends will work here, too, if you use the weight of the car to put a little tension on the ball joint. In any case, it's a good idea to leave the nut on the threads of the ball joint, but loosely. That way the joint can't come flying out of there and make one less member of your family.

Ball joint renewal, although easier than fitting new kingpins, can be dangerous if you don't know what you're doing. In most cases the weight of the car must be used to compress the front spring, with a jack or axle stand under the control arm. If you make a mistake and disconnect a ball joint that is receiving the force of the spring through the control arm, the spring can push the arm aside and come flying out from under the car. If your arm or leg or even your head happens to be in the way, something is going to get broken—and it won't be the spring. Before you tackle any ball joint replacement job you must have a service manual for your particular make and model of car and follow the instructions in it exactly.

Manufacturers such as Moog make just about any part that could possibly wear out or be damaged on a front end. The inner ends of the control arms pivot on bushings and you can get complete bushing kits to replace anything that is worn. On the older kingpin independent front ends, a bushing is at the outer end of each A-arm, pivoting it to the spindle support. All of these bushings are available, but their wearing rate seems to be very slow so they are seldom replaced. Ball joints don't wear as fast as some people would have you believe, either.

CHECKING BALL JOINTS

If you want to make an interesting survey sometime, just ask half-a-dozen mechanics how they check ball joints for wear. You will probably get six different answers. Better yet, have your car actually checked for ball joint wear at six different service stations. Probably every one of the attendants in the stations will tell you that your ball joints are worn out, and they may even go so far as to show you the excessive play by wiggling the wheel back and forth while they have the car jacked up in the air. Sometimes, of course, the information that your ball joints are worn out is done deliberately just to sell parts, but usually it's done through a misunderstanding of the nature of a ball joint and the amount of play that is permissible.

Almost any new car will have quite

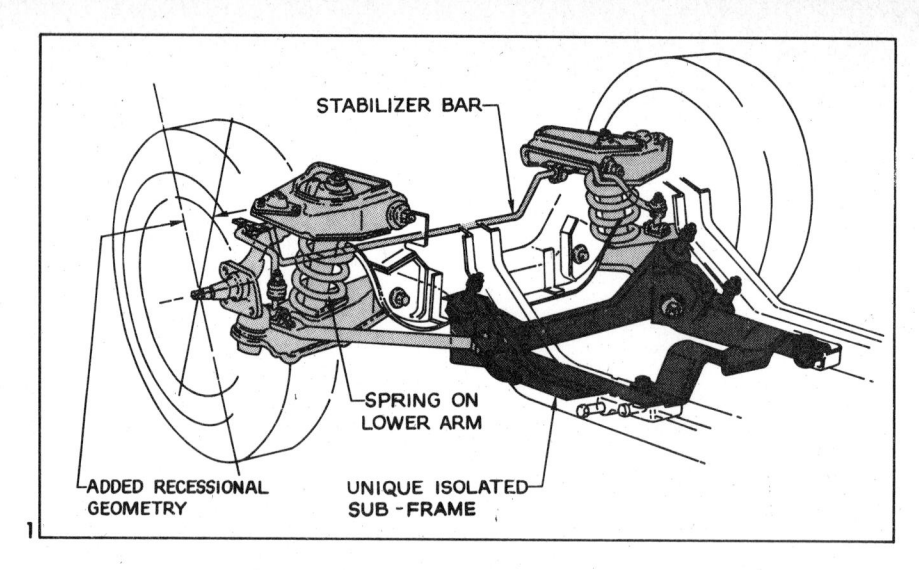

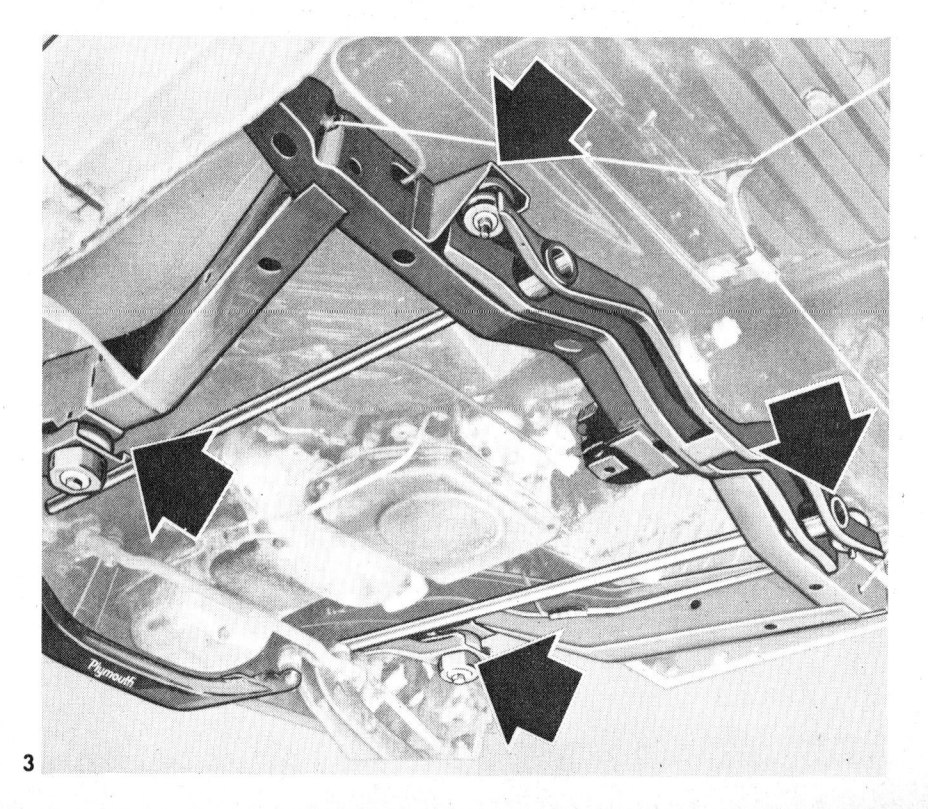

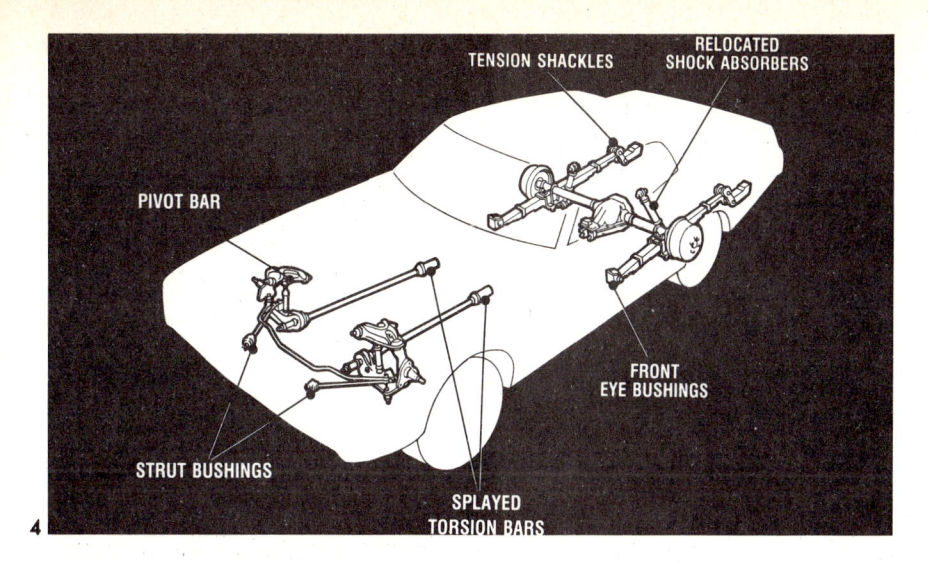

itself and raise the car until the wheel is clear of the ground. In that position the only weight that you will have on the lower ball joint is the weight of the wheel, brake drum, spindle and other parts in the wheel assembly. If you want to get fancy you can use a dial indicator with the base on the lower arm and the indicator stem directly in line with the ball joint stud. On a lower joint where the stud points down, you will have to use a magnetic base for the dial indicator, but it's the same principle. With pry bar underneath the tire pushing against the ground, you merely lift the wheel straight up and down so as to move the stud and ball up and down in the ball joint. If the up-and-down movement of the stud exceeds specifications, you should replace the ball joint.

In some cars the spring is on the upper arm, which means that the upper ball joint receives the load. That type of front end is easily recognizable because you can usually see large spring towers sticking up in the engine compartment when you lift the hood. On that type of front end you raise the car by jacking against the car frame, allowing the wheel to hang down with the spring extended at full length. Moog Industries recommends that you use a support wedge between the upper control arm and the frame of the car because, in some cases, allowing the suspension to hang down fully extended will put a bind on the control arms and will not free the ball joints. Once you have the car supported this way it's easy to check the actual play in the upper load-carrying ball joint with a pry bar under the tire the same as you did on the other arrangement of the spring. If the actual movement of the joint exceeds specifications, replace it; that's all there is to it.

You notice we have been stressing axial movement because this is what Moog Industries recommends. However, some manufacturers want you to check ball joint play by grabbing the bottom edge of the tire and moving the wheel in or out. There's nothing wrong with checking ball joint wear in this manner if you are careful to measure accurately. Still, the method can vary a lot with diameter of tires and wheels and is not as accurate as the axial play measurement. It comes in handy, though, if you want to scare somebody half to death by grabbing his tire and showing him how loose and wobbly it is. All that wobbling around doesn't mean a thing unless you actually measure the play in the joint itself.

The important joint to check is the load-carrying joint—the one in the control arm that receives the force of

1. The geometry of the new Mustang II's front end is made to allow for the wheels to move rearward as they move up on bumps. This "recessional" movement soaks up road shocks.

2. The Mustang II's new subframe front suspension is bolted to the chassis with rubber isolation pads on both sides for quiet ride.

3. Four rubber isolation bushings are used on the subframes and the torsion bar mounting crossmembers to dampen suspension vibrations.

4. The emphasis in '74 is on less noise and vibration. Dodge has made a number of suspension modifications in this direction to be more compatible with the new radial tires.

5. Sometimes obscure front end or driveline vibrations can only be reduced by attaching a dampening weight to the transmission.

a bit of play in its ball joints, enough so that you can jack up one wheel and wiggle it all over the place. It looks terrible but it really doesn't mean a thing. Specifications on the amount of play in the ball joint that is allowed can vary depending upon the car that you have. If you want to be a stickler for accuracy, look up the specifications for your car. In general, however, .050-inch of axial movement is all that should be allowed on the load-carrying ball joint. Some specifications say .100-inch and some may say less than .050-inch, but Moog engineers have found that .050-inch is a good maximum figure. If the play in the load-carrying ball joint exceeds that figure, then the joint should be replaced.

Chrysler Corp. tells us that .070-inch is OK on their '68 and later models. The 1967 and later Imperials are different. Their lower joints should not have any play. Check the specs carefully for your car, or you may be replacing ball joints when there is nothing wrong with the old ones. The best place for specs is a factory shop manual, but there are many independent manuals with reliable specs, such as Chilton, Motor, National, or other Petersen publications.

Checking ball joints for play is very simple. All you have to remember is that the control arm that receives the force of the spring or torsion bar is the arm that has the loaded ball joint. If the spring or torsion bar acts on the lower arm, which it does on most cars, then place a jack under the arm

CHASSIS, SUSPENSION & BRAKES/**39**

The Front End

the spring. But what about the other ball joint (follower joint), the one that does nothing but keep the steering knuckle from falling off the car? It doesn't carry any of the load, so it doesn't wear as fast as the load-carrying joint. Ordinarily you would not have to replace it even when the load-carrying joint is completely worn out. However, Moog Industries recommends that ball joints be replaced in pairs. If the load-carrying joint is worn out, replace the other one too, and then you know you've done a perfect job. If you want to check the play in the follower ball joint it can be easily done at the same time you check the load-carrying joint. Just wiggle the wheel around while you have the car jacked up, and see if you can observe any play in the joint itself. Because the follower ball joint locates the wheel, it should be replaced if you can see any play in it. A loose follower joint can give wheel alignment that changes with every bump in the road. Mostly, you will find that the follower joint does not have enough wear to need replacing.

Front ends for racing and hot rod applications are only limited by the imagination of the car builder. There probably aren't any two race cars or hot rods that were ever made with exactly the same front end, unless they happen to have been built on a production line. A knowledge of plane geometry will help in designing a front end for your race car. But many times the guy who doesn't know a thing about engineering, just goes ahead and comes up with a better front end than one that's been completely thought out.

If you are modifying the front end on a stock car or street job, what you do to it depends on where you're going to run it. In circle track racing with stock cars, a general rule is to lower the car as much as possible and stiffen up the suspension until it's almost solid. Weaker front springs on a drag car will allow it to settle more when it's standing still but will allow it to come up into the air more when you stand on the throttle. And this is what you want, so that you can get as much weight transfer as possible to the rear end. When modifying a front end for racing you have to be willing to experiment, and you have to be willing to change back to what you had before if the experiment doesn't work out properly.

For oval track racing, the experts

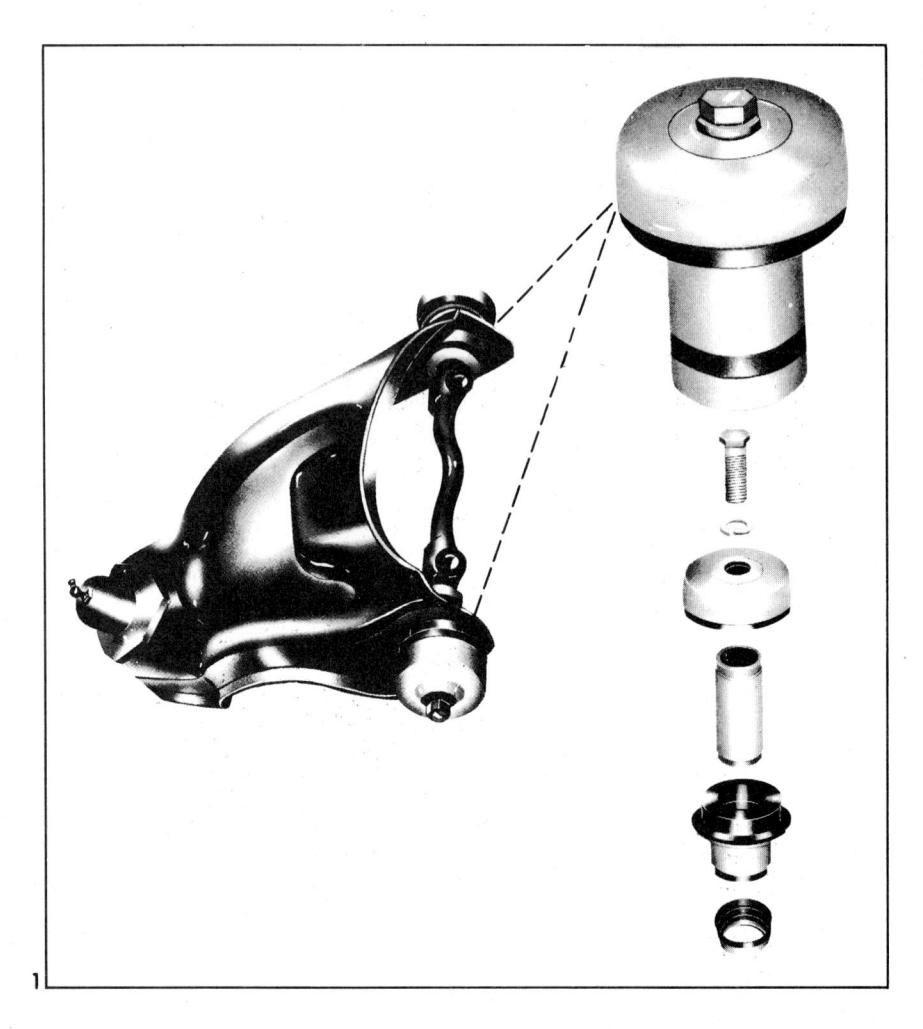

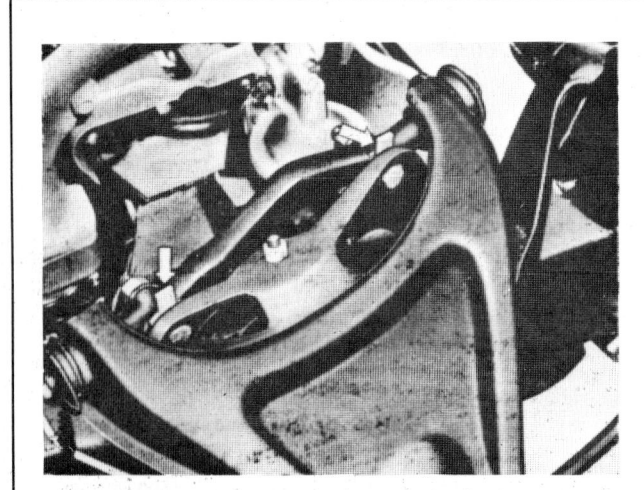

1

2

TO DECREASE POSITIVE CASTER: ADD SHIM AT "A".
TO DECREASE NEGATIVE CASTER: REMOVE SHIM AT "A".
TO INCREASE CAMBER: REMOVE SHIMS AT BOTH "A" AND "B"

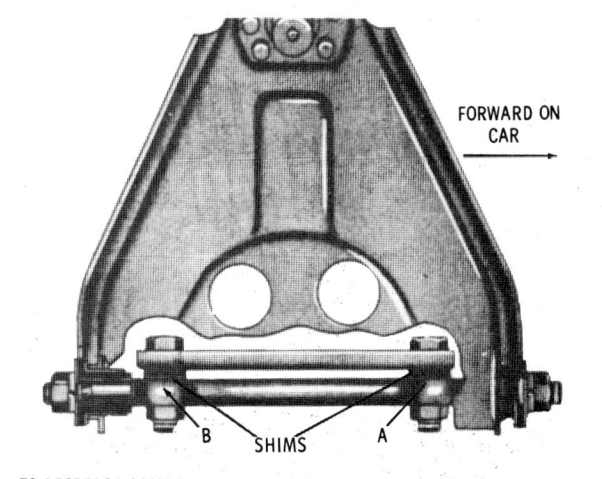

TO DECREASE CAMBER: ADD SHIMS AT BOTH "A" AND "B".
BY ADDING OR SUBTRACTING AN EQUAL AMOUNT OF SHIMS FROM "A" AND "B", CAMBER WILL CHANGE WITHOUT AFFECTING CASTER ADJUSTMENT.

40/CHASSIS, SUSPENSION & BRAKES

tell us that the right front wheel and tire should be kept perpendicular to the track surface for maximum traction. You can do this by setting the wheel with a lot of negative camber. If the range of adjustment isn't enough—and it usually isn't—shortening the upper A-arm will do it for you.

How do you know if you have exactly the right amount of negative camber? The pros recommend using a tire temperature gauge at several points across the width of the tread after a few hard laps. If the tread is cooler on one side than the other, change the camber to lean the wheel toward the cooler side. The idea is to make the whole width of the tire do the work, not just a part of it.

Caster should be changed, with more positive caster in the right front than the left. That will tend to make the car turn left, which is the only way to go on an oval track. To counteract the unequal camber and caster settings, Stock cars are set with toe-out of 1/8- to 1/16-in. instead of toe-in.

Many oval track cars use a big, tough stabilizer bar, but this can cause understeer, which is kind of frustrating when you have the wheels cramped all the way to the left and the car keeps plowing toward the fence. A lighter bar will allow more weight transfer to the right front, and help to create an oversteer condition.

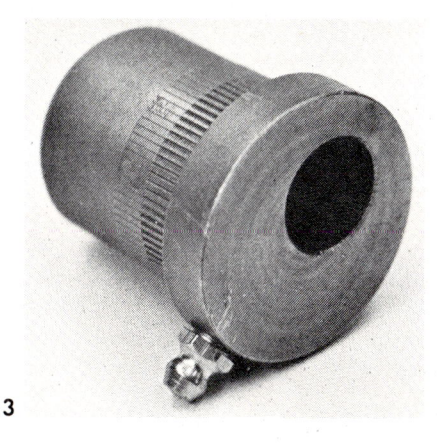

It's much better to spin out than to plow into the fence, if you have to make a split-second choice.

Weight-jacking or "wedging" has been done for a long time to all kinds of oval track cars for better traction in the turns. The term "wedge" comes from using small wedges in a leaf spring to put a twist into the car frame. On a cross-spring car, wedges will be used at the right side of the front spring perch, which raises the frame slightly at that corner and causes more weight to bear on the right front tire. Wedges are also put on the left side of the rear spring perch, so that more weight bears on the left rear.

Since the total weight of the car remains the same, putting more weight on the right front and left rear tires must lighten the left front and right rear. The result is extreme oversteer, which feels terrible when you are not used to it—but can give your car fantastic adhesion in the corners. The rear end will come around much faster when a car is wedged, up to a point. At that point, centrifugal force and weight transfer equal the load on the rear tires, and you can go like a rocket through the corners. Of course the left front wheel is so lightly loaded that it will be in the air most of the way through the corner on a midget—and barely touching on a bigger car—but that is the way to get speed in the corners, as long as you don't have to turn right.

There are no rules for setting up a chassis, just suggestions. What works for you may not work for anybody else. Worse yet, what works for you at one track may put you entirely out of the program at another.

The main thing is to be brave. Don't be afraid to try something just because all your friends tell you it won't work. The important thing in racing is to win races.

If you do go racing, don't expect the modifications you make to work equally well on the street, they won't. A sprint runner whose specialty is the 100-yard dash is never expected to be a great *mile* runner, and likewise your suspension shouldn't be asked to do too many jobs. There are no easy compromises between racing suspension and street suspension. What works great on an oval track would ruin a car for the road, and lift-chassis drag suspension isn't exactly the hot setup for freeway ramps. As it is in stock form, your automobile's front end does an excellent overall job. If you must make street modifications to it, just add the factory heavy-duty suspension components. Chances are the factory engineers know a little bit more about your front end than any of us.

1. A-arm bushings are vital parts of the front end, contributing to the safety, quietness, and handling. These special bushings by JAMCO are made so that the never need lubing.

2. Only an experienced front end expert should do your alignment, but you should learn how it's done. The caster and camber adjustments on most cars are made by using shims between the A-arm attaching bolts and the mounts on the frame.

3. These all-metal A-arm bushings are made for racing use. Since they are eccentric, they allow for more adjustment than stock bushings, to better suit a car for road-racing with different geometry and tires.

4. When a car has two tie-rods, you can adjust either one, but this will also change your steering wheel's position. Check this guide for the correct steering wheel placement.

CHASSIS, SUSPENSION & BRAKES/41

Wheel Alignment

The front wheels do much more than merely holding the car up. Here are the critical factors involved in proper steering and road holding.

Caster, camber, toe-in and toe-out—fancy words and mumbo-jumbo to sell you new tires? You don't need your wheels lined up, they're already straight—you can tell that just by looking at them, right? Wrong. Nevertheless, this attitude is still prevalent among many drivers. One of the factors contributing to this negative approach toward wheel alignment has been the difficulty in educating the driving public on how to take care of its automobiles. Those of us who drove for Uncle Sam recall the practice of visually checking all wheels before starting a vehicle. No one ever bothered to tell us exactly why we made that check. But the manual specified that a check of tire conditions and pressure be made each day. Although it is definitely a worthwhile practice, did you ever see a civilian driver bother to do it? Certainly, it would be a rare sight; yet this is one of the best ways to catch tire wear (a symptom of improper wheel alignment, among other things) in its early stages.

Too few of us realize that traveling 65 mph (or even today's 55 mph) on super highways can put a tremendous strain on the wheels and tires, if all four are not set properly. And how many drivers realize that the best alignment job in the world can be knocked out by the simple act of hitting a rut at moderate or high speeds, or banging the tire up against the curb while parking. This is not to say that wheel alignment is a delicate proposition about which little can be done, but don't blame an alignment man because your new treads disappear in a few thousand miles if the real reason is your poor driving habits.

Let's look at wheel alignment from the viewpoint of a skier—if his boards aren't properly aligned under him, he's going to take a bad spill, fast. And when he makes a highspeed turn, those skis had better relate to each other correctly or it's all over. Automobile drivers are more fortunate

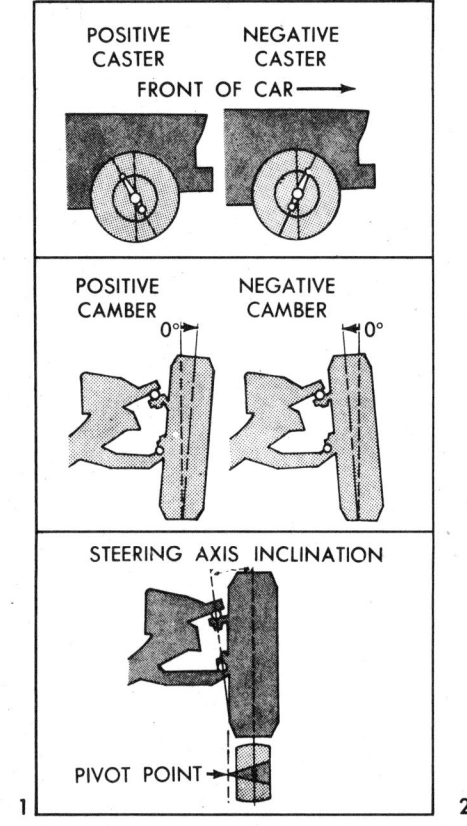

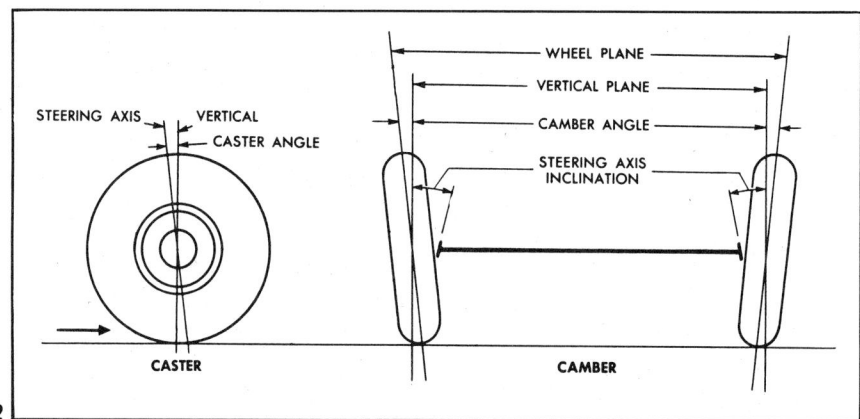

42/CHASSIS, SUSPENSION & BRAKES

in that the wheels are secured to the vehicle—if not, many of us would be off the road more often than on it. But even so, consider the damage involved in dragging one wheel around a turn if it's not lined up properly. Whenever you put more than one wheel on any sort of vehicle, you can assume that normal wear and tear, if nothing else, will eventually cause problems. And as parts wear, you can also assume that steering responsiveness will gradually suffer. Many motorists faithfully adhere to the notion that rotating their tires is a worthwhile idea, yet reject any suggestion that their caster or camber might need a periodic check.

THE ALIGNMENT SHOP

While alignment shops are all over the place, alignment procedures run the gamut from good to bad, and so do the qualifications of those who do the work. But wheel alignment can be a precision job, if the man behind the machine knows his business. Such a man is really more important to your front end than the equipment he uses; while good equipment is important for a correct alignment job, it's really worthless if the operator is just following a manual while he loosens *this* and tightens *that*. A good alignment specialist can look at your car and draw a pretty fair conclusion from his past experience as to exactly what he has to do to correct tire wear, steering, and handling. He'll take your car for a test drive before ever running it onto the rack, but once it's there, he understands its

1. Alignment specs are designed to put a slight tilt to your front end, but they really are just making up for other factors, and actually do make your front wheels go straight under normal driving conditions.

2. Both caster and camber affect a car's steerability and handling, and usually reflect the designer's compromise between handling in turns or straights, and ease of steering.

3. A modern independent front end is composed of a number of safety-vital parts. All of these must be checked before doing an alignment.

4. Most front ends are aligned by moving one of the A-arms (usually the upper) by small shims (arrows).

5. As demonstrated by this model, the A-arm's caster baseline is just straight up and down.

6. Removing a shim from the rear of the A-arm shifts the "tilt" of the spindle to the rear, which gives you positive caster.

7. When the same number of shims are removed or added at both points, it changes the spindle's angle in another plane, which is camber.

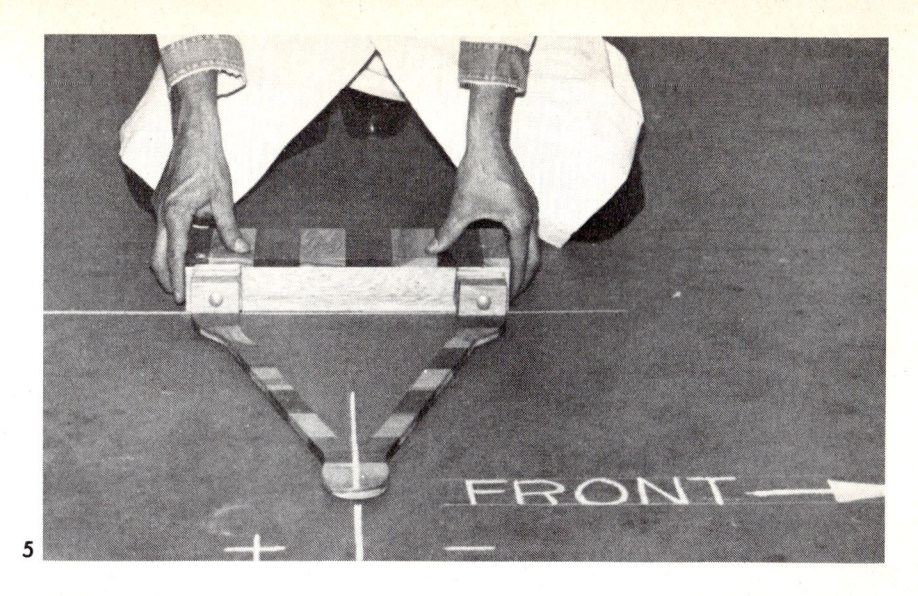

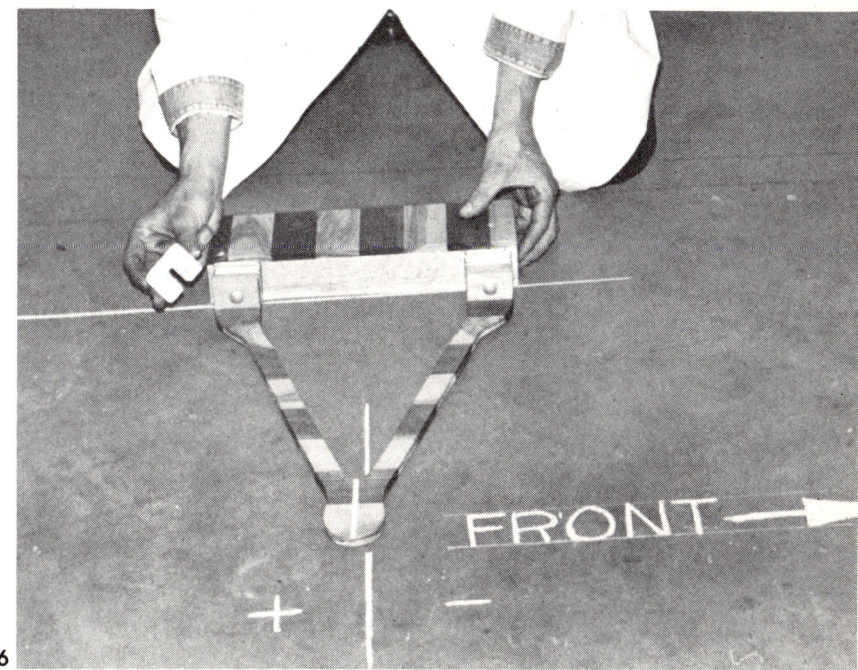

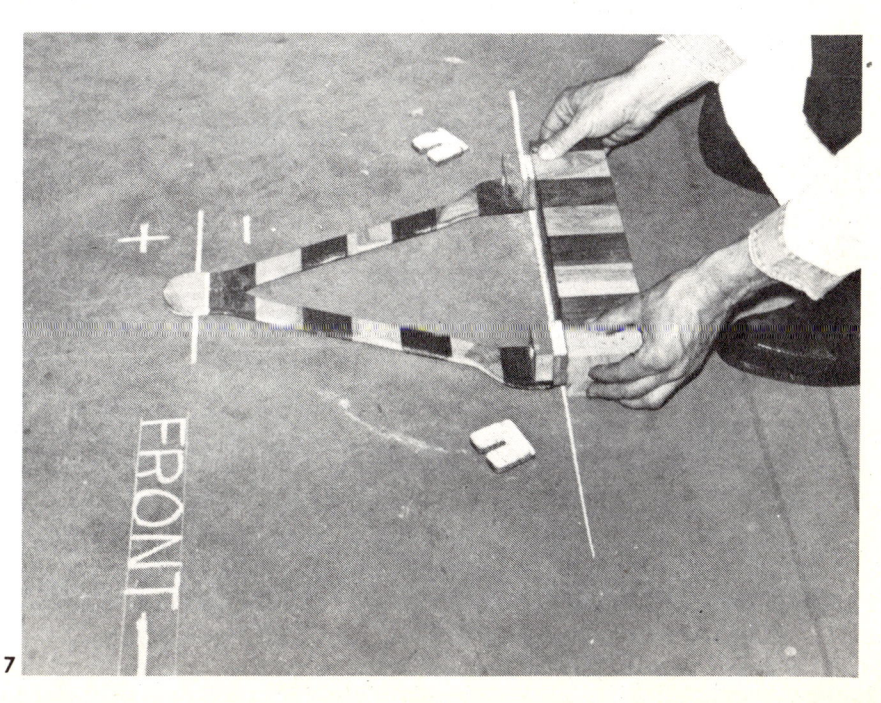

Wheel Alignment

problems and knows which adjustments are necessary to correct them. Finding such a wheel alignment man may sound like a pretty tall order—don't be misled by shiny new or complicated looking apparatus—but it can be done, and once you locate him, hang on tightly. He's worth his weight in gold to you. And while you're at it, make that daily trip around the car and take a good look.

The various factors involved in wheel alignment were explained in the front end chapter, but even if you can't do the job yourself, you ought to know what's involved in setting all of these factors correctly on your front end. Toe-in and toe-out are probably the easiest specs to set on your front end. All it takes is suitable measuring equipment and a few adjustments to the tie rod length. As with any alignment problem, the condition and wearing of your tires will be your first clue that something is awry. When there's a feathered edge on the *inside* of the front tires tread design, there's too much toe-in, meaning that the fronts of the tires are closer together than the rears. Almost all cars are supposed to have *some* toe-in, which essentially is designed to allow for the slack present in the steering gear and other front-

1. Since front-end designs differ from make to make, so do the methods of adjusting their alignment.

2. Adjusting the early Chevy kingpin front ends requires taking off the upper grease fitting and inserting an Allen wrench, which controls the eccentric upper spindle mount.

3. Chrylser Corp. cars which have torsion bar front suspension also use eccentric adjusters. You simply loosen the locknuts (A) and then turn the cambolts (B) to move the wheel/spindle; then tighten nuts.

4. Full-size late-model Fords are a special problem to align, unless you have a tool like this to hold the upper A-arm control shaft in place after you loosen it for your alignment adjustments.

5. Not all cars are aligned at the upper A-Arm. Most of the smaller Ford products, like this Maverick, have their eccentric adjusters on the lower arm for ease of adjustment.

6. On this Mustang with strut-type suspension, the caster is changed by lengthening or shortening the strut. Loosening one nut and tightening the other will bring the lower control arm backward or forward to give you the caster change you want.

7. It's important when doing front-end alignment that the steering wheel and brakes be locked when the car is on the rack. A simple clamp does it.

METHODS OF ADJUSTMENT

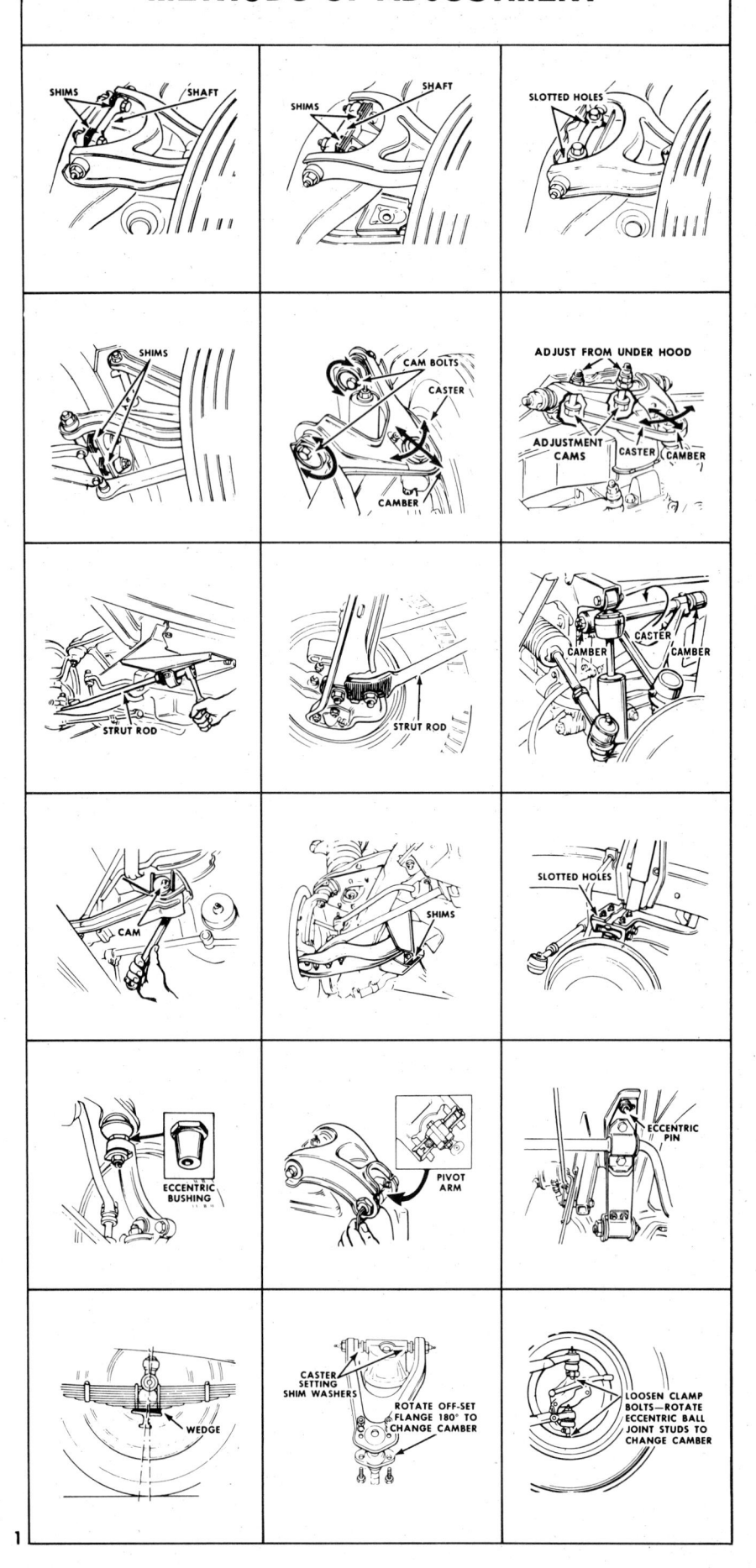

44/CHASSIS, SUSPENSION & BRAKES

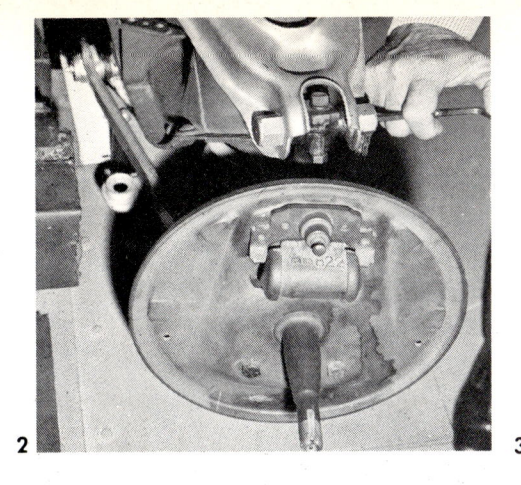

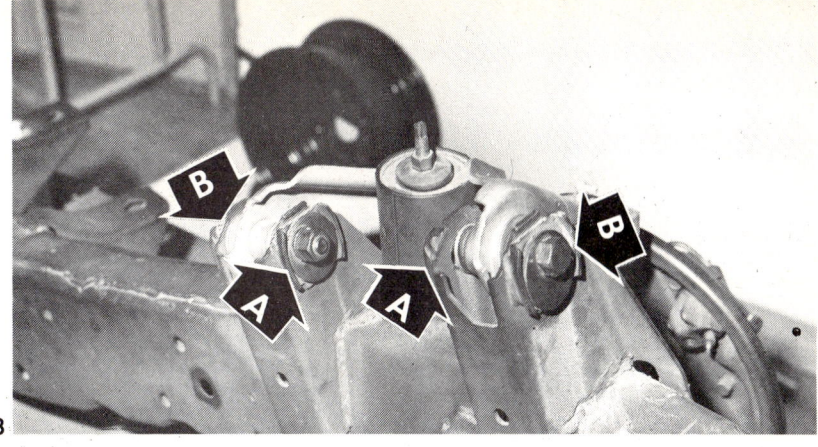

end components. When the car is going straight down the road, there really isn't any toe-in, the wheels are pointing straight ahead because the force of pushing them down the road has "spread" them apart at the front. So setting a little toe-in to start with allows for this spreading action and makes the wheels point straight when driving. Just as too much toe-in is wrong, toe-*out,* where tires are closer at the rear than at the front, is also wrong and will cause a feathered edge on the *outside* of the tread. Each tie rod on an independent front end has three basic parts, two male threaded ends and a female threaded centerpiece. By loosening the clamps, the centerpiece can be turned to effectively lengthen or shorten the tie rod as the ends thread in and out. Toe adjustments are simple. Making the tie rod shorter (where the tie rod is behind the spindles as it usually is) will give you toe-out, and making it longer will make the tires toe-in. But on an independent front end where there is a tie rod on each side of the car, you should make the same adjustments on each tie rod to keep the steering wheel in the correct center position.

TOE-IN—AND OUT

If you were really paying attention in the front end chapter, you may be wondering now whether this toe-in stays the same at all times. It doesn't, of course, due to the way the steering arms on the spindles are angled (the Ackerman effect). The inside wheel on a turn must turn in a smaller circle than the outside wheel. To do this, the wheels must assume a toe-*out* relationship which can be measured on a front-end aligner when the wheels are turned on the calibrated turntables. However, the wheels should return to their normal toe-in relationship when turned back to the straight-ahead position. If the difference in angle between the two front wheels on a turn (called the "steering geometry" or "cornering

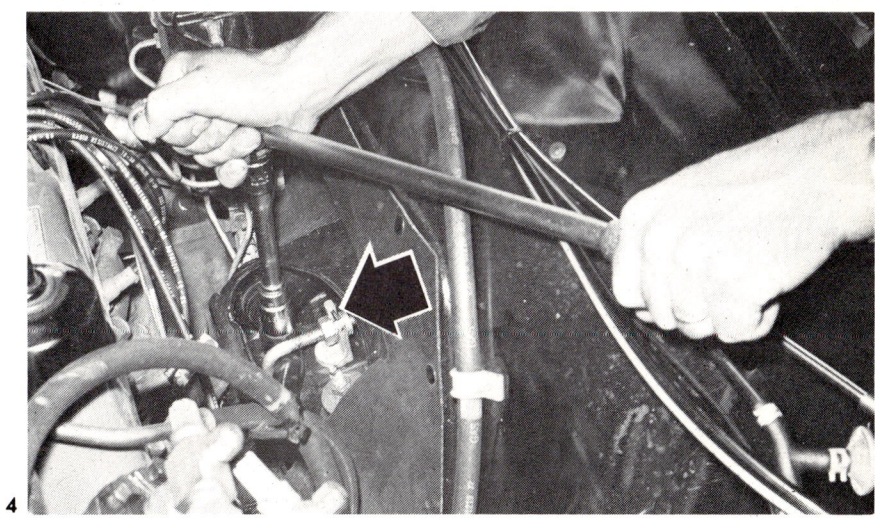

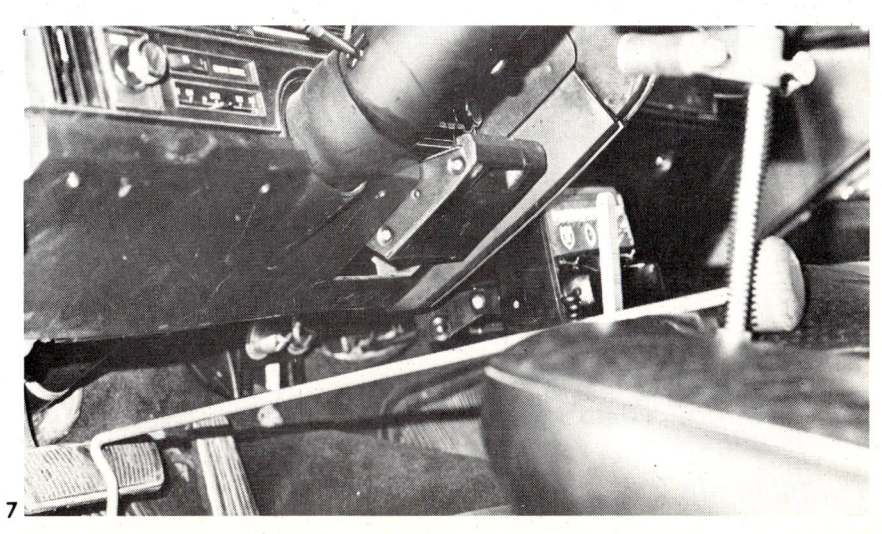

CHASSIS, SUSPENSION & BRAKES/45

Wheel Alignment

wheel relationship") is not according to spec, there's no adjustment that can be made except to replace any bent steering arms or tie rods.

Caster and camber adjustments are only slightly more complex to make than setting toe-in. If you have an antique car, truck or van which has a solid beam front axle, then the adjustments are really no harder to perform, but you'll find a lot less alignment shops that can do the work. To correct anything other than toe-in on a beam axle front end, the axle itself must be bent by chaining it to the alignment rack and using hydraulic jacks. Caster can be changed to a small extent by bending the radius rods (if so equipped) or shimming their mounting points on the frame. If it's a beam axle with two semi-elliptic leaf springs as found on some trucks and vans, you can change the caster by shimming between the leaf springs and their mounting pads on the axle. Adjusting toe-in on a beam axle is even simpler than an independent though, because there's only one tie rod to work with.

On the more common independent front end, there are several methods of setting caster and camber, depending on how the A-arms are attached to the frame. Usually the upper A-arm is attached to the frame by a shaft which can be shimmed either closer to or away from its mounting bracket on the frame, thus tilting the wheel as desired. The camber setting is designed to reduce tire scrub as the wheels are turned and to spread wheel loading evenly over the wheel bearings and spindle. Some symptoms of improper camber in your front end would be rapid tire wear and a tendency for the car to pull to the side with the greatest camber. When there's more wear on the outside of the treads, then there's too much positive camber, while negative wears the inside treads. Most cars are designed to have some positive camber, or outward tilt, on the top of the wheels to allow for the change of angle that occurs when a normal load of cargo or passengers is added. As with other aspects of front-end align-

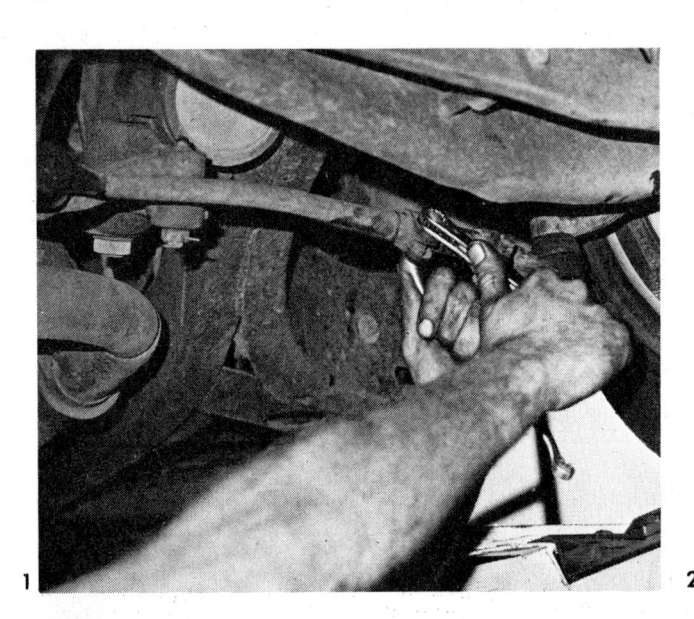

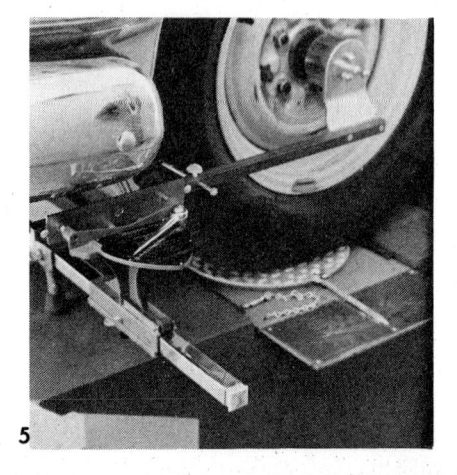

46/CHASSIS, SUSPENSION & BRAKES

ment, camber is designed to make the wheels operate close to perpendicular to the road when driving, with maximum, even contact across the tire tread.

There are usually two adjustment points on each upper A-arm. While camber is adjusted by shimming the same amount at each point, the caster can also be changed merely by placing more or less shims at one point than the other, thereby tilting the spindle either forward or back.

Just as the methods of adjustment may vary from one vehicle make to another, the equipment used to align a front end also varies from shop to shop. In good working order, they all do the same job, which is to align your front wheels to factory specs. However, if you took your car to several different shops, you might get different readings at each shop! Just find a good shop with a reputation and stick with it. We'll show you several different methods of alignment in this chapter, all of which do the job. Just remember that you shouldn't wait until your tires are almost bald before you think about having this important service performed.

1. Your toe settings are simple to make. Just loosen the (probably a bit rusty) clamps on the tie-rod adjustment sleeves on each tie-rod.

2. Both tie-rods must be adjusted equally for the steering wheel to remain centered. With an alignment system that has an electric monitor, toe is easily adjusted while watching readings on the screen.

3. Every alignment shop you go to will not have brand-new equipment, but remember that it's not the type of equipment, but the way that it's used that counts. Most systems use a gauge hung off the wheel spindle.

4. In the Bagge system, toe readings are easily taken from a gauge bar which connects the two wheels. Note the length of the pointer which will magnify readings for more accuracy.

5. The Bender alignment rack uses a combination of wheel turntables and gauges mounted on a bar which connects the two wheel up front.

6. A new system from the Stewart-Warner Alemite company locks onto the outside of the wheel rim for sensitive readings, and uses line-of-sight transits to read the specs.

7. Shooting either in front or to the rear of the wheels or even over the tops of the fenders, the Alemite aligner sights in on the crosshairs at the opposite wheel, and readings tell him exactly what alignment is.

8. Another interesting Alemite tool is this spreader bar, which locks in between the front wheels to simulate the road forces that separate them. With the spreader bar in place, all cars are adjusted to zero toe.

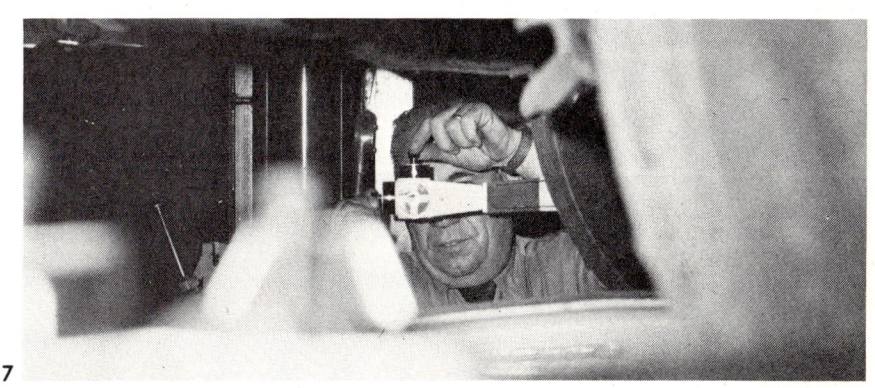

CHASSIS, SUSPENSION & BRAKES/47

Springs and Torsion Bars

Springing mechanisms vary throughout the auto industry, but they accomplish the same end result.

Springs have come a long way since the days when the royal coach was hung—or suspended, if you prefer—on great leather straps. As you can imagine, leather doesn't have all that much give to it and sway control was nonexistent, with the result that the coach pitched and rolled like a flat-bottom boat in a typhoon. Today, the modern passenger car is hung on a variety of springing mechanisms, including leaves, coils, and torsion bars. Often these are used in combination, such as leaf springs on the rear, with coils holding up the front. Which setup does the best job depends on the weight of the car, the type of suspension design and the particular engineer to whom you happen to be talking at the moment.

LEAF SPRINGS

Of the three basic types, the leaf spring has the widest application. Depending on the design of the suspension system, it can take a number of shapes: quarter-elliptical, semi-elliptical, or cantilever, to name a few. By selectively arranging the leaves it can even become its own shock absorber. But why is the leaf the most commonly used?...what makes it so universally applicable?

There are three primary answers to this compound question. One is tradition, another is versatility, and the third is that all-important factor: cost.

The use of leaf springs far predates the invention of the automobile. Stacks of leaves that look identical to their modern-day counterparts were used on wagons and stagecoaches over 100 years ago. And as the first cars were nothing more than self-propelled wagons, what could be more natural than to swipe a set off the old buckboard? They were tried and true. It was that dang, newfangled engine that was causing all the trouble. Not until much later, when cars became faster, did more sophisticated suspensions become necessary. At 6 mph almost anything will do.

Just because the leaf spring was first does not necessarily mean it is the best. In terms of energy stored per pound of spring weight, leaf springs are on the bottom of the list, with a figure of 300 in.-lbs. of energy stored per pound of spring. This falls far below the 700 in.-lbs. per pound that describes a coil spring and is less than a third of the 1000 figure that applies to torsion bars. But in terms of cost, leaf springs become much more interesting. Not only are the units themselves cheaper, but the suspension design incorporating them is generally simpler and, therefore, less costly.

If for no other reason than the fact that leaf springs have been designed into so many different cars, engineers have learned more about them than they've learned about coils or bars. And early in the game the leaf was refined to a high degree. For example, the Chevys of the late '20's utilized the friction between the leaves as part of the dampening system so that the springs in effect became their own shock absorbers. In later applications this has proven unnecessary and in fact undesirable, due to the harsh ride that results. Modern designers use everything from asbestos to zinc between the leaves to reduce friction and cut down on transmitted road noise.

Although the energy-storing capabilities of a leaf spring are less than the other types, it does offer one advantage not found in either a coil or torsion bar. It is possible to build a higher progressive rate into a leaf spring. That means the further the spring is deflected the more resistance it offers as more leaves are brought into play. Thus, it is possible with leaf springs to design a reasonably soft ride over minor road disturbances with enough reserve action to prevent the suspension from bottoming when the car encounters a severe "irregularity."

When speaking of springs, the term spring rate keeps cropping up. Spring rate is simply how much force is needed to bend a spring a given distance. If you have a spring with a rate of 300 lbs., that means to bend the spring 1 inch you must load it with 300 lbs. of either weight or impact force. To bend it 2 ins. you need 600 lbs., and so on until you reach the limit of the spring travel. A progressive rate spring might require 300 lbs. for the first inch, 400 lbs. for the second inch, and so forth.

There are a number of ways to vary the rate of a spring. In the case of leaf springs, the two most common methods are to increase the number of leaves, or increase the thickness of the leaves—or both. Generally speaking, the heavier single leaf is useful only on light cars such as the smaller-engine Camaro and the Chevy II. When the weight goes up you need to add more leaves to carry it. This is due to the fact that as you increase the thickness of a single leaf you run into a limitation of elasticity, even for spring steel. Elasticity is not the ability to stretch. What the word actually means is the ability to return to original shape after being deformed. A piece of window glass is very elastic, but not particularly flexible. When a flat spring leaf is bent, the material on the outside of the curve is stretched while the material on the inside is compressed. The thicker the leaf, the more stretch is

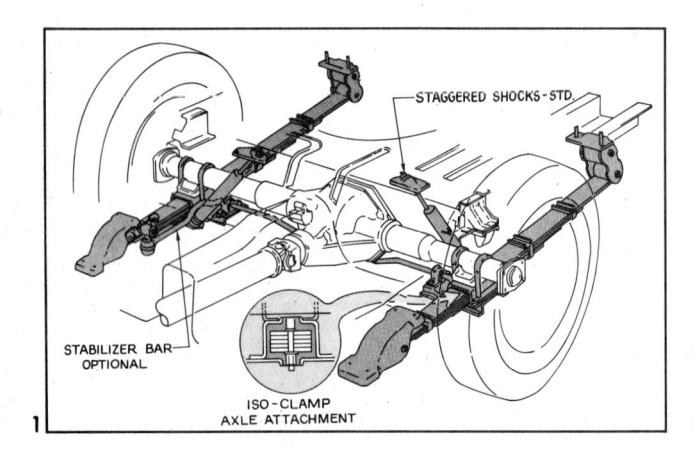

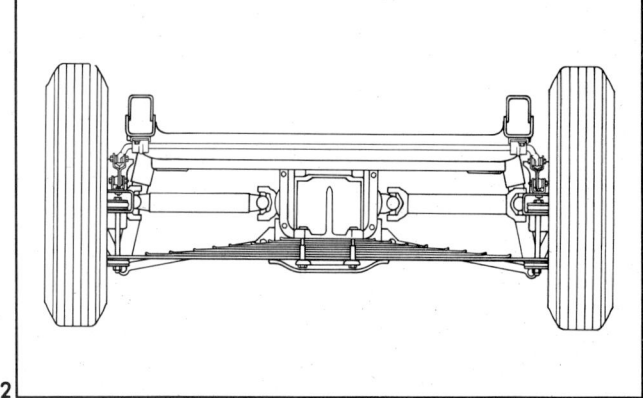

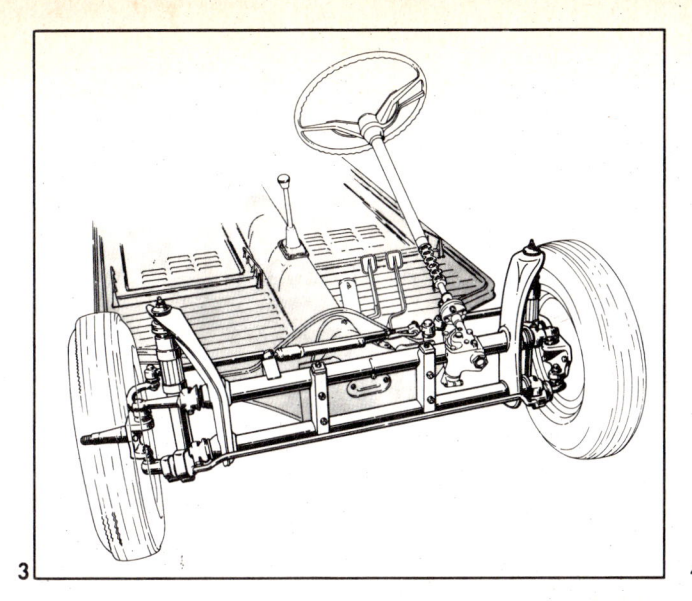

1. The leaf spring has been around since the first cars were built and it's still doing the job today. The new Mustang II uses sophisticated leaves in the rear with extra-big shackle bushings and lots of rubber for isolating road noises out.

2. The transverse leaf spring has been out of the suspension picture for over 20 years, except on Chevy's Corvette with the independent rear suspension ('63-up). It takes on a unique role here, actually working like two separate quarter-elliptic springs, one for each side.

3. The ubiquitous Volkswagen's four-trailing-arm front suspension uses two sets of transverse torsion bars. In each of the front tubes are sets of laminated steel leaves that permit controlled amounts of twist.

4. Many of today's American cars use coil springs all around for smooth ride quality, however the rear end must be anchored with several firm control arms and the shocks must be stiffened to make up for the lack of inter-leaf spring friction.

5. Devices to "restore sagging front ends" have been around for years, but they don't cure anything. They do make the ride stiffer and force the springs to bottom out sooner.

needed to bend a given amount. Therefore, as you increase the thickness you increase the distance and quickly reach a point called the elastic limit. If the leaf is bent any further it will not return to its original shape, and thus is not a spring any longer, but a piece of permanently bent steel.

Once you have decided to multiply the number of leaves to achieve the desired rate, there are still a number of variables, such as the arrangement of the leaves. Older cars (much older) used elliptical springs—two stacks of leaves joined in the shape of an ellipse. The stacks were tied together at their ends and hooked to the car at the center of each half. The design was a hangover from the horse and buggy era and was usable only as long as cars resembled surreys, because of the distance necessary between the frame and the axle to accommodate this stacking arrangement. Later it was found that by using thicker leaves—and more of them—the same effect could be achieved with a semi-elliptical design which was only half as high. This spring shape has proven so versatile that it is still found in one form or another on many of today's cars. A quarter-elliptical spring is half of a semi-elliptical: that is, the spring ends at the axle and extends only one direction from it. Except for rare instances years ago, quarter-elliptic springs have not been used for production cars, but are often seen on hot rods and race cars where space and weight are at a premium.

With the exception of the full elliptical shape, leaf springs are attached to the frame by means of shackles. These are connected to the main leaf of the spring at the shackle eye, which is a loop bent in the end of the leaf. A bolt is passed through the loop and held to the shackle with a nut. The bolt rests in a rubber bushing which serves two purposes. One, it permits the shackle to swing as the spring is flexed, which is an important movement. Without it the whole assembly would be rigid and would have no spring action. The second function of the bushing is to keep vibration and road noise from being passed from the spring to the frame of the car.

These are several ways to modify a leaf spring to make it stronger, softer, higher, or lower. Longer shackles are one common means of altering the height of the body in relation to the axle. At your local hamburger stand, you can see many examples of how to and how *not* to raise your car. For cars with leaf springs, just using longer spring shackles will raise the car, and shorter shackles do the opposite. But a word of caution: long shackles with several sets of holes for the spring eyebolt are sold by the thousands in speed shops today. They work fine for drag racing because the two rear springs can be set in different holes for preloading one side or the other. However, when used on the street to gain the "jacked up" look, they adversely affect handling. Unlike the drag racer, you have to go around corners, and these long shackles create lots of side-sway on corners.

INTERESTING NO-NO's

One "problem" that seems to befuddle the "pepper tree" set is that a set of custom rear spring shackles, say, 3 ins. longer than the stock counterpart, only raise the car approximately half as much, or about 1-½ ins. Shackles 4 ins. longer than stock will raise the car only about 2 ins. What is happening in the case of the 4-in. longer shackle is that while the back of the car rises 2 ins., the rear of the spring is depressed an equal amount. It's all a matter of sim-

CHASSIS, SUSPENSION & BRAKES/49

Springs

ple leverage, since the front end of the spring is attached to the chassis by its front anchor, while the axle is approximately midway back, between the anchor and the shackle. So, if you want to raise the rear of your car by 3 ins. (heaven forbid), then you must utilize rear shackles 6 ins. longer than stock (shudder!).

Obviously, the reverse is equally true. If you revert to decreasing the length of the rear shackles in order to lower your car's silhouette, a decrease of 2 ins. will drop the car's rear only 1 in. However, we're talking theory only; shortening a shackle will only serve to lessen its swing or arc, thereby reducing the effectiveness of the spring which can "give" only as much as the shackle can pivot.

Another popular method for jacking cars up is the use of air bags. They are great for racing, because you can change weight distribution just by adding air or letting it out. They go inside coil springs, and kits are sold to adapt them for leaf spring cars. But they weren't designed to raise a car 6 ins. or so, and when the bags are overloaded by pumping that much air into them, they wear out early.

Overloads or helper springs are sometimes used to beef-up the suspension to carry that 440 where the old flathead used to go. Incidentally, these are examples of the progressive spring, as the helpers don't come into play until the original spring has been depressed part way.

Another method of modifying the leaf is re-arching, sometimes called "torching." On the surface this seems simple enough. All you have to do is apply a torch to the spring, out near the shackle eye, and heat it until it is soft enough to be bent easily. The problem is that the heated area stays soft, relative to the rest of the spring, and has none of its original temper. This leads to early failure, which in a tight turn can get tricky. Few hot rodders have a tempering oven in their backyard, so detailed instructions on how hot, how long, and how to quench would be of little use. It is much easier to let the nearest spring shop do the job—and cheaper over the long haul.

COIL SPRINGS

As speeds increased and the desire for luxury cars grew, engineers turned to coil springs to provide the ride that the auto-buying public seemed to demand more and more.

Coil springs offer their own mixture of advantages and problems, and in most respects are more similar to torsion bars than they are to leaf springs. When a coil is compressed there is only a slight amount of bending involved. The real action is the twisting of the wire from which the spring is wound, and this twisting motion is the same thing that stores the energy in a torsion bar. From the standpoint of the principle of operation, the only difference between the two lies in the slight bending found in a coil.

In spite of working to a lower stress, the energy-storage capabilities of a coil spring are greater than those of a leaf type, although less than those of torsion bars. This should mean lower unsprung weight, since it requires less material to make a coil of equal strength to a leaf. But in practice it doesn't work that way. The complexity of the suspension system necessary with coils offsets the weight gain. Then too, coils demand a more sophisticated system of vibration dampening and sway control, and a lack of this technology in the early days led to the great swaying barges of the '40's and '50's.

On the plus side, coils lend themselves to a wider range of design due to the smaller space they occupy. They were instrumental in the development of the 2- and 4-wheel individual suspension systems. Space is further gained by locating the shock absorber inside the coil, enabling a more compact suspension package.

If you had the equipment to unwind the coil spring from the average car, you would probably be surprised at its length. Ten to 12 ft. is not uncommon, and this is another reason why coils are designed into a given car. Say the suspension requirements preclude the use of leaf springs; then the designer is left with the choice of coils or torsion bars. But for the same thickness as a coil, the bar would have to be 12 feet long! The obvious answer is to wind the bar into a coil, and that is exactly what is done in many situations.

The thickness of the metal used is the function of a long and pretty hairy set of formulae dealing with rate, pitch, and load, which say nothing more than the heavier the car, the thicker the metal must be.

Like most ideas, coils are at best a compromise. The improved ride characteristic is often offset by the increased cost of the more elaborate suspension systems needed to accommodate them. For the front, double control arms are nearly universal, and coils in conjunction with a solid front axle are rare, although not not unheard of. The Ford Bronco uses such a setup. Coils on the rear demand control arms, sometimes called torque arms, to stabilize the frame and axle. These arms transmit acceleration and braking forces to the frame and control axle torque reaction. Without them the car would be completely unstable, as coils lack even the little lateral stability inherent in leaf springs.

As with all other types of springs, coils must be mounted on rubber bushings. Metal-to-metal contact raises transmitted road noise inside the car to an intolerable level. These bushings are also found at the ends of the torque arms for the same reason. The spring bushings are located at the end of the coil and should be checked for wear when replacing or repairing the spring.

Modifications on coil springs include inserting spacers between the coils to lengthen the spring and raise the car, or to hopefully rejuvenate the tired and sagging spring. You should be warned, though, that those "twistin" spring raisers also stiffen the ride

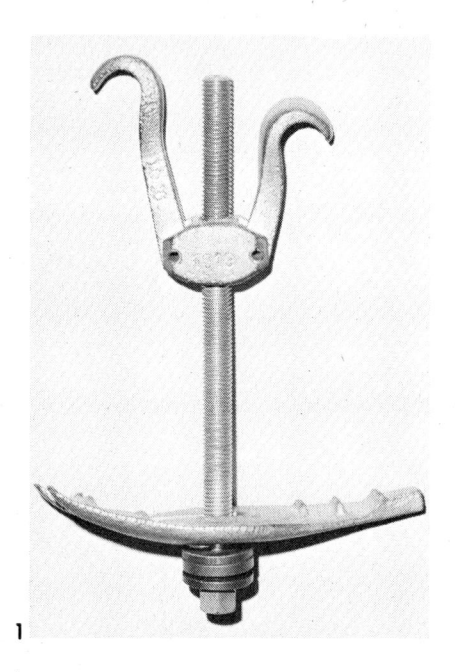

1. The only real cure for bad front springs is replacement, which is made easier and safer with a tool like this Alemite unit which goes inside the spring. Tightening the bolt compresses the spring.

2. You can see here how sagging coil or leaf springs can adversely affect your front-end alignment. The same goes for front and rear ends lowered on purpose for the "trick" look.

3. Not all vehicles use regular steel springs. Dunlop makes these rubber "Hydrolastic" suspension units for BMC cars. Using special rubber, and hydraulic fluid moved through orifices, these units replace both the springs and shocks.

4. Most racing cars use a combined coil spring/shock absorber that is adjustable for all track conditions.

5. Racing coil/shocks usually have several settings for shock firmness and the spring can be adjusted by turning a threaded collar.

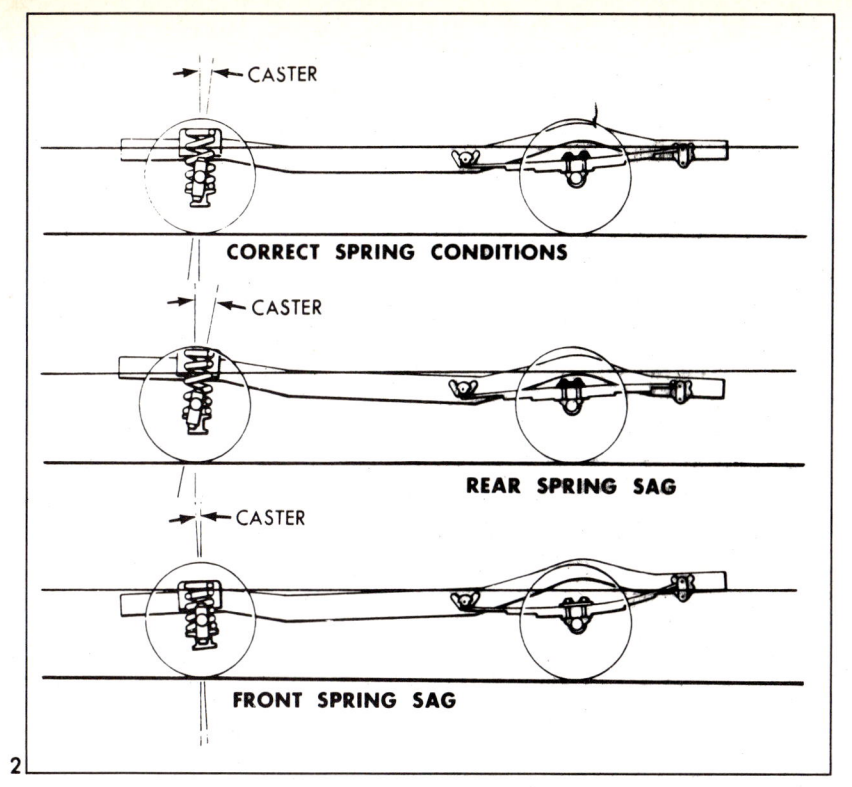

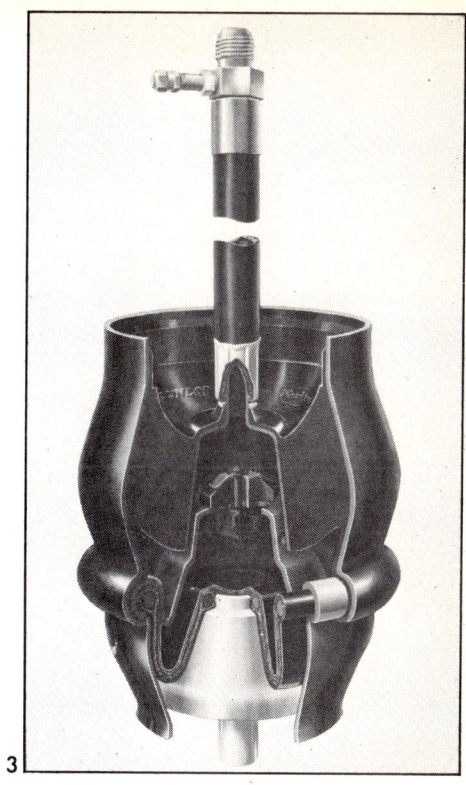

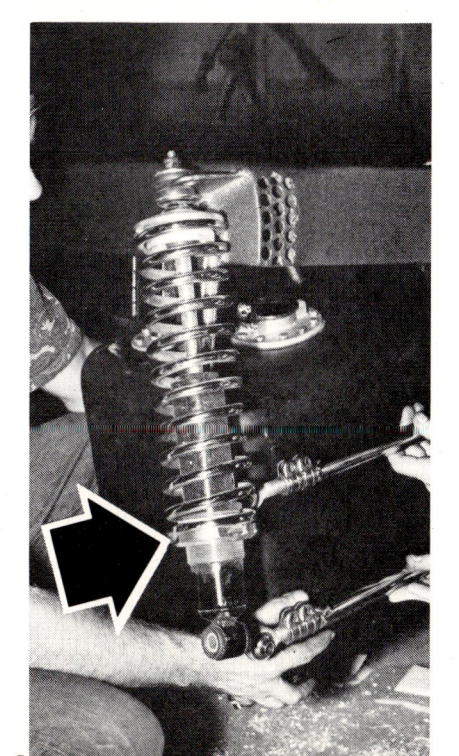

and make the front end bottom out sooner on bumps.

There are several methods of lowering. One way is by removing one or more coils by cutting. But don't make the mistake of trying to get a 2-inch drop by cutting out one coil when the coils are 2 inches apart. You will be disappointed to find the car sags more than you wanted. The reason for this is that by shortening the spring you have made a whole new unit that is not only smaller, but weaker, as well. This further demonstrates the similarities between coils and torsion bars, as we will see when we examine the effects of varying the length of a bar.

If you insist on changing the height of your vehicle, be advised that many states now have new laws regarding suspension modifications. Most of these laws specify that either *no* modifications are legal, or they restrict you to raising or lowering a car no more than 2 ins. With both leaf and coil springs, the best way to change ride height is with different model stock springs. If you want to lower the car, use the lighter-capacity springs from a six-cylinder "cheapie" model; this will also give you additional front-to-rear weight transfer for drag racing. If you still think that the jacked-up look is what you want, use the springs designed for a heavy-duty model with air-conditioning or a station wagon. These will generally raise the car a legal inch or two.

Heating the coils should be the last thing you think about—and then only long enough to decide it is a bad idea. As with leaves, heating removes the temper and turns that section of the coil into soft iron that is bound to fail sooner or later, with the heavy odds on sooner.

TORSION BARS

Torsion bars seem at first blush to be the answer to the car builder's dream. What could be simpler? Or stronger? Why doesn't everybody use them? Well, with all their virtues, bars have some drawbacks—and a big one is the lack of versatility. For example, once it is decided that the required load and rate dictates a coil spring, it is possible to vary the diameter and length to fit it into the space available. Not so with torsion bars. Here, when the lever length and maximum stress are fixed, so are the diameter and torsion bar length. In other words, when the slide rule says the bar must be so long and such-and-such a diameter, that is what it must be. Without changing the cross-sectional area of the bar, it can only be shortened by increasing the length of the operating lever or putting two or more bars in parallel. And often the parallel solution isn't as easy as it sounds. Due to the nature of the beast, in order to shorten a bar by half you would need to place eight bars in parallel to maintain the same rate. It isn't easy but it isn't impossible either, because that is exactly what Volkswagen does. But we'll get into that refinement a little later.

Torsion bars should be inspected when removed for nicks or scratches on the surface that create stress ris-

Springs

ers which lead to cracks. These cracks will quickly propagate through the spring steel of the bar and lead to failure. In addition to the seals used at the end of the bar, most torsion bars are coated with a heavy paint for protection. If small nicks are found and replacement of the bar is not feasible, you may polish out the scratch and shot-peen the area to remove the stress riser. Be sure to apply a new coat of paint to the polished area.

Most U.S. cars equipped with torsion bars have a height adjustment at the end of the bar that lets you raise or lower the car a limited amount. This is accomplished with an adjusting nut and is one of the features that makes torsion bars unique. Another is the inherent sway control of the bar that simplifies that area of design. But there are other design factors that make this type of spring less than perfect. For one thing, in a unibody construction, using bars positioned fore and aft, it is necessary to beef-up the chassis near the center of the car where the bar is anchored. In designs using transverse (side to side) bars—such as Volkswagen—this problem doesn't present itself to the designer.

Torsion bars offer one advantage over leaves and coils in that the height of the car may be altered without affecting the spring rate. As Chrysler products are the only ones on this side of the pond to make extensive use of bars, (GM's front-wheel-drive Cad Eldorado and Toronado are torsion bar-sprung—in the front—but are of fairly limited production), we will discuss a typical height adjustment on a late model Dodge. You must first make sure that there is nothing interfering with the static height such as passengers, low tires or a trunkful of old batteries. Park the car on a dead level surface and make sure the fuel tank is full. Clean out any mud, sticks or old gum wrappers from the bottom of the steering knuckle arm assemblies, and from the lowest area of the height-adjusting blades, which are directly below the center of the lower control arm inner pivots. Hop up and down on the bumper a few times to get the car settled in its normal position and then measure the distance from the lowest point of one adjusting blade to the floor, and from the lowest point of the steering knuckle on the same side to the floor. Subtract the second measurement from the first and your answer will be somewhere from 1 in. to 4 ins., depending on car model. Check that figure with the specifications for your car in the factory shop manual, and raise or lower the bar adjustment until they agree. The side-to-side difference should not be more than ⅛-in.

AIR/OIL SUSPENSION

One of the most novel suspension systems in use is one that doesn't use any springs at all. There are no coils, leaves or torsion bars in it. We are talking about the suspension on that funny-looking French car—the Citroen. Actually, the idea is so far removed from the standard concepts of suspension that it looks as if it might have evolved on some other planet. But it works.

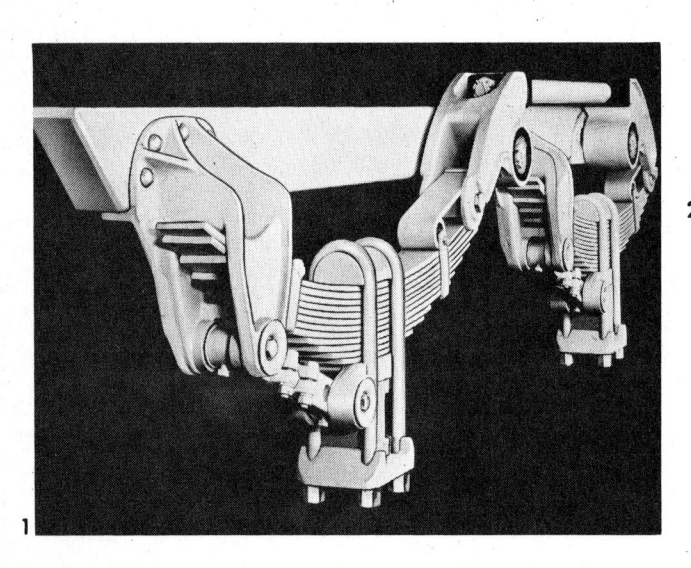

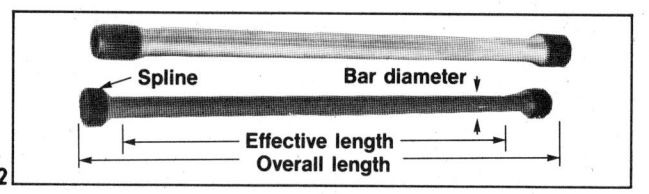

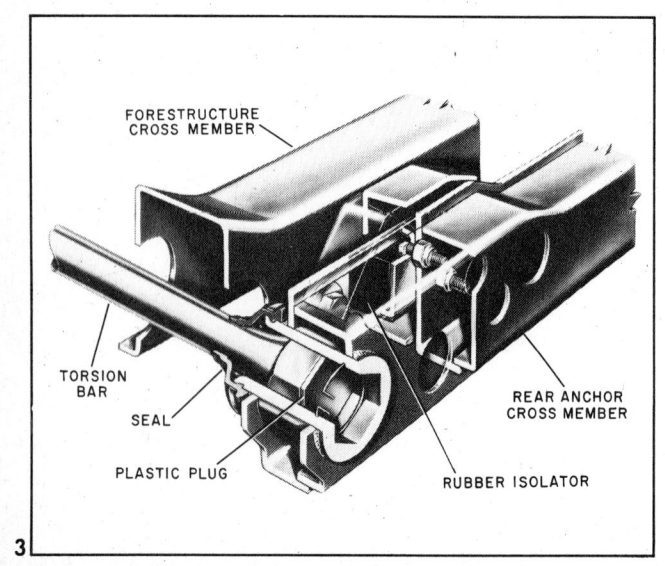

52/CHASSIS, SUSPENSION & BRAKES

The basic unit of the Citroen's air-oil suspension is a steel sphere about 4 ins. in diameter. There is one for each wheel. Inside the sphere is a rubber diaphragm dividing it into two hemispheres. On the top side of the diaphragm the space is filled with pressurized nitrogen, while on the other side, the hollow is filled with brake fluid. Although the internal pressure of the nitrogen is constant, the pressure on the fluid varies, as we will see in a minute. The wheel is connected via a series of levers to a piston which acts on the brake fluid in the bottom of the sphere.

When the wheel strikes a bump, the piston is driven into the brake fluid which, in turn, transmits the force to the nitrogen cushion. The fluid distributes the load evenly over the surface of the diaphragm. The nitrogen naturally resists this action and forces the wheel back to its original position at the earliest opportunity.

The fluid end of the system is connected by a maze of plumbing to a pump run by the engine. The output of this pump can be varied by the driver and this varies the pressure in the system. The effect of this is to raise or lower the car. When things get rough you can just touch the lever and go from 6 ins. of ground clearance up to 11 ins.

In the rear is a self-equalizing device that performs a number of functions. One is keeping the car level. If you suddenly load four people in the back seat, the rear of the car droops as any car would. But in a few seconds the back of the car starts to rise and soon it is level again. Another thing the system does is transfer pressure while you are cornering so that the outside wheels become more stiffly suspended than the inside pair which keeps the car very level in a turn. This works so well that the Citroen is one of the best handling passenger sedans in the world. But the real beauty of the air-oil is the combination of ride and good handling. While the car is handling almost like a sports car, it is riding like a Cadillac wishes it could.

The air-oil suspension is deceiving in appearance. All those tiny tubes and switches give you the impression that it would be fine for a scale model, but under a full-size car it wouldn't last. In practice the system has found increasing acceptance by the manufacturers of buses and heavy trucks. It has more than paid for itself by providing a smoother ride and therefore reducing damage to the goods in transit.

RUBBER SUSPENSION

If the air-oil system seems the way out, there is still another one on tap that is even more exotic—rubber in shear. The energy stored in a leaf spring is 300 in.-lbs. per pound of spring, but a rubber spring in shear can store 2000 in.-lbs. per pound of spring weight. This obviously makes it a much more efficient material and you wonder right away why it is not being used. It is, but so far the application of rubber springs has been limited to heavy vehicles such as trucks and buses and has not yet found favor with the passenger car designers.

Because of rubber's high energy storage capabilities, the weight of the spring is markedly reduced, which means the unsprung weight is lower. Other advantages of rubber are the possibility of achieving a rising rate characteristic (which is required to improve the performance of the suspension without the necessity of designing elaborate linkages), and its tendency to be its own dampener, which takes part of the load off the shocks. Rubber does take a small set after it is installed, but this happens within a couple of days and the suspension can be adjusted before the car leaves the factory.

Road noise transmission is lower with rubber springs than with any other kind, as you would expect when you remember that rubber bushings are used with steel springs for that very purpose.

One possible drawback which isn't likely to bother anybody but an Eskimo is that rubber will freeze. But it takes some pretty chilly weather to cause rubber to solidify.

Air bags have recently come into vogue and could be considered as

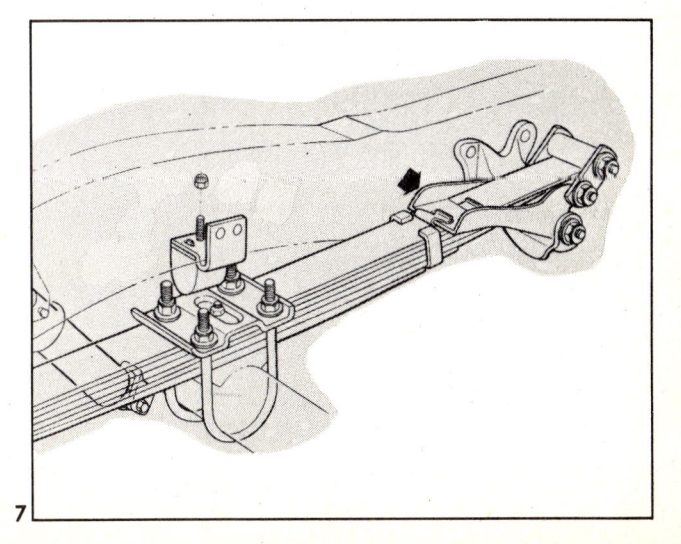

---

1. Big trucks use leaf springs like those on passenger cars, but they use more leaves, and often tie pairs of big springs together with these kind of pivoting center mounts.

2. A torsion bar is actually just like a coil spring that's been straightened out. The bar is made of spring steel and the type of steel as well as several dimensions will determine its "bounce" and capacity.

3. Torsion bars are most often seen domestically on the front end of Chrysler Corp. cars, where they are mounted parallel to the framerails and are anchored at the rear in a special "floating" crossmember.

4. The torsion-bar setup on this dragster is similar to a VW, in that the bar is actually several strips of flat steel, attached to the axle from its ends and adjusted in the middle with a clamp which provides the controlled amount of twist.

5. To give the softness of a coil spring with the stability of the standard leaf-rear setup, carmakers have gone increasingly to the use of rubber in spring mounting. This new Mustang II is a good example; the white areas here represent rubber.

6. Springs don't always have to be mounted outboard at the wheels. This road racer uses a lever-type control arm to operate coil/shocks mounted inboard, out of the airstream.

7. This '68 Ford pickup rear spring uses an unusual rear shackle, which works like an overload device. When the spring deflects a certain amount, the lever (arrow) on the shackle will exert extra pressure on the spring.

CHASSIS, SUSPENSION & BRAKES/53

Springs

overloads, except that when they are inflated they act on the spring through its whole cycle, not near full compression as overload springs do. Considering the success of the air-oil suspension, the bags seem to be only half a solution. Then there is the problem of leaks. Even the best bags seem to have a limited duration of usefulness.

SUSPENSIONS FOR OFF-ROAD VEHICLES

In the last few years, off-road racing has become popular and, with its vigorous demands on suspensions, it has shed new light on the entire subject. By trial and error, a great deal has been learned about going fast over rough ground, and one of the things learned is that very few stock suspension setups are satisfactory. Even the venerable VW that serves so well in fun machines must be reworked if you want it to survive the distance.

One of the tricks that improves the performance of the VW front ends is cutting of the stoppers located between the trailing arms. This increases the wheel travel from 5¼ to around 7 ins., which means the wheel can travel further before it hits the stop and transfers the shock to the chassis.

Increased wheel travel also improves the handling of an off-road car by keeping the wheels in contact with the ground more of the time. When a car strikes an obstacle and bottoms the suspension, the force generally bounces the car into the air. They are a little tough to steer up there. If the wheel can give and soak up the shock, the car just rolls over the rock, stump, cactus, or whatever while keeping all four wheels where they belong: on the surface.

The VW assembly is well suited for the outback. A number of design ideas make it so, and not the least of these is the trailing link principle. Basically, the trailing link means the wheel is suspended behind the axle, or in this case the pivot point. When the wheel hits a rock it travels in an arc upward and toward the rear of the car. This gives the wheel a fraction of a second longer to roll over the rock than it would have if its motion were limited to the vertical.

Another trick that improves both ride and handling on a buggy is the removal of two of the stack of eight torsion leaves from the front end. Remember we said it would take eight bars in parallel to do the work of one bar shortened by half? Well, that's just what VW has done. The front wheels are tied to a stack of eight flat torsion bars bound together as a single unit. Because a dune buggy is quite a bit lighter than a sedan, the removal of two of these leaves brings the spring rate into better agreement with the new vehicle weight.

WORKING ON SPRINGS

Eventually, the best of springs succumb to the pounding of the road and need a leaf replaced or new liners between the leaves. This is especially true with older cars. One of the first steps in rebuilding a hot rod should be to remove and disassemble all the springs. Inspect them for wear and cracks, and pay special attention to the bushings which will almost certainly need replacing. New spring liners or lubrication will also definitely be in order. Removing leaf springs from later models is a simple matter.

Place a jack under the frame (not the axle) and raise it until the wheels almost clear the ground and all load has been removed from the spring. Remove the nuts from the U-bolts that hold the spring to the axle and then take out the shackle bolts. There is a certain amount of preload in a leaf spring, but the shackles should have a sufficient arc of travel to accommodate this. On the older

1. When coil/shocks are used on a solid axle, such as at the front of this drag car, a control rod (arrow) must be added to prevent sway, as the shocks have pivoting mounts at both the axle and chassis ends.

2. There are several ways to locate a rear axle when coil springs are used. Either four control arms can be used (two upper and two lower) or just two lowers can be used along with a Panhard (control) rod for necessary lateral stability.

3. Old leaf springs can be at least partially rejuvenated by taking them apart, wirebrushing the leaves clean, putting greased cheesecloth between the leaves and reassembling. Although the spring tension won't be brought back to new, you can regain some stiffness by wrapping the leaves with windings of electrical tape.

4. If you're looking for softness in a leaf spring's action rather than firmness, you can insert thin strips of Teflon or similar plastic between the leaves and reassemble.

5. New Chrysler Corp. cars have a special tension-type shackle, which keeps the spring under load at all times. A special tool is needed to safely remove these type springs.

54/CHASSIS, SUSPENSION & BRAKES

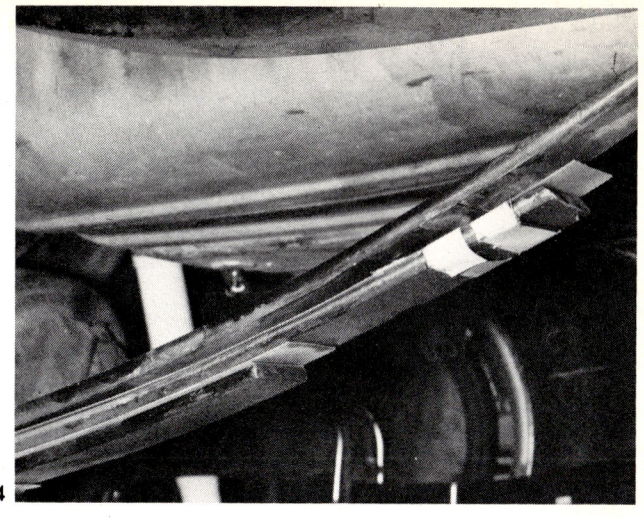

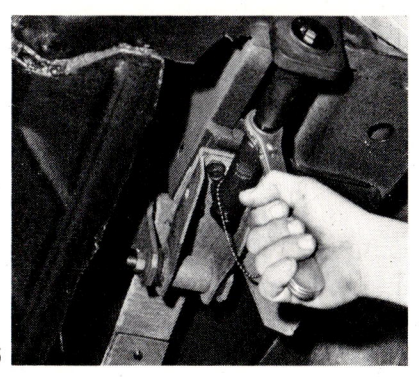

transverse leaf springs with short shackles, one must use a spreader when removing the shackle bolts.

Commercial spring shops employ a hydraulic spreader for this operation and it is safer to let them handle this job. If you prefer doing it yourself, you can make a spreader using the screw jack principle, but make sure the ends are forked to engage the spring securely. Under no circumstances should you try to use a bumper jack. There is a great deal of force stored in a short amount of spring travel, and if the jack slips it will be moving out like an AA fueler.

The older, high-arched springs are pre-loaded two ways, and you should remember both of them. The first is in the mounting which we described, and the second is in the leaves themselves. In order to fit the center bolt through the leaves, they must be compressed since, at root, they do not fit closely together, as do later models. This means that if you were to merely unscrew the nut from the center bolt, the stored energy would be released suddenly when you reached the end of the threads. In practice, this occurs before the end of the bolt is reached because the force is so great, and three or more threads will be stripped off. A couple of broken fingers—and often more—can be expected when this happens.

Before loosening the nut, clamp the spring on either side of the center bolt with 8-in. C-clamps turned down tight. This will hold the spring in shape so that you can remove the nut and the bolt. Then loosen the clamps, slowly working from one to the other, a turn or two at a time, until the spring is relaxed.

Vintage leaf springs are not the only ones that can pose problems for the uninitiated. Coils, too, must be treated with respect when you remove them. If you just jack up the car and start unscrewing things, you are really asking for it. When you get to the last bolt holding the coil in place, the stored energy of the spring will be released all at once and the spring will do about three laps around your garage at eyeball height. To prevent this it is necessary to invest in a simple tool. There are different models for the various makes of cars but they are essentially the same.

The correct, safe procedure is to jack up the car and set it on jack stands high enough for the A-frame to clear the floor jack when the frame is in the extreme down position. Take off the tire and wheel and remove the shock and stabilizer link if it has one. Then wheel in the floor jack and raise the lower A-arm a little to disconnect the lower ball joint. At this point you break out the handy-dandy spring tool and bolt it in the lower A-frame, using two flat washers to distribute the load. Make sure the bolts are properly threaded, as this is the little gimmick that is going to keep the spring from going into orbit. Now you can lower the floor jack, and the tool will hold the spring in what is called the "first" safety position. With a pry bar you can slip it to the "second" safety position, which releases the spring tension but still holds it in place. From there you can slide the spring out by hand. Replacement is accomplished by simply reversing the order of these instructions.

Removing and replacing torsion bars, while lacking the danger element of coils and some leaf springs, should nevertheless follow procedure to avoid damage to the components. The first step is to remove the upper control arm rebound bumper. Then place your jack under the center crossmember with a broad support between it and the jack. This spreads the load and prevents damage to the crossmember. When the car is raised, the front suspension will be completely unloaded. If you use a hoist to raise the car, position it so that the same effect is achieved. Release the load from the torsion bar by backing off the anchor adjusting bolt.

On the rear of the bar is a snap ring and it is the next thing to go. Here again you need a special but simple tool that will vary from one model to the next. It is a clamp that grips the bar and is held in place with a pair of Allen screws. Below the clamp is a striking pad and a handle for positioning the tool. This is clamped to the bar and then the bar is driven backward through the rear anchor. After the bar has cleared the anchor points, remove the tool and take off the rear anchor balloon seal. This will make it easier to remove the bar. Exercise care when sliding the bar through the rear anchor so as not to damage the seal. Before replacing the bar, check the seal for wear; then check the hex openings in the anchors and the hex ends of the bar for dirt or grit. Relube both ends of the bar and follow the reverse of the removal procedure to reinstall. Be sure to check the suspension height when the job is finished. The upper control arm rebound bumper should be tightened to 200 in.-lbs.

Now that you've accumulated the necessary data—the whys and the wherefores of springing action—it's time to spring into action yourself ... with confidence in your ability, and the rewards of a self-satisfying repair/rework job in store.

CHASSIS, SUSPENSION & BRAKES/55

Shock Absorbers

Usually taken for granted, shocks play a highly important role.

Absorbing shock is primarily a function of the springs that attach the suspension system to the frame or chassis of the car. The shock absorber, as we know it, is given the job of controlling the action of the spring.

If you strike a crystal drinking glass it will emit a sound that is created by its harmonic vibration. However, should you apply the lightest of pressure with your finger against the glass, both the sound and the vibration will cease. You have duplicated the major function of the modern day automotive shock absorber.

The earliest cars did not use anything other than springs to attach the axle and wheels to the frame of the car. A carry-over from the horse and buggy, it was soon realized that adequate control of a motor vehicle at the speeds they were then going would require stiffer springs. Unfortunately, the stiffer springs that were needed for control did nothing at all for the comfort. You had a choice: go slow in comfort or fast in agony. You could not have both features in the same automobile.

Engineers of the day were well aware of the problems inherent in the leaf springs that were used by virtually all of the manufacturers. Once put in motion by the wheel hitting a bump or hole in the road, the spring continued to react and counterreact. The wheel would bounce up and down until the internal friction of the spring leaves and the subtle damping characteristics of the tire brought the spring back to its normal position. Since the road conditions of the day left much to be desired, the wheel would inevitably hit another bump, or series of bumps, before the spring ever returned to its normal position. This resulted in a vehicle that had its wheels off the ground as much as they were on.

Stiffer springs would cut down on this natural tendency to bounce along, but only at the sacrifice of comfort. The wheels would still leave the ground on contact with a bump, but the car would be absorbing a large percentage of the shock since the stiffer spring would not flex over the smaller bumps. Control was somewhat better since the wheel/car relationship was not so sporadic, but something better was needed.

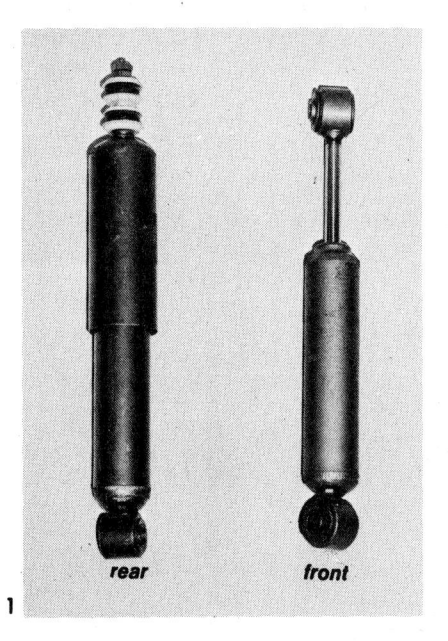

The earliest damping devices took the form of friction discs that attached to the spring and to the car chassis through levers. The discs were held together by a bolt through the center, or a series of bolts around the outside, that could be tightened or loosened to provide varying amounts of resistance. When the wheel came across an irregularity in the road surface that was severe enough to move the spring, the friction of the damping device would resist the movement of the spring in both directions. In this way it served to stop the wheel from bouncing much more quickly, since it absorbed the energy that the spring previously had to absorb by itself.

With the adaption of these devices it was found that the spring itself could be much more flexible and thus provide a smoother ride. Control of the vehicle was taken care of by the friction damper since it kept the wheels in contact with the ground for longer periods of time.

These early developers were reaching for the same goals that are today being sought by the automotive industry: a suspension system that will give a maximum of control as well as a smooth, effortless ride for the passengers. The first is for safety, the

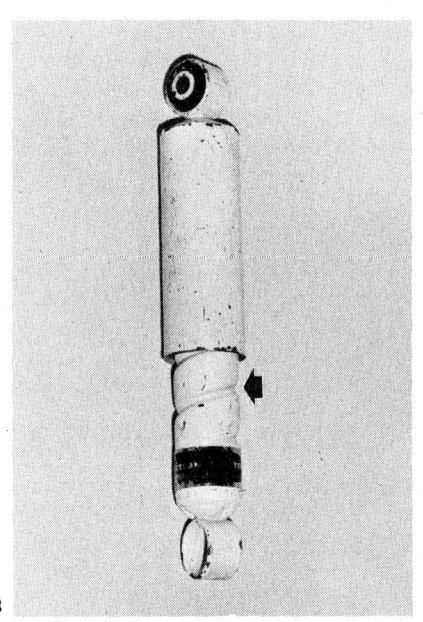

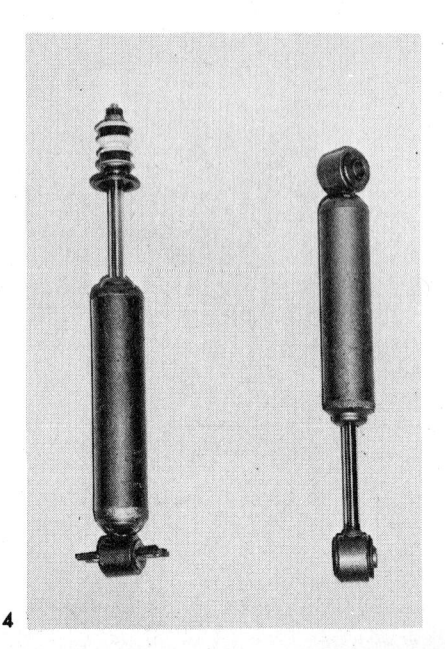

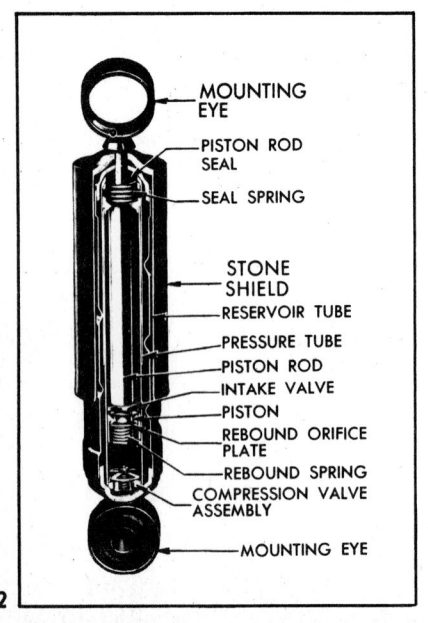

56/CHASSIS, SUSPENSION & BRAKES

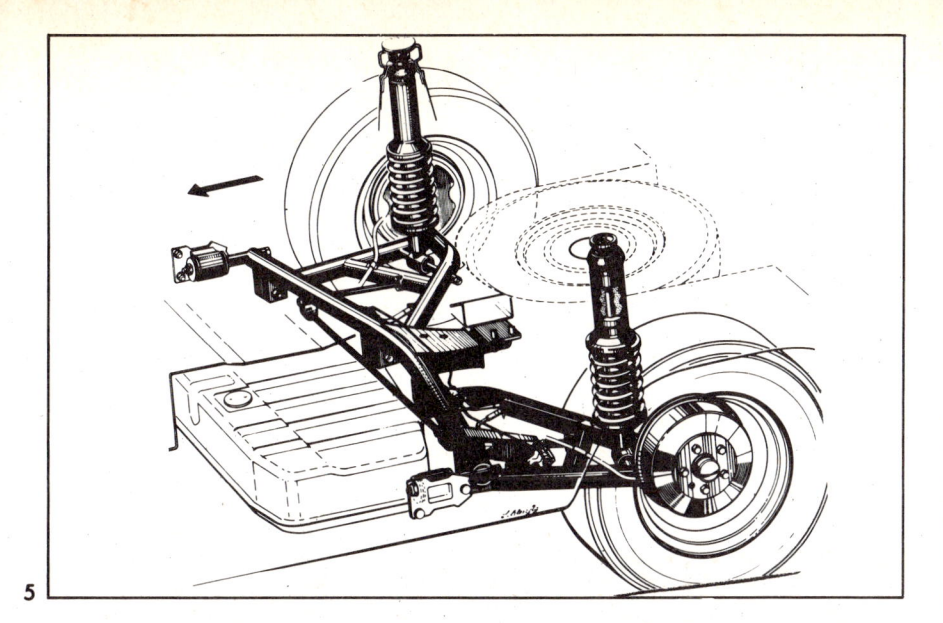

pass liquid via small internal orifices.

Present day shock absorbers are nearly all identical externally, although they differ internally according to intended usage. Not unlike the bicycle pump, they consist of a sealed cylinder that contains the fluid reservoir and the piston end of the actuating rod. The rod extends out one end of the cylinder and is generally used as a mounting point. The other mounting point is attached to the closed end of the cylinder.

As the actuating rod is pushed into, or pulled out of the cylinder by the action of the car's suspension, the piston attached to the end inside the cylinder is subjected to the laws of hydraulics that then resist the movement to a degree determined by the sizes of the valves and orifices. The larger the valves, the less the resistance will be, providing that a fluid of the same consistency is used.

The reservoir that surrounds the cylinder is necessary since the actuating rod displaces volume in the upper cylinder that would otherwise be filled with fluid. As the piston moves within the cylinder, fluid flows to and from the reservoir through valves operated by the change in hydraulic pressure. By juggling valve and orifice sizes, engineers can provide a dampening rate to suit the requirements of any type of vehicle.

When fluid flows through an orifice, the pressure increases as the square of the speed. If an orifice is designed

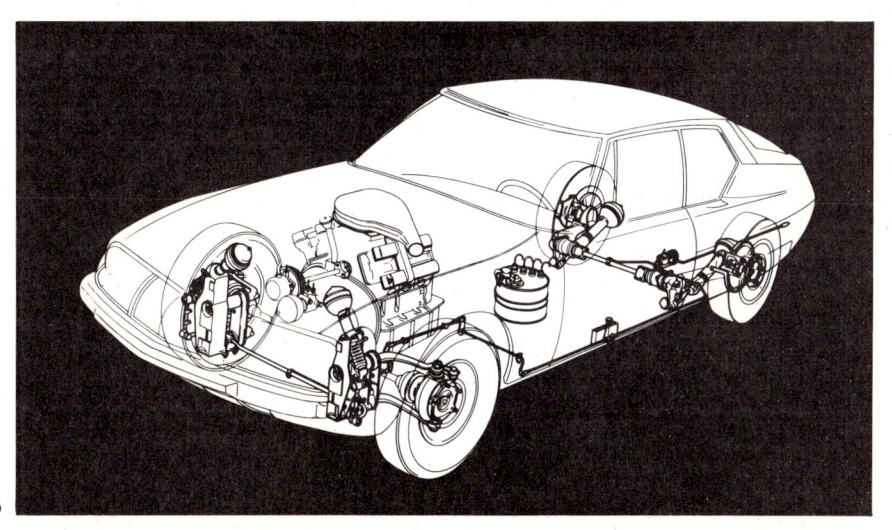

second for salability—goals that the present-day hydraulic shock absorber comes close to achieving.

Over the years many types of hydraulic shock absorbers have been used, each with varying degrees of success. All work on the same principle of forcing fluid through a restriction in order to resist an outside force supplied by the tension of whatever spring method was used. Units operated by a lever or series of levers were popular for many years and worked well. Often they would comprise a functional part of the suspension system by using the operating levers as control arms to attach the wheels. The length of the operating lever would also affect the dampening rate of the unit by changing the leverage to the internal pistons. A modern day door closer is a miniature lever-operated shock absorber and even bears a close physical resemblance to automotive units. Today, however, the type that is predominant on passenger cars is the direct acting telescopic type, to which we will confine our present discussion.

HOW A DIRECT ACTING SHOCK ABSORBER WORKS

Perhaps when you were young, you and your friends rode your bicycles to a nearby lake on hot, sticky summer days. Once there, you probably had a few water fights, using the tire pumps from your bicycles. You just put the end of the pump in the water and drew the handle out slowly. When you "fired" it by forcing the handle back in, the water spurted out at your opponent. Then you refilled the pump and "fired" at him.

A "loaded" bicycle pump is essentially the same as the most widely used modern day shock absorber. Admittedly, it would be impractical to stop and refill it after every bump, but in theory at least, the filling operation by the side of the lake corresponds to what happens when a shock has been compressed and the spring is trying to force the wheel back toward the ground. The violent energy that the spring has inherited from a bump in the road is calmed down by the reluctance of the shock absorber to

1. Most ordinary shocks are built in in two different forms. Front shocks usually have a rod and cylinder, and rear shocks have two telescoping sections, a cylinder and a cover. Front shocks do without the cover because of their greater heat.

2. This cutaway shows the makeup of a typical shock absorber. Oil flowing through controlled orifices provides the spring dampening action.

3. Often you will see a shock with a spiral groove around the cylinder. This is designed to prevent aeration of the shock's hydraulic fluid.

4. Most shocks are mounted with the cylinder at the bottom, but since the suspension-half of a shock is unsprung weight, a shock with the cylinder at the top should reduce unsprung weight and improve handling.

5. Many smaller foreign cars use a MacPherson-strut front suspension, in which the spring and shock are an integral unit. They work well, but can be expensive to replace.

6. The luxurious (and expensive) Citroen SM uses no springs or shocks at all. Self-levelling suspension is achieved with a hydro-pneumatic pump and air/oil cylinders at each wheel. Even the ride height of the car is adjustable to five positions.

CHASSIS, SUSPENSION & BRAKES/57

Shock Absorbers

to provide restriction at high speeds (sharp blows), the same orifice at low speed will not create the necessary dampening. For this reason valves that will open progressively as pressures increase are nearly always used. To further prevent the restriction from becoming excessive at high fluid speeds, this valve usually incorporates a relief valve that stays closed at low speed.

In many countries throughout the world the term "shock absorber" is considered to be a misnomer. The springing system is the shock absorber, and the item that we are referring to is merely a device that dampens the movement of the spring, just as the touch of a finger will stop the ringing of a glass. For this reason they are referred to as "dampers" in England and Europe, and "cushions" in the land of the rising sun. Perhaps the Japanese are closer to the truth than their more experienced automotive counterparts, since the units do cushion the spring.

Actually, though, they are all correct if you look over the wide range of types available. Some are only dampers that could be compressed by a small child and have their dampening characteristics limited to the return stroke. Others offer resistance in both directions in varying percentage ratios, determined by the particular application. So rather than siding with any of them as far as the proper terminology, let's stick with "shock absorbers,"—wrong though it may be—and worry more about how they work, and what types should be used for what conditions.

As already stated, the shock absorber will absorb some of the shock if it is designed that way. Many applications, especially those on luxurious passenger cars, are designed to soften the initial shock that would otherwise be taken entirely by the spring, so that very flexible springs giving an extremely comfortable ride under normal conditions can be used. Were you to hold one of these units and compress it by hand it would move very easily. However, if you put it in a vise and gave it a sharp blow, such as it would receive going over a rough road, it would offer more resistance. This is possible since, as the speed of the movement is increased, the liquid reaches a point where it cannot get through the internal orifice as quickly as the shock wishes it to. Under normal highway conditions the liquid moves quite readily and has little if any restricting effect. But, when it receives a sharp blow, it provides restriction. This supplies an inherent ability to conform to road conditions.

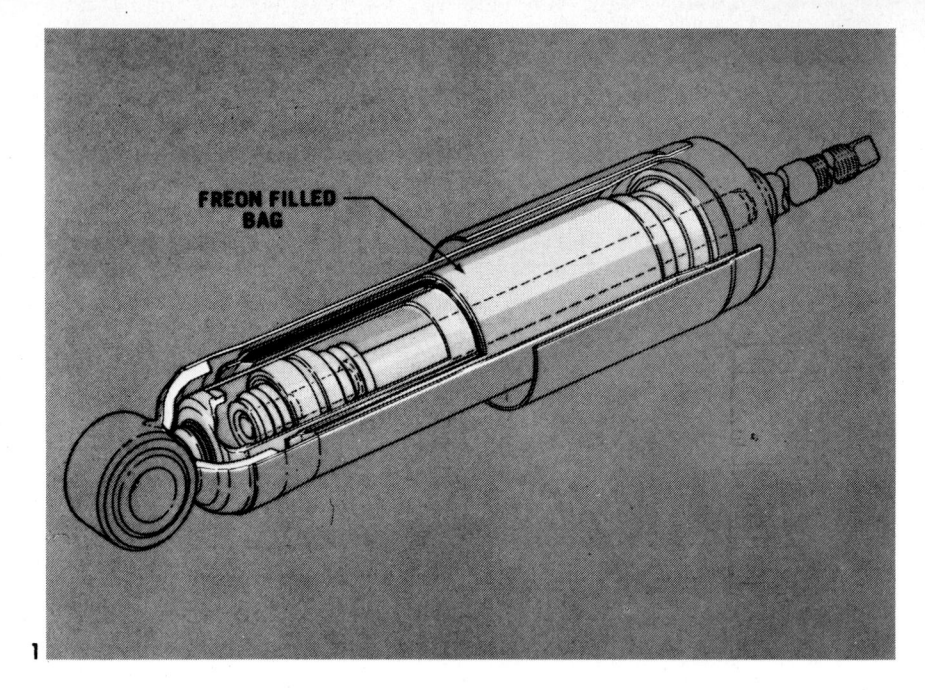

The majority of shock absorber units are permanently sealed by the manufacturer, so internal modifications are impossible. Some of the competition types are rebuildable, though, thus offering an infinite number of dampening rates that can be suited to special vehicles or particularly unusual road conditions.

Since the rate at which the damper affects the suspension system depends on the ability of the fluid inside the unit to pass through the internal valves, changes can be made to either the fluid or the valves. A thicker fluid will pass more slowly—a thinner one more quickly. Substitution of one or the other will lower or raise the speed at which the liquid will pass through the respective orifices.

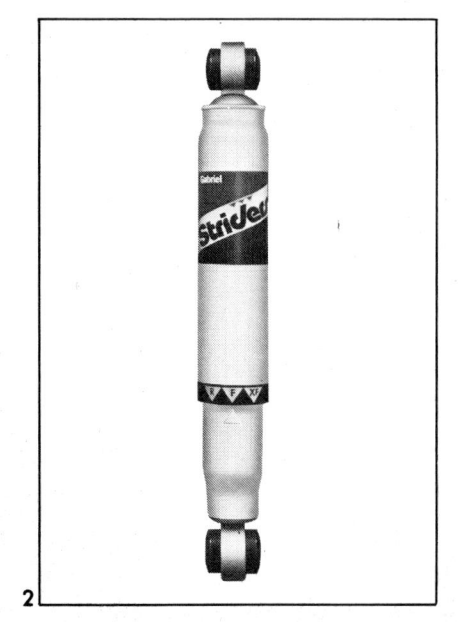

Changing the fluid alone, however, will change the dampening on both the compression and rebound strokes the same amount. By modifying one or the other of the internal valves, the rebound/compression relationship can be changed. Figures for such units are given in percentages, so a unit that is equal in resistance in both directions will be identified as having a 50/50 ratio. Passenger cars designed for smooth riding may vary from 60/40 to 80/20. The larger number represents the amount of resistance on the rebound stroke.

When a vehicle fitted with a set of 60/40 units hits a bump of the type found at a railroad crossing or "dippy" intersection, the initial resistance to compression of the spring will be assisted by the shock absorber at a 10% lesser rate than it would be if the units were of the 50/50 type. Once the energy has been absorbed by the spring and shock absorber, the rebound stroke will begin. As the

58/CHASSIS, SUSPENSION & BRAKES

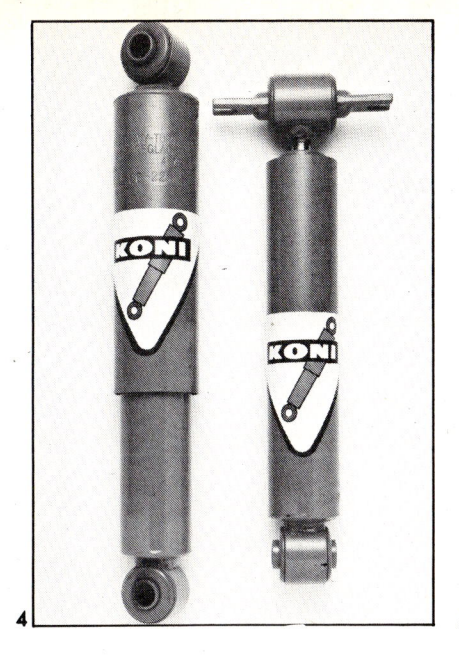

spring forces the wheel back toward the ground, the shock absorber resists on the rebound stroke at the 60 figure. The greater amount of resistance on the rebound stroke is necessary since the shock is now controlling the release of the energy stored in the spring when it was compressed by the bump. The shock is trying to keep the spring compressed, or fighting it, whereas on the compression stroke the shock was helping by resisting compression.

Since springs of any kind will not work efficiently without a shock absorber (even some engine valve springs have them), and since shock absorbers will not work at all without a spring, they are closely interrelated. The type of spring, the strength of it, the application, and method of application are all factors that will determine the ultimate efficiency.

The energy absorbed by the spring is passed on to the shock absorber in the form of heat. This heat can have adverse effects on the fluid being used within the unit and thereby reduce its damping qualities. In some applications, such as Jeeps and off-road vehicles, the shock will get so hot that to touch it would cause a serious burn. Racing cars will often duct cool air to the shocks just as they duct it to the brakes.

The length of a given spring and the amount of wheel travel that the particular suspension system allows are important considerations in the mounting of a shock unit. If the unit does not have as much maximum travel as the suspension system itself is capable of, a hard jolt could well break it. If the travel of the unit is more than that of the system, the extra length is wasted since it will not utilize its complete stroke. The angle at which the unit is mounted between the suspension and the chassis must allow the full travel or suffer poor operation because the unit moves less than the suspension.

Two ins. of suspension travel will move a vertically mounted shock two ins. One that is mounted at a 45° angle will not move that far—important considerations if accessory units are installed at home on a hot rod or other special purpose vehicle.

The weight of any motor vehicle with conventional suspension systems can be divided into two types: sprung weight and unsprung weight. Sprung weight is that weight which is supported by the springs, and unsprung weight is that which moves with the springs—wheel, suspension arms, etc. Half of the shock absorber, the half bolted to the chassis, is sprung weight since it never moves. The other half will go up and down with the wheel and is therefore unsprung.

Since the spring must both support the car and force the wheel back on the ground after each bump, the lighter the unsprung weight the less work the spring will have to do. The less work it has to do, the lighter it can be. The lighter it is, the better the ride under normal conditions, and the more important becomes the job of the shock absorber unit. Some manufacturers even mount the shock absorber with the heaviest portion, the cylinder, attached to the body, and the rod that operates the piston attached to the suspension. This makes the cylinder a part of the sprung weight, and the unsprung weight is therefore reduced.

1. The shocks used in Thunderbird's new "Posi-Ride" rear suspension use an extra compression control valve and a Freon-filled plastic bag that completely avoids aeration problems.

2. There are a number of adjustable shocks on the market today, but one of the few American shocks with a lifetime guarantee is the new Gabriel Strider, with three ride settings.

3. Shocks are often double-up for racing use, such as on this NASCAR Grand National car, where they are used with long travel arms, custom A-arms, brakes, spindles and hubs.

4. Perhaps the best-known of the adjustable shocks are the Dutch-made Konis, long familiar accessories on race cars and sporty street cars.

5. The most common suspension unit in road and drag racing cars is the coil/shock, like this Chapman unit. Ride height is adjustable by means of threaded collars(arrows).

6. Championship cars require their own special types of shocks. These Konis used on some Indy cars are doubly-adjustable, in that springs can be adjusted by a collar and the shock rate by a knob on the bottom.

7. Since the angle a shock is used at can determine its stiffness, too, it's a simple matter for some racers to make shock mounts adjustable. The closer to vertical you mount shocks, the stiffer their action.

CHASSIS, SUSPENSION & BRAKES/59

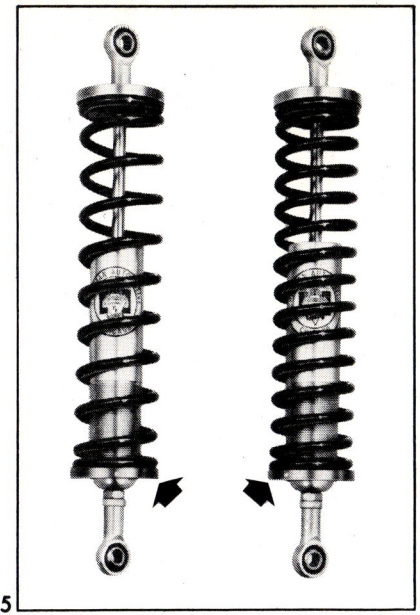

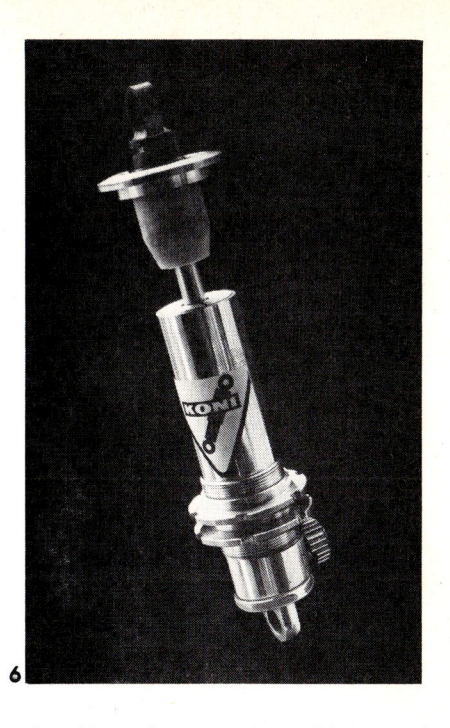

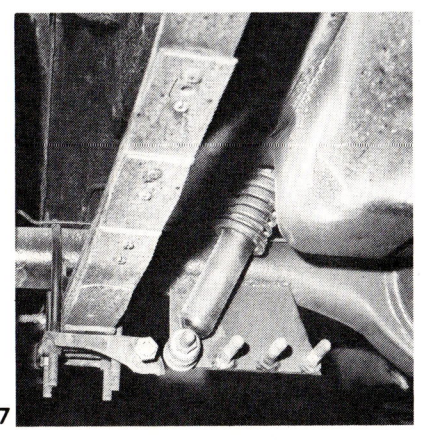

Shock Absorbers

SPECIAL-PURPOSE SHOCKS

Manufacturers of standard passenger car shock absorbers also have developed units for special uses such as towing and racing. The nature of the use involved usually means an individualized installation that should be done, or at least supervised, by people experienced in the field.

Pulling a heavy trailer or boat behind a car not designed to do the job can be a hazardous undertaking. The weight of even the best-balanced trailers will compress the rear springs and shock absorbers to a point where the car no longer has any rear suspension travel left to absorb road jolts. With several thousand pounds trailing along behind the car, proper suspension control becomes even more important than on a car only.

The usual practice is to install what are commonly called "overloads." These are specially built shock absorber units that are enclosed in a coil spring. The complete unit is generally installed in place of the existing shock unit. The additional spring increases the total spring poundage, and the dampening rate in the unit is changed to suit. Under heavy load, the extra springing will keep the rear from dragging and still provide good suspension control. Unloaded, the ride may be a little harder than standard, but not to the point of being uncomfortable.

Racing cars rely on shock absorbers to keep the tires in contact with the road surface with little or no concern for the comfort that would require a compromise in the design of the unit. High-speed handling is of prime importance, and the advancements made in the racing field in the past years have greatly increased control. Shock absorbers used on racing cars are usually of the type that allow adjustment of the dampening rate to suit conditions. Some of them must be removed from the car, while others can be adjusted in a few seconds while in position on the car's suspension.

This very same feature has found its way into some accessory units for passenger cars and may well be a standard item on new cars in the future. Even if the units were never adjusted by the owner, the new car dealer would be able to set the car up for any special conditions that might exist in his area.

The adjustment is confined to changing the rate of the dampening on the bump stroke and does not affect the rebound rate. This actually serves to assist the spring if adjusted to a harder position, or limit the amount of dampening if adjusted to a softer setting. There are various methods employed, but all do essentially the same thing: they change the path of the shock fluid through larger or smaller orifices. For harder dampening, smaller orifices are used. For softer dampening, larger ones are used. Although usually adjusted manually, there are examples that have been electrically controlled from inside the car. If the driver of a car so equipped comes across an unusually bumpy section of road, he can instantly adjust the bump rate to suit the conditions.

Another type of adjustable shock that has come into extensive use in the past few years is the air shock. These have a rubber boot or bag between the upper and lower sections and these bags are connected to a filling valve (just like a tire valve) by plastic tubing. The valve is usually located in the trunk or at the rear bumper for easy filling. The shocks are generally used on the rear only and operate like overload springs. The similarity is reflected when you plan to carry a heavy load or tow a trailer. In that case, you would just stop at a filling station and add some air pressure to the shocks, to raise the rear of the vehicle. Although originally designed for overload use, air shocks find their most frequent use today as a means to provide clearance for big rear tires or simply to get the "jacked-up" look. While they're not as dangerous as long spring shackles, air shocks have their limits. Remember, when you jack a car way up in the air you're raising the center of gravity, which will put additional loads on the outside tires during cornering. While the extra load can no doubt be covered adequately by the larger tires, it is true that the ultimate cornering power and handling must suffer. As overload devices, air shocks work great because unlike add-on mechanical springs, you let most of the air out after you're through towing in order to return the car to a normal ride.

Racing stock cars of the type raced at Daytona, Charlotte, and the other

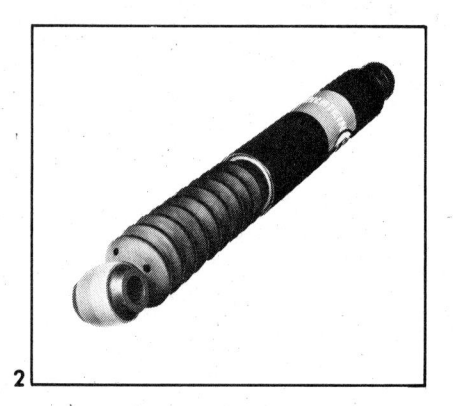

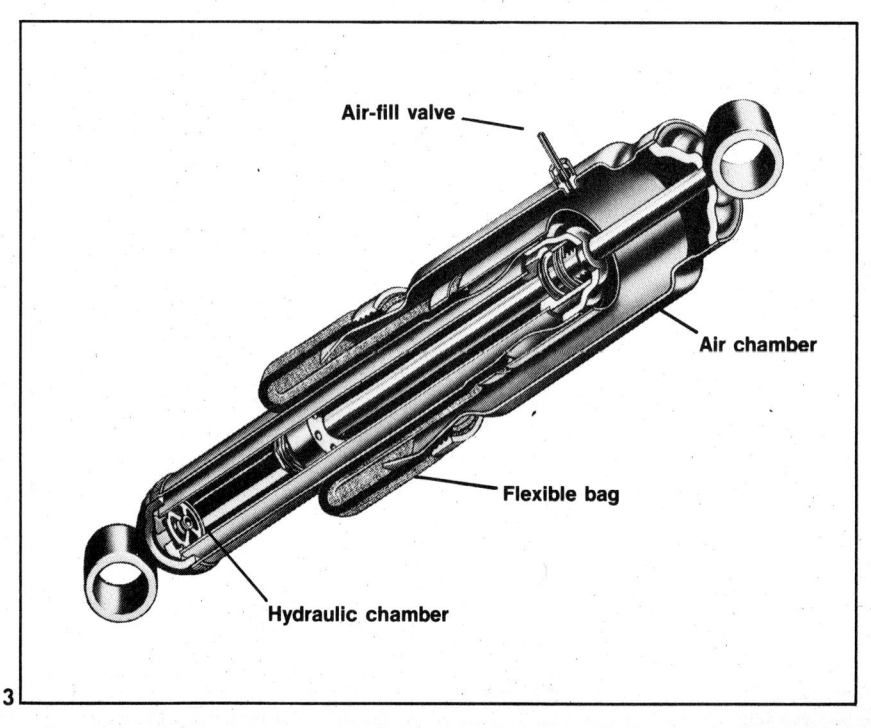

60/CHASSIS, SUSPENSION & BRAKES

big car tracks have recently reached speeds thought impossible five years ago. To keep the chassis up to the speeds, drastic measures had to be taken in the suspension department, particularly with regard to shock absorbing units. Spring control on such heavy vehicles, going as fast as they are capable of going, is more important than horsepower. What good is the horsepower, if the car will not remain stable at near-200-mph speeds?

Because of the tremendous loads involved, and the fact that no suitable units existed, accepted practice has been to use two heavy-duty shock absorbers on each wheel, thereby doubling the dampening rate. These are used in conjunction with heavier springs in order to resist the tremendous centrifugal force experienced on banked curves.

Drag racing developments have brought about many innovations that ultimately find their way into production cars, and the staggered mounting of shock absorbers is one of the latest to find favor with the manufacturers. When a car accelerates, the rear axle has a tendency to turn in the opposite direction to the wheels. By mounting one shock absorber behind the axle and the other in front of the axle, this tendency is resisted. There are other ways of preventing this axle "wind up," but in all but a few cases the simple reinstallation of the shock unit accomplishes axle control.

Although the direct acting hydraulic shock absorber has emerged as the most popular type with cost-conscious, new car manufacturers and cost-no-object racing men, it is by no means the only avenue of spring control that has been investigated. Sealed gas cylinders have been used, and various other air bag concepts have been explored, but for one reason or another these have been dropped in favor of the current popular type.

One interesting concept some years ago had rubber, in a series of different hardnesses, acting as both the springing medium and the damper. By careful selection, the rebound values of separate compounds of rubber could be arranged to provide excellent wheel control. A combination of the different compounds, combined with controlled friction between each of them, offered great possibilities but was never developed beyond its infant stage. Perhaps the future will see more experiments along these lines, as the list of synthetic rubbers lengthens with the aid of space age accoutrements.

Regardless of the future of spring control technology, one very important fact emerges from our present knowledge of the shock absorber. It is vitally important to the control of the car—and it will not last indefinitely. It should be an item that is periodically checked and replaced when necessary, just like spark plugs, oil filters and brakes. Only special custom shocks can be repaired; most are replaced when worn. Shocks will seldom ever "go bad" overnight. It is a gradual wear process that may not be noticed until it is too late.

Don't wait that long!

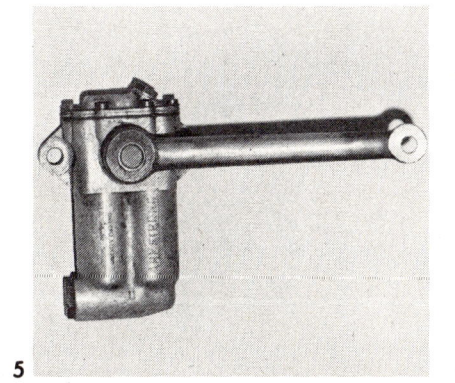

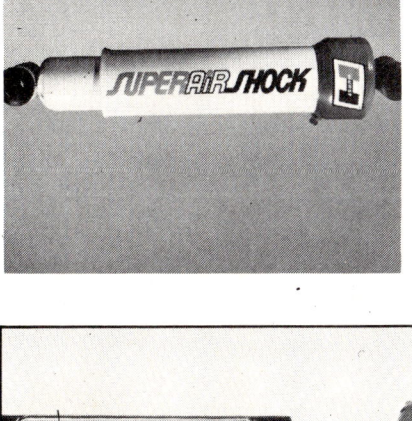

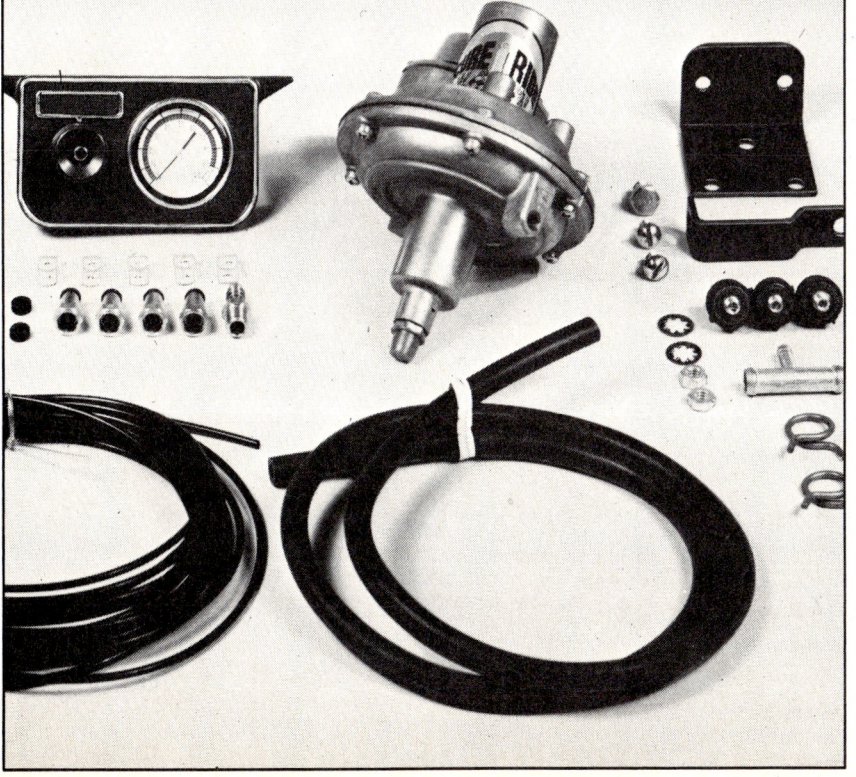

1. This truck setup for off-road racing features an unusual shock arrangement. One vertical shock is to control the springs, while the rear shock dampens axle windup.

2. Gaining favor lately with the off-road racing crowd is the Bilstein shock. Of single-tube construction, there is little fluid foaming and nitrogen gas is sealed in under high pressure. Bilsteins are also OEM on such cars as Mercedes and Porsche.

3. For those who want to carry an occasional load, tow a trailer or just beef up a tail-dragger, there are a variety of air-filled shocks on the market. Most use an air bag on the shocks, which are filled from the rear bumper or inside the trunk for extra load-carrying capacity.

4. Hurst's new "super" air shock can handle up to 175 psi and has no puncturable air bag. The plunger rod on this shock is a hefty ½-in. thick.

5. Aluminum lever-type shocks found on many small foreign sports cars can be rebuilt, unlike most other shocks. Also, changing the viscosity of the oil/fluid changes the shock rate. Although not recommended for the street, some road racers fill their lever shocks with STP!

6. As an accessory to their air shocks, the Cure-Ride Co. makes this miniature air compressor (run by the engine's vacuum) and controls so you can adjust the air shocks' height from the dash. Compressor is also good for inflating air mattresses.

CHASSIS, SUSPENSION & BRAKES/61

The Steering System
What happens between the steering wheel and the road.

Think back, if you can, to your first hot rod—not your first car, but the "soap box" racer you built from scrap wood and some "borrowed" baby carriage wheels. Steering was no problem, right? You made the 2 x 4 front axle pivot on a bolt at the front of the "frame," and steering was just a matter of putting your feet on the ends of the axles; or if you wanted to keep your feet in, you shortened your mother's clothesline and used the rope to steer. It seemed logical enough at the time; after all, didn't all those wagons in the cowboy movies steer something like that? Thankfully, steering gear design has progressed steadily since those wagons went out of favor and "the contraption" was invented.

On a wagon, the horses did the turning. A self-propelled vehicle which is *driven* by the rear wheels instead of *pulled* required a different concept. The pivoting axle couldn't have worked on an automobile because in a tight turn, as the axle became almost parallel to the frame, the front of the car would have been extremely unstable. A German inventor named Lankensperger came to the rescue in the 19th Century, though, when he designed a stationary axle on which the wheels steered. It was patented in English-seaking countries by Rudolph Ackerman, and has been called Ackerman steering ever since. Early cars used a crude Ackerman steering setup with a "tiller" in the cockpit for steering. A bumpy road gave you quite a workout, since the rough-riding suspensions pulled the tiller out of your hand all the time. It also was not too positive in terms of control, and was barely adequate for even the slow speeds of the day.

Faster cars required better handling for those poor roads. And when "balloon" tires and front-wheel brakes were introduced, steering became even harder, and led to the development of the steering box. Essentially, the driver steered a wheel at one end of a shaft, at the other end of which was a set of gears that transferred the motion, through arms and rods, to the wheels.

DRAG LINK STEERING

Naturally, the early steering gearboxes were fairly simple by today's standards. Most cars used the fore-and-aft drag link type of steering, so familiar to hot rodders because of its application on pre-1949 members of the Ford family. With this type of linkage, the short shaft from the steering box was connected to a pitman arm that hung down from the box and was connected, as were most of the steering linkage components, by a spring-loaded ball joint, to the drag link (no, it wasn't a racing

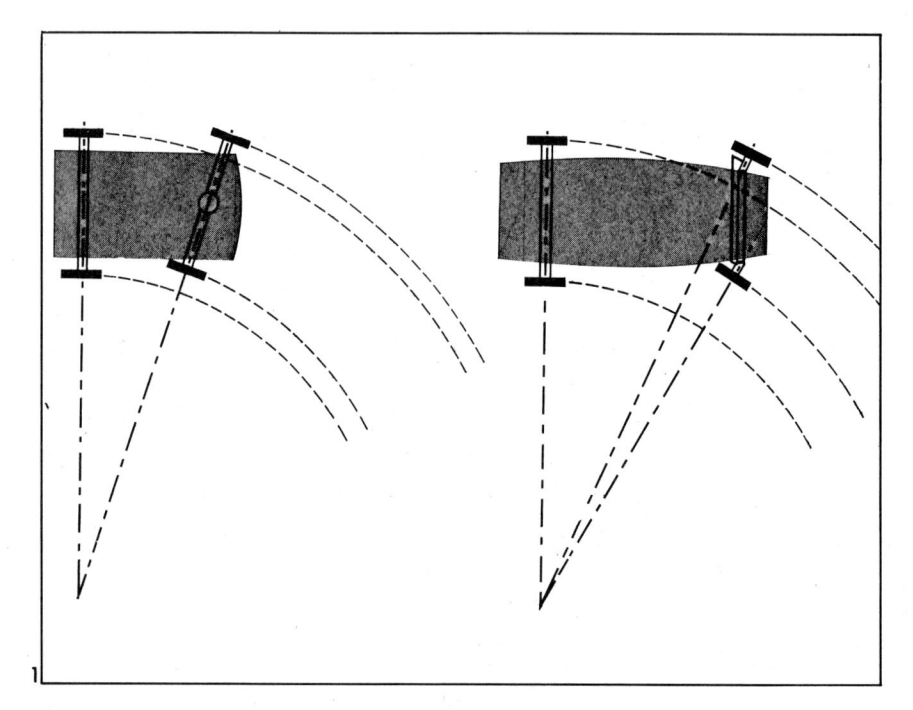

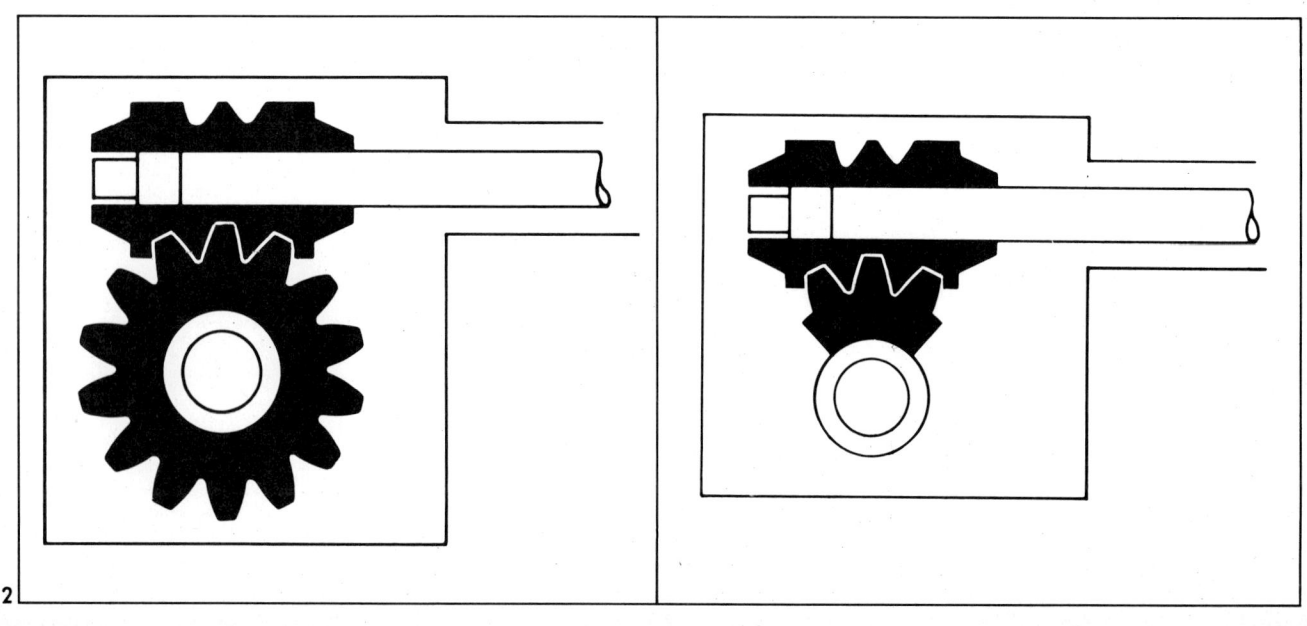

62/CHASSIS, SUSPENSION & BRAKES

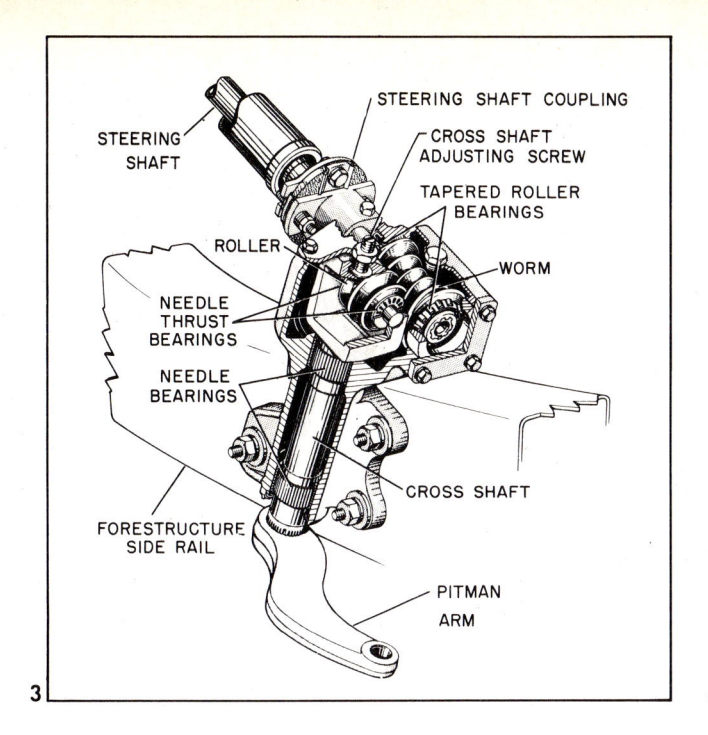

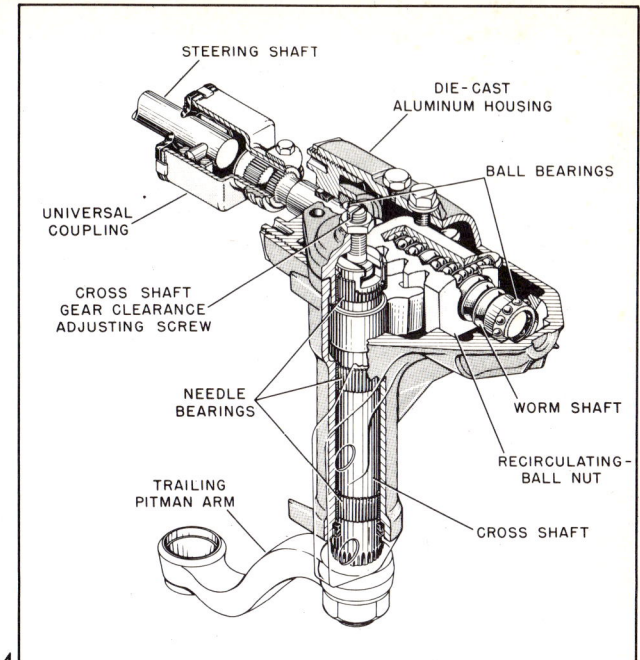

part!). The drag link paralleled the frame and ran forward to connect to an arm that steered the left front wheel. The two front wheels were connected by a tie-rod so that they would steer together, and the gear ratio in the box and the leverages of the various linkages determined the overall steering ratio.

WORM AND SECTOR, WORM AND WHEEL DESIGNS

Most of the design changes for the subsequent 40 or 50 years were concentrated within the gearbox itself, as a multitude of gearing methods were tried in an effort to come up with the best compromise among handling, driving effort, and friction. Up until the '20's, two designs that were very common were the worm and wheel, and a variation, the worm and sector. The worm gear was, and still is, almost universal in its use on the steering column shaft. In the worm and wheel design, as the name implies, a toothed wheel meshed with the teeth on the worm, and a shaft connected this wheel with the pitman arm. The worm and sector was simply the same system, but instead of using a wheel, just a piece-of-pie portion of the wheel was used, since within the turning limits of the front wheels most of the wheel-gear was useless.

Friction proved to be the common enemy of all steering designs, and these early types were no exceptions. Most of the loads in the box were concentrated on the gears at their mesh points, and constant lubrication was a necessary drawback. They also required frequent adjustment, and proper alignment became difficult at the mesh point because it was found that the gears wore unevenly. That is, they most often wore out in the straight-ahead position, where they received the most use.

Once the gears were worn, you could adjust them only so much before the gears would bind. The worm and wheel type did at least have the advantage that the wheel could be removed and reinstalled with fresh teeth at the mesh point.

ROSS STEERING

The introduction in 1923 of the Ross cam and lever steering gear was a solid step forward in terms of reduced friction and wear. One long groove (the cam) spiralled around the end of the steering shaft and a lever on the pitman shaft had a peg on it that fit this groove. As the steering wheel was turned, the peg was forced to ride up or down the shaft in the groove, and this action turned the pitman shaft and arm.

A later feature of the popular Ross steering, one which has been utilized in most cars ever since, was variable pitch on the groove. By making the spirals wider apart at the middle, steering could be made faster in the straight-ahead position for more sensitive driver control and handling. At the ends of the spiral, they had to be made closer together to make tight turns easier. One of the first rules you learn in physics or mechanical engineering is that when you gain some advantage by leverage or gearing, you lose something at the same time in speed or required effort. In parking, or other circumstances where the steering is turned to its limits, a fast angle on the cam would give the driver a real workout going from hard left to hard right and back. Where the spirals were closer together, more turns were required but the effort was reduced, and fast action was considered to be less important in parking.

Another very important factor in steering gear design that the Ross unit incorporated was irreversibility, which may be a mouthful but nevertheless necessary. With the old tiller steering, there was a question of who was steering whom, since every road shock and bump jerked the lever out of the driver's hands. This turned out to be a problem with wheel steering also, as some of the simpler designs of steering gears produced a similar effect. The Ross steering was a good compromise; it was almost irreversible. It was difficult for motion to be passed from the wheels back up through the steering wheel, but

1. Compared to the early wagon-type center-pivot steering at left, the modern steering at right requires the inside wheel on a turn to turn sharper than the outside wheel. This is the Ackerman effect, which means the wheels have to toe out on turns even turning on a common center.

2. By comparing these drawings, you'll see how the development of the worm-and-sector steering box (right) made it possible for a smaller and lighter assembly to be built.

3. The worm-and-roller design was a step forward in reducing friction, and was used in Detroit by Dodge up to just a few years ago.

4. The modern steering box utilizes recirculating ball bearings to take the friction loads and needle-type bearings on the cross-shaft for much easier steering, even with faster ratios. Since no one seems to have come up with a better system, this design has been in use for over 20 years, and is on most cars today.

CHASSIS, SUSPENSION & BRAKES/63

The Steering System

enough was felt at the wheel to give the driver that important "feel of the road" which gives him confidence in his control.

WORM AND ROLLER

Friction was still a factor to be reckoned with, though, as cars got heavier, tires got bigger and tire pressures became lower for a better ride. It wasn't just that it was becoming harder to steer the car, but friction and wear within the gearbox were increasing again with these greater loads. So the people over at the Saginaw Steering Division of General Motors started making worm and roller steering in 1926 for the heavy Cadillacs. Basically, the worm on the steering shaft was hourglass-shaped; it was thicker at the ends than in the middle. Instead of a curved sector meshing with it, there was a roller, like a single large gear tooth, which was perpendicular to the steering shaft. It was mounted in roller bearings in a yoke that was part of the pitman arm shaft. These bearings took much of the load and the big roller distributed the wear more evenly. The design was so efficient that it is still used today.

RECIRCULATING-BALL STEERING GEAR

By far the most widely used steering gear today is the recirculating-ball type, introduced on the 1940 Cadillac. Another development by Saginaw, it was basically an improvement of the screw-and-nut design that had been around for many years. A long worm gear was on the bottom of the steering shaft, on which a large, coarse-threaded nut was fitted. The nut was inside a collar or sleeve that could slide back and forth inside the box, and this sleeve had teeth on one side that meshed with a sector gear on the pitman shaft. As the steering shaft was turned, the nut moved up and down the worm gear threads and pushed the sleeve up and down with it, so that the teeth on the sleeve moved the sector and turned the pitman arm.

Actually, it was a lot less complicated than it sounds, and had a number of features that have appealed to later engineers. One of the best features was its irreversibility; only enough road feel came back through the steering for good control. And it considerably reduced the driver effort involved in steering even such boat anchors as the 16-cyl. Cadillacs on which it was used.

That old specter of friction is the area modern engineers have so improved in this basically good design, which is where the recirculating balls come in. The grooves in the worm and inside the nut were machined for ball bearings, so that, in a sense, the balls performed the function of threads and absorbed the steering gear loads and friction. As the car was steered to the right, the balls would circulate in one direction, and in the opposite direction during a left-hand turn. Two tubes connected four holes in the nut/sleeve unit so that the balls could circulate over and over again and distribute the wear evenly among all of them.

Friction was reduced so much that steering was made much easier without having to slow down the gear ratio, which as we have said results in more lock-to-lock turns for the driver. Except for power steering, this represents the furthest advancement of steering gear design thus far, at least on domestic cars.

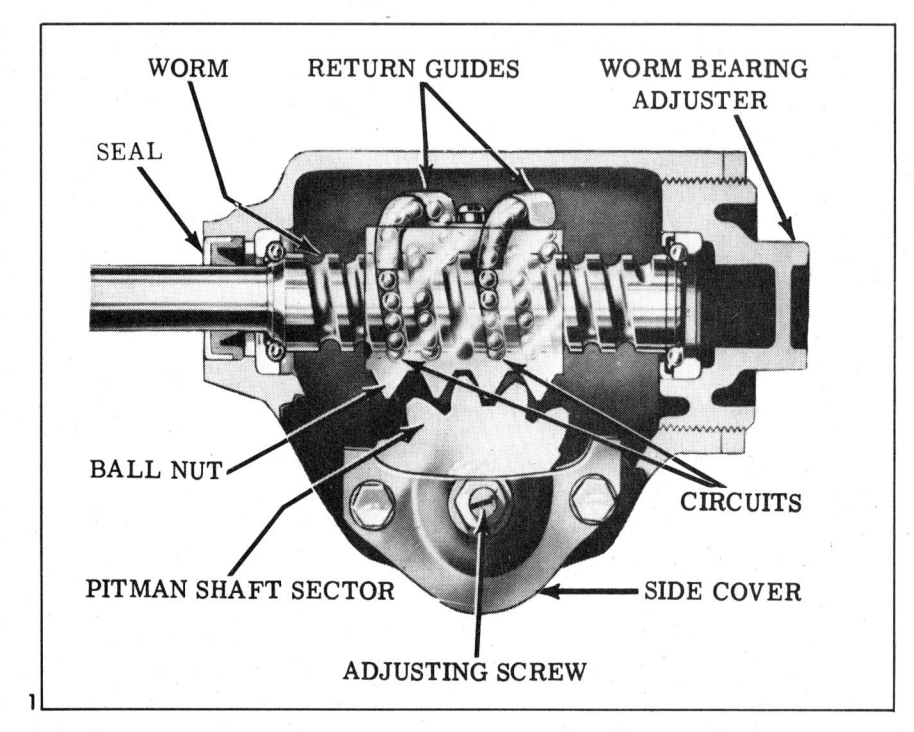

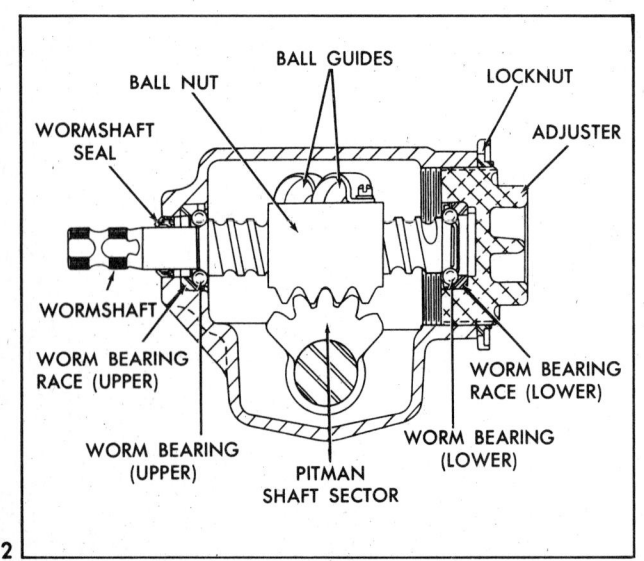

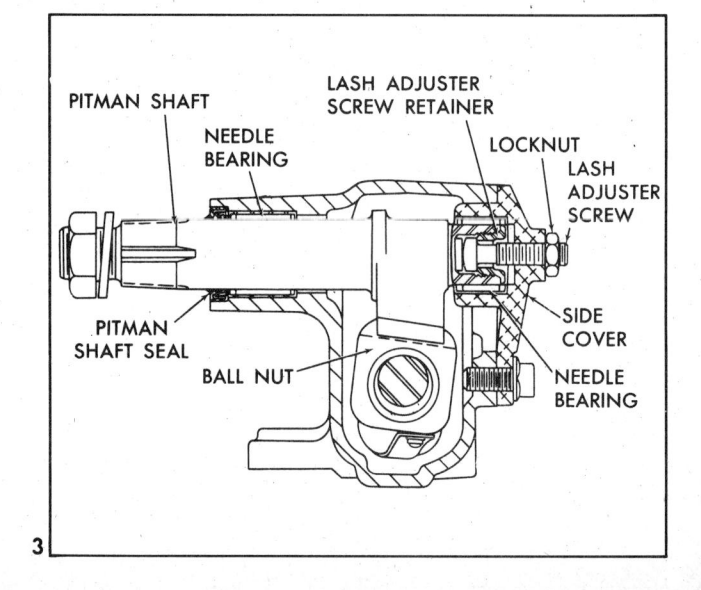

64/CHASSIS, SUSPENSION & BRAKES

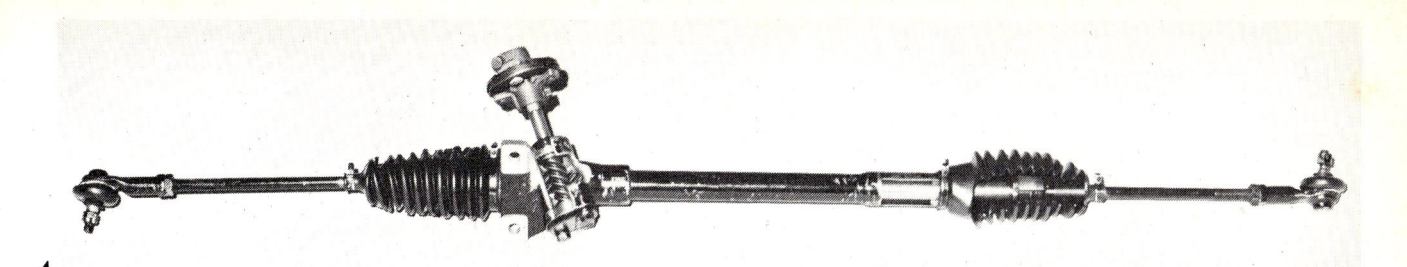

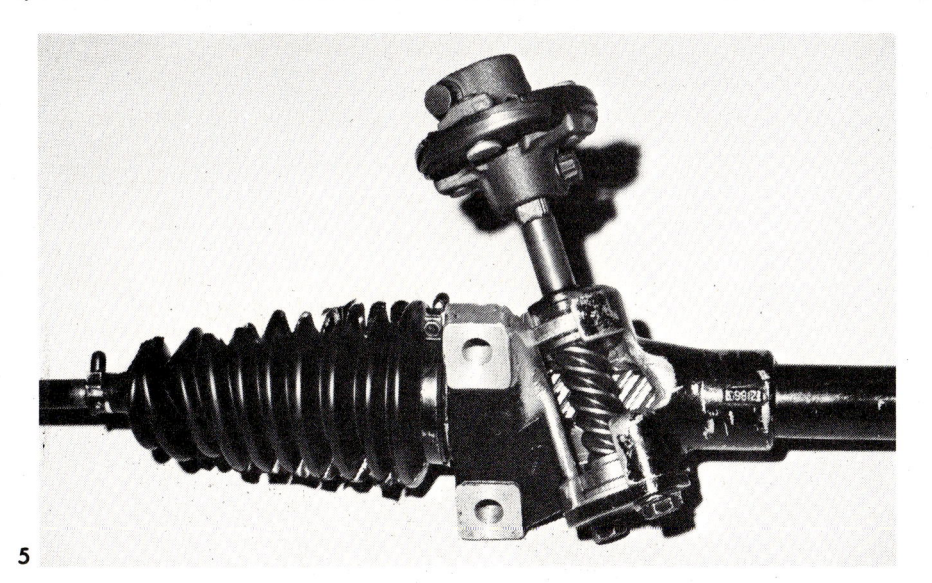

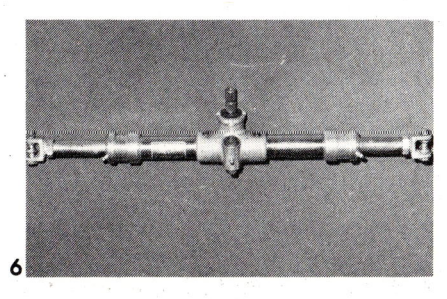

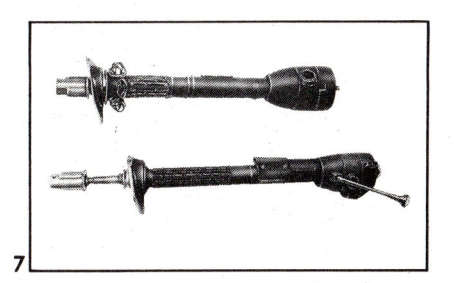

RACK AND PINION STEERING

Across the Atlantic "river," car manufacturers through the years have utilized some of the same steering systems as we have, though the light weight and smaller size of their cars have permitted the use of generally faster steering ratios. Perhaps the most interesting and different design is the rack and pinion type, seldom found on American cars, but common on most foreign sports cars and many different kinds of race cars.

In this case, the gear on the steering column is similar to the pinion gear in a differential—cut on an angle, and meshed with a steel bar (the rack) toothed on one side. The rack is mounted parallel to the front axle, and as the steering wheel is turned, it operates directly on the steering linkage without the use of a pitman arm or drag link. It's fast, simple to work on, and lightweight because it eliminates some of the usual linkage, which are the reasons it has been such a favorite on race cars and sports cars. Its one drawback is that it has very little inherent irreversibility, but in a racing machine the driver isn't worried about comfort or parking ability and is usually interested in more feedback or road feel than the average driver. Rack and pinion steering is thus a natural. Its quick action has made it the standard system on most imported sports cars, which are small and light, but hasn't found much favor with Detroit because it would require too much driver effort on our bigger and heavier automobiles.

For passenger car installations a compromise is often made by using a shock absorber-type damper on the linkage to reduce the reversibility. Since the damper's action is proportional to the amount of force put on it, small road shocks (desirable road feel) can be felt throughout the steering, but fast, hard, driver-jerking bumps are dampened.

After the development of the recirculating-ball steering gear, most of the changes in domestic steering have been concentrated on the linkage rather than the box itself. When independent front suspension was introduced in the mid-1930's, different linkages had to be designed. First of all, the tie-rod had to be split, so that it wouldn't be stressed when one wheel moved and the other didn't; thus, ordinary drag link and tie-rod steering was out for these cars. A short drag link from the pitman arm connected to a usually centrally mounted bell-crank, pivoting on the frame at the other end, and the now-two tie-rods attached to the bell-crank. As the steering box moved the bell-crank, it moved the two tie-rods, which had swivel ball joints at each end and were designed to swing in the same arc as did the wheels and

1. Ball bearings constantly riding in the grooves of the wormshaft are what make the recirculating-ball steering box virtually trouble-free.

2. In this side view of the modern recirculating-ball steering box, you can see how even gear contact can be maintained between the ball nut and the sector gear throughout its travel up or down the threaded wormshaft.

3. Since wear is usually minimal in the recirculating-ball steering box, adjustments are rarely necessary. A fine adjustment on the pitman shaft is possible with a lash screw and lock nut, which is usually at the top of the box for accessibility.

4. Something new, at least to the domestic-car scene, is the rack-and-pinion steering design. Used on many small imported cars, it's now used here on Pinto and the Mustang II. Its advantages include lightweight, positive feel, and a simpler system that eliminates several of the slop-prone parts of other linkage designs.

5. Cutaway demonstrates the true simplicity of the rack-and-pinion design. A threaded "pinion" gear works on a toothed "rack", to which short tie-rods are attached directly.

6. Although not seen until recently on passenger cars here, the "R&P" steering has been used to advantage on racing cars for years. This is a custom-built Gordon Schroeder unit from a USAC champ (Indy) racer.

7. While steering box designs have remained basic, the column has gone through many changes since 1967 to conform to federal safety standards. All cars must have a column that can collapse safely in an accident. This '74 Chrysler unit uses slotted mesh metal that under impact curls back over a mandrel on the floor.

CHASSIS, SUSPENSION & BRAKES/65

The Steering System

the A-arms.

The typical idler arm steering setup today has the steering box mounted so that the pitman arm is underneath it and swings left and right rather than forward and back, as with the older drag link-type steering. It connects to a relay rod, which runs to the other side of the frame where it connects to the idler arm, and the two tie-rods are connected to the relay rod. A description of the system sounds like that old song, "kneebone connected to the shinbone, shinbone connected to anklebone," right? Sorry about that. Just focus on the illustrations, and suffice it to say that it works.

MAINTENANCE

In most cases, you won't have too many complaints about the steering gear on your car, mainly because modern steering systems are well designed and relatively trouble-free. And besides, you'll probably be giving all your attention to good stuff like the engine and suspension. Taking care of your steering amounts to no more than periodic checking, keeping it full of grease or 90W oil and adjustments when necessary. Rarely will you ever want to *rebuild* a steering box. It would prove to be a pain in the neck. Most guys are content to visit their friendly/unfriendly neighborhood junkyard for a replacement unit if something goes seriously wrong with it. You could buy a good used steering box and column for what it would cost to replace even one of the gears in your present box with a new factory unit. But, as with anything you buy used or from a wrecking yard, you have to be careful or you'll wind up spending good bucks for an item that is pure guano.

If you do buy steering in a junkyard, check it over as carefully as you would select a used transmission, even to taking off the box cover and washing it with solvent so you can inspect the teeth on the gears. Inspect the box for defects, cracks, welds, etc., and if it's still in a car, try it out to see if it binds or has any play in it. If you're getting one from another model or year than your own car, see how many turns it is from lock to lock so you can determine if it has the ratio you want.

Before you start thinking about throwing out your steering and replacing it, check into it thoroughly, and even before attacking your steering box, try to determine first if it isn't something else which may be affecting the handling or steering. Things like poor shocks, unbalanced wheels, a misaligned front end, bad wheel bearings or improper tire pressure can produce the same symptoms as a defective steering gear.

If everything else checks out, then inspect your tie-rod ends and idler arm. As trouble-free and long lasting as these parts are, they wear out long before your steering box. Jack up the front end or put the car on a hoist and push up and down on the idler arm. If it's loose, pull it off and inspect it. Usually there is a bushing in the end that should be replaced. Tie-rod maintenance involves pushing up and down on the end of the tie-rod, checking for play just as with the idler arm. To remove them you may have to borrow a mechanic's "tuning fork" or "pickle fork," which is a heavy steel bar forked at the end. It's machined at an angle, like a wedge, so that you can put the fork between the tie-rod end and the steering arm. Hitting the end of the bar with a hammer forces the stud of the tie-rod end out of its socket in the steering arm. Above all, the most important thing to remember when doing any work on the front suspension or steering is to *never* leave out the cotter pins. The life you save will be your own.

ADJUSTING EARLY FORD DRAG LINK STEERING

If you have good reason to suspect there is play within the steering box itself, the adjustments are not difficult. For those of you lucky enough to own an early Ford, here is how it's done, using the Ford as a typical example of early drag link steering. Three adjustments that can be made are: end-play in the sector shaft; end-play in the worm shaft; and correct mesh between the worm and sector. For all adjustments, the front end should be jacked up and the drag link disconnected from the pitman

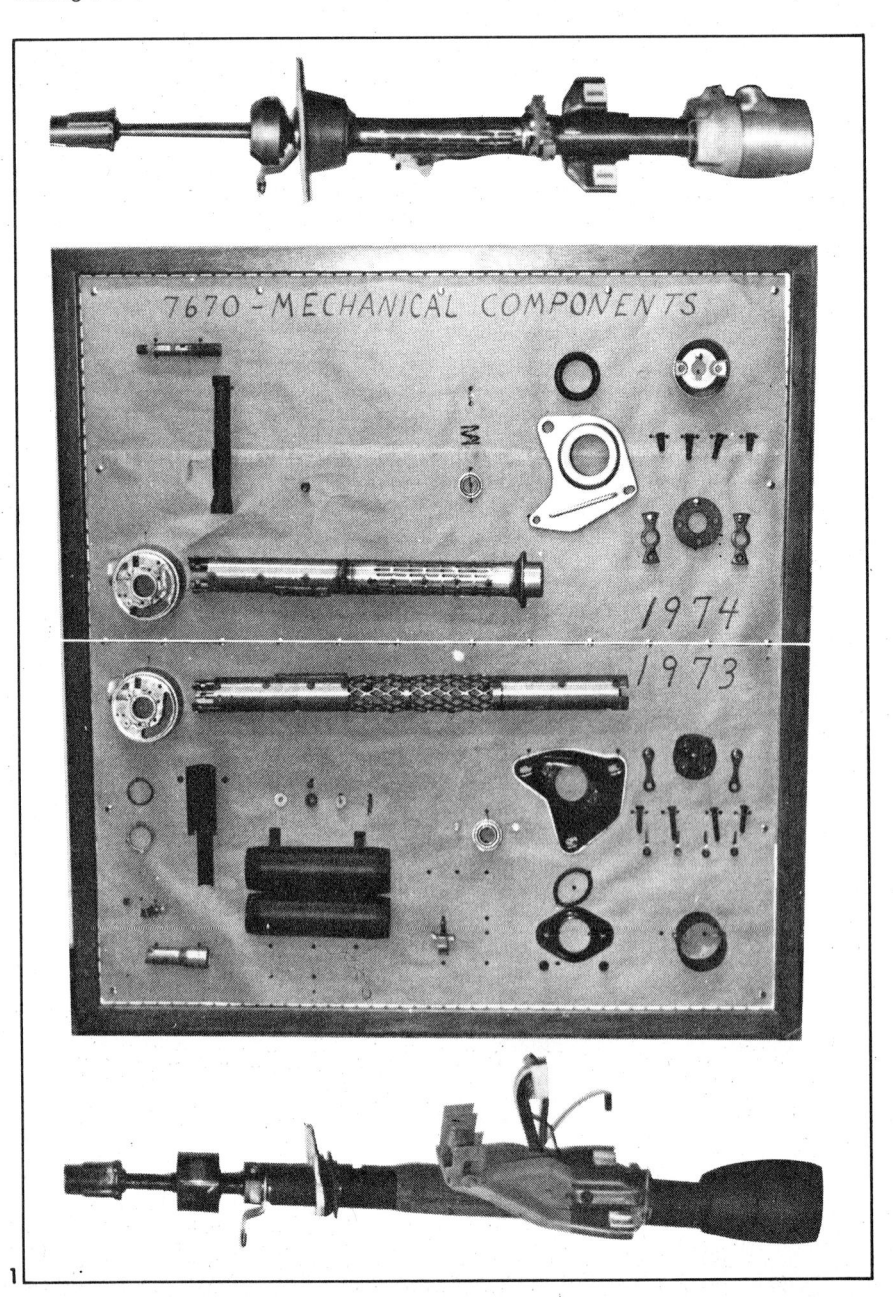

66/CHASSIS, SUSPENSION & BRAKES

arm. To adjust end-play in the sector shaft, turn the steering wheel to either extreme, then back 1/8-turn. Pull back and forth on the pitman arm as if to move the shaft in and out of the box. If there is play, adjust the sector thrust screw, which you will find on the engine side of the box. Retighten the lock nut on it, and check for play.

Now check for end-play in the steering shaft by pulling up on the steering wheel; you shouldn't notice any play or extra clearance between the steering wheel and the end of the steering column. Just below the shaft/box mating, you will find the housing clamp bolt, 180° around from the topside lubricant hole, which you will have to loosen before taking up any play you may have noticed. Loosen the lock nut on the worm adjusting screw, then tighten the screw with a box wrench. Back off 1/6-turn, retighten the lock nut and check for stiffness in the steering.

Unlike the end-play of the two shafts, checking and adjustment of the gear mesh must be done only while the steering is in the *center* of its right and left travel. Move the pitman arm back and forth by hand (fore and aft) to check for play between the gears. Loosen the three nuts that hold the box cover 1/4-turn. The topmost one (with the steering in the car) has the eccentric adjuster nut under it on the same stud. The outside nut should be loosened 1/2-turn; then you can slowly and carefully adjust the eccentric, turning it clockwise and checking for play as you go. When there's no play, tighten the outside nut first, then the three other cover nuts.

RECIRCULATING-BALL ADJUSTMENTS

For the late-model crowd, here's the "skinny" on adjusting the recirculating-ball steering. Here you have only two adjustments to make for end-play on each of the shafts. You won't have to worry about worm/nut mesh because the use of the steel balls between the teeth eliminates wear in most cases. Jacking up the car and disconnecting the pitman arm from the linkage is still the first step. Remember, when working on this type of steering system when the linkage is off, *don't* turn the steering wheel *hard* over to either extreme or you may damage the steel balls. If you suspect that the car may have been in a front-end collision at one time, then loosen the steering column support mount that is under or behind the dashboard to eliminate the possibility of a misaligned shaft during the adjustments. If your car has flexible U-joints in the steering shaft, you don't have to worry about this.

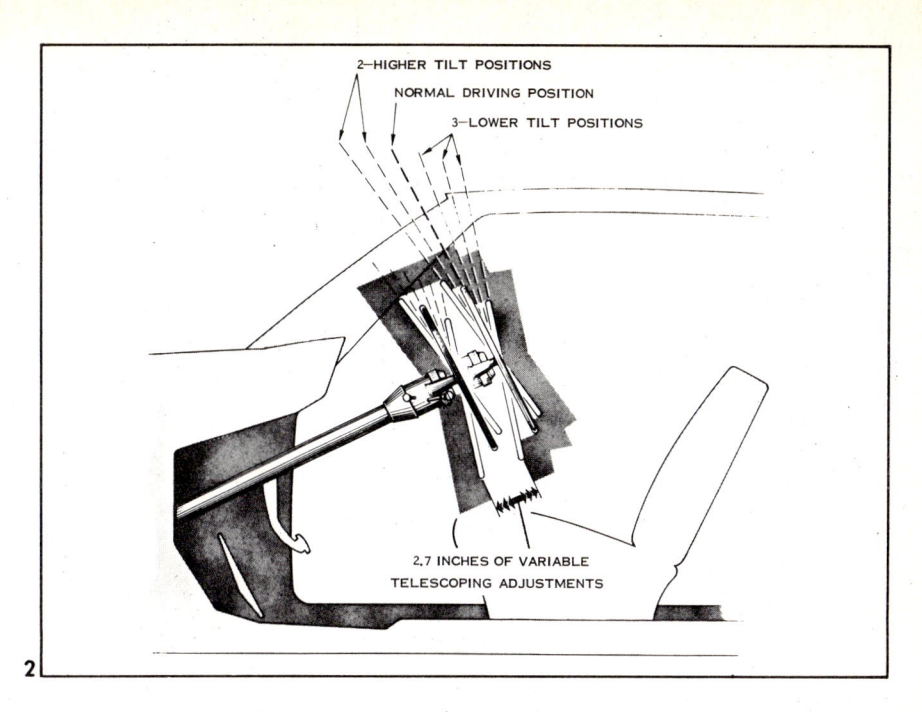

With the steering about one turn from the full left or full right, back off the lock nut on the pitman shaft (opposite side of box from pitman arm) and loosen the adjuster a few turns counterclockwise to take the mesh load off the gears. Now pull up and down on the steering wheel to check for end-play in the steering shaft. Play can be taken out by another lock nut/adjuster combination found at the bottom end of the steering box. The large lock nut can be loosened by tapping it with a hammer and punch in the notches provided, if you don't have a wrench that big. Always check for lost motion again after tightening the lock nut following an adjustment.

Now you can adjust the end-play in the pitman shaft and at the same time take care of lash where the sector gear meshes with the teeth on the underside of the ball/nut mechanism. Since the gears are cut at an angle, end-play adjustment of the pitman shaft controls the mesh between them, too. Turning the adjuster *clockwise* will take up the lash, but make sure you don't overtighten it. These adjustments of late-model steering gears will only rarely be needed, but by all rights they should be made with the use of a pounds-pressure gauge on the steering wheel to measure drag or bind. Assuming that you don't have such a gauge, though, you can do it yourself as outlined above, or have it done at your dealer.

Lubrication for the steering box (about SAE 90W) can be purchased at most parts stores or you can have it put in at a garage, since you don't need very much. Some steering boxes use chassis grease. If there is no filler plug on the box, or if it has a grease-gun type lube fitting, it probably should have chassis grease. Using 90W in a box designed for chassis grease will result in a big mess, because the 90W will probably leak out profusely.

REMOVING THE STEERING BOX AND COLUMN

If all of the above has failed to correct any problems you suspect are coming from the box, you haven't much choice but to replace the unit. It may look like it's going to be a beast of a job (it really isn't), but keep telling yourself that you need the exercise, or consider it as a challenge. Naturally, you first have to take that steering wheel off, and for this you're going to need a steering wheel puller or gear puller because it's on there pretty tight. You'll need it to pull the pitman arm from its shaft for the same reason.

After disconnecting the electrical and shift linkage connections from the mast jacket—which is the column or tube covering the steering shaft—you can unbolt the box from the frame, the mast jacket from the dash bracket, and pull the mast jacket into the inside of the car and off. The shift arms on it can be worked through the

1. With the steering-lock ignitions and energy-absorption features, the steering column becomes an engineer's challenge. Comparing '74 (top) and '73 Dodge units, you can see how the new multiple-slot/mandrel-type not only works better, but eliminates several parts for easier servicing.

2. One of the few steering column features that isn't a government requirement is a tilt-and-telescope wheel, an option on some late-model cars. It really is a luxury, but it's great for reducing driver fatigue and providing a "custom-fit" feel.

CHASSIS, SUSPENSION & BRAKES/67

The Steering System

flexible sealing around the steering column at the firewall. Now the box itself and the steering shaft can be removed from the frame. On many late-model cars, there is a fabric and metal U-joint just above the steering box which really makes it easy to remove the steering. You simply undo the joint and you can remove the steering box and do it without touching the column.

Because safety is so important, the collapsible steering column has become a standard item on new cars. Some have a steel mesh section in the middle that folds up in a crash, while later versions utilize two sections held together with plastic pins that shear under impact, telescoping the two sections. When working with such a column, be careful not to collapse it by accident (no pun intended). Don't yank on it too hard, and don't use a hammer on the shaft to loosen the steering wheel when removing it.

MODIFICATIONS

If your experience with hot rodding has brought you past the simple hop-up or bolt-in engine swap, then you've probably had a problem with steering at one time or another. Big engine/little car swaps or the scratch-building of a street rod usually involve some modification of the linkage or the relocation of the steering box. For the swapper, the problem is generally one of trying to get clearance between the new powerplant and the steering box of the car, which always seems to be right where you and your exhaust manifolds don't want it. Often the easiest and best solution in the long run, if the interference isn't too great, is a set of tubing headers that cautiously avoid the steering box. As luck would have it, though, you've already spent more money than you have on the engine, right? So you're stuck with the cast iron manifolds and now you'll just have to move that box. This problem can crop up even if you're using the car's original engine, when you're setting the engine back.

For most of the engine swaps into later-model cars, all you want to do is move the box, since the design and operation of the steering gear should be adequate for your needs, and you'll want to keep it. The number of ways of doing this is as varied as the swaps, but none is beyond the reach of the average swapper. With relation to the engine, the problem is most often one of lateral clearance, and moving the box further to the left of the motor will do the trick. If the box was originally mounted to the inside of the frame, just cutting the frame so that the box mounts within the rail is usually enough. But it's vitally important that any frame weakness as a result of such cutting be made up by extra-heavy gussets and welding. It takes something like 400 lbs. of pressure to turn the front wheels at rest, so keep in mind that the box mount must be super-strong. A better way, perhaps, is to mount the steering box on *top* of the frame rail. Then you can gain more clearance by moving it outboard with a small extension or platform welded on the frame.

Relocation of the steering box usually brings with it a few related problems too, like the steering column. Even moving the box a small amount can create an alignment problem for the column. When the major change is one of vertical-plane angle, you can shim the column/dashboard mount to make up for it, or make up a new mount. When direction of the column is changed laterally, or the clearance problem is at the column instead of the box, the best way out is one or two U-joints in the steering column, like those that many new cars have. Take a look at some NASCAR Modifieds. Often working with large, late engines, early bodies and special frames, some have as many as three U-joints in the steering shaft. Remember, though, that if you install more than one (and two should be the limit), the column is going to need some kind of support to hold it up the middle. Too many U-joints in there and steering will be like playing golf with a garden hose for a club! You can find these U-joints (aircraft) through various surplus houses in your locale, through Eelco, P.O. Box 4095, Inglewood, Calif. or Earl's Supply Co., 14611 Hawthorne Blvd., Lawndale, Calif. 92060.

In cases where the steering has been moved back on the frame, you may have to shorten the steering column as a result. If the relocation wasn't a drastic one, a custom steering wheel is all you need. They look real pretty in metalflake or the popular wood-rimmed style, and come in many different diameters. If you've moved your steering forward, one of the dished-type wheels will maintain the rim in the same position for driving. They are also built in either flat-spoke style or reverse-dish, which gives more room at the wheel and adds a little "early" flavor to your street machine.

The street rod builder has a whole different situation to deal with than the late-model swapper. He can generally choose the type of steering he wants, and in the case of the scratch-built car, he has no stock unit to rework and *has* to choose one. Once you burden down the front end of your early rod with a big late-model engine and transmission—especially if you're using an automatic—that fast-ratio early Ford box can steer like a truck with both

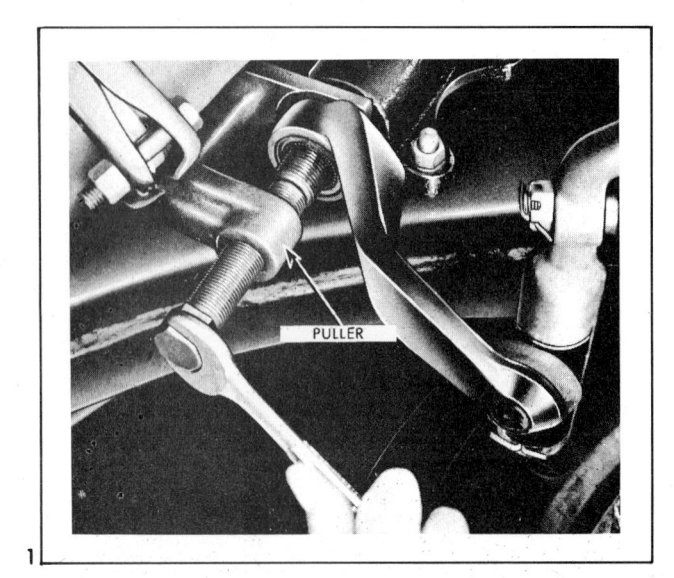

68/CHASSIS, SUSPENSION & BRAKES

front tires flat. So the updating route is the only way to go. The only formula for choosing late-model steering for a rod is to try to match the unit to the weight of the car by using the steering from a car whose front-end weight is similar to that of the rod.

The thing to look for is how the pitman arm works and in what direction. The best way to go is to get a box whose arm swings in the same fore-and-aft direction as the early drag link steering box, so that adaptation of the new unit to the existing linkage is easy. A setup that has been very popular, especially for the lightweight T-buckets, is one of the Corvair boxes, most of which are aluminum. At first it seems like a poor choice because the pitman arm points up instead of down, but a little machine work will take care of that. By machining the box so that the steering shaft can be swapped end for end, you come up with a unit that works very much like the early Ford.

After disassembling the gearbox, you'll notice that there is a seal where the steering shaft originally came out, and at the other end is the nut for adjusting the worm bearings. A 15/16-in.-diameter Welch plug (freeze plug) will fill the hole where the shaft came out, replacing the seal. Drill and ream a 15/16-in. precision hole in the adjuster nut and you're in business. Put a stock seal in this new hole, wash up the pieces and put the gears back inside, but this time with the shaft coming out of the adjuster nut. Now the stock mounting holes are on the bottom, easing fabrication of a frame mount, and the pitman arm hangs down just where you want it.

Also popular for early street iron are the late-model pickup steering boxes. Ford pickup boxes of early '50's vintage are particularly easy to use because they mount just like the early Ford units. By trimming the ears on the flat mounting flange of the box so that only three bolt holes are used, it can be fitted inside the frame channel and bolted in merely by drilling new holes in the frame.

An easily available unit that is light and smooth-operating is that found on the compact vans, like the earlier Ford Econoline and Dodge A-100. However, they utilize a trailing pitman arm, so in order for it to steer in the right direction, the pitman arm must be installed pointing straight up. This can be a great help in keeping the drag link straight when you're using a dropped axle.

MODIFICATIONS FOR FASTER STEERING

Existing steering can be modified for a faster or slower ratio by the use of special pitman or steering arms. A longer pitman arm provides a faster steering ratio, with the opposite being true for a short pitman arm. Sometimes careful scrounging can unearth one from another year or model to fit your bill, like using an early Ford arm on a '48 Ford box to quicken it up. Late-model Corvettes use special steering arms with two holes for the tie-rods to mount in. Utilizing the forward holes changes the steering ratio from the standard ratio of about 20:1 to a faster 17.6:1. They should not be moved, however, on models equipped with power steering, because of interference with the tie-rod.

Some cars have steering arms that bolt to the steering knuckle instead of being made in one piece with it. To quicken the steering, find an arm from another year of the same make car that is shorter. In this case the leverage principle works opposite. A shorter steering arm has the same effect on quickening the steering as a longer pitman arm.

When measuring the length of any arm, do not measure along the arm, or your calculations won't work. *Ignore* the shape of the arm and imagine two lines running straight through the holes in each end of the arm. The distance straight across between those two lines will be the effective length of the arm. Compare with other arms measured the same way, and you will know if the new arm will give you faster or slower steering. Remember, a longer pitman arm gives faster steering, and a shorter pitman arm slows the steering. On steering arms, go shorter for faster steering and longer for slower.

Speed equipment houses often have special arms you can buy for your car for faster steering, such as the Eelco units for Corvairs and the VW units made by Crown Mfg. Co., 858 Production Place, Newport Beach, Calif. If at all possible, though, *don't* modify your existing pitman arm—you're playing with your life. Never bend it, whether hot or cold; if you have to, make a new one from flamecut steel plate. When you do, you can make it any length and drill several holes in it so you can change the ratio just by mounting the drag link in a different hole. The top can be splined for the pitman shaft at a machine shop, or you can weld the splined section from the old one into a hole in the new arm. Remember, though, any part of the suspension or steering that you've cut and welded should be magnafluxed for your own protection, especially on a race car. If you don't have a magnaflux certificate for it, a suspicious-looking welded part could get you turned down at an NHRA safety inspection, too.

The more you delve into the design and construction of various parts of the automobile, the more you begin to respect the job that your car does, as you discover the many complications that had to be accounted for in its development. You should by now have a basic understanding of the principles of steering gear design. Whether you just plan on giving your '55 Chevy chassis the once-over, or you dream of building a nifty little T-bucket roadster, the information here should steer you straight.

1. Chances are that your steering system will never need big repairs while you own the car. While most such repairs may best be left to a professional, there are minor jobs you can do with a few tools. Pullers like these are useful for removing pitman arms or tie-rod ends.

2. If your car didn't come with an optional tilt-wheel, Grant makes one for most cars from '68 up. Although it doesn't telescope, it offers five tilt positions, and a little class.

3. If any slop does accrue in your steering system, the first suspect part should be the idler arm, which should be rebushed or replaced. Kits like that at left are available to convert your idler arm from simple bushings to ball-bearings, for easier steering with less slop.

4. If your front end checks out to be in good shape and you still don't like the road feel (as with many of the utility four-wheel drives), you can install a steering stabilizer (shock absorber) on your tie-rod.

CHASSIS, SUSPENSION & BRAKES/69

Power Steering Systems

Rarely a choice back in the '50's, power assist steering is sold on more than half of today's domestic cars.

Although power steering is not a new concept (the 1903 Columbia electric truck used an electric steering booster), little effort was put into its development until the '50's. Its first serious application by Detroit was as an option on the 1951 DeSotos and Chryslers, and the next year on the Cad-Olds-Buick lineup at GM. Many improvements in pumps, valves and steering gear have come about since then, and today the majority of new cars sold are equipped with power steering.

LINKAGE-TYPE POWER STEERING

Basically there are two types of power steering systems that have been used on passenger cars: linkage-type and integral-type. The linkage-type consisted of an oil pump, sometimes driven off the rear of the generator, with hoses carrying the oil or fluid to a valve assembly and hydraulic piston that acted on the tie-rods to assist in steering the car. It was primarily a booster, and was merely added to a car with a standard steering box and linkage. The integral-type, however, required a whole new steering box, with the valving and assist action all working within the box itself. The linkage-type has now been almost entirely phased out in favor of the integral power steering system.

Actually, those *early* Chrysler and GM power steering systems were of the integral-type, although nothing like the ones we have today. They were big, bulky and expensive... too expensive in fact to have become at that time the popular, mass-produced accessory the engineers thought they could be. Since the linkage-type required no special steering box and the hydraulic cylinder didn't take up any room in the engine compartment, it was cheap enough to be offered on all models, not just the more expensive cars. It became the standard for power steering for the next decade.

In the typical installation, the pump was driven off the back of the generator or by a separate crank-driven belt. The pump had to have enough capacity to do the job at low engine speeds in parking situations, but it was found that pumps burned up by overheating the fluid when it pumped madly at highway speeds. Something had to be done to cut down the flow at high speeds, yet provide adequate flow at low speeds, so a pressure regulating relief valve was incorporated into the pump body. When the pump output exceeded maximum specifications, the relief valve released the flow of oil back into the return line into the pump so that excessive pressure was not built up and steering boost was provided only when needed.

It wouldn't have been difficult for engineers to have designed a power steering system that required no driver effort at all, but this would have brought on that old spector of "road feel" and driver senses. A certain amount of resistance had to be designed into the system so that the driver felt he was doing at least *some* of the steering. Most of the early model linkage-type power steerings required a wheel rim effort of from 4 to 7 lbs.

VALVING IN THE LINKAGE-TYPE SYSTEM

Although Ford began the linkage steering trend in 1954, it was Saginaw (GM) that came out a year later with a unit that incorporated the steering valve into the power cylinder where it connected to the regular linkage. From the inside, the steering valve, which controls which way the cylinder is going to push on the linkage, operates something like a miniature automatic transmission. The

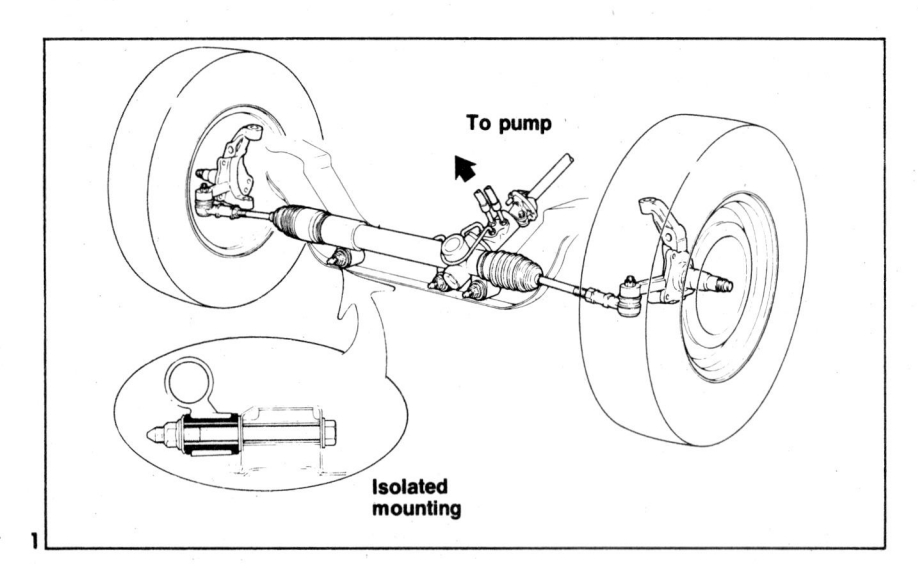

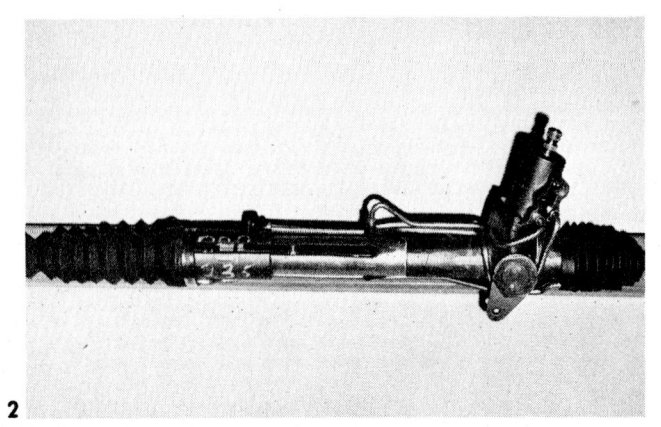

70/CHASSIS, SUSPENSION & BRAKES

feel? Remember when we were talking about manual steering and we described how a hydraulic cylinder could be used as a shock absorber on the steering gear? Well, the hydraulic cylinder in the linkage-type power steering functions the same way, but unfortunately it works *too* well. Some of these early systems gave the driver the feeling he was driving on butter with bald tires.

INTEGRAL POWER STEERING

While several designs of integral power steering were still being tried all along on the more expensive cars, the down-to-earth Fords and Chevys used the linkage-type right up until as recently as 1964. But in 1965, both Ford and Chevy made the switch to the more refined and less bulky integral-type power steering system, although Chevrolet still used the linkage-type on both the Chevy II and the Corvette.

The main problem for any power steering system is to design a control or steering valve assembly that has the proper amount of sensitivity and road feel, is simple enough to remain trouble-free for years, and does all of these things within a small package. The earlier integral power attempts had utilized a control valve that was actuated (told whether to move left or right) by the lower thrust bearing on the steering box worm shaft. As the driver turned the steering wheel—the theory went—a certain amount of thrust was put on this lower bearing, and because of the direction in which the nut moved on the worm, the

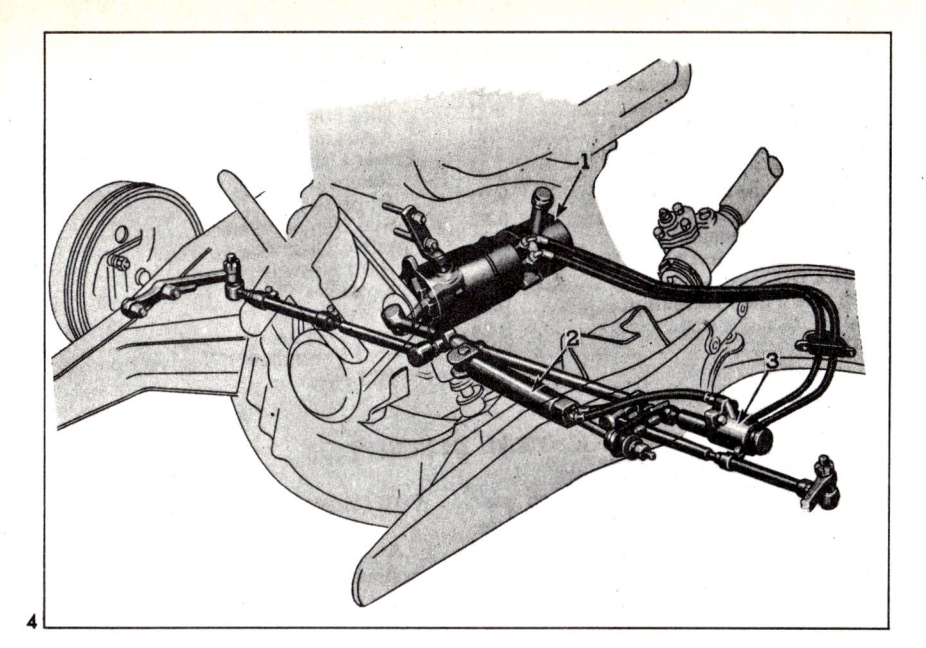

heart of it is the spool valve, which is like a small cam with round lobes. Spring-loaded, as it is moved to the right or left, the "lobes" cover and uncover oil passages in the valve body. For instance, when the driver exerts a predetermined amount of effort on the steering gear for a left turn, the spool valve moves to the right against the pressure of its centering springs. This uncovers passages that permit the fluid to be channeled into the right side of the booster cylinder, forcing it and the steering linkage to turn the wheels to the left.

The geometry of the front end is such that the wheels tend to follow a straight track and to return to the straight-ahead position after a turn. With power steering, the springs on the spool valve force it back to the center of its body when the driver stops holding the wheel to the left. This cuts the fluid flow to the cylinder and stops the assist action, so the steering gear can return to the center of its travel.

The linkage-type power steering system was adequate for the cars it was being used on, but it had a few disadvantages. If you drove a '55 Chevy with power steering and then jumped into a new Chevy with power steering, you'd notice the main difference right away. The earlier design had required 4 to 7 lbs. of wheel effort, while the cars of today require only about 3 lbs. And as easy as modern power steering is in terms of wheel resistance, you would notice that the newer ones *feel* better; they feed back more of the road to the driver for a better sense of control. But why should the easier (and faster ratio) late steering give more road

1. The newest thing in power systems is the power rack-and-pinion that is optional on the new Mustang II. Up to now only available on very costly European cars, it's the only one in this country. It's compact, direct and rugged, and has good road feel.

2. Steel lines from the pinion part of the box carry fluid to either side of the sealed rack's center, and the fluid pushes the rack left or right in response to signals from box.

3. With the optional power assist, the Mustang II rack-and-pinion has an 18:1 ratio with good road feel and less overall weight than the conventional-type power steering.

4. When power-assist steering first became popular in the 1950's, most were of the linkage type, with the pump mounted off the generator. The Comet and Maverick are among the few cars to still use this system.

5. With the pump (A) on its own belt and mounted close to the steering box (B), the modern integral-type power steering system has shorter hoses and a lot fewer parts than the old linkage type. Many of the newer cars also have a fluid cooler (C) to fight today's underhood temperatures.

CHASSIS, SUSPENSION & BRAKES/71

Power Steering Systems

thrust was different for right and left turns and varied according to the amount of effort that the driver exerted. The trouble was that the bearing—along with the control valve—was located at the lower end of the steering column and box, and made for a bulky system.

The 1965 integral systems, which have been continued virtually unchanged in basic design, could be made into a smaller unit because the valve assembly was mounted in the upper end of the steering box, where it mated to the column. The secret of these units is the way in which the valves are actuated. Basically, within the column, the worm shaft and the shaft from the steering wheel are linked by a short *torsion* bar. This torsion bar is connected at its lower end to the worm shaft and also is pinned to the valve body, which is mounted in teflon ring seals inside the upper end of the steering box. To the *upper* end of the torsion bar are pinned the stub shaft and the lower end of the shaft from the steering wheel.

So the valve body and the valve itself (pinned to the stub shaft) are attached to opposite ends of the torsion bar. When the driver turns the steering wheel, the torque on the shaft twists the torsion bar slightly, which changes the relationship between the spool valve and the valve body, controlling the opening and closing of fluid passages.

Another feature in which the new integral systems saved space in the engine room over the linkage-type was the design of the power piston assembly. While the older types had used a separate and necessarily bulkier hydraulic cylinder, this unit utilized a seal and a teflon ring to make the recirculating ball/nut mechanism act as a hydraulic piston. In other words, the ball/nut fit within the steering box housing with a tight fit made by the teflon, which performed the function of a piston ring. As the twisting of the torsion bar caused the valve to channel the flow of oil to either the upper or lower side of this "power piston," it was forced up or down the worm gear, instead of the driver supplying all the force.

Except for the pump and the two oil lines, the late integral-type power steering is all one self-contained unit in the steering box. And having the hydraulic cylinder action located within the box solved the problems some of the earlier cars had had with the hoses. They had been forced to use long hoses that stretched from the engine-mounted pump all the way down under the car to the power cylinder, and along the way those vulnerable hoses had to be routed out of the exhaust heat and harm's way. The integral system, however, needed only two short hoses from the pump to the box, since the pump was usually on the same side of the engine as the steering box.

VARIABLE ASSIST

It wasn't too long after the introduction of these integral steering units (it is interesting to note that Ford and Mercury thought enough of the GM-Saginaw boxes to use them on the FoMoCo line) that those die-hard drivers who had spurned power steering before because it lacked good "feel," finally decided to switch rather than fight with manual steering on their new cars. What made them

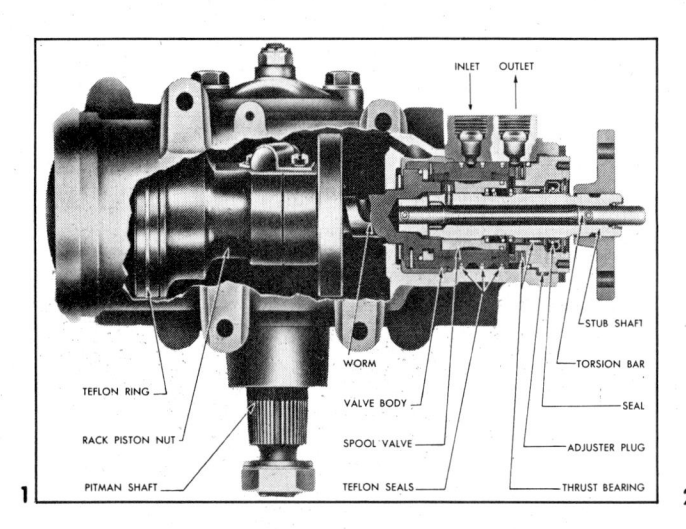

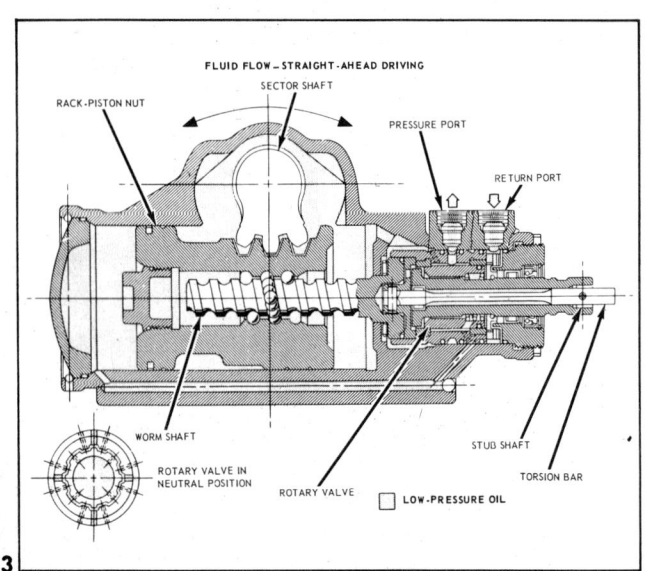

72/CHASSIS, SUSPENSION & BRAKES

decide that it wasn't so bad after all was the variable assist feature of the new integral units.

The torsion bar has a better sense of how much assist should be applied than did the older linkage systems, while still incorporating less wheel rim effort than the linkage types. Up to a predetermined effort of about 1 or 2 lbs., the steering is entirely manual; above that the valve opens and allows some assist. Above 3 or 4 lbs.' rim effort it supplies full assist, in such circumstances as parking. But on the highway the effect is not noticed unless you start to make a turn, so there is enough of that manual-like road feel to satisfy most of today's drivers.

The late Chrysler Corp. power steering units are also of the integral variety, but use a somewhat different steering valve. It relies, as did the earlier GM integral units, on actuation by the thrust bearing on the wormshaft, but this time the upper bearing is the one doing it. When the steering wheel is turned one way or the other, the wormshaft actually moves up or down a small amount. This small amount is multiplied by a pivot lever and transferred to the spool valve. This pivot lever is mounted lengthwise within a coil spring and is side-loaded by ''reaction springs'' which impart some road feel to the action of the assist components by exerting a ''centering'' force.

PUMPS

So far we have discussed the design of power steering boxes and linkages, but you should know something about the pumps that supply them, too. The main difference between the pumps used on different makes is the design of the fins used to push the fluid around within the pump and build up pressure. One of the most common is the vane-type used by GM and some American Motors and Chrysler Corp. cars. All the pumps use a rotor that spins inside of the pump housing or body. With the vane-type unit, a number of blades are fitted to slots in the rotor, with the slots being deep enough for the vanes to slide in or out of the slots. The inside of the pump body itself has an out-of-round or oval shape to it, so that there is more room for the blades to slide out when they pass the ''stretched-out'' portions around the rotor. Centrifugal force keeps the blades or vanes in contact with the walls of the body at all times, though they move in and out of their slots as the rotor turns. In one revolution of the rotor, there are two places where the vanes are loose and they pick up fluid, and also two places where they are forced in by the walls of the body, therefore putting pressure on the fluid.

A variation on this type of pump is the increasingly popular roller-type, which has been used in the past by Ford and is now used by both American Motors and Chrysler on some of their cars. The inside contour of the pump is again oval-shaped, but in this case the rotor has a set of wide V-grooves cut into it. Steel rollers ride in these grooves and, like the vanes of the Saginaw pump, they follow the inside contour of the pump body as centrifugal force pushes them out at the ends of the oval. They trap fluid in the same way as the vanes and when they pass the narrow portions of the body, they pressurize the fluid and force it out through two outlets. A good feature of the oval or elliptical shape inside the housing, which makes for two inlets and two outlets since there are two pickup and two compression areas, is that the pressure and side loads on the rotor shaft are more equally distributed than would be the case if the rotor were just mounted off-center in a round housing—which would leave a compression or pressure area on only one side, as some early pumps had been designed.

New cars from Dearborn use another variation on the vane-type pump, known as the slipper-type, although any of the pumps used today could be referred to as slipper-type. Also rotating within an elliptical or roughly oval-shaped chamber within the pump body, the rotor of the slipper-type pump has several wide

1. The Teflon ring seal in Saginaw power steering box is the key to making the ball-nut mechanism do the work of a piston under fluid pressure.

2. This cutaway of a late Ford power steering box shows how the ball-nut mechanism works just like a piston in a cylinder. The circled area is where an assemblage of O-rings, seals and valves controls the fluid flow.

3. In this view of a Saginaw power steering box, the dark areas are filled with pressured fluid. Since the unit is shown in straight-ahead operation, fluid pressure is low.

4. Since all the fluid in a power steering box is under pressure, and in hard turns considerable pressure, more care must be given to sealing. This Ford box uses two large rubber oil seals where the sector shaft comes out the bottom of the box.

5. Ford uses a slipper-type pump on which the fluid reservoir is integral with the pump. Eight spring-loaded seals (slippers) do the pumping.

6. Most power steering pumps have balanced loads on the shaft because of the elliptical shape of the pump housing and having two fluid inlets and two outlets opposite each other.

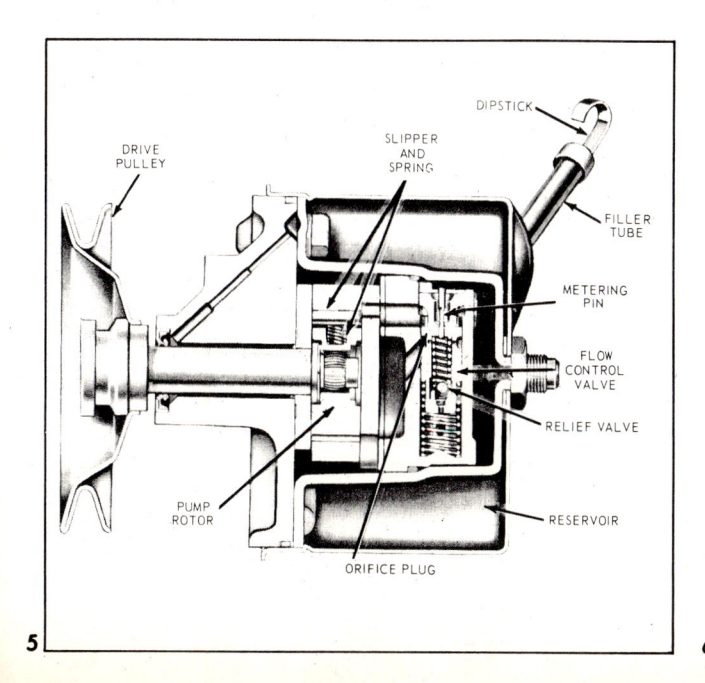

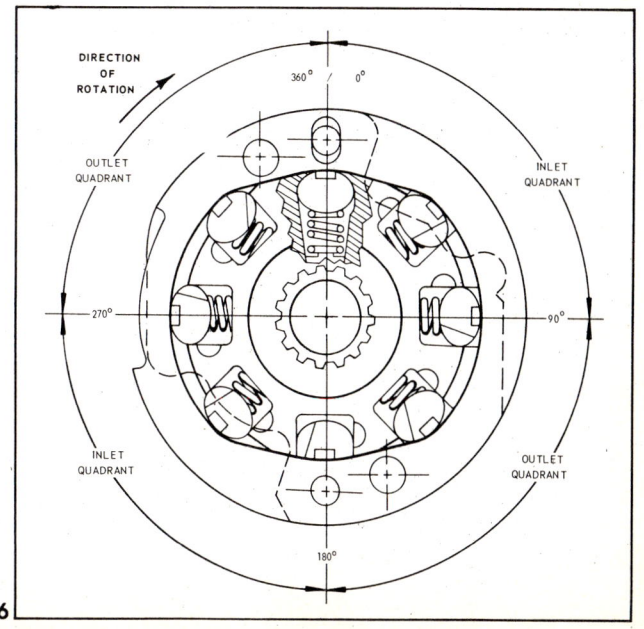

Power Steering Systems

slots cut into it that are fitted with springs topped by scrubber-type "slippers." The springs keep the slippers in contact with the inner contour of the body, and the whole rotating assembly might remind you of a spring-loaded hone spinning within a cylinder on your engine. For many years, Chrysler used this type of pump, and in fact everybody but General Motors has used it at one time or another, but Ford was the only major manufacturer using it in the past few years.

MAINTENANCE

Since for both the linkage- and integral-type of power steering, the basic steering gear is the same as that for the manual steering of the same car, most of what we outlined in the previous chapter applies to power steering as well. Service procedures for adjusting the linkage and steering box are much the same, and there are few special or extra requirements.

Even more so than with manual steering, it is not advisable for the average amateur mechanic to disassemble or try to rebuild a power steering system. The hydraulic parts of the system are precisely fitted to each other at the factory and it's easy to ruin their efficiency by taking them apart and putting them back together, unless you know exactly what you're doing. With any kind of steering, power or manual, most of the troubles you may blame on your steering gear are the fault of some other part of the front end, anyway. Improper tire pressure, misaligned front end, dragging brakes, bad ball joints or bent suspension components can all cause symptoms for which you might at first suspect the steering gear. But luckily, the steering gear on your car is built to last, with practically no service, and you shouldn't have any trouble with it in normal usage.

Again, if you are having trouble and you've determined that it definitely is the power steering, your best bet is to replace the offending part or have it serviced by someone who is qualified and experienced.

If anything does go wrong with your power steering, it is probably the pump, which seems to do the most work and wear out sooner. Your local dealer should be able to check the output of your pump for you with special flow and pressure gauges. At any rate, there are a few simple service procedures that you can do yourself, and in fact will probably mean the difference between a lemon and a long-lasting, trouble-free system . . . if you don't neglect them.

FLUID LEVEL

There is no ordinary heavy-grease lubrication of the steering box with power steering. It and all the other components are continuously lubricated by the flow of oil (fluid) through the system. Hence, maintaining the proper fluid level is the first and foremost rule to remember. Type A automatic transmission fluid is the one most generally used, and should be added to the pump reservoir when the oil is hot and the engine is shut off. Check the pump's dipstick just as you would check your engine oil dipstick. While transmission fluid is the most common lubricant for power steering pumps, manufacturers now specify on some makes that only special power steering fluid should be used, so check your owners manual on this.

If you have noticed that the fluid level is down quite a bit when you filled the reservoir, or suspect for some other reason that there is air in the hydraulic system, then you should bleed the power steering. Don't worry, it's a lot easier than bleeding your brakes, and no smelly fluid runs down your sleeve either. Simply add enough fluid to get the correct dipstick reading and let it sit for a few minutes. Run the engine for a few seconds to circulate the fluid, then shut it off and check the dipstick again. Repeat this procedure until the oil level seems to remain constant. Now jack up the front end so the front wheels are off the ground. With the engine kept running at a fast idle (1500 rpm) turn the steering wheel to the left and to the right, being careful not to hit the extreme stops too hard. Lower the car and again turn the wheels each way, then shut the engine off and check the fluid again. That's all there is to it. Remember that a lot of foam in the oil is an indication that there is air in the system, as is the case if the oil is milky.

PROPER BELT TENSION

Besides the fluid level, proper tension on the belt that drives the pump is one of the few but important maintenance checks to be made on a power steering system. These two factors probably account for the majority of noisy turns. If you've ever owned or driven a car with power steering, the noise that it can make is nerve-rattling. It can really boggle your mind when you've got dad's car and you're trying to sneak quietly into

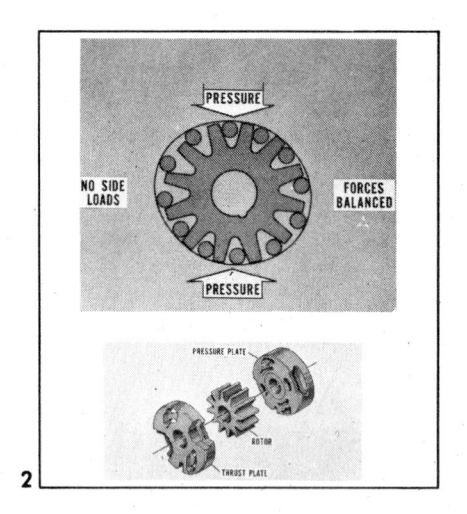

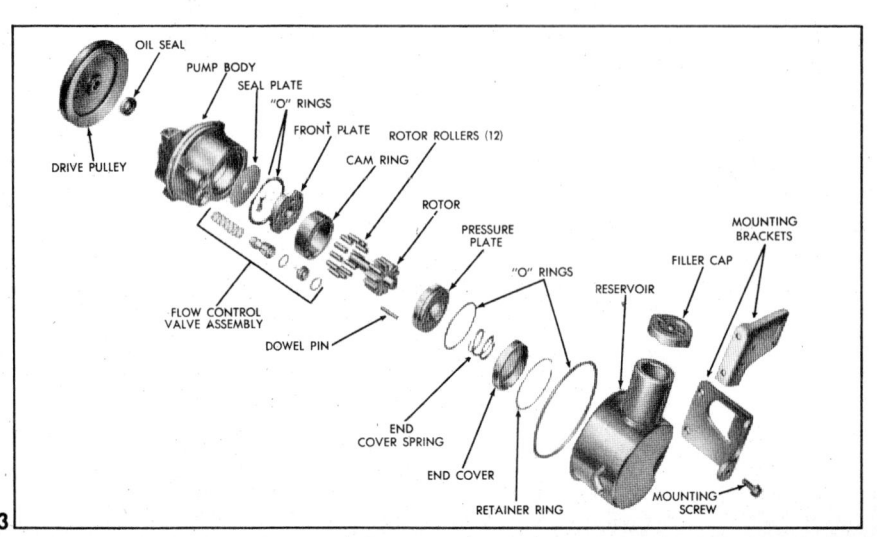

74/CHASSIS, SUSPENSION & BRAKES

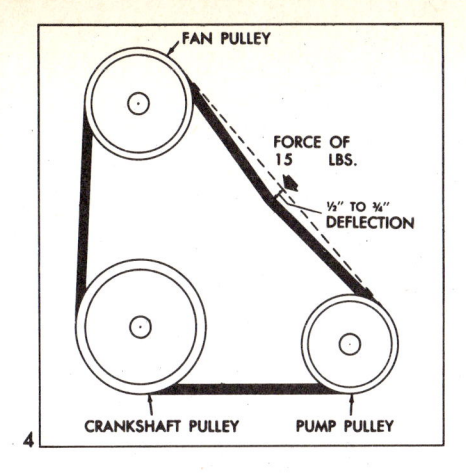

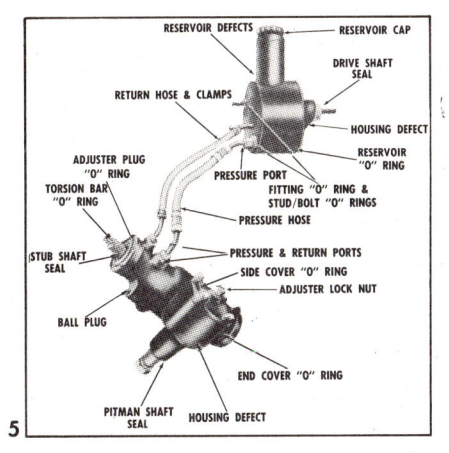

the driveway at 3 a.m. after a long night at the drive-in. Assuming that your belt is in good condition, or properly dressed with about a miniskirt's amount of fan belt dressing, you can adjust the tension to factory specs. Some manufacturers recommend gauging the tension by pressing the belt in between two of the pulleys and they list a certain amount (like ½-in. or ¾-in.) of deflection as indicating correct tension. Other manufacturers suggest using a special gauge to measure the tension. If you don't have such a device—and you probably don't—have it checked at a garage or dealership.

RATIOS

You can count on the steering ratio in a power steering box to be quicker than the manual box for the same car. As we mentioned in the previous chapter, lowering (speeding up) the ratio in a steering box brings a corresponding rise in the effort required to turn the car. This is why the slowing down of steering has paralleled the increasing weight, bulk, and tire sizes of Detroit cars. Although many performance buffs sneered at the turns-lock-to-lock figures and talked about sports cars, the Fords and Chevys had to steer easily enough even for the little old lady from Carbuncle, Miss. *Power* steering, however, opened a whole new world for the engineers. The ratio could be made faster, because the pump did the work when you had to parallel-park, and the handling, driver control, and even safety of the car could be improved.

Unfortunately, Detroit sat on its rear axle for over 10 years before they started really taking advantage of this opportunity. Early power steering ratios were as high as 25:1 or 30:1, and only recently have the manufacturers dared to drop down below 20:1, although Chrysler Corp. cars have been generally faster steering than other makes. A good ratio would seem to be between 15:1 and 18:1, but of course it must be remembered that the ratio can't be made too fast or the car would be too hard to steer if the power system failed and the car had to be steered manually.

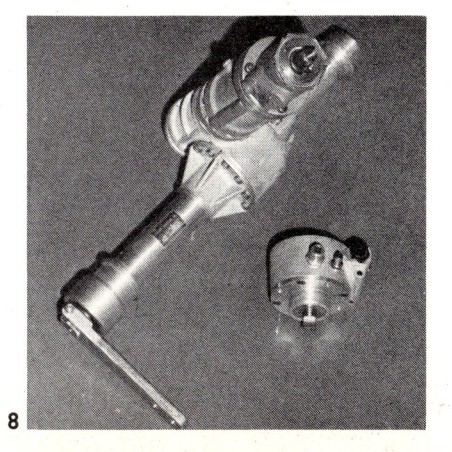

Although power steering doesn't have too many possibilities as far as modifications go, it's interesting to note that it is showing up with increasing frequency on circle track and off-road cars. Whether big stock car or nimble little sand racer, power steering's two major advantages— quick ratio and reduction of driver fatigue—are bound to be utilized on more and more racing machinery in the future. And now that Detroit is coming around with better ratios, especially on its muscle cars, those handling-conscious car buyers might even stop talking about imported sports cars.

1. Most Chrysler products use the compact roller-type power steering pump, with the flow-control valve (arrow) below the pumping portion.

2. Centrifugal force in the roller type pump forces the rollers to move towards the outside of the pump, so they can pick up oil from the inlets. But when they are forced in by the elliptical shape of the housing, the oil is forced through the outlet ports. Having two of each port keeps the forces on the shaft balanced.

3. Exploded view of the roller pump shows how really simple it is. There are the usual O-rings, springs and seals, but the basic parts include the flow control valve, rotor and rollers, the elliptical cam ring and the front plate and pressure plate.

4. Most power steering systems run for years without problems, provided that belt tension and fluid level are kept to manufacturer's specs. Check your owner's or shop manual for the amount of belt tension and proper way to check steering fluid level.

5. Perhaps the only problem you may have with a power steering system is fluid leaks. We don't mean to alarm you, but these are some of the areas to watch for leaks, early signs of some problem in pump, lines, or box.

6. Contrary to popular theory, not all power steering pumps can use regular automatic transmission oil. Chrysler Corp. has their own special power steering system lubricant.

7. Hot rodders used to think of power steering in the same way as automatic transmissions, they were for old folks only. But now with the better variable-ratio units, they're realizing its advantages in such cases as this engine swap where a big engine and fat tires posed a steering load for this pickup truck.

8. Power steering is no longer a stranger to the racetracks, either. This lightweight, compact unit from Gordon Schroeder is fast finding favor with oval-track drivers who no longer need Popeye arms to wheel their huge tires around fast turns.

CHASSIS, SUSPENSION & BRAKES/75

Keys to Better Handling

There's more to handling than merely pulling on a racing helmet.

In virtually every road test magazine article, reference will be made to the way that a car handles. Car A handles better than car B, and car C is better than both of them. But how can one, reading an evaluation written by someone else, relate words to the actions of the car in question?

The way that a car reacts to the movements of the controls by the driver, the feel of controllability and predictability that it transmits, all combine to create a degree of confidence in the driver. The more confidence the driver has in his knowledge of what actions cause what reactions—and the consistency of those reactions—the better the car "handles."

Good handling is not limited to high cornering speeds. A car that is easy to park, easy to back up, and requires a minimum of steering wheel movement to continue in a straight line, is also a good handler. One that is not affected by crosswinds can be said to handle better than one that handles well when there is no wind but is all over the road at the slightest breeze. Cars like that—that handle well under some conditions and poorly under others—really are not "good" handling cars. You cannot stay home from work just because a little rain has fallen or a breeze is blowing. A good handling car must handle well under all conditions.

Ideally, the ultimate handling car would be one with four tires of equal size and pressure with each carrying 25% of the total weight of the vehicle. The center of gravity would be at ground level and the relationship of all four wheels would always remain the same. This design concept rules out suspension of any kind, but keeps the wheels perpendicular to the road surface at all times. No engine or brakes could be used since the torque that they could transmit to the tire contact area would reduce the cornering power. This is the ideal. However, since it has some features that are a little impractical, compromises must still be made.

Notice that all features in this "ideal" car were chosen to complement one thing—the tires. This one item has more influence on the behavior of an automobile than any other. Whether going in a straight line, cornering or stopping, the tires are the contact with the road surface. Where they go, so goes the car.

Tires are inherently flexible, and when side loads are transmitted to them, such as when turning a corner, they deform and create what is called a "slip angle." This angle is the difference between the direction in which the tires are pointing and the direction in which the car is actually traveling. The tire is not actually slipping, but is rather twisting at the point of contact. This slip angle is created at both the front and rear, with the front wheels generally having the larger angle because they are steerable.

When the modern car is designed, whether a passenger or racing car, great care is taken to see that the tire contact area is not drastically varied in size or loading by weight distribution, center of gravity, roll centers, suspension geometry and the other inherent factors. Each one of these factors can move the complete vehicle concept further and further away from the ideal.

WEIGHT DISTRIBUTION

Due to the intended use of modern passenger cars, a constant weight distribution is virtually impossible to achieve. A single-seater racing car that will always carry the same amount of weight (except for fuel consumption) can be set up to figures that the designers feel is best. However, a passenger car that can carry one, two, three, four or more passengers—not to mention luggage for all of them—will have weight distribution figures directly related to the amount of load at the time. Since the average car is driven a large percentage of the time with only the driver aboard, most new cars are at their most favorable settings with the weight of the driver alone. While alone, the driver would be more likely to push the car to the limit, so this is also a definite safety advantage.

WEIGHT TRANSFER

During cornering, centrifugal force transfers weight from the inside wheels to those on the outside. This transfer loads the outside tires and unloads the inside—with the result that traction is no longer equal on both sides of the car. In extreme cases, the weight transfer may create enough body roll to lift the inside wheels clear of the road.

Understandably, efforts to limit the amount of weight transfer will result in a better handling car since the less weight transfer, the more tire contact area on the road. Factors that affect the amount are items such as center of gravity, height of the roll center (the higher the roll center, the less the body will roll), the type of suspension system and the ability of the tires to resist sliding.

76/CHASSIS, SUSPENSION & BRAKES

1. **Even with lower speed limits on the highways, driving can still be fun when you have a car equipped for good handling. And you don't need an expensive sports car to enjoy it, either. Properly set up, even little Pintos and Vegas can be gratifying.**

2. **The roll center is an extremely important facet of handling, and is fixed by the type of suspension. But it is only important in how it is related to the center of gravity. A high CG coupled with a low roll axis (line drawn between front and rear roll centers) would have considerable lean on corners. Conversely, with a high roll center and low CG, leaning would be less and handling improved.**

3. **Oversteer and understeer are the most common terms used to describe a car's handling abilities, and it is generally conceded that a slight amount of understeer is desirable for best results in all kinds of driving. These are some of the steps you can take to mechanically channel a car's chassis towards this goal.**

4. **Among the rear suspension features of the new Mustang II is staggering of the rear shocks. As on Z28's, the right shock is mounted ahead of the axle and the left behind, so the shocks do double-duty in helping to prevent axle windup on acceleration.**

CENTER OF GRAVITY

Directly related to weight is the center of gravity. The location of this theoretical point will determine the amount of weight transfer during cornering and therefore the amount of the total load that each tire must take. Were it at ground level and halfway between the axles on the centerline of the car, there would be no weight transfer at all. Unfortunately, this cannot be; the point must be clear of the ground and somewhere in the mass of the automobile. The closer to the ground the better, but design restrictions usually raise it higher than would be liked. The location will be affected by load just as the weight distribution is. If the load is uneven enough to move the point off the centerline of the car, cornering ability will be increased in one direction, and decreased in the other.

For many years, Indianapolis cars—and the Sprint and Midget cars used on oval dirt tracks—have intentionally been loaded on the left side, either by offsetting the engine, the body, or by controlling weight distribution through the "wedging" or "weight-jacking" principle. Since they only have to turn left, the cornering ability in that direction is the most important. On many dirt track cars the driver can "jack" the weight during a race, causing the chassis to run "flat" or with as much "wedge" as the driver feels he needs. If and when track conditions change, he can alter the cornering characteristics of the car from the driver's seat. Sometimes the wedging is done in the garage before the race, and the driver does not have a control for changing it while the machine is in motion.

ROLL CENTER

As a car negotiates a corner, its natural tendency is to roll over. Because of weight transfer, the weight on the inside wheels is reduced and the weight on the outside ones is increased. The theoretical point about which the mass rotates is called the roll center. Unlike the center of gravity, which is a single point somewhere near the center of the car, the roll center runs the length of the car. The rear point will generally be higher than the front, so a side view of this

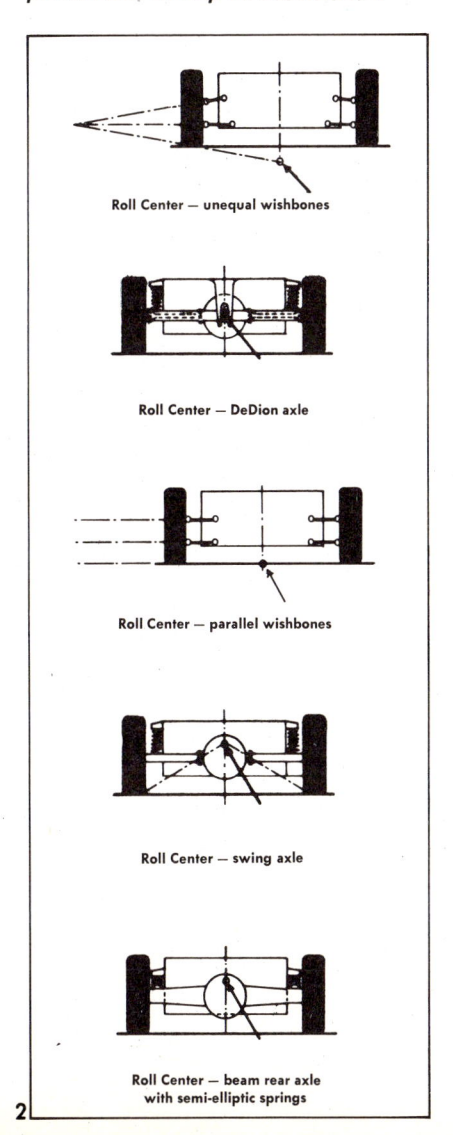

Roll Center — unequal wishbones

Roll Center — DeDion axle

Roll Center — parallel wishbones

Roll Center — swing axle

Roll Center — beam rear axle with semi-elliptic springs

CHASSIS FEATURE (Adjust as indicated)	FOR MORE UNDERSTEER	FOR MORE OVERSTEER
Front tire pressure	Lower	Higher
Rear tire pressure	Higher	Lower
Front tire section	Smaller	Larger
Rear tire section	Larger	Smaller
Front wheel camber	More positive	More negative
Rear wheel camber	More negative	More positive
Front springs	Stiffer	Softer
Rear springs	Softer	Stiffer
Front anti-roll bar	Thicker	Thinner
Rear anti-roll bar	Thinner	Thicker
Front track	Narrower	Wider
Rear track	Wider	Narrower
Weight distribution	More forward	More rearward
Rear deck spoiler	Higher	Lower

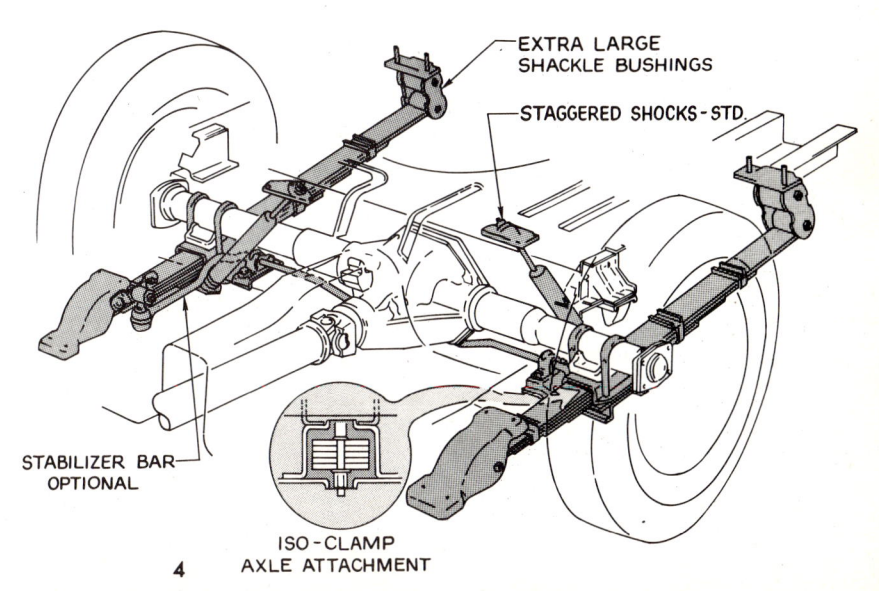

EXTRA LARGE SHACKLE BUSHINGS

STAGGERED SHOCKS - STD.

STABILIZER BAR OPTIONAL

ISO-CLAMP AXLE ATTACHMENT

CHASSIS, SUSPENSION & BRAKES/77

Better Handling

theoretical line would find it slanting downward toward the front. General practice is to have the front point about 3 to 4 ins. above the ground and the rear about 5 ins. above.

Similar handling results can be had with either high or low roll centers, but the lower ones seem to have fewer disadvantages although they create more body roll. As the point is raised, the body roll is decreased but tire wear, due to more wheel deflection, is increased. Suspension design plays a very important part in the location of these points, as we shall learn in the following discussion.

SUSPENSION GEOMETRY

The dictionary defines geometry as "a branch of mathematics that deals with the measurement, properties, and relationships of points, lines, angles, surfaces and solids." Applied to an automobile's suspension, these related points, lines, and angles are primarily responsible for keeping the tire contact patch in complete contact with the road surface.

Since the wheel must be attached to the frame through pivot points of some kind, up-and-down movement of the wheel will take the path of an arc around those pivot points. This causes the wheel, and the tire, to continually change attitude in relation to the road surface. With a solid rear axle this is not so. The wheels remain perpendicular to the road surface at all times, except for the effect that movement of one wheel has on the other. On the front of most cars, however, the wheels are independently suspended, causing the reaction known as camber change. The less the camber changes, the more the tire remains in contact.

Camber change is nothing more than wheel lean. While the wheels attached to a solid axle remain essentially perpendicular to the road surface, independently suspended wheels will lean. The amount of lean is determined by the suspension geometry. As the wheel leans, the sidewall distorts and the effective contact area of the tire is reduced.

Therefore, a suspension geometry that keeps the wheel as near vertical and perpendicular to the road surface as possible will provide more tire contact area, and therefore better grip. Wheel lean of any kind only detracts from the efficiency of the tire.

In designing the front suspension, there are two ways for the engineer to go. He can attach the wheel to the frame through either equal length or unequal length control arms. The equal length, providing they are parallel, will move the wheel up and down with no camber change at all. This would seem to be ideal, since the tire contact patch will not be distorted and therefore change its area. However, in general practice this advantage is offset by the fact that the wheel is forced to move in and out from its static position by the movement of the suspension. This causes tire scrubbing that rapidly wears out the best of tires. In racing, this type of design can be used to advantage because of the limited life of racing tires anyway. In addition, it is felt by some racing car designers that camber change in high-speed cars will be prevented by the gyroscopic effect of the turning wheel. This could conceivably prevent the suspension from working because the wheel would refuse to tilt.

Modern day passenger car choice is usually the unequal length control arm type that keeps the contact patch in the same place and tilts the top of the wheel. Generally, the top of the wheel will tilt in toward the car, but on the new Buick it does the opposite. Here the arrangement of the unequal length control arms tilts the top of the wheel outward. Both sys-

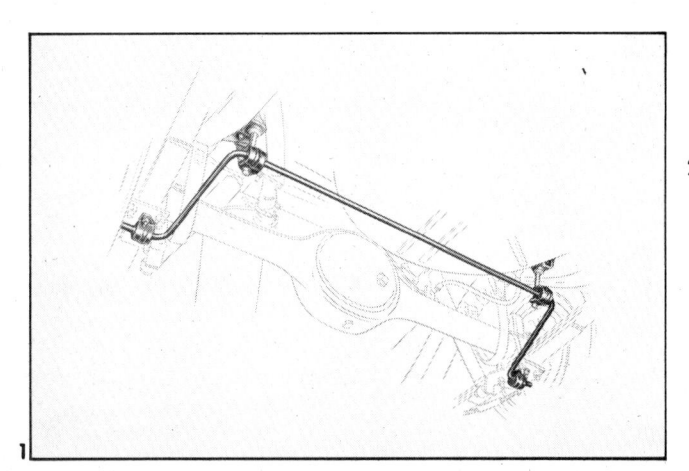

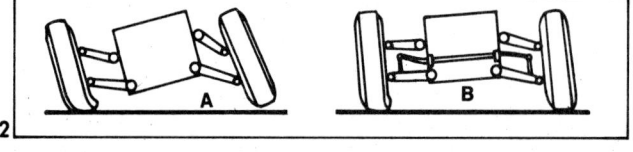

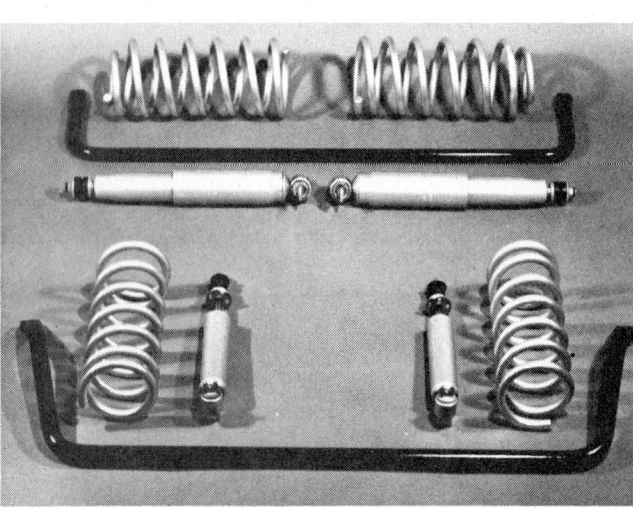

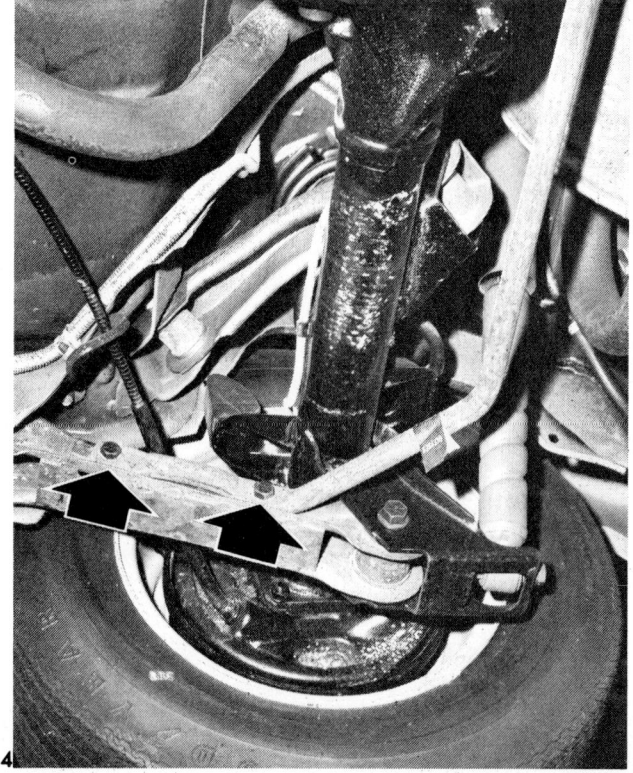

78/CHASSIS, SUSPENSION & BRAKES

1. Probably the best modification that can be made to your car is the addition of anti-sway bars, sometimes also called just "sway" bars.

2. Sway bars work like torsion bars, allowing the wheels to move up and down together, but when the wheels try to move independently, such as when cornering hard, they restrict the movement and improve cornering. In drawing A, a car without a front sway bar lifts the outside tire on a hard corner, while in B the sway bar limits the roll and keeps the tires more squarely on the road.

3. If your springs and shocks are in poor condition, it's foolish to add a sway bar in search of Can-Am handling. That's why sway bars are often offered in kits along with heavy-duty springs and shocks.

4. Factory and aftermarket sway bars are available for almost all cars, including those with coil springs in the rear, where the bar bolts directly to the lower control arms rather than rubber bushings on frame.

5. Another type of "sway" bar is the Panhard rod or "track rod," which serves to keep the chassis centered over the rear axle, especially on cars with coil springs in the rear.

6. Better than a simple track rod is this arrangement, known as Watt's linkage. James Watt developed it for his steam engine, but as applied to automobiles the pivoting link in the center allows the rear end to stay centered even when the chassis moves.

7. Most production cars that have coil rear springs use four control arms, because the angle of the upper arms keeps the axle centered in a lateral plane, just like a track rod.

8. This Ronnie Kaplan-built Pro Stock drag car has an imaginative method of axle location. Besides the standard Watt's linkage for lateral location (A), there are also Watt's linkages on each side of the axle (B) for locating the rear end in a fore'n'aft plane while allowing the rear end to move strictly straight up and down, as the center links can turn on the axle housing.

tems provide good tire contact and long tire life.

ROLL STIFFNESS

Poor handling qualities that result from compromises taken in the original design can often be corrected by increasing the roll stiffness. Low roll centers and excessive camber changes due to suspension geometry and the like, will be improved if an additional springing medium in the form of an anti-roll bar, at either end or both, is fitted. On passenger cars it is usually called a stabilizer bar.

Without increasing the total spring rate of the suspension system, and the harsh ride that would go with it, anti-roll bars can increase cornering ability in several ways. In the front they are a simple bar that attaches to the suspension arm for each wheel. It reduces the amount of camber change by pitting the forces imposed on each wheel against the forces of the other. At the same time it reduces body roll by creating a firmer attachment between wheels and the mass of the automobile. Unfortunately the wheels are no longer truly independently suspended, since the bar attaches them solidly together. Were the bar too stiff for a particular car, the cornering capabilities could be lessened.

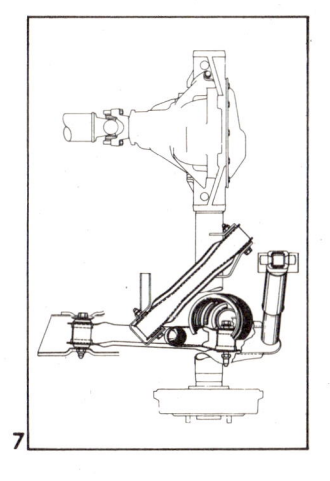

Anti-roll bars can also be fitted to the rear, but due to the nature of most cars with solid rear axles they are unnecessary. In the few cases where they are used, such as the newer pony cars and high-performance types, it is essential that the stiffness relationship between the front and the rear be correct.

UNDERSTEER & OVERSTEER

As we have already seen, the tires create slip angles during cornering. There is generally a difference in the angles between the front and rear, and this difference creates the basic handling characteristics of the car. If the front angle is greater, the car is said to understeer. If the rear angle is greater, it is termed oversteer. In some cases, where the angles are the same, the car is said to possess neutral steer characteristics.

Common among passenger cars as well as racing cars, understeer is perhaps better described as "pushing the front end." If while rounding a corner, the steering wheel must be

CHASSIS, SUSPENSION & BRAKES/79

Better Handling

progressively turned into the corner to maintain the chosen radius and keep the car on the road, it is evidence of understeer. It can be caused by things other than design. If it is excessive, it may be that the tire pressure is too low. Increasing the pressure of the front tires will usually reduce the understeer since it limits the distortion of the tire and creates a more stable contact area. At the same time it may be that the tire pressure in the rear was too high and the basic ratio between the front and rear slip angles was changed because of it.

As may be expected, oversteer is the direct opposite of understeer. If the rear slip angle is greater than the front, the car will seem to want to spin when going through a corner. The steering wheel must be turned away from the inside of the corner in order to keep from running off the inside of the road. This condition can also be altered by changing tire pressures but is usually only prevalent in production-type cars at very high cornering speeds. Many racing cars will exhibit understeer capabilities and then the condition becomes one of oversteer. This is due to the fact that at very high speeds oversteer is somewhat easier to control.

As can be seen from the causes and cures for each, the choice of tires and tire pressures can have an effect. If a car is very close to the line on understeer, a change of tires could well make it into an oversteering car. In fact, racing cars will have adjustments built into their chassis so that they can, in conjunction with different sizes or types of tires, change the chassis characteristics to suit a particular race course or driver's style. On an ultra-fast type of course, slight understeering characteristics are desirable but may not be the answer to fast lap times if there are a number of slow corners. On slower corners, an oversteering car can better be steered with the combination of steering wheel and throttle, whereas an understeering car would push the front end off the road if too much throttle were applied.

NEUTRAL STEER

Seldom achieved, neutral steer describes a car that has slip angles so near to being identical, that both ends exhibit the same characteristics. In theory, this could be any car that has a very slight understeer. While cornering with the power applied, the slip angle of the rear wheels will be increased. If the amount it is increased brings it up to the same angle as the front, the car will be cornering with neutral steer. It is a delicate balance. Too much power and the car will oversteer; too little, and it will revert to understeer.

Four-wheel-drive cars, a type that have seen brief use in single-seater racing, are good candidates for neutral steer characteristics, since the power is applied to both the front and rear wheels in equal amounts with close to identical slip angle changes. This makes chassis adjustment a theoretically easier task since applying power has less of a changing effect than it does with a 2-wheel drive.

All three terms—understeer, oversteer, and neutral steer—refer to how the chassis and suspension react to cornering. The driver can control the amount of any of them by proper use of the controls. In a racing situation, with a car set up with a slight understeer tendency, a typical 90° corner will be taken in three distinct stages. As the car enters the corner it is still in the process of slowing down, so the weight bias is toward the front. This exaggerates any understeer characteristics, with the result that the wheels must generally be turned sharper into the corner. This has a side benefit of scrubbing off some speed but is still a definite understeer condition. As the car approaches the middle of the corner, the driver begins to apply power, and the slip angle in the rear increases to a point that creates neutral steer. Too much too soon will switch the car to a definite oversteer—a condition that requires correction and a loss of time. With the car in the correct position in the corner during this neutral steer period, the throttle pressure can gradually be increased until the car oversteers a slight amount. The exit from the corner will be under hard acceleration in a slight oversteer that is slowly being reduced to zero by the fact that the front wheels are being straightened out, and the previous weight transfer to the outside wheels is decreased.

FRONT WHEEL STEERING

That the front wheels steer the car will come as a surprise to very few. However, word that the rear wheels are also responsible for some directional control will usually raise an eyebrow or two. But first, let's take a closer look at what goes on up front.

When traveling in a straight line, the front wheels are essentially parallel. When turning a corner this is not

---

1. Traction bars used on drag cars prevent rear axle windup and put the torque to work on the chassis. From rear-end expert Pepe Estrada we've borrowed this formula for finding the correct length bar. This is an empirical formula to make the bar halfway from the rear end to the CG.

2. Although more of a subjective factor, good steering control and feel is a part of handling. One of the changes that Chevy made to its highly-rated Monte Carlo was adding a dampener (like a shock absorber) to the steering system to take out any undesirable feedback.

3. Setting up a car to handle means making lots of adjustments. Getting the proper load on each wheel with coil springs is made easier with AirLift air bags inside the coils, allowing individual adjustments by varying the air in each bag.

4. With special adapter springs, AirLift air bags can also be used with leaf springs, for overload use or weight-jacking for handling.

5. There are many different methods of reducing wheel hop and axle windup. In this unusual setup, a heavy-duty shock absorber has been attached to the rear of a leaf spring to dampen its flexing on acceleration.

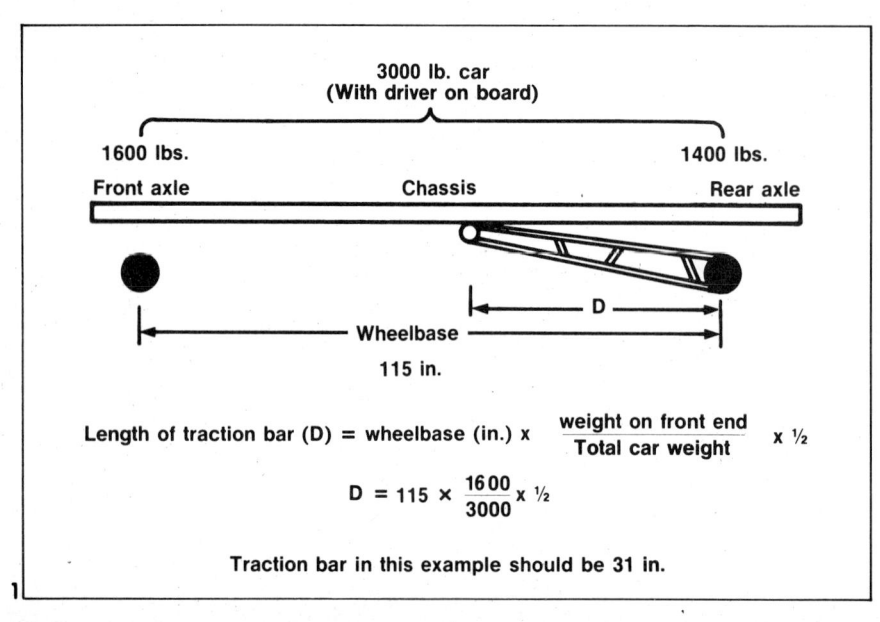

3000 lb. car (With driver on board)

1600 lbs. Front axle — 1400 lbs. Rear axle

Chassis

Wheelbase 115 in.

D

Length of traction bar (D) = wheelbase (in.) × $\dfrac{\text{weight on front end}}{\text{Total car weight}}$ × ½

$$D = 115 \times \dfrac{1600}{3000} \times \tfrac{1}{2}$$

Traction bar in this example should be 31 in.

the case. One of the wheels will turn more than the other; which one depends on the particular type of car. Since the outer wheel actually has farther to travel than the inner, it is running on a larger radius. The Ackerman principle therefore calls for the outer wheel to turn fewer degrees than the inner for the same amount of steering wheel movement. Were they to travel on the same radius, the outer tire would have more traction because of weight transfer and tend to drag the inner tire sideways as the turn is made. Strangely, as speeds go up, and the outer wheel obtains more of the load; slip angles of the two wheels differ. This brought about application of the anti-Ackerman principle.

With the outer tire doing more of the actual controlling, it was favored over the inner. By giving it more turn than the inner, the slip angle is increased, and the cornering improved. Both Ackerman and anti-Ackerman are applied in present-day cars, the anti-Ackerman being more popular in high-performance types.

REAR WHEEL STEERING

As we have seen, when a turn is made, the weight of the car is moved to the outside wheels. As this occurs, the outside spring is compressed and the load on the inside spring is reduced. The whole axle then twists, moving the outside wheel and causing the rear axle to steer the rear end of the car into the corner.

The amount of axle twist, and the resultant amount of steering effect, can be controlled by the amount of camber (bend) in the rear leaf springs. The front half of a leaf spring, from the point at which the axle attaches to the front mounting eye, is like a flexible connecting link. The greater the camber of the spring, the greater will be the change in its effective length when cornering forces cause it to straighten out. If it is nearly straight to begin with, there will be very little change in length, and therefore very little axle twist that causes the steering effect.

Ideally, a flat spring will contribute favorably to steering. In addition, a flat spring will provide more lateral stability due to its reluctance to swing sideways as readily as a cambered spring. A cambered spring will be susceptible to straight-line sway and, under cornering load, will move the outside rear wheel rearward, causing the rear wheels to steer the car to the outside of the corner, the exact opposite of what is desired.

UNSPRUNG WEIGHT

As far as the suspension designers are concerned, the total weight of an automobile is divided into two types: sprung and unsprung. There is always concern for the total weight of the complete car, but as little as possible unsprung weight makes the task of building-in good handling much easier. The tires, wheels and suspension components that attach them to the main body/chassis structure comprise the unsprung weight. The remainder of the car is sprung weight. Put another way, all items that move with the movement of the

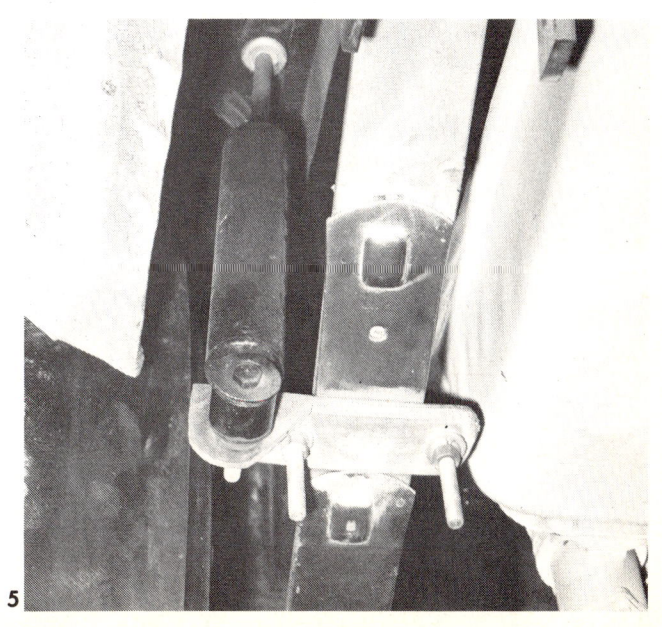

CHASSIS, SUSPENSION & BRAKES/81

Better Handling

wheel are unsprung. This will also include the portion of shock absorbers and anti-sway bars that are attached to the suspension system. The portions that attach to the frame are sprung.

The less the unsprung weight, the easier the job of the suspension. Light components can be kept in contact with the ground much more easily than heavier counterparts. Movement of the wheel and related assemblies must be stopped before the springs can return the tire to the surface. The lighter it is, the less the momentum to be controlled: This allows the use of softer springs for a smoother ride.

With all of the features that the design engineer tries to incorporate to assist the handling of the complete vehicle, compromises are inevitable. How many compromises are made, and which features are favored, will determine the ultimate handling characteristics of the car. Some of the components on newer cars may be of a dual-purpose variety, available as an option for different types of handling. A basic chassis may be available with a soft, plush ride at the expense of good high-speed handling, while its Super Sport counterpart will sacrifice the soft ride for cornering performance. A typical example might be an early Mustang—available with either a low-horsepower 6-cyl. engine with softish suspension, or an out-and-out racing power plant with handling to match. Through a choice of options, a middle-of-the-road version is also available. Take your pick.

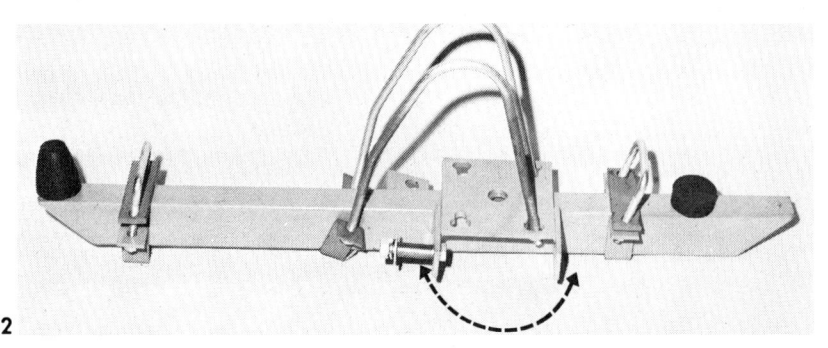

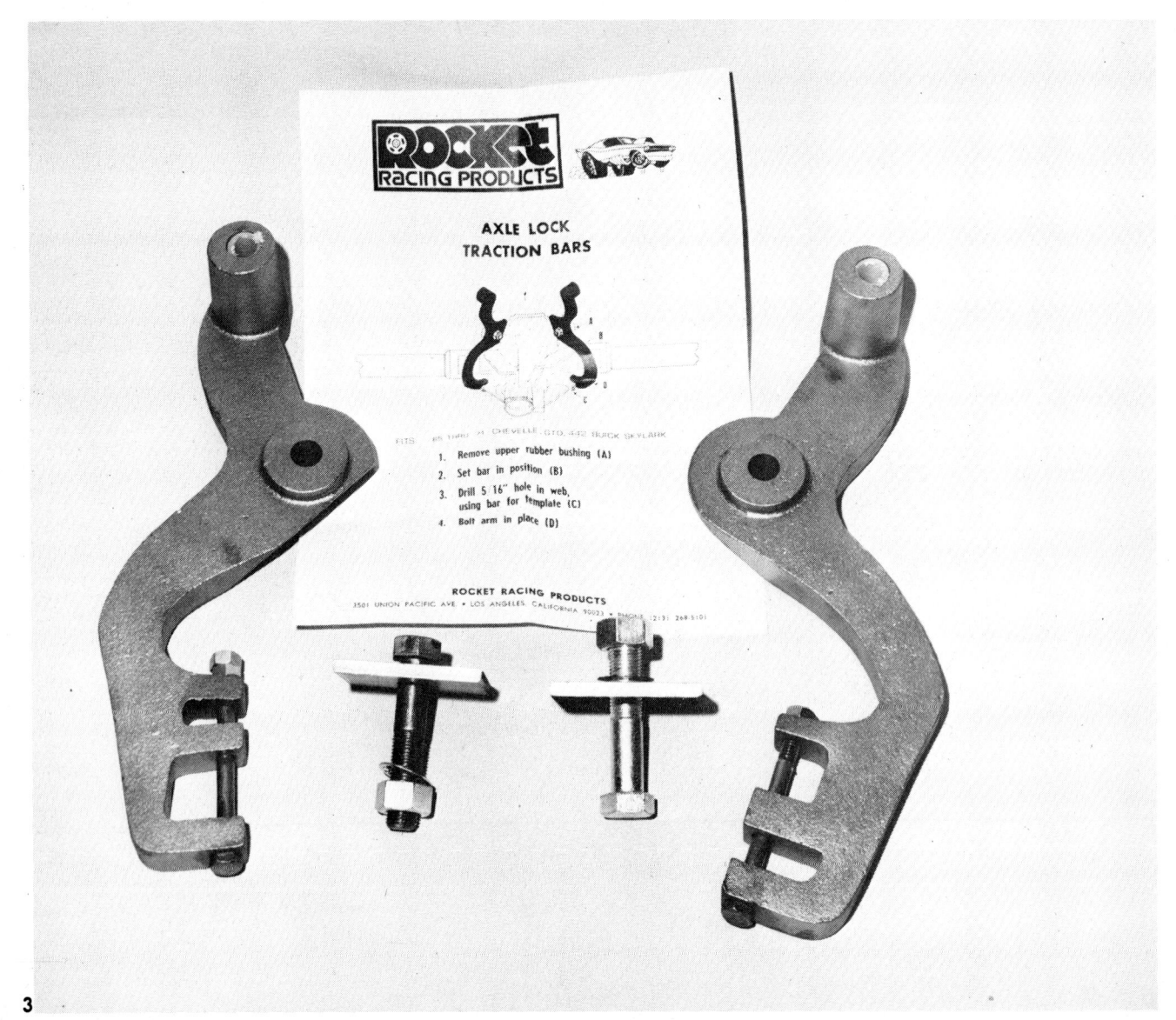

82/CHASSIS, SUSPENSION & BRAKES

But compromises must still be made. The designer must work within the limits of currently acceptable space considerations, type and location of driving components, and lastly, styling. Current trends call for lower and lower cars with the result that wheel travel is limited. In addition, suspension geometry will have to be arrived at with arms and linkages that must fit in very limited spaces. Good handling, which is a very great challenge when the designer has a free hand in total design, is even more difficult to achieve when the vehicle is as complex as the modern passenger automobile.

IMPROVING HANDLING

In many cases handling can be changed for the better, but not actually improved. A good deal of the handling capabilities of any vehicle are dependent upon the way it is driven. A change that better suits the car to the driver's technique is in essence an improvement, even though it might not suit other drivers. What's good for the goose is not necessarily good for the gander.

Cars such as the 6-cyl. Mustang mentioned earlier can be improved by adapting the very items that differentiate it from its racier cousin. Suspension geometry will not have to be altered since most items that make one car handle better than the other are of the bolt-on types anyway. Springs, shock absorbers, sway bars and, probably most important, the type and size of the tires, are all items that should be added. Little guesswork will be involved in improvements on this type of car since, one by one, the features of the better handling car can be bolted on to the other.

What if there is no direct counterpart in the same line? This is a distinct possiblity with cars that are close to being a decade old. There were very few good handling cars 10 years ago, and until the advent of the pony cars and Super Sport varieties, you had to have an imported sports car to be able to zip around a corner without enough tire squealing to attract the attention of everyone within a block and a half. These cars probably can't be brought up to the standards of the current crop of good handlers, but they can be improved.

One must remember that body roll and weight transfer are contributing factors in cornering ability, and that these areas should be tackled first. At the time the car was produced, there were probably some heavy-duty options made available for use on police cars or taxi cabs. These would usually include such features as anti-sway bars, heavy-duty shock absorbers and stiffer springs. Before trying to adapt some accessory item, check for some original pieces. If you can find a dealer who has any in his attic he will probably be delighted to get rid of all he has.

Probably the largest single improvement will come in the selection of tires and wheels. Wheels are mentioned since the most suitable tires will probably be too wide for the rims. The combination of the tires and the heavy-duty items will be about all that can be done reasonably. Any changes to the basic geometry, weight distribution, and center of gravity will not fall within the "economically feasible" category. This is on cars that are primarily for street use; drag racing modifications are another matter.

1. For Mopars and other cars which have a pinion snubber on the frame or rear end, an adjustable snubber allows you to prevent windup when you want to by spacing the snubber close enough that the rear end can only twist a small amount.

2. If you do buy the spring-mounted type traction bars, try to get ones like this Rocket item which allows you to mount the shocks either in front or behind the axle, so you can stagger the shocks for handling.

3. Traction bars are also available for coil-sprung cars which relocate the upper control arms for better weight transfer upon acceleration.

4. With spring-mounted bars, it's best to leave the clamps off for most street driving. They work on the dragstrip but leave the ride a little stiff on the street.

5. Actually, you can make your own traction bar quite easily by welding some plates and a length of tubing to your stock rear spring plates and adding a suspension snubber in front.

Brake Hydraulics

There's much more to it than meets the foot.

There are many ways to transmit force and leverage from point A to point B, which is really all that the hydraulic part of a brake system does. If point B is far enough away from you, then you can send quite a bit of force to it with a bomb, but only once.

You can get design-happy, too, and transmit force with cables, levers, bellcranks and all kinds of fancy mechanisms, but in brake design none of these methods are as good as using a hydraulic line with hydraulic fluid between two cylinders. The cylinder attached to the pedal that your foot pushes is called the master cylinder. When you push on the brake pedal, fluid is forced out of the cylinder, through the lines, and into the wheel cylinders.

Let's say you step on the brake pedal with about 100 lbs. of force. The pedal is not directly connected to the master cylinder but works through a leverage principle to multiply the amount of force you put on the pedal. If the ratio of leverage on the pedal is 5:1, your 100-lb. big foot will be multiplied into 500 lbs. of force applied to the master cylinder piston. All hydraulic systems—whether they are for brakes or actuation of controls on a tractor, an airplane or a rocket—work because force can be multiplied while pressure remains the same. If the piston in our master cylinder has an area of one sq. in. and we are applying 500 lbs. of total force to it, then the pressure, sometimes called unit pressure, is 500 pounds per square inch. If we attach lines to the master cylinder so that the pressure can be transmitted, then we will have 500 psi anywhere in the system.

You must remember that there is no air in the system at all. It is completely filled with hydraulic fluid, and the fluid itself flows very little when the brake pedal is depressed. If nothing gives at the end where the force is applied, which in the case of a brake system would be the brake shoes themselves, then the hydraulic fluid does not move at all. You can understand this better if you blow into an ordinary soda straw, with your finger holding the other end shut. You are creating quite a bit of pressure in the straw and against your finger, but you aren't moving any air at all. If you get a leak, then you are going to move a lot of air, or fluid in the brakes. But then you wouldn't have any brakes, just a big mess.

With our theoretical 500 psi of brake pressure in our hydraulic system, we can apply as much force as we want to the brake shoes. If we have a large, heavy car that is difficult to stop, then we can make the area of the wheel cylinder piston 2 sq. ins.

With our 500 pounds' system pressure this will give us 1000 lbs. of force on the brake shoe. If we have too much pressure, making the brakes lock up all the time, then we can use a wheel cylinder piston with an area of only ½ sq. in. With 500 psi system pressure this will give us a force on the brake shoe of 250 lbs.

By varying the area of the pistons in the master cylinder and the wheel cylinders we can get any combination of forces that are necessary to do the job of stopping the car. On a car with double-ended wheel cylinders you may even find two different sizes of pistons in the same cylinder. If you were designing a brake system and you wanted the car to stop easier so that the driver didn't have to push on the pedal so hard, you could make the area of the wheel cylinder pistons larger or you could make the area of the master cylinder piston smaller. The right combination of piston sizes will give a brake that stops with very little pedal pressure but doesn't lock the wheels so that the vehicle becomes uncontrollable. Let's take a closer look now at a master cylinder and how it functions.

MASTER CYLINDERS

A master cylinder is basically just a piston sliding in a cylinder so that it creates hydraulic pressure, but actually it has a lot of little design features that make it work much better than a simple hydraulic cylinder. At the front end of the master cylinder piston is the primary cup, which seals against the piston walls so that fluid is forced out through the lines when—

1. *The basic hydraulic brake system includes a master hydraulic cylinder operated by the brake pedal, and hydraulic lines that carry the fluid pressure to individual "slave" or wheel cylinders, which do the work of pushing the friction shoes against the drums to stop the car.*

2. *Although for a given leverage in the pedal linkage the hydraulic fluid pressure is the same throughout a system, different size cylinders at the wheels give different amounts of braking force. This is why most cars have larger diameter wheel cylinders in front, since the front brakes have to do 60% of the braking work.*

3. *The standard master cylinder is a hydraulic cylinder with an integral fluid reservoir. It is here that the pressure is generated to operate your brakes. The check valve at the front is designed to hold residual pressure in the lines (about 10 psi) to keep the wheel cylinders snugged against the brake shoes.*

4. *All cars today are required to have a dual braking system, and the heart of the system is a dual master cylinder like this. The two piston assemblies are connected, but can operate independently if one or the other fails. If a car has disc brakes in front, then only the rear port will have a residual check valve.*

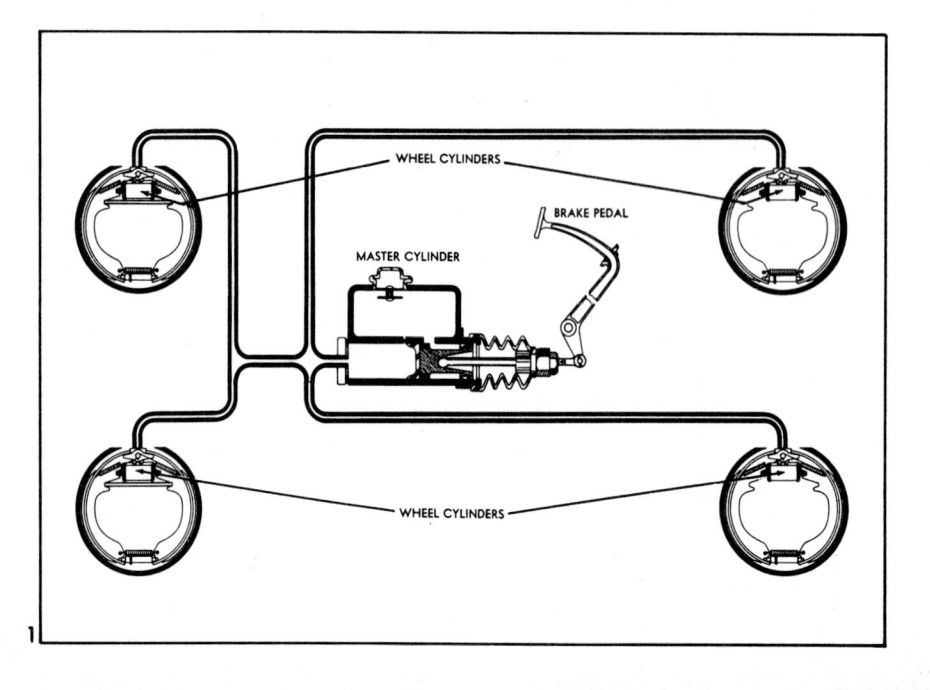

84/CHASSIS, SUSPENSION & BRAKES

EFFECT OF WHEEL CYLINDER SIZE ON FINAL BRAKE PRESSURE

Pedal — 100 lbs. force
Pivot point
2 in.
14 in.
Master cylinder
700 lbs. force
Bore—1 sq. in.
Master cylinder pushrod
Pressure *per square inch* is always the same

½ sq. in. bore — 350 lbs. force
1 sq. in. bore — 700 lbs. force
2 sq. in. bore — 1,400 lbs. force

2

COVER BOLT — GASKET — BODY — OUTLET PORT — INLET PORT — CUP — ROD — BOOT — STOP — WASHER — PISTON — SPRING — SEAL — VALVE — CUP

3

DISC BRAKES
RETURN SPRING (SECONDARY)
BLEEDER
SECONDARY BRAKE FLUID RESERVOIR
FILLER CAP
RETAINER
PRIMARY SYSTEM BRAKE FLUID RESERVOIR
RETURN SPRING (PRIMARY)
BOOT
PUSH ROD
RETURN SPRING (SECONDARY)
SPRING
TUBE SEAT (SECONDARY) BRAKE OUTLET PORT
RESIDUAL CHECK VALVE
SECONDARY PISTON ASSEMBLY
(PRIMARY) BRAKE OUTLET PORT
PRIMARY PISTON ASSEMBLY

4

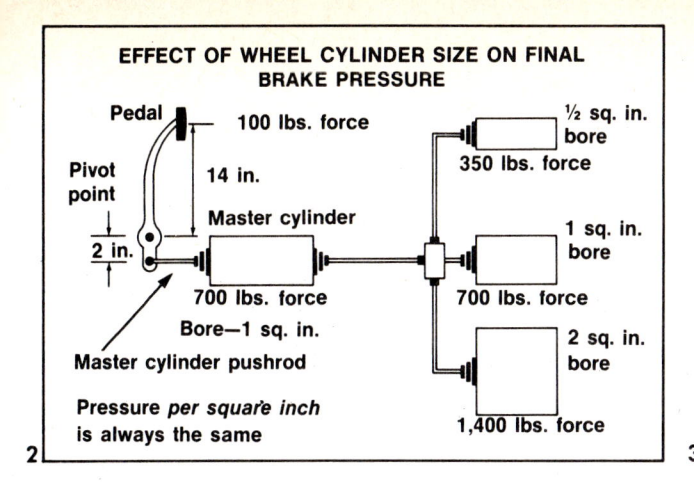

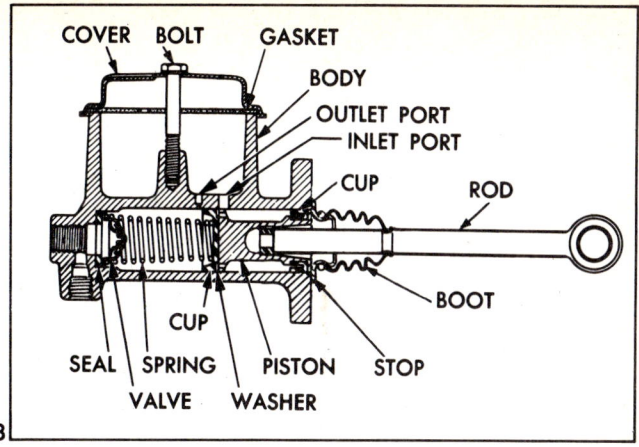

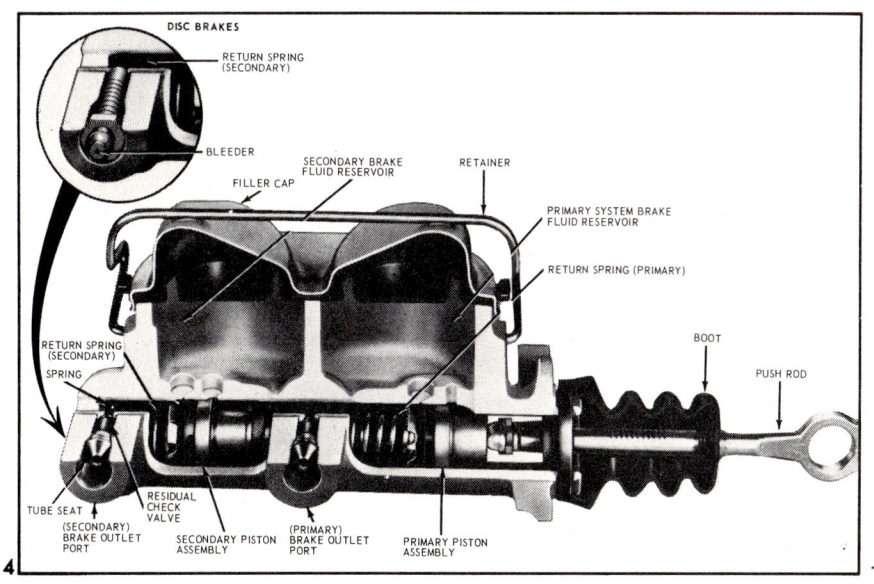

ever the piston is pushed. The primary cup is not attached to the piston. It stays against it on the braking stroke merely because of the force of the hydraulic pressure. On the return stroke, a large spring pushes the primary cup and the piston to the off position, thereby keeping the cup seated against the front face of the piston.

If you examine one of the piston return springs carefully you will see that it is designed to push only on the center portion of the primary cup. The outer portion of the primary cup can flex to let fluid through little holes in the piston into the forward portion of the cylinder. If the piston is stroked rapidly back and forth, the piston and primary cup will return faster than the fluid. Fluid rushes through the small holes in the front of the piston, passes the lip of the primary cup and overfills the front portion of the cylinder. You have probably done this at one time or another just by pumping the brake pedal. When you do, the applied position of the brake pedal becomes higher because you have pumped more fluid into the brake line. Because there is fluid on both sides of the front portion of the piston, a secondary cup at the rear of the piston keeps this fluid from leaking to the outside. When you see fluid dripping out of a master cylinder, it is this secondary cup that is leaking. Fluid enters the area between the primary and secondary cups through a large port in the cylinder.

If we do pump up the brakes to get more fluid into the lines and make the brake pedal higher, this fluid has to get out somehow when we take our foot off of the brake. If it didn't get out we would be driving around stinking up the whole neighborhood with burning brake lining. The excess fluid in the lines returns to the reservoir in the master cylinder through the compensating port, which should just clear the forward lip of the primary cup when the piston and cup are in the fully retracted position.

At the front of the master cylinder or somewhere near the outlet port is a small check valve which will allow most of the fluid to return to the cylinder, but not quite all of it. This check valve maintains about 10 lbs. of pressure in the hydraulic lines and wheel cylinders, preventing air from being drawn into the wheel cylinders on the return stroke of the master cylinder, and keeping the wheel cylinder pistons from vibrating away from the brake shoes.

The forward stroke of the master cylinder piston is limited by the movement of the brake shoes. When they hit the drum nothing can move anymore, the hydraulic pressure builds up as the piston stops moving. On the return stroke the piston is mechanically stopped at the rear of the cylinder by a washer and snap ring.

In the normal operation of a master cylinder, a certain amount of fluid leaves the reservoir and goes out into the lines. In order for this fluid to leave and reenter easily there has to be an air vent in the top of the cylinder so we don't get an air lock. For many years this vent was direct to atmosphere and it worked fine, except that the moisture in the air would contaminate the brake fluid and cause the gummy residue that we see in so many master cylinders. Late style master cylinders still have the air vent in the filler cap, but underneath the cap is a diaphragm-type gasket which can move down as fluid leaves or up when fluid reenters the reservoir. With this system there is no direct contact between the fluid and the air, and the fluid lasts a lot longer because it doesn't get contaminated.

In a dual master cylinder everything works exactly the same as in a single cylinder, except that the front piston is activated by hydraulic pressure instead of a pushrod. Also, there is an extra bolt somewhere in the cylinder, either screwed down from inside the fluid reservoir or from outside underneath the cylinder, which acts as a stop to limit the rearward motion of the front piston.

The check valves in a dual piston master cylinder are usually in the fluid outlets, because that's an easy place to put them. Drum brakes use a check valve, but disc brakes have only a plain hole with a tube seat. If you have a combination drum and

CHASSIS, SUSPENSION & BRAKES/85

Brake Hydraulics

disc system, the outlet to the drums will have a check valve, but that to the discs will not. Cadillac throws us a little curve. In 1968 they dropped the check valve from the drum outlet on most models, evidently feeling that they didn't need it. However, the check valve is still in the outlet to the drum brakes on Cadillac's larger cars, such as limousines and specially built commercial chassis.

When one-half of a dual system fails, you get a lower pedal, but the remaining system will continue to work. If the system fails that is connected to the front part of a dual master cylinder, then the front piston will go forward until it bottoms out, allowing the rear piston to build up pressure. If the rear hydraulic piston system fails, there will be no hydraulic pressure to activate the front piston. In that case, a stop on the rear piston pushes against the front piston to operate it.

Another type of master cylinder usually seen only on trucks and imports is the combined brake and clutch cylinder. There's nothing mysterious here—it's just two cylinders with a common reservoir. Clutch hydraulic systems work pretty much the same as a brake hydraulic system. Usually both master cylinder and slave cylinder pistons are the same size because any leverage needed has been achieved through the mechanical arrangement of the levers. The hydraulic system is only used to transmit the force and is not needed to gain any leverage. Sometimes the leverage you get from a hydraulic system is too great, and we get wheel lockup. If it occurs on the rear wheels, a proportioning valve will help.

PROPORTIONING VALVE

Because disc brakes are not self-energizing, they require a lot of hydraulic pressure to stop a car. When you have the same size master cylinder operating a combined drum and disc system, it follows that the pressure to the drum brakes is going to be more than needed. Also, the drum brakes do not need as much pressure because they are on the rear of the car, which is very lightly loaded when stopping, because of weight transfer to the front.

Test drivers found they could lock up the rear wheels on a combined drum and disc system without even trying, so the engineers had to go back to the drawing board. What they came up with was a proportioning valve. It's a little gadget in the hydraulic line to the rear brakes. If you make normal stops, the valve does nothing, but when you really mash the pedal, the valve comes in anywhere from 200-400 lbs. (depending on the car) and proportions the hydraulic pressure to the rear brakes. It is not a cutoff or limiting valve. It allows the pressure to go as high as necessary, but only as a percentage of the pressure to the front disc brakes.

The proportioning valve works so well that now it is appearing on cars without disc brakes, to help keep their rear wheels from sliding. The metering valve is another story. It's only on the disc brake jobs.

METERING VALVE

Whenever discs and drums are used on the same car, it is difficult to make both systems come on at the same time. Drum brakes have clearance between the shoes and the drums, and the hydraulic fluid has to move the brake shoes to take up that space before the brakes are applied. Disc brakes do not have any clearance to be taken up because the pucks are out against the disc, lightly brushing it at all times. So when discs and drums are used in combination, the discs start braking first.

To keep the front disc brakes from coming on too soon, a metering valve is used in the line between the master cylinder and the front calipers. The metering valve will not allow any hydraulic pressure to be applied to the front calipers until the pressure has risen to 75-100 lbs. Delaying the application of the front brakes until 75 lbs. pressure has built up allows the rear brake shoes to go out against the drums. However, 75 lbs. is not enough pressure to actually make the rear brakes do any braking. It just allows them to catch up to the front. As the pressure in the system rises above 75 lbs., the metering valve allows fluid to pass and, all four wheels brake at the same time. The way that the wheel cylinders work is the next phase of our subject.

WHEEL CYLINDERS

Take a medium-size piece of cast iron, make a straight polished bore through it, put cups in the middle, pistons on the end, and you have a wheel cylinder . . . it's as simple as that. The hydraulic line from the master cylinder connects to the middle of the wheel cylinder and the fluid is admitted under pressure between the two cups. Each cup has its own piston and the hydraulic pressure tries to push the pistons out of the cylinder. Some kind of a connecting link runs from the piston to a tab on the brake shoe and the piston transmits pressure through the shoe to the drum and stops the car, or so we hope.

Filling a master cylinder is easy—you just pour fluid in and start pumping on the brake pedal. Fluid will fill the cylinder and go out through the lines to the wheel cylinders. But when the fluid reaches the wheel cylinders you're going to have one heck of a big air lock unless you have some means of letting the air out of the cylinder so that the fluid can get in. This is done through a bleeder fitting, which is usually mounted at the highest point on the cylinder so that all the air can be eliminated. Once the wheel cylinders are filled and all the air is out of the system it is never necessary to bleed the wheels again unless you get a leak somewhere or

1. The rear piston in a dual master cylinder operates the front brakes. If for some reason you lost pressure in the front brake system, the rear piston would move forward until it hit the secondary piston, and pushing it mechanically rather than hydraulically, would apply the rear brakes.

2. Most dual master cylinders have stops for each piston, usually a screw for the floating piston, and a cir-clip or retainer for the rear.

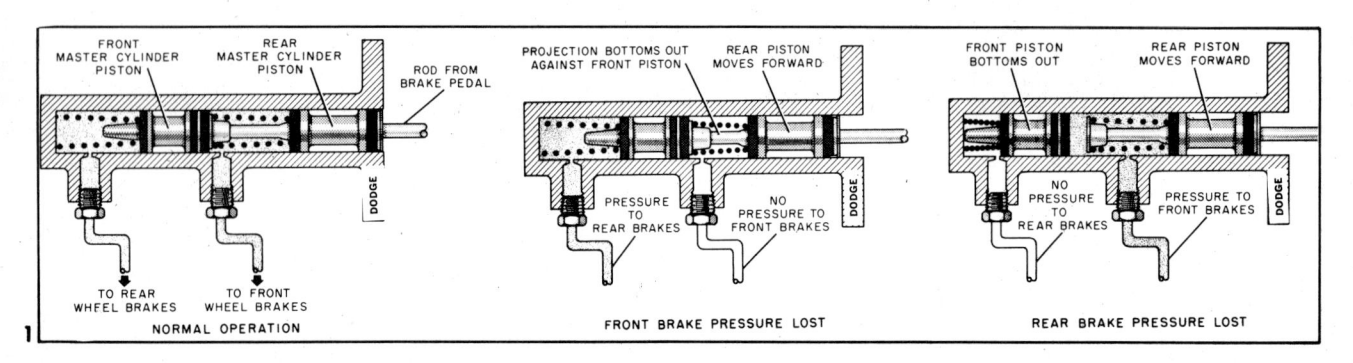

1. NORMAL OPERATION — FRONT MASTER CYLINDER PISTON, REAR MASTER CYLINDER PISTON, ROD FROM BRAKE PEDAL, TO REAR WHEEL BRAKES, TO FRONT WHEEL BRAKES (DODGE)

FRONT BRAKE PRESSURE LOST — PROJECTION BOTTOMS OUT AGAINST FRONT PISTON, REAR PISTON MOVES FORWARD, PRESSURE TO REAR BRAKES, NO PRESSURE TO FRONT BRAKES (DODGE)

REAR BRAKE PRESSURE LOST — FRONT PISTON BOTTOMS OUT, REAR PISTON MOVES FORWARD, NO PRESSURE TO REAR BRAKES, PRESSURE TO FRONT BRAKES (DODGE)

86/CHASSIS, SUSPENSION & BRAKES

something is wrong which allows air to pass into the system.

Most wheel cylinders have a spring between the two cups. The spring doesn't seem to be necessary in the operation of the cylinder because the hydraulic pressure alone is enough to keep the cups out against the pistons. However, during the assembly period before hydraulic fluid is admitted to the cylinder, the spring is helpful because it keeps the cups in the right position.

Some cylinders use expanders on each end of the spring. With expanders the force of the spring is directed to the lip of the cup and helps to keep the cup out against the cylinder and prevents leaks. The EIS Company uses expanders in their wheel cylinder kits even though the original equipment wheel cylinders might not have been equipped with expanders. The EIS cup has a small projection in the center which helps to locate the expander and keep it from getting up on one lip of the cup or from rubbing against the cylinder wall. Expanders definitely do help to prevent leaks but at the same time they can result in an aluminum piston running so dry that it will seize against the cast iron cylinder bore. The ideal situation would be to have just enough leakage so that the piston was lubricated. Unfortunately, you can't train a wheel cylinder cup to leak just the right amount. If they leak at all they will probably leak enough to ruin the brake shoes. The EIS engineers evidently feel that expanders are the only way to go. They also make sintered iron, self-lubricating pistons to solve the sticking problem.

Most of the cylinders that you see will be double-ended and have a straight bore the same size all the way through the cylinder. Some brake designs, however, particularly those which have individual anchors for each shoe, will use a cylinder with a step bore. The small end of the cylinder is used for the trailing shoe, which isn't very efficient anyway because it is not self-energizing. A step-bore wheel cylinder kit will of course have two different sizes of replacement cups and pistons.

Another odd design is the baffle cylinder, seen on Ford vehicles. The baffle is a partition in the cylinder. It has metered holes that control the speed of application of the secondary (rear) shoe on the front wheels. In a duo-servo brake without the baffle, sudden application of the brake forces both shoes out away from their anchor post. When the primary (front) shoe hits the drum, it rotates with the drum, forcing the secondary shoe in the direction of drum rotation and up against the anchor with a force that can bend anchors.

With the baffle in the cylinder, the primary shoe gets a head start. It goes out first, wraps into the drum, and transmits force to the secondary shoe before the secondary shoe has a chance to be pushed off the anchor post. In the baffle cylinder, the cup spring acts on the forward cup only, with no spring between the baffle and the rear cup. The system works, but it makes you wonder why they didn't just make their anchors a little stronger, instead of going to all that trouble with the baffle.

DISC BRAKE CALIPERS

Hydraulic theory is the same whether the brake is disc or drum. It's just that on disc brakes a few little tricks have been designed into the system. The return spring on drum brakes pulls the shoes back against the adjuster and when enough wear occurs on the linings, the adjuster is set up either by hand or automatically by the self-adjusting brake.

Designing return springs and adjusters into a disc brake would not be too difficult, but it would increase the cost of the brake. Designers got around this on the caliper-type of disc brake by using what is known as seal retraction. In a drum brake, the shoes are firmly attached to the backing plate and they do the braking by pushing on the drum. In a disc brake the caliper is firmly attached to the steering knuckle and hangs over the disc like a horseshoe. When the driver steps on the brake, the action is not so much of a push as it is a squeeze. The brake calipers can have any number of pistons and even have more than one caliper per wheel.

Most of the calipers that first appeared on American cars a few years ago had four opposing pistons in each caliper. Because the hydraulic pressure is equal throughout the system, one piston cannot overcome the other and therefore they squeeze equally from both sides. It's just as if you picked up a book between your thumb and forefinger; if somebody tries to pull the book out of your hands you squeeze harder and prevent them from doing so. On a car, if the two pistons squeeze the disc hard enough they will stop the car.

The early disc brake calipers had small pistons, so they used four. The pistons themselves do not push on the brake disc. A metal shoe with lining either riveted or bonded to it hangs loose between the pistons and the disc and acts as a friction agent just like an ordinary drum brake shoe. Many years ago, the Crosley car used pucks or pads that screwed onto the piston itself. That design transmits too much heat through the piston and has a tendency to boil the brake fluid. Almost all later cars use a shoe and lining that hangs loose between the disc and the pistons for air circulation to pass off some of the heat.

After the pistons move out of their bores and force the brake shoe against the disc, there's no spring to bring them back. In fact some pistons have a very light spring behind them that helps to push them out toward the disc. This light spring works the same way that the residual pressure does in a drum brake hydraulic system, keeping the pistons out close to the discs so that the brake pedal doesn't go all the way to the floor when you put your foot on it. When your foot is off the brake, the pressure in the hydraulic system drops to zero because a disc brake system has no residual pressure valve in the master cylinder.

When the pressure drops to zero, it is the seals around the pistons that pull them back from the brake shoes and thus relieve the pressure on the disc. The seals are made with a rectangular cross section and fit into a groove usually in the caliper housing.

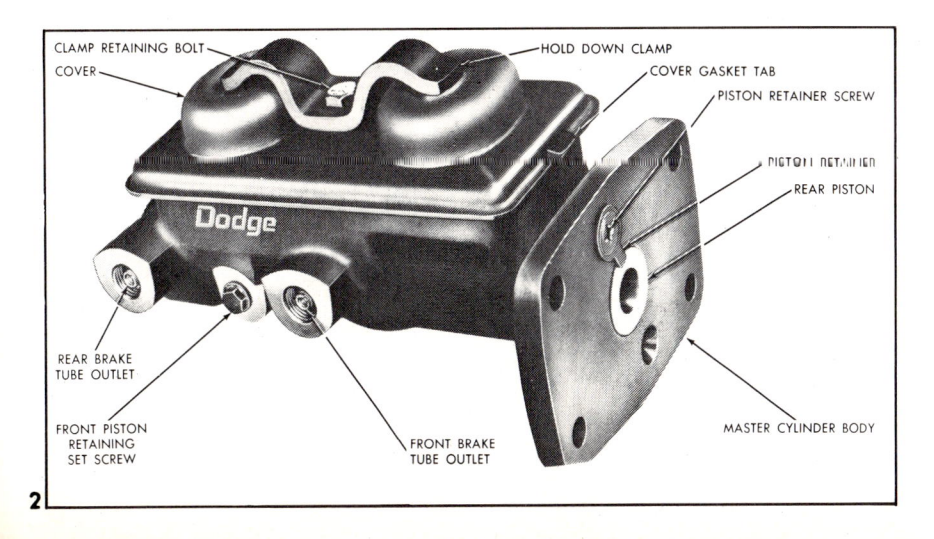

CHASSIS, SUSPENSION & BRAKES/87

Brake Hydraulics

The thickness of the seal is greater than it needs to be for just sealing alone. When you put your foot on the brake and the piston moves out, the seal does not slide immediately the way a cup does in a drum brake wheel cylinder. Instead of sliding, the seal bends and stretches around its whole diameter. It tries to hold onto the piston while the hydraulic pressure is pushing the piston out of the cylinder. The piston only has to move a few thousandths of an inch to push the brake shoes against the disc. In most brake applications the seals will not change their position relative to the piston or the housing. They just stretch a little. When you take your foot off the brake, the tension of the rubber pulls the seal back to normal and they retract the pistons away from the brake shoes. It sounds goofy, but it does work.

If you study this seal retraction, you can see that it depends upon the seal being a little bit sticky where it contacts the piston. If the piston can slide freely through the seal, then the seal will not have the bending action to pull the piston back. That happens often, and is the reason that the pucks never really pull completely free of the disc.

The square section seal also results in automatic adjustment. The seal will only bend as far as the piston goes out against the disc. If the brake shoes wear to the point where the piston will stroke beyond the elastic limit of the seal, then the piston will slide through the seal to take up the excess clearance between the shoe and the disc. When everything is new the self-adjusting feature works fine, but when the seals get old and the surface of the piston gets a little bit rough, then the piston may not slide through the seal as easily. This means that the seal is going to be stretched more than it should be, and when the brakes are released, the piston will be retracted too far. The brake pedal goes down further than it should and defies the best efforts of mechanics to get it to come up higher. The only right way to correct this situation is to replace all the seals, and the fluid, and to clean everything.

Another thing that causes low pedal on disc brakes is the springiness of the caliper. Some calipers are of such weak construction that they actually bend when the brakes are applied. One manufacturer came out with a bulletin explaining that while it was possible to push the brake pedal all the way to the floor it wasn't necessary to push it that far to stop the car. After years of driving a car with drum brakes which have a good, hard pedal, it's a little bit difficult to get used to a brake that feels like you're stepping on a wet sponge. With the introduction of the single-piston caliper, discs are finally reaching the point where it's a good idea to have them on your car.

In any disc brake, the only force that the caliper and its mounting brackets should be required to take is the force of the disc rotation. The hydraulic force of the piston pushing against the disc should be balanced within the caliper so that the caliper is not pushed to one side or the other. In a caliper with opposing pistons, equal hydraulic pressure throughout the system automatically balances the forces so the caliper is not pushed to one side. In a single-piston disc brake, the hydraulic action takes place all on one side of the disc. The caliper still fits down over the disc just like a horseshoe, but instead of pushing against another piston on the other side of the disc the caliper just pushes against itself. This system won't work with a rigidly mounted caliper; something would have to give and it would have a tendency to bend everything. The solution is to let the caliper float back and forth on bushings so that it can center itself over the disc no matter how hard you push on the brake. In the old 4-piston design, the slightest wobble in the disc would make the brake pedal do a dance underneath the driver's foot. In the single-piston floating caliper design all that slight disc wobble does is move the caliper around without affecting the brake pedal. Whatever brake you have, they all let the guy behind you know that you are coming to a halt, by turning on a big red light.

STOPLIGHT SWITCHES

When the driver stomps on the brake pedal, hydraulic system pressure goes from a low residual to several hundred pounds. A hydraulic stoplight switch is a small device screwed into the master cylinder or into a fitting somewhere near the master cylinder. The switch has two terminals on the outside, a couple of points on the inside, and makes the connection between the two terminals whenever the hydraulic system pressure goes up. Because the stoplight switch goes on at the same time as the brakes, it does not tell you that the car in front is going to stop, but only that he is already stopping.

Almost any hydraulic stoplight switch will work on any car as far as screwing it into the hydraulic system. The terminals for the wire leads are something else. There have been more different kinds of push-on, screw-on, flip-on, or just plain loose stoplight switch terminals than you

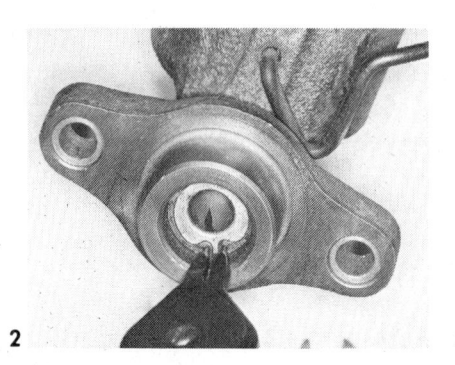

---

1. First step in rebuilding a master cylinder is removing the stop screw for the floating (secondary) piston.

2. On most master cylinders, cir-clip holds the primary piston inside the bore and must be removed for rebuild.

3. Being careful not to cock the pistons in the bore, you can now remove the cylinder's internals.

4. After disassembly, this is what you have. All of the parts, including the master cylinder and cover, should be thoroughly cleaned and inspected. Pay attention when you take it all apart, so you don't mix up springs.

5. Check the bore with a penlight flashlight for defects in the bore finish. If defects show up even after honing, the cylinder must be replaced. Brake hones are adjusted with knob.

6. After honing the bore, wash the cylinder out with alcohol. Cleaned pistons should be fitted with new seals from a rebuilding kit, coated with brake cylinder assembly lube, and slipped back into the bore.

7. Unless you want to spend a long time bleeding them on the car, dual master cylinders are best bled on the bench with clean fluid and two short steel lines like these.

88/CHASSIS, SUSPENSION & BRAKES

could dream up if you were in the middle of a psychedelic trance. There doesn't seem to be any good reason for the multiplicity of terminals, unless each switch designer thought that all the ones before him were no good and wanted to design his own. Some of them certainly are no good and seem to develop loose or corroded wire terminals without any urging. If both of your stoplights are not working, the first place to look is the switch. And the first thing to do is wiggle the terminals on it so that you obtain a better electrical connection.

The stoplight switch does not have to be hydraulic. General Motors vehicles used mechanical stoplight switches for years, and in most late cars of all makes, the switch is mechanical. The mechanical switch is either a lever or plunger of some kind designed to work off the brake pedal. The plunger type is usually adjustable and can be set so that the brake lights will come on at the slightest touch of the pedal.

Turn signal systems on modern vehicles all use the stoplight filament or bulb for signaling. If the driver should signal and brake at the same time, the steady source of current from the stoplight switch would cancel out the pulsating current coming from the turn signal switch. Rather than tell drivers not to step on the brake when they are going to make a turn, the manufacturers have wired all stoplights so that they are automatically shut off by the turn signal's switch on the side that is being used for signaling. A car that uses stoplights separate from the rear turn signals would have no connection between the turn signal wiring and the stoplight wiring. The stoplight switch used to be the only electrical part of the hydraulic brake system, but nowadays with the big emphasis on safety there is also a warning switch or brake failure light switch.

BRAKE WARNING LIGHT SWITCHES

When you turn the ignition switch to the "on" position, on many cars there is a red light on the instrument panel that glows brightly with the letters *brake* on it. It doesn't mean for you to hit the brakes; it just signifies that if you expect to get anywhere very fast, you had better release the parking brake before you pull away. What most people don't realize is that a red brake light will also come on (in many cases the same light) if there is any imbalance of pressure between the front and rear brakes on a dual master cylinder system. This seemingly miraculous deed is done by the warning light switch, a little gadget mounted somewhere near the master cylinder with several hydraulic fittings and one electrical lead. The switch itself is nothing but a cylinder with a free-moving piston. The hydraulic line to the front brakes is connected to one end of the piston, and the hydraulic lines to the rear brakes at its other end. Since hydraulic pressure is equal in front and rear systems, nothing will happen so long as you don't have any leaks. If a leak or failure should occur in either system, the force of hydraulic pressure from the other system will move the piston along the cylinder until it contacts a little terminal, thus making a ground circuit to turn on the brake light on the instrument panel.

General Motors has self-centering switches. If you step on the brake and half of the system has low pressure, the lights will come on. But when you take your foot off the brake, the light will go off. The result with such a warning device is that the driver usually thinks the light is there just to tell him when he stepped on the brake. Ford and American Motors, evidently feeling that the driver might pay more attention to the light if it stayed on, have designed their warning light switches so that once it's on, it stays on, and it's quite an

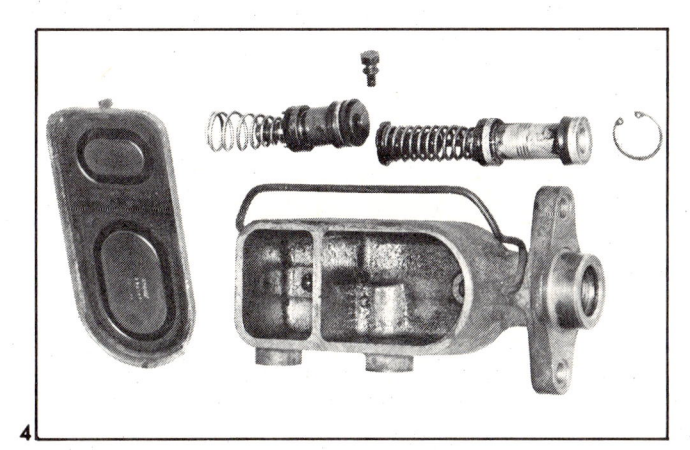

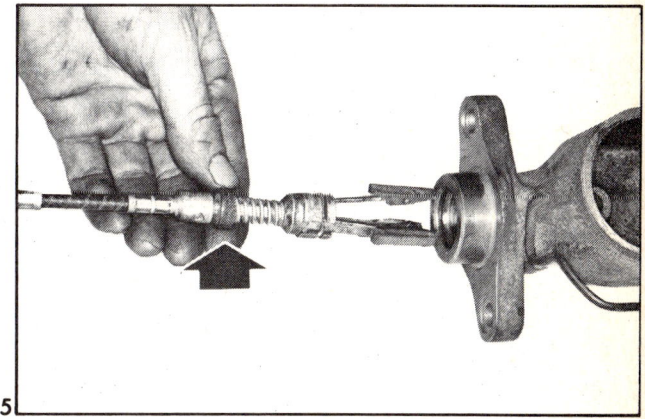

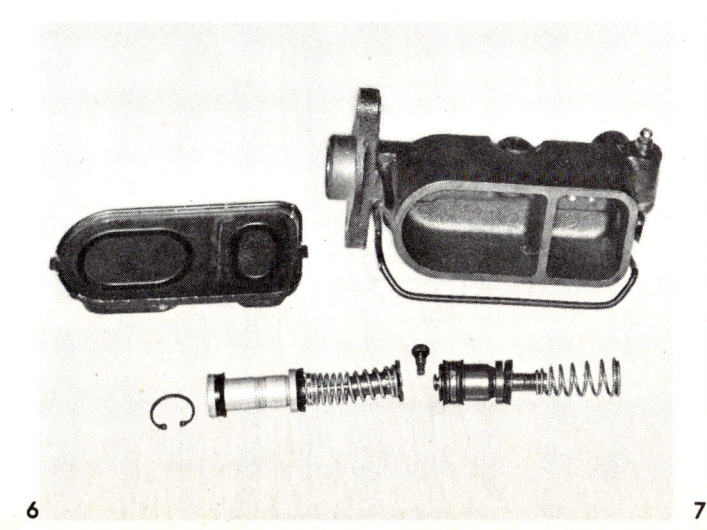

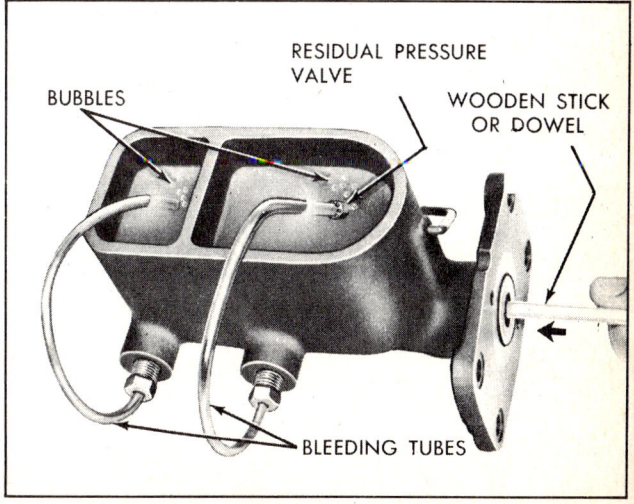

4

5

6

7

RESIDUAL PRESSURE VALVE
BUBBLES
WOODEN STICK OR DOWEL
BLEEDING TUBES

CHASSIS, SUSPENSION & BRAKES/89

Brake Hydraulics

involved procedure to switch it back off. We'll cover that later when we tell you about bleeding. Right now let's talk about how the fluid goes to the right places.

HOSES AND LINES

About the only way you can tell if a brake hose should be replaced is to take a look at the rubber covering on the outside of it. If it looks old, dried up, or even cracked, it's a good idea to replace the hose. Brake hoses don't wear out slowly, they burst; but they are so well made that this rarely happens. If you do have to replace a brake hose, you must be sure of three things: 1) the length, 2) the type of fittings, and 3) the method of attachment to the car frame and also to the wheel cylinder or caliper. Some wheel cylinders are identical, except that one will take a hose and the other takes tubing and a nut. There are no adapters or anything that you can do to convert a wheel cylinder from a hose fitting to a tubing fitting. The threads and the seat in the cylinder itself must be correct for the particular application.

Never under any circumstances should the design of either brake hose or brake line fittings be changed just because you can't find the right fitting. If the cylinder is designed to accept a brake hose and a washer, then either buy the right parts or don't put it together. If you are repairing a car that needs a new brake tube, there is only one way to go. You should buy ready-made, steel brake line with the steel nuts already installed and the tubing already flared. Auto parts houses have these steel lines already made up in various lengths.

Steel brake lines are always double flared to keep them from cracking. You may have read books that tell you how to do double flaring. The job is not anywhere near as easy as you may have heard. It's so difficult to get a good flare on steel tubing—one you feel you could trust your life with—that the purchase of ready-made brake line is the only way to go.

When you buy a new brake hose or line, you should never assume that it is clean. Look through it with a flashlight, or pour alcohol through the line and blow it out to be sure there is nothing in it that will contaminate the fluid. The best fluid can be ruined by dirt or even the smallest amount of water.

BRAKE FLUID

If it weren't for the terrific amount of heat generated by brakes, you could use water in brake lines without any trouble at all until the temperature went down to freezing. Those are the two major problems with brake fluid: it can't boil and it can't freeze no matter how much you heat up the brakes or how cold the weather is. Before the Society of Automotive Engineers developed the specifications for brake fluid, a manufacturer could put just about anything into a can, add a label that said "brake fluid"—and it would end up in your master cylinder. Brake fluid specifications came into prominence right after World War II. At that time engineers figured that a boiling point for brake fluid of 235° F. was adequate. Later on somebody found out that by stopping a car often enough and fast enough you can easily heat the brake fluid up to 250° or more. About 1957, SAE dropped their original specification for moderate-duty brake fluid, leaving only the heavy-duty specification, number 70R1, which boils at 302° F.

Cars kept growing larger, wheels kept growing smaller, which let less air in to cool the brakes, and the result was that the 70R3 specification was established with a boiling point of 374° F. If you want to buy the best drum brake fluid, buy one that is labeled as meeting specification 70R3 or J1703A (a new number for the same specification). Both exceed the 70R1 spec. If you want an inexpensive fluid for drum brakes, 70R1 may still be available, but it will be discontinued when present stocks are sold. Eventually, the 70R3 number will disappear, leaving only J1703A, sometimes shown on cans as J1703.

In disc brakes, you should use fluid that has a boiling point higher than the SAE specs. It appears that SAE has not come around to assigning a specification number to disc brake fluids. The only way you can tell if you have one of them is to read the can very carefully. Usually somewhere on the can is the notification that the fluid is for disc brakes, or maybe the actual boiling point of the fluid is given.

The Department of Transportation has recently set its own standards for brake fluids, with DOT-2 being the designation for standard drum fluid. Fluids equally suited for both drum and disc systems are tabbed DOT-3, which means they have a 460° boiling point. An even higher-rated fluid (DOT-4) is for heavy-duty disc applications, but so far only Girling makes a fluid that meets these specs, and it is not widely available yet.

Some companies do not identify their fluids on the can. They even use confusing names or numbers so that it is impossible to tell which of the fluids they make is the best one. If

1. This is what the other part of your hydraulic braking system, the wheel cylinder, is like inside. You can see from this cutaway how the fluid comes in from the brake line and forces the two pistons out to push the shoes into the drums.

2. Most wheel cylinders follow this design. Components are: 4, body; 1, 9, rubber boots; 2,8, pistons; 3,7, cups; 6, spring and expanders; and 5, bleeder screw. Note how the lips on the cups face to the center.

3. Wheel cylinders should be gone through as part of any complete brake job. After pulling the boots, cups, pistons and spring, hone the bore using brake fluid or honing fluid on the tool. It shouldn't take much honing to clean out any corrosion or glaze from the cylinder's bore.

4. If a cylinder's bore gets too large, it will leak under pressure, causing a dangerous loss of brakes. Brake shops often use gauges like these to check them. The gauges are made .005-in. oversize, and if the gauge fits loosely in the bore after honing, cylinder must be replaced.

5. After honing, the cylinder must be washed out with alcohol and wiped with a clean, lint-free rag.

6. Wheel cylinder rebuilding kits are inexpensive brake insurance and contain all the parts needed except the metal piston. When thoroughly cleaned, your old pistons are OK.

7. Install the cup, piston, boot and shoe link for one side of the cylinder, then install the spring with expanders attached.

8. Your cleaned pistons and all of the new parts should be coated with clean new fluid before assembly.

9. To hold the assembled cylinder together (against the spring pressure from inside) a special spring clamp is used until the shoes and retractor springs can be reinstalled.

the guy on the other side of the parts counter doesn't know, let the price be your guide.

Ford disc brake fluids have been colored blue so that you will be alerted when you take the top off a master cylinder. All of the fluids will mix with one another without doing any actual damage to the system. However, the boiling point of any of the disc brake fluids will be lowered quite a bit if you add 374° fluid. It doesn't do any good, either, to add disc brake fluid to a system that is filled with 374° fluid. If you want to raise the boiling point of your fluid by converting to disc brake fluid, the only way to do it is to remove all of the fluid from all of the lines and cylinders and start over again with the kind of fluid you want.

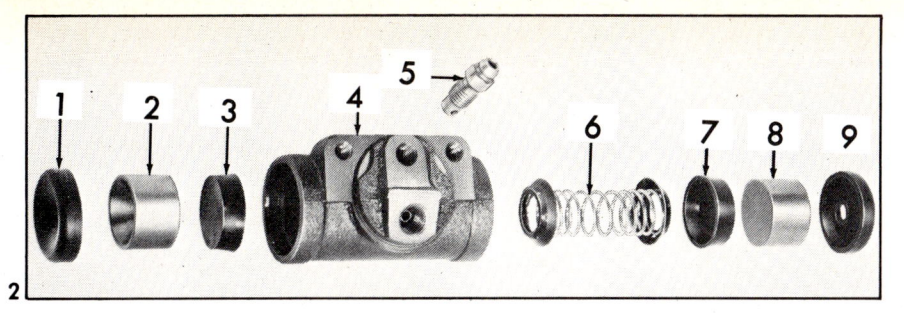

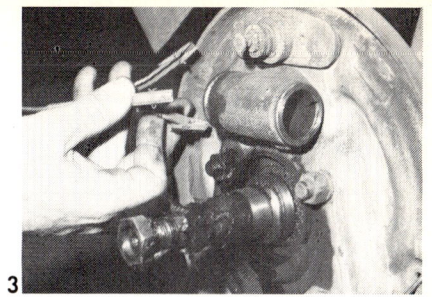

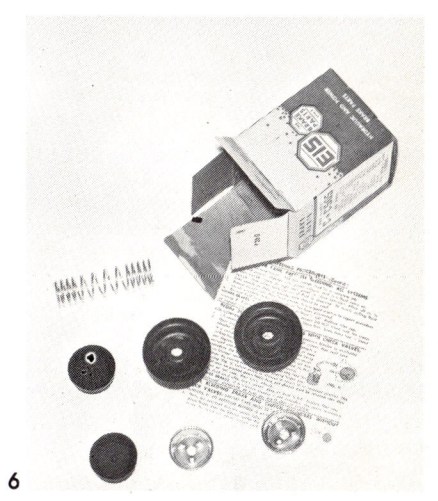

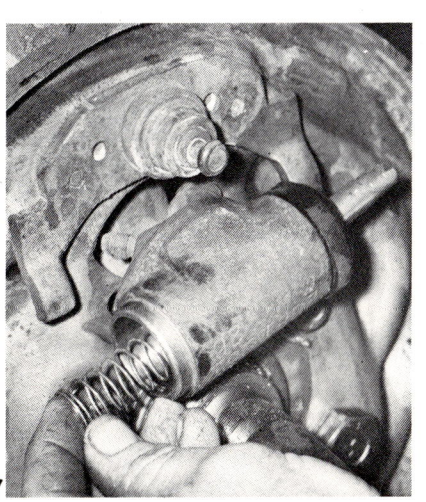

Removing fluid from any hydraulic brake system is not just a simple matter of opening the bleeder fitting on the wheel cylinders and letting it drain. In order to rid the system of any air, the bleeder fitting has to be at the top of the cylinder. Most of the fluid is at the bottom of the cylinder, so you cannot drain a wheel cylinder unless you take it apart completely, and wipe it dry.

Should you use one of the special fluids on the market made for flushing out the brake system? If you are willing to take extra precautions, the flushing fluids are a good idea on an old car. Extra precautions mean that you must be very careful to get all of the flushing liquid out of the system by flushing it out with brake fluid. SAE says to forget the flushing liquid, because they feel that nobody is going to get it all out of the system, and they are probably right. On a later model car, which hasn't had many years to build up deposits in the lines, flushing fluid should not be necessary at all. Just use a new brake fluid.

This flushing of the lines and hoses must be done before the wheel cylinders are reassembled, because it is impossible to do any flushing through a bleeder fitting. The correct procedure for brake system flushing is to either remove all wheel cylinders, or remove the pistons and cups, leaving the wheel cylinders in place on the backing plate. Remove the cover from the master cylinder and pump the brake pedal until there is nothing coming out of the ends of the lines except air. Then fill the master cylinder with the flushing liquid and flush it completely through the system. Continue to pour fresh flushing liquid into the master cylinder and pump the brake pedal until the fluid comes out the ends of all the lines just as clean as it is when you pour it into the cylinder.

Next you should remove the master cylinder and either rebuild it or install a new cylinder. Fill the new master

CHASSIS, SUSPENSION & BRAKES/91

Brake Hydraulics

cylinder with fresh brake fluid and pump the brake pedal until you have a pure stream of new brake fluid out of the ends of each line at each wheel. At that point you are ready to rebuild all of the wheel cylinders; then bleed the brakes and you're done.

Brake fluid or flushing fluid should not be used twice. Never pour anything into a master cylinder except fresh fluid right out of the can it came in. If you accidentally leave the top off a can of brake fluid over the weekend or a few days, throw it away when you discover your error. In the short time the top has been off, the fluid will have absorbed enough moisture out of the air to lower its boiling point to where it would be dangerous to put in your car.

If you know much about the actual way brake jobs are done in a garage, you will probably feel that much of the foregoing is nit-picking theory that nobody follows. Unfortunately, it's true. Many brake jobs are done without any regard for the recommendations of the manufacturers. Probably not one car in 10,000 has ever had its hydraulic systems completely flushed. When a new or rebuilt wheel cylinder is installed, it is common practice to add only enough fluid to the master cylinder to make up for what is lost during bleeding. If there is any dirt in the line, or contaminated fluid, it goes right into the new cylinder and stays there. It's a tribute to our hydraulic brake designers that brakes work under such conditions.

It's very difficult to have any automobile manufacturer tell you how long your brakes are going to last. If you ask them when you should change the shoes or the brake fluid, they will say to do it "as needed." With the brake fluid manufacturers, it's a different story. Some of them feel that brake fluid should be changed once a year, but in order to change it properly you have to flush the system with clean fluid and rebuild all the cylinders. It takes a lot of time if you do it yourself and it's very expensive if you pay somebody else to do it. The result is that usually the only fluid a hydraulic system receives is whatever is needed to raise the level in the master cylinder when you pull the top off and look in. The level in the master cylinder should not drop appreciably, even after many months, unless you have a leak somewhere.

HYDRAULIC LEAKS

Brake lining checks are usually done by pulling one drum off and eyeballing the lining. The assumption is that lining wears more or less equally on all four wheels. Leaks, however, do not necessarily develop in all four wheels at the same time. Therefore, if you want to check for leaks at the wheel cylinders, you should pull off each drum and peel back the dust boot on the ends of the cylinders to see if any fluid has bypassed the cups. A little bit of fluid in the dust boot is all right. It helps to lubricate the piston. But if any fluid runs out of the boot when you peel it back, it's time for a wheel cylinder overhaul. Of course if you see any collection of corrosion underneath the boot, you don't just pop the boot back on and let it go at that. Corrosion can cause a sticking piston, so the wheel cylinder should be rebuilt.

If, after peeling the boots back, you don't find any corrosion or leakage, you're not through yet. Take a spring tool and pop the springs off the shoes and move the shoes out away from the cylinder pistons. With the shoes out of the way you should be able to put your fingers on the dust boots and move the pistons back and forth easily in the cylinder. Don't move them too much! You're not trying to pump water out of a well, you just want to know if the pistons are free. If they are sticking, then the only thing you can do is rebuild the offending cylinder.

The same type of leak inspection applies to the master cylinder. You crawl under the car, or under the instrument panel, peel back the boot, and if you get an eyeful of liquid it's time to rebuild the cylinder.

There's another type of leak that shows up in a master cylinder only if you know how to check it. If you remember how a master cylinder works, the primary cup is surrounded by fluid on both sides. It is only the secondary cup that keeps the fluid from leaking to the outside of the cylinder. If the primary cup is leaking you will feel the pedal slowly going down to the floor under the pressure of your foot. Sometimes an internal leak will not show up under heavy foot pressure, but only when you are just pushing enough to make the brakes work. If you feel a leak in the primary cup, the only way to fix it is to remove the master cylinder and rebuild it or install a new cylinder.

Disassembly of either master cylinders or wheel cylinders is not difficult. You won't have any trouble if you work carefully, but when you pry the snap ring out of the end of a master cylinder to remove the piston, cover the end of the cylinder with a rag or with your hand so that the ring doesn't fly up and hit you in the eye. On all dual master cylinders, you must remove the little bolt that is the stop for the forward piston. If you don't see where it's screwed in from outside the cylinder, look down in the fluid reservoir and you'll probably find it in there.

After getting all the parts out of a wheel or master cylinder, you should clean it thoroughly with alcohol, blow it dry with compressed air and inspect it with a strong light. If the cylinder is corroded, pitted or feels rough when you slide your finger along it, it should be honed very lightly or touched up with crocus cloth. When we say crocus cloth, we mean the very fine cloth used by jewelers, when working on expensive metals. Do not use emery cloth, sand paper or steel wool; they are all too coarse and will scratch the cylinder. If you use a hone and the cylinder does not clean up with just a few strokes, don't waste your time trying to rebore the cylinder by moving the hone back and forth for the next ten minutes. Throw the cylinder away and buy a new one.

The springs, cups and pistons should be dipped in clean brake fluid before you put them into the cylinder. The boots can be put on dry. After the cylinder is assembled, slip a wheel cylinder clamp onto it and then put your brake shoes and return springs back into their respective positions on the backing plate.

The parts that you use in both wheel cylinders and master cylinders should in most cases be exact duplicates of the pieces that came originally on the car. There is an exception to this rule, however. The EIS Co. has done considerable research on hydraulics. In many cases they have designed internal parts for wheel and master cylinders that are considerably better and longer lasting than the original equipment. A good example is their kit that is designed to be used in the Ford Motor Co. front wheel cylinders that have the little baffle inside the cylinder. The baffle makes it impossible to hone the cylinder properly because the hone will not go right up next to the baffle where the cup does when installed. EIS has solved this problem by making a wheel cylinder kit with different pistons that position the cup farther away from the baffle than the stock cup was. You can hone those baffle cylinders if you are going to put an EIS kit in them. If you are going to use an original equipment kit, do not hone the cylinder; you'll end up with nothing but a big leak.

EIS believes very much in expanders for cups. They use them in just about every wheel cylinder where they can be fitted. They also use a ribbed secondary cup on their master

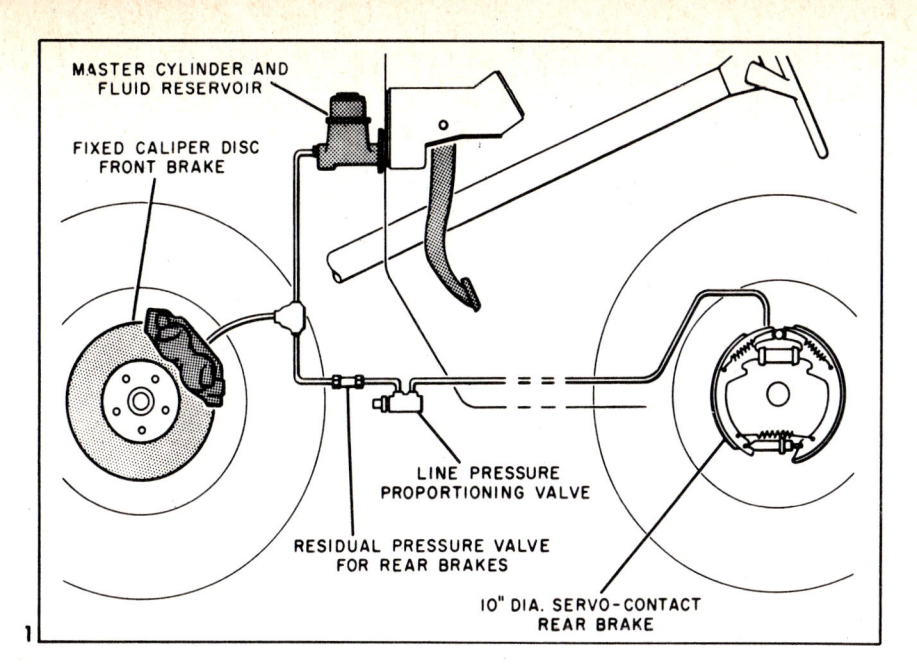

1. Most mixed disc-and-drum braking systems include a proportioning valve in the line to the rear drum brakes. The discs up front take more pedal pressure than the drums, so the valve limits pressure to the rears so they don't lock up on hard stops.

cylinder pistons. It's really the only way to go and it'll cure a lot of problems with leaking master cylinders.

Whether you are doing one, or four wheel cylinders, the procedure is still the same. After you put them all back together, then you have to take care of the bleeding.

BLEEDING BRAKES

Shop mechanics use a pressure bleeder, sometimes called a bleeder ball. It is a double-chamber tank with the air pressure in the tank separated from the brake fluid by a neoprene diaphragm. The diaphragm is necessary to keep the brake fluid from absorbing moisture in the air. Pressure bleeders operate somewhere around 10 to 50 lbs. of air pressure; just enough to push the fluid through the master cylinder and out to the wheel cylinders. All you do is hook up the pressure bleeder to the master cylinder and then go around and crack each bleeder screw until you get a steady stream without any bubbles. It isn't necessary to use any hoses or jars when you're bleeding with a pressure bleeder because you only crack the bleeder screw a quarter of a turn or less, just enough to let the air out until you get fluid only. You can hold a rag over the bleeder fitting so that you're not squirting fluid all over the place, and you can tell by the sound of the fluid coming through when the air is all out.

If the brake shoes have been adjusted properly and fit the drums correctly, the brake pedal should be hard and high when you step on it. On a single-piston master cylinder you should check for a little squirt of fluid out of the compensating port when you just touch the brake pedal, before you put the lid back on the master cylinder. If the squirt is there, then you know that the compensating port is open. Dual-piston master cylinders may not squirt, but you can check them with a small flashlight. You must have free-play in the brake pedal, so that the push-rod is not pressing against the piston when your foot is off the brake. If the pushrod is holding the piston in a little, it may close the compensating port, holding the brakes on.

If you don't have a pressure bleeder, then you will need a friend to help you, or a bleeder hose and a jar. The friend method is much quicker; all you do is have him put pressure on the brake pedal while you go around and open one bleeder fitting at a time to bleed the air off the cylinders. It may take several strokes of the master cylinder to get all the air out and your friend must add fluid to the master cylinder as it goes down. If your friends have all left you, then you hook up the bleeder hose to the bleeder fitting and crack the fitting open about half a turn. The end of the bleeder hose should be in a jar, ending beneath the surface of some clean brake fluid so that you won't have any chance of sucking air back into the wheel cylinder when you take your foot off the pedal. With the hose-and-jar setup you just go to the brake pedal and stroke it three or four times until you've run about a half-inch of fluid into the jar. Then tighten the bleeder fitting on that wheel and go to the next one.

If you're having this work done at a gas station, make sure they don't use one of those gallon brake fluid cans with the squirt pump on it. Unless it's brand new, all the air in the can has contaminated the fluid and lowered its boiling point.

Bleeding disc brake calipers is a little bit tricky. There usually is a metering valve in the line between the master cylinder and the front calipers. When bleeding with either the pressure tank or foot method, you must push or pull—depending upon the model—a little plunger on the metering valve, or install a clip to hold it open. This will allow fluid to run freely through the valve so that you can bleed the brakes.

A good way to bleed calipers is by the gravity method. Put a brake hose on the caliper and submerge it under the surface of some clean fluid in a jar and then open the bleeder screw. Because there is no residual pressure valve in the disc brake outlet on the master cylinder, fluid will usually drain right through the caliper and you can get all the air out that way. It's a good idea to tap the caliper with a plastic mallet while the fluid is running through. This will tend to break loose any bubbles of air that happen to be in the caliper lines.

After bleeding, do not forget to take the little clip off the metering valve. Some car makers are so afraid that a mechanic is going to leave the clip on the valve that they will not allow him to use such a tool.

There are a lot of little tricks that you can learn about bleeding. If you are installing or rebuilding a master cylinder without doing anything to the wheels, you should fill the master cylinder and bleed it on the bench; then when you hook it up to the car all that is necessary is to bleed at each fitting where it attaches to the master cylinder—and you're all done.

If you have rebuilt all the wheel cylinders, and are a sharp mechanic, a slick trick when you don't have a pressure bleeder is to open all the wheel cylinder bleeder screws about ¼-turn. Pump the master cylinder until you get fluid out of all four wheels. You don't have to watch each wheel; just listen, and feel the pedal. Then go around and tighten all four bleeder screws and you are done. It works well and it's fast. But it's also contrary to all accepted practice, and can get you in trouble if you are not experienced, so don't tell anybody we told you.

While you are bleeding, you are actually creating a leak in the hydraulic system. On late model cars with the brake warning light you may notice the red light on the instrument panel coming on when you are stroking the brake pedal. On General Motors cars

CHASSIS, SUSPENSION & BRAKES/93

Brake Hydraulics

the light should go off when you take your foot off the pedal because their switch is self-centering. The same light is used for the parking brake warning light, so before you spend several hours trying to fix a warning light that is on, release the parking brake and see if it goes out.

The Ford and American Motors switches are diabolical devices that stay on even after you take your foot off the brake pedal. To get the Ford light turned out you will have to center the valve in the brake warning light switch. That is done by creating a leak on one side of the switch and pushing steadily on the brake pedal until the light goes out. If you can't get the light to go out, then you are creating a leak on the wrong side of the switch. Tighten the fitting and go to the other side to make the leak. As soon as the light goes out you must remove your foot from the brake pedal immediately. If you keep pushing you'll shift the piston all the way to the other side and the light will come right back on again. If that happens, tighten up the fitting, go to the other side of the switch and create a leak all over again to center the switch.

Actually, there is an easier way. The Raybestos brake people have come out with a samll device known as a "differential switch lock," which is used to hold the valve mechanism of the brake light warning switch of 1965 to 1971 FoMoCo cars during the bleeding operation. The device screws into the warning light switch socket to prevent the pressure differential switch valve from being actuated, so there is no need for elaborate recentering techniques.

American Motors uses the same general method of centering the switch, except that they do not have a ramp on the piston for the little switch plunger. You must remove the plunger from the switch. If you try to center the piston without removing the plunger, you may bend it and then the whole thing is ruined. If you bleed an American Motors car (or any of their Jeep models) by the foot method, correct procedure is to remove the warning light switch plunger before you start. Otherwise, you may bend the plunger while doing the bleeding.

The only parts of the hydraulic system which should be repaired are wheel cylinders, master cylinders, hoses, or lines. If a proportioning valve, metering valve, or brake warning light goes bad, replace it with a new unit.

On some cars the designer had an awful time getting the master cylinder to line up with the foot pedals, and he had to make the thing run uphill. The result was he was left with an air pocket in the end of the master cylinder and no way to get rid of it unless he put a bleeder fitting there. If you see a bleeder fitting on a master cylinder, bleed it first before you go to the wheels.

When bleeding power brakes by the foot method, always do it with the engine off, and exhaust all the vacuum out of the unit by stroking the pedal before you start the bleeding procedure. When bleeding brakes by the foot method, it's not a good idea to stroke the master cylinder all the way down until you almost push the piston clear through the end of the cast iron. Long strokes on a master cylinder are particularly bad if it's old.

There may be a lot of dirt and sediment in the end of it and one long stroke is all it would take to put a big groove in a cup and cause one heck of a leak. It's surprising how few strokes it takes to pump enough fluid out through the lines to fill a wheel cylinder and get all the air out. Working on hydraulic brakes is really very simple and can be very satisfying when you add up all the money you save by doing it yourself.

ANTI-SKID BRAKES

The word "skid" can be interpreted a lot of different ways. What it means to you will depend upon what happened to your car the last time it went into a skid. If you went into a turn on a gravel road a little bit too fast and the rear end came around so that your car did a loop-the-loop and ended up in a ditch, that's what skidding means to you. If you have ever been on a steep hill trying to start up from a standstill on a rain-slickened pavement, and all your car did was sort of slither around, you may figure that you know what skidding is all about. On snow or ice, with or without tire chains, you can do a lot of sliding around before you even touch the brake. Under the circumstances you might think that an anti-skid brake is just what you need, but it isn't. An anti-skid brake is designed to minimize skidding caused by wheel locking. It is not something that will miraculously bring you out of a skid when you step on the pedal.

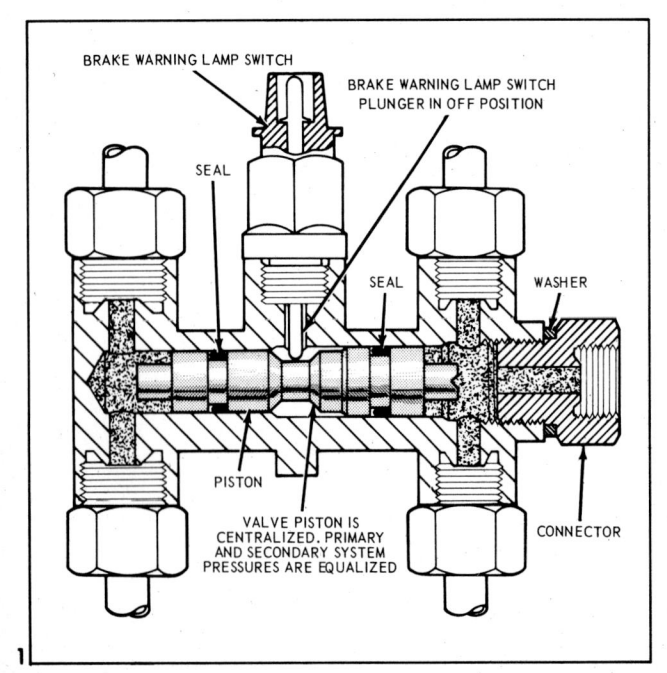

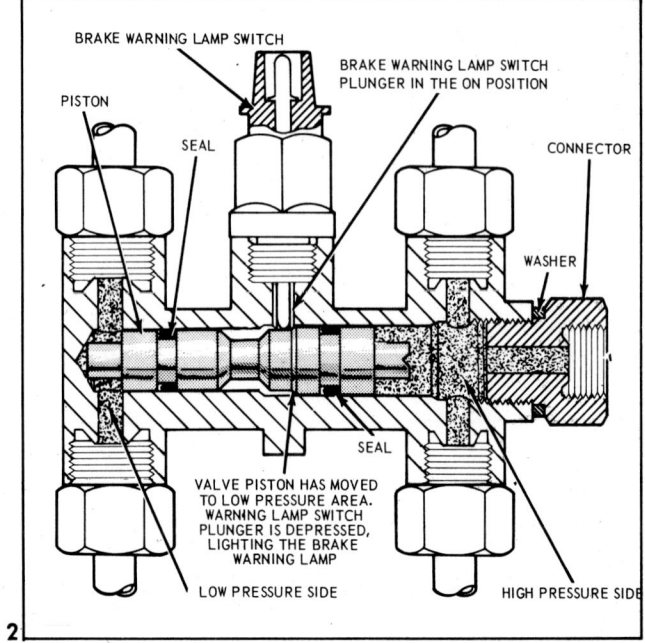

The anti-skid brake system that appeared on Lincoln and Thunderbird in 1969 works on the rear wheels only, and makes it impossible to lock them up. Anytime a wheel is locked up tight by the brakes, it ceases to be a wheel and becomes merely a single point in contact with the road which can slide in any direction. Rear wheels of a car have always had a tendency to lock up under severe braking because of the weight transfer. The problem became worse with the introduction of disc brakes, because you can step on the brake pedal a lot harder before you lock up a disc. Without the proportioning valve on drum/disc-equipped cars, the rear wheels would be locked up almost every time you made a severe stop. Anti-skid brake systems do a better job than the proportioning valve.

In an ordinary stop, just as in ordinary acceleration, the rear tires operate as if they were geared to the road surface, without any slippage. But in a maximum stop the tires will brake most efficiently if they are sliding about 10% to 20%. A wheel that is locked up does not stop anywhere near as well as one that is slipping 10% to 20%.

A driver who is alert, and has had a lot of practice, can apply the brakes in a maximum stop situation so that he gets the maximum deceleration of the car. He brakes by the seat of his pants, and he can do an excellent job of it, probably as well as any anti-skid braking system now in use. Race car drivers are particularly good at this. They have been around the course before, and know exactly to the nearest foot how far they can go into a corner before they have to apply the brakes.

A practiced stopping situation is one thing, but a panic stop is another game, even with the best driver. It is too easy to lock up the wheels, losing the best braking efficiency of the tires by going beyond the ideal slip ratio of 10% to 20%. Also, the ideal slip ratio does not translate into a single pressure factor that you can just apply to the brake and hold. As the car slows down, less pressure is needed to keep the ideal slip ratio. You can feel this in a car, when you find it necessary to back off the brakes slightly to maintain the same rate of deceleration as the car slows down.

What a car needs is a gadget that will apply the brakes with exactly the right amount of hydraulic pressure, so that the ideal 10-20% slip ratio is maintained. But we don't want to do this every stop. We would look silly driving around town making maximum stops every time we wanted to slow down a little.

What Ford's Sure-Track engineers and others have done is develop a system that works only when the driver steps on the pedal hard enough to decelerate the wheels faster than the ideal rate. It works on ice, dry pavement, gravel, or any kind of surface the car might be on, including an oil-slick test pad.

In each rear hub, behind the axle flange, is an electric sensor, consisting of a toothed ring attached to the axle and a coil of wire around a magnet attached to the backing plate. Current is fed to the coil of wire, which encircles the toothed ring. As the speed of rotation of the car wheel changes, it changes the strength of the magnetic field enveloping the toothed ring and the coil of wire. The signals from the sensors are sent through wires along the axle housing and frame to a control module under the glovebox.

At all times, the control module, which is a computer, knows exactly how fast the rear wheels are turning. If the system was built with ordinary electrical parts, it would have to sense the speed of the car from some other means, perhaps a fifth wheel, and then compare the car speed with the speed of the wheels to know if the wheels were locked up or not.

But the computer has a memory. The control module computer was told by Ford engineers exactly how much deceleration of the rear wheels to tolerate. If the driver pushes too hard on the pedal, approaching wheel lockup, the control module knows this by the signals it receives from the rear wheel sensors. The control module then sends a signal to the actuator, and the actuator takes over the braking of the rear wheels from the driver's control.

The actuator is operated by an electric solenoid and engine vacuum. When it is told to do so by the control module, it rapidly pulsates the hydraulic fluid in the lines to the rear brakes. This applying and releasing of the rear brakes has an average value that results in a 10% to 20% slip of the rear tires, for maximum resultant stopping power.

All kinds of electronic controls are built into the control module so that it won't be fooled by changing road conditions. The rate of pulsation can be as rapid as four cycles per second, if needed. The big secret about the control module is the ideal deceleration rate that is built into it for comparison with road conditions. Many factors were weighed in telling the control module what to do in every situation. Car total weight, the amount of weight on the rear wheels, and weight transfer in a stop were all figured into the complete computer control module.

They even have a red light on the instrument panel that glows if the Sure-Track system breaks down. It's the same light that comes on if there is a differential in pressure between the front and rear brake systems. But the beauty of Sure-Track is that if it fails, it doesn't affect the regular hydraulic braking system. The red light will come on to indicate that the system is not working, but that won't affect normal braking. The red light should not be ignored, however, because you won't know if the light was turned on by an inoperative Sure-Track or by a leak in the regular hydraulic system.

Sensitive drivers will have to be told about some of the peculiarities of Sure-Track. It clicks, and makes a few other noises when the ignition switch is turned on to start the engine. When the system is working during a stop, it can make other little noises that might cause the driver to think something is wrong with the rear end.

On dry pavement, most drivers will never know they have Sure-Track. It is in the wet or on snow that the system really pays off. When the pavement is slick, an expert driver will have to make all kinds of steering wheel corrections to make an ordinary car stop in a straight line. With Sure-Track, even a novice driver can make straight-line stops every time.

1. Along with dual braking systems, all late and new cars have a pressure differential switch like this to let you know if either front or rear systems fail. With normal pressure in both systems being equal, the valve piston is centered.

2. If either system fails, the valve piston will be forced to the weak side by the high pressure in the other system, pushing the plunger of the warning switch and lighting an indicator light on the dashboard.

3. Brake warning lights will also come on annoyingly when bleeding a system, and stay on afterwards, too. Raybestos makes this neat tool to screw into the differential switch before bleeding. It keeps the piston centered and the warning light off.

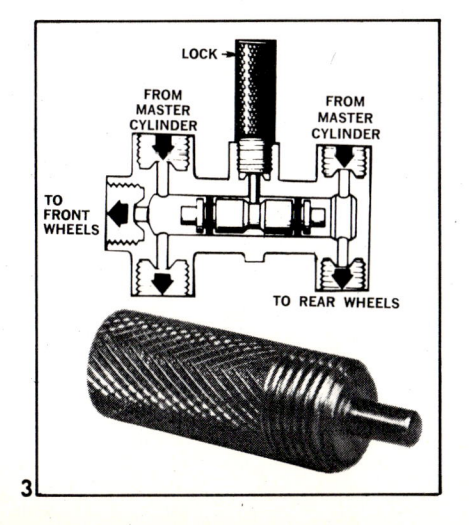

CHASSIS, SUSPENSION & BRAKES/95

Drum Brakes

Give your car a "brake"—stop here for the details.

While many of the world's car manufacturers are looking toward the greener pastures of disc braking systems, not all's lost—there is still some kick left in the ol' workhorse.

Legend has it that Ettore Bugatti, in squelching a criticism on his continuing use of mechanical brakes, was given to reply, "My cars are made to go, not stop!" Go they did . . . although the genius of the maestro also saw to it that his "children" stopped, which they did, and well.

The act of stopping somehow has never seemed to possess the same gut appeal for the auto enthusiast as its opposite—going. The basic fundamentals, designs, technologies and subtle nuances of engine and chassis construction have, throughout the years, been directed toward making an automobile go as fast and as safely as it can, irrespective of road conditions. Yet, when it comes to putting a stop to all this fun, then you're talking another tale . . . .that's not what all this work to build a high-speed car is all about . . . why it's made to go, not to stop!

It has been said that brakes began when wheels started turning. So you can hark back to the golden days of Egypt for the first crude braking devices . . . however, running up the rump of some hard working horse probably comprised much of that early "whoa" power. Sometime in the 16th century, the Germans devised a remote-controlled wooden post brake to stop their ore wagons, while further on down the line, in the 1800's, 30-car trains of wagons were controlled by thrusting pins between the spokes of the slow-turning wheels.

Not until the turn of the century (really the last decade of the 19th) were there any significant changes in brake design—aside from the devices produced by Westinghouse to stop heavily laden trains. The advent of the early motor cars necessitated an equally positive means of bringing them to a halt after their earth-shattering, 12-mph charges. Don't laugh: you must remember that these 4-hp monsters were really nothing more than motorized carriages designed for haul-by-horse. So when people like Ford, Olds, Daimler or Benz started putting the power to these rickety buggies, what stopping power they had was soon found wanting.

Obviously those early braking systems were extremely rudimentary. Most of them featured a kind of external contracting type of design that employed bands made of cast iron, wire rope, hemp, leather, elm or cotton belting to produce the needed friction. Means of transmitting the actuating power began as a simple lever which slowly evolved into a rather complex series of rods, shafts, cams and pivot points that all required constant adjustment to ensure even the lowest level of braking performance. As time went on, the problem of stopping the ever faster and heavier automobiles eventually led to the demise of external contracting brakes and a switch to the more powerful internal expanding shoe-to-drum designs.

Further refinements by the "middleteens" incorporated the use of new linings made of woven asbestos impregnated with bits of metal, and a gradual switch to a 4-wheel braking system brought on by various racing experiences here and abroad.

The Roaring Twenties saw the first U.S.-built passenger car equipped with hydraulic, not mechanical, brakes . . . an honor falling to the mighty Duesenberg. Most brakes during this period still depended upon mechanical linkage to synchronize and transmit the urge from the driver to the brake. Because women couldn't muster the necessary pull those old brakes needed, there began a drift toward a sort of self-energized type of drum brake.

By the '30's, the era of the mechanical brake was drawing to a close—Ford for a while, Bugatti forever, managed to thumb their noses—as the industry swung toward hydraulics while the clouds of war gathered over Europe.

As you might gather, the war years brought about many new automotive innovations, with a revolution in brake and lining technology just a matter of course. Big, heavy trucks, high-speed aircraft and lumbering armor—operating in some of the most god-forsaken spots under equally poor conditions—demanded and got brakes that could and would perform well anywhere in the world.

The termination of hostilities and the ever increasing trend to lower and lower automotive silhouettes put the drum brake and its designers to even more of a test. To come up with better and more consistent stopping power, increasing advances in metallurgy, hydraulics and lining makeup

1. Despite the growing success of disc brake systems, the refined and efficient drum brake is still the automotive standard for stopping.

2. Most cars today use self-energized, servo-action brakes. Servo-action merely means that both shoes are linked so that the action of one shoe is used to further multiply the work of the other (secondary) shoe. When the shoes "wrap-up", they conform closely to the surface of the drum for maximum braking contact area.

3. In the past, some cars have used the leading-shoe type of drum brake, like this '62 Chrysler. In this type each shoe has it's own wheel cylinder and there is no wrap-up effect.

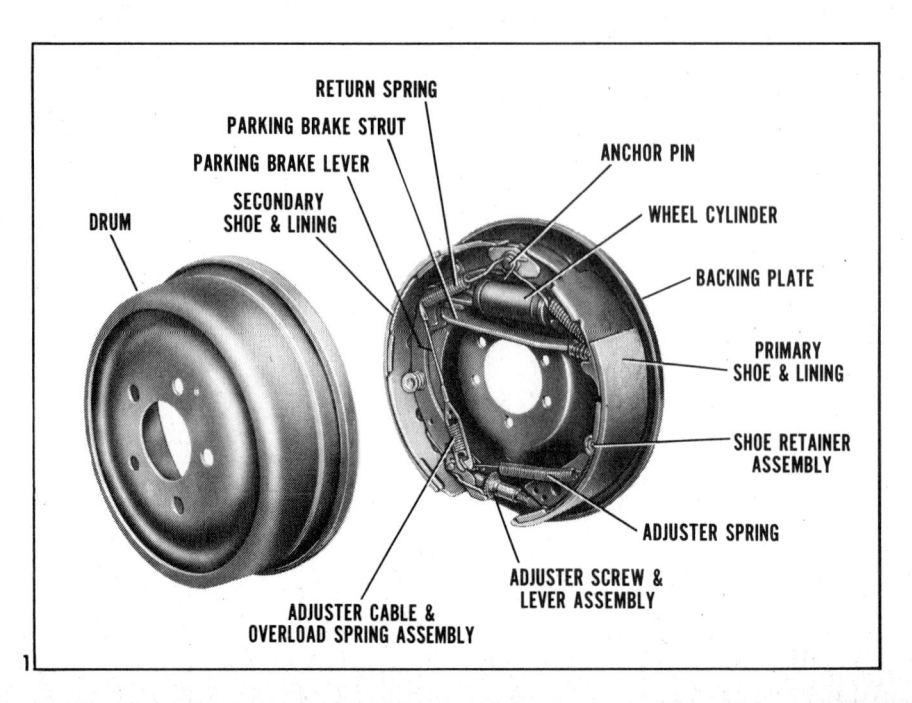

96/CHASSIS, SUSPENSION & BRAKES

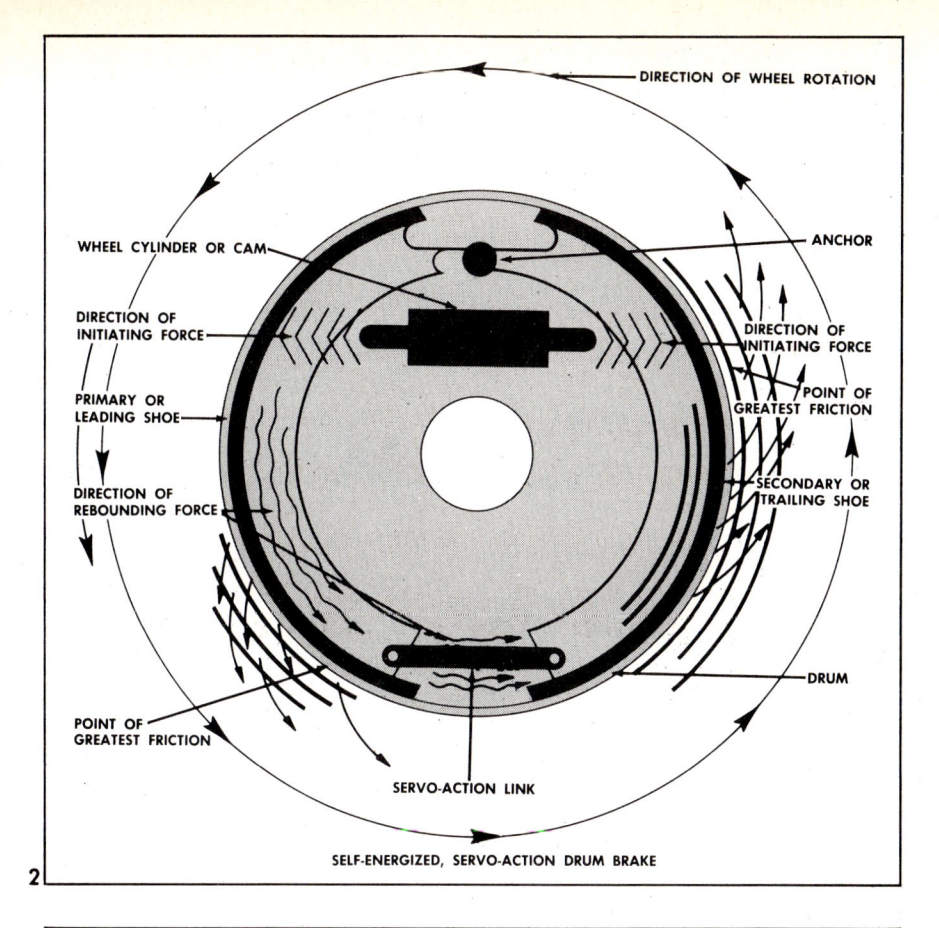

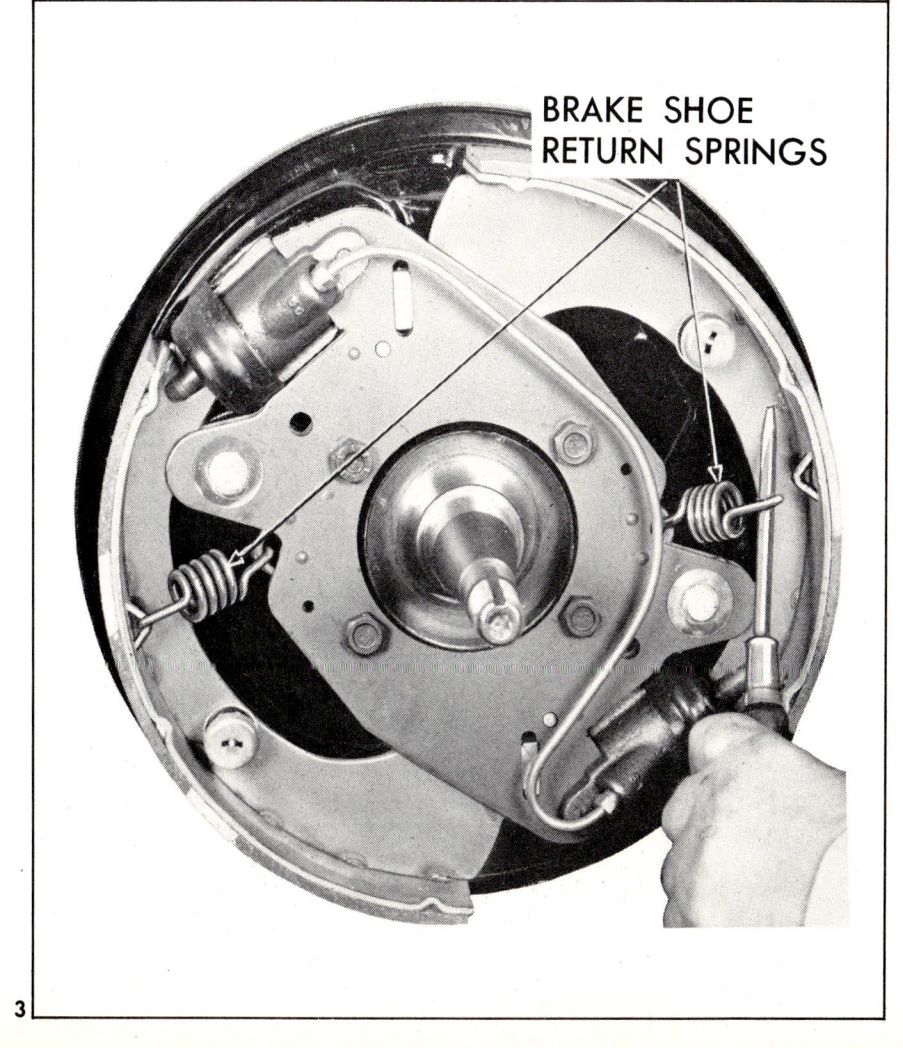

were soon offset by rising costs, wrap-around styling and the advent of a new type of external contracting brake... the disc. Yet as the '60's, with its experimentation in metallic linings, 2-piece drum castings, power-boosted hydraulic systems, multi-section shoes and non-self-energizing brake designs—have slipped by, there still remains that fight left in the old drum brake ... which should be reason enough to delve into this thing a little further.

BASIC DRUM BRAKE THEORY AND DESIGN

While the essential prerequisite of any braking system is to stop a moving vehicle, how it goes about it is the primary concern of basic brake design. Your car may be able to decelerate on a dime, but what good is it if in doing so you're fighting four locked wheels while ricocheting off various and sundry cars parked alongside the curb. It's for this reason that we'll pause for a while and discuss the basics of drum braking.

Although there is a vast array of styles and types of drum brakes, you induce friction (which drags you to a stop) either by the expansion or contraction of the brake shoe against the revolving drum. Comtemporary drum brakes employ expansion (the pressing outward of the brake shoe against the inside of the brake drum, while their disc counterparts use contraction (like squeezing) to produce a like effect. Yet there was, during the early days of automotive braking systems, a time when the most common form of brakes employed the contraction principle. As we have said, your car evolved from a carriage, and stopping a carriage during the latter part of the 19th century was accomplished literally by brake "shoes"... like a discarded pair of spats nailed firmly to a wooden block and operated by a long lever. When this arrangement was set in motion, the friction of the spats against the rotating wheel was evidently enough to get things stopped. This was probably your first "spat" brake; but we're not really interested in these. It's time to drum up a little interest in the other type... those that have internal expanding shoes.

Drum brakes are generally comprised of a number of similarities such as material make-up, lining design, shoe shapes, springs, backing plates, adjusters, the means of activation (wheel cylinders or cams) and many other minor innards. The basic difference with drum brakes is in design; that is, whether they energize themselves during the braking process or whether they derive all their energy from an outside power boosting device.

CHASSIS, SUSPENSION & BRAKES/97

Drum Brakes

To begin with, all brakes need a means to initiate a braking action which usually falls to the driver. Forget how that action is transmitted—be it by a wooden handle, a set of cables, steel rods, hydraulic fluid, compressed air or electric current. Once the impetus is broadcast from the driver's foot or hand to the point of input (the hydraulic wheel cylinder or mechanical cam), then some physical laws begin to make themselves felt. Initially brakes were activated by a 1:1 ratio, but that proved to be inadequate to get things slowed down. Something had to be designed to help the driver out. Presto-stoppo, *slow* and behold, there came upon the scene the commonly known "self-energizer" drum brake.

SELF-ENERGIZING BRAKES

In a basic discussion of brake operation, you must begin with a general understanding of the two types of ways to induce shoe pressure against the brake drum. If the shoe pressure is helped along by a reaction of shoe against drum, you have what is called self-energization. On the other hand, if 100% of the shoe pressure comes from a source outside the brake drum, then we're talking about a non-self-energizing brake.

Self-energizers were originally designed because the early braking systems couldn't scare up enough line pressure to adequately stop a moving vehicle, especially one driven by a woman. What was needed was a means to multiply the initial oomph to a point where the brakes stopped themselves . . . and it worked.

When the brake was operated, the shoes were forced against the rotating drum by the pressure from a wheel cylinder or cam attached to the backing plate. However, it was quickly found that the brake shoe would go with the spinning drum if some means weren't found to retain the shoe against the drum, hence an anchor point. The location of the anchoring pin became the foundation on which all self-energized brakes were and are now based, because as the brakes were applied, the friction generated by the shoes against the drum tried to twist the shoe around its anchoring point. This "leading shoe" generated a force much greater than that originally applied by the wheel cylinder or cam. In other words, the brake engineers began to use the weight of the drum's spinning motion as a lever to force the shoe against the drum in a one-two punch progression. The initiating force of the wheel cylinder or cam pushing the shoes into the turning drum, fol-

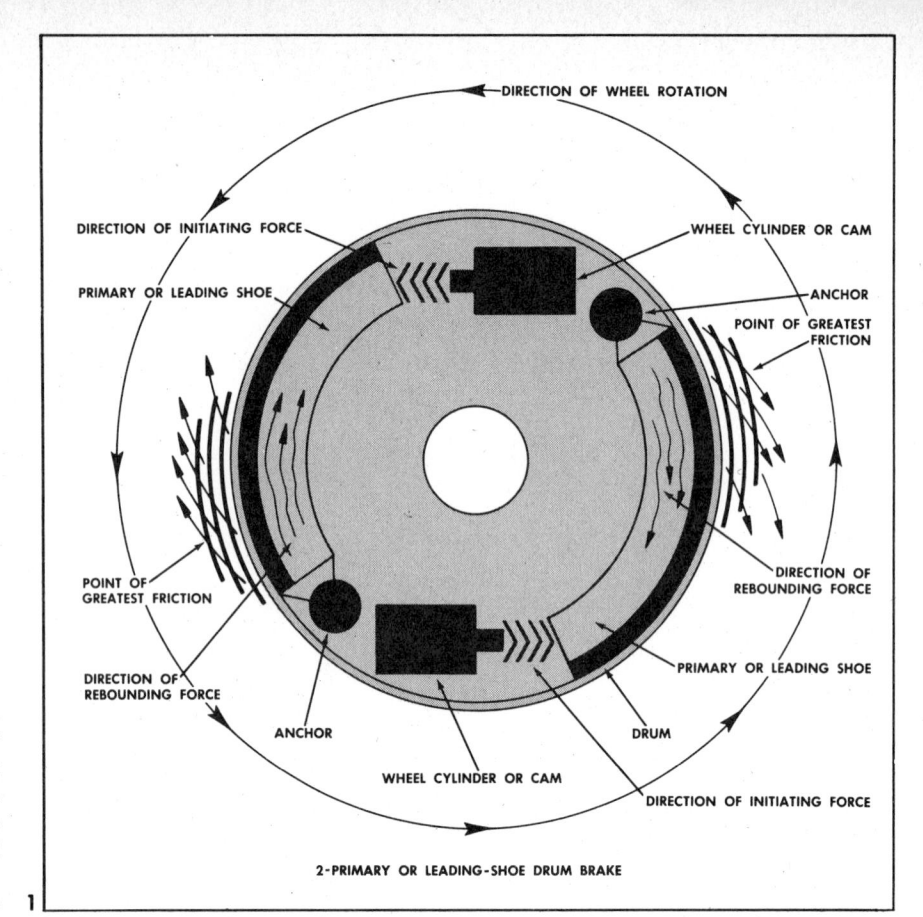

1

2-PRIMARY OR LEADING-SHOE DRUM BRAKE

2

98/CHASSIS, SUSPENSION & BRAKES

lowed by the frictional force of the leading shoe action, was the basic bang-bang of any self-energized braking system.

WHAT'S THIS SERVO THING?

Self-energized brakes can be classed into two distinct groups: servo-action and non-servo-action.

Servo-action brakes are typified by their reliance on a primary/secondary shoe relationship, with some kind of linking device needed to transmit the force from one shoe to the other. The primary shoe (the first punch) initiates the action by sending the rebounding force generated by the shoe's friction against the brake drum through a link usually serving double duty as an adjuster. From the link, the force travels up a secondary shoe, which (when attached to an anchor point) acts against the drum because the primary shoe is pushing on it and because it is self-energized. Because this secondary shoe does most of the braking, you'll find it covered with a greater amount of lining material. In short, servo action is merely a term for the linking of one shoe to the other as a means of multiplying (in either direction) the self-energizing process.

The other basic type of self-energized brake is what we know as a 2-primary shoe-er. Instead of having to rely on the secondary shoe to provide the majority of stopping power, brake designers began splitting the system by discarding the linking device (that ol' servo) and attaching in its place two anchor points to the backing plate, with a second wheel cylinder or cam so each shoe worked independently of the other. While the self-energizing principle remains the same (bang-bang), the brake now does twice the work, because both

1. The primary or leading-shoe brake is also self-energizing, but the the shoes work independently, and the self-energizing is away from the wheel cylinder and adjacent to the anchor points of the shoes.

2. Ford's little Courier mini-truck is one of the few modern cars with the dual-cylinder brakes. The only problem with two primary shoe brakes is that there is no self-energizing when driving the car in reverse.

3. This pre-'49 Ford brake typifies early drum brake designs which had self-energizing action on only the primary shoe, which is why that shoe has a bigger lining here. By contrast, later cars have the larger lining on the secondary shoe because the servo action makes it do much of the work.

4. A modern application of the leading-trailing design like the early Ford is Chevy's Vega rear brake. The braking power with this design is the same in either direction, given the same size linings on each shoe.

shoes are leading. It works like this . . .

As with the servos, the wheel cylinder or cam forces the brake shoe into the rotating drum, which (by its friction) locks the shoe firmly against the anchor point. As there is no linking device to transmit the pressure to the opposite shoe, the force ends up by pulling the heel of the primary or leading shoe up against the turning drum in typical self-energizing fashion. As you can see, by splitting the braking action into two equal but separate leading shoe systems, the effectiveness of the brake can be doubled. What's more, the brakes will usually provide greater wheel bearing life, increase the longevity of the lining, eliminate the need for different lining materials, and possibly reduce an ever-present tendency for chattering, squeaking or grabbing. But these two types of self-energizing brakes do

Drum Brakes

have their drawbacks.

Unfortunately, when it came to self-energized brakes, the pioneers in the field soon found all that glittered was not gold. Too much self-energizing in a leading shoe setup would wrap up the brake shoes to such an extent that they became tighter than a drum (pardon the pun). This produced an unenviable condition called locking brakes; locking brakes were, as they are to this day, both dangerous and damaging. To circumvent this self-destructive habit, a whole new set of principles concerning pivot pin placement, shoe lining degree of contact and anchor point location were conceived. By controlling the shoe's leverage against the drum, or varying this or that pin location, point of contact, and degree of attack, brake designers could come up with a happy medium of good stopping power coupled with an absence of any built-in over energizing.

When we discussed the principle of a 2-primary or leading shoe drum brake, we purposely left out a major drawback... and that's what it is. When backing up, a two-leading-shoe brake loses all its self-energization. The split cylinder/cam-to-anchor pin system allows the shoes to work in only one direction, unlike its servo-action cousin which, by the very nature of its linking device, works in either direction. Like we've said, self-energization multiplies a one-to-one line pressure many fold. But when you reverse this procedure, you'll find yourself with a 2-secondary or trailing shoe brake (non-self-energized and all) facing a one-to-one-er—with not enough leg power to get the job done—as you slide slowly into the sunset. For this reason, 2-primary or leading shoe brakes are used only up front, while the servos are saved for the rear. For a little on the non-self-energizers, be patient; they're next.

NON-SELF-ENERGIZERS

Back to the blackboard. Remember, the early brakes were what we called non-self-energizing in design. However, due to the need to stop heavier and faster cars, coupled with the desires of the little woman to get behind the wheel (and it was a *wheel* in those days), something had to be done to stop that Stutz... hence the self-energizing brake. But as speed and weights continued to climb, so did the need to find better, more consistent braking action. By the time the war came to a close, the state of the art in hydraulic designs had come to a point where power-assisting units could now be included on most braking systems, which consequently made non-self-energizing brakes quite practical. Those power boosters gave the driver enough poop to do the braking himself without having to leave it up to any self-energization.

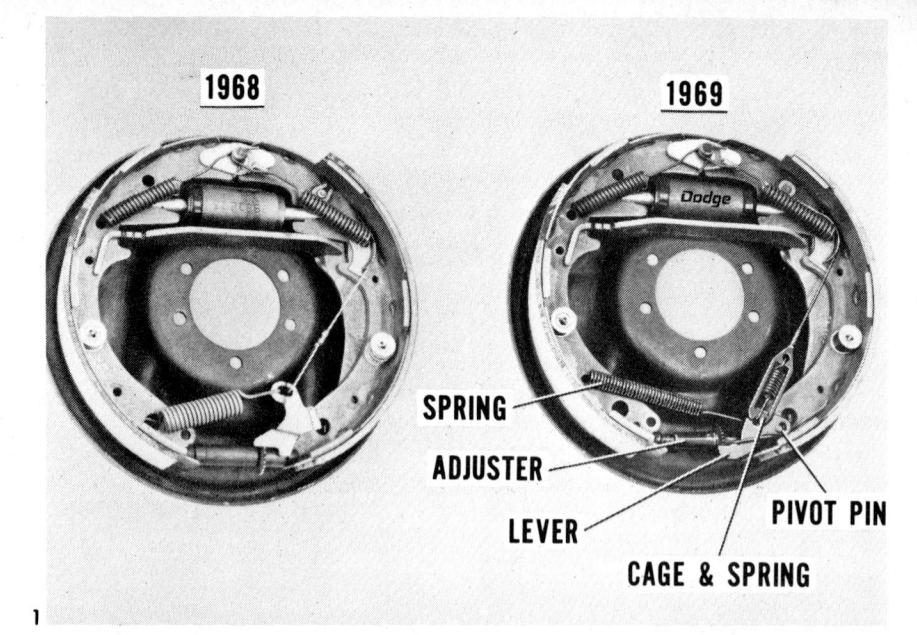

When contemplating a non-self-energizing, 2-trailing/secondary-shoe brake, just remember what we have discussed about a 2-leading/primary-shoe brake, but reverse its order of action. Better yet, look at the whole thing this way.

Run your hand over the nap of an ordinary living room rug. Now as you go with the grain, notice how smooth the action is, even as you bear down (and you've really got to bear down to get any brake-producing friction). On the other hand, when you move your hand against the flow of the nap, see how chattery it feels—along with the fact that it doesn't take very much pressure to achieve a braking friction. Well, the same holds true when you begin to compare a self-energizing to a non-self-energizing brake. By locating the brake shoes in a manner where the action goes with the grain, the stopping force is much smoother, more consistent, easier, and according to one prominent British brake expert, it's equal to any disc braking system on paper. Yet it seems that economics are playing an important role in the development of 2-trailing-shoe drum brakes. They're costly to produce... but this type of brake *is* out there (in Europe) for those who want to equip their car with it.

100/CHASSIS, SUSPENSION & BRAKES

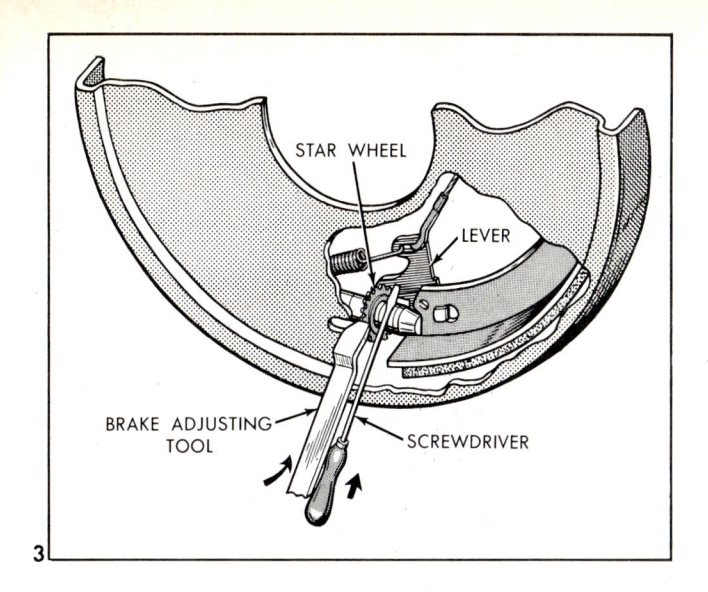

1. Self-adjusting brakes have been around since the '58 Edsel, but some people used to remove them because they over-adjusted. Dodge modified theirs in '69 for even adjustment and more consistent pedal height.

2. For more drum cooling with the wraparound styling of today's cars, brake engineers have been turning to finned drums for greater drum-to-air heat transfer.

3. Self-adjusting brakes such as most cars now have require two tools to adjust manually after a brake job. A small screwdriver or piece of thin welding rod is used to push the self-adjuster out of the way while you turn the adjusting star-wheel.

4. If your wheels are dynamically balanced, you should mark (circled) the wheel and the hub so that the wheel goes back the same way each time, as the drum is part of balance.

5. Ever wondered what those spring bands are around your brake drums? They dampen vibrations in the drum for smoother, quieter braking.

6. When Dodge went to cooling fins on their drums, they also changed the drum's shape to allow more air inside and prevent chattering by keeping the edges of the shoes off the drums.

7. Popular among hot rodders, drum brake swapping is an easy way to update your brakes without going to a disc system. This is a finned '67 GTO drum on the front of a '64 Chevy.

8. When doing brake service on your car for the first time, you may find flat steel Tinnerman nuts (arrows) on some of the studs. Don't worry about replacing them, they're just factory assembly-line aids.

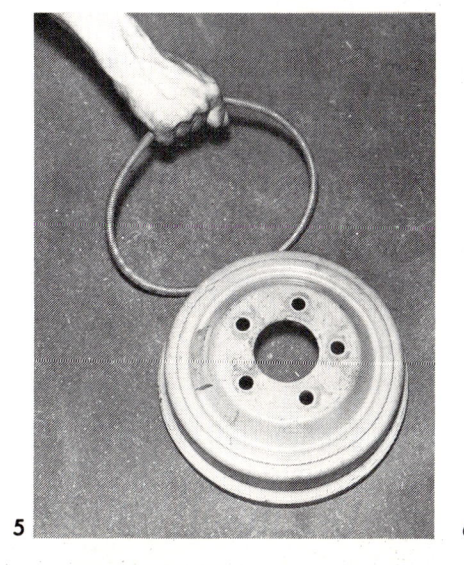

YOU'RE FADED!

While it's nice to be able to exert all kinds of pressure inside the brake drum, it doesn't mean a thing if the linings and drums can't stand the gaff of converting motion to heat, then dissipating that heat away from the braking surface and into the surrounding atmosphere.

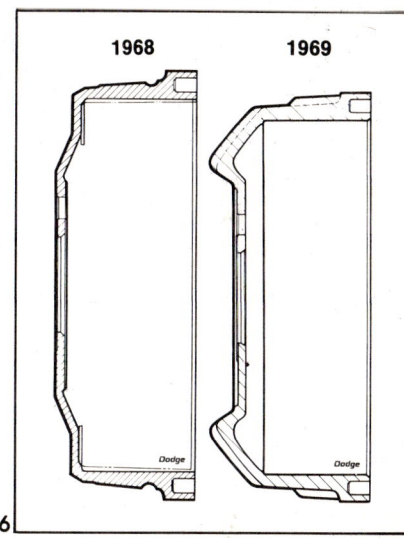

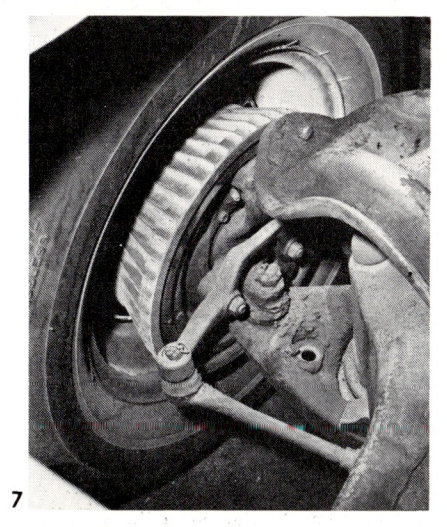

Obviously, heat is the drum brake's (any brake's for that matter) worst enemy; its ability to resist heat's ravages is of prime importance—and to do so successfully is harder than the Biblical place of eternal damnation.

When heat rears its ugly head to impede the braking process, it's known as fade. Finding a single cause for fade is something else, for fade is the result of a combination of events. First of all, as more heat is poured into the drum than can be sluffed off, the metal begins to lose its strength and rigidity. The outward pressure of the shoes, all the while, forces the drums to bow out and

CHASSIS, SUSPENSION & BRAKES/101

Drum Brakes

warp away from the shoes. This constant heating and cooling cycle, as the brakes are on, then off, eventually elongates the drums to a point where they're literally out-of-round, and cannot make full contact with the lining. Tied to this out-of-round condition is the brake lining's inability to retain its proper coefficient of friction (ability to bite) as it grows hotter and hotter. So as your drums grow and elongate, the lining glazes and loses its bite and you begin to run into that old black magic called fade.

Most of us have experienced heat-induced fade. In the wetter climes water will do the same thing. What happens here is that water leaking through the space between the backing plate and the brake drum begins to mix with the brake shoe dust and soak into the pores in the drums and lining. You can guess the rest. Those shoes and drums, lubricated with that mixture, get slipperier than greased slicks on a wet railroad track. It's a funny thing, but those self-energized brakes are the most susceptible to water-induced fade because they depend upon all that friction/leverage stuff. Non-self-energizers, due to their high-pressure design, are much more tolerant of wet drums and lining. They can more easily throw off the effects of a case of dripping drums.

So as the brakes either become too hot (you're now talking about +1200°) with the drums expanding away from the shoes and the lining turning to dust, or with water adding a bit of slip to an otherwise stabber-grabber, we might as well find a way or two to lick this problem . . . before your brakes just fade away.

WHAT'S TO COME OF DRUMS

How the engineers have combatted fade has been interesting because for the most part they've had their share of problems. Ideally, all they needed to do was to build a drum that would throw off heat as rapidly as it was produced by the friction of the shoes. This, so far, hasn't been easy. Drum design and construction has been tied to the fact that the best brake drum surface material was and is pearlitic grey cast iron. This high-quality, fine-grained material—a mixture of carbon, silicon, sulphur, phosphorus, chromium and manganese—has still proven (after years of success) to make the best mating surface. However, it just doesn't throw off the heat fast enough. Steel, aluminum and a wide variety of other combinations have been put through the experimental wringer but, in the end, brake designers return to pearl.

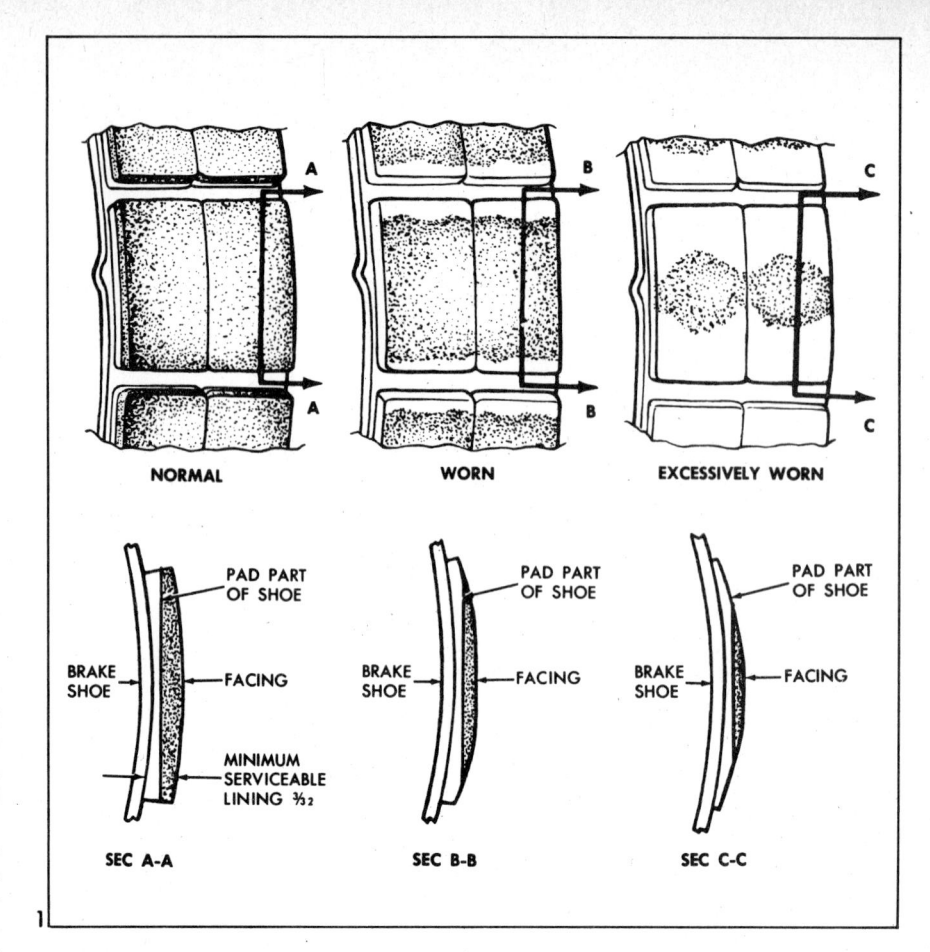

Some car manufacturers have tried to use drums made of aluminum and lined with pearlitic iron, but this process—while an improvement—is quite expensive (try $80 per copy for a combination aluminum/iron Lincoln brake drum). Another method would be to go to much larger, highly finned drums (like the grand prix cars of the '30's); however, this would fly in the face of our low-silhouetted, wrap-around automotive styling which precludes the use of anything so large for brake drums.

A LITTLE ON LININGS

To further combat the problem of fade, brake engineers have put a great deal of time and effort into brake lining research. There was once a time when brake lining was nothing more than the heel of a worn shoe, or some rope nailed to a lever that rubbed against a wheel. As the automobile was transformed from a buggy to a bomber, the linings had to keep pace. By the early '20's, woven cotton fabric—impregnated with various bits and pieces—had given way to molded asbestos interwoven with metallic bands as a means to combat the ever increasing demands of mighter motor cars. As always, the search for better, more heat-resistant lining compounds has been pursued. For example, within the last few years, there has been renewed inter-

1. You can tell by the look of your linings whether they are seated right or whether they are wearing wrong because the drum has warped.

2. Really worn drums are dangerous because they can flex away from the shoes under high braking pressures. Note the ridge left on the outside edge of this overly-abused drum.

3. When arcing a brake shoe on a special grinder, brake repairmen sometimes grind a groove down the center of the lining. Even though contact area may be reduced, braking can be improved due to the improved cooling and resistance to glaze.

4. Combination drum/shoe gauge can be used to determine whether a drum is warped or out-of-round, as well as whether it's too worn to turn.

5. When drums are within suggested tolerances, they can be turned on a brake lathe for a smooth, new finish. This is a finned aluminum drum with a pearlitic grey iron liner.

6. Manual adjustment of drum brakes is done through the backing plate with a screwdriver or special tool. After adjusting, the stock rubber plug should be replaced to keep dust and moisture out of the brakes.

7. Since the edges of brake shoes ride on the "nubs" of the backing plate, these areas should be lubed with high-temp grease in a rebuild.

8. Other than normal box, open, or socket wrenches, these are all the tools normally needed in overhauling drum brakes, and in a pinch other more common tools can be substituted.

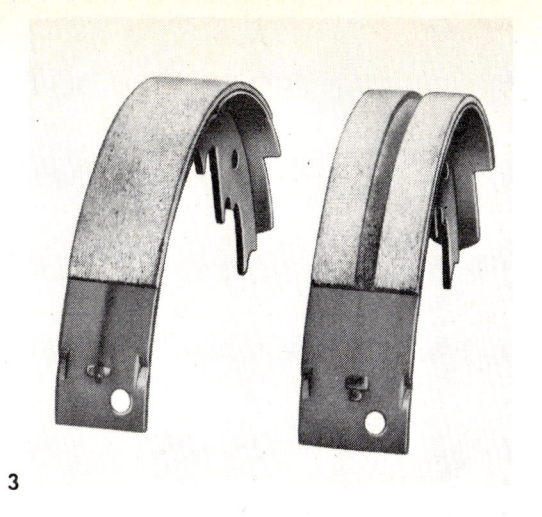

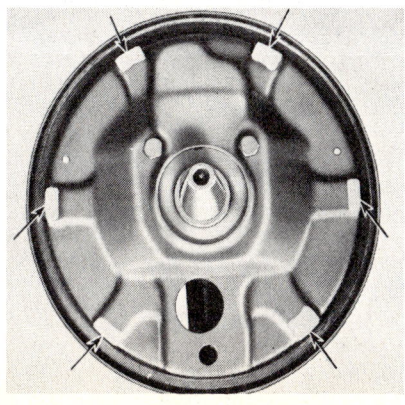

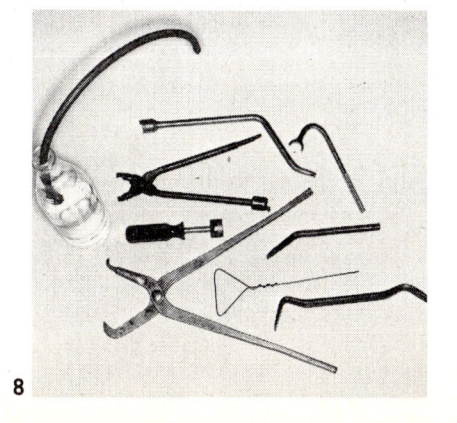

est in hard, metallic-segmented lining coupled with power-boosting master cylinder devices to provide smoother, fade-withstanding brakes, free from squeak or chattering.

Remember, as we discuss technology, keep in mind that linings must encompass these four characteristics: (a) prolonged resistance to wear; (b) ability to live under high temperatures; (c) smoothness of operation through reduced tendency of chatter or squeaking, and (d) retention of an excellent coefficient of friction. Like camshafts, there has really been no *one* answer—what brakes are asked to do by their users will greatly influence their design principles, size, and lining makeup.

RIVETING OUR ATTENTION

Another factor in brake linings is how they are attached to the brake shoe. As we have said before, they were originally nailed to some sort of wheel-fitting, half-moon shoe which in turn was attached to a kind of lever. Time continued its steady pace and lining technology followed suit—rivets replaced nails, and laminates were substituted for rivets. Obviously, the latter two methods of attaching brake linings to their shoes are to this day still quite popular, as well as controversial. Each method has its pros and cons . . . so we'll briefly touch upon both.

Riveted lining remains a favorite when it comes to holding the lining to the brake shoes. Rivets can be made from just about anything metallic. They are generally attached to the brake shoes through countersunk holes drilled in the brake lining. Definite and specific clearances as to rivet head and shank diameters are thoroughly formulated, with the same holding true as to numbers and placement in relation to severity of use and/or application.

When it comes to relining time, riveted lining has usually been the cheapest to purchase as you are just buying the lining, not the shoe. That is—unless the shoe is warped, the welds broken, rivet holes elongated or the pivots points badly distorted—you can generally reuse the shoes. Let's face it, all you have to do is to knock off the old, sneak on some new, slip in a rerivet job and be on your way. Brake shops try to get in as much rerivet work as they can because the lining is much easier to store in bulk and the time needed to turn out a first class brake job is much shorter. Another positive aspect of using riveted lining is that the very holes in which the rivets rest also indicate, by their depth, how much lining remains on the shoe. This plus a squeak-resisting tendency makes riv-

CHASSIS, SUSPENSION & BRAKES/103

Drum Brakes

eted lining a continuing favorite among automobile manufacturers and brake shops.

A BIT ON BONDING

Bonded lining, on the other hand, has become increasingly popular in brake shoe circles for a number of reasons, mostly stemming from longer lining life. Rivet heads take up quite a bit of lining area, both in the holes they rest in and the amount of depth the head uses in that hole. Someone figured that the head depth plus hole removes a little over a third of the total brake area throughout the life of the lining. Looking at it in another way, once the rivet head begins to protrude above the surface of the lining, then that lining must be changed or the metal-to-metal contact of drum-to-rivet will score and eventually ruin the drum.

But bonding does have its disadvantages. Bonded lining tends to squeak more than good riveted lining, and debonding those brake shoes can be a monumental task unless you have the right equipment. Just for this reason, bonding and rebonding should always be left up to the pros. Even the large majority of brake shops send out all their bonding work because of the knowhow, expense and time needed to go through the process of sweating off the lining, allowing the shoes to cool without warping, then rebonding on the fresh lining. Obviously this is, (and has always been) strictly a specialized shop operation, so forget about doing it yourself.

PIVOTS, PINS AND ANCHORS

A final aspect of drum brake design is pin, pivot, and anchor location. Much of the braking effect is accomplished by leverage, whether it be self-energizing or gained through high piston pressures. There are reams of formulas set up and followed by brake engineers that govern each and every pivot point location of the backing plate, anchor pin size, angle of lining attack, degree of lining contact, ad infinitum. All these variables of brake design control the precise workings of the unit. These formulas are the tuning processes, the subtle differences that separate one brake from another.

As you can see, it all boils down to the fact that those simple, old drum brakes aren't quite as simple as you would be led to believe. They're a rather complicated piece of braking mechanism and as such have undoubtedly caused many sleepless nights among overworked automotive designers.

Now that you've gotten through a short discourse on how and why drum brakes work the way they do, putting what we've said into practical use by doing our own down-and-dirty brake job should make it all worthwhile. Anyway, let's give it a whirl.

Elsewhere in this book are three pictorial features on drum, disc and metallic brakes. The photographs and illustrations will show many of the various parts and operations associated with these braking systems, and how the poor guy in the field gets them squared away.

A "QUEEK PEEK" INTO THE FUTURE

Detroit is in the midst of switching to disc brakes, on the front at least. The engineers claim it isn't production-feasible on a solid axle rear end, although the Europeans have been doing it for years. For 1974, power front disc brakes are standard equipment on many cars, while optional on most others. There are many reasons why the moguls of Motor City haven't gone completely to disc brakes, aside from discarding a tooling investment built up over a 50-year span of drum brake manufacture; so maybe we should explore a few of these reasons.

We touched briefly upon non-self-energized, or 2-trailing-shoe brakes—

1. On some cars like this Vega, the brakes can only be adjusted with the wheel off, through a hole in the drum. In this case, the hole has a plug that must be punched out first.

2. When there is no hole for your adjusting tool in either the drum or the backing plate, the shoes must be adjusted with a gauge before the drums and wheels are installed.

3. Any brake job should include a thorough check of hydraulic lines. Cracked hoses like this can rupture dangerously under panic conditions.

4. Some cars today are equipped with a proportioning valve to keep proper balance between front and rear brake pressures for straighter stops. You can often adapt one of these to any other car for the same improvements.

5. The parking brake mechanism is found on rear brakes only, and uses cables to pull on a pivoted lever which pushes both the secondary shoe and the primary (through a strut) shoe out against the drum.

6. After, and only after, adjusting your rear brakes, you can adjust the parking or "emergency" brake. Just use the adjusting nuts to take up any slack in the cables without drag.

on paper, at least, the equal of a disc brake system. However, a major hurdle in their further development is high production costs which may eventually stifle the switch to this smooth-stopping, consistently-operating drum brake.

Linings again come under closer

104/CHASSIS, SUSPENSION & BRAKES

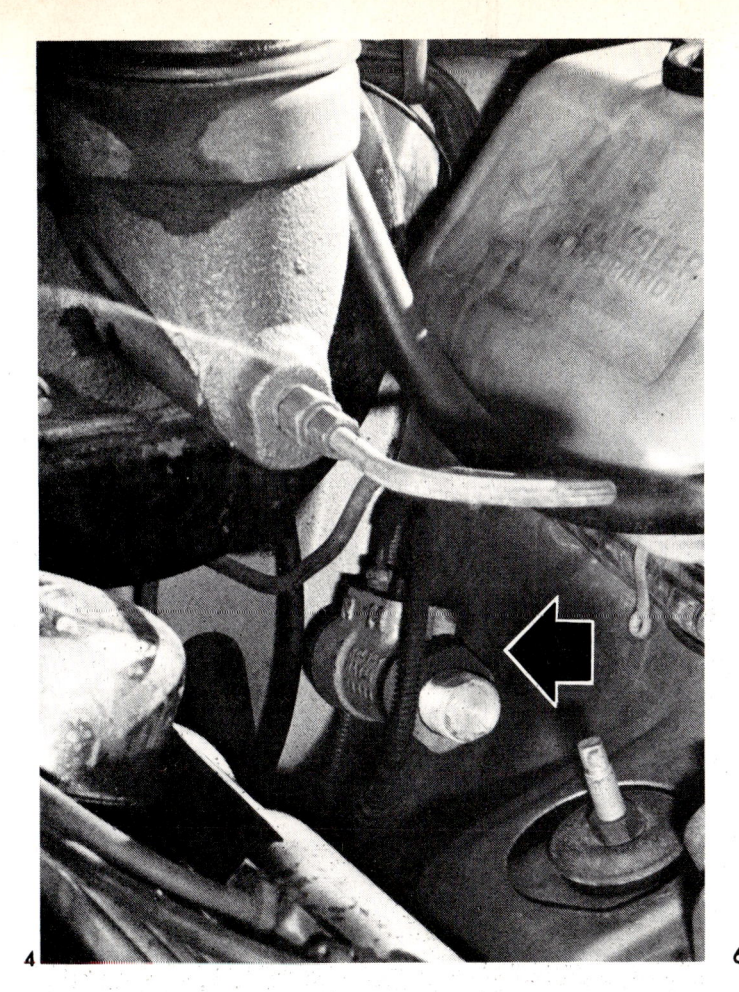

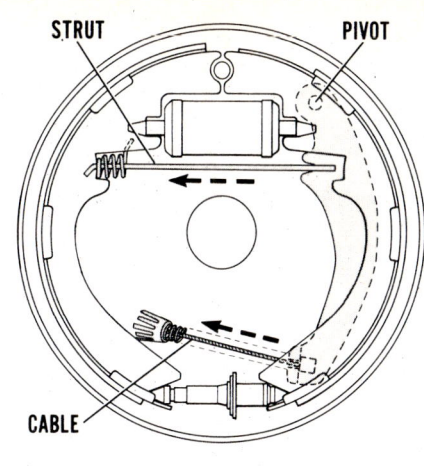

5 PARKING BRAKE

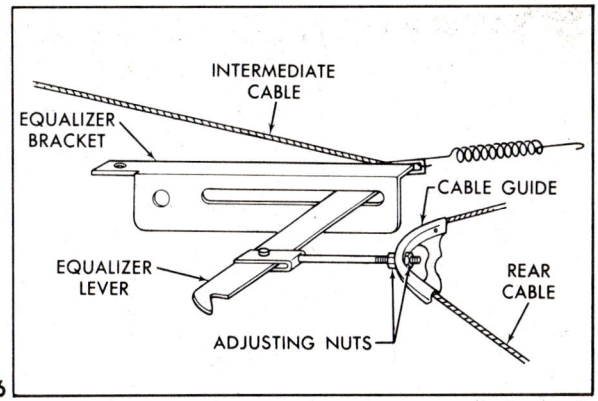

scrutiny because of a renewed interest in metallic linings, especially in heavy-duty or bad weather conditions. Metallic linings require a smoother drum surface than that needed by other types of linings. Up until a couple of years ago, grinding an ultra smooth surface was pretty costly. But a rolling process—using a special attachment anchored to a brake drum lathe—can roll flat the ridges left by the cutting tool, leaving a 15-20 micro-in. finish. This is just what the doctor ordered.

Metallic linings have been around for many years, but not until recently was the problem of premature drum wear solved satisfactorily. These new linings now available feature superior stopping power along with long lining life, like 50,000 miles or more. Actually, their greatest advantage is complete resistance to fade, in fact they work even better when hot. Just the ticket for high-performance cars and trucks or campers that may travel on long grades.

There are already segmented linings (of various combinations) on the market as well as a gaggle of new methods to facilitate their attachment on the shoe itself, such as clip- or slide-on designs.

There is even a little thunder on lining contact itself. Some people believe that full contact can be detrimental to good braking while helping to reduce the life expectancy of the brake lining. This controversy surrounds the actual grinding of the lining as to specific points to reduce contact, but it still seems to be a personal thing, left up to individual tastes, and nothing definite has been released by any manufacturer.

Drums themselves are undergoing continual testing, especially with an eye toward new space age compounds for better heat dissipation, a greater use of deep finning and lower-cost combination drums.

Probably as important as the continued developments in design and execution of drum brakes themselves is their servicing in the field.

When it comes to this aspect, there has been an on-and-off battle between the various brake manufacturers and the independent brake shops. It all centers around some kind of standardization policy concerning acceptable relining procedures. While the manufacturer is worried only about his particular unit, those specialty shops are constantly having to service any number of differing brakes. Consequently, there is a much needed reform push by those who speak in behalf of the brake shops for a general across-the-board way of relining and regrinding, no matter what type.

From its crude beginnings—as a shoe dragged against a turning wheel—to a technically complex piece of stopping mechanism, the drum brake has undergone countless changes and refinements, yet still remains relatively inexpensive to build, and easy to repair. Much has been done to improve stopping power under some pretty improbable road conditions, but much more needs to be done to make drum brakes equal to the vehicles they're asked to control. Whether Detroit will take up the challenge will be the story of the '70's.

Grinding to a halt is, unfortunately, the first indication given the "point A-to-B driver" that something is amiss in that all-important area between his car's wheels and suspension. There are plenty of drivers who will go to great lengths to stretch that last mile out of those weary brake linings, yet cry a mean blue streak when they find out they have gone beyond that point of no return with a set of scored drums as "goof positive." Cry as they will, the fact is that the most important safety accessories on any automobile are those hard-working brakes and when they get sick, it's a fool who neglects the patient. Curing the problem is a relatively inexpensive operation, yet when left too long it can turn into a wallet deflator.

CHASSIS, SUSPENSION & BRAKES/105

Overhauling Drum Brakes

Shoe relining and parts "freshening" is an at-home job. It's easy if done right.

We'll assume if you're reading this story that you're doing so because your brakes are acting up. Maybe your pedal is down to the floor, and squishy at that, or maybe you can hear that telltale grinding noise from the vicinity of your brakes as you screech to a halt, hoping for your sake that the guy in front of you hasn't got substantially better brakes himself. Instead of quibbling over whether you'll get a sponge rubber front bumper or a mushroom mooring anchor to solve your plight, we'll also assume that you're willing to "do yourself a favor" by doing the complete brake job you should have done 10,000 miles ago. So grab a star-wheel adjuster in one hand and a bleeder wrench in the other as we show'n'tell you through a drum brake overhaul.

Up in the air goes your car, not by a single, solitary bumper jack, but by something a lot more solid, like a good scissor jack, followed by plenty of cribbing on all four corners. Got 'er up? Good! Now we can start whipping the lug nuts off the rears and pulling the dust cap from the front spindles. With the dust cap off, it's just a matter of removing the cotter key from the spindle nut. With this done, give the nut a good twisting session, yank off the tire/wheel/drum combination, and the whole shebang will be at rest in your lap. Or you can get at the rears with a lug wrench first, (older cars require a wheel puller) then move progressively forward. The thing here is to try to find the drums most susceptible to wear as an initial procedure; then if they look all right, you can troubleshoot rather than do a complete brake job. As a rule of thumb, most pros start with the brake that is closest to the master cylinder. They figure the closer to the point of input, the more pressure applied to the wheel cylinders. By this line of reasoning, the left front should be the place to start, so we'll begin there. However, it's best to ask a pro about the wear characteristics of your particular car; he'll start you at the right place.

For the record, a quick eyeballing of the left front tells you right off you've got problems. In fact, the wear is to the point where the rivets are scoring the brake drum. The contact hasn't been severe enough to warrant any replacement worries, but as you slide your fingers across the braking surface, you can detect the gouges and scoring marks. While you're at it, closely inspect the drum's surface for any cracks, checking, and burned spots. Don't just stop there; be sure to see if the drums have begun to take on a barrel-shape or bell-mouth appearance. It's impossible to get even rudimentary braking performance if only a small portion of the drum and the lining come in contact with each other. A brake pro can tell in one glance if a drum will need turning, while chances are the backyard mechanic can't. Most of these guys have mikes for eyes, so as you wind your way to the local parts house, drop by a friendly brake shop and show them your drums. Their eyes, experience and a couple of measuring tools will tell them all they need to know . . . then be sure to take their advice.

Assuming you've got all four drums off (a couple look a little sour) take your time and check—might be a good idea to have a notebook in hand—which part goes where, especially shoe and spring location. OK, so you have a 2-primary (leading shoe) brake where the lining is all the same, but assuming you don't have this type, then check the shoes closely. Your primaries will be of a different color and size from the secondaries, which usually feature a shoe with a greater amount of lining. The important thing here is not to transpose brake shoe linings; this would, if done, lead to early brake failure. Another important thing to remember is where the two brake shoe return springs go. The heavier, beefier spring will be attached to the secondary shoe because it takes more pull to snap it off the drum. Be sure to keep all the parts and pieces in their own pile wheel-for-wheel and front halves and rear halves . . . those goodies are no longer interchangeable as they now have their own separate wear characteristics.

Removing the return springs is only complicated insofar as whether the spring system initiates from the anchor pin or is stretched between the brake shoes. Most of our brakes feature a centralized point (at the anchor pin) on which one end of the return

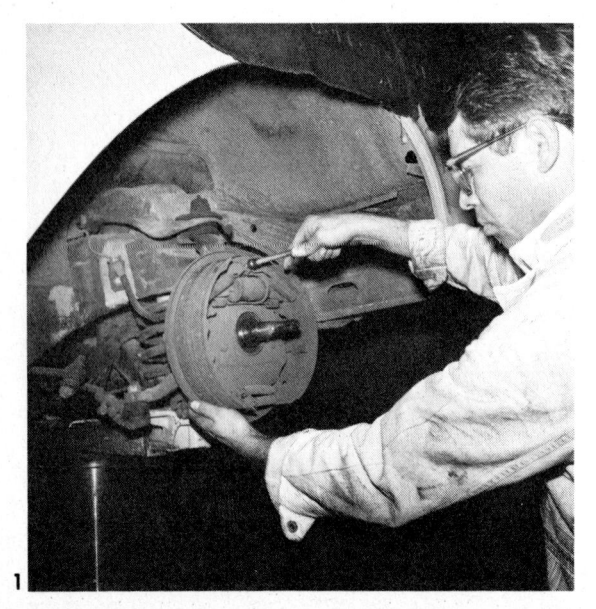

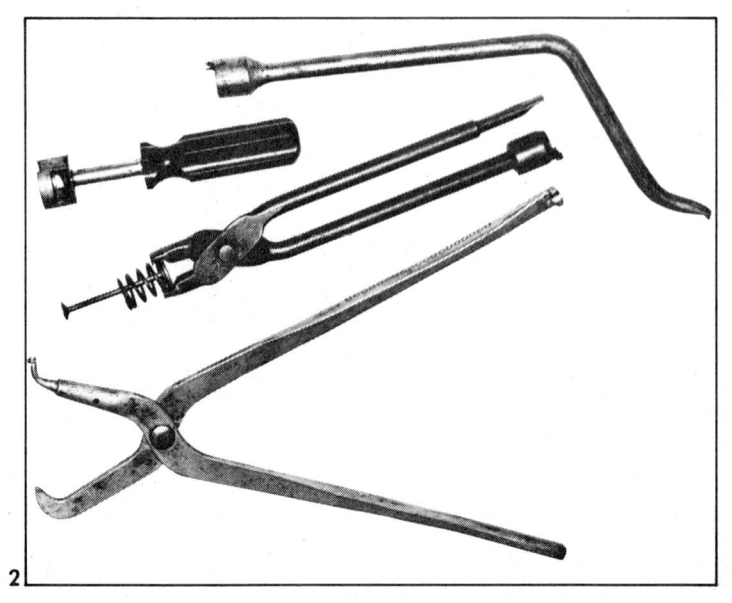

106/CHASSIS, SUSPENSION & BRAKES

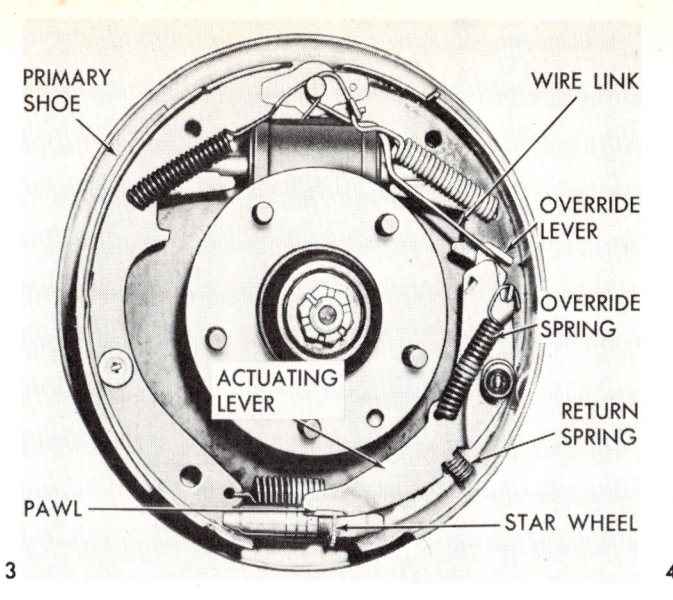

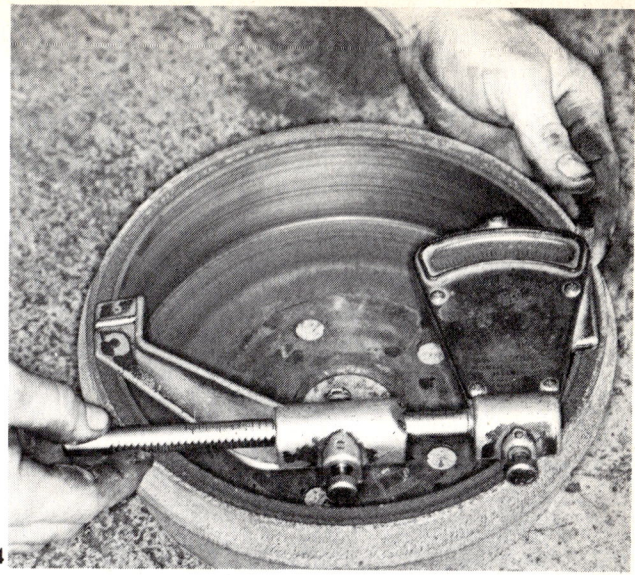

Labels on figure 3:
- PRIMARY SHOE
- WIRE LINK
- OVERRIDE LEVER
- OVERRIDE SPRING
- ACTUATING LEVER
- RETURN SPRING
- PAWL
- STAR WHEEL

1. Overhauling your drum brakes isn't as difficult as you may have thought and if you do a thorough job, you'll get many safe, dependable years of service out of them.

2. Few specialized tools are needed to do a basic brake reline. Some of those you'll find handy are, from the top: shoe return spring tool, shoe hold-down-spring removing tool, a combination tool, and a different type of equalizer spring pliers.

3. Not every drum brake you run into will look exactly like this example, but almost all today are the single anchor, Bendix servo-action type, most with self-adjusters like this.

4. The relationship of the drum size to the size of the linings is the most important factor in a good job. Before cutting, the drums are always measured to see if they're oversize.

5. If a drum is determined to be in the legal-to-cut range and isn't too far out of round, then it's either cut (A) or ground (B) on a brake drum lathe. Sometimes both types of finishing techniques are used.

spring is placed while the other is firmly attached to the brake shoe.

Getting the return springs off is a matter of what you want to use. If you care to spend a few bucks, you can pick up a specialized, all-purpose tool which can do about anything but play the "Flower Drum Song." These plier-like tools have a barrel-shaped end that fits over the anchor pin with a notched lip to engage the spring's shank. All you then have to do is to give the spring a twist and you're done. If, on the other hand, you're experiencing a sinking feeling in the wallet area, grab a pair of vise-grips, get hold of the shank end of that spring and yank 'em off.

However, you may be the guy with a set of early Ford brakes, or the user of some Chrysler products; in any event, these types of brakes feature return springs either spread between the shoes or affixed to various points around the backing plate. Here another portion of your all-everything, handy-dandy brake tool can shine. While the tooth end locates itself in some hole on the lining or shoe, the corkscrew end slides around and down the spring's shank and ends up at the retaining bend. Again put the squeeze on the handle and it's off. Of course, your vise-grips will work just as nicely, but not as easily.

Now when we get to the parking brake (we assume on the rear brakes) just disconnect the cable, remove the parking brake strut or spreader, twist or pull off the return springs and get to removing all the hold-down springs. Whether you do the job with that all-purpose tool again or a pair of common ol' pliers, either will suffice in grabbing and twisting (90°) the little retainer cap to unhook the spring from the shaft. With any luck the total brake shoe

CHASSIS, SUSPENSION & BRAKES/107

Drum Brakes

package—linkage, adjuster and all—will come off in unison. Hooray!

It's time now to open up your trunk (hopefully you have two cars), chalk a wheel placement on each drum (left front, right rear, etc.), grab all your worn shoes (you can get a trade-in on these), and hurry on down to town. There is always the possibility on arrival that the guy who grinds your drums will also sell you some lining. Initially a shop will mike your drums to check for elongation and/or depth of score. These are but two of the many maladies from which drums can suffer, but assuming yours are a bit out-of-round, a little metal has to be removed. If, by chance, the cure will take any more than .060-in. worth, forget it. Those brakes scare up all kinds of pressure and when coupled to lots of heat buildup, they'll warp and fade like right now. Let's say two of your drums check out within the maximum stock allowable tolerance of .010-in., but the other two need a quick .020-in. clean job to clear up the combination scoring and elongation. While they're being turned, you can now select what kind of replacement lining you'll need.

Remember, this lining must be oversized to the extent of compensating for the metal being removed, be it riveted or bonded, and should be cam ground to ensure a good fit. This clearance grinding is usually accomplished on a device called an arc grinder. The new lining is held in place on the shoe while the grinder, preset to a specific arc measured by the drum mike, hones the lining to provide a perfect shoe-to-drum fit. Performing this clearance cutting (.030-in. for VW's, .040-in. for most U.S. makes, .045-in. for late model Chevys from '66 on, due to a suspension idiosyncracy) allows the lining to seat itself more evenly, although many people will tell you to plan on at least 5000 miles of driving before they're fully seated. The only other things you'll need are a set of wheel cylinder kits, a quart of high-quality brake fluid and some alcohol, which is the same as shellac thinner. We mention the kits here because it's false economy not to rebuild your wheel cylinders while the brakes are apart. By the way, the chapter on hydraulics will tell you how to rebuild both your master and wheel cylinders, so we won't go into that subject at this time.

You're now on your way home, loaded with four good drums, fitted lining, wheel cylinder kits, various fluids and a healthy tube of silicon-based brake grease. The rest can be done in your garage.

Your first order of business is to give the backing plates a good cleaning followed by a liberal dab of brake grease at each contact point (this silicon-based grease resists the inroads of high temperatures and allows the shoes to slide freely against the backing plate). Disassemble and again, thoroughly grease up your star adjuster, making sure it revolves freely. With all the parts cleaned and lubed (if needed) you can begin the attachment proceedings. The fronts are relatively easy even if you've got self adjusters; the rears take a little more time. The parking or emergency brake paraphernalia tends to slow things down, so we'll start here.

Initially your attention should be directed toward the parking or emergency brake cable and its attachment to the backing plate. As the cable was disengaged during the removal of the shoes, it should now be reattached to the parking brake lever. Be sure it's well lubed and the actuating cable is free of any kinks or interference. Slacking off on the adjustment will make it a lot easier to put the shoes and drums on. As you remember, we said to make a mental note of which shoes went where, but if you didn't, you'll then have to determine what type of drum brake design you have. Most replacement lining sets are marked "primary" and "secondary" on the edges of the shoes. If it's a primary/secondary type of brake, then the primary shoe will be the front or leading shoe. On the other hand, if you're blessed with a 2-leading-shoe type of brake, shoe location is of little importance; they're both the same . . . and this holds true for some other designs as well.

Be that as it may, the two shoes with the adjuster, parking brake spreader bar and the self-adjusting mechanism should be installed as a unit. Then slip the package onto the anchors, tying the shoe to the backing plate with the hold-down springs. Now attach the shoe links, making sure they're properly seated or centered through the boot onto the piston. With them out of the way, you can install the return springs, ending the procedure with a couple of good whacks on the shoes to ensure their seating correctly against the backing plate with no slop. Everything should be working freely, including the self-adjusting unit.

There is no hard, fast rule in adjusting brakes because there are so

MAXIMUM DIAMETER (OPTIONAL LOCATION)

SEALING COMPOUND

many designs on the market. Some drums on cars originally equipped with self-adjusters have a plug in the drum held in by a little tab. With a punch and hammer you can knock out this plug and thereafter adjust the brakes with drums in place. One make allows no outside adjustment because they've not cut an adjustment window in the backing plate. If you're going to adjust this type of brake, figure on pulling the drums. Then you either guesstimate how much adjustment on the star wheel is enough to bring up the pedal, or go out and scrounge a brake shoe setting gauge (it looks like a crude caliper), measure the sweep of the drum, then adjust the shoes to fit this measurement while allowing a clearance of .005-in. between the lining and the drum.

On the other hand, you may be blessed with windows on the backing plate, but a self-adjusting mechanism is getting in your way. This adjustment arm must be pushed or pulled away from the star adjuster with a screwdriver or a piece of welding rod fashioned for such an occasion, followed by another screwdriver or an adjusting tool. If you're the proud owner of a not-so-complicated piece of braking power, it's just a matter of sticking a screwdriver or adjusting tool through the hole at the back of the backing plate or through the front of the brake drum (like pre-'68 VW's), moving the adjuster in an up-and-down motion while slowly revolving the drum. When contact is made (audio—a low "shuushing" sound), back off the adjuster anywhere from 10 to 20 notches. The automatic adjustment (if any) will take over from there. "But I don't have an automatic adjuster," you say! OK, do the same thing, but drive your car for a week or two, then readjust your brakes... by that time they should have seated properly. Then do a good bleeding job and you can be on your way.

One last reminder; if you depend on your parking or emergency brake for anything but looks, release the hand brake before you begin to adjust your rear brakes. Then start adjusting and bleeding the rears, followed by moving to the parking brake. Getting the feel of proper rear brake adjustment is sometimes hard because the rear axle itself has built-in drag and noise. So just back off the rear brakes completely and get used to the *normal* feel and sound of the rear axle drag before adjusting the shoes. All you have to do now is to crawl under the car, give the adjusting nut in the center of that half-moon connection a few turns (until you tighten it enough to hear the shoes clack) to remove any excess play from the cable. If you're the proud owner of an older Chrysler product, your parking brake is mounted on the tailshaft of the trans, and adjustment requires special tool.

Remember, take it easy for a while. New lining and drums work well, so well that they will tend to glaze if you overbrake them, ruining all that work and expense... so give them a little babying at first and you'll enjoy years of safe service.

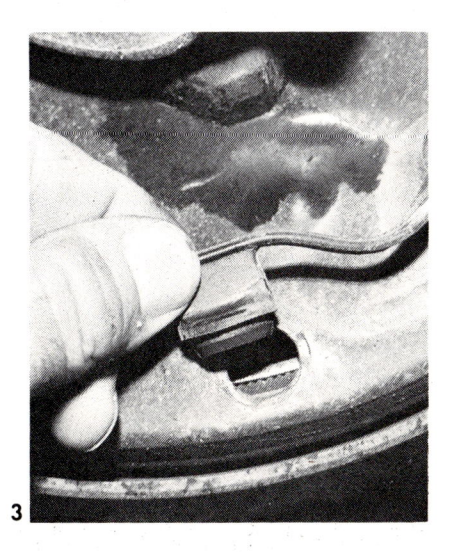

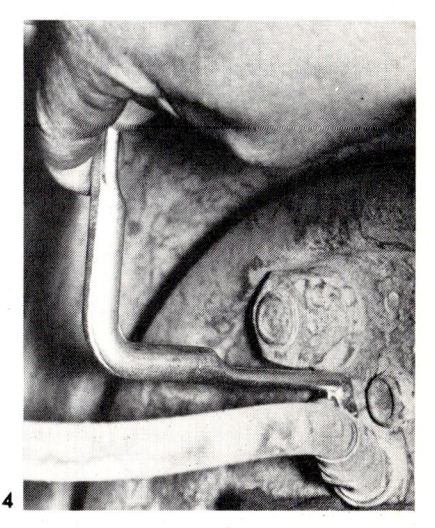

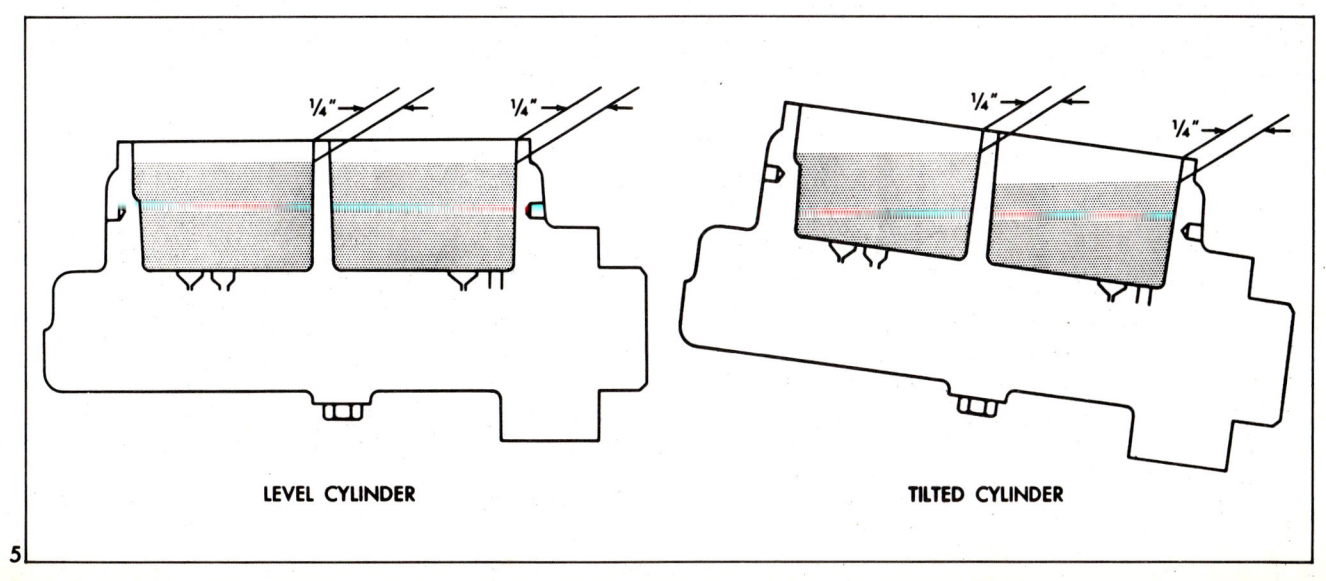

1. Many states have laws on how much a brake drum can be cut, since one that is too thin after cutting will flex under hard braking. New cars now come with the maximum (inside) diameter marked on the drum itself.

2. Although not often done, it's a good idea to seal the area around a wheel cylinder on the backing plate if you have taken it off to rebuild it. This prevents dust and moisture from entering the brakes.

3. Don't forget also to replace the rubber dust plug in the backing plate after adjusting the star-wheel.

4. Bleeding brakes can be a messy job, and access to the bleeder screw is not always the best, which is why this offset bleeder wrench is handy.

5. Between brake jobs, you can check the master cylinder fluid level on occasion. But never fill the master cylinder reservoir to the top, or there will be no room for expansion.

LEVEL CYLINDER   **TILTED CYLINDER**

CHASSIS, SUSPENSION & BRAKES/109

Drum Brakes

HOW-TO: Drum Brake Overhaul

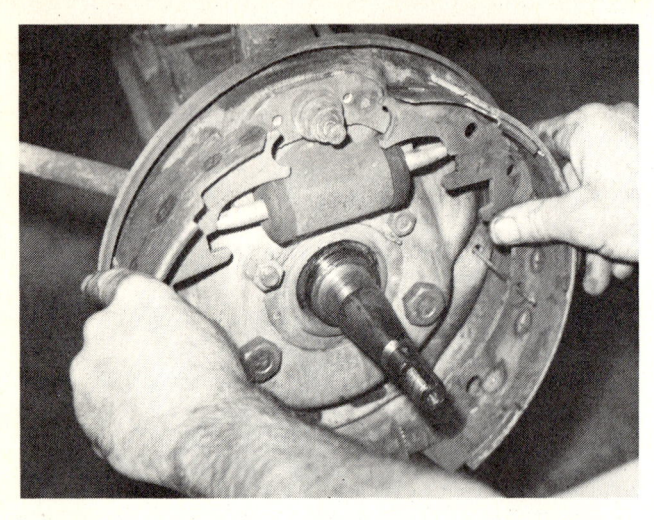

1. Once you've determined that your brakes are not what they should be, pull off and mark the drums and proceed to unclip the brake return springs and remove the shoes.

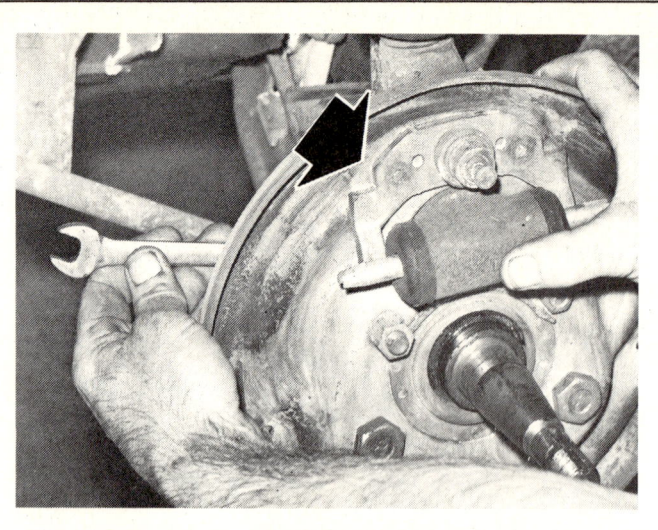

2. On most front drum brakes, you can't disassemble the wheel cylinder until you unbolt it from the backside of the backing plate to clear the cylinder stop (arrow).

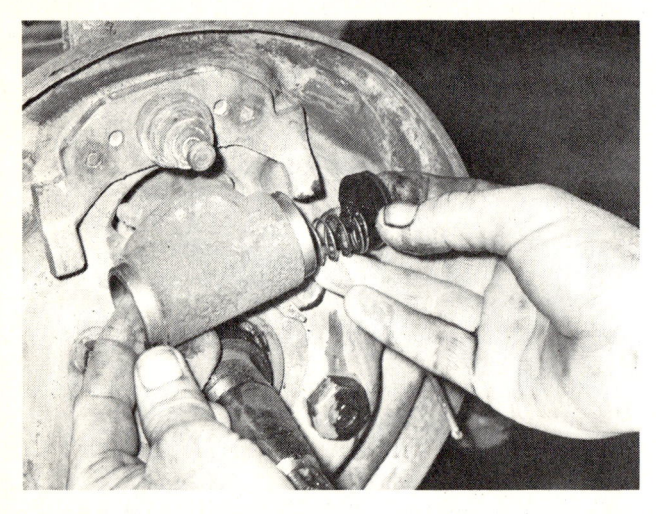

3. With the cylinder free of the backing plate and the piston retainers, you can pull off the shoe links and rubber dust boots for an inspection of the inside.

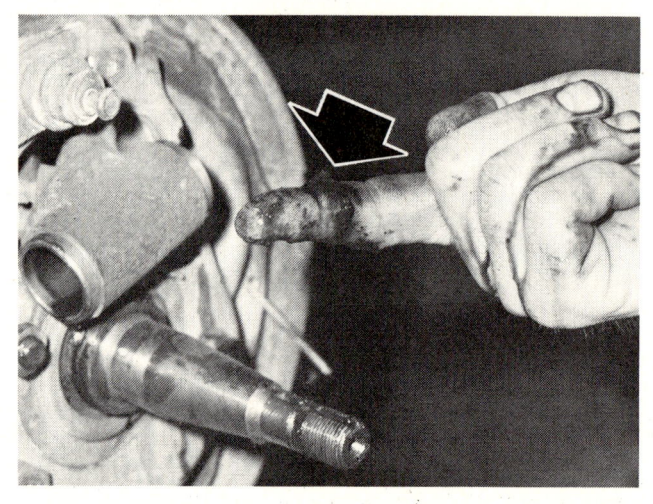

4. Wheel cylinders should receive new innards as part of any complete brake job, and this one's a perfect example of why. Look at the dirt from inside the cylinder.

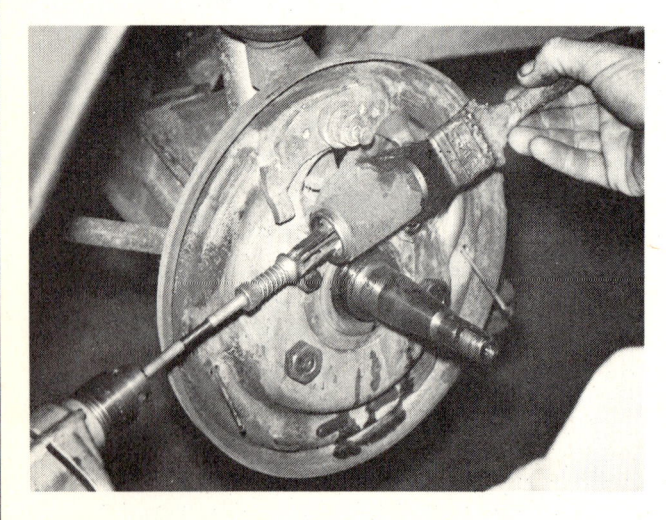

5. If there aren't any deep pits in the cylinder bore, you can clean it up with a wheel cylinder hone stuck in an electric drill. Use brake fluid as a hone lubricant.

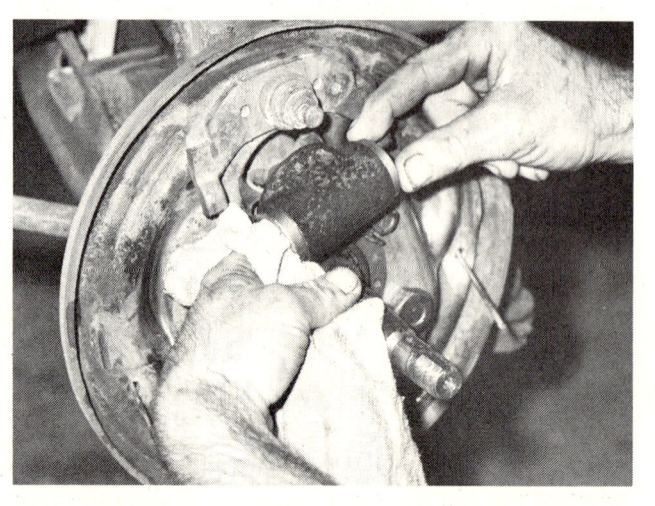

6. You must thoroughly clean out the newly-honed wheel cylinder with clean, lint-free rags to get rid of dirt and honing dust. Then wipe bore with clean brake fluid.

110/CHASSIS, SUSPENSION & BRAKES

7. New wheel cylinder "guts" come in a wheel cylinder rebuilding kit. After cleaning the old pistons, coat the new parts with brake fluid and install in bore.

8. If you're doing the job at home, take the drums to a brake shop to have them turned on a lathe for a true, new surface to take full advantage of the new linings.

9. Drums can be worn out-of-round from overheating or from a previous brake job that wasn't done properly. Note how brake lathe didn't hit warped portion of drum.

10. Brake drum/shoe gauges come in many forms, but in any case, the drums should be measured after cutting on a lathe to make sure they're within the legal limits.

11. Some brake shops reline their own shoes, but most get theirs from a rebuilder or parts store, just like you or me. First step in relining is removing old lining.

12. New linings are attached onto the thoroughly-cleaned shoes with a pneumatic riveter. Shoes with bonded-type linings are usually relined at a wholesale rebuilder.

Drum Brakes

HOW-TO: Drum Brake Overhaul

13. New shoes are always arced on a grinder to the exact curve of the newly-sized drums for full contact. Some brake shops grind a cooling slot in the shoes also.

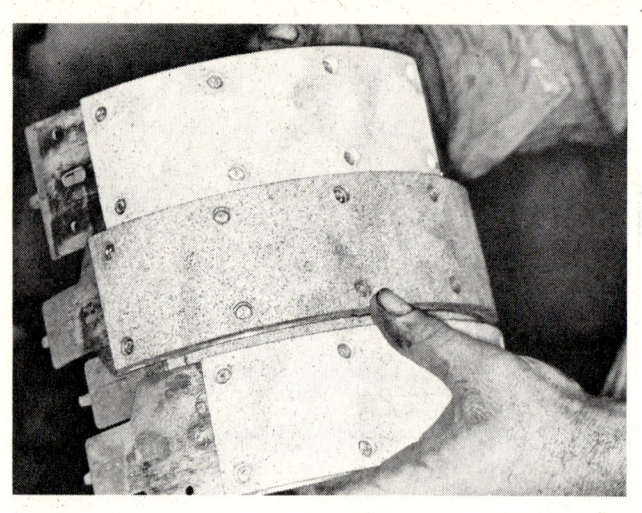

14. Shown here are two types of linings used. The light-colored linings are for the primary shoes, with softer material to help in wrap-up of the servo-action brakes.

15. With the wheel cylinder rebuilt, the entire backing plate and spindle should be cleaned off with wire brush and air blast. Put Lubriplate on shoe contact points.

16. Star-wheels (adjusters) can be tough to turn when they rust up, so prevent this by thorough cleaning of threads. Then lube with Lubriplate before assembly.

17. The new shoes are first attached to the backing plate with the hold-down springs and "nails." Although a special tool is used here, you can also use pliers.

18. With both shoes held on by their springs, you can start putting back the return springs, but make sure the self-adjuster cable (arrow) is in place first.

112/CHASSIS, SUSPENSION & BRAKES

19. Since the brake shoe return springs are super-strong (or should be), putting them on with pliers can be a painful experience. Use of the proper tool is safe, fast.

20. A good combination brake tool has the return spring remover-installer on one end of a long pair of pliers. The pliers end is used to install shoe-connecting spring.

21. With everything back in its rightful place, shoes can be adjusted preliminarily to the drum size so that you don't have to spend all day adjusting through drum.

22. As long as you had to pull the front drums to do the brake job, it's only common sense to now clean and pack the wheel bearings with new grease and adjust them.

23. With all the wheels and drums back on the car, you can now bleed the new brakes, after adding new fluid to master cylinder. Check level after bleeding two wheels.

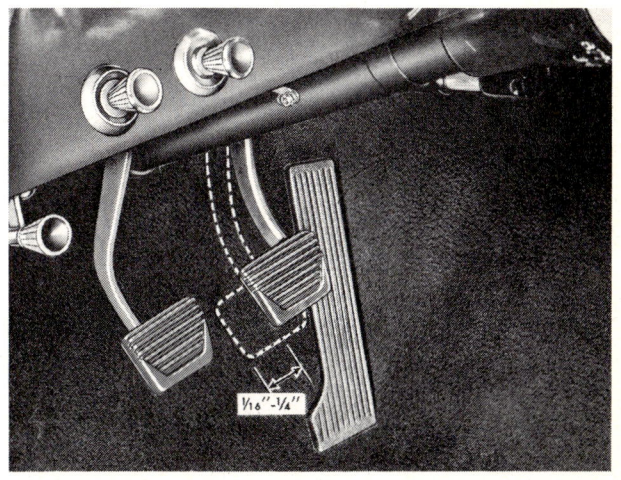

24. Check your owner's manual or service manual for the proper pedal height for your car. You should now have a firm, high pedal that starts working right away.

CHASSIS, SUSPENSION & BRAKES/113

High Performance Brake Relining

It used to be that hot rodders spent all their time worrying about how fast their car would *go*, but driving faster brings with the thrills a responsibility to be able to stop just as quickly. Hot rodders today have become increasingly aware of the performance of their chassis as well as what's under the hood, and of all the aspects of a chassis, brakes are the most important. This applies not only to the guy with a hot street machine with 400 hp, but equally to the weekend driver with a pickup saddled with a heavy camper.

It's interesting to learn that doubling the weight of a vehicle requires double the stopping power, but what most drivers don't realize is that doubling the speed requires *four* times the stopping power! Unfortunately, lessons learned in this area sometimes come with tragic penalties. How many times have you wished you had brakes that really stopped? Both camper owners and street machiners should be happy to learn that there is a way to improve braking performance and virtually eliminate fade, installing Velvetouch Metalik linings. You won't need to switch an all-drum car to discs with these linings.

An average, full-size car was tested by *Rod & Custom* magazine, and a first stop from 70 mph took 230 feet, with succeeding stops from the same speed of 288, 321, 360 and 380 feet. After that the brakes were completely gone! While you may never have to stop in repeated fashion from 70 mph, have you ever felt your brakes fade on a long down-grade or counted the number of stops you make from 35 mph in stop-and-go traffic? Just to show you what a difference true high performance brakes can make, the same car was tested after installing the Metalik linings. From the same speed of 70 mph, the driver made 13 stops one after the other, and with stopping distances ranging

HOW-TO: High Performance Brake Reline

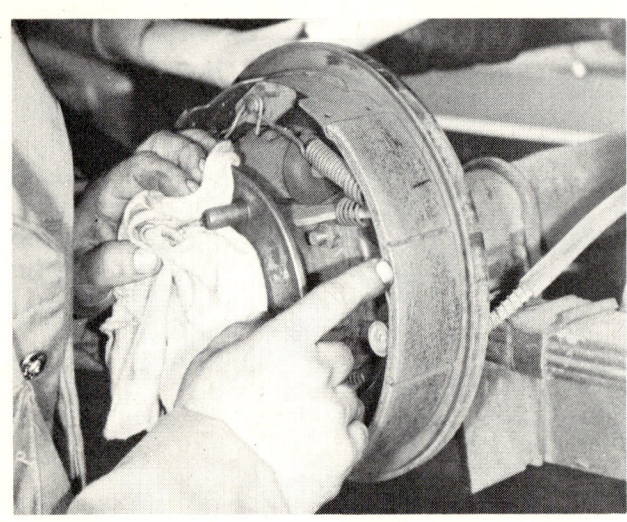

1. Metalik brake linings are segmented to allow for heat expansion and cooling under severe braking conditions. At some brake shops, Metalik brake guarantee is 50,000 miles.

2. The old brake linings are removed and discarded. This street'n'strip Mustang had used and abused these Metaliks for over two years and they still have some life left.

3. The drum is miked to see if it's out-of-round and to determine how much if any should be turned to restore a normal finish. The most that should be removed is .060-in.

4. Instead of a normal rough cut, drums used with Metalik linings must have a very smooth surface, so Gaspar makes one heavy cut and three very light ones for a fine finish.

from 195 feet to 225 feet, all stops were shorter than with the stock organic lining's *first* stop.

The Velvetouch Metalik is a soft metal; if you scratch its surface, graphite-like particles will come loose. Under severe braking conditions at higher speeds, ordinary lining material crystalizes and glazes, acting as a lubricant and lowering the coefficient of friction between lining and drum to practically zero. But when used under identical conditions, the molecules of the Metalik lining expand, improving the frictional grip between the two surfaces and even more important, this grip does not fade under repeated high-speed stops. The lining dissipates heat because it's segmented.

The Metalik lining has other distinct advantages, especially for the driver who's hard on his brakes. A changeover to Velvetouch will increase lining life to roughly double that of ordinary linings. Putting Velvetouch linings through a water bath has no ill effect on efficiency, and they should require fewer brake adjustments than standard linings.

When Velvetouch Metalik linings are installed, the self-adjusting mechanism must be removed because the linings should be completely clear of the drum after initial adjustment. If the self-adjuster is left in operation, there's a constant drag factor that wears down the Metalik linings rather quickly. Once installation is complete, drive the car with extreme caution at first because the brakes will only slow down the car without stopping it completely. Brake a number of times from 20 to 30 mph to heat up and seat the linings, then park the car and let the brakes cool. After this, you'll have about 75%, efficiency which rises to 100%, as seating becomes complete through repeated use—this process should take about 2 weeks.

While Metalik brake installation is quite similar to that of any other brake job, there are a few important and subtle differences, so we went to All-Star Tire in Paramount, Calif. where Gaspar Farace, who manages All-Star's brake department, installed a set of front discs and rear linings on a street 'n' strip 1969 Mustang for us. Follow Gaspar's tips and you'll be right in the brake of things. By the way, you can get the Velvetouch brakes through speed shops that carry Lakewood Industries equipment.

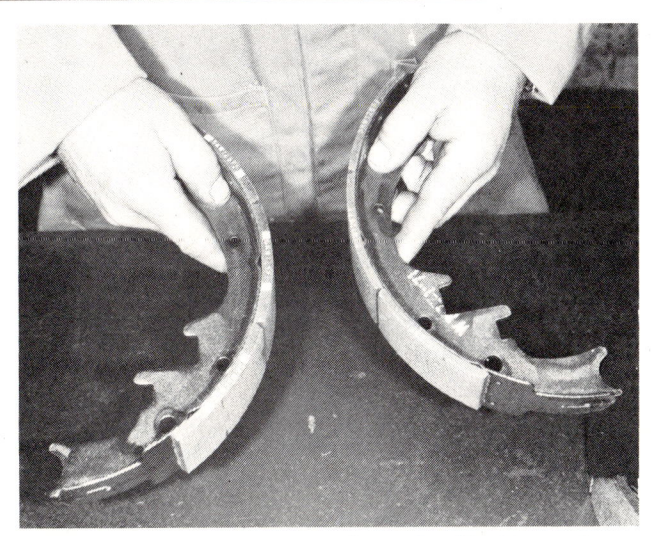

5. For a duo-servo system such as the Mustang, primary shoes are stamped Pri or For; secondary is stamped Sec or Rev. The forward shoe (right) is always the thinner one.

6. Although linings come pre-ground, Gaspar likes to make his own light arcing on the shoes for a perfect fit to a particular drum's inside diameter and contour.

7. If you're going to install the Velvetouch linings, every part of the system must be in top condition. All the Mustang's wheel cylinders were cleaned and rebuilt.

8. Heat-resistant lubricant is used on all brake friction points; ordinary lubricant may run or vaporize under the intense heat of severe braking with Metalik linings.

Brake Relining
HOW-TO: High Performance Brake Reline

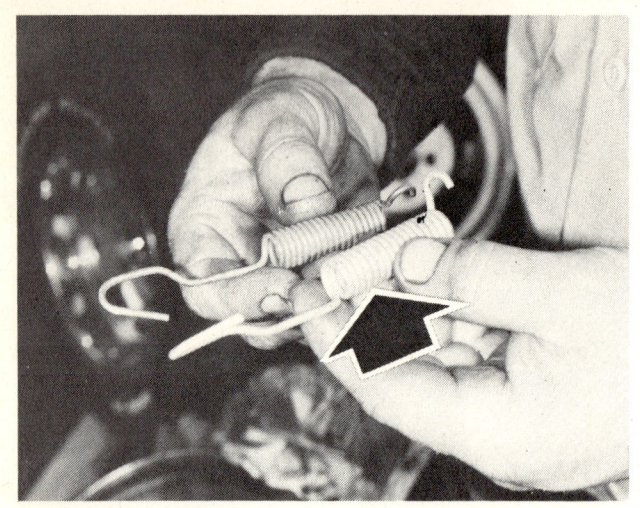

9. To help maintain proper shoe-to-drum clearance and prevent drag, heavy-duty shoe return springs (arrow) are used for reinstallation in place of stock-tension units.

10. The Velvetouch brakes are installed just like stock ones, except that the self-adjuster is not used and now the star-wheel is held in place by connector spring.

11. Here's how your completed installation should look. When drum is replaced, lining should be completely clear of drum after you've made proper shoe adjustment.

12. This Mustang has combined disc-and-drum system, so the front discs will get Metalik linings also. Gaspar is checking rotor thickness, critical to lining clearance.

13. The caliper is removed as for regular disc lining replacement. As with all disc brakes, the calipers are torqued (110-140 ft. lbs.) in place, and require air wrench.

14. You may have to spread the pads apart with a prybar to get the caliper pistons retracted enough to slide the caliper and pads off of the rotor.

116/CHASSIS, SUSPENSION & BRAKES

15. The caliper is still attached to its brake line, so it should be wired up to the car so it doesn't hang on the hose. Old pads are now discarded and rotor removed.

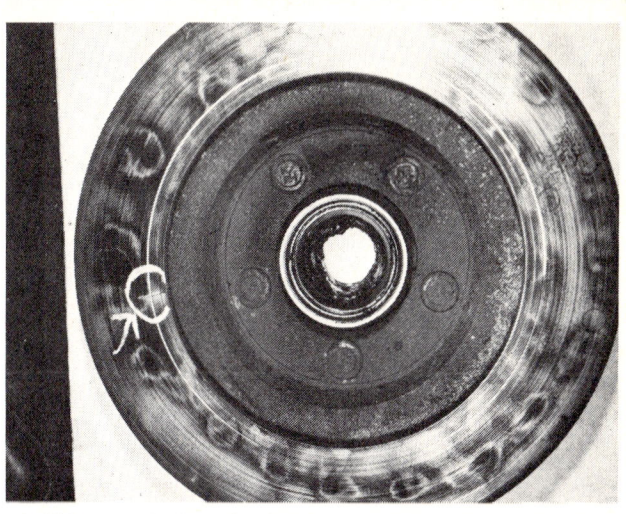

16. This rotor had received some extremely hard usage at the dragstrip; note the blued hardspots and a crack just starting. If the lathe won't clean it up, replace it.

17. Since the efficiency of Metalik linings depends on pad and rotor finish, Gaspar machines the rotor to remove the wear pattern developed with the old caliper pads.

18. New pads are chamfered on each end; this serves the same purpose as segmented lining, since the top layers of material are subject to greater expansion with heat.

19. In this case, Gaspar was able to save the rotor in the lathe, and while he was at it, he cut a cooling line in its face. Regreased bearings, new seals were installed.

20. Metalik pads are replaced in caliper just as standard ones would be. Once caliper is secured in place, you're ready to put the wheels on and seat the new linings.

CHASSIS, SUSPENSION & BRAKES/117

Disc Brakes

When it comes to stopping, drivers have been beating the drum for discs.

The little word "if" is why disc brakes are on your new car. Because *if* we didn't have wrap-around styling, *if* we didn't have wide, oval-type tires; *if* we didn't have solid, low profile wheels; *if* we didn't have modern hydraulic booster systems, and *if* we didn't depend upon lots of air to cool our burning drums, we wouldn't need to turn to disc brakes. But those "ifs" are here to stay and so is the "super squeezer," the disc brake.

Disc brakes are not new; they've been on the scene since the turn of the century (1902 to be exact), but the braking technologies of the early 1900's were not up to making them practical. They were merely another one of those far-out ideas.

Not until 36 years later—while Hitler rattled his swords—did a couple of Britishers, working on a brake skeleton in the closet, begin to fashion a practical way of stopping high-speed military aircraft . . . Their solution, the disc brake. Further experimentations during the war proved their ultimate practicality as trucks, tanks, and of course aircraft, found themselves stopping with discs. By war's end, the lesson learned in disc brake use soon saw its fruition in the willing form of automobile racing. The disc brake had come of age.

The handwriting was on the wall, and Detroit surprisingly was able to read it, although rather haltingly. First it was the builders of the bug-like Crosley. They chose to adapt the Goodyear-Hawley aircraft-inspired single-spot brake to their rather spartan offering. Across the country, in the land of the sun, Ted Halibrand, using Toby Cagle's patents, soon had his products on many of the top Indy cars. Things also looked fine in '49 as Chrysler took up the challenge with a combination disc/drum arrangement which attempted to mate the best of both braking systems in one, self-energizing disc brake. Unfortunately, Detroit dropped the ball. Their early efforts ran into a money and prejudice problem and while their interest waned, the Europeans (mostly British)—influenced by the racing success of Jaguar and Colin Chapman—recovered the fumble and began incorporating Girling and Dunlop disc brakes on many of their ultra high rollers.

It wasn't until the early '60's—when there was a dying gasp from Studebaker in the form of a curious mixture of Bendix discs up front and drums at the rear of their plastic-bodied Avanti—that U.S. auto makers showed any renewed interest in disc brakes. Seemingly out of the blue, the cost-conscious, conservative managers of Motor City found (after extensive testing) that discs were really for real. A revolution took place to equal the switch from mechanical to hydraulics some 30 years ago. All of a sudden Corvettes, Lincolns, Thunderbirds, Mustangs, Ramblers, Valiants and Avantis began sprouting discs like weeds in a lawn. With typical Detroit fanfare, the car-buying public was offered the disc/drum braking system. What had been just a year earlier a trickle offering to appease the purist, had now become a full blown gusher—with even the proverbial little old lady from Pasahogan getting into the act. A word to the wise. If you happen to have a little stock in a company manufacturing disc brakes or parts thereof, hold on as if playing caliper...it kinda looks like discs are going to be in the big leagues for a long time.

Now that we've agreed to the fact that Detroit is currently offering an almost unbelievable proliferation of disc/drum braking systems, the next step is to find out why. The story goes like this . . .

OBJECT: TO STOP

Drum brakes, by the very nature of the beasts, are sorry losers to a modern combination of tent-like front end sheetmetal and fat, lower-than-low profile tires on solid mag-style wheels. Somewhere, buried in all that iron, are four rather forlorn brake drums starving for heat-absorbing air. You see, we've come a long way from the days of high arching front and rear fenders (fall by a classic car, antique, or roadster show for a visual comparison)—or 18-in. wire wheels and tall, skinny front rubber.

Modern car esthetics (that'll drum up a little heat from the purists) has done its darndest to direct the breeze away from the outer brake surface. Try as they will—with fins galore, combination aluminum/steel drums, drilled and ducted backing plates, et al—brake experts could not and cannot overcome the effects of cold-air starved drum brakes. Oh sure, drums, if cool, will provide all the braking the typical American tires on the typical American car, hustled over the road by the typical American driver, need on the typical American road. However, the typical American braking system is on ragged edge under panic stop conditions and when subjected to any kind of continued use, like high-speed freeway flying or trailer-toting over twisting mountain roads, the trolls of fast-fading binders really begin to work their evil tricks. Obviously, Detroit—while blessing us with their outpouring of drag-inspired thunder-wagons—had to do something to get their little prodigies stopped . . . and the disc proved to be what is known in baseball as a "stopper."

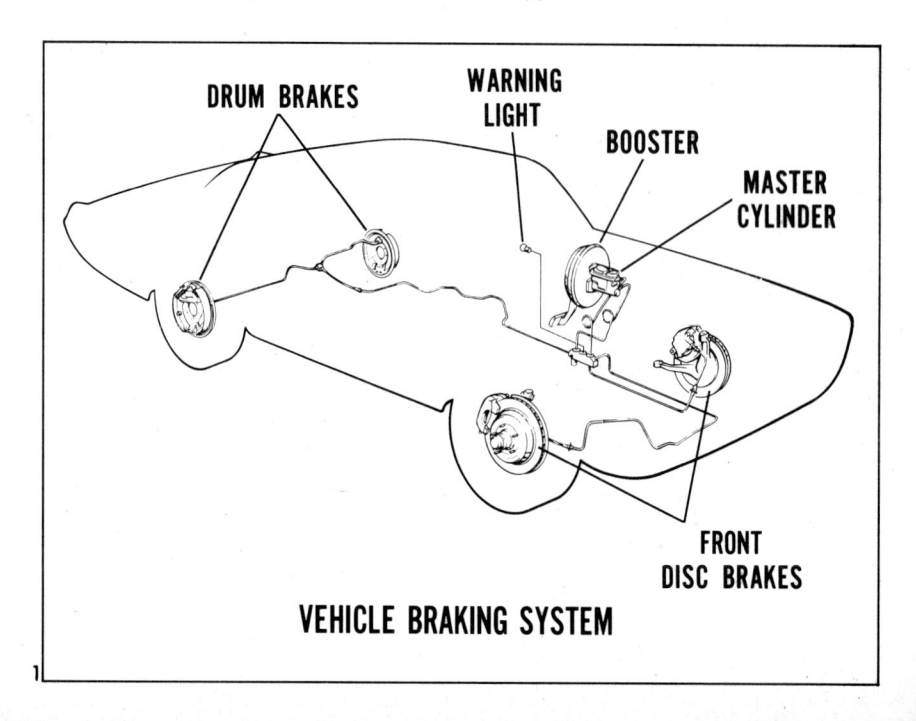

VEHICLE BRAKING SYSTEM — DRUM BRAKES, WARNING LIGHT, BOOSTER, MASTER CYLINDER, FRONT DISC BRAKES

118/CHASSIS, SUSPENSION & BRAKES

For the moment, discs do happen to be the stopper. Aside from their inherent simplicity, ability to resist heat-induced fade light weight and ease of maintenance, disc brakes offer a near-perfect solution to consistent braking action, under less-than-ideal weather or design conditions. Why? Because they are non-self-energized brakes.

The well known "discus commonus" is nothing more than a wheel-shaped, steel platter (some with a set of turbine-like vanes sandwiched in the center to induce a greater cooling effect). This disc or rotor is attached to and rotates with the turning wheel in a manner smacking of drum brake. Taking the place of a backing plate is a rotor splash shield to keep dirt, grease, road filth and other foreign material away from the braking surface of the disc. Doing the actual work is a vise-like, hydraulically operated device called a caliper which is usually mounted to a steering knuckle on a meaty bracket. Applying the actual squeeze-in pinching pressure to a biscuit-like pad or puck, bonded or riveted to a thin steel plate, are a set of pistons, housed within the confines of the caliper. How many pistons drive the pads (pucks, shoes, etc.) toward the rotor depends upon its intended use, but most modern passenger applications are being currently equipped with C-clamp style, full-floating single-piston calipers. Racing versions, on the other hand, can feature any number of multi-pistoned calipers attached to various points on the rotor. The thing is that these units bite fast-

1. Since most cars have disc brakes on the front only, this is a typical layout for a modern, Detroit car. All have the required differential switch and warning light, and because of higher pedal pressure requirements, most have a power booster as well.

2. What makes the disc brake unlike a drum brake is that stopping force is now exerted like a pincher that squeezes in on the rotating disc, while in a drum brake the force is applied outward against the drum. One of the disc brake's advantages is that being in the open, it runs cooler.

3. There are no retractor springs in a disc brake caliper. The piston is pulled back in the cylinder by the flexing of the boot and seal.

4. When the brakes are applied, the fluid pressure forces the piston in against the pad, which pinches in on the rotor and stops the wheel. It's the elastic action of the distorted piston seal and boot which pulls the piston back after releasing brakes.

5. When disc brakes first appeared in numbers on American cars in the mid-'60's, most designs were of the "fixed-caliper" type. The caliper was bolted solidly to the spindle and the pads came together inwardly to the rotor, or disc, of the brake.

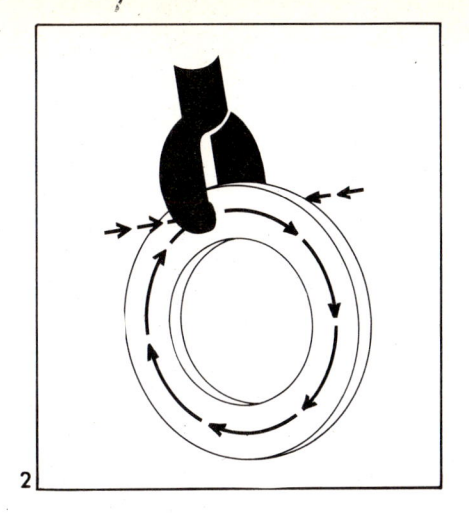

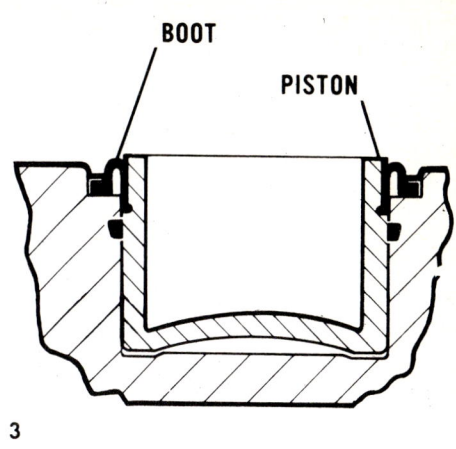

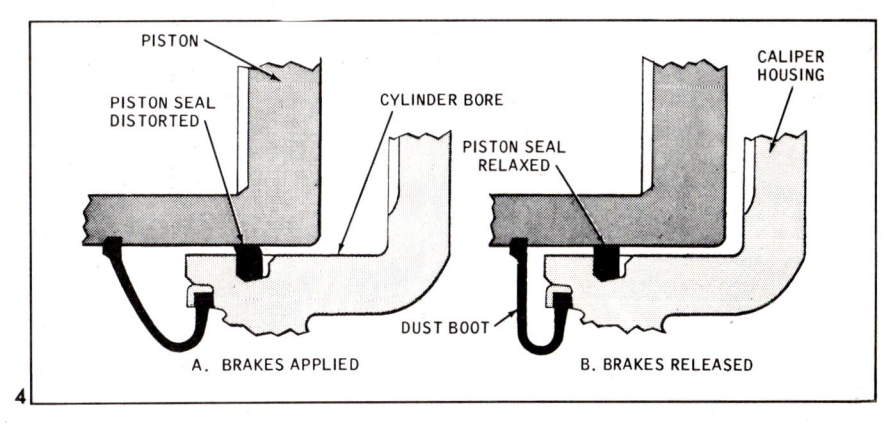

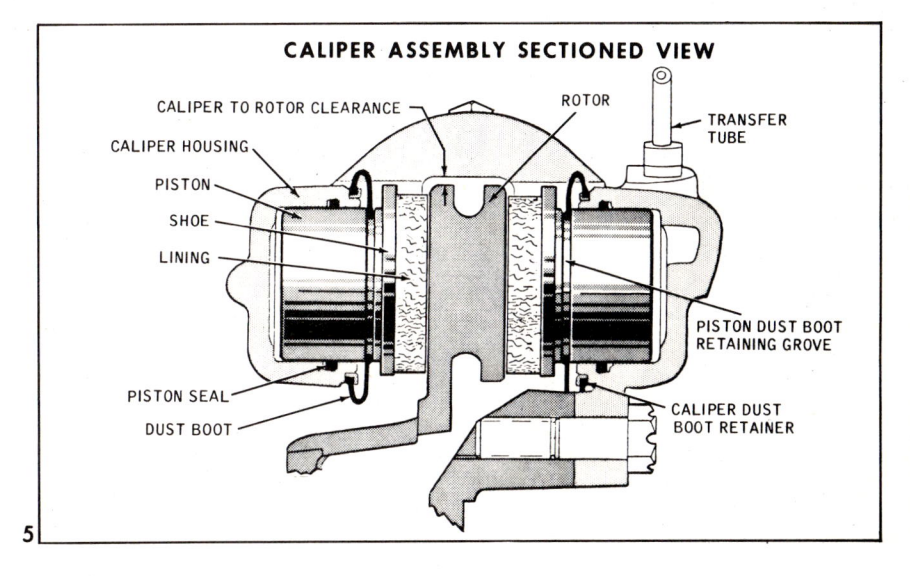

er and quicker than a bulldog on a mailman, and—by their utter simplicity—make you wonder why it took so long for our friends back in Michigan to start putting them on their products.

DISC BRAKING PRINCIPLES

A disc brake has the same effect as a 2-trailing-shoe brake. That means that disc brakes depend upon hydraulic pressure (and lots of it) plus great big pistons rather than any self-energizing to create the needed friction to get things stopped. As we stated in the Drum Brake chapter, self-energizers use a rebounding principle to self-increase brake producing pressure. The discs—by being non-self-energizing, and coming on all at once—tend to give a much more progressive braking action. That is, the harder you press on the brake pedal, the greater the braking effort at the point of pad-to-rotor contact. Consequently, disc braking is merely going-with-the-grain-type of drum braking, a boon to the users in foul braking conditions, a resister to erratic and fade situations, a relatively trouble-free means of stopping. But, it

Disc Brakes

takes a lot of line pressure against massive pistons to get the desired non-self-energized effect... the primary reason you'll get full-power boosting equipment in your split braking systems when buying a new car.

THE FAVORED FEATURES OF DISC BRAKES

As we said, disc brakes are inherently stable because they offer the user a non-self-energized braking action and—likewise—much cooler running. Now this isn't always held as an undisguised blessing because of new trends in pad lining makeup (especially metallic). These become more efficient the hotter they get. In fact, many brake designers keep the pads in slight contact with the rotor to fill a triple-purpose need: 1) to provide a self-cleaning action; 2) to keep the pads warm; 3) to give constant self-adjustment. There are special metallic linings with a healthy dose of copper and other minerals that still clamp like crazy even though they're well past the 1500° point. In racing applications, the rotor becomes so hot it glows like Rudolph's nose. Nevertheless, the street versions are relatively cool running. New lining developments to reduce squeak and grab at low temperatures have offset a main deterrent to disc brake usage.

Heat, the drum brake's worst enemy, tends to have another positive effect on the rotor, because the heat-induced growth of the metal is toward rather than away from the caliper. Because the braking pressure is equally divided on either side of the caliper, discs resist the persistent contact-reducing drum elongation caused by self-energized shoes pushing against the red-hot drums. You may eventually run into some rotor deflection (runout) but with the new floating calipers, "wobble" is not the problem it used to be.

OK, so discs are smooth acting and relatively cool running... what else is in their favor? Well, they're light and compact. For instance, to equal the heat absorption ability of, let's say, an 11-in., dual-piston, single-caliper disc brake, its drum counterpart would have to be a rather massive piece of braking power. Don't take my word for it, just pick up a back issue of any of the enthusiast magazines devoted to the road racing cult and check the hunks of finned tin bolted on the grand prix cars of the '30's, '40's and early '50's. One look should give you a pretty good idea what it took to stop these types of cars...and they weren't light, besides being far from compact. Agreed... those big, heavy, multi-lined drum brakes would do the job, considering the tire contact and suspension development, but with the post-war switch to lighter, quicker cars and a revolution in handling technologies, all those big drummers did was to increase unsprung weight—and that's a no-no in the handler's handbook.

Another aspect in brake performance is the shape and style of automotive wheel design. At one time, tall spokers were the rage; in fact, you didn't have a sports car unless it came stock with large-diameter wire wheels. Not only do wire wheels have a very pleasing esthetic effect, they also keep open to the brakes an easy avenue of cool air flowing past their surfaces. When you consider this, plus the fan-like effect of spinning spokes, the drum could stay relatively cool. Unfortunately, spokers are not as strong as solid wheels, they're much more expensive to manufacture and those stringy things between the rim and the hub must be retightened constantly—or you wind up with a Flexi-Flyer. Obviously these things weren't the answer to mass-production, so during the '30's, into and out of the '40's, wire wheels fell by the wayside.

By the '50's, only semi-limited production sports cars, possibly 50% of all-out racing machinery and a classic car here and there still used the old spokers. The rest of us had to be content with going on with solid rims,

1. After the fixed-caliper type came the improved "floating" caliper, in which the caliper was mounted on two special bolts and could self-center itself over the rotor during braking.

2. In this exploded view of the same floating caliper, you can see the special bushed pins it floats on.

3. In the floating caliper design, only the adapter was bolted to the spindle, the caliper could move to center itself by moving on the bolts and sleeves that hold it to adapter.

4. What is now referred to as the "third generation" caliper design is the sliding caliper, as typified by this '74 Mustang II. Here one half of the caliper is bolted solidly to the spindle, while the portion that houses the pistons is free to slide in machined ways (arrow). Only one screw need be removed to service the caliper, which has only 12 parts.

5. Because of the problems adapting disc brakes to rear axle housings, disc brakes are rare on all four corners of an American car. The '69 Camaro did offer it as an option, but few of these were sold and it was done mostly to justify Chevy using them on their Trans-Am cars.

6. All cars are required to have a pressure-differential warning switch with a dual-braking system, but on cars with front discs a proportioning valve must be added in the line to the rear drums, and often a metering valve is used in the front lines.

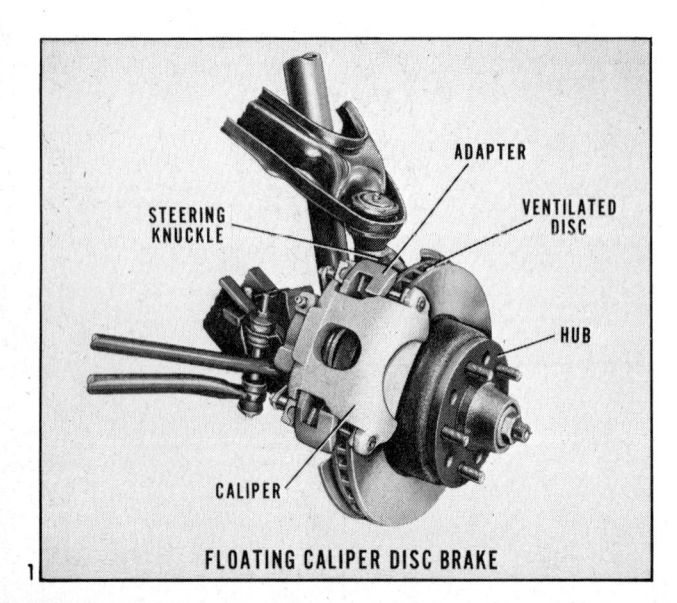

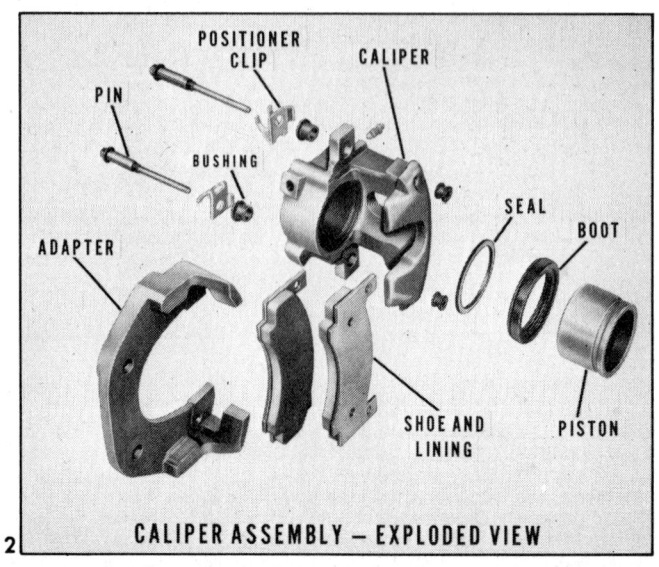

1 FLOATING CALIPER DISC BRAKE

2 CALIPER ASSEMBLY — EXPLODED VIEW

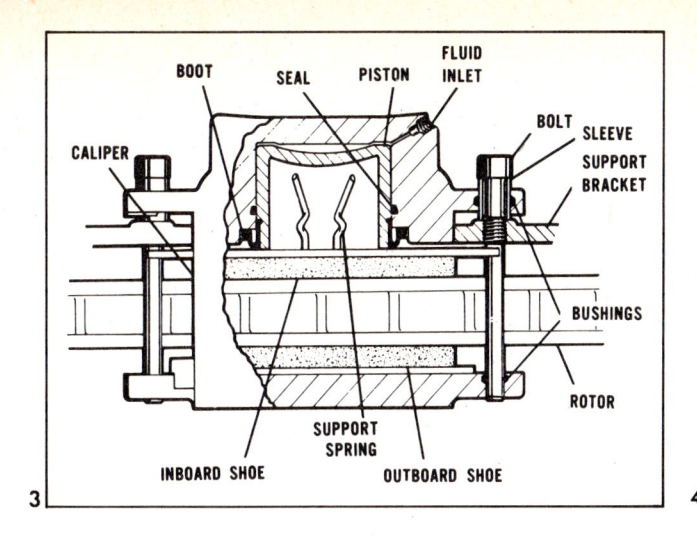

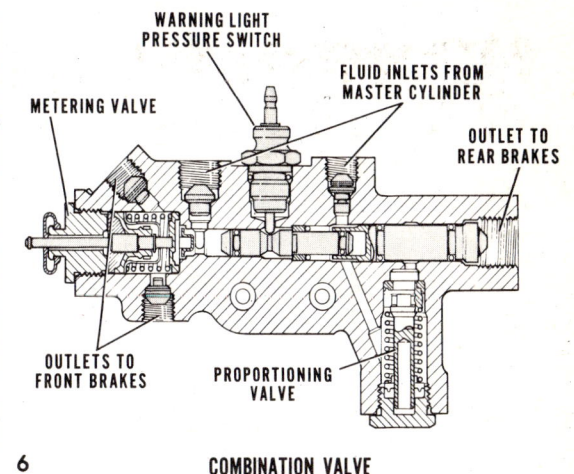

and the brakes, losing more air as the result, began to give ever-increasingly erratic performance. When the '60's, under the influence of ever-lower profiles, dropped the wheel size to a miniscule 13-14 ins., that about spelled the death knell to the drum brake. How in the heck could 10-in. drum brakes stop a 6000-lb. car traveling a solid 60 mph, after more than a few panic stops? The answer was simple. *They couldn't.* But discs could and did, and this feat was accepted as a further plus to their ability to function well under a variety of adverse conditions.

Not only did wheels become smaller, but they also became wider. Our big, ying-yangy cars needed to get as much contact with the pavement as they possibly could to give the driver even a modicum of stability. Wide tires, developed on the high-speed circle tracks of the South and Southeast, and their acceptance as a glamorous (as well as necessary) part of a car's suspension characteristics forced the wheel manufacturers to go to even wider wheels. Now you had a 2-pronged shrouding problem to just about end it all.

Furthermore, if wheel design didn't finish off the drums, the *coup de grace* was administered by such a case of front-end overhang that it would put a combination of Sophia Loren, Carol Doda, Dagmar and Raquel Welch to shame. No kidding, you know that those old drums are in there somewhere, but getting air to 'em was harder than a miser's heart on April 15. Fortunately, discs have the ability to function properly even with this further reduction of cooling air . . . another plus.

But probably the thing that ultimately sold Detroit on the disc brake was their inherent simplicity. In other words, the fewer moving parts through the elimination of springs, brake shoes, adjusters (most discs are self-adjusting), anchor points, etc., the less can go wrong and, the easier the units are to manufacture. If you've ever watched a disc brake reline job at a brake shop, it's purely a case of bip, bam, thank you, next customer—so the discs have to be easy to repair.

FIXIN' A DISC

While 99.9% of disc-type brakes fall into the category of being non-self-energized, they can be put into two separate camps as to style: the single, large piston, floating caliper or the multi-piston, rigid caliper. Up until '69 most disc brakes were of the latter design. However, the latest trend is away from the rigid-caliper type because of its susceptibility to malfunction due to excessive rotor runout (wobble) or the problem of over-flexing front suspensions. For example, a car during hard cornering could have its suspension tweak to the extent of actually pushing the rotor against the pistons and shoving them deep into their respective bores. The next time the brakes were applied, the excessive piston travel would give little or no braking effect, *unless* the driver had enough sense to pump the pedal to get his brakes back. Runout, or rotor wobble, is to discs or rotors what elongation is to drums. Excessive runout causes the pistons (on a rigid caliper) to pulsate against the rotor like a needle on a warped phonograph record and is commonly known as piston "knock back." Obviously, Detroit found it easier and probably cheaper to manufacture floating calipers than to lick the problem of flexing front suspension and runout-susceptible rotors.

The floating caliper is really nothing more than a built-in flexibility at the joint between the caliper and its retaining bracket. While GM cars feature two bolts shoed with O-rings to allow the caliper to slip back and

CHASSIS, SUSPENSION & BRAKES/121

Disc Brakes

forth, Ford products simply use rubber-motor-mount-like grommets to achieve a like lateral flexibility. With the caliper now acting in a C-clamp fashion (the piston as the screw-in portion, the outside pad like the immovable portion of the clamp), bouncing happily over the high and low spots of the rotor, Detroit has restored the needed consistency to its discs. In fact, many of the 1974 cars feature a new, "self-centering" floating caliper which has only 12 parts, easier servicing, and can be used with firmer linings without squeal.

As we have said, disc brakes operate on the squeeze-in or pinch principle of brake-producing friction with only an assortment of different caliper-to-rotor arrangements separating one type of disc brake from another. Although military uses were initiated prior to World War II, their civilian automotive counterparts fleetingly appeared at GM somewhere in the late '30's, were judged a total failure, then reappeared in '48 on, of all things, the diminutive Crosley, the much bulkier Chrysler Imperial and, of course, on a number of Indy-type racing cars. On the surface anyway, these three early applications should give us a pretty good cross section of postwar disc brake thinking.

CROSLEY'S HYDRA-DISC

Its basic simplicity was really startling. The 2-piece rotor sat to the inside of a stationary, dish-shaped backing plate which acted as a splash shield. Inserted between the split portion of the splash shield and the rotor was a single large pad attached to the caliper in semi wig-wag railroad style. The outside half of the 2-piece caliper carried a like, but immovable pad and when hydraulic pressure was applied to the inner pad, the caliper—in typical C-clamp fashion—produced braking friction.

Although the units were both non-adjustable and full-floating, the size of the pads in relation to the swept area of the rotor made it pretty obvious that this thing dissipated heat like water off a duck's back.

CHRYSLER'S SELF-ENERGIZING DISC

Another means to get all the braking it could was the rather unusual effort by Chrysler back in the early postwar period. Even then, the automotive stylists were reducing the wheel size to a point where the existing 12-in. brakes couldn't function up to their design capabilities. In defense, Chrysler went to a combination disc and drum arrangement which featured a self-energized, clutch-like principle. Operating in a split, non-rotating, cast iron housing, bolted to a wheel hub, were two pressure plates covered with bonded brake lining supported by a spider bracket attached to the axle. The inner plate carried two wheel cylinders which—when hydraulic pressure was applied—pushed against a set of lugs attached to the outer plate. To ensure equal pressure around the two discs, six steel balls housed in a ramp-like pocket were placed between the two pressure plates.

When the brake pedal was depressed, the single-acting wheel cylinders—on the inner plate, acting against the lugs—caused the outer plate to rotate enough to push the steel balls out of their ramped pockets and force the two plates apart, and against the vertical surface of the split housing. The self-energized aspect was caused by the fact that the outer plate could be carried around slightly by the revolving housing, although the front brakes used the action only in forward motion (the same as a 2-leading-shoe brake). The rear brakes, on the other hand, gave a self-energized effect in both directions (for braking in reverse or parking) by a unique way of anchoring the inner plate while in forward motion. The outer plate was free to self-energize—(or anchoring the outer plate during a reverse motion, with the inner plate now free to self-energize itself.) Unfortunately, this cross between the two worlds was not geared to mass production techniques and soon found itself pushing up daisies.

Discs or not, another word for them was spot. Spot-type disc brakes—like the early automotive adaptation of the Goodyear-Hawley aircraft brake by Ted Halibrand using a Cagle-patented design and lovingly described as "crab-like" in appearance—were usually a one-disc arrangement housed in a caliper that in turn was firmly secured to a healthy bracket. Rather than "pinching" the rotor, the spot brake pressed a single pad into the rotor. The rotor was half a brake drum in appearance, filling much of the air space between the wheel and spindle, its finned surface dissipating heat, its vertical machined surface absorbing the braking action. The bracket to which the single piston caliper was mounted was itself attached to the rear suspension rather than the axle housing because Halibrand had an open-tube, live-axle rear-end arrangement. As a reminder, braking a Championship-type racing car was strictly for positioning only and not for continued use, although many modified Halibrand units found their way to Europe and were used quite successfully on the early British-built Vanwalls.

But enough of this reminiscing; it's time to get to a short-snort discussion of some of the more common disc brakes and how to go about changing pads; a little on rotor refurbishing and very little on hydraulics—that's covered elsewhere in this book in its own chapter.

BENDIX—SERIES E

Bendix is found on American Motors, Buick (Special and Skylark excepted) and Chrysler "B" cars (Coronet, Charger, Belvedere; Satellite).

Bendix still supplies Detroit with a fair share of its disc braking systems. Basically the units are comprised of a 2-pad, 4-piston, non-floating caliper arrangement mounted to the steering knuckle on most applications. The rotors are attached to the front wheel hub by five studs and are kept clean

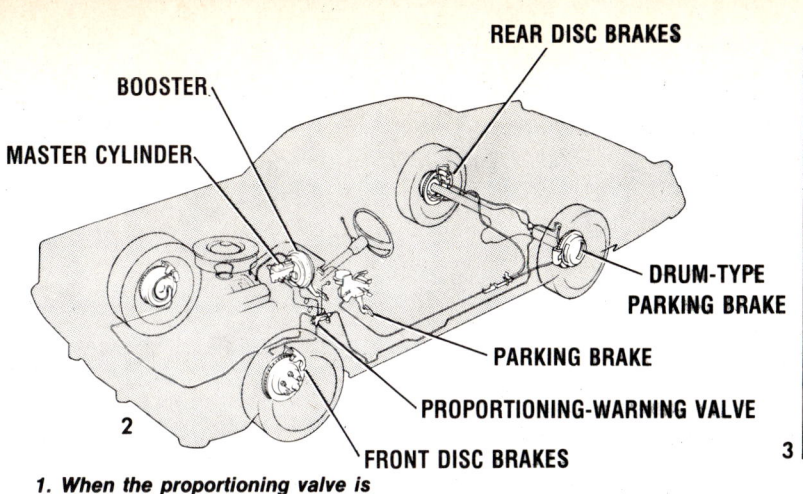

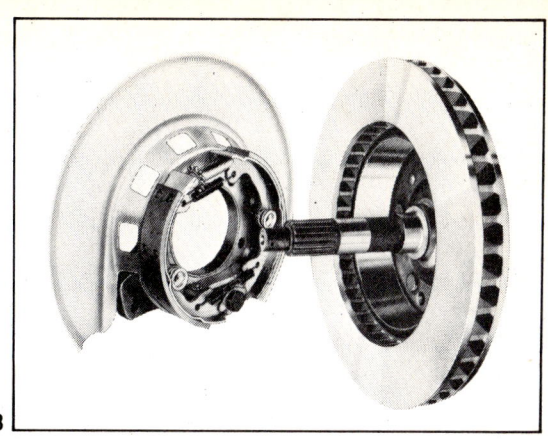

Figure labels (diagram 2):
- MASTER CYLINDER
- BOOSTER
- REAR DISC BRAKES
- DRUM-TYPE PARKING BRAKE
- PARKING BRAKE
- PROPORTIONING-WARNING VALVE
- FRONT DISC BRAKES

Figure labels (diagram 6):
- COOL ROTOR FIRST CONTACTS LINING HERE
- WITH BRAKE APPLIED FRICTION ON ROTOR CAUSES IT TO HEAT AS IT CONTACTS LININGS
- ROTOR IS HOTTER HERE
- ROTATION
- FRONT

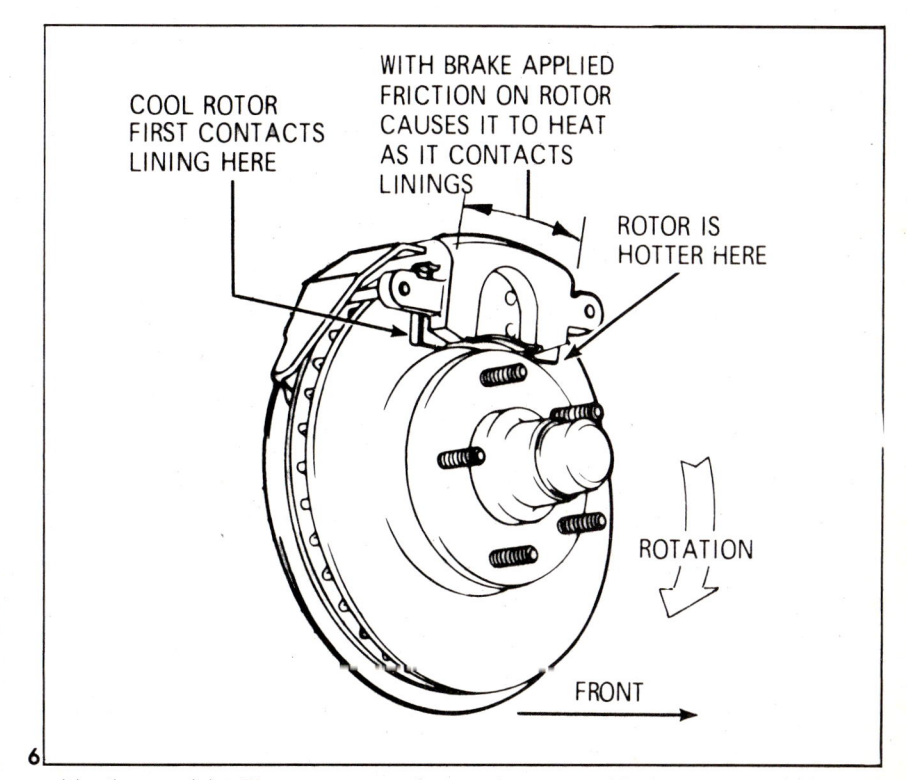

1. When the proportioning valve is separate from the warning valve, it is usually mounted next to the master cylinder in the rear brake line. As in this example, most disc-and-drum systems use a power booster.

2. The new '74 Chrysler Imperial is significant in that four-wheel discs are standard equipment now with a power booster and drum-type parking brake inside the rear disc rotors.

3. Corvette, the only other Detroit car with four-wheel disc brakes, also has a drum-type parking brake that works inside the rear rotors.

4. Most disc brake rotors for big and medium size cars are ventilated for cooling. The rotor has slots in it that pick up cool air as it moves, aiding in heat transfer off rotor.

5. On some small, light cars like the Chevy Vega, it was determined that there wasn't need for vents in the rotor (ventilated rotors are more expensive to make) and so a solid unit is used. What cooling they felt was needed is provided by the splash shield, which is formed into a scoop.

6. One of the advantages of a disc brake is that all of the rotor is not always in contact with the friction material. Once a portion of the rotor passes through the pads it has a full circle to cool off before contacting the friction material (pads) again.

by the slight rubbing action of the self-adjusting pads.

Anyway, figure your brakes are worth about 30,000 miles under normal driving conditions. Leave them any longer and you're running the risk of scoring the rotors. Bendix has two pad inspection ports at the top of the calipers, so just by removing a wheel at a time and visually checking the lining you can see where you stand. (Any less than 1/16-in. means you need new linings.)

The actual "R-and-R" on Bendix disc brakes is quite simple; just remember to change one set of pads at a time and make sure that your car is securely held in the air on jackstands or their equivalents.

Start by disconnecting the hydraulic lines from the retaining brackets, but don't loosen any of the fittings (saves you the trouble of having to bleed the brakes after you've finished with the pads). Then remove the bracket bolts, grab the lower edge of the caliper, shake up and down—as well as sideways—until the shims fall into your grubby palm. These shims ensure that the caliper is positioned parallel with the rotor so be sure to mark them "lower" as they aren't interchangeable with the top ones. Do the same with the uppers; shake well and mark "upper." Now hang the caliper from any part of the suspension with some baling wire, siphon about half the fluid from the master cylinder, and get to bottoming out the pistons with a couple of screwdrivers. Once they are slowly pushed back all the way in their respective bores, the

CHASSIS, SUSPENSION & BRAKES/123

Disc Brakes

worn brake pads should easily fall out.

With the pads now in the ash can, give the pad backing-plate-to-piston contact point a thin coat of Permatex Form A gasket #2...but watch out so you don't get it on anything else. Slip in the new pads, metal-back-to-piston, curved edge first, then spread the pads apart to clear and straddle the rotor. If for some reason you have mixed your "uppers" with your "lowers"—shims that is—side clearance should be .010-in. (measured with a feeler gauge) with the caliper retaining bolts tightened to 85 ft.-lbs. All that is left to do is to put the hydraulic lines back in their retaining brackets, depress the brake pedal a couple of times to seat the new lining, check the fluid level in the master cylinder ... then be on your way.

DELCO-MORAINE

A division of GM, D-M supplies brakes for Buick Special and Skylark, Chevy, Oldsmobile (except Toronado) and Pontiac.

Delco-Moraine is currently producing a full-floating disc brake which is being used on most of the (newer) cars. Its earlier models were very much in style and operation like the Bendix "E" which we have discussed; therefore pad removal and replacement follow the same line of procedure. Removing and replacing the friction pads on the full floater is a little more difficult than on the Bendix models, but still is relatively simple if you've got the tools and time.

We'll start by inspecting the lining within the single-piston, C-clamp styled, full-floating caliper, through the large inspection hole at the top of the caliper. Again, you must remove the front wheels, one at a time, then determine if the lining is less than the minimum (.020-in.) allowable. Any less than that and off comes the good ol' caliper.

First thing is to remove and "can" two-thirds of the brake fluid in the master cylinder (front reservoir) because when you depress the piston to get out the worn pads, the fluid will back up though the brake line and overflow all over your nice new firewall paint...and hydraulic fluid is an all-time paint remover. The next step is to place a 7-in., C-clamp over the caliper—screw end positioned on the outboard disc's steel backing plate—and screw in until the piston is fully bottomed and the pads are freed from the rotor. Now lift off the caliper without disconnecting the hydraulic lines, remove the C-clamp and start dislodging the pads and float-producing assembly (bushings, sleeves and bolts) with a special brake tool (Part No. J-22835).

You should now pretty well have it all apart, so it's time to begin cleaning the caliper, making sure no abrasives are used. While you're at it, check for any cracks, cuts, or leaks; don't use any compressed air for cleaning or drying, it'll dislodge the boots.

Now whomp away with your special tool. Make sure the float-producing assembly is given a silicon-based fluid bath, and check to see that the shoe lining end of the sleeves is flushed on the machined portion of the caliper's ears. Next, place the shoe support springs in the piston's center. Position the inboard pad assembly so that the bottom edge of the steel backing plate contacts the piston and spring ends (adjust if springs don't contact the center of the piston). Then press down on the ears at the top of the disc until it flushes on the piston. (When properly seated it shouldn't extend more than .001-in. beyond the edge of the shoe.) Next, folks, grab the outboard shoe, position it so that its ears are over the caliper's ears and the bottom is engaged in the caliper's cutout. With both pad assemblies installed, check to see that there is no clearance between the bottom of the outboard shoe and the caliper's abutment. Return now to the C-clamp to hold the unit to the rotor so you can make sure the caliper is centered on the rotor, with no more than .005-in. side clearance, using a pair of visegrips clinching the shoe's ears as the means for the adjustment. With the clinching (sounds like a love-in) at the end, you can remove the C-clamp, bolt down the caliper to the bracket (35 ft.-lbs.), and consider a day well spent.

KELSEY-HAYES FULL-FLOATING DISCS

K-H builds disc brakes for Cadillac dorado, Chrysler "A" cars (Barracuda, Dart, Signet, and Valiant), all FoMoCo cars, and the Oldsmobile Toronado.

This full-floating disc brake differs from the D-M units as to means of achieving the caliper's movement by depending upon four rubber bushings on two steel guide pins threaded to the bracket holding the caliper. If you happen to own a car equipped with the new K-H floating caliper brakes which has seen a good "thirty-thou" under its wheels, it's time to take a gander at the lining. On the other hand, K-H's older, 4-piston, 2-shoe, non-floating caliper disc brake "R-

124/CHASSIS, SUSPENSION & BRAKES

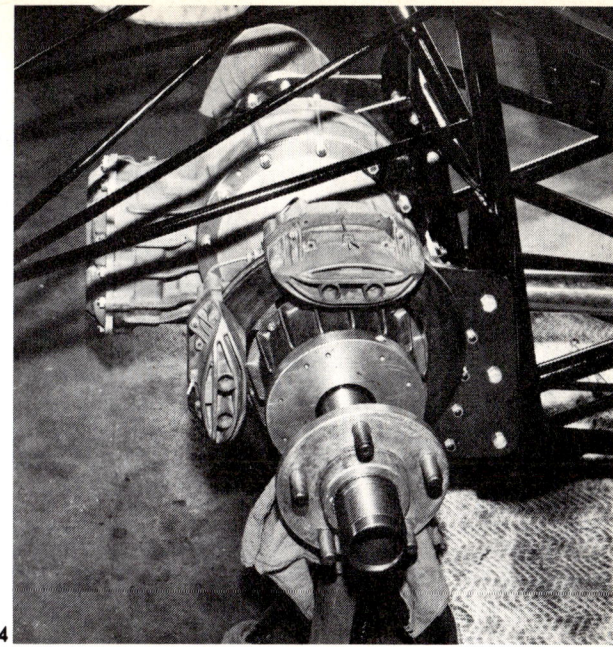

1. Although disc brakes have many advantages in heat dissipation, they still need fresh air. In racing cars like this Trans-Am Mustang, scoops and ducts are used to gather air.

2. In some racing applications like drag racing, the rotors are drilled out, not only to save a little weight but to add surface area for cooling.

3. This racing car uses a special caliper which allows using a larger than normal friction pad (arrows).

4. When you have to stop a fueler or funny car from 230 mph at the end of a ¼-mile run, you have specialized braking requirements. Most cars have to use two sets of calipers on each rotor, since brakes are on rear only.

5. Disc brakes are now so popular for race cars and hot rods that there are a number of kits on the market for adapting them, like this one by Hurst-Airheart for dual calipers.

and-R'' has been covered pictorially elsewhere in the book and gives you in living gray a visual instruction on how to do it.

With the car off the ground (preferably on jackstands) we'll start attacking K-H's new full floaters. Begin by pulling off the left front wheel, peek into the large inspection window and check to see if the lining is down to the minimum .100 in.; if so it's time to do a little unboltin'!

While high on the jackstands, remove the front wheels, caliper guide pins, positioners and rubber bushings that hold the "vise" on the steering knuckle. Now slowly slide the caliper (leaving all hydraulic lines, etc., alone!) out and away from the ventilated rotor. Next, hang the unit with the aid of a short piece of baling wire—just make sure it's not causing the brake line to kink—and start pulling the outboard shoe and lining plate, then the inboard shoe and the lining plate, away from the anchor. The outer bushing can now be pressed out of the bore with a proper tool and quickly discarded while the inners (flanged) are slid off the guide pins (the same for positioners) and also given the deep six.

With everything either in the trash barrel or hung to the suspension, check the caliper for any leaks around the boot, the mating surfaces of the abutments on the calipers and anchors for any rust or corrosion, and the braking surface of the rotor for any cracks, hot spots or deep scoring marks. If everything looks good we can get to putting it back together.

Because we threw away all the old positioners, inner and outer bushings, we'll have to get a new set of these along with the pad assembly. Now slowly begin to push the piston back into the bore until it's bottomed (hope you drained a good portion of the brake fluid out of the front reservoir of the master cylinder...or it's paint removin' time). Put the new inner guide pin bushing in the caliper with the flanged end on the inboard side. Shove in the flanges of the outboard bushings, working it into its proper position from the outboard side of the caliper. With this done, you can begin sliding the new pad assemblies into place, making sure that the metal portion of the pad is at the end of the

CHASSIS, SUSPENSION & BRAKES/125

Disc Brakes

caliper and anchor. By holding the outboard pad in its proper place, you can carefully slide the caliper into anchor position and over the rotor. Alignment of the anchor's—as well as the inboard and outboard pads'—guide pin holes should go off fairly easily. Then install the new positioners over the guide pins (open ends facing outside, stamped arrows pointing upward), which should be inserted through the bushings, caliper, anchor, inboard and outboard pads by pressing in on the end and threading into the anchor (tighten to 30-35 ft.-lbs.). Lastly, but not leastly, kick the brake pedal a few times to gain a firm pedal, check and refill the master cylinder (bleed if necessary), then sit down and have a tall cold one—you've really earned it.

BUDD

Budd discs were used on Chrysler's "C" cars (Imperial, Chrysler, Polara, Monaco, Fury) up to 1968.

The Budd disc brake is basically a system that incorporates a 2-pad, 4-piston, non-floating caliper over a 2-piece, ventilated rotor. Although it features a self-adjusting mechanism—by allowing the pads to brush the rotor—lining depth should never be allowed to get any closer than within .030-in. of the steel shoe, or a good case of scoring can be counted on. When you get your Budd-equipped car on a set of jackstands with the front wheels off for pad checking, the lining can be viewed through a large inspection window on the top of the brake's caliper.

With the car up on something (be sure it's sturdy) we can get to whipping off the anti-rattle spring, unbolting the caliper from its bracket, and lifting it up and away from the rotor. Best to attach it with some wire to the front suspension before lifting out the worn pads. Now carefully remove the pucks (one at a time) through that generous inspection window. Then insert a piston compression tool (Part No. C-3992, which appears more like a reverse-acting valve spring compressor) into the window, place it between the piston's insulator pads, and turn the star-shaped knob until the pistons are fully bottomed in their bores.

As in the case of the other brakes, go about checking for any fluid leak, structural damage and rotor wear.

If everything appears aces, then get to reinstalling the new pads. First of all, slide the pad assemblies into their proper positions one at a time. Next slide that good ol' piston compression tool between the pads so as to hold them apart, but loose enough to make removal easy. Now it's an easy matter of sliding the caliper over the rotor and into position for rebolting to the mounting bracket. (Tool should be loose enough to be forced out of the caliper by the rotor when it's lowered into place.) Tighten the caliper's mounting bolts from 80-90 ft.-lbs. All that is left is to lower your wheels, check your master cylinder for proper fluid level (about ⅛-in. from the top) make several 40-mph semi-panic stops (to remove any foreign materials), and call it a day.

A LITTLE ON ROTORS

While rotors (or discs) don't usually suffer the same proportionate maladies that brake drums do, they do get tired and do need to be checked along with the pads. Most rotors are not overly expensive ($15-$30), so it really doesn't shoot down the budget if you have to replace one or more. Yet, why waste money by letting a small cavity work itself into a pulled tooth when a little session on the disc lathe can square it away.

Most rotor problems fall into two basic categories: resurfacing—light ridges, rust, and scoring; or reconditioning—heavy ridges, rust, and scoring, out-of-parallel, and/or excessive runout (wobble). While the minor problems don't affect the modern generation of full-floating discers, your non-floating varieties have trou-

1. Disc brake swapping, to update older cars, has become increasingly popular with hot rodders. Here's a Maverick to which '70 Mustang disc brakes, spindles and all, have been adapted for better fade-free brakes.

2. Herbert & Meek, the engine swap people, have a number of kits for adapting late-model discs to early cars. This is a kit for full-size Chevy disc on '55-'57 Chevy spindles.

3. Knowing the extra pedal pressure required with disc brakes and yet not wanting to use a power booster, this engine swapper played it safe by bracing firewall-mounted cylinder.

4. Some GM cars, like this '72 Olds, have a plastic cap over the bleeder screw on the caliper. This is a good idea, keeping out dirt and water.

5. Another neat trick from Olds is the disc brake wear indicator they introduced on '72 Toronado. When a set of pads wears down to the danger point, an indicator (arrow) comes in contact with the rotor, making loud screeching noises during braking to warn you that linings are worn.

6. The friction material on disc brake pads is really no different from that on drum brake linings, and under severe conditions can fail through abuse. When the material is so worn that the rivets are cut, then metal is exposed to the rotor.

7. Here's a perfect case where the motorist's neglect cost plenty. The pads were allowed to wear to the metal, which scored and ruined the rotor. When changing the pads is so easy on disc brakes, there's little excuse for driving this long with the screech of bad linings. While a drum may only cost $15, this rotor cost the motorist $80 apiece!

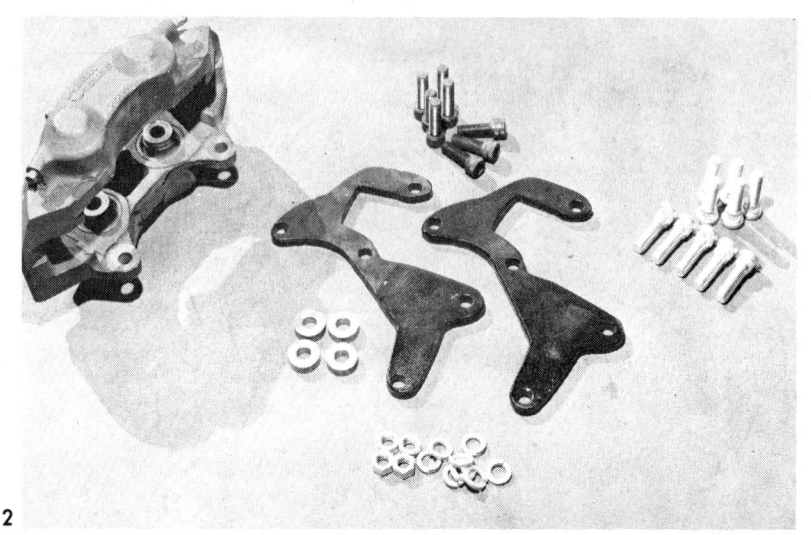

126/CHASSIS, SUSPENSION & BRAKES

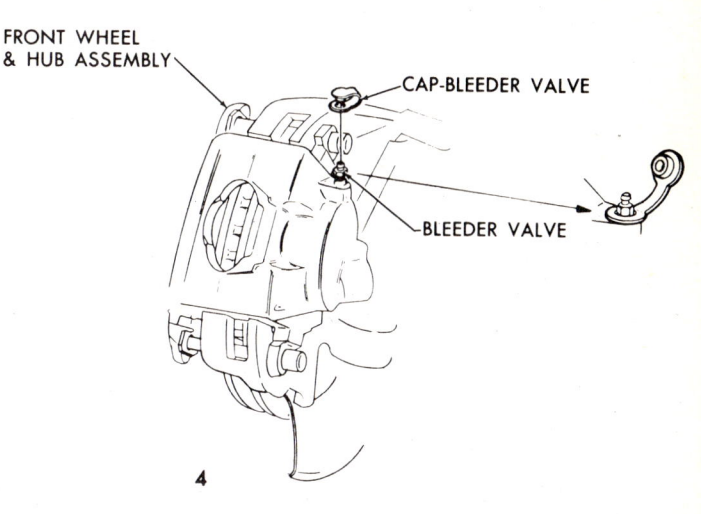

ble adjusting to rotor surface variations, with not too pleasant results. If visual inspection has shown obvious problems, or if you've managed to measure the rotor's thickness at 12 points around its edge to determine out-of-parallel (.005-in. most cars, .007-in. for Fords and Cadillacs), you've got to visit the brake shop. While you're at it, you might as well check for runout (wobble) by mounting a dial indicator to the end of the caliper or steering knuckle, then give the rotor a few turns. If you've adjusted the dial indicator so that it reads zero when you start, the maximum allowable tolerances run from .002 to .005-inch. Check a service manual for the specification for your car.

Anyhow, you'll need to have the truing process done outside. Unless you've got the wherewithal ($1500 for a good lathe) to do it yourself, figure on spending a little for the refurbishing...it's a heckuva lot cheaper than letting it go and later suffering from a real case of runout (the green variety) from your ever loving wallet.

SOME RACING 'N ROADSTERING

No doubt about it, disc brakes got their prime automotive baptism in the heady world of competition, road racin' style. While most Americans were fiddling as their drums burned, the Europeans (primarily British) got hot on the trail of discs. As early as 1952, a relatively unknown driver by the name of Stirling Moss slapped a load of Girlings on his racer and sped off to the wars. The Girlings he used were of a 3-piston design—the pucks themselves rested inside the piston bores. However, the Moss-induced punishment coupled with the fact that the pad area was inadequate, along with problems of boiling fluid and erratic braking soon found him switching to the more trouble-free Dunlop

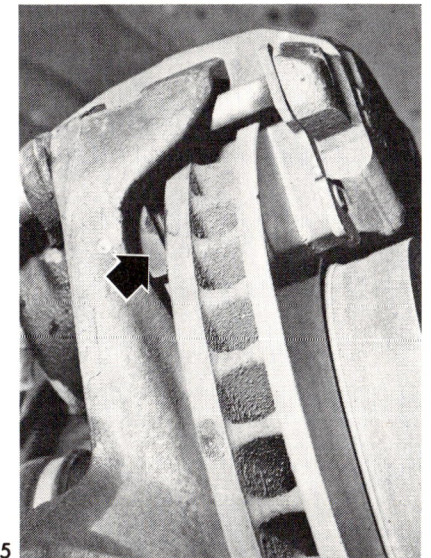

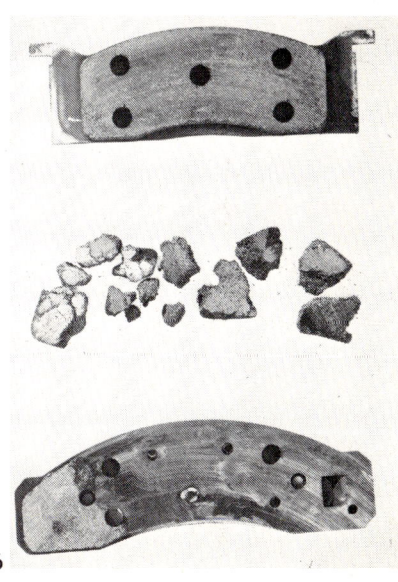

CHASSIS, SUSPENSION & BRAKES/127

Disc Brakes

design. By the time the '53 LeMans 24-hour race rolled around, Jaguar—with a Moss-driven, 50-lap Rheims victory under its belt, using 3-piston Dunlops—was ready. And 24 hours later, placing one and two, with all doubts erased... Jaguar—and others—knew that racing discs were here to stay.

Development continued with greater use of metallic, quick-change linings, ventilated rotors and 4-piston calipers. By the mid-'60's, the state of the art had reached the point where the braking efforts were such that the engine was hindering (reciprocating parts weren't slowing fast enough) rather than lending aid in stopping a high-speed vehicle.

The ultimate (for the time being) disc brake was the result of Ford figuring it was time to do some serious Ferrari racing. Ford had the horses (427 ins. of Holman-Moody, Stroppe) and the chassis (super-tuned by Phil Remington and Ken Miles) in probably the biggest, fastest, most powerful car of its type ever to hit the Mulsanne Straight. The only critical problem was the brakes. Getting the 2860-lb., 225-mph monster slowed down to navigate the 35-mph curve at the end of this 2½-mile-plus Le Mans saltflat required the brakes to absorb something in the order of 4,095,600 ft.-lbs. of kinetic energy, every 3.85 minutes for a solid 24 hours... and they did it. Basically the units featured 3-in.-thick ventilated rotors sprayed with a copper matrix which could be quick-changed like the pucks in the calipers. The calipers were a 3-piece arrangement with separate cylinders on each side of a bridge-like centerpiece. By the time Ford left Le Mans, its builders knew they had met the single, most critical challenge... the brakes.

OK, so you're all lathered up—like if they're good enough for the big boys, how about me and my little "T"...?

If you're in the market to build yourself a set of disc binders to go along with a tube-framed, glass-bodied T-bucket, people like Hurst-Airheart, Edco, Roadster Engineering and most of your local chassis shops carry a full line of rotors, anchors, brackets and bolts to get 'em attached to the early Ford hubs. The calipers are a different story. Those you'll have to find in either factory form from wrecks, junkyards, abandoned hulks, or will have to order via a speed or chassis shop. Naturally all your large manufacturers (Bendix, Budd, Delco-Moraine, Kelsey-Hayes, Girling, Dunlop, Lockheed, Hurst-Airheart, Halibrand, etc.) have them for sale; the thing is to make sure that the caliper and rotor are paired to the extent that the proper side clearances are maintained and that the supporting brackets are beefy enough to ensure good performance.

1. A good tip for VW owners with disc brakes is bending a length of coat hanger into a tool for removing the brake pads from the caliper.

2. Like drums, disc brake rotors that aren't worn too badly can be turned on a brake lathe to provide a new, flat surface for the linings.

3. Again just like a drum, a rotor must have a vibration dampener put on before turning in a lathe, even though it is not hollow like a drum.

4. You can only lathe-turn a rotor so much before the pads can't travel far enough to reach it, making the brakes dangerous. Rotors are marked now with their minimum safe thickness.

5. Here's a typical floating caliper disassembled. Although it looks very simple and uncomplicated, the newer sliding calipers have even less parts.

6. Dial indicator can be used to check a rotor for thickness changes around its circumference. These would cause a surging feeling in the brake pedal and variations over .005-in. would have to be corrected on lathe. The rotor should also not exhibit any more than .003-in. taper at any one point around its circumference.

128/CHASSIS, SUSPENSION & BRAKES

While you're at it, those deep-dished, racy-race wheels might cause a little clearance consternation both as to rotor and caliper fit. The thing is that the speed industry has caused these disc brake conversions to be almost a strictly bolt-on-operation, but watch out for wheel/brake interference. Make sure the custom wheels you buy are made to clear disc brakes, or you'll wind up having to make a spacer plate of some kind.

Well, consider you've been slipped the disc as a way of backing out of a tight situation... like what the drums have found themselves designed into. There is even an inkling that the future may hold some of the same surprises for the disc that the past did for the drums... but for the moment, discs are it.

By the broadsides from the brake industry, there doesn't seem to be much controversy over the merits of disc brakes. But while the idea of disc brakes on American cars, even as an option, is a relatively new concept, some of these discs have been around long enough to wear out their pads and/or rotors. How about yours? Ready for repair?

Happily, you—the backyard brakeman—don't need a small fortune's worth of tools to do it yourself. All that's required are a few basic hand tools, possibly a service manual covering your make and model year, good light and this photo story.

If, on your way, you come across a badly worn rotor, lower it into the nearest swill bucket—a new one costs only $20. Again, if it's a leaking caliper you happen to see, unbolt the offending item and hotfoot it over to your nearest brake shop. Calipers are rather tricky pieces of braking mechanism and should only be worked on by trained personnel equipped with the proper tools.

Mostly you'll find that your discs will be an unbolt, pull, replace, rebolt and bleed operation which can save you the price of a weekend of serious racing, or more importantly... a tragic accident.

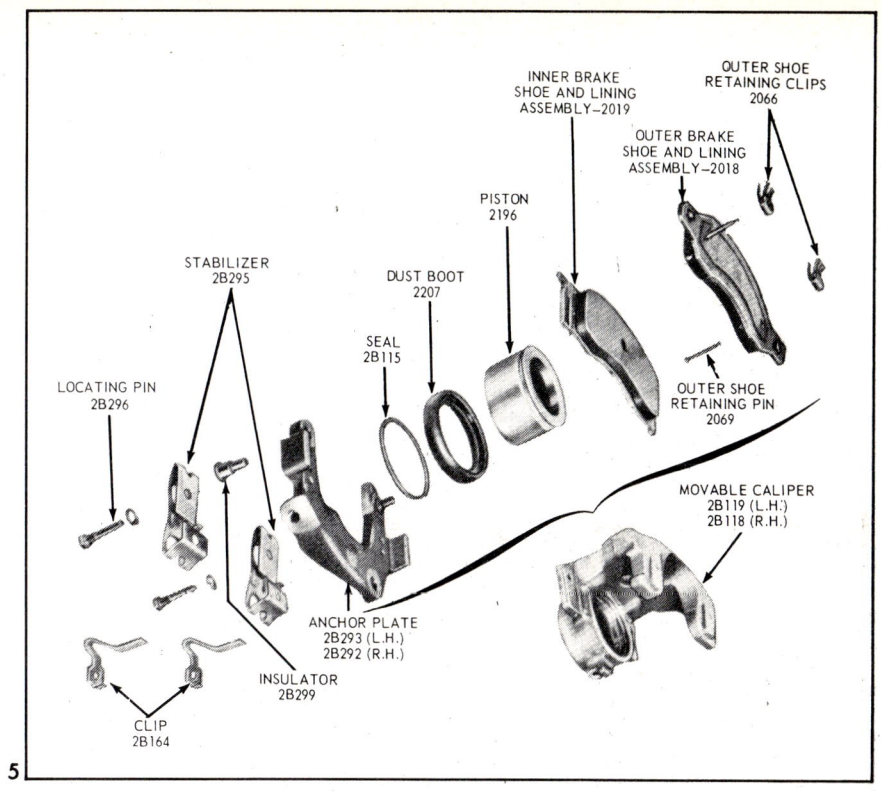

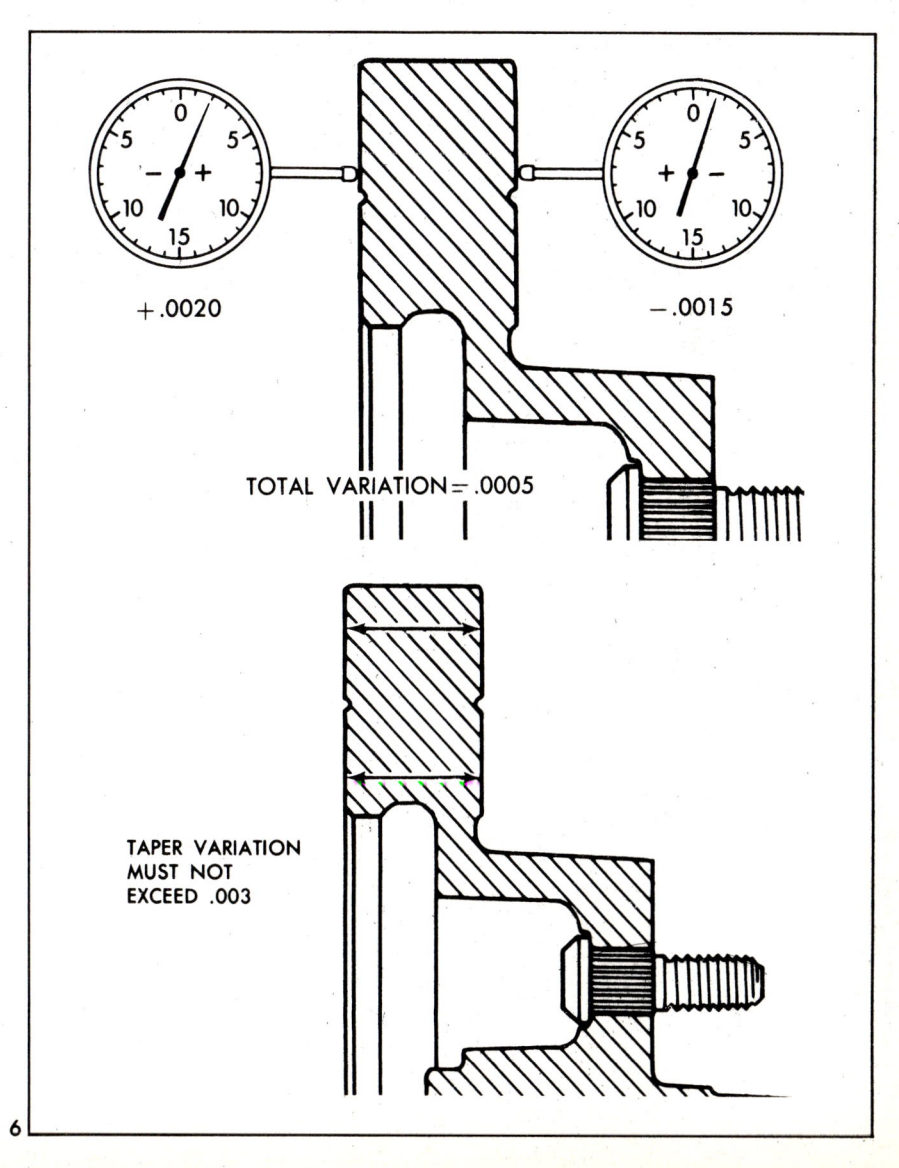

CHASSIS, SUSPENSION & BRAKES/129

Disc Brake Caliper Rebuilding

Replacing the friction pads on disc brakes has become so easy, compared to doing a drum brake overhaul, that there's no excuse for driving with worn-out linings. However, some drivers have heard so many good things about disc brakes that they assume the brakes are either indestructible or that they don't need replacement. These drivers don't find out until they get the $200 repair bill that "running on the rivets" is a lot more expensive than with drum brakes, since the rotors can cost as much as $75 each to replace, compared to perhaps only $20 for a new drum.

And since discs are so easy to replace, there's a temptation to assume that replacing the pads is *all* that's ever necessary in servicing disc brakes. This is another dangerous assumption, because there's a hydraulic system that needs to be looked at, just as with drum brake wheel cylinders. The backyard mechanic may be a little frightened of working on his calipers, since they are larger and slightly more complex than a wheel cylinder, but the rebuilding process is not substantially different.

When you do a complete brake job

HOW-TO: Caliper Rebuilding

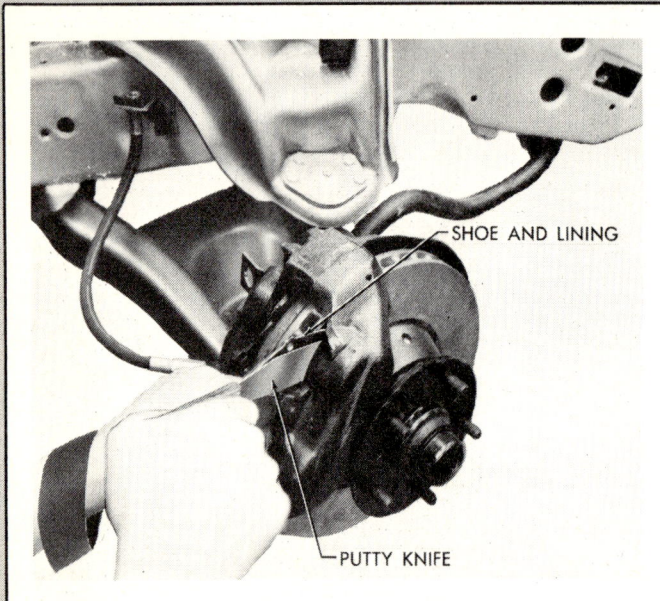

1. In some stubborn cases, you may need some kind of thin tool to slip between the pistons and the pad (putty knife) to retract the pistons enough to get the pads out.

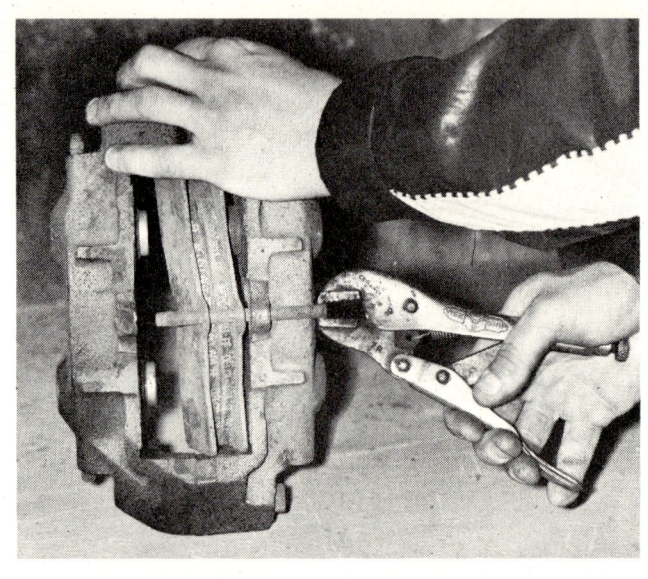

2. After removing the caliper from the spindle and the hydraulic line, pull the cotter pin from the retaining pin and remove the brake pad retaining pin.

3. The pads should come free of the caliper housing at this point, unless the brakes have not been used for a long time and are rusted in, which require prying.

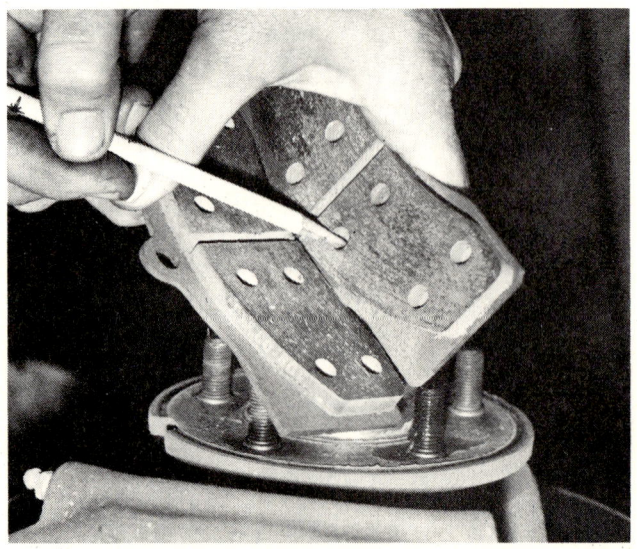

4. While bonded shoes or pads may go a little bit longer, you can't take a chance with riveted linings like these. If they're down close to the rivets, replace them.

130/CHASSIS, SUSPENSION & BRAKES

on a disc brake car, you should go through the calipers as well as replacing the pads, and there may even be cases where your pads are OK but the calipers are leaking or malfunctioning. In any case, the first step is to remove the pads, which on most calipers means pulling out a retaining pin of some kind, while on some newer cars it means taking the caliper off the spindle mount. If you are going to use the pads over again (assuming that they are in good shape and have plenty of material left) then mark them as to location. Since disc brake pads wear thinner at the leading edge than the trailing, they must go back into the caliper the way they came out for proper brake action.

Now's a good time to check out the caliper action. Using a flat tool placed across the pistons and with the caliper still attached to the spindle, pry against the pistons to see how freely they move in their bores. If there is no leakage past the seals and none of the pistons appear to be frozen in their bores due to corrosion, then the caliper can probably be used as is. If not, however, it's time for an overhaul that includes removing the calipers, taking the two halves apart and removing the pistons and seals, honing and cleaning the bores, and reassembling with new parts and plenty of clean brake fluid. Be sure also to use only fluid specified for *disc* brakes, since it has the higher boiling point required with your brakes. We've outlined here in pictures just how to go about this complete caliper rebuilding procedure with no tools out of reach of the weekend mechanic.

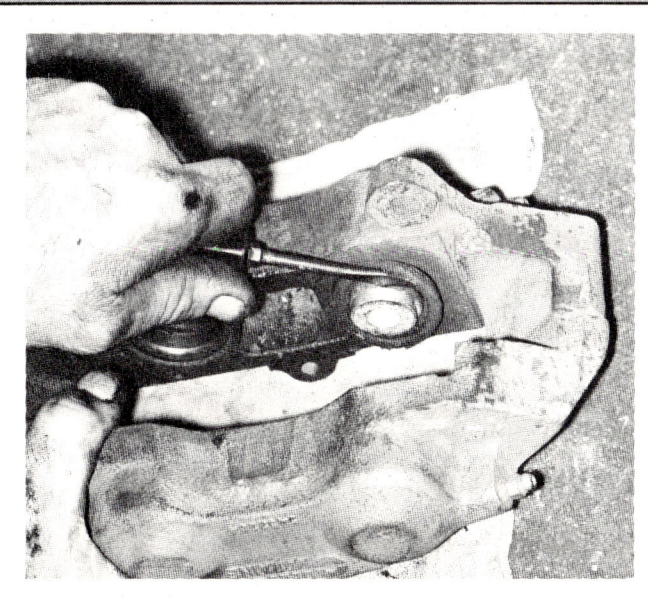

5. Your first step in disassembling the caliper itself is to pry the rubber boots out of the bores with a thin screwdriver, but be careful not to score the cylinders.

6. Use an air hose in the brake line hole to force the piston out of the bores. If it takes a lot of pressure to move them, put rags or wood in middle for protection.

7. The air pressure should pop the pistons out of their bores, but if not, cover them with a rag and pull them out with pliers, being careful not to ruin them.

8. The two halves of the caliper will have to be taken apart at this point. An air wrench or breaker bar will be helpful, as these bolts are torqued to 130 ft.-lbs.

Disc Brake Caliper Rebuilding

HOW-TO: Caliper Rebuilding

9. If there is discoloration in the bores, remove it by wiping crocus cloth in the bore, but minor pits will have to be honed Deep pitting means caliper must be replaced.

10. After honing or polishing with crocus cloth, wipe the bores out with clean rags and wash down with alcohol (denatured), then wipe again until bores are clean.

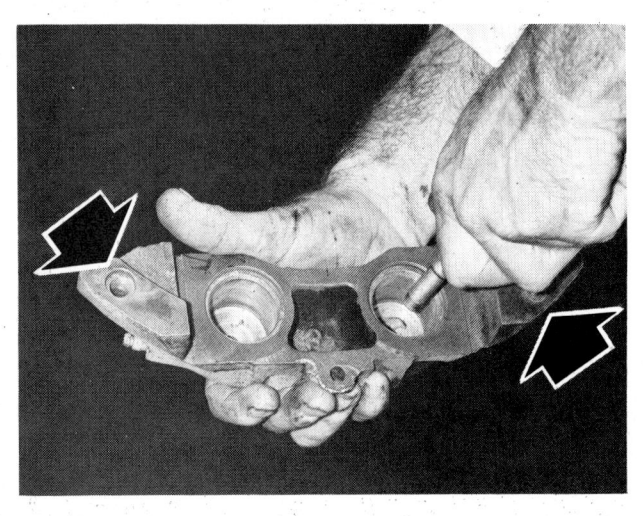

11. After cleaning with denatured alcohol, use an air line to blow dust and cleaning fluid out of the caliper. Also clean the O-ring sealing indentations well (arrows).

12. When you're sure the bores are completely clean, you can wipe them down with clean, new brake fluid (of the disc brake type only) or brake cylinder assembly fluid.

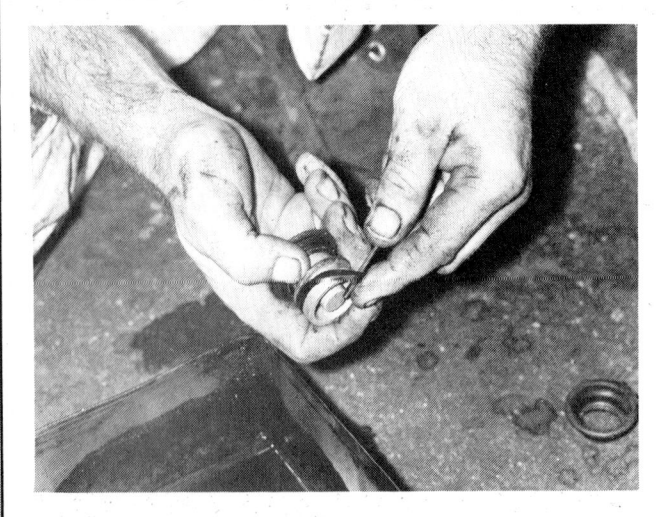

13. Now back to the pistons. With a small screwdriver, take off the seals and boots (being careful not to cut the pistons) and wash pistons in clean denatured alcohol.

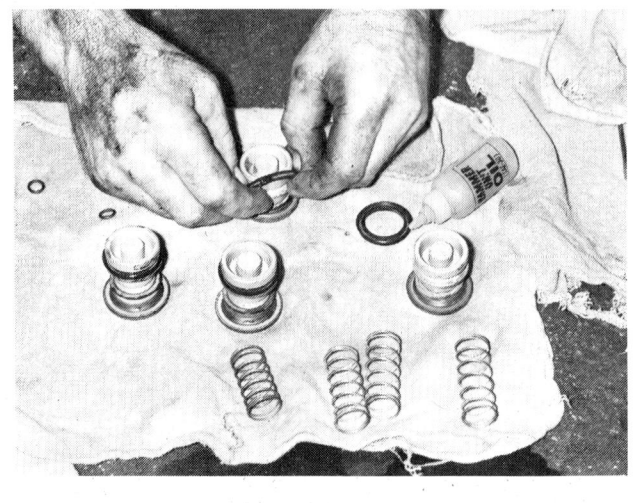

14. With your rebuilding kit, you should have all the springs and seals needed. Lubricate the seals with brake fluid and install with lip toward large end of piston.

132/CHASSIS, SUSPENSION & BRAKES

15. Lubricated with brake fluid, the large end of piston goes into bore first, over the spring, with the piston boot in place on the smaller end of the piston.

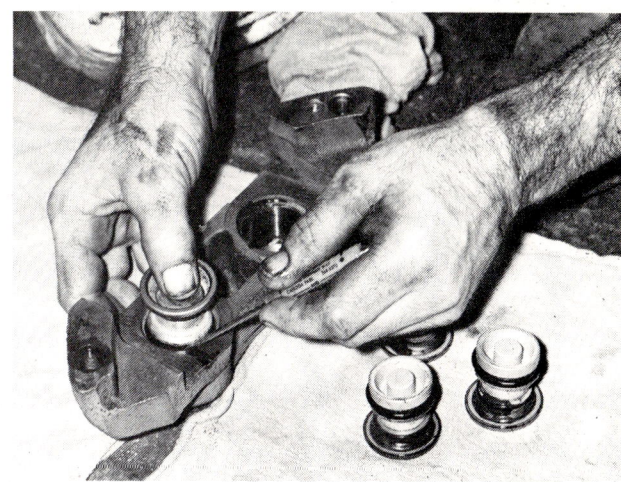

16. You may need a small, dull screwdriver to help you get the piston seal to slip into the bore without the seal coming out of its groove and twisting in the bore.

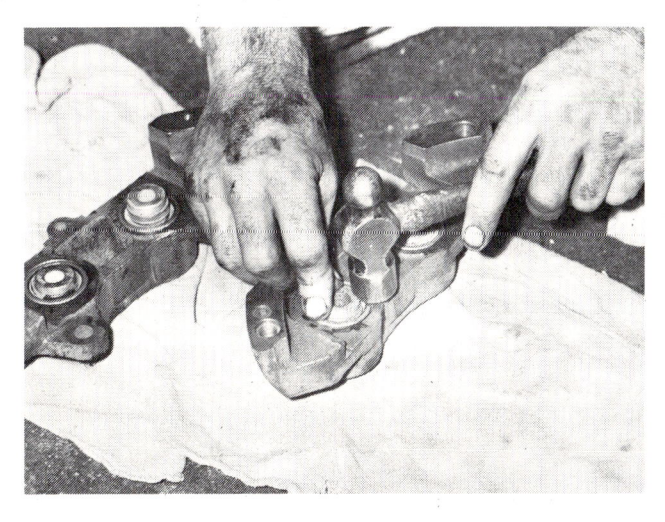

17. After making sure that piston is fully seated and is flush with the end of the bore when fully depressed, you can now tap down the edges of the boot to seat it in.

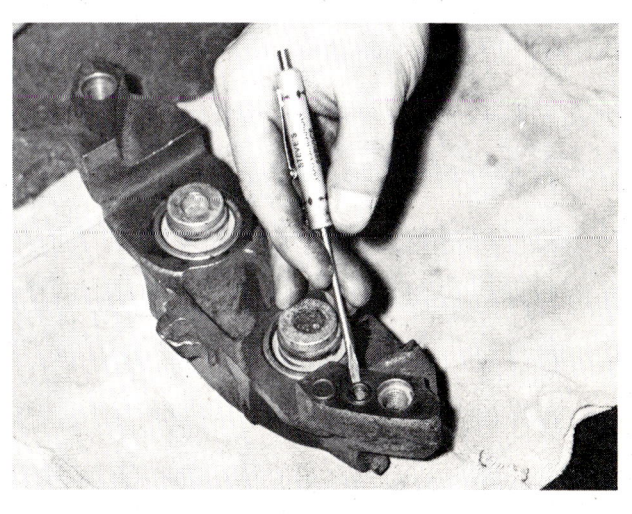

18. At this point, almost ready to reassemble caliper, you must be certain that new transfer passage O-rings are in place and lubed with fresh brake fluid.

19. Alternating from one end to the other, tighten the caliper housing bolts a little at a time, until you get to the 130 ft.-lbs. spec. Lube bolts with brake fluid.

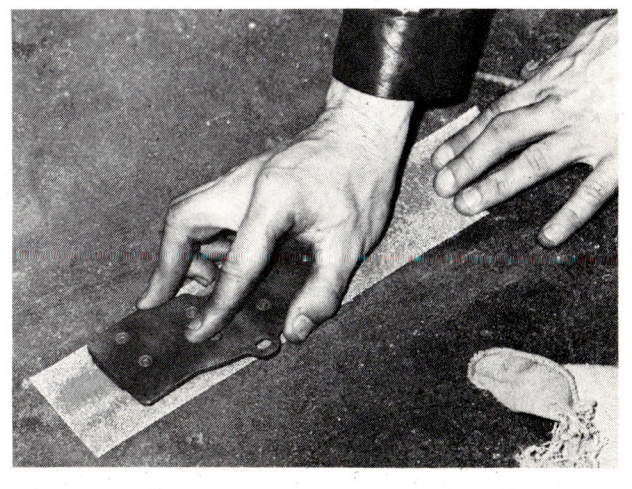

20. If you are using the old pads again, sand off the glaze against a flat surface. Put the calipers and pads back on the car, bleed the system, and you're done!

Power Brake Units

Here are the systems that take the stomp out of stopping.

Power brakes operate through known physical laws regarding the atmosphere that surrounds us. Although we are seldom aware of it, air has weight. At sea level, it exerts a pressure of 14.7 lbs. on each square inch. The amount of air bearing down on this small an area derives its weight from the fact that it is actually a column of air many hundreds of miles long, reaching to the outer atmosphere of the earth. In common terms this weight is referred to as atmospheric pressure, and its weight is measured in pounds per square inch (psi).

Vacuum is the absence of air and therefore the absence of any pressure. If a chamber is divided in the center by a floating valve or diaphragm, and a vacuum is applied to both sides, the valve will remain stationary. However, if air, and its accompanying pressure of 15 psi, is introduced to one of the chambers, the piston will move toward the side that is still under vacuum. Attach the piston to a rod on the vacuum side and the chamber can be made to do work. Attach the rod to a hydraulic cylinder and this work can be multiplied even further.

Essentially, this is how the power brakes on automobiles operate. A power brake assembly is introduced into a normal hydraulic brake system to do work for the driver. Where it is installed, how large it is, and its particular type may vary, but the principle is always the same.

The cylinder in the case of the power brake unit is usually shaped more like two pie plates put together than like a cylinder. Inside there will be a disc-like diaphragm that separates the two sides. The vacuum is supplied by the engine from the intake manifold since this always contains vacuum created by the intake strokes of the pistons. The brake pedal operates valves which regulate the amount of atmosphere that will be let into the pressure side of the chamber. As the pedal is depressed, the valve that allows the atmosphere to enter opens as the vacuum valve closes. The harder the pedal is pressed, the more the atmospheric valve opens and the greater the pressure against the diaphragm. This is the more common type and is termed a vacuum suspended booster system.

In some cases an atmospheric suspended unit is used. This type works in exactly the same way with the exception that the chamber contains atmosphere until such time as the brakes are applied. Operation of the valves then allows vacuum to enter one side of the chamber. The following descriptions of the various types will be limited to vacuum suspended units since they are most common. Virtually all functions will be similar in the atmospheric suspended type of brake.

INTEGRAL TYPE

With the known assist available from the power unit, the only choice left to the engineer is the location in the system. The integral type, which is used on most passenger cars, places the hydraulic master cylinder on the vacuum side of the chamber and the brake pedal on the other. The movement of the diaphragm moves a rod connected directly to the piston in the master cylinder and applies pressure to the brake cylinders at the wheels. As pressure develops in the hydraulic system, and the braking force is applied to the wheels, the resistance is backed up through the master cylinder and power brake unit, giving the driver a "feel" of the amount of braking taking place. The harder the brakes are applied, the greater will be the "feel" at the pedal. Were this not the case, it would be impossible to regulate the amount of braking needed to bring the car smoothly to a stop.

When the driver stops depressing the pedal and keeps it in a particular position, the atmospheric valve will close so that pressure on the hydraulic system can equalize and a constant braking can take place. When the driver releases the brake pedal, the vacuum valve is again opened and vacuum is applied to

1. The ultra-basics of a power brake system is a diaphragm housed between the master cylinder and the brake pedal. This diaphragm gets vacuum from the intake manifold to boost hydraulic pressure in the system.

2. While most systems today push on the master cylinder directly, some older types push the brake pedal into the master cylinder with lever action on the pedal assembly.

3. In the reaction lever-type unit, force from the master cylinder is applied to a set of levers through a bridging mechanism. The reaction back to the driver's foot is low until the spring deflects to allow the levers to contact the valve mechanism.

4. Another type of booster uses a rubber disc instead of levers. When a certain reaction load is reached, force from master cylinder becomes great enough to push disc outward to where it contacts head of pushrod, then reaction load is divided between power piston and the driver's foot.

5. Vacuum in a power brake booster keeps both chamber halves at low pressure until brakes are applied. Depressing the brake makes the input rod open the atmospheric valve and admit air to the rear chamber. The difference in pressures on each side of the diaphragm forces the power piston forward to work on the brakes.

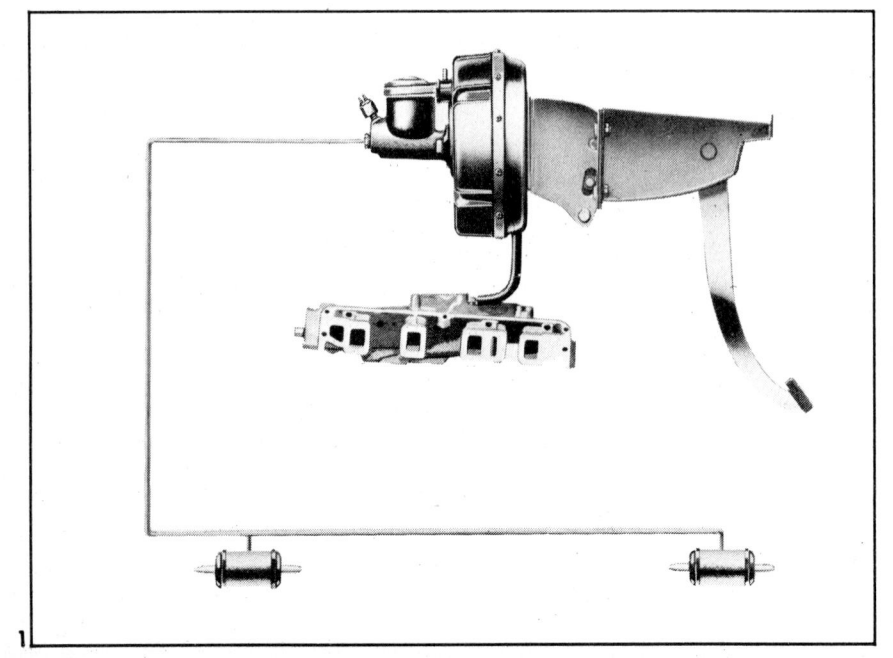

134/CHASSIS, SUSPENSION & BRAKES

both sides of the diaphragm. This releases the brakes.

MULTIPLIER TYPE

Older cars with hydraulic braking systems lend themselves to the adaptation of the multiplier type of power unit. Instead of the power unit being operated by the brake pedal and then operating the master cylinder, the brake pedal operates the master cylinder as it would in a car without power brakes. The master cylinder then applies pressure to the atmospheric valve in the power unit. In an identical manner to the integral unit, the diaphragm moves toward the vacuum side of the chamber and operates another hydraulic cylinder that produces high pressure in the brake lines leading to the wheel cylinders. It is called a multiplier because that is

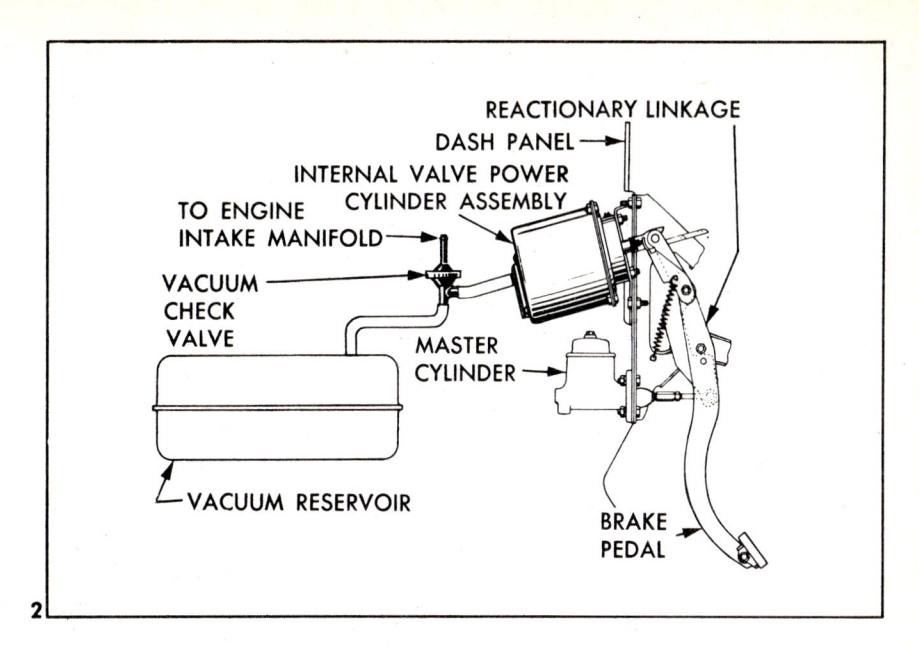

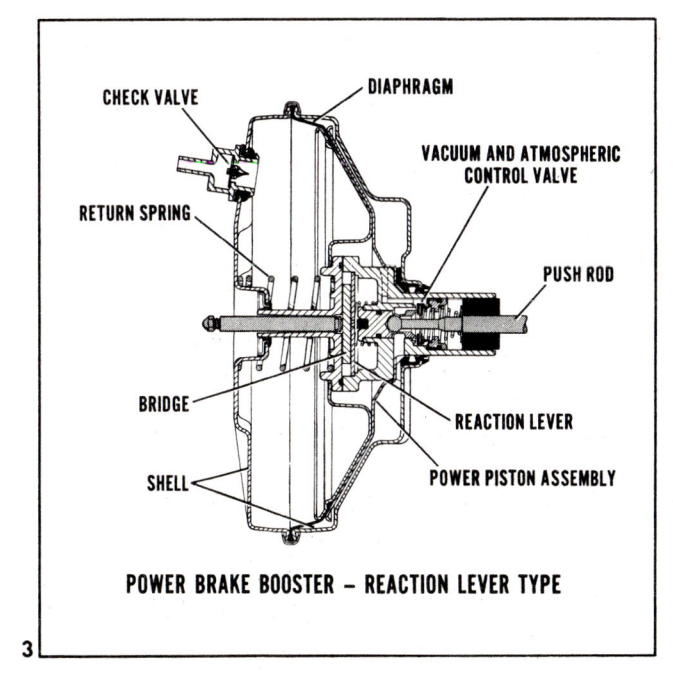

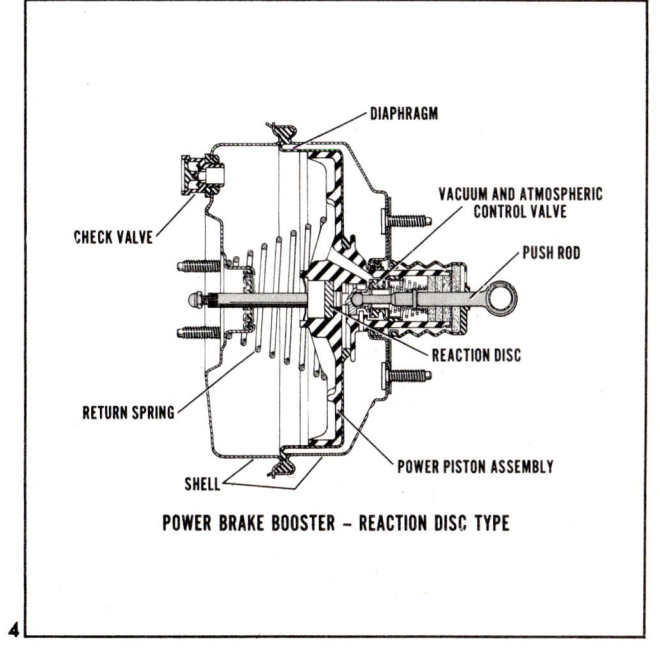

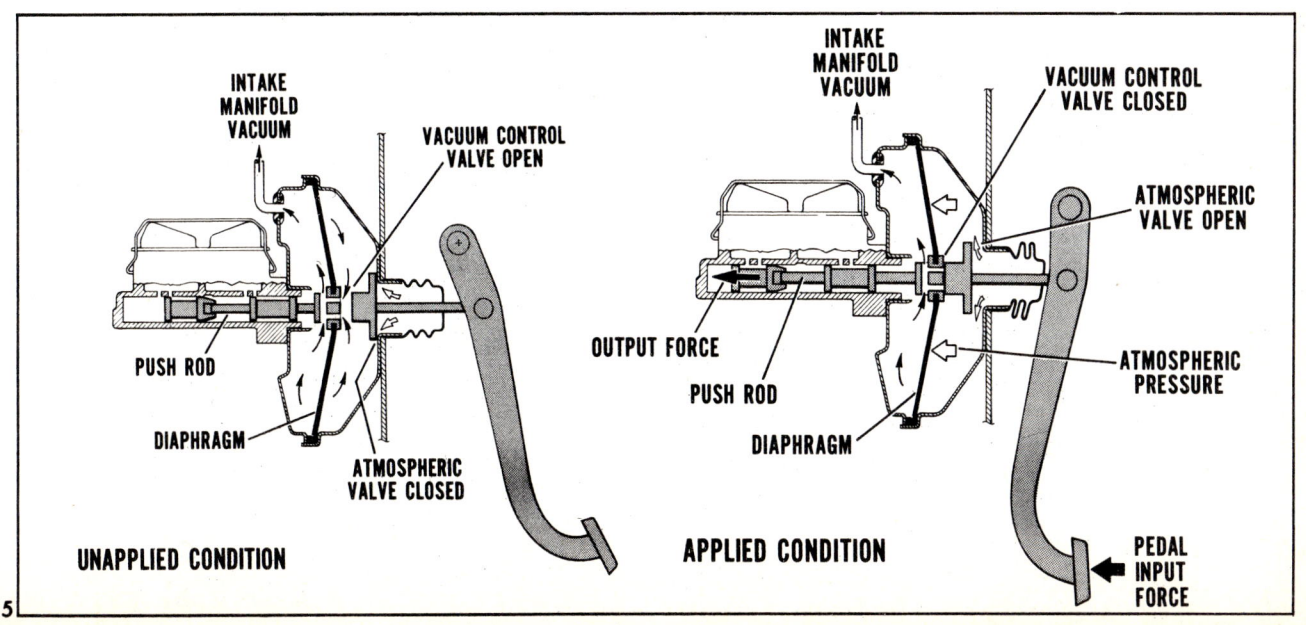

Power Brake Units

what it does; it multiplies the pressure produced by the master cylinder.

The hydraulic cylinder on the power unit is actually two hydraulic cylinders in one housing. As the pressure is forced from the master cylinder at the brake pedal to the cylinder on the unit, it simultaneously closes the vacuum valve and opens the atmospheric valve. Since the cylinder on the unit does not multiply the force it receives, but only forwards it to the wheel cylinders, it requires a longer stroke in order to transmit the pressure. In order to accommodate this added stroke, the diaphragm to which it is connected is moved far to one side of the chamber by a large diameter spring whenever vacuum is applied to both sides.

As the pedal is depressed and atmospheric pressure is allowed to enter one side of the chamber, the force of the spring is overcome, and the diaphragm moves toward the other side. It is attached directly to the actuating rod of the hydraulic cylinder, so pressure is therefore exerted through the brake lines to the brakes at each wheel.

Included in the control valve is a diaphragm that will still be under the influence of the vacuum even though the chamber has been shut off from it. On the other side of this diaphragm, atmospheric pressure being admitted to the chamber will force it upward and resistance will back up through the first stage of the hydraulic cylinder to the master cylinder, and ultimately to the driver's foot. This provides the brake "feel." When the driver holds the brake pedal in a steady position, the diaphragm in the chamber will quickly equalize in pressure, and the resultant equalization in pressure in the control valve diaphragm will close the atmospheric diaphragm.

Releasing the brake pedal will open the vacuum valves to both sides of the diaphragm, and the diaphragm spring will return it to its first position.

The same pressure differential technique can be used in an even more simplified manner in the power assist type of unit. In place of a chamber containing a diaphragm and valves to admit either vacuum or atmospheric pressure, a simple bellows attaches directly to a lever operated by the brake pedal. As the brake

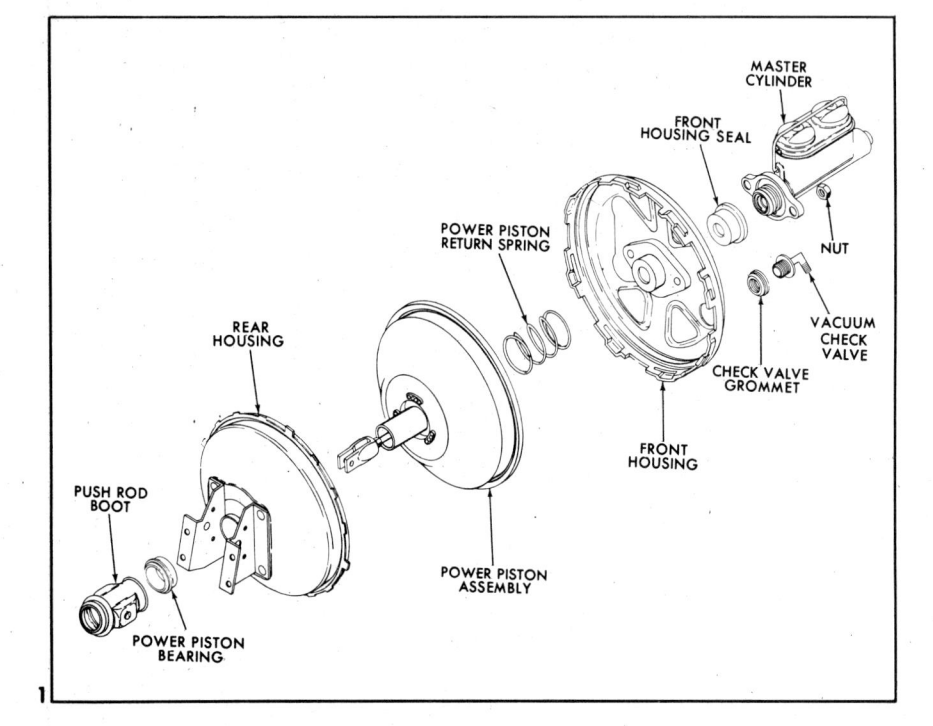

1. Broken down into its components, the modern vacuum-assisted booster is simple, really. Remember that the power piston is actually a flexible diaphragm that does all the work.

2. A check valve is present in the vacuum supply line to all boosters. This keeps dirt and engine fumes out of the chamber and allows a reserve of vacuum to be stored so car can stop well even if the engine dies.

3. This is a cross section of an older Ford bellows unit. When vacuum is introduced to one side of chamber, it collapses and pulls the pedal.

4. This is a Bendix unit as it is with the brake off. The power piston (diaphragm) is to one side of the chamber and doesn't put any pressure on the master cylinder pushrod.

5. When the brakes are applied, the power piston moves to the other side of the chamber, pushing the pushrod into the cylinder to apply brakes.

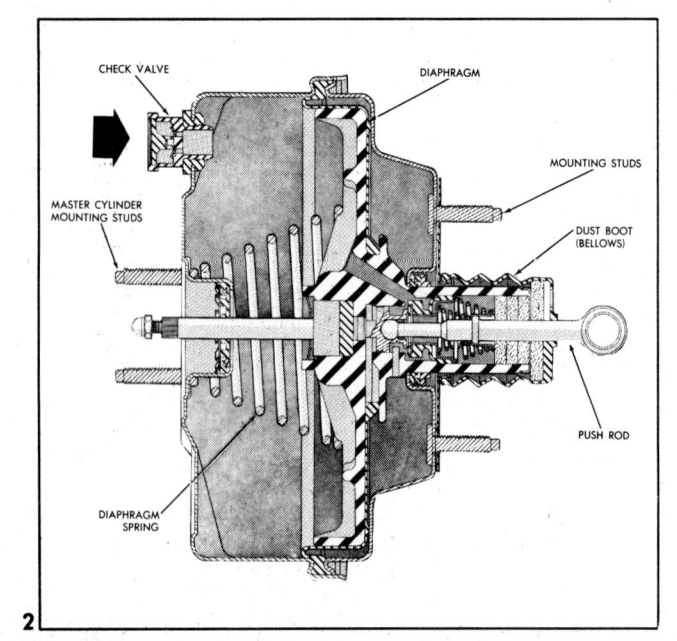

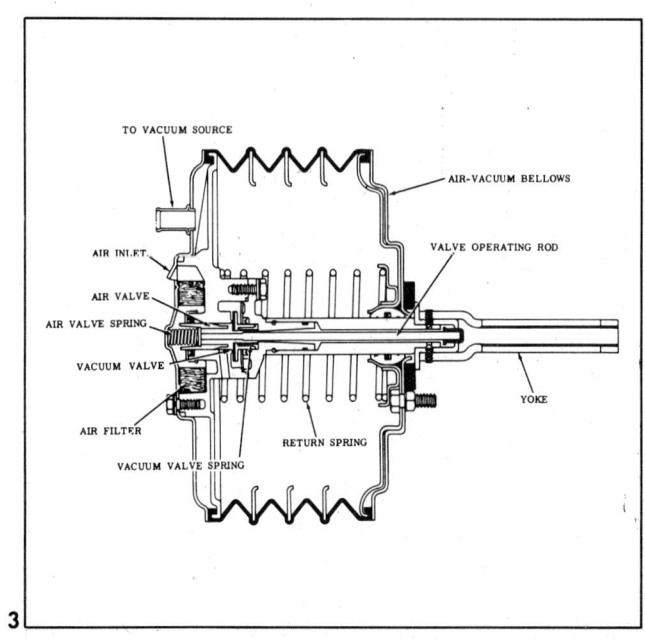

136/CHASSIS, SUSPENSION & BRAKES

CHASSIS, SUSPENSION & BRAKES/137

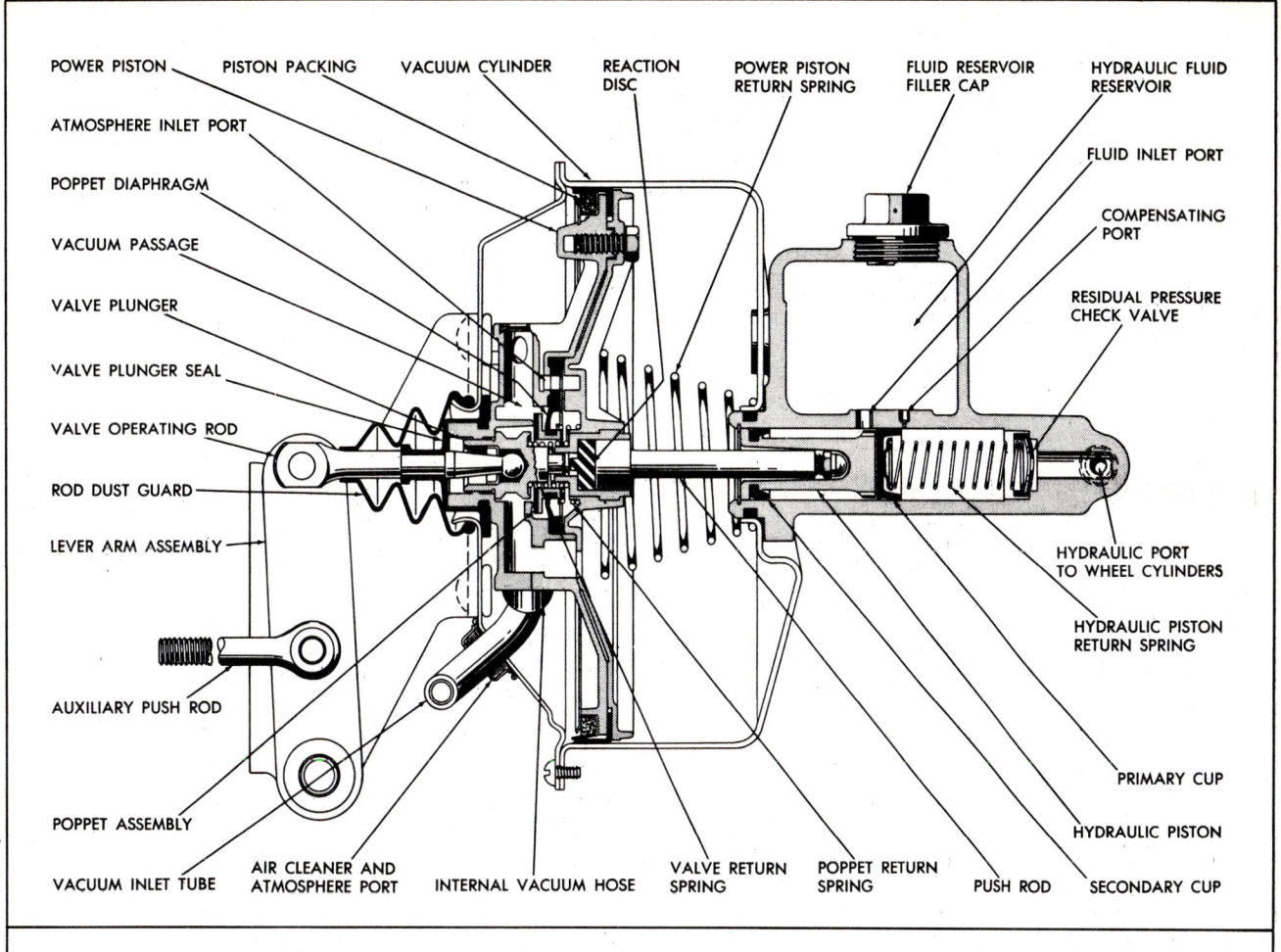

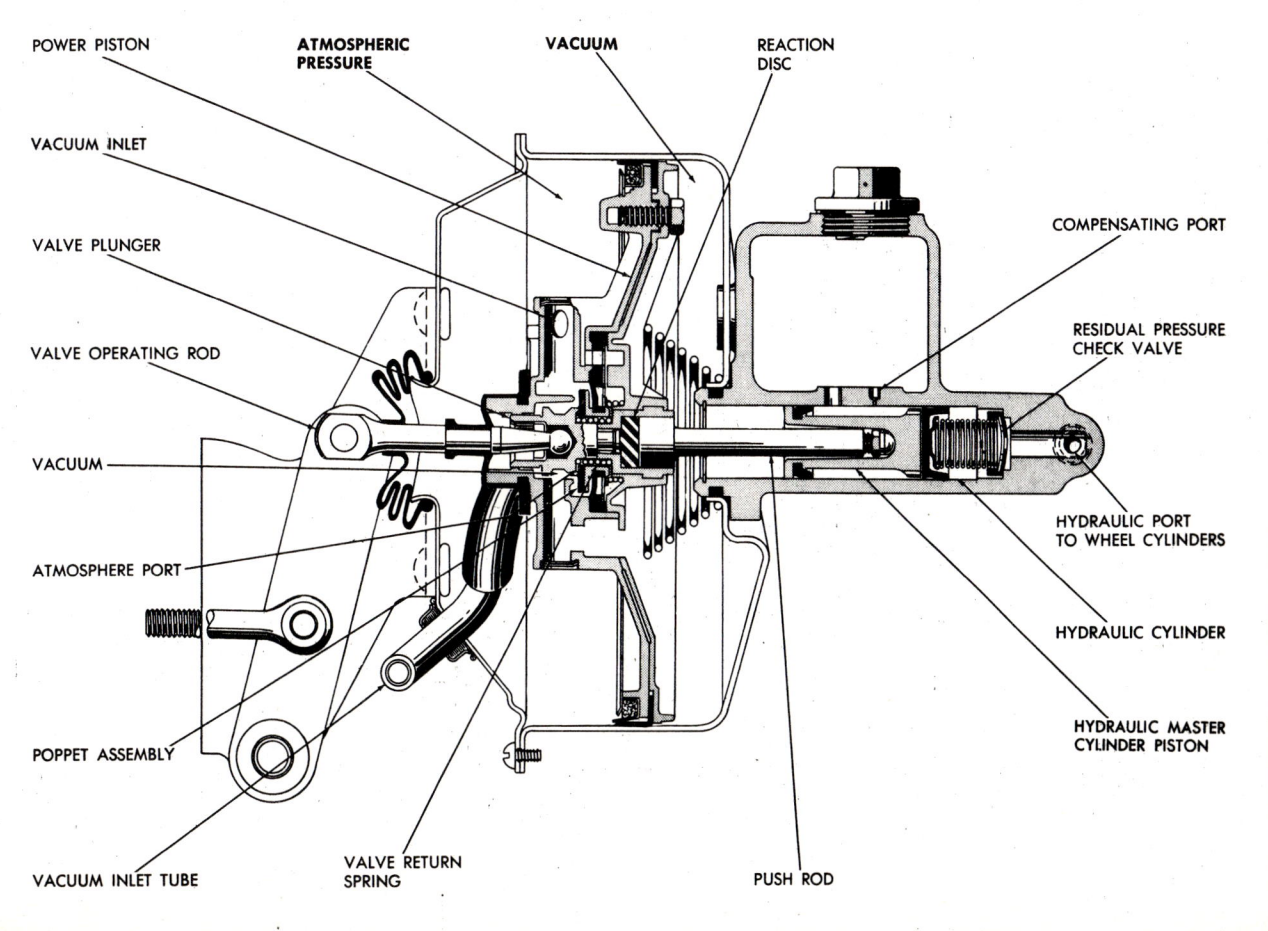

Power Brake Units

pedal is depressed, it opens a valve that admits a vacuum into the bellows and consequently the bellows collapse. As they collapse, they pull on the opposite end of the lever and the combined force of this and the pressure on the brake pedal operates the master cylinder.

When the driver holds the pedal in a steady position, the reaction back through the master cylinder operates a secondary lever that closes the vacuum valve. This provides brake "feel" much the same as in the other systems. As the pressure is removed from the pedal, the vacuum valve closes completely and the atmospheric valve opens to fill, and once again expand, the bellows. Sometimes the "brake off" position is assisted by an auxiliary spring attached to the pedal.

This system includes a vacuum reserve manifold vacuum and will operate the bellows even when the engine is not running. Should the reserve tank be empty the brakes will still function, but considerably more pressure is required to stop the car.

As is the case with so many late model components, power units are replaced as an assembly rather than being repaired. Earlier vehicles had units that could be disassembled and the faulty parts replaced, but today this is not done. Not only is the modern unit virtually trouble-free, it is less expensive to replace than to repair

However, before jumping in and replacing the unit when experienceing brake trouble, check thoroughly to see that the unit is actually the problem. It could well be that the hydraulic system itself is to blame, or the shoes may need adjustment. As already stated, power units seldom fail and the other components of the system could well be at fault.

Apart from a mechanical failure within the unit, the only thing that can cause trouble is a vacuum leak. Check the vacuum line for an audible hiss whenever the brake pedal is depressed. Press it several times since a slight hiss at first touch is not abnormal. If it continues, however, you may have found the cause of your troubles. Internal leaks of any kind may not be determined from external examination, and will require replacement anyway.

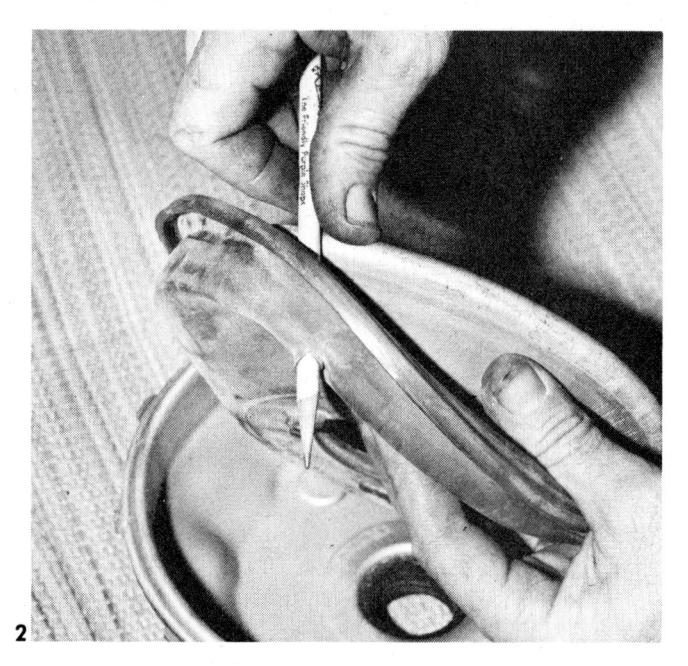

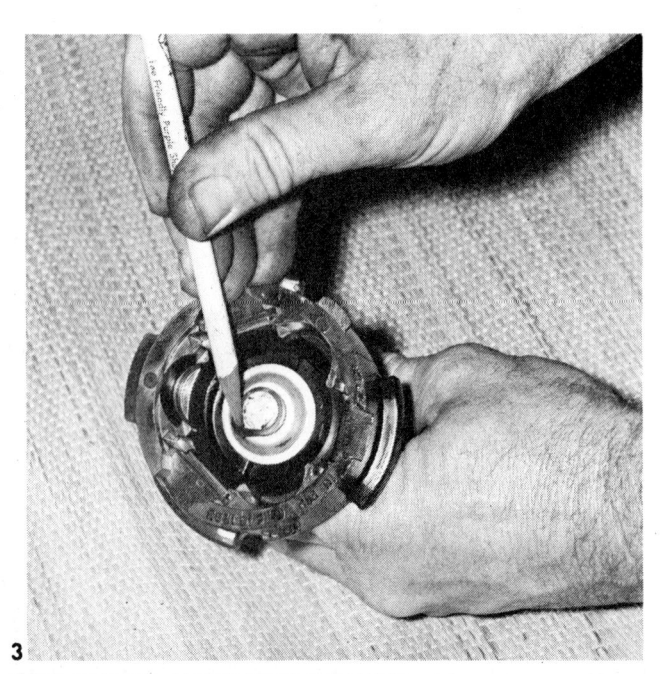

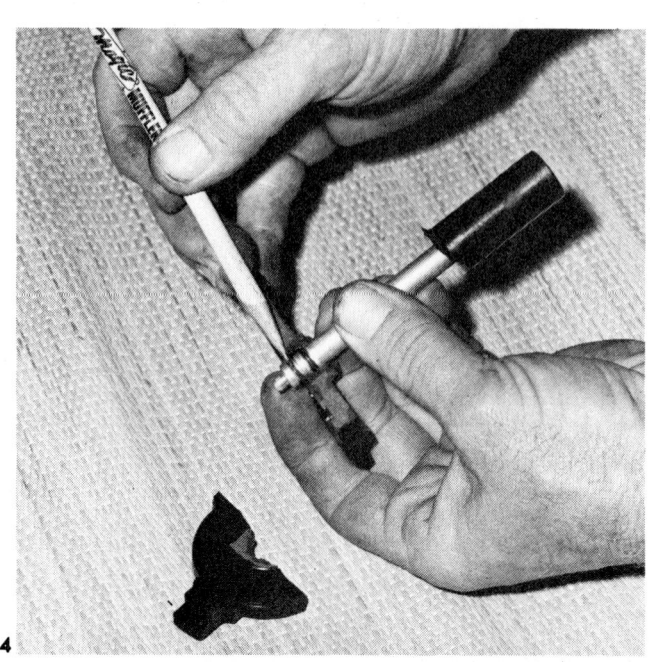

To check for a leak in the unit itself, shut the engine off and depress the brake pedal several times. After

repeated use the vacuum should be used up and the power assist will disappear. Should the brakes fail to have any assist once the engine is shut off, this is an indication that the unit is not storing vacuum. It is possible that there is a small leak that only affects braking during repeated stop-and-go driving, and the unit should be replaced. Again, it may only be a loose fitting so check them all very carefully before replacing any major components.

With an understanding of how the particular unit operates and which fluid lines go where, the automobile enthusiast can replace a defective unit with a minimum of tools. Probably the single most important adjustment is the height of the master cylinder pushrod. Incorrectly adjusted, the brakes will be inoperative. Check a service manual for the particular car prior to replacing the power unit.

Older cars that may not originally have been intended to be fitted with a power system, will often have the power unit mounted on a bracket forward of the firewall. This was a concession to the existing body panels. Later cars that had power brakes "designed in" will usually mount the unit directly on the firewall. The older ones are generally more accessible, while the later ones will have a simpler mounting arrangement, even though it may be necessary to get up under the dashboard to remove them. In either case, once the unit is located and its type established, it is an easy matter to locate the attaching points.

1. This is a Cadillac power unit disassembled for repair. Note that the reaction retainer (arrow) is broken; the symptoms of this were very sensitive brakes that would lock up at slightest pedal pressure.

2. The slightest crack or leak in a power piston will mean that you have no power assist at all, since this will void the valving and allow atmospheric pressure to run through the housing and into the engine.

3. Power brake units are seldom rebuilt at home, but repair kits are available although hard to find. In a kit will be all new seals for the vacuum piston. Any truly complete brake job includes replacing these.

4. Other seals that need replacing at regular intervals include these O-rings on reaction retainer rod.

5. Here's a cutaway of a typical dual master cylinder, power brake unit, valve operating rod, and boot. Note the return springs centering the power piston diaphragm.

6. It's easy to adapt power brakes to an older vehicle when the new unit is used with it's own master cylinder and connected to the pedal linkage the same way. Power brakes are now a favorite update of engine swappers.

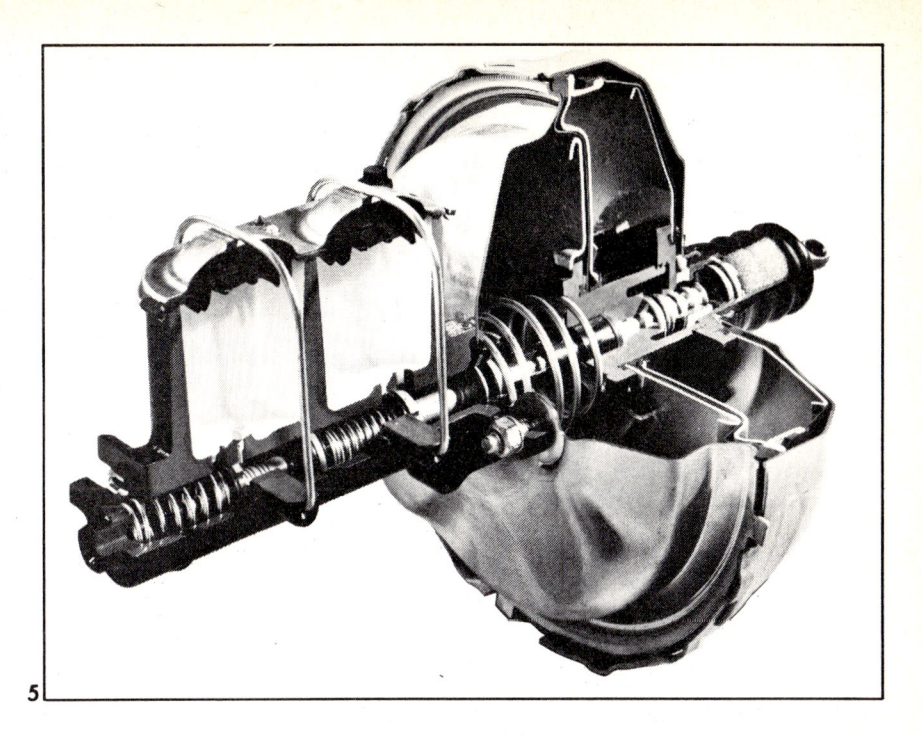

Wheels and Tires

Everything you've wanted to ask about them, and some things you haven't.

As the average automotive enthusiast thumbs through the publications that deal with his specialty interest, he is constantly bombarded with both editorial and advertising ink concerning the wheel-tire combination, enough to rival even the celebrated "cam wars" of years back, in terms of attention. But, as was the case with the camshaft, the basics of wheels and tires are usually a mystery to the average guy—with high-pressure advertising, fancy product names and gimmicks giving him the impression that they are made by "magic." The multi-million-dollar wheel and tire market today is truly a *caveat emptor* jungle.

In the youth of the automotive industry, things were a lot simpler. You bought what was available, which wasn't much, and tried to get along with it. The early motorist had to be a daring soul to begin with, and usually started out on a trip with as many as eight spare tires with him to cope with the expected flats. They were of the "clincher" variety, meaning that the tire had to be stretched over the wheel and bolted onto the rim with clamps and pumped to about 50 lbs. pressure and, needless to say, they were a bear to change. Shortly after the turn of the century, though, things began to look up. The straight-sided tire was introduced and tires started to appear on the market with tread patterns, where they had previously been smooth.

Then came demountable rims, which unbolted from the wheels and stayed with the tire, so when you changed one of those frequent flats you just bolted on a new rim and tire. It might surprise you to know that these early tires were all *white*, because it wasn't until carbon-black was introduced into the tire manufacturing process a few years later that they took on that familiar black color they've had ever since. About the 1920's, wood-spoke wheels disappeared in favor of steel wire wheels, and as tires improved, the wheels were made smaller and smaller in diameter.

The cords for these tires were cotton for the most part and, as the cord fabric was made stronger, tire pressure was dropped in an effort to make the ride more comfortable. Changes in wheel design and construction have paralleled the development of tires all along, and when steel disc wheels came in during the mid-1930's, it was to accommodate the lower pressure tires. The "drop-center" rim on these wheels, which had a ledge-like edge on each side of the tire mounting surface, was necessary to hold the tires onto the wheel at the lower pressures. The idea has been utilized ever since.

While the ride was thus being improved by tire developments, cars were at the same time getting heavier and faster. And as the automobile came to be relied on more and more as basic transportation, tire mileage became very important. In short, it had to be improved. Unfortunately, as has been the case with a number of technological achievements, it took a war to spur the development of better tires. Cord design had been a slow-moving field before World II, and it was the poor heat control of cotton cord fabric that was bugging the engineers. What they came up with was rayon, which turned out to be so

140/CHASSIS, SUSPENSION & BRAKES

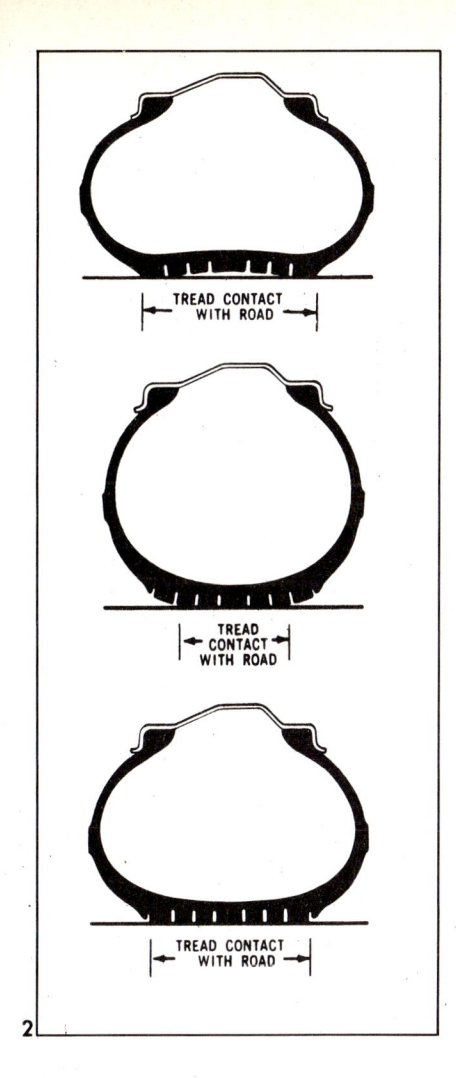

1. Shopping for tires or mag wheels can be a confusing problem today, what with the plethora of brands and sizes on the current market.

2. Proper tire inflation has a lot to do with how a set of tires will handle and how long they will last.

3. The construction differences in radials, conventionals and biased tires are in the cord angles, but these changes make all the difference in driving and length of tread life.

good that it supplanted cotton almost entirely, even after the war. When developing military tires that had to work under adverse conditions, they discovered that rayon had superior heat-resistance, and it's been used since then.

Another fast-moving type of transportation—aviation—was responsible for the development of another important cord material, nylon. Airplanes needed tires that were lighter and could withstand the abuse and high temperatures of takeoffs and landings at high speed. First developed seriously in 1948, nylon was found to be stronger, lighter and *cooler* running, an extremely important feature. While being stronger than rayon, it is also more flexible, but this leads us to one of the few disadvantages of nylon for passenger car tires.

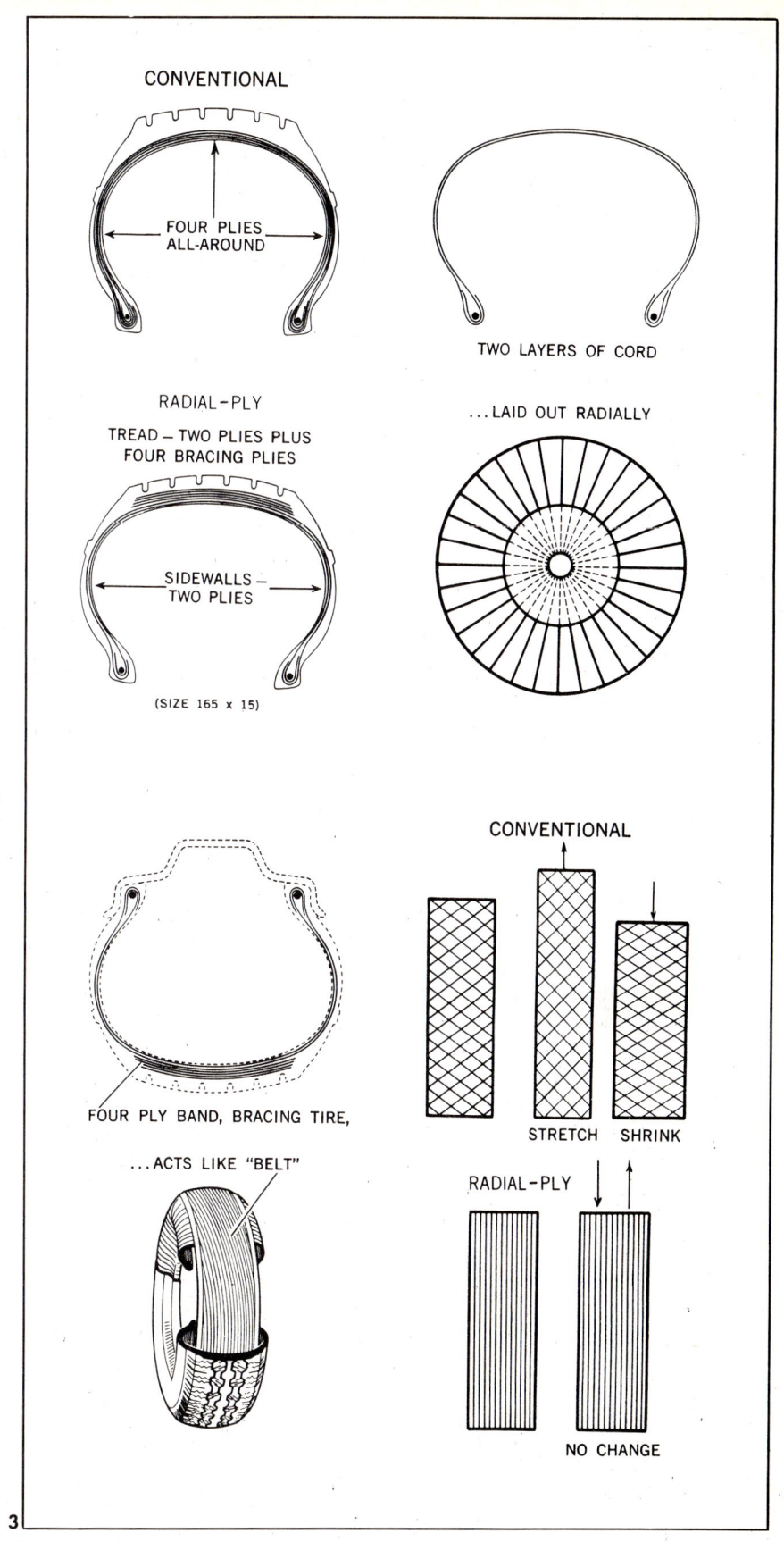

Nylon has the characteristic that it flexes a little more when it has warmed up to its operating temperature, and when a "hot" set of tires are parked in the garage overnight, a small flat spot "sets up" on the bottom of the tires. When the car is driven again with the tires cold, the flat spots produce a slightly annoying thumping noise, which disappears after a few miles of driving, or some-

CHASSIS, SUSPENSION & BRAKES/141

Wheels and Tires

times a few blocks, depending on the climate. You might ask, "If nylon tires are so good, why don't all the Detroit car makers use them?" This thumping just described is the main reason. The difficulty is that dealers have felt prospective car buyers while test-driving a new car might think the car was doing the thumping instead of the cold tires. This characteristic is probably more noticeable in extremely cold weather, but the thump has been subdued some by new construction techniques.

THE TUBELESS TIRE

Over the years, tire manufacturers have come up with an incredible array of devices and gimmicks to lessen the hazard of a flat tire. There was a time when a flat tire on the highway was extremely dangerous, with the front end of the car swerving all over the road. Gummy solutions, special tubes, dual tubes and other devices have been tried but, strangely enough, the most practical aid has proven to be the elimination of the tube! Well, not really. The tag of "tubeless" is actually a misnomer in a way, because the tube hasn't been eliminated, just made into a permanent part of the tire itself. The tubeless tire has a liner of special very soft rubber bonded to its inside, taking the place of the tube. The *wheel* now has become part of the air-holding body, and it had to be improved so that air wouldn't leak out, either from the rim flanges or through the rivets that hold the wheel center to the rim.

Although there are countless things encountered on the road which can damage a tire, the majority of flats are caused by nails, glass, and other pointed objects. When a tube-type tire is punctured, the air-holding body, or tube, deflates suddenly because the tube can back away from the object which caused the puncture, and "explode" within the tire. But with a modern tubeless tire, the inner liner is soft enough to provide a seal around the intruding nail, and as long as the nail remains in the tire, the car can be driven safely to the nearest service station. And when a tubeless tire *does* go flat, it doesn't go instantly; it's slow enough to allow you to safely pull over to the side of the road when you first notice it. Besides these safety features of the tubeless tire, they also run cooler, are lighter, experience no chafing of the tube against the tire or the rim, and are much easier to service.

HOW MANY PLIES?

Despite its safety features, the tubeless tire was introduced to the public amidst widespread skepticism. Somehow, people just thought it couldn't be safe if something was taken away from the tire. But experience bore out its virtues and it was accepted completely after a few years. The general public has always been slow to accept changes, but no other change has caused the tire manufacturers so much grief as the switch in 1961 from 4-ply tires to 2-ply.

The average car or tire buyer has never known enough about how tires are constructed to really understand what he is buying. He has always figured that if it only has two plies, it must be only half as strong as one with four plies, right? Wrong. A 2-ply tire has a 4-ply rating, which means that it can support the same load as a 4-ply tire with a 4-ply rating. Many present-day 4-ply tires actually have an 8-ply rating.

Improvements in cord construction and fabric materials have made it possible for the same load to be carried by a lesser amount of plies. By now you have realized that *heat* is public enemy No. 1 to your tires, but what you may not realize is why there is so much heat generated in them. Braking, acceleration, and simple road friction all contribute to the demise of a tire carcass, but a major cause of heat is friction *within* the tire. When you look at a newly mounted tire before it is installed on your car, it looks and feels firm and seems as round as it could be. But on the car, no tire is really round, or firm. It has to be relatively soft, and run at comparatively low pressure for a smooth ride, since the tire is actually the final link between your suspension system and the road, absorbing many of the minor road shocks. To do this it has to flex, and it is the flexing of a tire, either in the tread or sidewall, that creates heat. As a tire rolls, it has to distort and deform from its roundness as it contacts the road, causing a rippling of the tire fabric. There is then friction generated between the plies of fabric as the tire ripples, causing heat. The more plies there are, the more friction is generated as the plies rub against each other. So to cut the heat and increase tire mileage, you have to cut down on the number of plies, but you can only do this when you have improved the cord strength or fabric design so that the load can be carried safely.

In short, this has been the history of the tire business. When cheap, poor quality cotton was used for cord fabric back in 1920, tires had to have eight plies to support a car, light as cars were then. In fact, although the weight of the average passenger car has increased steadily since the horse-and-buggy days, tires have had a steady *decline* in the number of plies, and as the number of plies has decreased the tire mileage has *increased*. Tires have gone from eight plies with cheap cotton, to six plies with improved cotton, to four plies with rayon, to two plies with present-

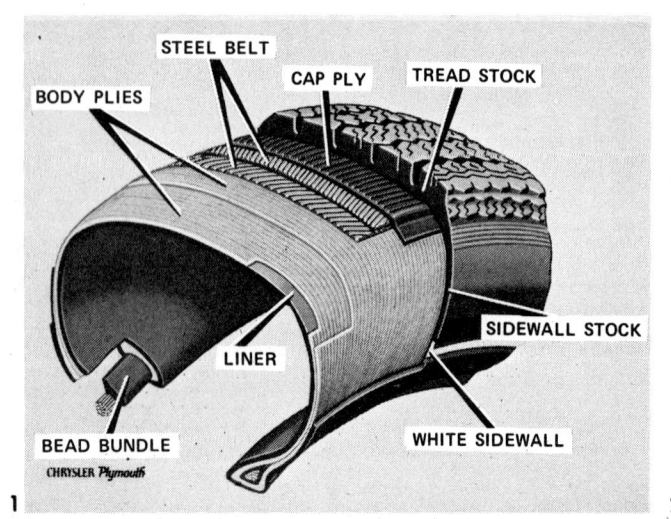

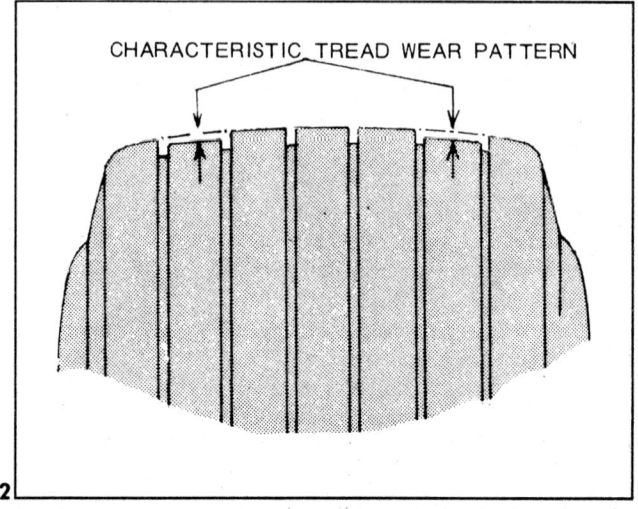

142/CHASSIS, SUSPENSION & BRAKES

1. Steel-belted radials have become all the rage in Detroit this year, with radials being optional on many new cars. These found on Chrysler products have a two-ply polyester cord body enclosed by two steel belts under a cap ply. Radial benefits are longer tread life, improved handling, and perhaps even better gas mileage.

2. If you've got 'glass-belted tires and noticed that the second and sixth treads are wearing out before the others, it's not your alignment, but a characteristic of these tires, especially those in wide sizes.

3. Since 1968, new tires have to have these tread-wear indicators. When a tire needs to be replaced, a band of solid rubber appears across treads.

4. Since your tires are the final contact between your chassis and the road, they are the indicators when you suspect a mechanical problem. The way they are wearing tells you about your car and your driving.

5. Static imbalance in tires/wheels can be corrected on a simple bubble balancer, but the more serious type of imbalance, dynamic, shows up at speed and must be analyzed with a "wheelspin" type of balancer.

day improved rayon and nylon. To predict a single-ply tire for the future wouldn't seem out of line!

Seriously, every time a breakthrough was made in cord material, the number of plies (and at the same time the heat they generate amongst them) could be dropped and tire mileage increased. Besides the heat factor, the modern 2-ply/4-ply rated tire is more flexible than its 4-ply counterpart, making it less subject to rupture by objects on the road.

RADIALS AND BELTED TIRES

Since the tubeless, 2-ply nylon tire, the greatest advancements in tires have been made in other directions, mostly in performance. The tire moguls seem to be borrowing more and more from their racing tire experiences. The modern wide-tread, low-profile, high-performance passenger car tire is a direct descendant of the revolutionary 1963 Indy tires designed by Mickey Thompson and built by Firestone for his Chevy-powered entry. The design was quickly copied by everyone, adapted to virtually all types of road and sports car racing machines, and in the past few years has entrenched itself on high-performance production cars. On the Indy cars they provided lower unsprung weight, a lower center of gravity, less frontal area in some cases, and substantially increased traction and handling. They have done much the same for passenger cars since 1966.

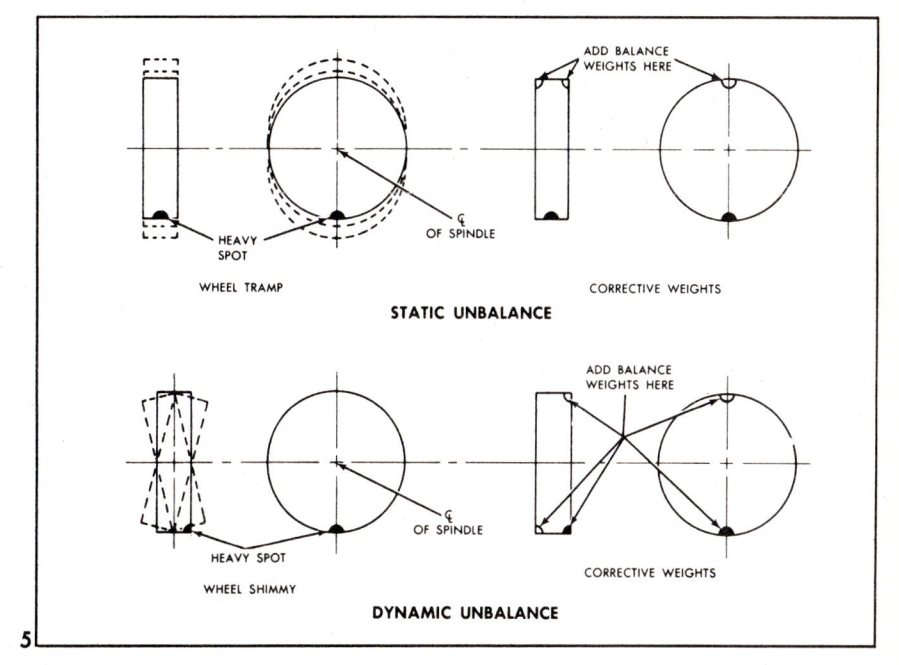

So finally we come to today, and everyone's buzzing about two other developments of recent years—the radial tire and the polyester-belted cord tire, which in some cases go hand in hand. Actually, the radial tire isn't that new—they've been using them in Europe for some time—but our tire manufacturers were slow to pick up on the idea. What makes the radial a different tire is its cord *angle*. Conventional passenger car tires have the cord plies running *with* the rotation of the tire, but at an angle to each other, usually between 32° and 38°. The radial tire cord angle is 90°; in other words the two (or more) main plies run at right angles to the rotation of the tire, from bead to bead.

This type of cord direction gives great flexibility to the tire, but something has to be done to firm up the tread portion so it isn't "squishy." So the tire makers belted 'em right in the tread. By adding several tread-width belts of cord material just under the tread, and running *with* the rotation

CHASSIS, SUSPENSION & BRAKES/143

Wheels and Tires

(i.e., 90° to the main radial plies), everything seemed to work better than had been expected. While the sidewall of the radial has only two "unbiased" plies and is quite flexible, the tread portion of the tire is exceptionally firm, which gives it the handling quality it is known for. The sidewall is flexible enough for a decent ride, but the tread can stay in contact with the road better than a conventional bias-ply tire for improved cornering. And since there aren't the usual biased plies to cause heat buildup, and the tread doesn't squirm on corners (the conventional tire wears *eight* times as much on corners as it does on a straight road), tire mileage is one of the strongest features of the radial, up to as much as twice the ordinary tire's mileage.

Naturally, there are a few disadvantages to the radial, otherwise we'd all have them by now. First of all, they're expensive, because they require special construction techniques and equipment and can't be built on standard tire machinery. When radials were first introduced in this country, people complained that although the radial cornered better, it gave no warning when it came to the limit of its holding ability. A driver can feel when a conventional tire is going to lose traction or slide. This no-warning problem has been subdued in newer model radials. About the only other drawback to the radial is a slightly harsher ride below 40 mph, above which it smooths out beautifully.

Radials, because of their different cord angle, can't be built on regular tire machinery, as we've said. For a long time the cost factor kept American tire manufacturers from jumping on the radial bandwagon, but this has all changed in the past two years or so. Now almost everyone makes not only radials but steel-belted tires for greater advantages of long life, handling and safety. This year marks the first time radials have been offered, even as optional equipment, on many of Detroit's offerings. Chrysler Corp., for example, offers steel-belted, polyester-cord radials across the board on their cars for '74 and even guarantees them on a warranty basis for 40,000 miles.

Spawned as something like a compromise between the radial and regular bias-ply tires, most of the original equipment and aftermarket tires today are known as "belted construction." What this means is that the manufacturers have mated the stiff under-the-tread belt of a radial to a conventional tire. Two standard plies are used in the sidewall construction, but under the tread are those same two cords plus two plies of fiberglass or polyester material. These can be built on regular tire equipment, but offer some of the wear-resistance and handling qualities of the radial.

THE SIZE ASPECT

Tires, naturally, come in all sizes and shapes. Formerly, a typical tire size may have been 8.00x14, while today may be listed as a G78-14. These new ways of identifying tires actually tell you more about a tire than the old system, it just takes some getting used to. In the example above, the G stands for the tire size and there are sizes from D up to huge L-series monsters. The 14 of course represents the rim diameter that this tire fits, and the 78 tells you some new information, the tire "aspect ratio." The aspect ratio has to do with the tire's cross-sectional area, and means that in this case the tread is 78% as high as it is wide. The lower the aspect number, the lower the "profile" of the tire. In the past few years, high-performance tires have become *the* thing and aspect ratios have continually plunged to the point where 70 and 60-series tires are common and a few companies have recently come out with 50-series tires whose tread is twice as wide as it is high. These babies are really wide, low-profile items!

BASIC HOW-TO'S FOR TIRES AND WHEELS

The days of the "tire-iron derby" have just about disappeared from the tire-mounting and repairing scene, and today it's a lot easier to take your new skins down to the local gas station for mounting. Even the poorest-equipped service station has a time- and labor-saving mounting machine, but there are a few things you should know about the procedure, even if someone else is going

144/CHASSIS, SUSPENSION & BRAKES

lbs. won't seat the beads, then deflate and try again, using more of the tire lubricant.

BALANCING

If you just putt-putt around town picking up groceries, you don't have to worry about wheel balancing, but if you do any high-speed or highway driving, balancing is something you should look into. Basically there are two kinds of wheel balance—static and dynamic. The symptom of static imbalance is a slight wheel hop or "wheel tramp," while dynamic imbalance usually shows up as a shimmy or vibration. In any case, the problem is an easy one to solve, and requires only that you bring the car to a front-end shop or properly equipped service station and pay the man about $3 per wheel.

Tires and wheels can be balanced either on the car or off, but the first method is preferred because this way the brake drum is balanced with the wheel. Before balancing, check to see that your lugs are properly tightened, since a loose lug nut could cause lateral runout of the wheel. Balancing on the car is quite simple: An adapter ring is attached to the wheel, and the balancer fits on that like a hubcap. The wheel and tire are rotated by a portable machine that spins them with a small wheel and electric motor. As the wheel is spinning, the operator can juggle the control knobs of the balancer to show him exactly how much weight to add and where to add it on the rim. An important thing to remember, after the job, is that the parts are only in balance when assembled as they were when the balancing was done. You can ensure that the wheel will always be replaced the correct way by putting a dab of paint on the end of one of the lug studs and a corresponding mark on the wheel next to

to do the dirty work for you.

To avoid damaging the tube when mounting a tube-type tire, get one bead of the tire on the rim before you put the tube inside it. The bead sections of the tire and drop-center area on the rim should first be coated with tire lubricant. Slip the tube inside the half-mounted tire, pull the valve stem through the hole in the rim and secure it with a threaded holder, then mount the other bead on the rim. Inflate the tube to seat the beads of the tire, and deflate the tube completely by taking out the valve core; then you can reinflate to the proper pressure. The deflation and reinflation after the beads are seated takes out any folds or kinks in the tube that may have been incurred while the tire was trying to seat.

Naturally, you don't have to worry about such things with a tubeless tire, but they have their own idiosyncrasies. Since the wheel is part of the air-holding body, you should check it over carefully before mounting a tire. Straighten out any dents in the rim then wire-brush or sand-smooth the bead seating areas, and check the rivets and/or welded areas for possible air leaks. Some "mag" wheels are a little porous in their casting, and consequently can leak with tubeless tires, in which case you'll have to put a tube inside them....check wheel manufacturer's recommendations before you buy.

After securing the tubeless-type valve stem in the rim, and lubricating the bead seats with tire lubricant, you can mount both beads. To make the beads touch the flanges so the tire can be inflated, you will probably have to squeeze the center of the tread with a steel band or bead expander, a tool that any service station will have. Don't put any more than about 10 lbs. pressure in the tire before removing the expander, and if 40

1. When a dynamic balance job is done on the car, then your brake drum and lugs are all balanced with the wheel, but you must remember in servicing the car to always put the wheel back on the same way, or balance is off.

2. Stewart-Warner Alemite makes a handy little stick-on speedometer for testing tire/wheel balance. You can check out a complaint of shimmy at a certain speed right in the shop.

3. Chevrolet now runs its tires and wheels through a computerized spin balancer to closely match tires and wheels to each other's balance.

4. The spin balancer allows testing a tire at simulated high speeds for a precise job, but usually calls for weights to be placed on both sides of the rim, while bubble-balanced wheels can have the weights all on the inside where they don't show.

CHASSIS, SUSPENSION & BRAKES/145

Wheels and Tires

the lug. You should balance your wheels whenever mounting new tires, and if you change a tire and don't want to rebalance it, mount it on the rear of the car where the imbalance will not affect the overall performance as much as on the front end.

CARE AND FEEDING OF WHEEL BEARINGS

Adjustment and lubrication of your wheel bearings are important aspects of car maintenance and can save you from Excedrin headache No. 452—which is paying for new ones. There are several types of anti-friction bearings used in automotive wheel bearings, but most are either ball- or roller-type, and maintenance procedures are basically the same. You should check them about every 5000 miles, and whenever you do a brake overhaul job.

Jack up the front end of the car, remove the hubcaps, and take off the dust caps (which can be pried off with a screwdriver on most cars, although some screw on like the early Ford caps). You will only be concerned, however, with your front wheel bearings, since the rear ones are not wheel bearings but *axle* bearings, and need not be disturbed unless you suspect some real trouble. When these axle bearings have to be removed, a hydraulic press is required to remove them from the axle shaft and to install new bearings.

On the front, first straighten and remove the cotter pin, then take off the nut and washer. By grabbing the tire and jiggling it, the outer wheel bearing will fall out into your hand; then you can pull the whole tire/wheel/drum assembly off the spindle. With a section of an old broom handle or similar tool, you can go through the center of the hub and tap out the inner grease seal and remove the inner wheel bearing. Remember that dirt is the biggest enemy of any automotive part, so clean the bearings thoroughly with solvent or gas. You can dry them with an air hose, but don't spin the bearings when they are dry or they may be damaged.

Whether ball or roller bearings, check them over for pits, roughness or other damage, and if the grease you cleaned out of them was very black and smelled burned, then they have probably been damaged by running under excessive heat. Be sure not to overlook the races either, and if you replace a bearing, replace the races along with it. If they check out OK, you can pack them with fresh wheel bearing grease, either by hand or with the aid of one of the several types of packing tools. Always use the same type of grease; don't mix the three popular types—the black grease (moly-base), the light yellow (lithium-base) or the dark green (sodium-base)—because they are chemically incompatible. When packing the old tried-and-true hand way, don't just coat the bearing with grease; work the lubricant into the inner parts. With your palm full of grease, keep pushing the bearing into it with a sliding motion, until you see the grease coming out the other side of the bearing assembly.

Naturally, assembly is important, because adjusting the bearings either too tightly or too loosely can cause failure. Use new grease seals after putting the inner bearings back in place, then slip the tire/wheel/drum assembly back onto the spindle and reinstall the washer and nut. There are two ways of adjusting the bearing nut: by feel or with a torque wrench. Bring the nut up finger-tight and then turn it with a wrench a little at a time as you spin the wheel until you feel a binding. Then back off the nut to the next spot where the holes are lined up for the cotter pin. And use *new* cotter pins each time; they're inexpensive insurance. If you have access to a shop manual and a torque wrench, you can be a bit more precise about it and tighten the bearing to factory specs while spinning the wheel. Even if the holes in the spindle and the nut line up, turn the nut back to the next slot for the final adjustment. Sometimes specifications give a final torque figure, but it is usually in inch-pounds, and we don't expect you to have a torque wrench that will read accurately that low.

You can adjust almost any wheel bearing that ever lived if you remember two simple rules: 1) Ball bearings should be set up with a slight preload; 2) Tapered roller bearings should be adjusted to zero end-play with no preload.

The ball bearings used in wheel hubs are designed to take thrust. They must have a slight preload so that the balls will not run on the edge of the circular groove instead of in it. Chevy recommends tightening the nut to 33 ft.-lbs. while rotating the wheel, and backing off 1/6- to 1/12-turn, whichever is necessary to make the cotter key hole line up.

Tapered roller bearings must be set up with zero preload so that the rollers are not forced to take uneven loads. If tapered rollers are slightly loose (end-play .000 to .005-inch) they merely move along the race a little, and it doesn't affect their load-carrying ability.

Before they switched to the tapered roller bearing, General Motors cars had more than their share of front

146/CHASSIS, SUSPENSION & BRAKES

wheel bearing trouble. One secret for making those bearings live longer is to use a lightweight grease, one that is almost light enough to pour like oil. When the bearing gets warm during normal running, a lightweight grease will run and keep the bearing lubricated. A heavy grease will be thrown off at high speed and never get back on the races where it is needed. The new moly greases which are black will do a good job of preserving bearings, too.

FIXING FLATS

Although tires have improved so much over the years that flats and blowouts aren't too common any more, the average motorist usually does have one sometime. Fixing the

1. Uniroyal offered some interesting tires a few years ago called Masters. One tire was designed for the front of a car (at left) with nine tread rows for steering, and a special rear tire, asymmetrical in tread, was for the rear and designed to push.

2. Street custom wheels aren't made of magnesium anymore, but mag-style wheels are more popular than ever. Offering good looks, light weight, and the ability to carry the larger tires, they come in all sizes, styles and prices. The best quality wheels are stamped "Meets SEMA specs."

3. The offset of a mag wheel has a lot to do with whether it will fit your car's fenderwells. Check offset of custom wheels before you buy them and compare with the available fender clearance and your stock wheels.

4. One of the drawbacks of custom wheels is shopping for a shop that can mount them. Most service stations won't mount them because air-powered tire machines can break the alloy wheels. Any non-steel wheel should be mounted on a manual tire machine.

tube of a tube-type tire is basically pretty simple, and the standard hot patch method should be familiar to everyone. But tubeless tires require somewhat different procedures. There are a number of repair methods and there is some controversy over which is the best type.

For any repair, the first step is to locate the leak by inflating the tire on the wheel and holding it in a tank of water to check for bubbles of escaping air. For a small hole, up to 1/16-in. diameter, you can seal it without taking the tire off the rim. Clean the hole with a small rasp, being careful not to enlarge the hole, and with only about 5 lbs. of pressure in the tire, inject a thin rubber plug or a substance such as Firestone Resealer. Wait about 15 minutes before reinflating to normal pressure. For holes up to 3/16-in., the hot patch is a much more positive repair, but must be done with the tire taken completely off the rim.

Clean an area on the inside of the tire around the damage, slightly larger than the patch—roughing it up with a rasp—then clean the inside of the hole with rubber solvent and fill it with resealer. Center the hot patch over the hole and hold it in place with a clamp, then ignite the patch. Let it cool for 15 mins., remove the clamp and brush away any ashes that may be left inside the tire. The cold patch is a similar repair method, but vulcanizes by chemical action rather than heat. The area around the hole is treated with self-vulcanizing fluid and should be allowed to dry for 5 mins. The foil backing of the patch can be removed and the patch then "stitched" down with a ticking wheel, which is a tool with a toothed wheel on it that you roll back and forth over the patch.

There are several types of puncture-sealing rubber plugs, but the best appear to be those with a flat head on them. Some have to be inserted from the inside of the tire, requiring demounting, but with the use of special inserting tools they can be used from the outside also. Again, the hole must be cleaned out with a rasp but not enlarged, and this time glue is inserted into the puncture. Whether working from the inside or outside of the tire, you should apply glue to the head of the plug also, as it not only seals but lubricates the plug as it goes in. When the flat head is seated up against the inside of the tire, you can trim off the excess on the outside with a razor blade, just above the tread. Don't stretch the plug while trimming it.

Probably no other aspect of tire maintenance is so easy to care for, yet is so neglected, as proper air pressure. Other than good front-end alignment, it probably has the greatest influence on tire mileage. Overinflation will produce a harsh ride and wear out the center of the tread before the edges. Too little pressure, though, is the most damaging, and can cause poor mileage and even early failure. Low pressure will cause the tire to sag, and the edges of the tread will wear out before the middle, which is squeezed up away from the road a little as the sidewalls sag out further to the sides of the tread. Place a hardcover book on its binding on a table and open it two or three inches; the center of the binding lifts up just the way the center of the tire tread does. Even at normal pressure, your sidewalls flex about 400 times a minute at 30 mph, and when underinflated they flex even more, enough sometimes to cause damage to the tire fabric from the heat and constant internal friction.

A tire pressure gauge is an inexpensive tool that every motorist should have in the glove compartment of his car. Maintaining correct pressure is simply a matter of adding air at a gas station if it's low, or letting it out if it's too high, but there *are* a few cautions. First of all, check your pressure when the tires are *cold,* because heat from driving just one mile or so will increase the air pressure and falsify your reading. But don't assume from this that you should let some air *out* to compensate when the tires get hot, because you shouldn't. The tire "protects itself" when it changes pressure with temperature, because at highway temperatures it hardens up and rolls easier, reducing some of the friction. However, if you plan some sustained high-speed driving or extra load carrying, you can raise the pressure

CHASSIS, SUSPENSION & BRAKES/147

Wheels and Tires

about four pounds, being careful not to exceed the recommended maximum, which is molded into the tire sidewall.

THE RACING LOOK FOR THE STREET

If a survey were taken, probably the most common after-market addition to a car today would be a set of "mag" wheels and high-performance or wide-tread tires. Just one look at the cars in any drive-in stand, anywhere in the country, is enough to make you want to buy stock in Goodyear and American Racing Equipment. The custom wheel and tire phenomenon is here to stay. Within its realm, any car—big or small, slow or fast—can be made to look customized, dragsterized, or whatever your taste desires. Unfortunately though, some people see a funny car in a magazine or some of the ridiculous garbage wagons that travel the show car circuit, and decide that that's what they have to have for their own car. Custom wheels and tires are fine—they look great and can improve handling—but there are a number of important factors that the average street machine owner never takes into account when shopping for them.

Most "mag" wheels today are not magnesium but aluminum alloy, with only the true racing wheels being genuine magnesium. Yet the most highly touted advantage of these wheels is their light weight. While just about every street rodder buys the wheels for looks, if you ask him why he bought them he'll probably say hastily that "they reduce unsprung weight so they improve my handling." Although it is true that reducing unsprung weight will improve handling, most of the wheels on the market don't weigh much less than a stock steel wheel. Probably the lightest street wheels are the 1-piece cast aluminum ones, but they are also the most expensive. The less costly 2-piece wheels (alloy center welded to steel rim) weigh about the same as a stocker—some even more than a steel wheel because their design requires more metal. And whenever someone adds custom wheels to his machine, a set of big tires usually goes with them, and the wider they are, the better he likes them. What he doesn't realize is that he should also check into the weight of the *tires* he buys, not just the wheels. In 9 cases out of 10 he is probably picking up more unsprung weight with the big tires than he shed by using the alloy wheels!

Ever since Mickey Thompson brought out those wide, low-profile tires at Indy in 1963, there has been a progression of increasingly wider and lower tires in use in many forms of motorsports. Thompson used them because they improved cornering power and roadholding ability, and up to a point, a wide, low-profile tire will do the same for a passenger car. But while the racing machine is designed for these super doughnuts, your '49 Ford street machine isn't. There is a point where a larger tire is going to increase the unsprung weight of the car to where the suspension is overtaxed and overall handling suffers.

Another factor to consider is the wheel rim offset. Your stock steel wheels are designed so that weight-fulcrum of the front end (the wheel bearings) is centered over the tread of the tire and the load distributed evenly. With a wide alloy or reversed steel wheel, the tire is offset, or moved out so that the tire sticks out of the fender well a little, making it look even wider. While this does increase the front wheel track (which is the width between the front tires) and improves cornering, it also puts a greater load on the wheel bearings, which are now *not* over the center of the tread. The bearings may wear a lot faster with the loads all to one side. And the more offset and the wider the tire, the less fender clearance you will have at the rear. Just watch a Corvette sporting big sneakers come off the line hard at the drags. If he hasn't raised the body, you'll see smoke, not from the tires burning, but from the fiberglass burning as the body rears back from the weight transfer and the slicks get together with the wheel wells for a hot time. Pony cars suffer from this same malady of wheel-wellitis, and the cure consists of cutting away the inner lip of the fender, or completely radiusing the wheel well, which looks good anyway, but requires some bodywork. If you have the right bolt pattern on your drums, you may want to try a set of Olds Toronado wheels, which set the tires further inside the well than a stock wheel, and could save some chopping.

Even if you can't afford big tires, you may want to use a set of slightly wider rims with your original tires for improved handling. The American Tire and Rim Association recommends a flange-to-flange width of 75% of the tire section width. Most passenger car wheels are 70%-80%. Going to a wheel *wider* than 75% (with the same tire) will make the tire act like a racing tire, and although there is an increase in ride harshness and tire wear, cornering power is increased. Just the opposite is true for a narrower rim—there will be a *softer* ride because of the sidewall flex, but some stability will be lost. For this reason there are maximum and minimum widths to use for a given application; for instance, don't try mounting a set of 10-in. wide tires on a wheel less than 8 ins. wide, or a 12-in. supertire on a mag narrower than 10 ins.

The idea of a 12-in. tire on a street machine brings us to another subject, that of using racing tires on the street. This is a growing practice but a dangerous one. We've all seen jacked-up street funny cars with slicks or other impressive-looking rubber on them, but if these guys could

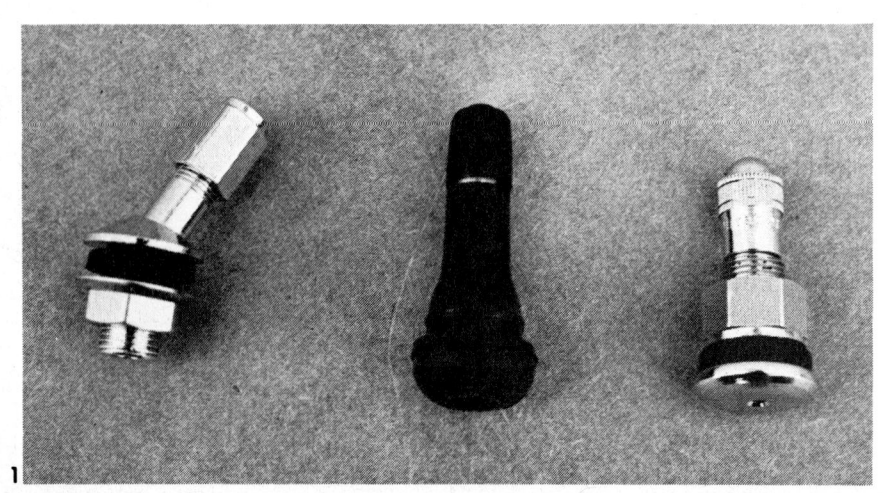

148/CHASSIS, SUSPENSION & BRAKES

see a cross section of such a racing tire compared to a passenger car tire, they'd think twice about using them. Racing tires, especially drag slicks, are not made to encounter wet roads, and so have little or no tread. A street tire must have good grooves in it so that water has a place to squish into when driving in the rain. In many states there is a required tread depth for tires, so in these areas racing tires are illegal on the street as well as being dangerous.

Cut an ordinary tire in half (not one from your father's station wagon, though) and look at how thick the tread and sidewalls are made. *Racing tires have just enough rubber under the tread to last a few races and the sidewalls are paper-thin, since the tire has to be as light as possible.* There are no curbs to scrape against on a race track, no railroad rails to ride over, nor any of the many other hazards a passenger car tire carcass faces. And lastly, many race tires are made to run at high inflation pressures, like 50 or 60 lbs., and this—coupled with their low cord angle—can make a new car using them on the street ride like a truck. Next time you see one of those boulevard Q-ships with 12-in. tires plainly marked "For Racing Purposes Only," don't envy the owner, pity him.

A good set of high-performance passenger car tires, like the Goodyear Polyglas items, and whatever quality-brand wheels fit both your pocketbook and your fancy, will give you the desired looks, handling, tire mileage and road hazard guarantee that you need, without the attending ills outlined above. A good investment, they also perk up the looks of just about any car, and—being bolt-on equipment—are the perfect way to personalize your stormer.

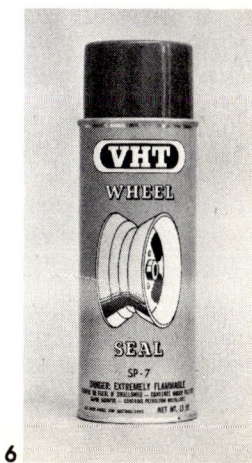

1. Just about every tire today is a tubeless type and requires valve stems, of which there are many types. The standard rubber ones should be replaced when your tires are changed but the all-metal ones are reusable. They're available in lengths and at different angles to fit any wheel.

2. An important consideration when buying custom wheels is whether they will fit another car you may later switch to. Some of the more expensive wheels have adapters or special lugs for quick changes in bolt patterns.

3. It's been said over and over in enthusiast magazines, but it bears repetition: Don't use racing tires on the street! Not only is it illegal in most states, these tires can be dangerous because of their very thin carcass, meant for smooth racetracks and not the abuse of everyday roads.

4. When installing custom wheels, you'll have to remove the Tinnerman nuts (stud clips) from the brake drums in order for the wheels to sit flush on the brake drums. In some cases a drum's balance weights may have to be removed also, which means the drum should be rebalanced with the wheel, on a dynamic balancer.

5. There are a variety of devices to theft-proof your custom wheels, of which the best are the keyless, case-hardened type. But with any of the mag wheel locks, losing the key can be a hassle if you have a flat!

6. Being somewhat porous, mag wheels sometimes leak air very slowly with tubeless tires. If this happens try some Cragar Wheel-Seal on the rim. If that doesn't work, you'll have to install tubes in the tires, which is not a good practice for a tubeless tire, since more heat is created.

CHASSIS, SUSPENSION & BRAKES/149

Driveshafts and U-Joints

Here's what delivers the power from the front to the back.

After the chassis builder has faced the complexities of his engine and either a manual or automatic transmission, he is faced with the problem of transferring his power and torque to the ground. In 99 out of 100 cases, the transfer medium is a shaft; the driveshaft. And why do we devote an entire chapter to something as simple as a driveshaft? Simply because about 90% of the automobiles *ever built* have used a driveshaft, clear back to the beginning of (automotive) time. So maybe if we shed a little light on what a driveshaft does, you just might discover that it isn't nearly as simple as you thought.

Very early horseless carriages did not use a driveshaft, but instead used spur gears, chains or belts to couple the engine to the driving wheels. As time went on, however, and the differential had to be introduced to the rear axle to augment steering requirements, and since the engine had moved from an under-seat location to an up-front position, the driveshaft or propellor shaft was employed. The so-called "torque tube" was also introduced about this time, and one of its most successful users was good old Henry Ford in his Model T. In fact, Ford's torque tube worked so well that it remained the basis of his driveline through the 1948 model year.

The torque tube is a hollow tube that connects the rear of the transmission to the front of the differential, and it houses a smaller, solid shaft which is the driveshaft itself. The function of the torque tube is to rigidly locate the rear axle, provide a housing for the driveshaft and its U-joint, and to transmit the "push" or motive force from the drive axle to the chassis. Still another function, and the one from which the name is derived, is to absorb the torque of the pinion gear, preventing it from climbing the ring gear instead of turning the wheels. Torque, like water, wants to follow the path of least resistance; the torque tube prevents this.

Better ways to control torque, and easier means of servicing U-joints, came along after World War II, and the torque tube last saw the light of day on the Chevy for '54, except for a brief resurgence in '61 on the Pontiac Tempest which lasted only through '63.

While both Chevy and Ford have called their system torque tube drive, there was a difference between the Ford and Chevy. Technically speaking, the Chevy driveline was not a true torque tube drive, because the rear springs absorbed some of the rear-end torque and, although it was a closed drive system, the front of the torque tube did not actually push on or "drive" the car.

The torque tube drive has been almost entirely abandoned by Detroit since the late '50's because it was heavy, bulky and hard to service, since the shaft was enclosed in the tube (ever work on a mid-1950's Buick?), and with its single U-joint couldn't make up the larger driveline angles necessitated by the big styling changes going on then.

HOTCHKISS

With the passing of the torque tube from the automotive scene, we enter the era of the Hotchkiss or "open" driveline. In a typical Hotchkiss system, the U-joints and hollow driveshaft are right out in the open. Nowadays, semi-elliptic rear leaf springs—or control arms on coil-sprung suspensions—are employed to locate the rear axle and absorb the pinion torque. If you've peeked under many cars, you may have noticed some variations in the way different car manufacturers have applied the open driveshaft. Most use a one-piece, hollow tube with a slip yoke and a U-joint up front, and a second U-joint at the rear connecting the driveshaft to the pinion yoke of the differential.

Chrysler used to use a ball-and-trunnion type of U-joint on most of their cars, instead of the more conventional splined slip yoke. This is the type of joint that is protected from water and dirt by a grease cover or boot. It necks down to a solid shaft about 1-in. in diameter before it goes through the boot into the housing. A pin is pressed through the shaft. Balls are fitted on each end of the pin so they can roll back and forth in machined rollways within the housing. The housing is bolted to the transmission tailshaft flange and transfers power to the shaft through the balls and the pin.

TWO-PIECE DRIVESHAFTS

Some of our longer-wheelbase cars have still another U-joint near the center of the driveshaft. Because driveshafts must run in near-perfect

150/CHASSIS, SUSPENSION & BRAKES

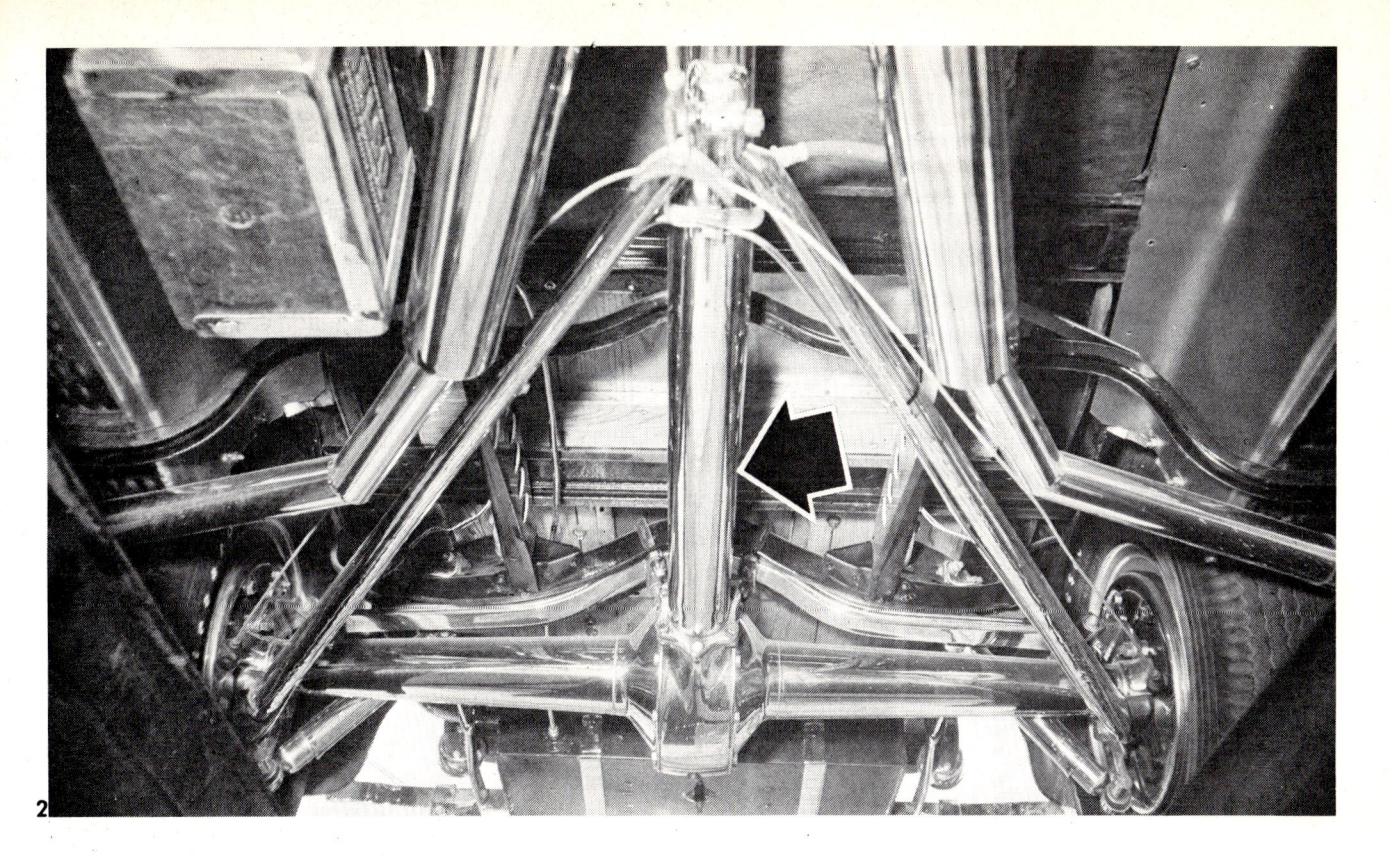

balance, it's logical that the shorter they are, the easier they are to balance. On big cars, as some long-wheelbase Chryslers and Cadillacs, a central U-joint in effect extends the reach of the transmission tailshaft, allowing the effective driveshaft length to be relatively short. Only the section of shaft between the central U-joint and the rear end must move up and down as the rear wheels traverse road roughness. The central U-joint is also occasionally employed by Detroit designers to keep a car's road height and overall height down low, for the

1. Whether hot rod or stocker, your driveline is an important, although often forgotten, element of a chassis. This rodder is taking no chances on his giving trouble, he's taking the driveshaft out for balancing and new U-joints. Note the two driveshaft safety loops that prevent accidents in case of failure of the U-joints.

2. Driveshafts used to be enclosed in a torque tube (arrow), which had a solid driveshaft inside and pivot ball/socket arrangement at the front. Torque tube and radius rods took all the rear-end torque instead of the springs or control arms.

3. One step forward in providing for lower floorpans to go with modern styling was the two-piece driveshaft. With the front half acting like an extension of the transmission, the effective driveshaft length was short.

4. It's best with any driveshaft to make some alignment marks before removing it for service, so that it can be put back the same way. This is a typical one-piece driveshaft with two U-joints and a slip yoke.

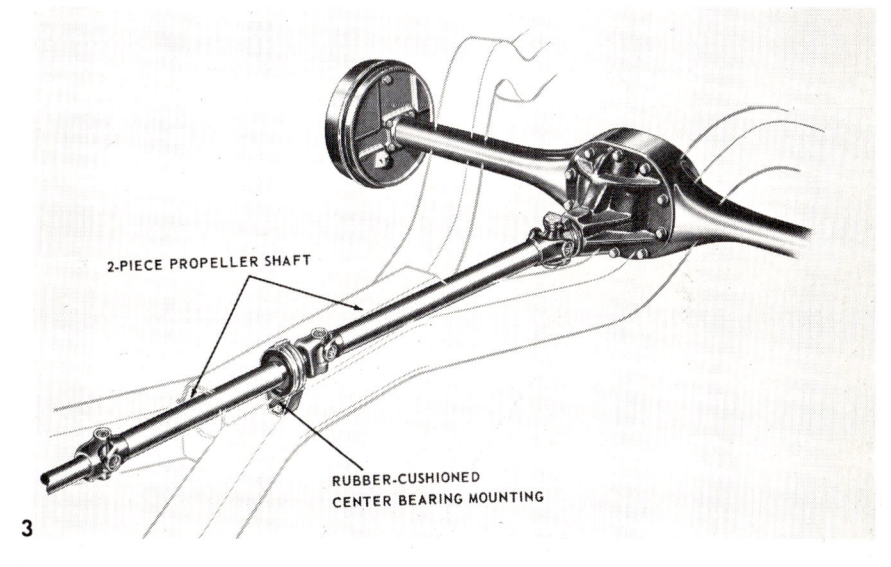

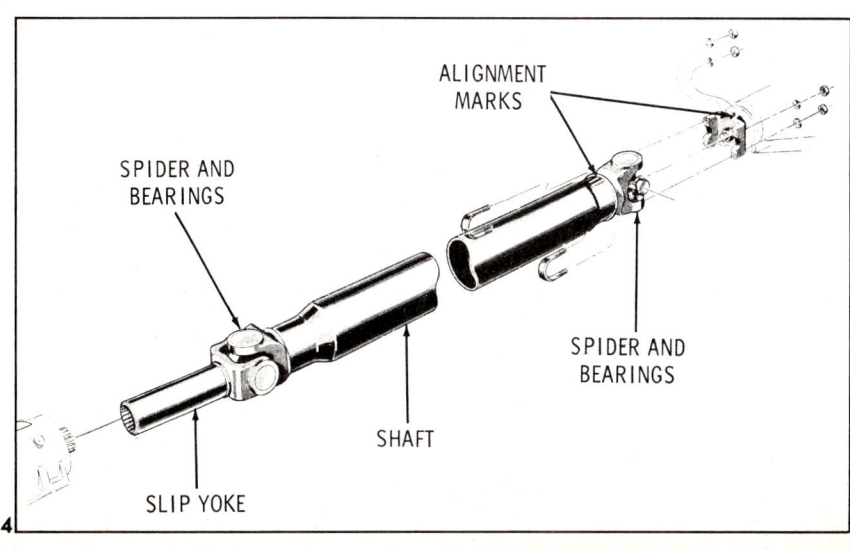

CHASSIS, SUSPENSION & BRAKES/151

Driveshafts and U-Joints

driveshaft can "bend" or "bow" downward as it spans the distance from the transmission to the rear end, keeping floor height at a minimum.

UNIVERSAL JOINTS

About 400 years ago an Italian inventor, Jerome Cardan, put the first universal joint to work. A hundred years later, an Englishman named Robert Hooke made improvements to Cardan's U-joint and came up with something closely resembling the "cross-and-yoke" U-joint design we're all familiar with today. It was crude and fragile by today's standards, but since horsepower in those days had four feet, U-joints did not transmit great gobs of power and it served its purpose at the time.

Hooke's basic U-joint design worked just fine in the very early automobiles which had 5, 10, or even 15 hp. But as output rose through the years, the U-joint had to be improved to handle the increasing abuse, reaching us today as the needle bearing cross-and-yoke design so familiar on the modern open driveshaft.

The cross-and-yoke U-joints found on modern cars are just about what their name implies. They consist of a steel cross with the ends of each arm or "trunnion" machined to a bearing race. The bearing races fit into bearing cups surrounded by needle bearings. The cups themselves are bolted to the pinion yoke or pressed into either of the driveshaft yokes, or perhaps into the splined slip yoke.

The ball-and-trunnion joint found on many MoPars requires a different procedure for service. Remove the front grease cover by bending the retaining tabs, and slide the main body back so you can remove the balls. Clean and inspect all the parts, but if you're going to replace the unit, it has to be done in an arbor press. It takes considerable pressure to press the pin out of the shaft, and if you use a hammer on it you'll probably peen over the end of the pin, and then you'll really have fun trying to get it out! Let a machine shop put the new one in, too, because a centering tool is required, ensuring that the pin is no more than .006-in. longer on one side than the other. When greasing for assembly, put half of the grease on the driveshaft side of the pin and half on the transmission side. Replace the cover by bending the tabs back in their slots in the body.

The constant-velocity joint looks just like two cross-and-yoke joints, but is disassembled differently. Most of them have the snap rings on the inside of the yoke and have to be removed with a special tool. When pressing out the bearings, they may not come all the way out, so insert a spacer between the bearing and the ridge at the center of the yoke and press again. It makes the unit easier to work on if you press out bearings on the linking yoke first, so that the two halves of the shaft can be worked on individually. After assembly with new parts, hit the yoke with a plastic hammer to seat the snap rings, and twist the cross to make sure you don't have any binding.

For those cars with 2-piece driveshafts, the center bearing and support should also be checked. On most cars, though, removing the center bearing from the front shaft will probably damage the bearings, so don't remove it unless you're sure it's in need of replacement. First, the large nut which holds the front shaft to the yoke for the center U-joint must be removed. Having marked the alignment of the pieces, of course, slide off the front shaft, and use a gear puller to take the center bearing off. In some cases the replacement unit will consist of the whole assembly, which is preferred, instead of just the bearing alone.

CONSTANT VELOCITY JOINTS

One phenomenon of the U-joint is that when it is functioning at an angle, the relative speed of the shafts on either side of the joint will fluctuate. That is, the total rpm's of both shafts is the same, but one will actually speed up then slow down, relative to the other one, with each revolution. The yokes on driveshafts are placed at a 90° angle to one another to cancel out most of these fluctuations and the resultant vibration when running at high rpm.

Since we can now see that one U-joint effectively cancels the other, what about two-piece driveshafts that employ *three* U-joints? This means one of the U-joints doesn't have a mate to cancel out its fluctuations. The problem is solved by the use of a constant-velocity or C-V joint on the rear shaft. It is a pair of cross-and-yoke U-joints connected by another short yoke to form a "fluctuation can-

1. Keeping driveshaft angles correct makes all the difference in U-joint life. The angles for your vehicle can be found in a factory manual.

2. When your rear springs compress, it makes quite a difference in your pinion and driveshaft angles. This is why it's important to install some kind of overload spring if you're going to carry heavy loads or pull a trailer. You customizers who lower cars for looks should think about it.

3. The axles of an independent rear end have U-joints just like standard driveshaft. In VW's case, they went to two constant-velocity U-joints in each axle to help the wheels stay nearly vertical during their travel and eliminate some drivetrain vibes.

4. Factory mechanics have tools like this Chrysler angle indicator to find driveshaft angles quickly.

5. You can do your own driveshaft angle-checking with a tool like this, available in big hardware stores. It also has a level and a ruler and can be used for many other jobs.

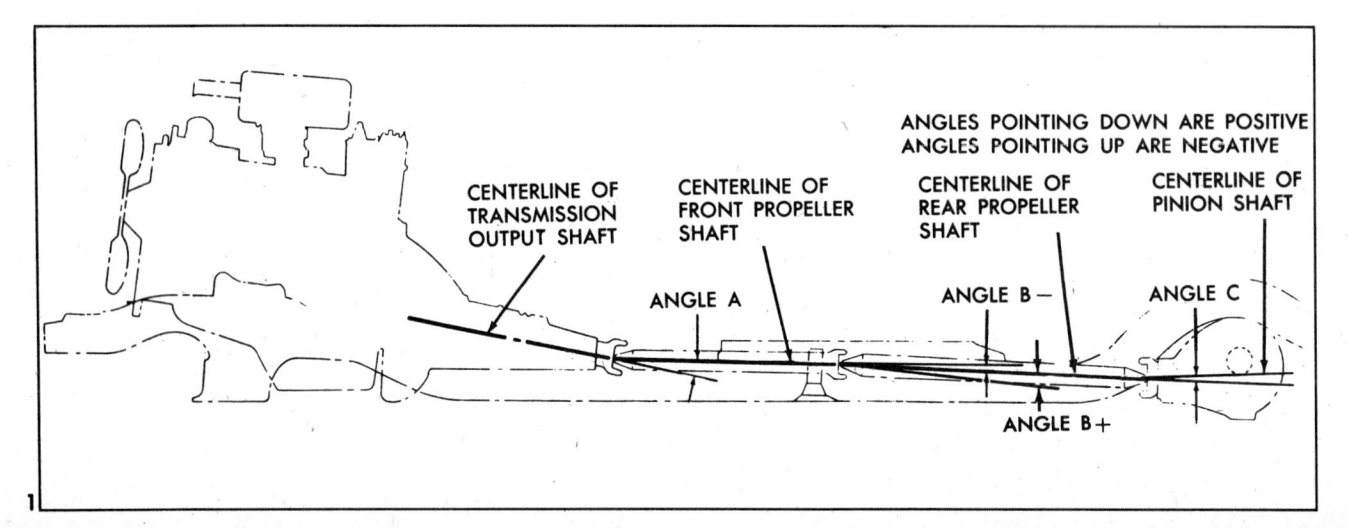

ANGLES POINTING DOWN ARE POSITIVE
ANGLES POINTING UP ARE NEGATIVE

CENTERLINE OF TRANSMISSION OUTPUT SHAFT
CENTERLINE OF FRONT PROPELLER SHAFT
CENTERLINE OF REAR PROPELLER SHAFT
CENTERLINE OF PINION SHAFT

ANGLE A
ANGLE B −
ANGLE C
ANGLE B +

152/CHASSIS, SUSPENSION & BRAKES

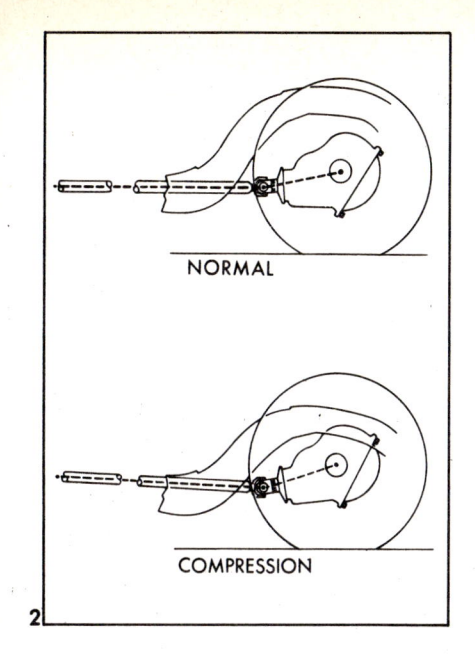

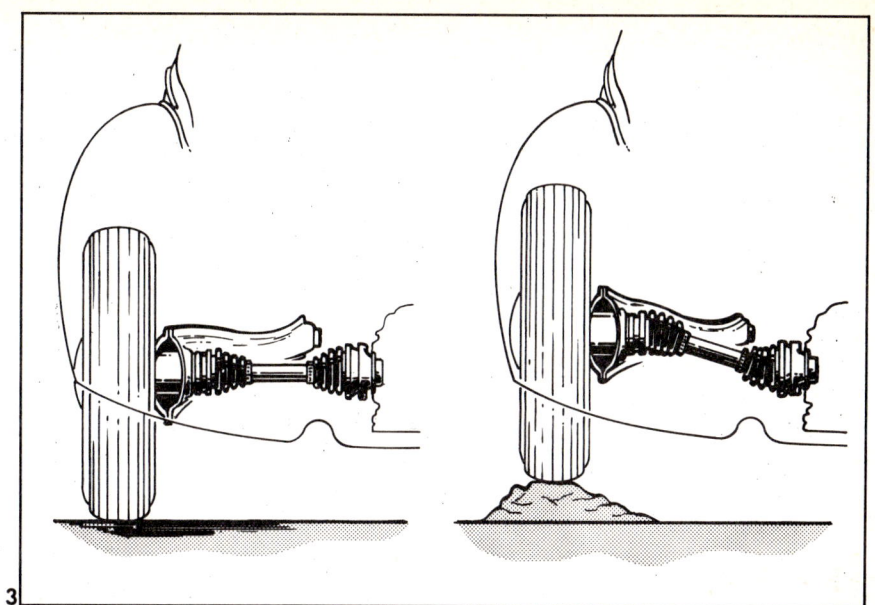

celer" U-joint fluctuation is also handled in a manner similar to the way it's handled on an engine's crankshaft. A harmonic balancer, or vibration dampener, is placed around the driveshaft. Most high-performance Chrysler products from '65 use a vibration dampener and they seem to require very little maintenance.

MAINTENANCE

The best maintenance is always preventive maintenance. Any U-joint that employs a grease fitting should be lubricated at the mileage specified in the owner's manual. Too, driveshaft and U-joint angles are very critical, and they should be kept within the tolerances outlined in the factory shop manual. Sagging springs, overload springs, heavy-duty or air-filled shock absorbers, or the addition of a trailer or other load that adds weight to the rear of the vehicle—these are just a few of the things that can create an overly great U-joint angle.

Oddly enough, driveshafts are not designed to run in a perfectly straight line, since the U-joints need to "work" slightly in order to keep lubricant working through the needle bearings. As your rear axle moves up and down, the angles change and the U-joint obediently compensates. Keeping the angles as low as possible makes the U-joint work less, last longer, and eat up less power. A pinion angle indicator is a gauge used to find the correct angle between the pinion and driveshaft. If you don't have one or don't know how to use one, you'll be better off in the hands of a competent front end and chassis repairman.

It's always a good idea to check your U-joints whenever you check your brakes or replace your tires and shock absorbers. Typical U-joints

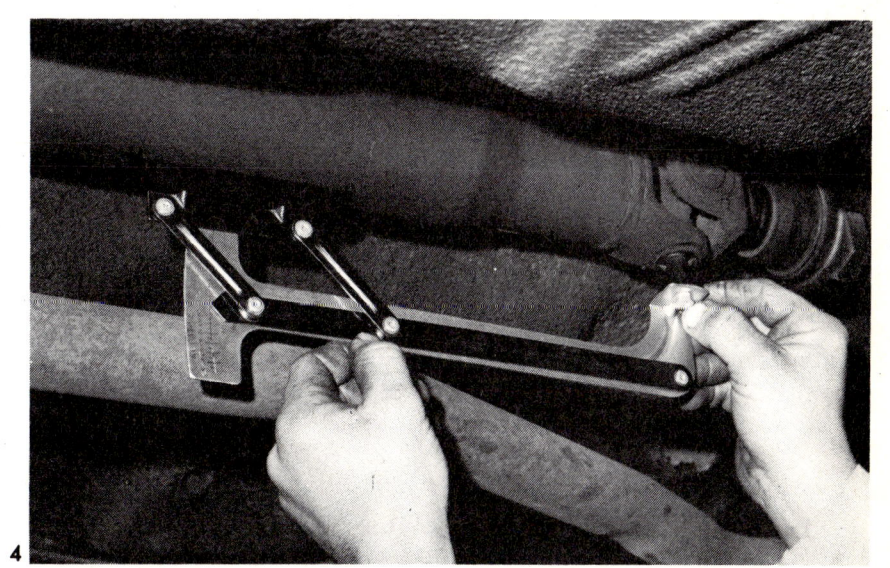

CHASSIS, SUSPENSION & BRAKES/153

Driveshafts and U-Joints

should last about 50,000 miles in normal use, but they should be inspected, cleaned, and lubed at about every 25,000 miles.

The best way to work on a driveshaft is to get it out from under the car. However, before you start, there are a few things you should gather together to make the job easier. First, call the parts house to make sure they have the U-joint kit and the grease seals you'll need for your particular make and model of car. Find some U-joint grease and have access to a large vise, and a factory shop manual for your car. If you have a splined slip yoke, find a plastic Dixie cup and a piece of gasket material about 8 ins. by 8 ins., and either some electricians' tape or two large rubber bands. If yours is the "ball-and-trunnion" front U-joint, or you have a two-piece driveshaft (with its three U-joints), make sure an auto machine shop is open the day you'll be doing your work.

Block the front wheels and, with the transmission in neutral and the parking brake off, jack stand the chassis high enough off the floor so that the rear wheels are hanging free.

ANGLES

An important part of any maintenance of the driveline is checking the various angles. If the driveshaft or U-joint angles are incorrect due to spring sag or a frame distortion, vibration can be severe. Checking and correcting these angles will prolong the life of the U-joints considerably. Basically, the front U-joint angle should be the same as the rear for smooth power flow through the driveline. But, because of body design limitations and sometimes crowded engine compartments, the front angles are usually harder to change. On cars with the distributor at the rear of the engine, close to the firewall, you can't lower the back of the transmission too much. Also, because of close quarters between the transmission and the floor tunnel, raising the transmission is also limited. These problems should be taken into consideration by the rodder contemplating an engine swap.

Thus the rear angles are the ones most often changed, although the rear transmission mount can be shimmed for small changes. The ideal situation, of course, is a straight driveline under normal conditions. You'll have to check your factory service manual for the exact specifications for your particular car, but in most cases the front angle, between the driveshaft centerline and the transmission shaft centerline, should equal the rear angle, between the centerline of the driveshaft and the pinion shaft centerline.

There are several methods of correcting driveline angles, depending on the type of rear suspension used. For cars with Hotchkiss-drive leaf springs, about the only way is by shimming under the rear spring pads on the rear end. Coil sprung cars, however, can be shimmed in several places, and it is therefore easier to get the exact angle you want. Upper and lower control arms can be shimmed, either at the rear end or, more commonly, where they mount to the frame. On cars with 2-piece driveshafts, the center bearing support mount may also have to be shimmed to get perfect alignment. As with the U-joints themselves, noise and vibration should give you a clue that it's time for your driveline to have a physical.

U-JOINT REMOVAL

A ball-and-trunnion joint is unbolted from the transmission and left on the studs. Then the cross-and-yoke is unbolted at the rear end, allowing the ball-and-trunnion to be pulled off the studs.

If you have a splined-yoke U-joint, take a look at the underside of the car floor just above the transmission tailshaft. If it's oil-stained, it's a good bet you'll need a rear transmission seal. This is no big thing as long as the driveshaft has been removed. A large screwdriver or a slide hammer can be used to get the old seal out, and a large socket or seal driver, and a hammer, will suffice to get the new seal in.

Assuming you found the rear transmission seal to be good, you can now trim about 1 in. off the top of that Dixie cup you were wondering about. Take it, the square of gasket material, and the tape or rubber bands along with you under the car.

Unbolt the rear bearing cups from the pinion yoke and set the cups carefully out of the way so the needle bearings don't get lost. Next, unbolt the center support bearing from the crossmember, if your car has one. If it doesn't have one, use the time to give thanks for being so lucky.

As soon as you slide the splined

154/CHASSIS, SUSPENSION & BRAKES

1. The independent rear drive on this Formula A road racing machine has rubber "doughnut" cushions in the axle shafts. As well as acting like U-joints, they cushion power loads.

2. If you have access to a vise, you can change U-joints. The yoke can be pressed out by using a small socket on one side and a large one on the opposite side. Squeezing them in the vise forces the bearing cups out.

3. If you're using your old U-joint, then it should be cleaned and lubed. If you're getting a new one, get one like this with a grease fitting.

4. With the old bearing cups out of the shaft, you can install the new yoke and push new bearing cups in.

5. When pressing new bearing cups into a driveshaft, only press them just far enough in to get the clips into the grooves, whether they're the inside or outside type.

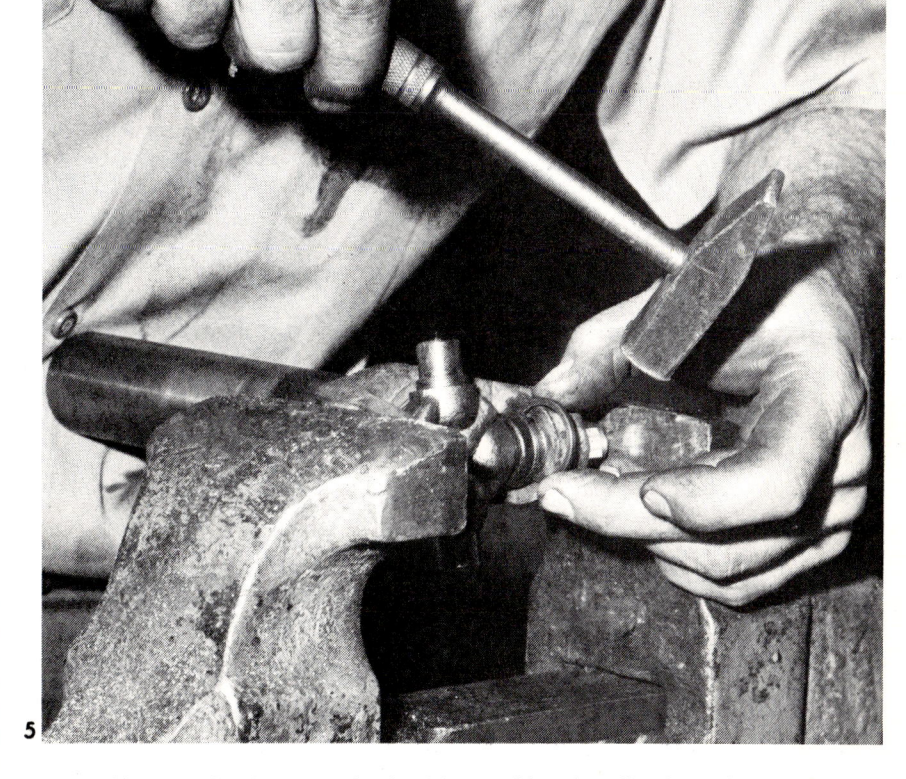

slip yoke off the transmission tailshaft, shove the Dixie cup in, open end first. This will keep the transmission oil off you and the floor. Now wrap the gasket material around the seal surface of the slip yoke and either tape it or rubber band it in place. This will keep the delicate seal surface protected from dinging or scratching. By the way, don't *ever* put a driveshaft tube in a vise; it's easily damaged.

To disassemble a cross-and-yoke U-joint you must first take off the clips that hold it together. C-clips are generally on the outside and are easily seen and easily removed. Just squeeze the inside parts together with a pair of duckbill or needlenose pliers and remove the clip. C-clips that are on the inside are harder to see and even harder to remove. Find one end or the other and tap it around the cup with a small drift punch or screwdriver, and a hammer. It *should* pop right out. While you're working at it, you'll probably think of a lot of names for it besides C-clip!

If your U-joint is still factory-original, it may not have any clips at all. Sometimes a nylon seal is used in place of a clip and when this is the case, the U-joint has been lubricated for life. The seal may need replacing, but don't try to take it out unless you're sure it does. Once the seal is broken or removed, it can't be used again. Most replacement kits for these joints come with conventional clips which can be removed and replaced several times.

After the clips have been removed, remove the bearing cups. To do this, select a couple of sockets, one just a little smaller around than the cup, and one that will fit inside the cup. Use one of the cups that was bolted to the pinion yoke to get the right size sockets. Place the yoke in a vise with the small socket on one bearing cup and the large socket on the opposite side of the yoke to receive the bearing cup when it is pushed out. It probably won't come out all the way, but with a pair of channel lock pliers or vise grips, just wiggle it a little while pulling on it. Reverse the sockets for the other cup.

CHASSIS, SUSPENSION & BRAKES/155

Driveshafts and U-Joints

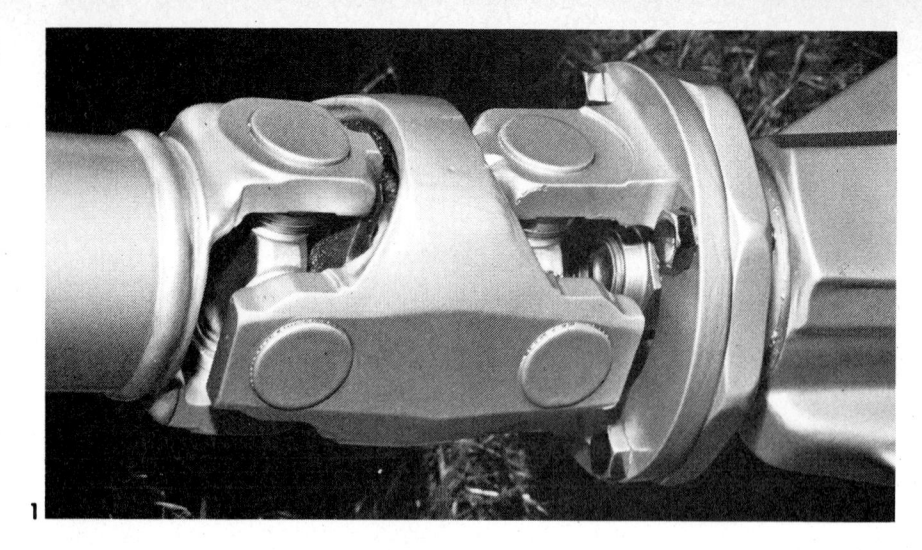

CLEANING U-JOINTS

To clean U-joints, take out the needle bearings (carefully!) and clean them and the cross in solvent. Be careful not to lose any of the needles. Do not clean the cups in solvent unless you can remove and replace the little rubber seals. If you have to, just use a clean rag to wipe the cups out as best you can.

Once all the parts are clean, check them closely for cracks or wear. Look very closely at the bearing surfaces. If anything seems to need replacing, always replace the whole joint. Do not attempt to mix the pieces from one U-joint to another—not even new ones. Some joints, even with the selfsame part numbers, may have slightly different trunnion diameters or bearing sizes.

Whenever possible, try to get a replacement U-joint with a grease fitting on it. Always read the instruction sheet that comes with a U-joint kit. The new joint may function better and/or last longer if it is installed in a certain way. Heavy-duty U-joints are always worth their somewhat higher cost, if you plan on a lot of hard usage.

Dab a little U-joint grease in each cup before reassembly; it will help hold the needle bearings in. If the cross has a grease fitting, shoot some grease to it until it oozes out the holes in the ends of the trunnions. This forces any air and solvent out. Put the joint back together just the way you took it apart (unless the instructions say something different), and be careful not to ruin the seals by pushing the cups in any farther than needed to seat the clips.

The constant-velocity or fluctuation-canceler type of joints look like two regular cross-and-yoke U-joints, but you need special tools, or you have to take them to someone who does. This also applies to the center support bearing on a two-piece driveshaft.

CLEANING BALL & TRUNNION

Remove the grease seal by bending back the tabs that hold it on. Slide the housing back, but keep your fingers on the ends of the pin where the little buttons are. Those buttons have spacers or shims under them that look like ordinary flat washers. Don't mix them up or lose them. They accurately center the pin and shaft in the housing. Don't attempt to hammer on any part of a ball-and-trunnion U-joint. After cleaning in solvent, inspect all the pieces for wear or cracks. If anything needs replacing, the whole unit must go to a machine shop to have the pin pressed out. It must be pressed back in, also, to within .006-in. of center, and re-shimmed in the housing. Keep the joint clean and grease it regularly, and you'll get a lot of use out of it. But, when it needs complete replacement, let a specialist do it.

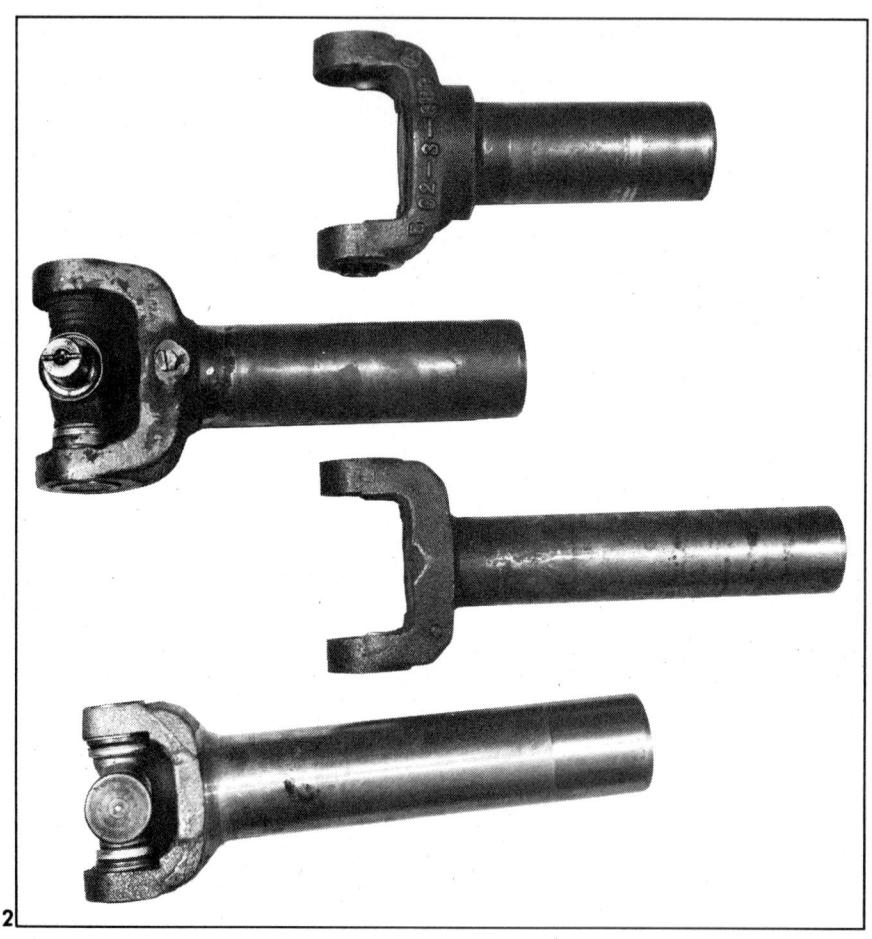

MODIFICATIONS

Now that you have that 427 Chrysler "wedge" crammed into your Pinto, or that fresh L-88 is almost in your Nova, there are a few last things before you can get that newly acquired power to the ground. If an engine swap has been kept "in the family"—GM into GM, Ford into Ford, etc.—the driveshaft won't present too much of a problem. A little shaft shortening or swapping U-joint yokes will solve most of the difficulties. Pinion yokes can, in some cases, simply be swapped just as easily as the slip yoke can. Such a swap is easy if you're also changing ring and pinion gears or rebuilding the differential.

If you're a little short of the folding green (and who isn't), but you feel you need a super-strong driveshaft,

1. The rear U-joint on this Olds is typical of constant-velocity ones used to allow for a flatter floor, without hassles of two-piece shaft.

2. Because of an engine or trans swap, someday you may have to mate two different driveshafts. This is made a little easier with the number of different slip yokes available.

3. If it's the rear end you want to swap, sometimes it's more convenient to change the pinion yoke to fit the driveshaft. These special yokes are: (top) Pontiac to Chevy U-joint; (right) Chrysler to Chevy U-joint; (bottom) stock Pontiac yoke; (left) Chrysler to Pontiac U-joint. All of these are custom-made for rear-end swapping.

4. Lakewood has come up with a neat aid for the hot rodder, the two-size U-joint. With two sizes of bearings, this one fits a Chevy driveshaft to a beefy Olds or Pontiac rear end.

it's time to fall by a wrecking yard. Reasonably late model muscle cars have real beefy driveshafts, like one from a '68 street Hemi, if your swap is all-Chrysler. A 455 Olds or Pontiac shaft should stand up under whatever you've put into your GM car, or one from a 427 or 454 Chevy. The driveshaft from a Boss 429 Mustang should stand the gaff of any all-Ford swap. If nothing else, consider just about any V-8-powered pickup or van; their shafts are usually heftier than their passenger car counterparts. Actually, keeping a driveshaft entirely within the family isn't that important, for even if you have to have both ends changed on, say, an Olds shaft to fit into your Chrysler-powered Ford, it'll still be less expensive than having a complete driveshaft tailor made to your requirements. However, because you'll never know what a wrecking yard shaft might have been through in its younger days, check any used shaft pretty carefully and have the yokes magnafluxed. It's cheap insurance.

Finding the length needed for a special driveshaft is not difficult. Start by making sure the engine and trans are where they'll permanently go, and that your rear end is all bolted up. Put the right slip yoke on the tailshaft of the trans and push it in as far as it will go. Now, pull it out 2-ins. Take the trusty tape and measure carefully between the center of the bearing cup hole in the yoke, and the place where the bearing cup is bolted to the pinion yoke. Measuring the proper distance this way will allow for half of the rear bearing size and slip joint movement.

Almost any work done on a driveshaft tube should be done by a competent machine shop. Putting on a different yoke, altering the length of the shaft, or beefing up a stock shaft, all will effect the final balance of the shaft. All cutting, welding, etc., should be done while the shaft tube is chucked in a lathe, and after the job's done, the final assembly should be balanced.

A driveshaft that is out of balance is not only hard on U-joints, transmission, and pinion bearings—to say nothing of vibrations felt throughout the car—it's downright dangerous. Remember that a shaft has to work very hard to transmit all that horsepower coming from under the hood. That's why it's best to have a professional make sure a shaft is strong, straight, and in balance. A driveshaft safety loop is good insurance in the event the driveshaft itself or front U-joint "goes away," which could easily flip the car or cause whirling pieces to penetrate the floorpan with dangerous results. The loop is great for the average street machine too, and they do look trick if visible from beside the car. The driveshaft safety loop won't give you horsepower, but it'll ease your mind.

BALANCING

If you've modified your car's driveline, or noise and vibration exist in a stock driveline even after you've checked everything, you should have the unit balanced. Chances are, if you found a good machine shop that did a lot of driveshaft work, they do balancing also. The operation isn't expensive, and should smooth out any minor irregularities in the driveline, if maintenance or modifications have been done properly.

Minor imbalance, however, can be corrected in your backyard, if you can't locate a shop that can electronically balance it for you. First jack up the car so that the rear wheels can rotate freely, and have someone "drive" the car at about 45 mph. While the shaft is rotating, get under the car and very slowly bring a piece of chalk or crayon up to the shaft, using a piece of 2 x 4 or something to guide and steady your hand. Stop after you have made the slightest contact with the driveshaft, and shut the car off. Now put two screw-type hose clamps over the driveshaft so that their heads (the part where the screw is) are opposite (180°) the small chalk mark, which represents the "heavy" side of the shaft. Check

CHASSIS, SUSPENSION & BRAKES/157

Driveshafts and U-Joints

for vibration at 60-70 mph (still securely supported on jack stands). If there is still a problem, try rotating the clamps a small amount at a time, and check after each time. If this doesn't seem to be helping at all, the vibration may be coming from your engine and not the driveline. It's a crude method, of course, and time consuming, but anything's worth a try if you can't get it done on a machine.

Lastly, a few tips that may keep away those "bugs" that Hertz and Avis are always talking about. As with most of your stock drivetrain, engine, etc., the driveshaft and U-joints of your car were originally balanced at the factory, and unless you know for sure that you're going to have it rebalanced, don't upset that balance. When cutting or modifying, be sure to make alignment marks beforehand, and also when taking apart U-joints for lubrication. You may find a washer or two spotwelded on some part of your driveshaft; if so, they were put there during the balancing and taking them off would upset the balance, although a machinist may take them off or relocate them during the rebalancing of a modified shaft.

The factory balance can also be disturbed by an accumulation of mud and grease on the shaft, so make sure it's clean. And if you have plans to have the car undercoated, be sure to cover up the driveshaft and U-joints. If you don't think that tar-like stuff is heavy, ask somebody running a Junior Stocker why he spent so many hours scraping it off the underbelly of his Nomad.

4-WHEEL DRIVE

Over the past several years there has been a tremendous increase in the popularity of 4-wheel drive vehicles. The rigs are great for splashing across streams, plowing through mud, and bouncing around in the desert. To accomplish this, most 4X4's are set up pretty high off the ground, which necessitates some steep U-joint angles. To put power to the front wheels, in addition to conventional rear-wheel drive, means employing a transfer case behind the trans so there's someplace for the front driveshaft to come from. This means the 4X4 has twice the usual number of U-joints, and since most 4X4's eventually get fitted with huge ground-clawing tires, each joint is put under a far heavier strain than a similar joint in an ordinary car. Naturally, off-roading means the joints put up with more than their fair share of water, mud, and sand, which isn't the best way to keep them clean and well lubricated.

There are, however, a few things you can do to help keep your 4X4's driveshafts and U-joints operating clean and with efficiency. One is to install a pair of lockable, free-running hubs on the front wheels—if your rig isn't one with a full-time system. Free-running front hubs will keep your front axles, front differential gears, and driveshaft disengaged from the wheels when running on pavement. The hubs not only help cut down on friction and drag, but the front U-joints simply sit still and do not work needlessly. Another good idea is to check and see if your 4X4 came from the factory with permanently-sealed U-joints and, if it did, replace them with heavy-duty joints having a grease fitting. When off-roading, carry a tool box with a grease gun, a couple of spare U-joints, and enough tools to remove and replace them.

The grease gun doesn't have to be a big, heavy, and expensive one, as long as it will develop enough pressure to force out any water and dirt as it forces replacement grease in. The best time to give the U-joints a going over with the gun is after you stop each day to camp, or on a shorter excursion just before you hit the blacktop for home.

Once at home, and while you're hosing the 4X4 down to get the grime off, squirt the underside, too. When it's as clean as hose pressure will make it, check both driveshafts for any dings or dents you may have picked up out in the boondocks. Driveshaft trouble, in the form of breakage or imbalance, can start with the smallest of dents or a deep scratch. If you give your driveshafts and U-joints reasonable care, you'll maintain peace of mind as you wail across the outback.

1. The only proper way to shorten or modify a driveshaft is in a lathe. Here the factory weld at the rear yoke is being cut away. Then the end can be slipped out and pressed into the shortened shaft for perfect fit and alignment. The new weld should be made on the lathe also.

2. Preliminary straightness checks on a driveshaft can be made with a simple pair of V-blocks by using a dial indicator to check runout.

3. Minor imbalances in a shaft can be corrected on the car by using two hose clamps as mentioned in text.

4. Before any driveshaft, especially a modified one, can be balanced it must be straightened. This is done by first finding the high side. Hold a piece of chalk near the spinning shaft until it just touches the high side. Do this several times and the chalk marks will indicate high side.

5. After you have "chalked" a shaft several times, the marks will show where the high side is. This area is then shrunk by heating it with torch and rapidly cooling with a wet rag.

6. Once the driveshaft is straight enough that the dial indicator shows minimal runout, the shaft can be put on the balancer. Until you know the exact weight to be added, pieces of clay are used to test balance.

7. When the balancer shows that the shaft is spinning true, the amount of clay used is weighed and the same amount of metal is welded on shaft.

CHASSIS, SUSPENSION & BRAKES/159

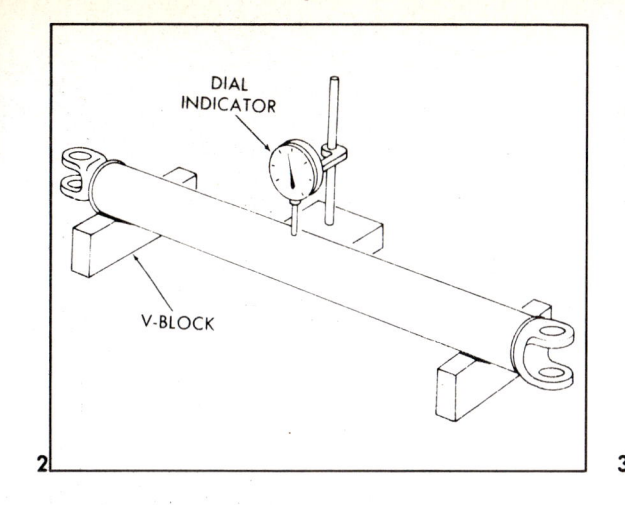

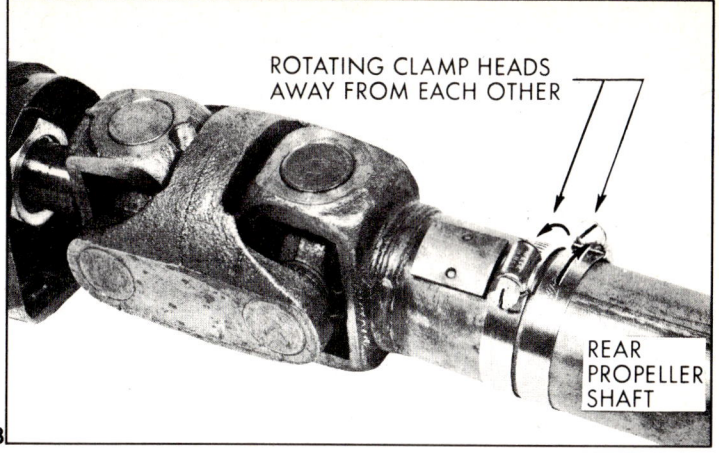

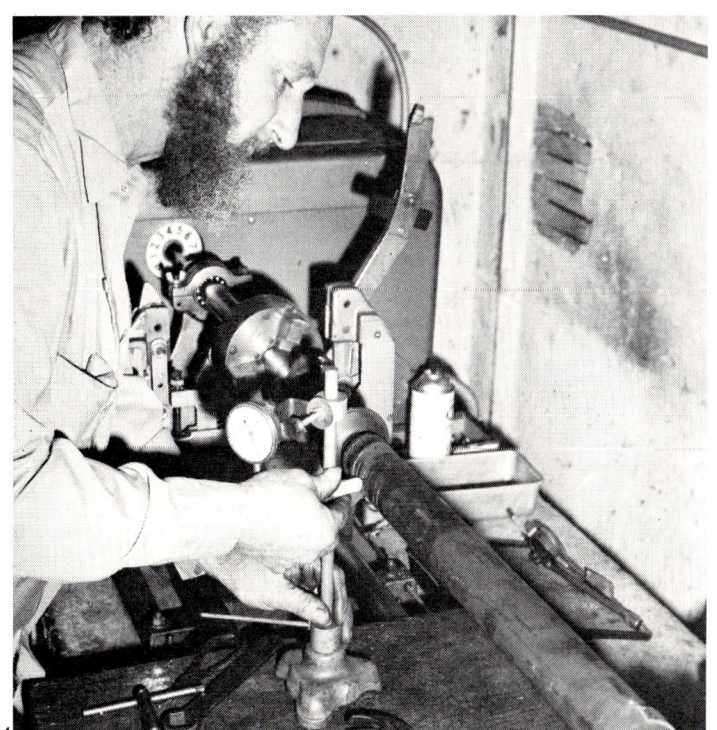

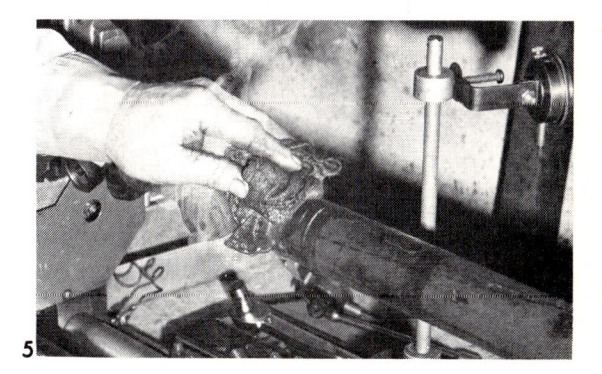

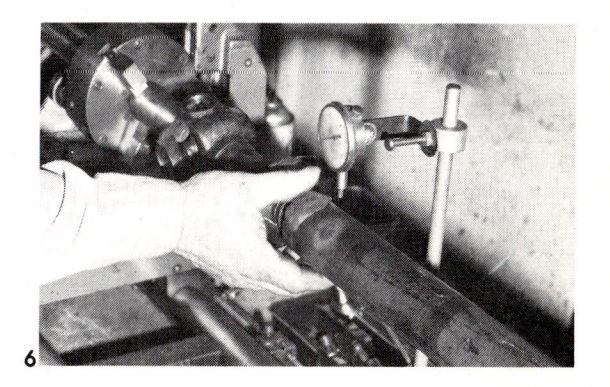

The Rearend

The latest on how a differential works, types of axles, setting up gears, gear wear patterns, and ratios.

Here we are walking around on the moon and mankind is still saddled with the same basic type of automobile final drive invented before the turn of the century. True, there are some relatively sophisticated rear-end designs, but by and large it is still a matter of an unsprung housing, two axles, and a differential. The economics of mass production being what they are, it is amazing that modern rear ends are as good as they are. Fortunately for the average motorist, the demands of high performance have been felt by Detroit designers, and the rear axle assembly of practically every passenger car is now created with a substantial margin of "beef" to take abnormal driving conditions.

That the rear end has undergone varied changes through the years is apparent, but why the changes have been made is seldom expressed. Early builders used the bicycle-type of final drive—a simple chain and sprocket to a plain live rear axle. An efficient method, but the solid rear axles proved a problem to turning, which meant that some kind of differential was necessary. During the turn, the inside wheel covers less ground than the outside wheel.

Cars of the early 1900's were often equipped with the popular bevelgear-driven rear end, a type of right-angle drive common to many forms of machinery. As automotive performance increased, the need for better rear ends created the spiralbevel-gear and worm-gear drives. The hypoid-gear drive common to the modern car has become popular with Detroit engineers and is now the industry standard. Whatever the type of gear used—bevel, worm, or hypoid—the requirement is constant: to transmit torque through a 90° angle. At the same time, this juncture is an ideal place to increase leverage to the rear wheels through relative gear ratios.

The bevel gear was dropped because of very high noise and limited service. Only one gear tooth is in contact at a time—and this a harsh, instant contact. The spiral bevel is a much better design, as the teeth are brought into contact through a sliding movement. This means there is more than a single gear tooth in contact and the overall design is far quieter. The traditional Model A Ford closed driveline is a typical example of the spiral bevel gear, having a short pinion shaft integral with the rather small diameter pinion gear. There are usually two bearings for pinion shaft support, but a single bearing is sometimes used. When there are two bearings, both of them might be on the same side of the pinion, separated by a washer, or they can be set up in a straddle mount, with one bearing on each side. Older hot rodders will recognize this as a definition of a famous series of Halibrand quick-change boxes, the straddle mount design being stronger and more popular.

As a general guide, the spiral-bevel-type rear end places the pinion shaft centerline on a plane with the axle centerline. By placing the pinion on a lower plane and changing the pitch of the gears, it is possible to have a quieter gear train with increased tooth contact. Because there is greater tooth mesh, the load is spread out more and tooth fracture is minimized. Of consideration to the engineer is the possibility of a lower floorboard hump since the driveshaft will be 3 or 4 ins. lower at rear-end contact. The hypoid gear just described is common on the modern passenger car and has been refined to a great state of reliability. Further advancements in metallurgy may help make this design unbeatable for mass-production.

The worm gear, popular in some forms of steering boxes, has been used for heavy-duty purposes but tends to generate abnormal heat.

This heat problem is controlled by lubricant and by dissimilar metals (where the drive worm might be steel and the ring gear bronze, etc.). By the very nature of the worm gear running beneath the ring gear (check an old Model T truck for a perfect example), it is possible to obtain very high gear ratios without losing input shaft diameter (strength) and without re-

1. A lot of devices have come and gone in the search for a perfect rear-end differential, and what we have today has evolved into a refined and practical package. These are some prototypes of the '50's Dual-Drive, an early limited-slip approach.

2. The modern rear end is rugged, efficient in power transfer, and generally requires no major service in the life of a car, other than adding a bit of lube or changing a bearing.

3. In case you've wondered how the outer axle bearings are lubricated, the gear lube is tossed around the differential by the gears and flows out the housing to the axle bearings, then flows back to the differential.

4. The oil seal, retainer and its gasket all help to keep lubricant from going past the bearing, where it might ruin the rear brakes.

5. Not all axle bearings are located the same way. The three basic types of rear ends include: semi-floating, three-quarter floating, and the full floating. The semi-floating is the most common type, while the three-quarter and full floating are used primarily in trucks, because they can handle higher bearing loads.

6. Since towing a car doesn't do the rear axle any good, racers who have to flat-tow a car use free-wheeling tow hubs like these NMW units. They bolt between the wheel and the axle and prevent the differential turning.

160/CHASSIS, SUSPENSION & BRAKES

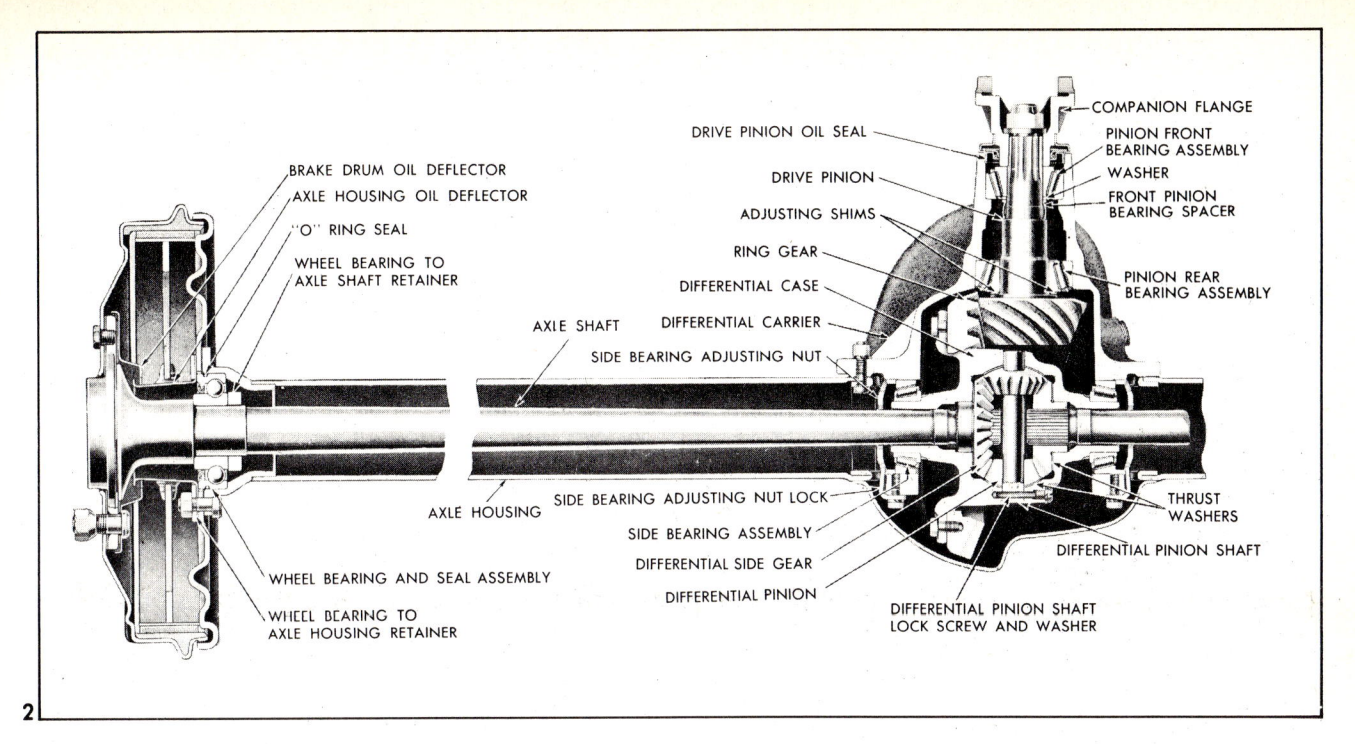

Figure 2

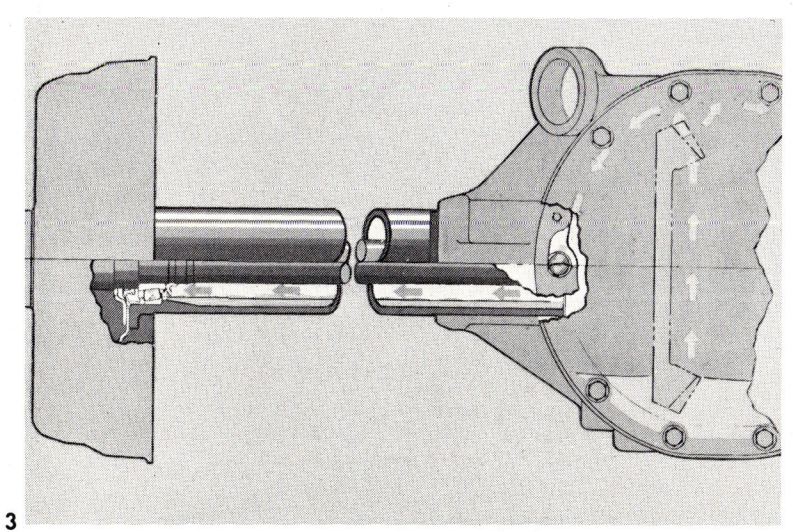

- BRAKE DRUM OIL DEFLECTOR
- AXLE HOUSING OIL DEFLECTOR
- "O" RING SEAL
- WHEEL BEARING TO AXLE SHAFT RETAINER
- AXLE SHAFT
- AXLE HOUSING
- WHEEL BEARING AND SEAL ASSEMBLY
- WHEEL BEARING TO AXLE HOUSING RETAINER
- DRIVE PINION OIL SEAL
- DRIVE PINION
- ADJUSTING SHIMS
- RING GEAR
- DIFFERENTIAL CASE
- DIFFERENTIAL CARRIER
- SIDE BEARING ADJUSTING NUT
- SIDE BEARING ADJUSTING NUT LOCK
- SIDE BEARING ASSEMBLY
- DIFFERENTIAL SIDE GEAR
- DIFFERENTIAL PINION
- DIFFERENTIAL PINION SHAFT LOCK SCREW AND WASHER
- COMPANION FLANGE
- PINION FRONT BEARING ASSEMBLY
- WASHER
- FRONT PINION BEARING SPACER
- PINION REAR BEARING ASSEMBLY
- THRUST WASHERS
- DIFFERENTIAL PINION SHAFT

Figure 4

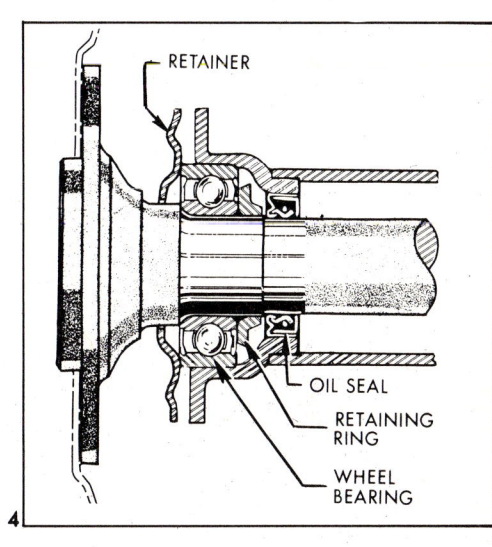

- RETAINER
- OIL SEAL
- RETAINING RING
- WHEEL BEARING

Figure 5

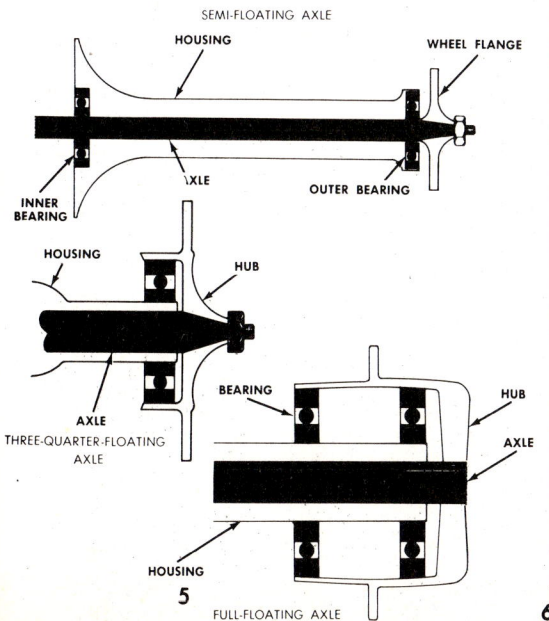

SEMI-FLOATING AXLE
- HOUSING
- WHEEL FLANGE
- INNER BEARING
- AXLE
- OUTER BEARING

THREE-QUARTER-FLOATING AXLE
- HOUSING
- HUB

FULL-FLOATING AXLE
- BEARING
- HUB
- AXLE
- HOUSING

CHASSIS, SUSPENSION & BRAKES/161

The Rearend

sorting to very large diameter ring gears. This problem of space vs. strength led to the creation of the double-reduction drive rear end, which uses a standard pinion, with the ring gear mounted on a short shaft. The short shaft turns a small gear which meshes with a large gear on the differential. Gear reduction is obtained through the ring and pinion, and also through the second gearset—quite compact for the results, but still very large. The use of planetary gears, now common to automatic transmissions, was long ago introduced into rear end gearing as part of the 2-speed package (remember the Columbia, Ford fans?) and could be controlled by the driver. Strength and reliability were causes for the 2-speed axle demise, a death encouraged by very good transmission overdrives; more flexible engines.

So far, so good. The engine torque is now changed in direction to make the wheels turn, but still the old chain and sprocket would work as well. What is needed is a device to allow either wheel to rotate at a different speed than the other while the power is still being applied. Here enters the differential.

WHY A DIFFERENTIAL?

The typical differential will contain a ring gear, housing, spider or pin, pinions, and side- or axle-shaft gears. Such a differential is in operation to drive the car whenever it is running, although differential action usually takes place on turns only. The ring gear is bolted or riveted to the differential case, the case enclosing the other gears. Splined axle shafts fit into side gears that rotate on plane with the ring gear, connected by four differential pinion or spider gears. These spider gears are like idlers, in that they are held on individual shafts inside the housing and only touch the side gears. This is the heart of a differential—and it's secret.

When the car is going straight, the spider gears do not rotate on their own shafts, but turn both side gears with equal torque from the main pinion gear. However, when the car turns a corner, the inside axle is making fewer revolutions than the differential housing. Because of this, the housing forces the idler pinions to run along the side gear (the case is turning faster), which in turn advances the opposite side gear the same amount. To see how this spider gear action works, put the car in gear and jack up the rear end. As one wheel is rotated, the opposite wheel will rotate the same amount in the opposite direction. The spider gears are idling and thus changing rotational direction completely.

The differential has a singular problem, however—a sticky situation that has plagued performance enthusiasts for many years. Engine torque tends to travel the path of least resistance. This means that one wheel in the mud will spin while the other on dry pavement is stationary. To make matters worse, this wheel will spin twice as fast as the differential.

The locking differential overcomes this tendency, but it has not proven a really reputable unit until the last two decades. Known by a number of different trade names, such as Positraction, Equa-lok, Sure-Grip, No-Spin, etc., the general principle is the same: keep the power going to both wheels all the time. This is accomplished a number of ways—through the addition of pinion thrust rings (side gear rings), clutch discs and clutch plates.

The Chrysler Sure-Grip is a typical unit, using clutch plates, discs and pinion thrust members. Here the pinion shafts are separate, one shaft for each two opposite pinion gears. On either side of the pinion gears are circular thrust members, followed in order by alternating clutch discs and plates. Normal friction of the road, wheel inertia and gear friction make the pinions resist moving. This resistance causes the pinion shafts to slide, or "work up" V-shaped ramps in the differential case. At the lowest point of these case V's, the pinion shafts are together. As the shafts are forced apart by the ramp angle, the pinion gears contact the thrust rings, which in turn put pressure on the clutch discs. In effect, both sides of the differential case become secondary clutches, with varying pressures possible. As the pressure increases, the tendency for one wheel to spin on ice or mud decreases. Drag racers use these types of differentials to help control individual wheelspin during acceleration. When turning a corner, the pressure is overcome and the differential can work normally. Clutch pressure can be adjusted and will have a direct effect upon both wheelspin control and turning ease. The stronger the pressure on these clutches, the less wheelspin and greater the resistance to turning.

TYPES OF AXLES

The types of rear axles in current use by vehicle engineers include all three of the popular styles—semi-floating, three-quarter-floating and full-floating. As a guide, consider the word floating to describe how the axle is carried inside the axle housing.

Almost all modern cars use a semi-floating axle. The outer bearing is attached directly to the axle, usually

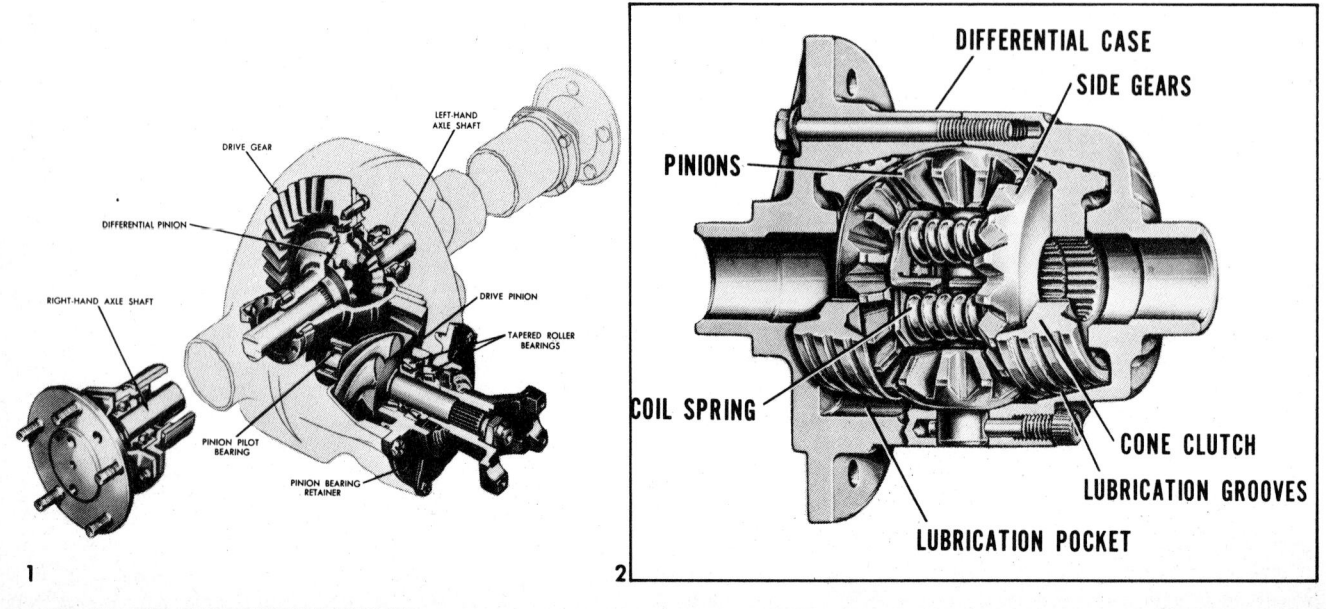

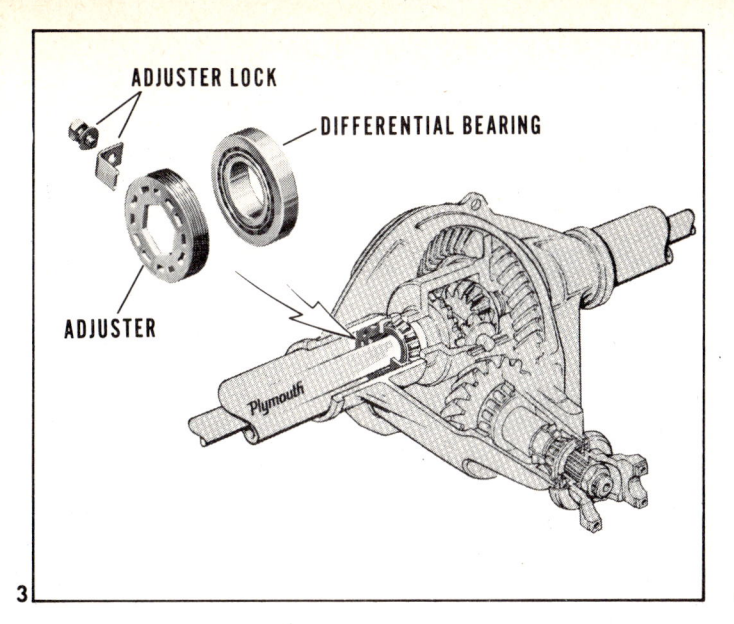

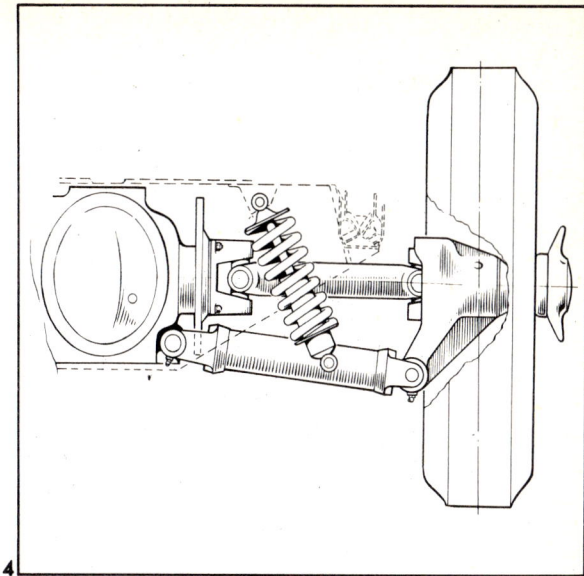

1. Torque that is passed to the rear end through the driveshaft twists the pinon gear which twists the ring or drive gear. Differential pinions allow one axle to turn faster when cornering, or tires would skid.

2. A variety of limited-slip devices are used by the different automakers. This is a cone-type Mopar Sure-Grip. All limited-slip units attempt to deliver full traction to both wheels at all times except when cornering. It's a great help on ice and snow.

3. Adjusting the bearings to get the ring and pinion gears to mesh right is always a time-consuming job. New Plymouths with small 7¼-in. axle will be a little easier to adjust because of new threaded adjusters for preload and backlash, instead of spacers.

4. The Jaguar rear end is an example of independent rear suspension, in which the differential is mounted solidly to the frame (to reduce the unsprung weight), the brakes are mounted inboard (for same reasons), while the wheels have individual springs and are driven by driveshafts.

5. The only American car with an independent rear end is the Corvette. Although the brakes are mounted at the wheels, unsprung weight is still less than with a normal rear end and ride and handling are improved.

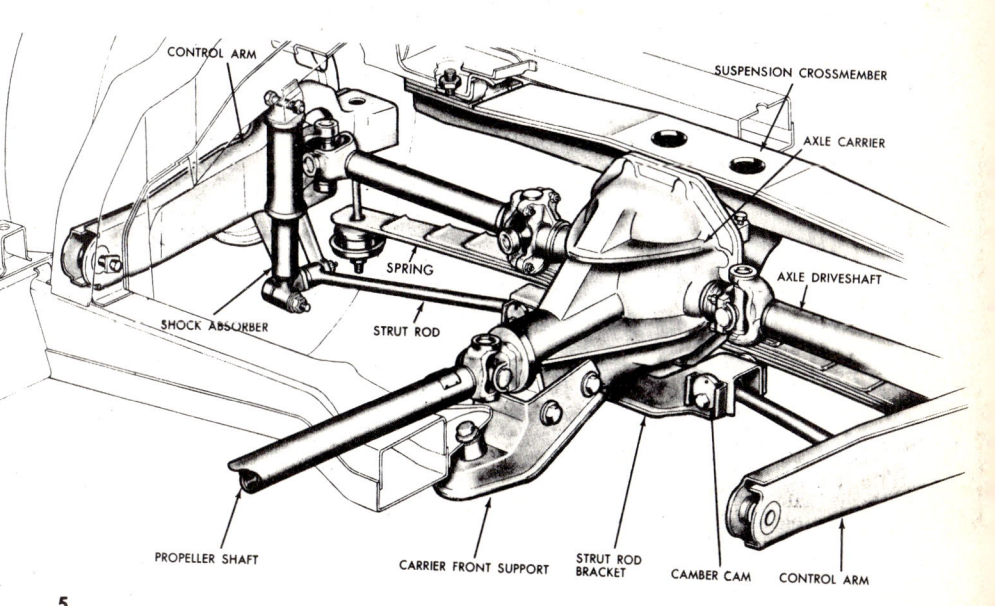

being pressed on. A semi-floating axle carries on its outer end all the torque and bending forces as well as the weight of the car. In fact, the whole weight that the wheel supports is carried by the short length of axle between the bearing and the hub. Even though the semi-floating axle carries all the weight and forces on its outer end, it still qualifies for the title "semi" because its inner half floats in splines in the differential carrier. The bending and side-thrust forces imposed by the pinion on the ring gear are taken by the carrier bearings, relieving the inner end of the axle from any force but torque. If the inner bearings were mounted on the axle itself, all the forces would be taken by the axle, and we would have a "plain live" axle, a design that doesn't live very long and is not used today.

The three-quarter-floating axle is common to closed driveline Fords of pre-1949. The outer axle bearing is in the hub, and supports the weight of the car. The axle holds the hub in place, and takes all the bending and torque forces except the weight of the car. Hot rodders long ago discovered that a broken axle in this type rear end was free to slip from the housing along with the attached wheel. Special retainers—U-shaped steel clips—were fashioned to bolt against the brake backing plates. Looping over the brake drum, they would retain the drum and wheel when an axle severed. Other designs of safety hubs went inside the brake drum and bolted to the rear-end housing. They didn't do anything until an axle broke, and then they kept the wheel and hub in place so the driver could coast safely to a stop.

The full-floating axle is common to heavy-duty applications, such as trucks and NASCAR stockers. A full-floating axle is splined on both ends, and transmits only torque. It is recognizable by the large ring of bolts in the center of the hub. Remove the bolts, and the axle can be slipped out. The car can be towed or pushed with the axles removed, because the axles have nothing to do with retaining the hub or holding up the car's weight.

Forces that act on these types of rear axle designs have much to do with which type is best for specific forms of automotive competition. With semi-floating axle, the shaft must be strong enough to carry bending loads as well as torque. The pre-'49 Ford axles were prone to break well in-

CHASSIS, SUSPENSION & BRAKES/163

The Rearend

board from torque, while Ramblers of the late 1950's would lose axles from loads. Forces acting on the wheel plane due to traction, braking or vehicle weight, cause a leverage equal to the overhang of the axle beyond the outer bearing which will tend to bend the shaft. These forces are greatly magnified when the vehicle is moving.

For the serious enthusiast, there are two ways of determining the greatest torque a shaft may have to carry. The first is to multiply maximum engine torque by the overall bottom gear ratio, then halve the result (the differential divides the torque). The second method is to calculate in reverse from the tire adhesion limit, with the greatest torque being that which will cause wheelspin on dry pavement. This torque will be 60% of the wheel load multiplied by the tire rolling radius.

Race car builders know that axle shafts must be made of quality materials and tailored for the job. There can be no sudden change in section where stress may build up, with the area next to the outer bearing critical. Interestingly, it has been found that shafts can be reworked by cutting and welding, and be capable of sustaining high drag racing loads. Special axles are machined for dragsters and expensive oval track cars.

Rear-end inner bearings are usually of the tapered roller variety, with ball bearings at the wheels. The outer bearings have a tendency to fail on heavier cars with semi-floating axles, simply because of the great load requirements. This failure may not necessarily be due to wear, but can be caused strictly from load. During shipment to sales points the cars are often tied down snugly. Vehicle weight shifts slightly on the rear bearings, causing them to wear locally. Some dealerships automatically install new outer bearings before the car is sold, to avert an early buyer complaint.

Rear end seals and gaskets can be a source of frustration on the older car, and should be kept in prime condition. Lubrication for the outer bearings in semi-floating designs comes from the gear cavity, flowing down the turning axle to the bearing. It cannot go further because of the cover flange seal and gasket. Similar seals are utilized around the pinion shaft. As a good rule of thumb, always replace seals and gaskets when bearings are replaced or serviced. Three-quarter and full-floating hubs are lubricated independently of the rear end.

In addition to the types of differential and axle assemblies, there are many sophisticated housing designs, ideas that are really segments of suspension characteristics. Any standard rear end will be necessarily heavy, which gives a poor unsprung-to-sprung weight ratio resulting in a variety of hops, tramps and other road-induced vibrations There are a number of ways to control the flailing of this weight mass—through roll center design, shock absorber location (as far outboard as possible and inclined at a trial-and-error angle), torque bars, and so forth.

Roll centers have a tremendous effect upon a car's handling as well as its ride qualities. Roll center is the point about which the sprung mass rotates under side load. This center will vary considerably in height relative to the type of rear-end design, which includes housing as well as springing mechanisms.

Unequal wishbones, which are common to some types of race cars, will produce a center well below the road surface, because of the converging angles of the wishbones. Parallel, equal-length wishbones will have a roll center directly at the road level. Vertical slides, like that of the Morgan and Lancia cars, work in a plane the same as parallel, equal-length wishbones and have the same roll center. A DeDion rear axle will have the roll center in the exact center of the rear end, while swing axles such as Corvair and Volkswagen (and early Mercedes-Benz) have a roll center near the top of the differential case. It is interesting that these latter designs have the center in practically the same place as the traditional solid housing rear end. Late Mercedes-Benz cars have a low-pivot swing axle, which effectively lowers the roll center to roughly that of the DeDion.

The DeDion axle is really a mixture of the traditional solid housing and

1. Ring and pinion gearsets have progressed from the early straight bevel gears and the spiral bevel to the modern hypoid type, which is the strongest and most quiet-running.

2. The heart of a differential is the ring and pinion gearset. The gear ratio is determined by dividing the number of teeth on the ring gear by by the number of teeth on the pinion.

3. Ring and pinion gears are mated and lapped at the factory to find the proper bearing and spacer sizes for them. The operator is in a soundproof room so he can detect unusual noise.

4. The Corvair was an unusual car in many ways, not the least of which was the drive layout. The engine was mounted behind the rear wheels and connected to the rear end, which was actually a transmission and a rear end, that was independent as well.

5. Of the two basic types of rear ends, the Hotchkiss and Salisbury, the most common today is the latter. As shown here, the differential gear bearings and all are contained in a housing that is part of the whole rear end. The gears have to be worked on through a cover on the back. With the Hotchkiss type, the gearset is in a removeable carrier and can be set up or adjusted on the bench.

6. A few years ago Dana Corp. came out with this rear end for Mercury's Cougar. Rare today, it was basically a redesign of their truck 2-speed unit. It works like an overdrive, so it would be handy today for mileage.

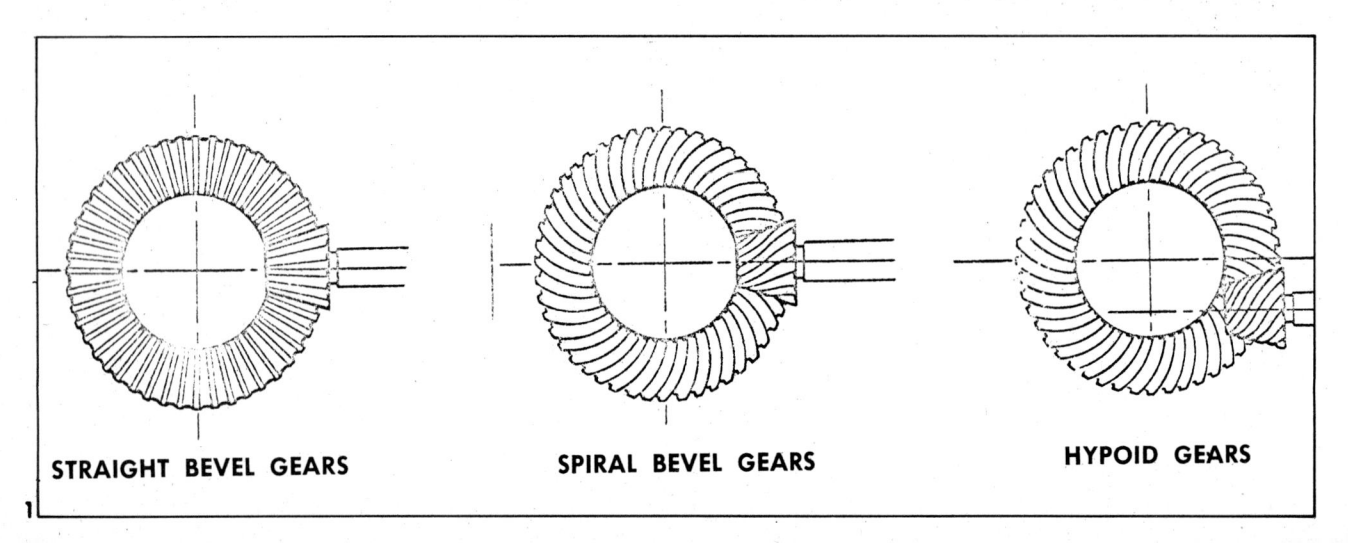

STRAIGHT BEVEL GEARS **SPIRAL BEVEL GEARS** **HYPOID GEARS**

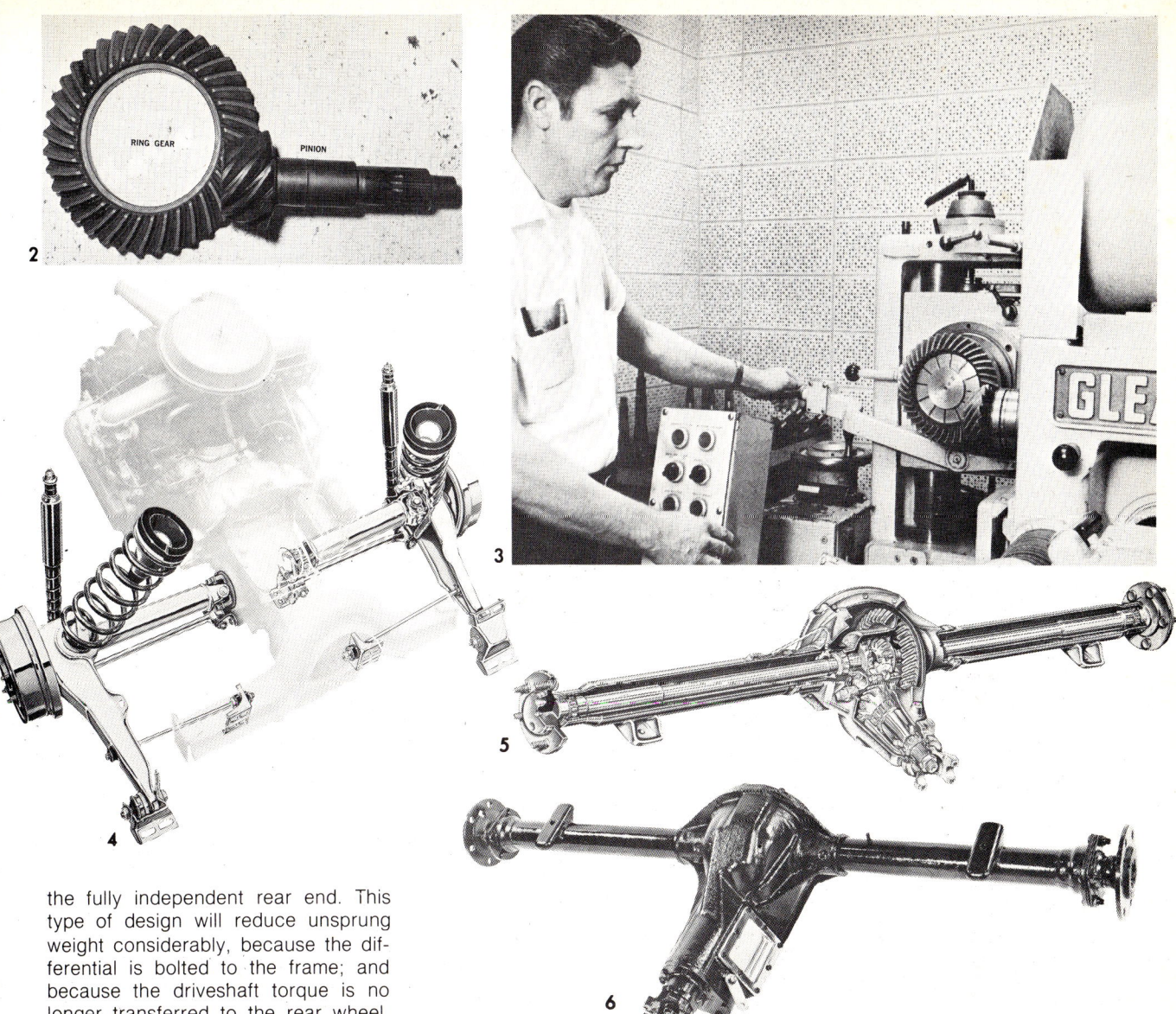

the fully independent rear end. This type of design will reduce unsprung weight considerably, because the differential is bolted to the frame; and because the driveshaft torque is no longer transferred to the rear wheel, there will be no individual wheel breakaway during acceleration.

DeDion axles use a regular beam of some type to connect the two wheels, with suspension off this beam. At either beam end are carriers for the hub, with connections to the frame-mounted differential through sliding splines on the individual drive axles. DeDion axles are of two types—one with inboard brakes to further reduce unsprung weight, and the other with outboard brakes. The obvious advantage of mounting the brakes alongside the differential housing, other than weight, is in brake reaction forces. Locating arms aren't necessary to transmit this force to the frame, and this design therefore requires less strength and bulk.

Simpler to construct is the independent rear suspension, using any of the several types of axle design, from swing axle to full independent. Advantages of the independent suspension are many, including: reduced unsprung weight; no driveshaft torque effect; elimination of tramps, hops, etc.; reduction of sideways push with single wheel bump or rebound which cuts down on rear-end steering effects; and more space above the rear end for storage.

With the independently suspended rear end, unsprung weight is cut a bit over 50%, while the DeDion only reduces it 40%. This is with inboard brakes; outboard brakes reduce the figures about 15%, or 35% and 25%, respectively. Unfortunately, not all independent rear ends have been fully designed for the car. That is, such a rear end will have a direct effect upon roll center, and center position has an effect upon handling, etc. The Mercedes 300-SL was a good example of this. As fine as the car was, the high rear roll center was not compatible with the low front roll center, with a consequent tendency of the rear end to "come around." This led directly to the current low-pivot swing axle in M-B cars.

The swing axle may have the inboard pivot point at the exact center of the rear end, as in VW and Renault, and to some extent in the M-B. Or the pivot points may be outside the differential as in Corvair, Tempest and race cars using the special Hewland transaxle. With a swing axle, the wheels swing through an arc about the inner universal joint. To some extent this gives an independent nature to each rear wheel, and the differential can be mounted to the frame. However, the wheels tend to tuck under during cornering, a factor used by automotive critics to force a design change in the Corvair. Since 1965, the Corvair has had a full independent suspension rather than swing axle.

In the full independent suspension, the wheels are free to rise and fall in a perpendicular plane. To do this requires a fixed plane hub carrier fixed to the suspension arms and an extra universal joint in the axle shaft. The full independent suspension may have inboard or outboard brakes, also, with the former exemplified by the Ja-

CHASSIS, SUSPENSION & BRAKES/165

The Rearend

guar XKE and Mark X cars and the latter by the Corvette.

No matter what kind of rear end is used, there is a requirement for axle location. In the simplest form, such as the Chevy II, the rear end is both sprung and located by a single leaf spring on either side. This spring keeps the rear end from alignment stray, restricts torque windup and absorbs bumps. When any other type of springing is used—such as coils, torsion bars or transverse leaf—some type of extra control is necessary. With coils this will include a side sway bar and torque bars. With torsion bars, the bar arms may be one part of the linkage, but with the transverse spring, the torque bars may be substituted by a closed driveline tube (older Fords, Chevys, and Buicks). For general use, factory-designed locaters are sufficient, but for increased performance, stronger locaters (or additional units) are usually required. Generally, independent rear suspension locaters are strong enough.

TROUBLESHOOTING THE FINAL DRIVE

Nothing can be quite so frustrating to the amateur mechanic as an assumed rear-end noise. Assumed, because the noise can be caused by tires, wheel bearings, wheels and bolts, bearings, the exhaust pipe, transmission, driveshaft, universal joints, differential gears and axles. Trying to isolate a problem will take the amateur several times longer than applying the cure. Fortunately, repair is usually a matter of parts replacement or minor adjustment. In the case of ring and pinion gear setup, special tools are required, and this particular problem might best be left to the professional. However, knowing how to talk shop never strained customer/mechanic relations.

Axles—The axle itself can be a source of some unusual noises, very difficult to locate. If there is a vibration on the upper speed range, usually above 55 mph, a good prospect is a bent or off-center axle. Production tolerances sometimes pass an axle that is off-center. The shaft will then whip in the housing and is a nuisance. It can be trued-up by slight machining, but the best solution is replacement. Race cars are especially intolerant of this particular condition.

A bent axle, which is very possible in the semi-floating axle designs, can produce the same symptoms. Excessive end-play in the axle (set at one side only) can cause a thumping noise on a rough road and during cornering.

Bearings—Even new cars can experience bearing troubles, and these can be varied. Most common are outer bearing failures. Unfortunately, the only difference between an outer and inner bearing noise is magnitude. The inner bearings and pinion bearings will seem more solid, or muffled. Bearing noise will be a continued grinding noise that increases in volume in direct proportion to car speed.

Usually an outer bearing will cause a rough spot on the bearing race. Somtimes this roughness can be felt by jacking up the car and slowly rotating the wheel.

Wheels—There are many causes of abnormal sounds from a wheel, including loose or "working" hubcaps, loose lug nuts, worn keyways in drum or axle, excessive axle end-play and broken wheels.

Third Member—The differential and carrier assembly noises are sounds unto themselves. The bearings will grind or sizzle as mentioned above. A ring and pinion set up too tightly will have too little backlash and cause a continuous whine, but gear noises may vary considerably.

If the ring gear is loose and creeping on its carrier, it will normally make a sharp, metallic sound when changing from reverse to a forward gear (this takes up maximum slack). If there is a thumping sound during cornering, look for a broken or nicked differential side gear.

The wrong kind of rear-end grease, gear teeth scoring and incorrect pinion/ring gear mesh will all cause a gear noise during engine load. During coasting, or deceleration, a heavy and irregular noise indicates wrong pinion adjustment or scored gear teeth caused by excessive end-play in the pinion bearing.

Broken Axles—This one is easy to find. There is a clacking noise and the car quits going (unless it has a limited slip differential). The causes are driver, grabbing clutch, vehicle overload, wrong wheel bearing adjustment or housing misalignment. If alignment is the problem, a new housing is usually required. The rest of the problems are easily overcome, except maybe the driver, who must overcome himself.

Broken Side Gear—Bent axle, worn thrust washers, or excessive axle housing deflection can all cause the side gear to break.

Broken Differential Case—Causes

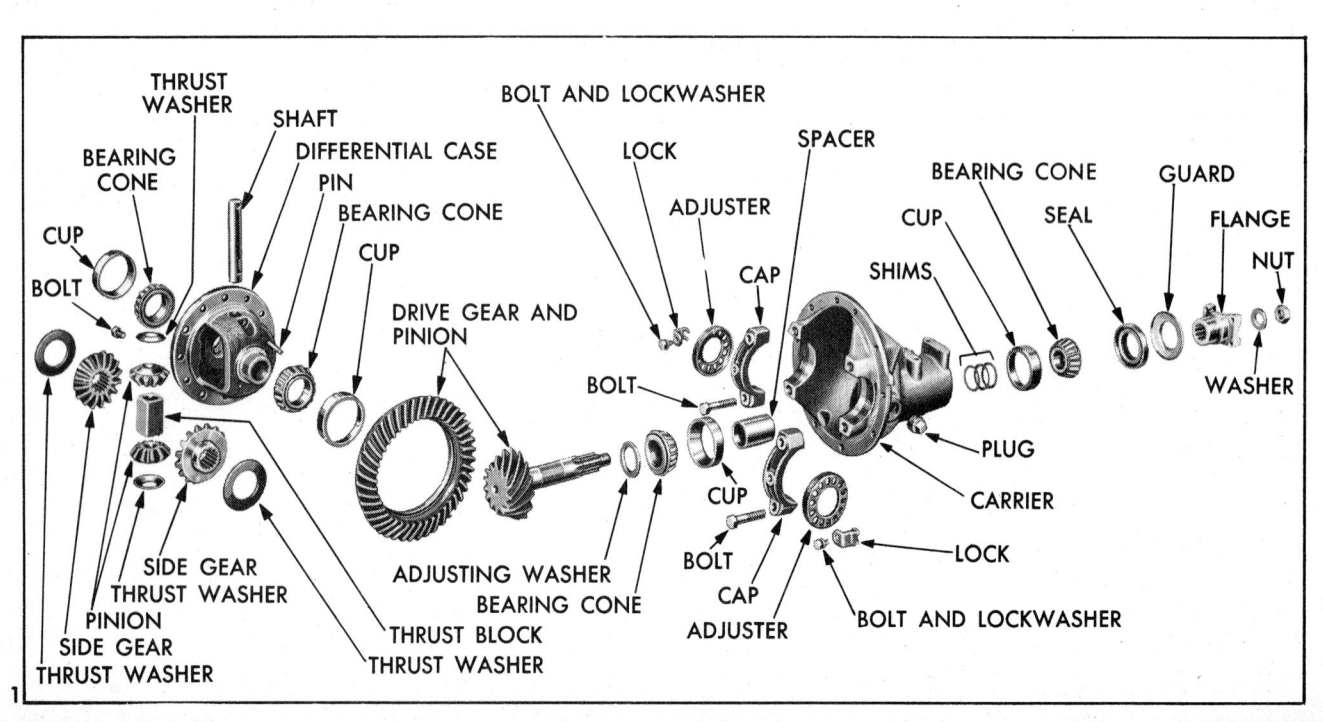

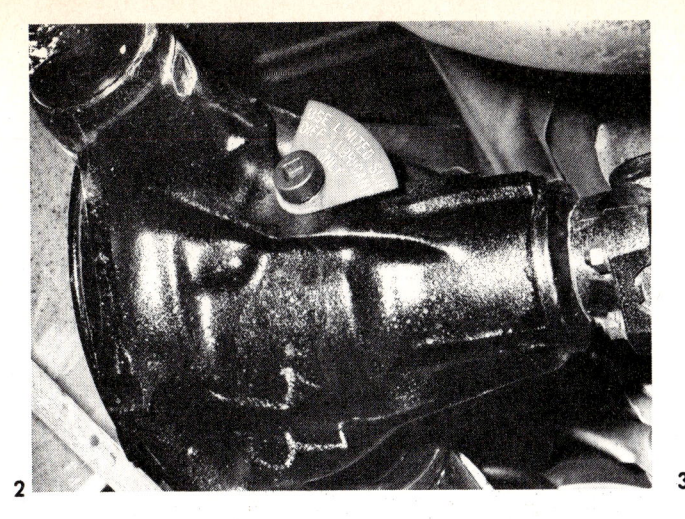

1. This is an exploded view of a non-limited-slip Chrysler rear end. This assembly is typical of Hotchkiss types with removeable center sections.

2. If you have a limited-slip unit in your rear end, be sure to use only the lubricant recommended for it.

3. The DeDion type rear end is like a cross between an independent and a typical solid axle. The wheels were connected by a solid bar (arrow), but the differential and brakes were on the chassis, cutting unsprung weight.

4. With the Hotchkiss type rear end the gears are contained in a "third member," which can unbolt from the housing for repairs or adjustments.

5. Some people would like to get rid of the rear end altogether. This is Jack Chrisman's '72 funny car. With a SOHC Ford 427 mounted in the rear of the chassis and sideways, he used gears and a large chain to drive the rear wheels like a go-kart, with a solid straight axle between wheels.

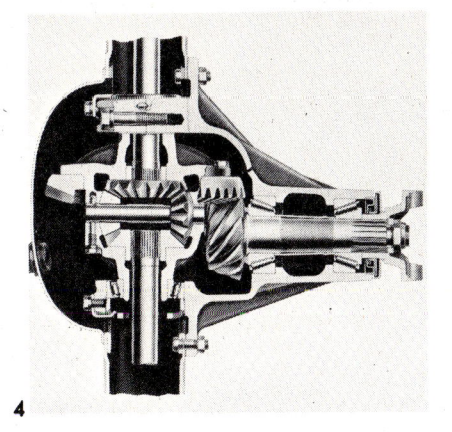

are driver, overload, wrong adjustment of differential bearings, or too much drive gear clearance.

Scored Differential Gears—Wrong lubricant or excessive loading.

Broken Ring and Pinion Gears—Driver, wrong adjustment, overloading, alternate slick and dry pavement.

Lubrication Loss—Too much lubricant in the rear end will allow pressure to build up and blow lube out the vent or past seals and cap screws. If the housing vent is plugged, pressure will also build. On some General Motors cars, the filler plug is vented. This vent will be closed if the plug is tightened too much.

When axle seals are worn, broken or hardened, oil will leak out onto the backing plates and cause the brakes to grab. If there is oil thrown on the flooring near the third member nose, the pinion bearing seal is faulty. Rarely, the housing will crack or there will be sand holes in the third member casting, causing leaks.

Overheating—This can be caused by wrong lubricant or too low an oil level. Also suspect tight bearings, not enough clearance between ring and pinion gear, and excessive wear in the gear teeth.

SETTING UP REAR GEARS

Setting up the rear end of an automobile has become as precise a science as correct carburetor jetting. It seems that all too many mechanics (those generally referred to as backyard or hot rod types) have overlooked this important fact. That's a shame, because the use of gears actually created for racing requires even more precision than standard gears.

With the old-type straight bevel gears, super alignment wasn't a big deal: you could be off as much as 1/64-in. and nobody cared. However, as the angle of the load-carrying gears increased, the requirement for perfect alignment also rose. If the oblique gears aren't matched just right, noise and wear problems are paramount.

The hypoid-type rear end includes gear angularity in the 50° range. This means that manufacturer recommendations must be adhered to without exception. Since rear-end gears give such outstanding service, it is not uncommon to go the life of an automobile without requiring third member work. The enthusiast, however, who must contend with varying ring and pinion gear ratios has learned to appreciate the exacting science of setting up a rear end.

There are many special tools produced for rear end gear work, usually made to fit a specific model carrier, and there are some special tools made just for racing gears. If the rear end is just for ordinary street driving, it may be set in the most basic manner, but the rules which follow on general setup and assembly should be applied for best results.

The modern Chrysler rear end is a typical unit, strong enough to take punishment from the biggest engines and simple enough for low-cost mass production. All MoPar product rear ends will interchange from 1957 up to the present. This business of interchange, from complete housing to individual pieces, will hold constant with most marques. Chrysler has a large and small diameter pinion on their V-8 cars—as do most other makes—with the large unit going to the big, high-horsepower cars. On Chrysler, the number 2070742 or 1634985 stamped on the left side of the third member housing indicates the large pinion (from 1960). The small pinion is identified by number 2070741 or 1820657. This is a lighter duty unit and the gears are difficult to obtain. Ratios for the big pinion are

CHASSIS, SUSPENSION & BRAKES/167

The Rearend

2.76 to 5.18, while the small unit stops at 4.89.

Cost of Chrysler gears are similar to the total market, with factory units above 4.30 costing about $25 more than the standard units below 4.11. For street use, something in the 3.54 range is applicable. The dual purpose car would use 3.90 to 4.11, and dragsters will use very high gear ratios of 2.90 to 3.25.

The very first step in working on any rear end is cleaning and inspecting the third member. Look for cracks, particles of metal in the old lubrication that might indicate bearing or gear tooth wear, and any evidence of external damage. Be especially careful to locate and remove burrs or nicks on the various machined and contacted surfaces.

Since the limited-slip differential is a standard unit plus a few extra parts, we'll follow that type through repair and setup. In the case of the Chrysler Sure-Grip, look for the right curvature of the clutches. Excessive heat or abuse will cause clutches to score on either the curved or flat discs. If there is any question as to condition, always install new parts. Before separating halves of any locking differential, always make matching alignment marks on both halves to aid in the proper reassembly.

There will be little things to look for in any particular rear end—that's why it is wise to consult a local mechanic before disassembly. One such minor (but very important) point with the Sure-Grip is the location of axle shaft thrust spacers at the center of the crossed pinion shafts. During the constant working of the shafts, the spacers take quite a beating, enough to cause the lockpin to fail. As the pin fails, the thrust spacers will tend to peen over. In an emergency, this simple pin can be made from a short stub of ordinary welding rod.

While the Sure-Grip is being reassembled, line up the retainer and clutch plate splines by inserting both axles. Move each axle back and forth slightly as the housing bolts are lightly tightened. The pinion shaft-to-housing cap clearance is important, and for racing should be set at .006-in. Too much clearance means an excessively worn disc; too little clearance means one of the flat plates (usually the thick one) must be dressed down slightly. With the right clearance and the splines aligned, tighten the housing cap bolts to factory specs (45 ft.-lbs.) while the axles are still in place.

Always check ring gear flange runout with a dial indicator. If this runout exceeds the maximum—.003-in. is a

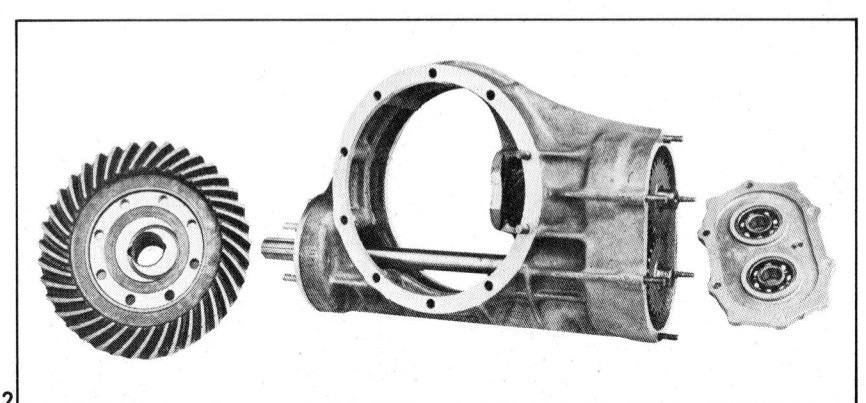

1. Race cars, whether for the drags, circle track or road racing, need a rear that's light, strong and with a capacity to change gearing easily. This bill has been filled in many cases with a Halibrand like this.

2. Still popular with the street rod set is the early Halibrand quick change center section designed to be used with early Ford axle housings. Simply removing the back cover and slipping out the two straight-cut gears gives ratio changes in minutes.

3. Most popular with rear-engined road racing cars is a transaxle with five speeds like this Hewland unit. It's strong, light and allows the independent suspension and inboard disc brakes these cars all use.

4. Most dragsters have come back to using standard rear ends, although considerably braced for competition. Note the large stiffening rib added to the rear of this fueler's housing.

5. When Mickey Thompson decided to beef up his Chevy truck rear end for serious off-road racing, he not only braced the housing, but added a steel tank to the center to hold extra lubricant and added scoops (arrow) to duct air by for even more cooling.

good max—chances are good the housing is faulty and should be remachined or replaced.

If there is the slightest indication of bearing wear or breakdown, they should be replaced. In Chrysler products, the pinion adjusting washer is located between the pinion gear teeth and the rear vearing. The back bearing is pressed in place and no amount of sledge hammering or cussing is going to remove it.

If the rear end has been working well, as far as the depth of ring and pinion gear mesh is concerned, the markings on the new pinion gear face may be used as a guide. However, these markings can be confusing. If the marking is a minus (-1, -2, etc.) then *add* this amount in thousandths of an inch to the thickness of the adjusting washer to retain proper mesh. For example: The pinion reads -2 and the original adjusting washer is .086-in. thick. Add .002-in., for a total of .088-in. to obtain the final washer thickness. The best way to set up any rear end in this critical measurement is by using the special setup tools.

Front pinion bearing preload shims are available in increments of .002-in. between .010- and .026-in.. At first, the original shims should be replaced on the pinion shaft and the shaft nut pulled down to specs (240 ft.-lbs. on Chrysler). A small torque wrench is then used to rotate the shaft, with new bearings having a reading of 20 to 30 in.-lbs. through a full 360° rotation. Used bearings will read between 3 and 15 in.-lbs. If the preload registers more than 30 in.-lbs., a thicker shim is needed under the front bearing. Less than 20 in.-lbs. preloads with new bearings means a thinner shim is necessary. An important point for the rear end used in drag racing! After the exact preload is found, add a .002-in. shim to allow for expansion due to the greater heat generated.

Assemble the ring gear to the carrier, and adjust the differential nuts by turning the large threaded caps until tight. Back the caps off ⅛-turn and set the backlash at .008-in., or .004-in. for drag racing. This backlash is especially critical in cars with standard transmissions. If more than .004-in., the instantaneous load tends to cause immediate gear failure! An automatic transmission preloads the axles, doing away with this problem.

It is wise to paint the ring gear teeth with white grease or red lead, then rotate the pinion several times to get a depth mesh pattern. As the pinion gear teeth contact the ring gear teeth, a valid pattern will emerge and will show whether the correct adjusting washer has been used behind the rear pinion bearing, and whether the ring gear is running true. This is strictly a safety check, and may not be necessary if special tools such as the Precision-American GS-II have been used.

When the correct adjustments have been made for depth mesh, the contact pattern is well centered on the drive and coast sides of the ring gear teeth, perhaps slightly toward the inner, or toe, end. Although the pattern will appear small, under actual use the contact area is considerably larger. If improper tooth contact is evident, the pinion should be adjusted either forward or backward, maintaining the backlash within limits.

As a guide to axle end play, keep it down to .006-in. for pure drag strip machinery, .015-in. for the street with Sure-Grip, and .010-in. with a standard rear end. For lubrication, use exactly what the manufacturer recommends, which would be 90W for street use. For hard street use, or any form of racing, you must use a super-heavy-duty lube like Torco 140W or Valvoline 140W.

Installation of outer bearings will call for a good chisel and a hefty press. The bearings are held to the axle by collars. Split the collars with the chisel, then remove both collar and bearing. The new collar must be pressed in place, something most machine shops can do in two minutes for a couple of bucks. Don't forget to include a new grease seal behind the new bearing!

Axle end-play is adjusted with shims at one side of the rear end only, and this adjustment must be observed. Generally, the original shims may be replaced if nothing special is done to the third member and the bearings remain unchanged.

Special gearsets in racing ratios require extra attention to setup and maintenance. Several of the high-performance gear companies make special tools for setting up ring and pinion sets, but these tools are often inaccurate. You can't afford any inaccuracy in a racing rear end that represents many hundreds of dollars

CHASSIS, SUSPENSION & BRAKES/169

The Rearend

invested, so rely on the actual tooth contact pattern for setting up a rear end. Look at the accompanying illustrations and adjust your gearset to give you the right pattern. Also, never drive on the street or flat-tow your race car with ratios lower than 4.56.

QUICK-CHANGE REARS

More than 10,000 quick-change rear-end center sections have been sold in the past 20 years. Of that number, more than 90% are still in existence and use. Because a quick-change is many things to the hot rodder, the specialized gearboxes go from one owner to the next, seldom ending in the trash barrel. Unlike some other forms of speed equipment, resale price remains high.

Most quick-changes are manufactured by Ted Halibrand, but there are other names in the field, although most utilize Halibrand gears, bearings, shafts, etc. The Model A and standard V-8 are the most common quick-changes, both being used extensively for street and racing. However, modern race car builders rely on the much stronger Championship quick-change, with a special transaxle also available.

Failure of a quick-change usually comes from gears or bearings; the housing is not usually a problem. However, if the smaller Model A or V-8 gearboxes are used behind a powerful racing ohv, there is the pissibility of splitting the case. Failure is normally the result of age, fatigue, lack of lubrication, misalignment, incorrect parts, or lack of proper maintenance.

The average quick-change sold for street use can easily be modified by the owner to bring it up to competition standards. The first thing to consider is chamfering of the ring and pinion, The top edges of these gear teeth are very sharp and tend to tear any contacting metal, leading to eventual gear failure. A small grinding stone may be used to round off these sharp edges.

Pressure buildup caused by the thrashing gears can be relieved by a small hole drilled in the case top. Often, especially in old, used units, the studs will have torn loose in the alloy case. Heli-Coils or a similar thread repair and new studs may be used, as well as Loc-Tite. You must definitely drill all bolts and studs for safety wire.

Check each part for burrs and nicks. Because the machining tolerances are held close, a burr will often cause just enough misalignment for trouble. This can be especially critical on the bolt flange mating surface of the ring gear. The ring gear may have a square lip at the mating surface edge of the locating center hole. This lip should be chamfered, as the carrier housing mating area is often radiused.

If bearings and/or splines are loose, they may be hard chromed and reused. The plating buildup will be just enough and is an excellent surface agent. Shot-peening the ring and pinion and lower shaft is a good policy to follow.

Sprint and Championship housings have precision-fitted side plates with threaded holes to help in removal. A correct size bolt is screwed into the housing and tightened until the plate pops loose; never use a screwdriver to pry the plate off. Use heat to remove a press-fit. The entire area surrounding the piece should be heated, then the piece itself tapped lightly with a soft hammer.

Occasionally the straddle bearing mount in the V-8, Sprint or Championship housing will be broken. This is invariably caused by lack of lubrication or misalignment. The broken piece can be welded in place, and after cooling naturally, the case can be remachined and checked for

170/CHASSIS, SUSPENSION & BRAKES

alignment. All mating surfaces are 90° to bearing races.

There have been other makes of quick-change rear ends made through the years, including Cyclone, Klentz and the current CAE. One design was made for the modern rear end with the transfer case ahead of the third member, but by and large the majority of quick-changes available are Halibrand. To this end Halibrand Engineering (Torrance, Calif.) maintains a complete repair facility for all past models.

1. When picking a rear end for its strength, find the one with the most teeth in contact at the spider gears. At left is a stock set of spiders, compare them to the "Monster Spiders" at right by Pepe Estrada. The more tooth area in contact at any one time means less pressure per square inch.

2. Another strength factor in any rear end is the number of spider or side gears. Both the Mopar (at right) and the GTO high-performance rear ends are cone-type limited-slip units, but the GTO is stronger because it has four spiders rather than just two.

3. Not just any ratio will fit in a given carrier. There are certain series of ratios. Both of these cases are Eaton posis, but the 3-Series at right will only take ratios up to a 3.70, while the 4-Series can take gears from 3.90 all the way to 6.14!

4. Even big Ford rears like this one require beefing to live under the pressure of drag racing. Some of the modifications necessary include using aircraft Allen bolts on the left cap and a billet bearing-adjuster nut.

5. One of the most popular rear ends for swapping is the Mopar Dana 60. This one in a racing '57 Chevy is ready to take on heavy horsepower.

Lenco Equipment Co. of San Diego now makes a street/strip quick-change unit that bolts to existing late-model rear ends and allows you to save wear and tear on your engine during the week, while still keeping the low ratio you need for weekends at the track.

RATIO RAZZLE-DAZZLE

The rear-end gears are lower because the numbers are higher. Sound familiar? And confusing? Don't feel alone, because long-time automotive enthusiasts are constantly getting confused over this point about gear ratios.

The closer to the number 1 (one) the gear is, the *higher* it is considered. This means the engine rpm in direct drive will more nearly approach wheel rpm, or the wheels will turn higher rpm for a given engine rpm.

The further the gear ratio is from the number 1, the *lower* the gear. That is, the wheels will turn fewer rpm than the engine, and this all has to do with the effects of leverage.

The ring and pinion gears can be considered the same as a lever and fulcrum. The closer to the end of a lever the fulcrum, the less effort is required at the long end to move an object. The larger the ring gear (that is, the greater the difference between the number of teeth on the pinion gear and the teeth on the ring gear) or the smaller the pinion, the greater the leverage. That's why a 4.11:1 rear end gear will start a car rolling easier than a 2.92:1 gear.

Trying to select the correct rear-end ratio is a big problem to the new enthusiast. For drag racing, especially when a close ratio 4-speed transmission is used, the rear-end gears will be rather low (high numerically), with ratios into the 5's not uncommon. However, such ratios would be foolhardy on a street machine, where something as low as 4.11:1 is sometimes considered impractical. For the car that will be driven primarily in city traffic and see occasional drag race duty, the 3.70 or 3.90 rear end has proven most popular.

The standard transmission's rear end will be lower than the automatic's because the overall starting ratio of the combined gears must be considered. That is, multiplying the low gear standard transmission ratio times the rear-end ratio may give a starting ratio of 14:1. However, multiplying the automatic low gear times the rear-end gear times the torque converter factor may give a starting gear ratio of 20:1. This is why the automatic is so popular for heavy-duty use with campers and why the rear-end gears may be higher.

Obviously, the lower the gear, the quicker the car will get off the mark, but the higher will be the engine rpm at cruising speeds. The higher the gear, the less leverage for starting, but the lower engine rpm at cruising speeds (with consequent better gasoline mileage and lower noise level). The only way to have a good low rear-end gear for traffic and/or racing, and still have a good highway ratio, is through the use of the familiar overdrive unit.

FINAL DRIVE OVERDRIVES

The overdrive is not a new concept to automobiles, but in the past it has been restricted almost exclusively to the transmission. While the 2-speed

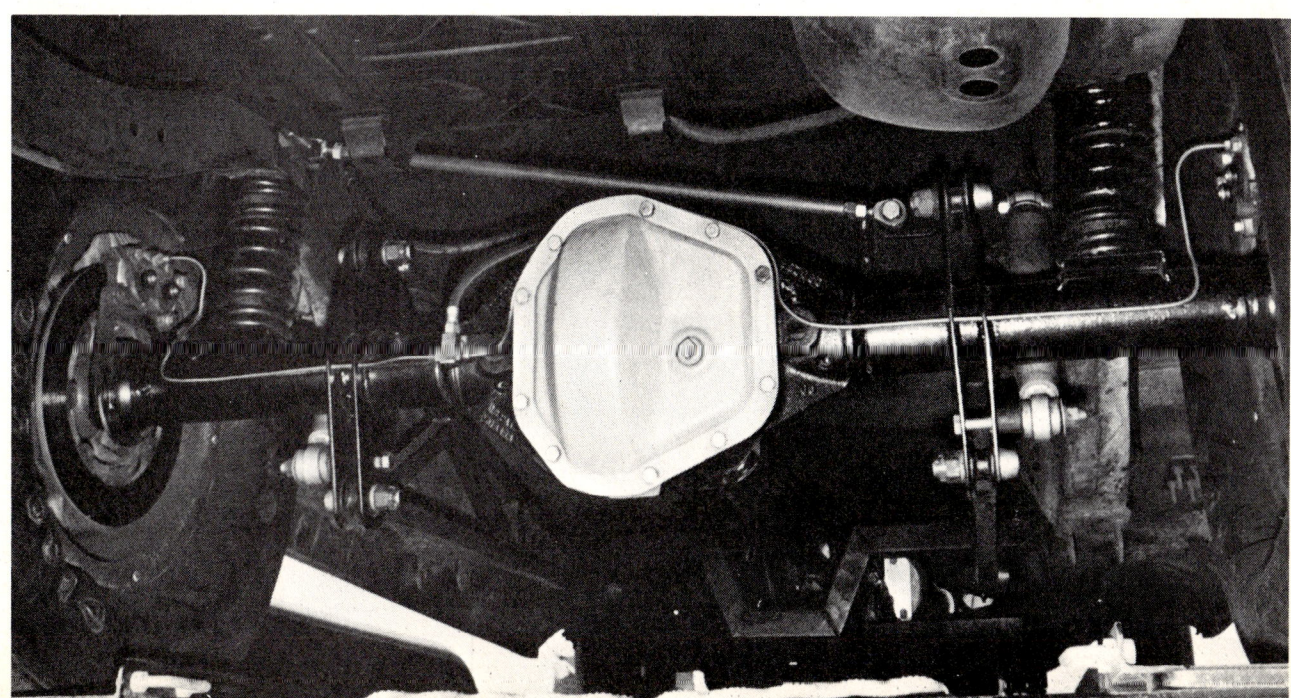

CHASSIS, SUSPENSION & BRAKES/171

The Rearend

rear axles used several years ago (and still used with heavy-duty vehicles) are a form of overdrive, it has been easier to incorporate overdrive gears in the transmission rather than in the final drive. Things are beginning to change back again.

Third-member overdrives are already on the market through Hone-O-Matic (Santa Fe Springs, Calif.), and are being used extensively by 4-wheel-drive devotees and camper truck owners. In development stages are two more rear end overdrives—one a planetary gearset from Borg-Warner and the other a form of 2-speed rear axle from Dana Spicer.

Dana built and installed six 2-speed axles for test vehicles several years ago. In this design, shifting must be done while the driveline is at rest. With an automatic, the transmission is absorbing power even when the lever is in neutral position, putting a strain on the driveline even at idle, so the engine is turned off and the trans placed in park before shifting. The rear gears aren't synchronous, and the only way to make a moving change is by manipulation of throttle foot and shifting hand to avoid "crash" shifts. It is possible that synchronous gears will be fitted if the unit is ever made production line.

Installed in the test cars, the overdrive ratio gives a high gear speed of 70 mph at 3000 rpm—which means the overdrive is .675 of the direct drive (4.27:1), or 2.88:1. Obviously this is just the ticket for drag racing enthusiasts, but it has far greater possibilities.

Suppose you live in a traffic congested city. You know that jackrabbit starts are often necessary just to keep out of harm's way, and you can't get 'em with a road cruising gear. Or perhaps you own a pickup and slide-in coach camper. Enough rear-end gear to handle the back roads and mountain inclines will be atrocious on the open highway, and gasoline mileage will be miserable. But if you change from a 4:11:1 down to a comfortable 2.60 or so, and still retain all the final drive strength required for the camper, you'd probably leap at the chance to buy such a unit.

The Dana Corp. 2-speed fits right into this category of heavy-duty applications, since the rear end is a redesign of a truck item. While it is heavy, which means more unsprung weight, chances are it can be incorporated in an alloy third-member housing to reduce unsprung weight. However, the only way this unit is going to see the light of production is for enough people to show an interest. We won't hazard a guess as to cost, but in production form it would probably be about as much extra as the big engine options.

The Borg-Warner overdrive is somewhat different in concept. Built into an alloy case to begin with, the B-W unit is also in the developmental stages and test cars are equipped with the housing bolted directly to the production third-member case. Borg-Warner is using a planetary gearset coupled with clutch discs and plates very similar to an automatic transmission. This allows smooth hydraulic speed changes, changes that can take place while the vehicle is moving. A vacuum line to the engine senses an immediate change in throttle setting, which means the throttle foot has automatic control over the final drive O.D. When cruising along in high gear/overdrive, if the throttle is suddenly opened for more speed, the overdrive shifts back to direct gear. Still more throttle and an automatic-equipped car would shift down once more to passing gear.

With a 30% overdrive, which is common for most passenger car applications, the B-W unit can be incorporated into the third-member housing also. It is probably slightly heavier than the Dana 2-speed, but the difference would be negligible. Production plans for the B-W design are not yet finalized, but chances are it will be included in some of the performance cars if engineering and advertising have their say.

1. An inexpensive process for axle strengthening you can do yourself is to pack them in dry ice for a day or two and let them thaw out gradually. This cold-stabilizing is good for any steel castings such as cases, yokes etc., but not for bolts or gears.

2. Available at motorcycle shops, Petrochem's Chain Life is excellent assembly lube for rear-end gears and clutch plates for limited-slip units.

3. Most important in assembling a rear end is the gear contact pattern. What you have to do is assemble the rear end and adjust the pinion shims and ring gear bearing adjusters until the pattern is closest to ideal.

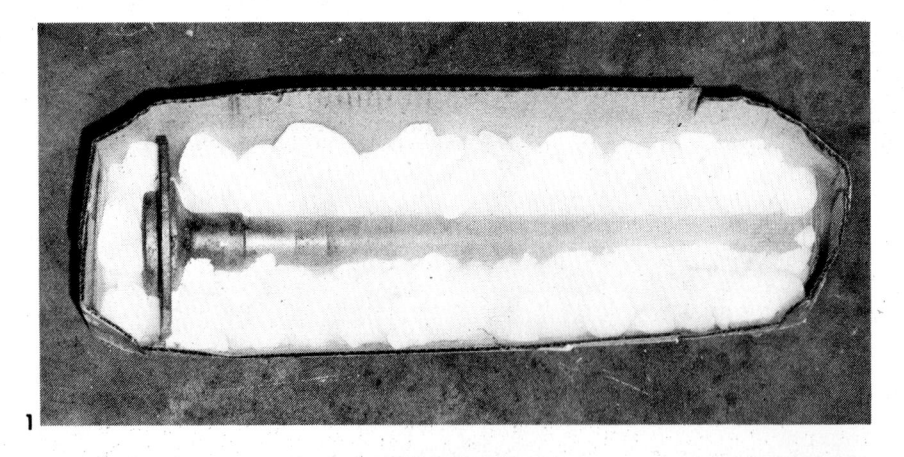

RING AND PINION PATTERNS

Getting the proper ring and pinion gear contact pattern is probably the most important factor in rear-end life. After installing new gears, you swab some white lead or Schiefer's Mark-Torque on the gears and begin turning to check their mesh pattern. Always turn the ring gear, not the pinion, and turn them back and forth several times. It's impossible to get a classic new-gear pattern on used gears, so settle for a compromise. But whether new or used, there must always be *some* toe/face contact and *never* any heel/face contact or you will break the ring gear. Lumpiness or clicking is caused by a crossed pattern, and edge contact on pinion will always produce a noisy rear end. The basic drawings come from years of rear-end work at Pepe's Gear Shop in Paramount, Calif. and apply to a Halibrand quick-change, as well as common hypoid-type rear ends.

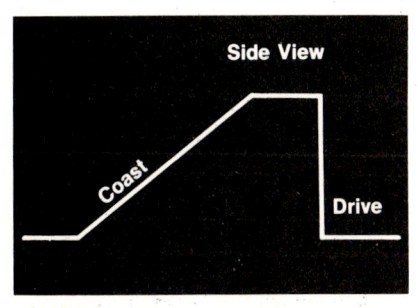

1. The load on a ring gear must be shared by both the drive and coast sides and should be roughly equal.

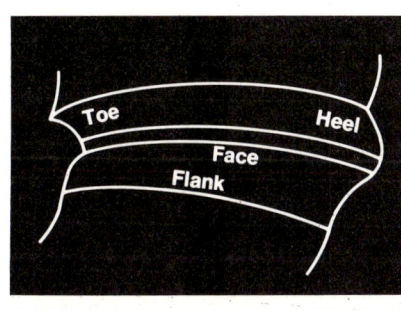

2. The part of ring gear on inside is the toe, while on the tooth, the face is the top and flank the bottom.

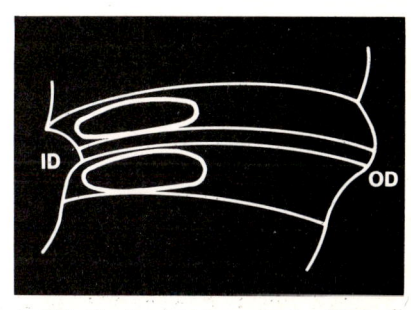

3. This is the ideal contact pattern in checking new gears, equal-length and somewhat biased toward pinion.

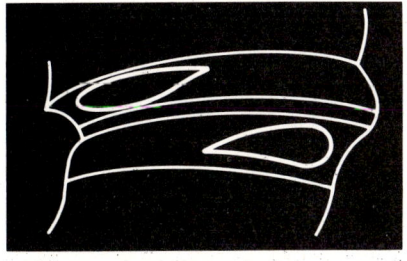

4. This crossed pattern means the pinion is too far back. This will probably crack the pinion teeth.

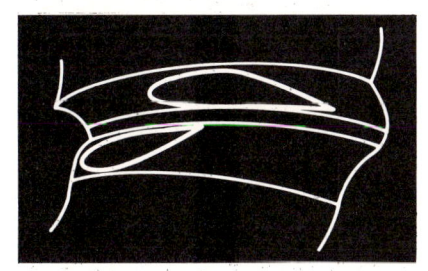

5. This crossed pattern means the pinion is too far forward and will probably crack the ring gear teeth.

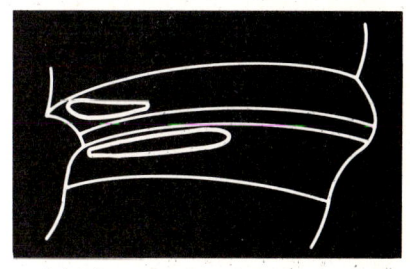

6. This pattern shows all contact at the tooth face, and means the pinion is too far forward and biased.

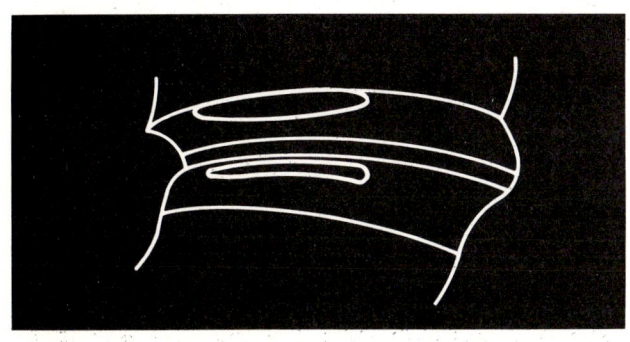

7. This is what is known as a "lame" pattern. It means the gears are mismatched and can't be corrected at all.

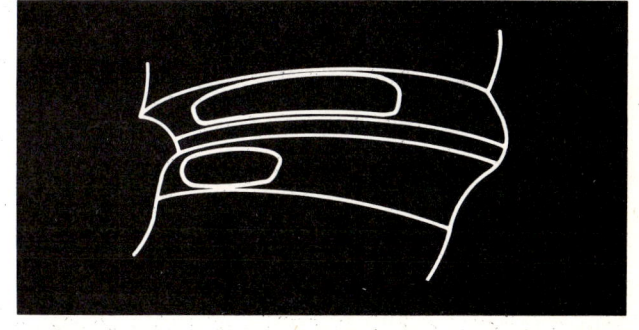

8. When using the low ratios like 5.86 or 6.20, you have to bias in favor of the (small and weak) pinion gear.

USED GEARS

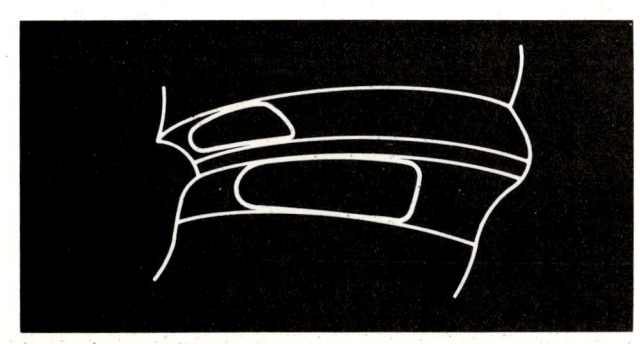

9. This is a good pattern for used gears. With used ones look more closely at the coast side than the drive side.

10. This is a poor pattern, but typical for used gears because they tend to cross up as the gears wear in.

FRONT-DRIVE SYSTEMS
Eldorado/Toronado
A decade old, this big GM system is still the finest of its kind.

Until the new crop of mini-cars arrived, America produced only two front-wheel-drive cars since the fabled Cord. They are the Oldsmobile Toronado, which debuted in 1966, and the Cadillac Eldorado, which appeared one year later. Both are still with us a decade later, though with the current flurry of downsizing it would appear that GM will not long continue making them.

Though they use different engines, the Toronado and Eldorado share the same transaxle, a massive affair mounted beside the engine. The torque converter is mounted in its normal position behind the engine. From it a hefty silent chain drives the automatic gearbox, which sits longitudinally but reversed back-to-front. The differential is directly in front of the transmission, and from it driveshafts extend out to the front wheels.

Because of their beautiful styling, unique drivetrain and the fact that they will soon cease to be manufactured in the rush for gasoline economy, these big cars are good bets as future collector's cars. Someone who recognized this potential is the owner of the car shown here, an immaculate white '71 Eldo with 108,000 miles on it. He had no desire to trade in the car on a newer Cadillac; he just wanted the front suspension returned to "like-new" condition. We show you how the job was done at Vanowen Brake & Wheel, 11576 Vanowen St., N. Hollywood, CA 91605. The shop's owner, Bill Chisholm, has forgotten more about suspensions and alignment than most people will ever want to know, and he shared his expertise with us.

This Eldo would not hold a wheel alignment, which indicated that it had worn bushings and bearings. Everything was replaced, at a cost of over $500 for the parts alone. If you have the tools and inclination, you can follow this procedure and save on labor costs (except for the final alignment, which must be done by a pro shop), but these parts don't come cheap.

HOW-TO: Eldorado Suspension Rebuild

1. The Eldo is a heavy car, and you don't want it coming down on you at an inconvenient time. Jacks are fine, but for real insurance Vanowen Brake & Wheel puts these timbers under the frame. That way an accident can't cause a crippling injury.

2. After removing the road wheel, the brake caliper is removed and hung up by a wire, so it will be out of the way (arrows). It is not necessary to disconnect the brake hydraulic line. The disc rotor then slips off the spindle.

3. After removing its nut, the ball-jointed tie rod end slips out of the wheel carrier casting. Note that the shaft of the ball joint is tapered. If it's stuck, tap the side of the carrier with a small sledge; never bang on the ball joint shaft.

4. Unless you're lucky, some persuasion will be needed to separate the upper A-arm ball joint from the wheel carrier. Remove the nut, then use a hand sledge to rap on the side of the carrier. The vibrations will shock the joint free.

HOW-TO: Eldorado Suspension Rebuild

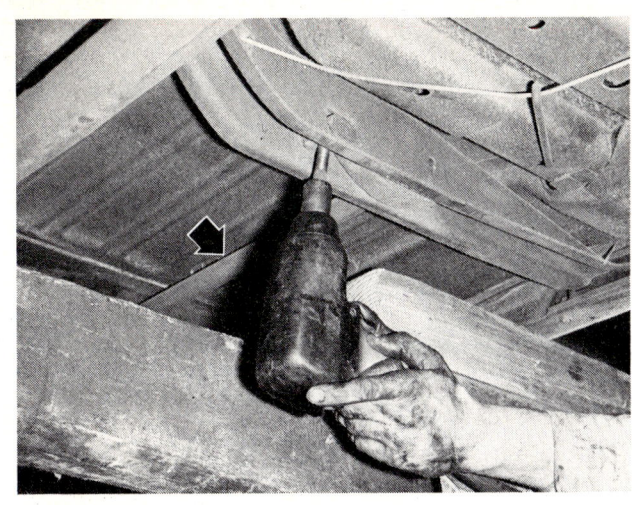

5. Before working on the lower A-arm, it is imperative to remove as much tension as possible from the torsion bar (arrow). Remove this bolt, which adjusts the bar's preload. Keep a jack under the A-arm, as some preload will still remain.

6. After removing its upper bolt and lower nut, the shock can be lifted clear. The lower A-arm will then want to move down, because the shock was acting as a restraint. Keep a jack or block under the arm until the wheel carrier has been removed.

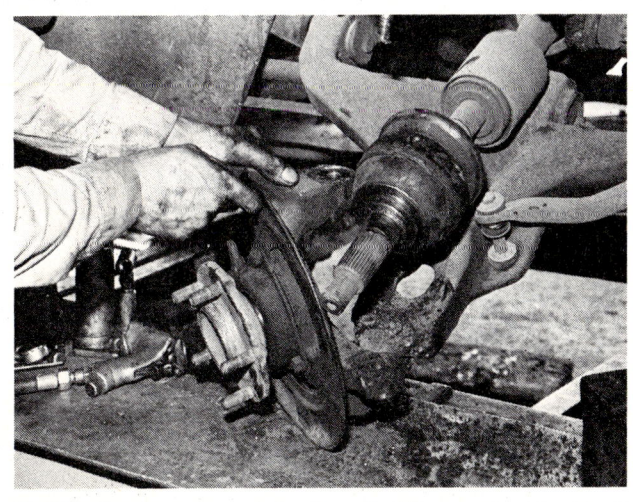

7. With the A-arm constrained so that it cannot whip downward, break the ball joint that connects it to the wheel carrier. Remove the spindle nut and slide the carrier with its brake backing plate and spindle off the splined axle.

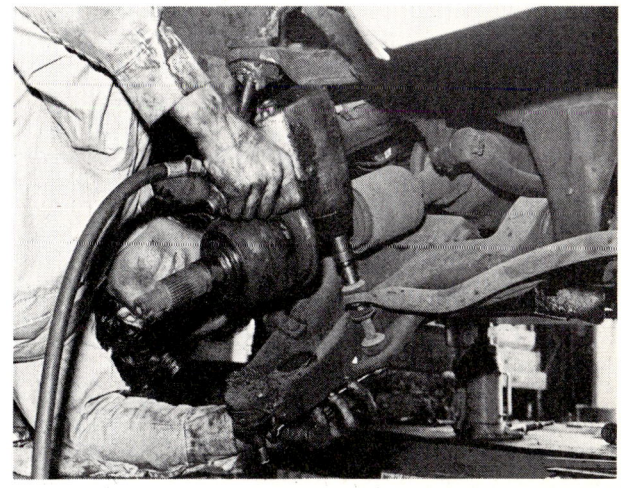

8. The end of the hefty stabilizer bar is then disconnected from the lower A-arm. If the other lower A-arm is not hanging free, this stabilizer bar will be under tension and will therefore want to snap up when it's released. Be careful.

9. Six bolts attach the axle's inner flange to the transaxle. An air-operated wrench is handy for tight spots like this, since there isn't room for a normal wrench handle. You'll probably need a big handle and long extension.

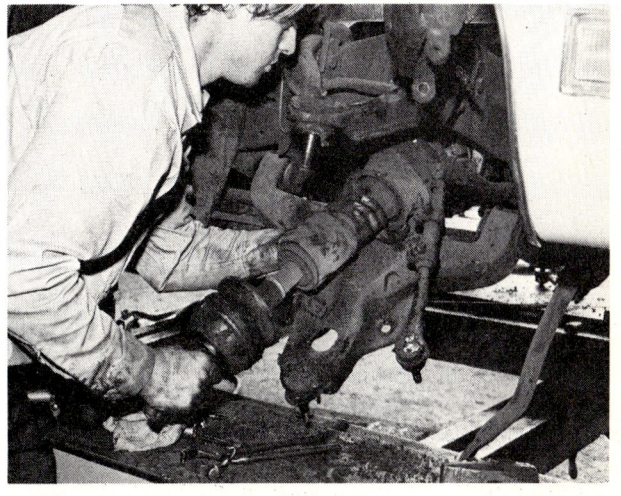

10. The driveshaft is then carefully lifted out. It has two large constant-velocity joints with a torsional vibration dampener in between. The dampener rarely gives trouble, but the constant-velocity joints often need replacing.

CHASSIS, SUSPENSION & BRAKES/175

Eldorado/Toronado

HOW-TO: Eldorado Suspension Rebuild

11. The purpose of a rubber dust seal is to keep grease in. It not only lubricates the joint but keeps dirt and water out. A torn boot allows water to wash out the grease, greatly accelerating wear. A joint won't last long under these conditions.

12. Two of these odd-shaped bolts with integral eccentric cams are used to attach the upper A-arm to the frame. Turning the two bolts in unison adjusts camber, while turning them in opposite directions adjusts caster.

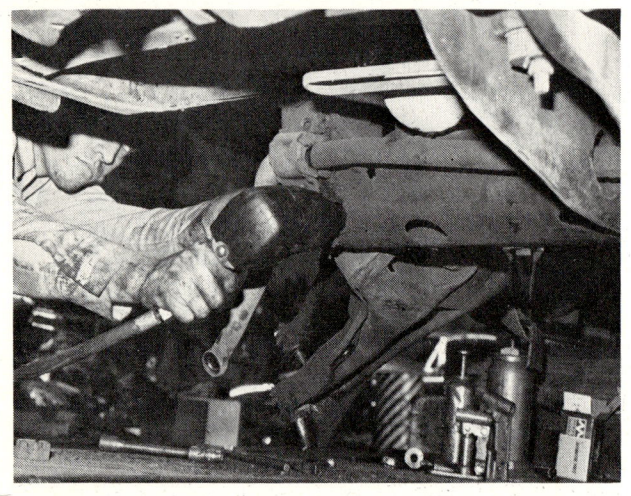

13. The lower A-arm must next be removed, because its ball joint and two bushings will be replaced. Access to the nut on the forward part of the A-arm is attained through this hole conveniently provided in the frame. Thank you, GM.

14. The rear bolt is then removed, and the A-arm slides forward off the torsion bar. A line scribed or painted on the bar and A-arm socket will assist you upon reassembly. If you want to be neat, take the A-arm and clean it thoroughly.

15. After unbolting and removing the wheel bearing retainer cap, the spindle is separated from the wheel carrier. A puller such as this one is almost always necessary in order to remove the pressed-on inner bearing race from the spindle.

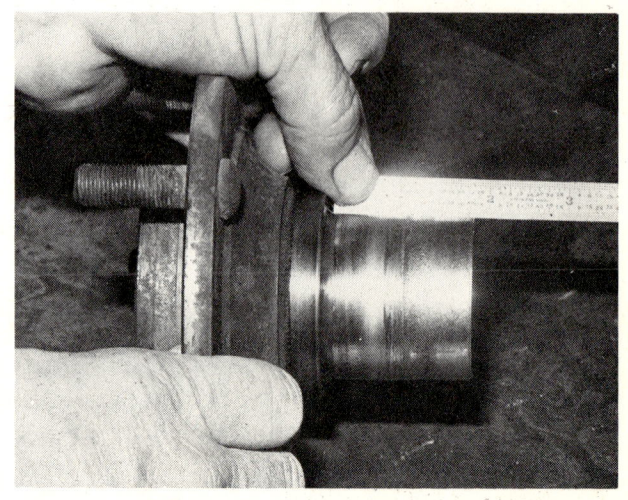

16. On this particular spindle the previous bearing had been improperly seated and the inner race had eventually begun to spin. The straightedge shows the wear caused on the spindle seating surface, which necessitated spindle replacement.

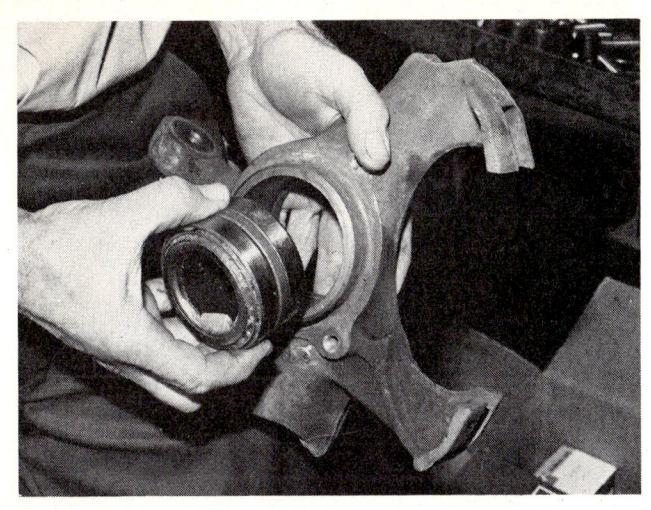

17. After a thorough cleaning, the carrier is fitted with a new bearing. Final seating will be done by the spindle nut. On the Eldorado, this one large bearing replaces the inner and outer wheel bearings found on conventional-drive cars.

18. The thick rubber bushings are now removed from the upper and lower A-arms. The bushings are press-fitted, so removal requires some persuasion from a hammer. Be careful not to damage the inner seating surfaces of the A-arms.

19. These bushings are designed to be gripped tightly at their inner and outer surfaces. In that way, during suspension flexing they act both as small springs and as dampeners. A loose bushing will not operate properly at either job.

20. The A-arm mounting areas should be scrupulously cleaned before installing the new bushings. Press them in like this. The small section of pipe here acts as a spacer. Don't pound the bushing in with a hammer or it won't seat properly.

21. The original ball joints were riveted in the A-arms at the factory. It is necessary to break the rivets with an air hammer (you can substitute lots of work with a cold chisel) to remove the joint. A good ball joint has no play in it.

22. These ball joints show the effects of long wear. Lower A-arm joint is at left, upper ball joint at right. If neglected long enough, a ball joint can wear sufficiently to pull apart and collapse the suspension—with disastrous results.

Eldorado/Toronado

HOW-TO: Eldorado Suspension Rebuild

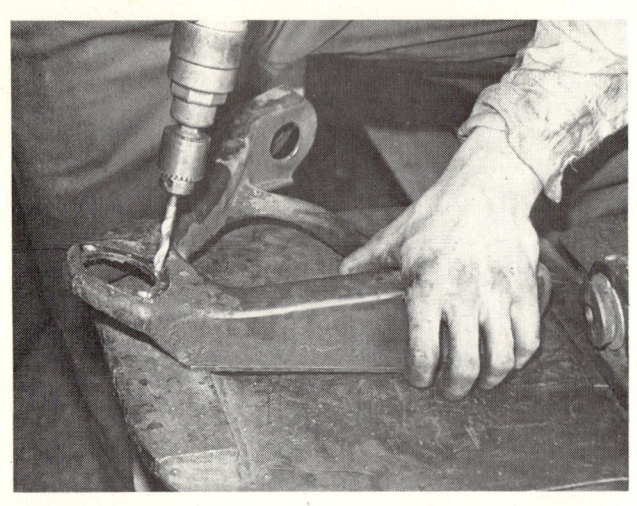

23. The replacement ball joints will be bolted in, not riveted, so the mounting holes must be enlarged slightly with a drill. This process also trues the distortion which was caused by removing the original rivets.

24. The new ball joint is a heavier-duty unit than the original joint, since the owner desires to keep this car indefinitely. Note how clean the upper A-arm now is; it's typical of the high-quality work done at Vanowen Brake & Wheel.

25. The new ball joint will certainly be good for another 100,000 miles (and perhaps a lot more), but only if it is regularly lubricated with the proper grease. At least at the next replacement there won't be any rivets to remove.

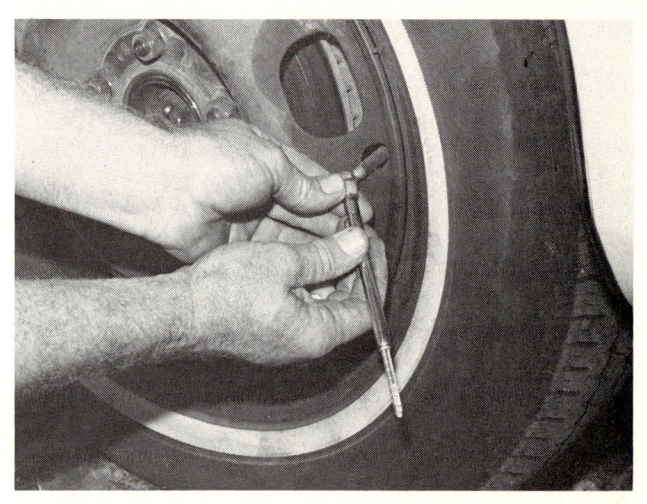

26. After suspension reassembly, the first step in alignment is to check inflation pressure. Proper pressure depends upon the tire manufacturer and actual load carried by the tire, but both front tires should be the same and carry the same pressure.

27. As another check on proper height before making any adjustments, Vanowen Brake & Wheel uses this homemade tool to measure rim height. Height should be the same on both sides. Device can spot an oversize or undersize tire.

28. Once inflation pressure and tire size are correct, measuring from the ground to the center of the spindle nut will reveal a wheel that's the wrong size. It's elementary, but you'd be surprised at what's found on some cars.

178/CHASSIS, SUSPENSION & BRAKES

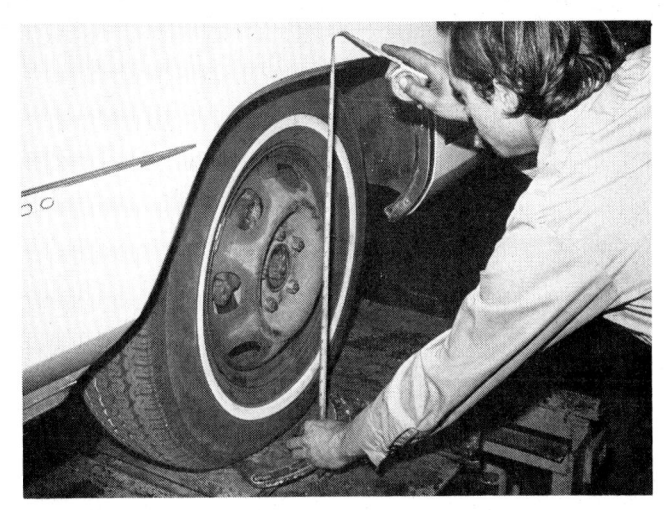

29. Yet another measurement is taken from the ground to the fender opening. The two sides are compared to obtain data for adjusting the torsion bars. Again, both sides should be equal unless one side will be carrying additional weight.

30. After adjusting the torsion bars to obtain the desired riding height, caster and camber measurements are taken. They will almost certainly be different from any taken before the suspension rebuild, so they must be checked carefully.

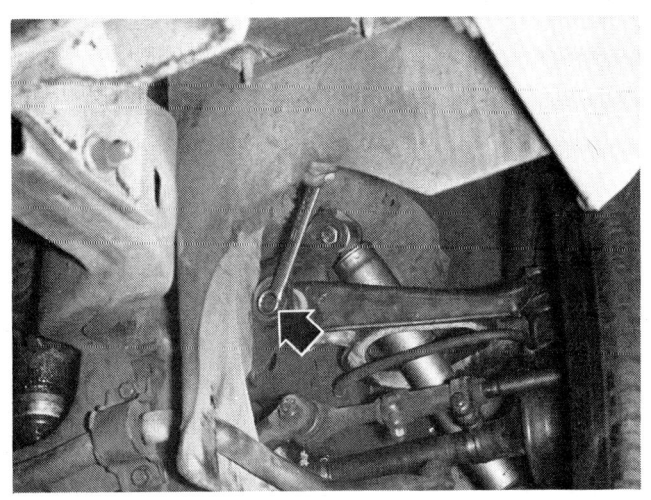

31. Now is the time to tweak those eccentric bolts in the upper A-arms, the ones that control both caster and camber. Fortunately for the alignment shop, those bolts provide a wide range of adjustment and are easy to reach (arrow).

32. Toe-in is the last wheel adjustment made. Some alignment shops do this with mirrors, but Vanowen Brake & Wheel uses an older and more accurate method. Front tire is rotated against a knife edge, which lightly scribes a line around tread.

33. The toe-in bar or trammel, with gradations and movable markers at either end, is then moved into position. Distance between the scribe lines is measured at both front and rear of tires; difference between the two measurements is the toe-in.

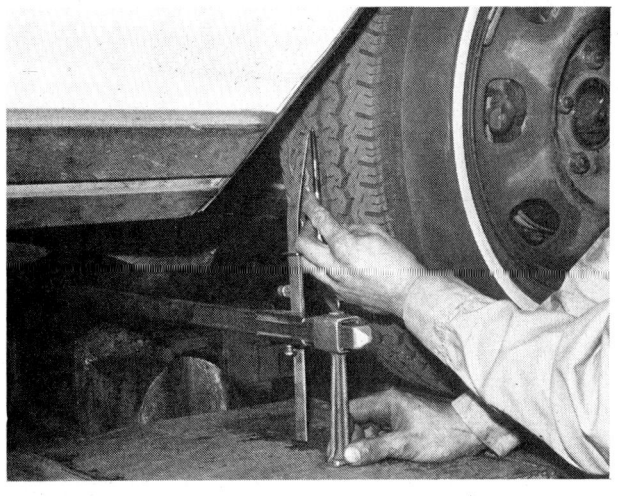

34. At the rear of the tire, the pen here is on the scribe line, while the pointer shows the distance measured between the lines at the front. One half the difference is the toe-in for each wheel, which is adjusted at the steering links.

CHASSIS, SUSPENSION & BRAKES/179

FRONT-DRIVE SYSTEMS

Ford Fiesta

Meet Ford's entry in the front-drive race—
from a ground-level viewpoint.

They've been a long time coming, but mini-cars from U.S. manufacturers are now upon us. Now, there's nothing new about small foreign cars in America, or even small cars from U.S. subsidiaries and affiliates overseas. Chrysler has sold Crickets from England, Simcas from France and Colts and Arrows from Japan. Ford has marketed English Cortinas and German Capris, while GM has pushed German Opels, English Vauxhalls and Japanese Izusu pickup trucks. What makes the new crop of mini-cars different is their efficiently square shape and unusual drivetrain—specifically, a transverse engine with front-wheel drive.

THE TRANSVERSE ENGINE

The BMC Morris Mini and its nameplate twin, the Austin 850, were the first cars to popularize this engine layout, back in the early '60's. Since then it has been picked up by many other automakers, notably Volkswagen and Fiat. Now the Ford Fiesta has it, as well as the brand-new Dodge Omni and Plymouth Horizon, which are reported on separately elsewhere in this book. The downsized GM compacts coming along in the next year or two will also have front-wheel drive, almost certainly with a transverse engine.

Why the comparatively sudden rush to this unusual configuration? In a word, *size.* If you shrink the size of a car but can't shrink the size of the human beings who have to occupy it, then something's got to give. What has given in this new breed of minicar is the space occupied by the engine, transmission, differential and driveshaft. By putting all the drivetrain components at one end of the car, there is no need for a driveshaft. The floor of the car can then be low and flat, greatly adding to the available interior room.

A transverse engine is practically impossible to achieve with a big car, since it has a big engine, but a little engine in a little car is so small it will not only fit sideways easily, but still leave enough room so that the clutch and transmission can fit right in beside it, all between the front wheels. This greatly shortens the hood length, allowing the passenger compartment to be much larger for a given wheelbase size.

Or, stated another way, it allows the car to become much smaller for a given passenger volume, which allows it to become lighter. And the

1. Front-wheel drive pulls Fiesta around corners with alacrity. Fiesta is the first front-wheel-drive passenger car Ford has ever marketed.

2. Transverse engine layout has clutch, gearbox, differential and final drive all clustered together between the front wheels. Note that the right axle is longer than the left one.

3. In real life, the Fiesta engine compartment looks almost as crowded with emissions equipment as the under-hood area of much larger cars.

4. Front suspension shows MacPherson strut, trailing links and easily removable disc brakes. Small phenolic bearings atop coil spring cups allow springs to turn with steering action.

5. Rear suspension has sturdy tube axle, track rod and husky trailing links. Drum brakes are self-adjusting. Axle is raised in the center to allow exhaust pipe to pass underneath it.

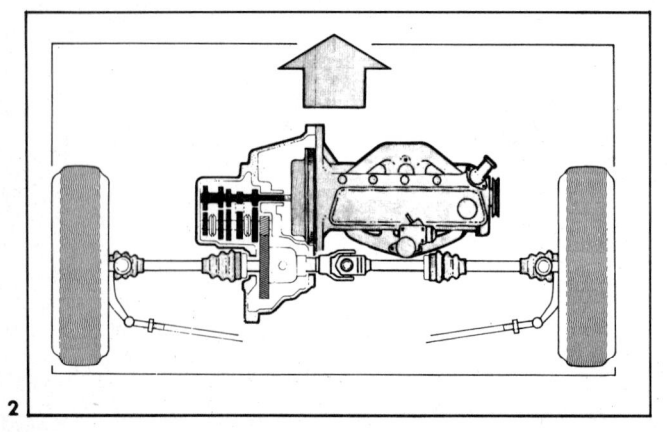

180/CHASSIS, SUSPENSION & BRAKES

lighter a car is, the cheaper it is to manufacture and the better will be its fuel economy. These are very compelling reasons, the latter one particularly so since the federal government has started dictating a fleet-averaged mileage figure which each manufacturer must achieve.

Since the Fiesta is the first transverse-engined, front-drive mini-car from a U.S. subsidiary to be marketed in this country, let's take a closer look at it. With all of Ford's economic power behind it, the Fiesta is obviously destined for sales stardom, and it will serve as the model for the type of car which will be found in rapidly increasing numbers on our highways in the future.

FORD'S WORLD CAR

The Fiesta is the first car from Ford since the Model T to be designed as a world-market car. Ford sells cars in practically every country of the world and has manufacturing operations in many of them. The Fiesta was intended to be a car which could be manufactured and assembled simultaneously in several countries and sold anywhere. This may sound quite logical and sensible now, but it should be remembered that American-built Fords are basically unsuitable for use anywhere else (LTD's don't go over very well in Europe or Japan), and the Capri was the first European Ford which had any appeal over here. The Fiesta is assembled in England, Germany and Spain, and it is the German-built version that is being imported into the U.S.

The Fiesta has already become a sales star in Europe, where it was available a year before being introduced into the U.S. Not only did it set a sales record for the first year of production that topped any other new car in history, but with it Ford now claims to be the best-selling marque in Europe, outselling VW and Fiat.

SUSPENSION, STEERING AND BRAKES

Set on a short 90-in. wheelbase, the Fiesta has small 12-in. wheels. The rubber moguls had better get busy, because there's going to be a big demand for these little tires soon. The standard wheel/tire combination is a 145SR12 Michelin steel-belted radial mounted on a steel wheel with a 4-in. rim, but optional is a 155SR12 Michelin on a 4½-in. steel wheel. A further option is a very handsome 4½-in. cast aluminum wheel with the bigger Michelin.

Front suspension is by MacPherson strut, which is appropriate on a Ford, since Earle MacPherson was a Ford engineer at the time he devised this suspension system two decades ago. It is a simple arrangement, and on the Fiesta it has been specifically designed to be easily serviced. The ball joint connecting the control arm to the strut can be easily unbolted, while unbolting four more bolts allows each complete strut to be removed. Toe-in is changed by adjusting the ends of the steering tie rods, but caster and camber are fixed in this suspension and no adjustments are provided. However, in the how-to section immediately following this article, we show how the Fiesta's caster and camber *can* be adjusted.

A notable point about the Fiesta's front suspension is its negative-offset geometry, which places the center of the tire's contact patch inboard of the pivot axis of the front wheel. Also used on front-wheel-drive Volkswagens, this arrangement has several advantages. One is its tendency to keep the tire rolling straight ahead in the event of a blowout rather than pulling suddenly to one side.

Something new on MacPherson struts is a fabric-and-phenolic bearing between the upper coil spring cup of each strut and the strut perch on the inner fenderwell. This bearing allows the coil spring to rotate freely when the front wheels are turned, eliminating spring windup and promoting easier and smoother steering.

The advantages of independent rear suspension have been touted so highly by certain manufacturers that it seems surprising that independent rear suspension is not used with every front-wheel-drive car. Springing each rear wheel independently would be an easy design task, since the wheels don't have to steer or drive—just support the car's weight. But like several other front-wheel-drive cars (notably Sweden's Saab), the Fiesta has a rigid rear axle. A sturdy steel tube is the basis, sprung by coils, lo-

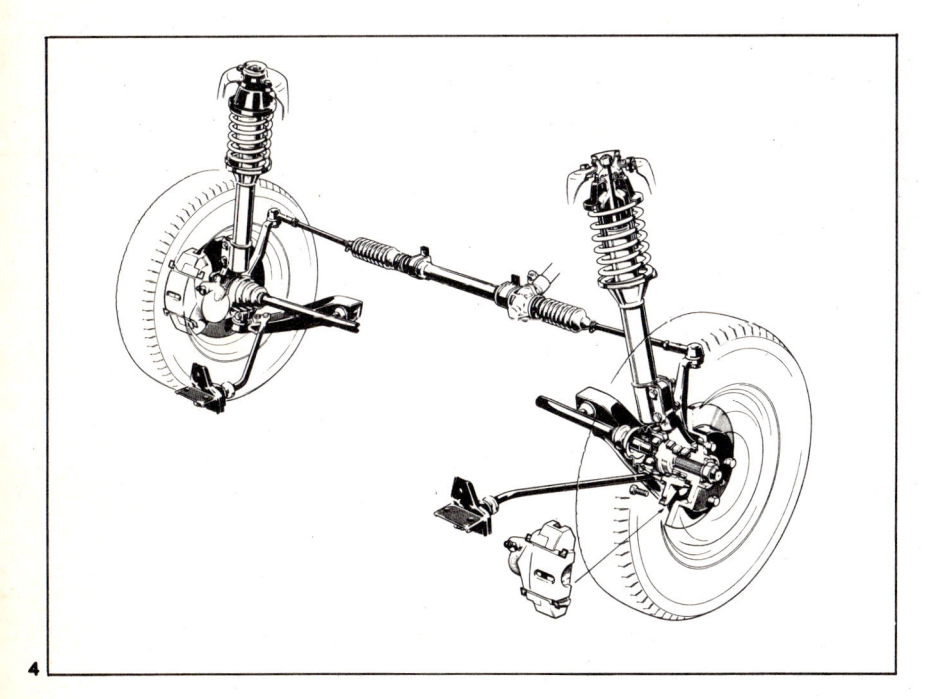

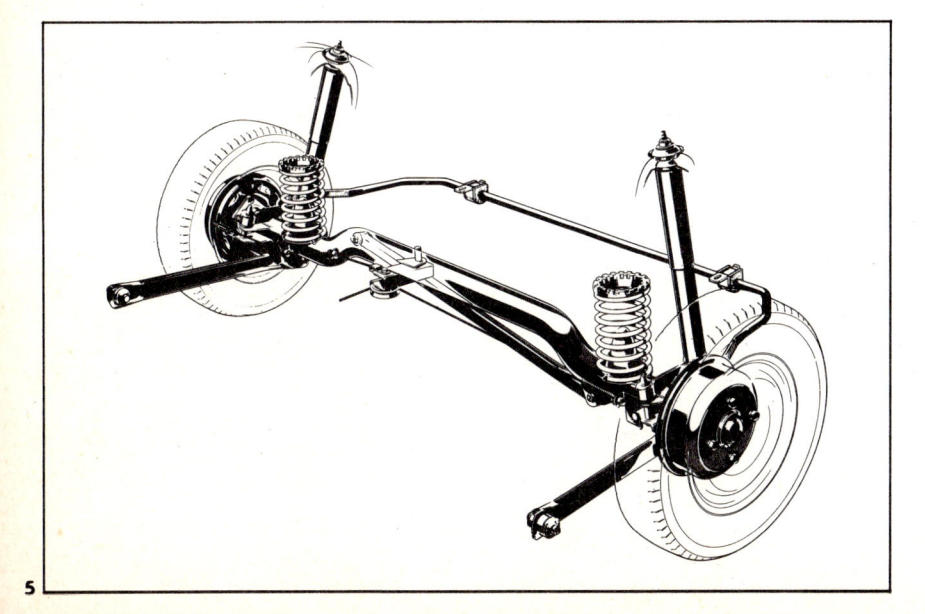

CHASSIS, SUSPENSION & BRAKES/181

Ford Fiesta

cated transversely by a track bar and located in a fore-and-aft plane by a pair of trailing links. On Sport versions of the Fiesta, an anti-roll bar is added at the rear.

Steering is by rack-and-pinion. The steering column has a collapsible center section for crash protection. The mounting brackets for the rack are rubber insulated to minimize the amount of road vibration that gets through to the steering wheel.

The Fiesta's braking is thorough but conventional by modern standards. The front brakes are 8.7-in. discs, while the rear brakes are 7-in. drums with self-adjusting shoes. The dual hydraulic system links one front brake with the opposite rear brake, so that in the remote event of a hydraulic failure, the remaining circuit will give balanced braking. The standard braking system is unassisted, but a power-assisted system is optional. The front discs are attached to the hubs with the same lug bolts which hold the front wheels on; only a single small machine screw retains each rotor when the wheel is removed. Since the lug bolts transmit braking and driving forces as well as locate the drum and wheel on the hub, it is very important that the proper type of lug bolt be used and that it be torqued properly. The optional aluminum wheels use a different type of lug bolt than the standard steel wheels, and the two types of bolt must never be interchanged.

ENGINE AND DRIVELINE

While the manufacture of many Fiesta components is done in Germany and the final assembly of all Fiestas destined for sale in the U.S. is done at Ford of Europe's plant in Saarlouis, Germany, the major driveline components are made elsewhere. Engines come from England, carburetors and distributors from Belfast, Ireland and transaxles from Bordeaux, France.

The engine is an inline 4-banger of conservative design. In contrast to some of the exotic engines found in other mini-cars, the Fiesta powerplant has an iron block and iron head, pushrod-operated overhead valves, a mechanical fuel pump and a single 2-bbl., 2-stage Weber carb. With a bore and stroke of 81x78mm it displaces 1600cc (97.6 cu. ins.)—quite a bit more than the 957cc and 1117cc engines used in European Fiestas. With a compression ratio of 8.5:1 the power output is 66 hp at 5000 rpm, but specially prepared English rally Fiestas already offer 110-hp versions of this engine. The performance of the American Fiesta is so good with the stock engine, however, that there are probably no plans to increase either the displacement or the power rating of this engine for quite some time to come.

The clutch is a conventional cable-operated device with a single dry plate and automatic adjustment of the cable.

The transmission has four forward speeds, all with synchromesh, and the manual transmission is the only one available. The gearsets, differential and final drive are all carried inside a 2-piece aluminum housing. The differential and final drive gears are behind and slightly below the transmission gears. However, 4th gear is not the conventional direct drive—it has a 0.88:1 overdrive ratio. Combined with the 3.58:1 ratio of the final drive gears, this means that the overall gear reduction in 4th gear is

1. Removing the rear floorboards reveals the spare tire and a small cubbyhole or locker for valuables or oddments. The big board hinged to the top of the rear seat is a blind which, when lowered, shields articles stored in the trunk from prying eyes.

2. With the floorboards in place and the rear seat lowered, the blind cleverly becomes a flap to limit the movement of luggage. Cargo capacity in this form is a generous 29 cu. ft.

3. Interior of the Fiesta can be plain Jane or Ghia fancy, depending on how much you want to spend. This is the Sport option, which has gaily striped seats, a tachometer and 4-spoke wheel.

4. Outline comparison with Pinto shows how Ford has maintained interior room while drastically cutting exterior size and trimming excess weight.

5. Handsome optional cast aluminum wheels are wider than standard steel wheels, carry bigger Michelin radials.

6. Big sunroof is another option. The tinted panel can be propped open at its aft end for ventilation or removed entirely and replaced with a metal panel. For a car with as much glass area as the Fiesta, this sunroof is a surprising but welcome option.

182/CHASSIS, SUSPENSION & BRAKES

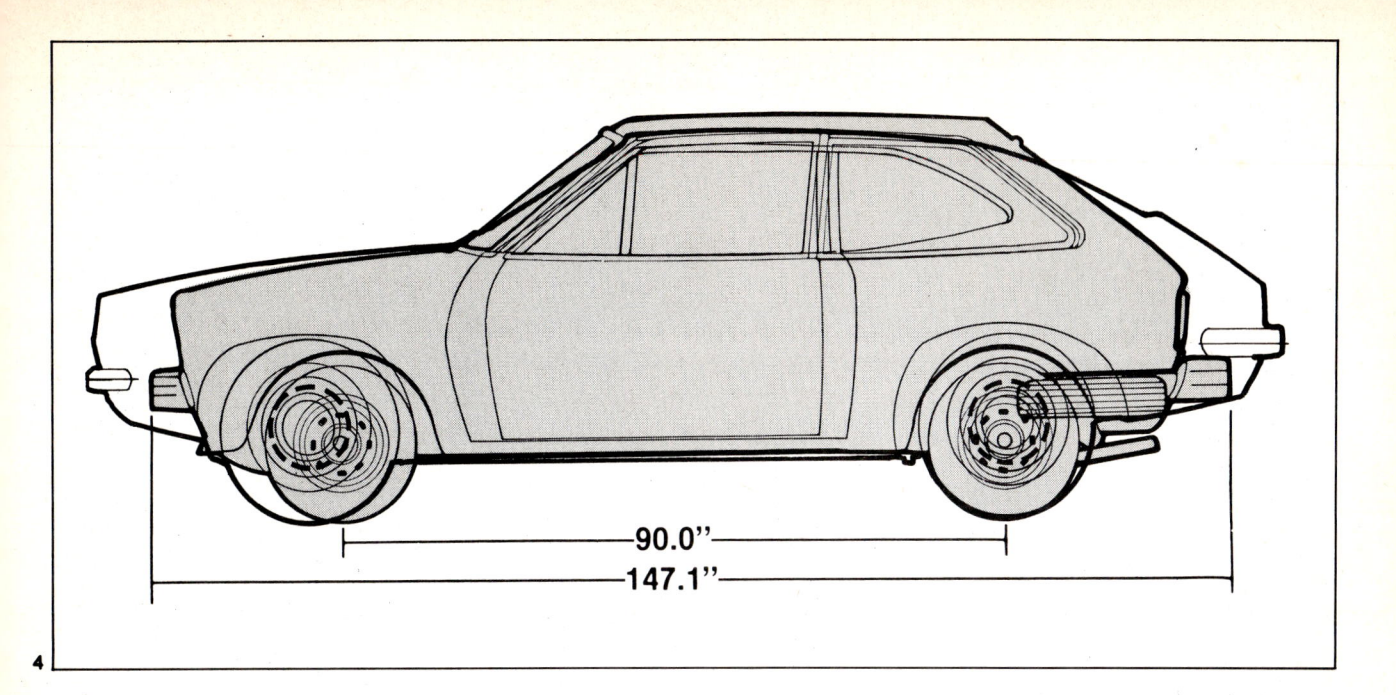

3.15:1. That constitutes rather tall gearing for a mini-car.

In a conventional front-engined, rear-wheel-drive car the final drive unit uses hypoid gears, because it must change the direction of power transmission through 90°; that is, from the driveshaft to the rear wheels. Hypoid gears have a lot of sliding action and require the use of a special extreme-pressure lubricant. In the Fiesta transaxle, since there is no need to change the direction of power transmission (that is, the engine is already rotating in the same plane as the front wheels), the final drive gear has helical teeth, the same as those on the transmission gears. All the gears in the transaxle can thus share a common lubricant. This helical gear also does not require mesh adjustment upon assembly. These are some of the minor but very real advantages of the transverse engine layout.

Since the final drive gear is not located on the vehicle centerline, the two driveshafts out to the front wheels are not of equal length. The short left shaft has a constant-velocity joint just outboard of the gear, while the long right shaft is in two sections. The inner portion of the right shaft is supported by a steady bearing at its outboard side, then connected to an outer shaft with its two constant-velocity joints.

SIZE COMPARISON

The payoff for all this clever engineering is in the Fiesta's compact size. The best way to get an idea of the Fiesta's dimensions is to compare it not to a Rabbit, Fiat or similar modern mini-car, but to that familiar Ford subcompact, the Pinto. In practically every interior dimension the 1978 Pinto 3-door hatchback Runabout and the Fiesta (all Fiestas are 3-door hatchbacks) are almost identical. In the front seat, the Fiesta has 0.3-in. more headroom, the same legroom, 2.2 ins. less shoulder room and 1.3 ins. less hiproom. In the rear seat, so often a cramped hellhole in previous mini-cars, the Fiesta has 1 in. more headroom, a whopping 5 ins. more legroom, exactly the same shoulder room and 1.8 ins. more hiproom. The Pinto fuel tank is larger—13 gals. vs. 10 gals.—but the Pinto needs a larger tank, since its fuel economy is not as good as a Fiesta's. With their rear seats folded down, both cars have the same cargo volume: 29 cu. ft.; but the Fiesta adds a small concealed compartment under the floorboards next to the spare tire. Also, the legroom of the Fiesta is more generous than these comparative figures indicate, since it has no transmission tunnel.

It is the difference in exterior dimensions that is startling. The Fiesta has a shorter wheelbase (90 ins. vs. 94.5 ins.), is 1.7 ins. *taller,* almost 8 ins. narrower, over 22 ins. shorter and at 1775 lbs. is no less than 700 lbs. lighter than the Pinto. With a slightly larger interior, the Fiesta is almost 2 ft. shorter and more than a *third of a ton* lighter than a Pinto. What this size and weight reduction mean in terms of increased maneuverability and fuel economy can easily be imagined.

OPTIONS

The Fiesta has a long list of options, most of which are collected into Decor, Sport and Ghia groups; your nearest Ford dealer will be happy to fill you in on these. Other notable goodies are those aluminum wheels, a flip-up sunroof, rear window washer/wiper, swing-open front vent windows, power brakes, air conditioning, stereo AM/FM, tinted glass, heavy-duty mechanical package and a two-stage base coat/clear coat paint. In fact, the only option which might be desired but is unavailable is an automatic transmission.

However nice the options are, it is the basic design of the Fiesta which is the real news and which will make or break this car in the long run. Ford has an enormous commitment to the Fiesta, and its sensible, efficient design is right on for the temper of our times.

CHASSIS, SUSPENSION & BRAKES/183

Ford Fiesta

HOW-TO: Fiesta Wheel Alignment

1. This view of the Fiesta front suspension shows the control arm, trailing link, driveshaft and shock/strut of the MacPherson layout. It's very well suited to a light car.

2. This front Cardan joint from a Fiat is almost identical to that found in the Fiesta. It's absolutely tiny when compared to the same type of joint used on an Eldorado.

3. This staked spindle nut is poor practice compared to the traditional castellated nut and cotter pin. It's cheaper initially, but cannot be adjusted without ruining the threads.

4. Staked spindle nuts are supposed to be used only once and discarded whenever the spindle is adjusted. As this Fiat nut shows, however, some mechanics reuse them. Not good!

5. Wheel bolt torque is important on all front-wheel-drive cars. Ford specifies 52 to 74 ft.-lbs., but Bill Chisholm at Vanowen Brake & Wheel found these varied from 20 to 45 ft.-lbs.

6. Improper, uneven bolt torque made this uneven wear pattern on the inside of the right front wheel. Since Fiesta bolts both fasten and locate, a loose one can cause wheel failure.

184/CHASSIS, SUSPENSION & BRAKES

7. After reinstalling wheel and torquing to specs come caster, camber measurements. Typical of small front-wheel-drive cars, Fiesta has small caster angle but large positive camber.

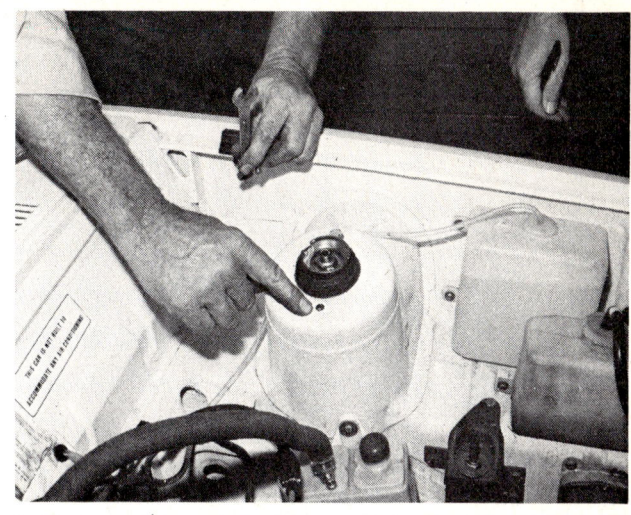

8. Fiesta camber angle is not supposed to be adjustable, but it can be done by slotting the two mounting holes at the top of the strut tower, allowing strut's angle to be changed.

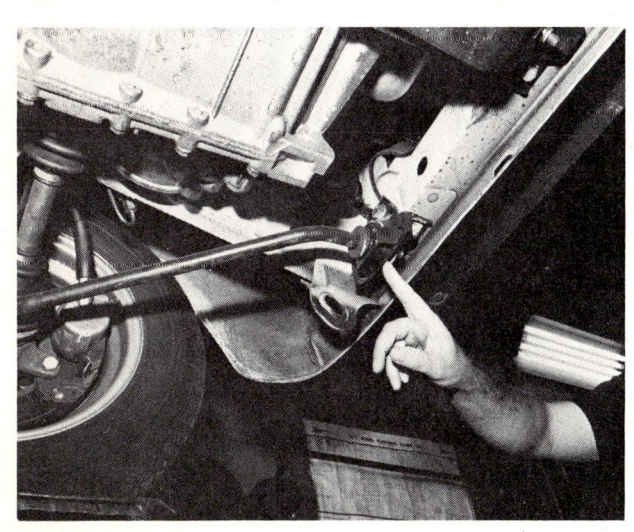

9. Caster angle on the Fiesta is not supposed to be adjustable either, but it can be changed by adding or subtracting shims at the forward mounting point of the trailing link.

10. After scribing lines on the Fiesta's front tires (see Eldorado how-to), Bill lines up the toe-in bar and measures distance between the scribe lines at the front of the tires.

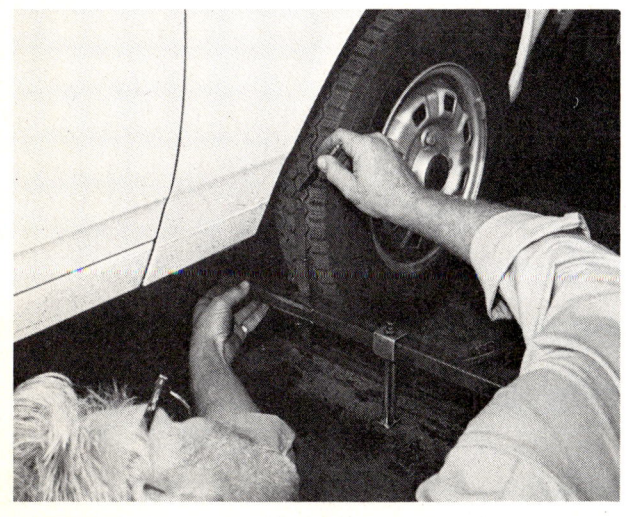

11. Holding the front measurement, the toe-in bar is moved to the rear of the tires and the distance between the scribe lines is noted. Half the difference is the toe-in.

12. Adjustment for toe-in is provided at the end of the steering links. Fiesta's static toe-out condition changes to dynamic toe-in condition as front wheels "pull in" while driving.

CHASSIS, SUSPENSION & BRAKES/**185**

FRONT-DRIVE SYSTEMS

Dodge Omni/Plymouth Horizon

The shape of things to come in domestic subcompacts is front-wheel drive.

A new kind of car for America" is how Chrysler Corp. describes their new Dodge Omni and Plymouth Horizon. Whatever your first impression is, get used to such new-breed subcompacts, because the future is here now. You'll be seeing a lot more such vehicles on our roads soon. With the rising costs of fuel, maintenance and the raw materials that go into building cars, it's time we stopped being the world's best example of opulent wastrels. The government is forcing the issue by making auto manufacturers meet fleet averages for fuel economy, which means that U.S. automakers will have to sell more and more small cars to make up for every big car they are currently selling.

The new Chrysler small cars are not unlike their imported competition in many ways, but they are the first of the new breed to be built in America and tailored specifically for the American road system and driver rather than for Europe. Like the Volkswagen Rabbit, Ford Fiesta and Fiat's most popular European cars, the Dodge Omni and Plymouth Horizon are small, boxy cars with front-wheel drive and small 4-cylinder engines mounted transversely in front. This type of layout has tremendous advantages in terms of efficient space utilization, fuel economy, low overall weight, good handling and steering responsiveness combined with comfortable seating capacity for four adults.

While the Omni and Horizon represent the first American-built cars of this design, they are certainly not the last. Chrysler expects to sell somewhere in the area of 200,000 units the first year, and the other Detroit manufacturers are said to be close behind with their own designs for 1980's-style subcompacts.

When you sit down with a clean sheet of paper to design a small car, after due consideration of interior space, weight and drivetrain layout, then the transverse-engine/front-wheel-drive configuration, which has been used in English and European cars for some time, becomes more and more logical. As one Chrysler engineer put it, "A unit-body small car is basically a two-box structure. You have to have a box for the engine and a box for the passengers, and the bigger you make the passenger box, the smaller the engine box has to be."

Placing the engine sideways up front allows considerable shortening of the engine compartment—as long as you have a small enough 4-cylinder engine to fit sideways. Conventional rear-wheel drive would, of course, be out of the question with such an engine placement, since the engine's drive would be at right angles to the direction of the driveshaft. Thus the front-wheel-drive layout affords more interior space and passenger footroom by eliminating the driveshaft tunnel in the floor.

More importantly, front drive also puts the full weight of the engine and transmission where it belongs, over the drive wheels. Up until now, the only American small car with the engine over the drive wheels was the ill-fated 1960-1969 Corvair, which was rear-engined and rear-wheel drive. Having the engine/transmission over the driving wheels puts the vehicle's center of gravity where it is most needed for good traction and stability in crosswind situations. These are two of the areas, incidentally, where our conventional small cars have been deficient. The stability factor will be most appreciated on the highway, where other small cars are blown side-to-side by winds and passing trucks. The traction factor will obviously be a great benefit in winter driving conditions (when proper winter tires are employed up front).

In addition to the practical features outlined above, with these two new cars Chrysler has also attempted to make the American consumer feel at home in a small car. He doesn't have to sacrifice the comfort he is used to

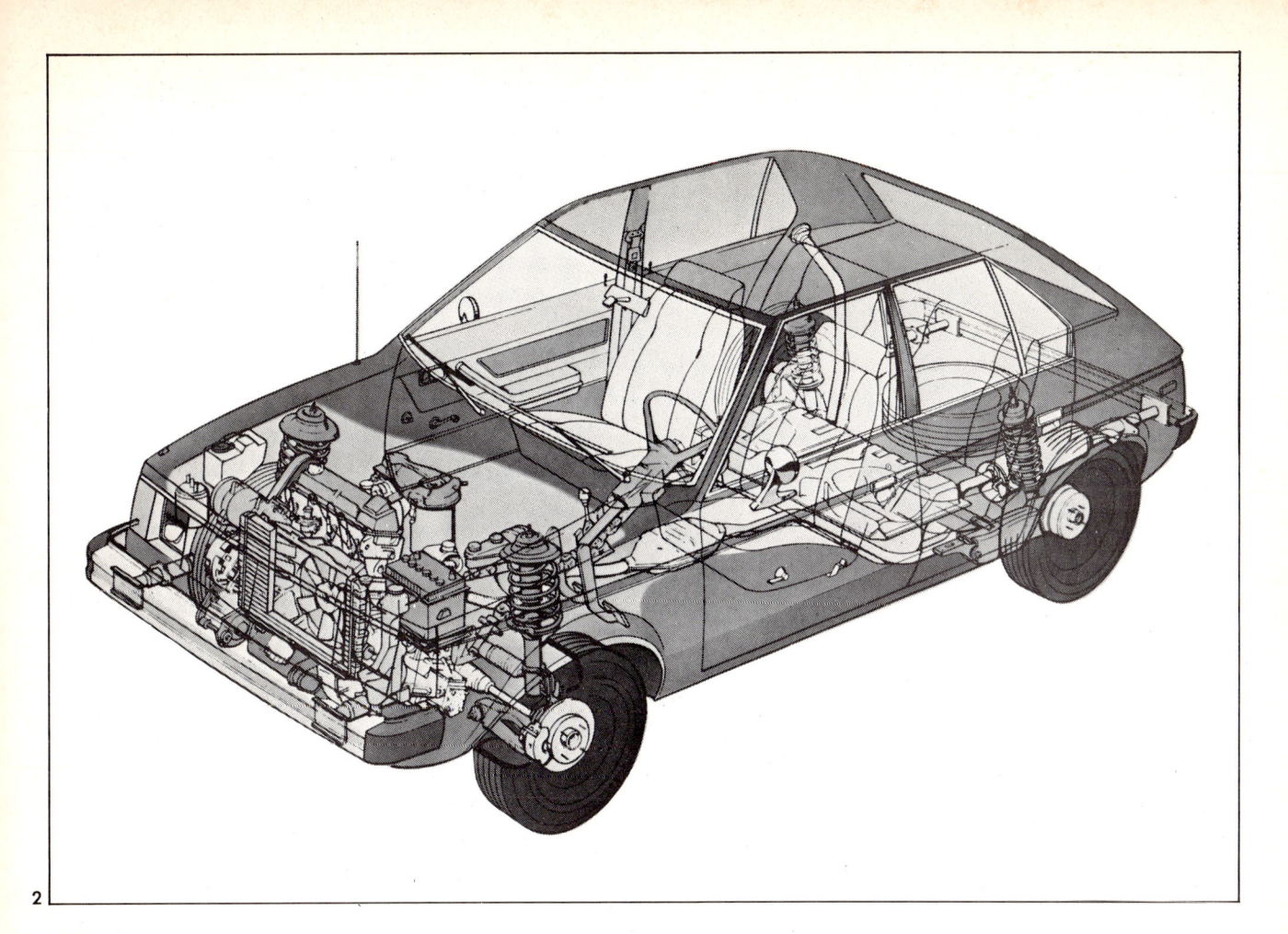

1. *Nimble, efficient and clean—these are the qualities of the new Dodge Omni and Plymouth Horizon front-wheel-drive cars, qualities we'll all be looking for in the cars of the 1980's.*

2. *The transverse engine location of the Chrysler L-cars means more room inside the 99-in.-wheelbase compacts. Omni and Horizon are roomier, softer-riding and more luxurious than their imported subcompact competitors.*

3. *Contributing much to the excellent handling of these cars are the anti-sway characteristics front and rear, the negative scrub radius, radials and forward center of gravity.*

with conventional and bigger cars. Chrysler knew this approach would be necessary in order to lure American buyers into smaller cars, and so the Omni and Horizon are designed to have the soft ride and low noise characteristics of a bigger car. Options include premium levels of interior and exterior luxury appointments to make them attractive and comfortable. Some of the other cars of this type have been European-harsh in ride and Spartan in their choice of dress-up or comfort features.

How the Chrysler engineers and their clean-sheet-of-paper approach achieved the parameters of ride, comfort, low weight, good handling manners and passenger room should be of interest to our *Basic Chassis*

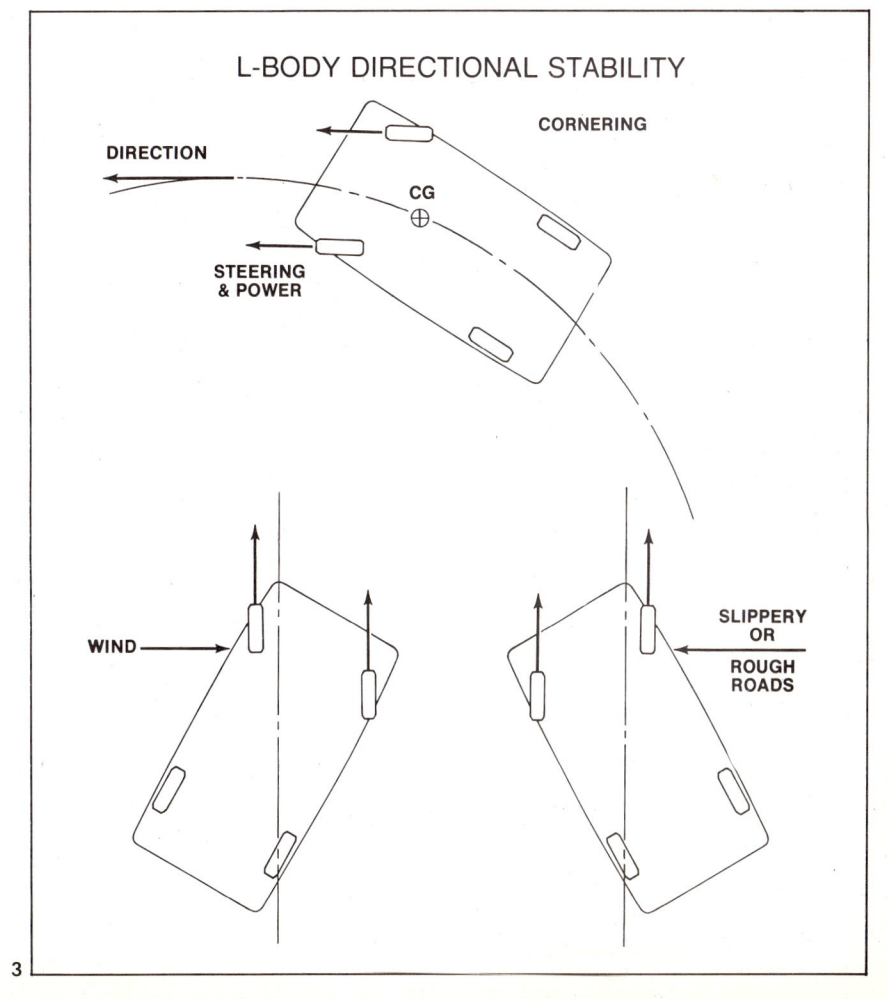

CHASSIS, SUSPENSION & BRAKES/**187**

Omni/Horizon

book readers. Chrysler has been working on the L-cars, the Horizon and Omni, for several years. However, so much engineering time went into the body, chassis and suspension for this wholly new car that there wasn't time for development of its own 4-cylinder engine. The Omni and Horizon both employ the proven 1.7-liter, overhead-cam 4-cylinder engine used in the Volkswagen Rabbit. Chrysler purchases the iron-block/aluminum-head engines from VW and adds its own ignition, carburetion and accessory drives.

The 4-speed manual transaxle with its weight-saving magnesium case is also a VW item, but Chrysler designed and built its own Torqueflite-like automatic transaxle. This was something the Chrysler marketing boys felt was a necessary development expense if their L-car was to appeal to the bulk of American consumers. The engine has a forged steel crank and rods, floating piston pins and a sintered iron timing belt sprocket on the cam. The addition of the Chrysler induction system (rather than VW fuel injection) with a Holley-Weber staged 2-bbl. carb and Chrysler's electronic Lean-Burn ignition system with Hall-effect distributor retains good engine serviceability consistent with an acceptable level of performance while meeting emissions standards.

The suspension requirements were perhaps the toughest for the Chrysler engineers to meet. They had to design a front and rear suspension system that worked with the front-wheel-drive concept, combining the best in both ride quality and handling. Let's start with the power output from the engine. Power flows through the transaxle from side gears to right and left output shafts, which have external flanges. These flanges serve as the attachment points for the left and right driveshafts that go out to the wheels. Constant-velocity U-joints are used on each shaft for smoothness, and each front wheel is driven by a splined shaft. This shaft extends through the splined hub like a conventional spindle, but rotates within the steering knuckle. On a conventional front end, the steering knuckle and spindle are all one piece.

Attached to the front end of the unit-body's underside is a stamped steel crossmember which supports the lower control arms at their inboard ends. The outboard ends of these control arms attach to the bottoms of the steering knuckles with standard, permanently lubricated ball joints. The upper ends of the steering knuckles, where you would expect to find an upper A-arm on a conventional front suspension, are attached to some specially designed shock-absorbing struts. Chrysler calls them Iso-Struts. The Iso-Struts are fixed at the steering knuckle end so that they cannot change angle or pivot. Thus they hold the steering knuckle and wheel in alignment with regard to wheel camber. Camber adjustment is provided, however, by the two bolts holding the eccentric Iso-Strut to the steering knuckle.

The use of the Iso-Struts as primary load-bearing members in the front suspension eliminates the need for the upper control arms, bushings and upper ball joints found in a conventional system. The upper end of the struts connects to the monocoque body/frame with a central stud, which passes through "compliant rubber" bushings. The use of these rubber bushings throughout the cars is the way the engineers could build in good handling while retaining the kind of ride Americans demand.

The telescoping struts are the shock-absorbing part of the suspension team; they combine with special

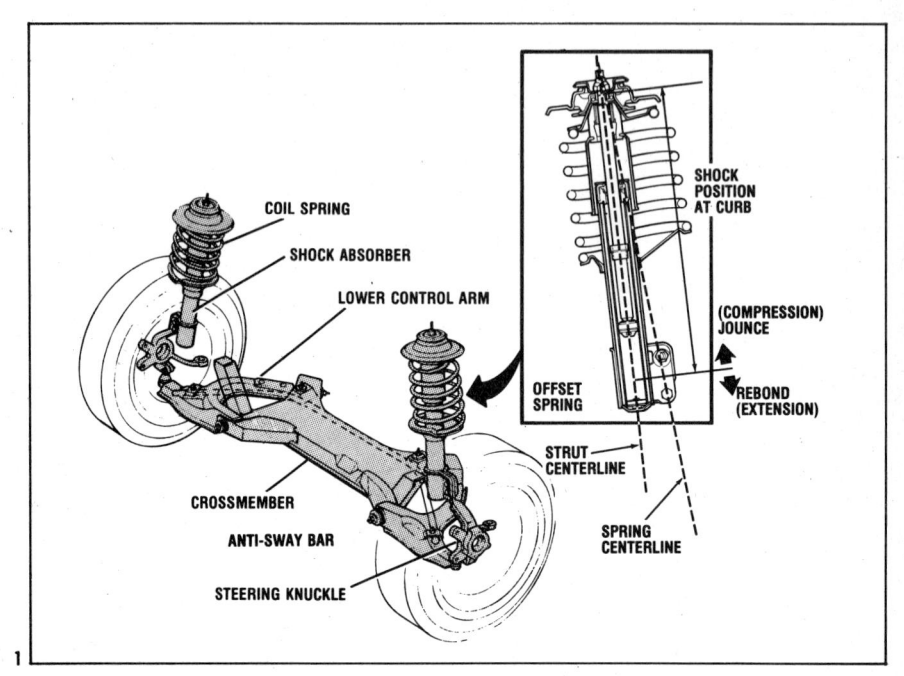

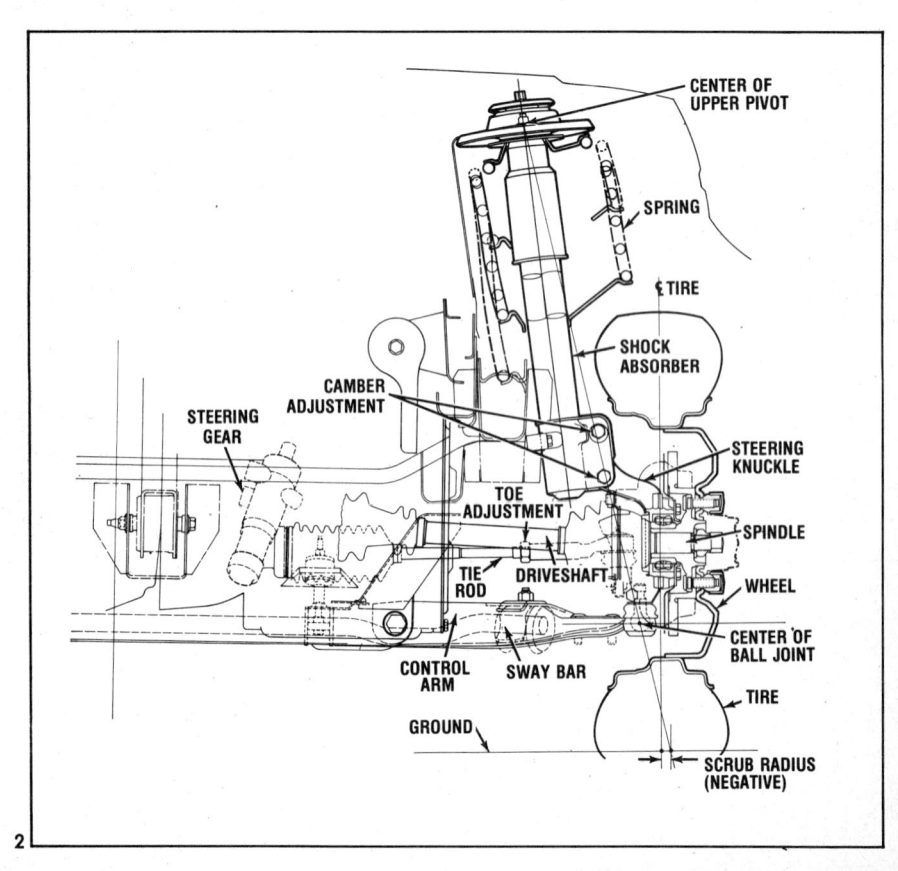

188/CHASSIS, SUSPENSION & BRAKES

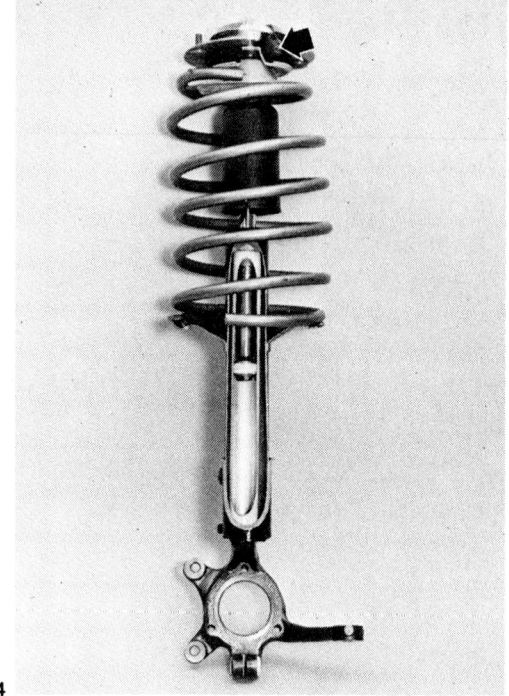

1. The front suspension is unusual for a strut-type front end, with full lower control arms and no caster struts. The sturdy, stamped-steel crossmember bolts to the unit-body.

2. There's a lot to study in this drawing, but notice especially the inclination of the coil springs and how the "spindle" drives the wheel through the steering knuckle. You can see how the tie rods, driveshafts and control arms are designed to pivot at approximately the same point.

3. The non-concentric springs make up for side loads on the hydraulic struts. They mount in compliant rubber bushings to the shock/spring towers.

4. You can see how the Omni steering knuckle differs from a conventional spindle. Cutaway model shows internal parts of the struts, and arrow indicates the rubber bushing between body and top of the strut's spring retainer.

5. Omni and Horizon both come with rack-and-pinion steering standard, while this Saginaw power unit is available as an extra-cost option.

low-rate coil springs. These springs mount around the struts. The lower end of the coil rests on a collar attached to the unsprung or moving section of the strut. The upper ends of the coil springs fit into rubber-bushed cups at the top of the spring/shock towers in the front sheetmetal. The lower A-arms attach to the crossmember with the same compliant rubber bushings that produced good ride characteristics in the Aspen/Volaré and Chrylser's luxury LeBaron.

You might wonder how it is possible to get away with using a low-rate coil spring and still have reasonable roll resistance and handling. These essentially soft springs were computer-matched to the roll resistance of the front anti-sway bar, which is also mounted in rubber at each end and at two places on the crossmember. These springs were also matched to the dampening characteristics and jounce/rebound limits of the Iso-Struts.

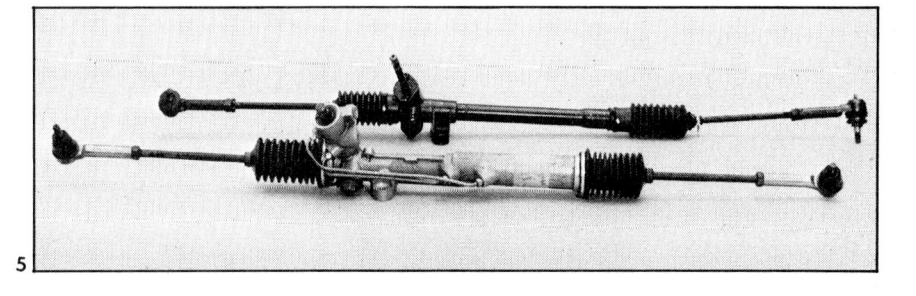

There's another interesting aspect to these springs: They are mounted not concentrically around the struts, but at an angle instead. Since the struts themselves are not vertical but are inclined from the tops of the steering knuckles toward the spring towers, the weight of the vehicle would normally put a considerable side load on the piston and rod inside the strut. By placing the spring at an angle to the strut, the load of the spring can counteract the side loads, resulting in much longer strut life and reduced ride friction. The travel of the strut is limited by a soft-jounce bumper built into the upper end of the strut assembly, which limits extreme vertical travel.

Free jounce travel, or the amount the suspension can move at each wheel *before* resistance is encountered, is 2.4 ins., considerably more than on a VW Rabbit. That's one of the reasons the Omni and Horizon ride better on rough roads than their competition. The *full* jounce travel available at each wheel is 3.6 ins.; combine this with the 3.2-in. full rebound travel and you have a total travel of almost 7 ins. plus a considerable suspension movement before things even *begin* to bottom out on the rubber.

These front hydraulic struts are built for Chrysler by Monroe, and due to the reduction in side loads within the strut, they should last considerably longer than conventional struts. Chrysler claims they are as durable as the coil springs that surround them. Another feature of the Iso-Struts is that they are *removable* for repair or replacement. On most of the import cars that use a similar MacPherson strut front suspension, the strut is part of the wheel spindle and cannot be replaced separately; it must be rebuilt. This often requires special tools and procedures that can run the repair bill up to four times what it would cost to replace a pair of conventional shock absorbers.

As you can imagine, the steering system on the Omni and Horizon is something new also. Both cars use a rack-and-pinion steering box which is mounted in rubber to the front cross-

CHASSIS, SUSPENSION & BRAKES/**189**

Omni/Horizon

member. Also contributing to a reduction in undesirable vibration feedback to the driver's hands is a special steering column silencer, another example of the rubber that Chrysler engineers use for sound suppression through the body to make the L-cars appealing. Most cars with unit-construction body/frame have a higher noise and vibration level than cars with a separate, isolated frame, but of course unit construction is a necessity in a subcompact to achieve the desired weight parameters.

There are two rack-and-pinions available: a standard manual box built by Burman and Sons, Ltd. of England, and an optional power-assisted unit built for Chrysler by the Saginaw Gear Division of GM. The rack-and-pinion connects to the steering column with a jointed, exposed shaft with two small cross-and-yoke U-joints. The latter are necessary to angle the steering so that it clears the engine and transaxle.

The quick steering response of the R&P on these 99-in.-wheelbase cars results in a turning radius of only 34 ft. and steering wheel lock-to-lock figures of 4 for the manual box and 3.2 for the power-assisted unit. At each side of the rack, there is a one-piece tie rod end and tie rod that attaches to the steering knuckles at the outside and to the threaded rods from the rack on the inboard ends, where adjustment is provided for setting the toe-out (.2-in. to 0). The steering gear ratio, for those of you who are interested, is 22:1 for the manual version and 18:1 for the power-assisted version.

Something about the steering and front suspension geometry that seems to be unique to this new breed of front-wheel-drive small cars is negative scrub radius. If you've studied the previous chapters of this book, you know that it is common for the ball joint centerline to intersect the center of a tire's contact patch. In other words, most independent suspensions are designed so that a line drawn through the centers of both the upper and lower ball joints will intersect the tire/road contact patch at about the center. This has always been considered ideal for the minimum loads on the front wheel bearings (assuming that the wheel design centered the tire between the inner and outer wheel bearings) and lowest steering effort consistent with good road feel. Scrub radius is a suspension term that's not usually discussed, because it isn't something that is readily adjusted like caster, camber or toe-in/toe-out. The scrub radius would be considered zero when the kingpin or ball joint centerline intersects the *center* of the tire patch. If it landed outboard of the tire center it would be *negative* scrub radius, and it would be *positive* scrub radius if it landed inboard.

If you have ever put wide tires and wider alloy wheels or "reversed" steel wheels on the front of a car, you probably induced positive scrub radius without knowing it. This leads to accelerated wheel bearing wear and more steering wheel feedback, because the wheel is further out and thus acts as a longer lever against the spindle.

What the front-wheel-drive engineers have done is move the

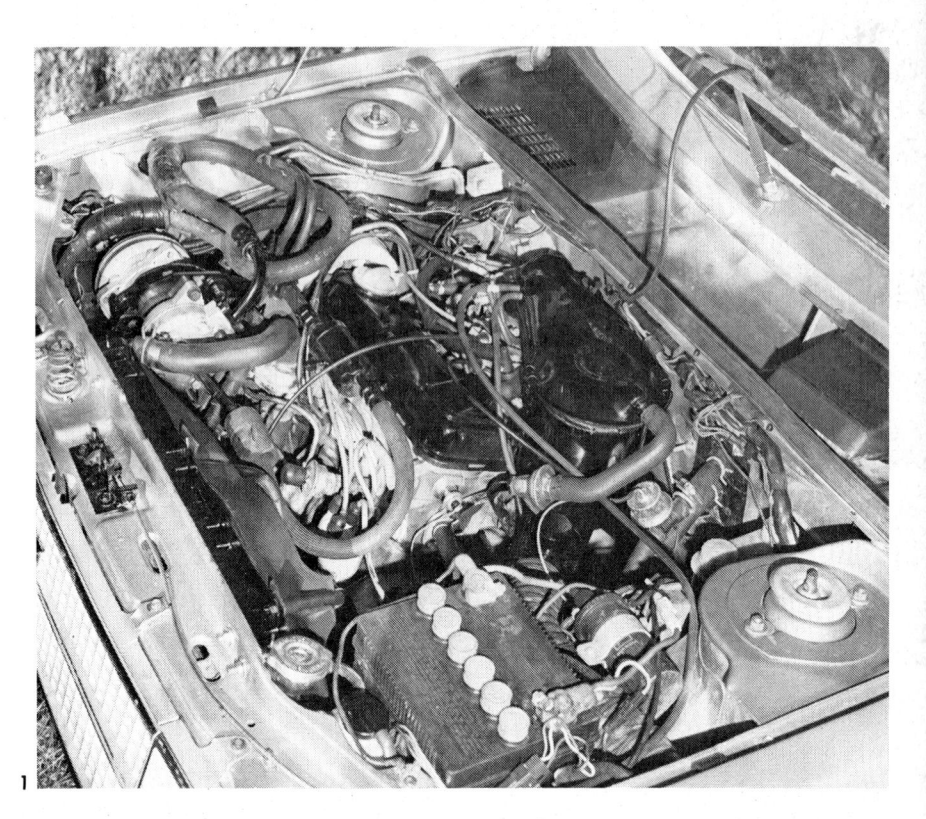

190/CHASSIS, SUSPENSION & BRAKES

centerline/patch intersection to attain a negative scrub radius. This has a number of handling benefits. In the event of a front tire failure, it would counteract some of the tendency to swerve, as well as enhancing straight-line braking and directional stability. It stands to reason that if the wheel/tire acts *less* like a lever against the spindle, then less road feedback from bumps will be felt at the steering wheel. Another plus is that the car will track more nearly straight under such annoying driving conditions as traveling on a road with two different surfaces, i.e. when the left wheels are on smooth pavement and the right wheels on a rougher or gravelly shoulder. This technique or design characteristic seems to be almost universal on the new front-wheel-drive cars, but we wonder why it wouldn't work just as well on conventional cars.

Since there is no driveshaft to the rear end in a front-wheel-drive car, the engineers had considerable freedom in designing a rear suspension system. They could have chosen a solid tube axle like the Ford Fiesta or VW Rabbit or made it a fully independent setup.

The Chrysler engineers compro-

1. Equipped with smog controls and air conditioning, the ohc VW four is almost lost under the hood. Chrysler builds its own electronic Lean-Burn ignition system and carburetion for the VW-supplied Rabbit engines. Though it looks crowded, most common components are easily serviced.

2. This factory display chassis shows a "Superman" view of the workings of the transverse engine and drive system. Nothing extends back from the engine except the exhaust pipe, which is spring-loaded to prevent cracking, a problem with some front-drive cars.

3. Pavement-eye view shows how the CV-jointed driveshafts exit from the magnesium-cased transaxle. Note the arms-forward layout of the anti-sway bar, opposite of most domestic cars.

4. Rear wheels are suspended by the same type of coil/struts used at the front, but they also attach to trailing arms that mount in oval bushings at the front (arrow), just ahead of I-beam.

5. The two rear lower control or trailing arms are connected just aft of their pivot points by a long I-beam that serves as an anti-sway bar by resisting the twisting leverage of the arms, making it semi-independent.

6. No effort has been spared to pare extra weight from Omni and Horizon, including the brake system. The cast aluminum master cylinder mounts a polyethylene plastic reservoir.

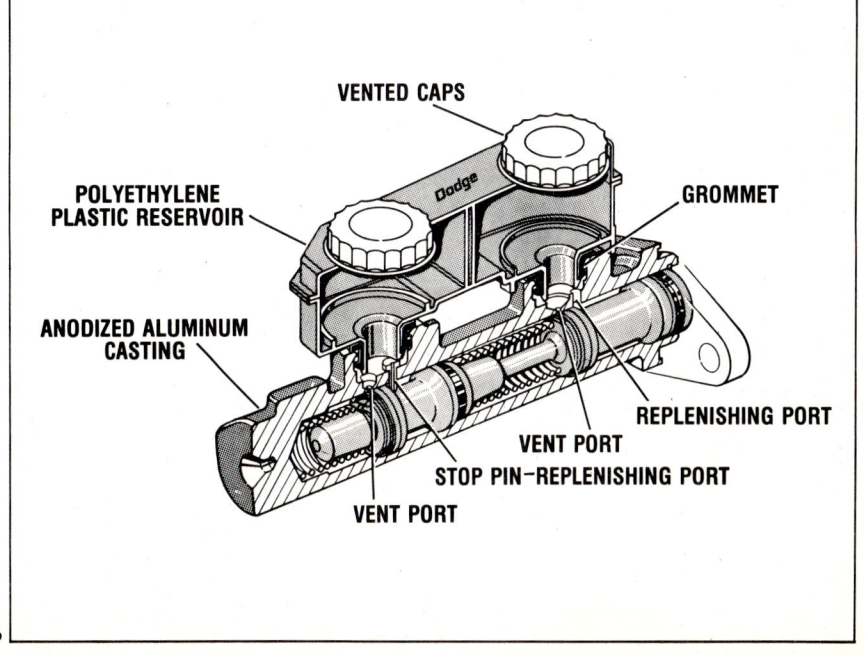

Omni/Horizon

mised and came up with a semi-independent system. The rear wheels and drum brakes attach to trailing arms that lead forward to hinge on the chassis/body within oval rubber bushings. The springing and shock control are handled by the same type of hydraulic struts and coil springs as are used up front on the two L-cars. The two trailing or lower control arms are connected just aft of their rubber oval bushings by a length of I-beam.

This may seem to constitute a solid, non-independent type of suspension, but it doesn't—quite. You see, an I-beam *will* flex and bend, whereas a length of round tubing will not, so the I-beam is really acting like an anti-sway bar between the two rear wheels. Up to a certain point (the twisting limit of the I-beam used), each rear wheel can move up or down almost independently of the opposite wheel. As with the rates of the front springs and sway bar, roll resistance of the I-beam at the rear allowed the Chrysler engineers to computer-select a pair of low-rate rear coil springs that complemented the I-beam and provided an excellent ride without harshness.

The VW Rabbit uses an I-beam at the rear also, but it is directly connected from one wheel to the other, straight across. Thus the wheels don't have any leverage to work against the beam to make it act like an anti-sway bar. On the Omni and Horizon, the beam's location near the front of the lower control arms gives the wheels some leverage so that they can twist the beam.

The Chrysler L-car brakes are interesting too. No effort was spared to bring these cars down to the weight parameters the designers had set for themselves, and even the braking system came in for dietary scrutiny. As a result, the Omni and Horizon master cylinders are built of anodized aluminum rather than cast iron, and the fluid reservoir is made of a high-molecular-weight polyethylene plastic. Many imports have had such master cylinders, but these are the first American-built cars to use them.

Disc front brakes, drum rears and an optional power booster could describe the braking system of most modern cars, but here again the Omni and Horizon are different. The 9-in., non-vented front brake rotors are stopped by a single-piston floating caliper using new semi-metallic linings. These molded, resin-bonded metallic shoes offer excellent fade resistance while maintaining adequate pad life. The rear drums are just shy of 8 ins. in diameter and use standard asbestos-type bonded shoes.

The braking system is of course a split or dual-master system to comply with federal regulations, but instead of splitting the brakes into front or rear halves, the Omni and Horizon have a *diagonal* split. The right front and left rear brakes are on one circuit and the left front and right rear are on the other circuit. This, say the Chrysler engineers, would make the car stop and handle better on varied road surfaces if one of the two circuits were to fail.

The small-car market in this country should be interesting in the next few years. General Motors is said to be building a front-wheel-drive small car for 1979 introduction, and Ford, depending on the continued success of its European Fiesta, should be bringing out a domestic model in 1980. Chrysler already has the jump on them, and judging by the way the suspension engineers have done their homework on the Omni and Horizon, the Ford and GM cars will have to be truly exceptional in the ride and handling department to top them.

1. Note how the permanently lubed ball joint is riveted to the A-arms. Upper end of steering knuckle is bolted to the strut. The front disc brakes are standard on the L-cars.

2. Chrysler has done more with the basic box shape of an efficient small car than most of the Europeans. Omni and Horizon are clean and even slightly aerodynamic for cars whose parameters were maximum interior room within a minimum exterior-size package.

3. The "woodie" trim on this Omni gives a station wagon look, but the only body style available is this efficient 4-door hatchback.

192/CHASSIS, SUSPENSION & BRAKES